P9-CMR-024

Paul Merkley
August 1999

BRANCHING OUT

BRANCHING OUT

The Transformation of the Canadian Jewish Community

GERALD TULCHINSKY

Published in 1998 by Stoddart Publishing Co. Limited
34 Lesmill Road, Toronto, Canada M3B 2T6
180 Varick Street, 9th Floor, New York, New York 10014

Distributed in Canada by:
General Distribution Services Ltd.
325 Humber College Boulevard, Toronto, Ontario M9W 7C3
Tel. (416) 213-1919 Fax (416) 213-1917
Email customer.service@ccmailgw.genpub.com

Distributed in the United States by:
General Distribution Services Inc.
85 River Rock Drive, Suite 202, Buffalo, New York 14207
Toll-free Tel. 1-800-805-1083 Toll-free Fax 1-800-481-6207
Email gdsinc@genpub.com

02 01 00 99 98 1 2 3 4 5

Canadian Cataloguing in Publication Data

Tulchinsky, Gerald, 1933–
Branching out : the transformation of the Canadian Jewish community

ISBN 0-7737-3084-2

1. Jews — Canada — History.
I. Title.

FC106.J5T84 1998 971'.004924 C98-931471-5
F1035.J5T84 1998

Editor: Sarah Swartz
Cover Design: Angel Guerra
Text Design: Kinetics Design & Illustration

Printed and bound in Canada

We gratefully acknowledge the Canada Council for the Arts and the Ontario Arts Council for their support of our publishing program.

This book offers a tribute to the Canadians who took up arms against the Fascists, in the Mackenzie-Papineau Battalion and other units of the International Brigades in Spain 1936–38, in the Allied armies throughout the world 1939–45, and in the forces defending Israel 1947–48. It is dedicated to the memory of Hananiah Meir Caiserman and Louis Rosenberg, who gave distinguished service to the Canadian Jewish community.

Of Remembrance

Go catch the echoes of the ticks of time;
Spy the interstices between its sands;

Uncover the shadow of the dial; fish
Out of the waters of the water-clock
The shape and image of first memory.

— *Abraham M. Klein*

Contents

Acknowledgements

I could not have written this book without the aid and support of my family, especially my wife, Ruth, who helped me to organize my research, accompanied me on research trips, entered many drafts of these chapters on our ancient word processor, kept track of files, tried to keep my desk tidy, and served as a tough-minded critic. She put up with dark moods when the going was rough and did without several summer vacations. My daughters, Ellen and Laura, contributed voluntarily to this work, Laura as a part-time researcher and editor and Ellen by translating several Yiddish texts into English. Steve, my son, kept urging me on, cheered the arrival of chapters, and helped in numerous other ways. Other family members, including my mother — now ninety-four — took an abiding interest and offered advice, none of which I dared to ignore.

Colleagues assisted me generously, especially Jack Granatstein, who, at frequent lunches in Kingston and Toronto and in response to many telephone calls, patiently heard me out, asked searching questions, and made many valuable suggestions. Jack criticized and commented helpfully on chapters and read my rough first completed draft. Throughout this project's duration, he gave me strong encouragement and vital moral support. So did Linda McKnight of Westwood Creative Artists. Irving Abella, Donald Akenson, Pierre Anctil, Michael Behiels, Michael Bliss, Gérard Bouchard, Mesh Butovsky, Ramsay Cook, Irwin Cotler, Esther Delisle, Ruth Dukas, Sidney Eisen, Jack English, Gerald Friesen, Adam Fuerstenberg, Louis Greenspan, Annette Hayward, Norman Hillmer, Lucien Karchmar, Arthur Kruger, Frank

Lewis, Sheva Medjuck, John Meisel, Les Monkman, Bryan Palmer, Hélène Pelletier-Baillargeon, James Pritchard, Ira Robinson, Paul Rutherford, Jonathan Sarna, Jack Saywell, Donald Swainson, Shelley Tenenbaum, Harold Troper, Marguerite Van Die, Mary Vipond, Harold Waller, Tracey Ware, Morton Weinfeld, Mel Wiebe, Barbara Wilson, and Ruth Wisse generously answered my appeals for information and guidance. Christopher Armstrong, Jack Cohen, Alan Davies, Richard Dennis, Louis Greenspan, Michiel Horn, Eddy Kaplansky, Cecil Law, Daniel Levy, Sol Littman, Marion Marks, Lesley Marrus-Barsky, Marion Meyer, Myron Momryk, Deena Nathanson, Marilyn Nefsky, Shloime Perel, Janine Stingel, Harold Troper, and Laura Wolfson allowed me to read and cite from manuscripts of their works-in-progress. Yossi Katz and Irit Amit gave me a wonderful tour of Asher Pierce's farm, Tel Asher, in Israel. Daniel Levy wrote the sidebar on Two-Gun Cohen, Eddy Kaplansky the one on Reuben "Red" Schiff, and Lynne Ginsburg the one on her family.

Harry Arthurs gave me access to the Dworkin papers and Dan Usher made available the letters of his uncle Moses Usher, an RCAF flight lieutenant who was killed in action during the Second World War. Bryan Palmer generously provided me with copies of the correspondence of Maurice Spector from his own research, and Jack Granatstein gave me his notes on the 1943 Cartier riding by-election. Ben-Zion Shapiro kindly allowed me to consult his letters written from Israel in 1951–52.

Barbara Wilson, David Bercuson, Jack English, James Pritchard, Brian McKillop, Lawrence Tapper, and Jack Granatstein read and commented on an earlier version of Chapter 8. I owe an enormous debt to the following busy colleagues who were generous enough to read my penultimate manuscript and did not spare the knife, pointing out errors and suggesting that I revise my thinking on many points: David Bercuson, Michael Bliss, Michael Brown, Maurice Careless, Ramsay Cook, Louis Greenspan, Ben Kayfetz, Daniel Levy, Paul-André Linteau, Royden Loewen, Ian McKay, Ira Robinson, Jonathan Sarna, Geoff Smith, Harold Troper, Harold Waller, and Morton Weinfeld. Irving Abella took time off from his busy schedule of work on Jewish public affairs to read and comment constructively on an early draft. Sarah Swartz also read the entire manuscript and provided many excellent suggestions for improving the text, as did Janice Weaver, and Donald Bastian and Natalia Denesiuk at Stoddart.

No historian could get very far without guidance from archivists and librarians, and I have been lucky in encountering some of the best in the world: Lawrence Tapper, Myron Momryk, Barbara Wilson, and the rest of the staff at the National Archives of Canada; Janice Rosen and Phyllis Kimia of the Canadian Jewish Congress National Archives (Montreal); Stephen

Speisman of the Ontario Jewish Archives; Harry Gutkin and Bonnie Tregobov of the Jewish Historical Society of Western Canada; Barry Hyman of the Public Archives of Manitoba; Lois Yorke of the Public Archives of Nova Scotia; Jean Dryden at the United Church Archives in Toronto; staff at the Glenbow Museum and Archives in Calgary; Jack Switzer of the Jewish Historical Society of Southern Alberta; René Rogers and Gabrielle Scardellato at the Multicultural History Society of Ontario; George Henderson of the Queen's University Archives; and staff at the American Jewish Historical Society Archives, the Tamiment Institute at New York University, and the Public Archives of Ontario. Former Canadian Jewish Congress official Ben Kayfetz, a walking archive of detailed information on an amazingly wide variety of Canadian Jewish topics, has been wonderfully helpful to me, as he is to all others. Yoram Mayorek at the Central Zionist Archives in Jerusalem was always generous with his time. I owe all of them so much.

I had the benefit of generous research grants from the Social Sciences and Humanities Research Council of Canada and the Queen's University Advisory Research Council and Principal's Development Fund, which allowed me to hire researchers who helped me enormously: Shawn Dolansky, Larry Gamulka, David Hartman, Richard Kicksee, Heather McInnis, Hannah Pickard, Danielle Pivnick, Jodi Rice, Sonia Riddoch, and Tamara Vander Walle. Librarians at Queen's often went beyond the call of duty for me: David Wang, William Morley, Lorraine Helsby, Bonnie Brooks, Donna Blake, Diane Cook, Thelma Fernando, and Barbara St. Remy. Vyvien Vella, calm and patient amidst many storms, did the final word processing with professional expertise and abiding good humour. In the Queen's history department, Norma St. John, Cindy Fehr, Judy Van Houser, Debby Stirton, Yvonne Place, and Margaret Nash helped me in countless ways. But this is not all.

Many years ago, my uncle Yitzchak Tulchinsky, while showing me around his beloved Tel Aviv, urged me to — I remember his exact words — "do something for the Jewish people." Having fled outbreaks of violent antisemitism in Bucharest in March 1942 with his wife and two-year-old daughter, he and some friends hurriedly bought an old rust bucket, the *Mircea*, in the nearby port of Constanza, hired a crew, and set out on the Black Sea towards Turkey and the Dardanelles in the hope of reaching refuge in Palestine. After several misadventures at sea — including having to cope with a boozy captain — they were permitted to proceed through the Dardanelles. Seeing, through his binoculars I assume, as they neared the Turkish coast that their boat was about to be shelled by a suspicious army shore unit, my uncle, in desperation, grabbed his little daughter (my cousin, Ala, now herself a grandmother) and held her aloft for the soldiers to see, he hoped, through *their* binoculars. They held their fire! Forced to come ashore, the refugees were interrogated and then released. Now in the Mediterranean, they were captured and briefly detained by Italian military forces occupying the Dodecanese Islands, where a kindly army medical doctor gave them first aid, food, and milk for the children.

After setting sail again, while hugging the eastern Mediterranean shore, they were captured by the Royal Navy and conveyed under guard to Palestine, where my uncle was locked up for some months but later allowed to join his wife and daughter, who in the meantime had been set free.

When he made his plea to me in Israel in 1952, I vaguely understood that somehow I should comply; but at age nineteen, I did not know how. Many years later, this is my answer.

Other forces were at work then and later: my strong Zionist family; friends in Young Judaea; instructors at the Machon l'Madrichei Hutz L'Aretz (Institute for Youth Leaders from Abroad) in Jerusalem; instructors at university; and colleagues at Loyola (now Concordia), the University of Saskatchewan, and Queen's University.

I wish to thank my students, from whom I have demanded so much, and who have taught me much more in return.

Dear friends like Moishe and Esther Langer, Shirley and Cyril Kalfin, Istvan and Bea Anhalt, David and Lynne Ginsburg, Marion and Gerry Marks, and Marion and Henry Meyer offered encouragement. Gidi and Toni Shimoni, Anne and Arie Lamdan, and Ted and Joan Tulchinsky provided frequent and bounteous hospitality during my research visits in Israel. They and all of the others named above, besides in her own special way my one-year-old granddaughter, Hannah Rachael May, helped and inspired me to write this book.

None of the above, of course, are in any way responsible for the shortcomings of this book. They are mine alone.

KINGSTON, ONTARIO
JUNE 1998

Preface

Covenant, Torah, Diaspora, and Israel mark the co-ordinates of the Jewish experience on the stage of world history. The unique relationship between God and the Jewish people struck by Abraham at Moriah and confirmed through Moses at Sinai has reverberated through history as the founding idea of Judaism. The Torah, handed to Moses and conveyed to the fractious Hebrew former slaves, established a behavioural code that through subsequent written documents, especially the Mishna and, later, the Talmud, elaborated on the principles underlying the binding law of the Halacha.

These texts and their commentaries over the centuries became the vehicle of daily religious observance that marked Jewish life, thought, and study since the destruction of Solomon's Temple in Jerusalem. The ensuing Babylonian exile and subsequent return of the Jewish remnants to Palestine led to the building of the Second Temple on the ruins of Solomon's in Jerusalem.

The wars of the Maccabees against the Hellenic conquerors and their culture were followed by the conquest of Judaea by the Roman armies, which led to the civil war among the Jews, the destruction of the Temple, and the dispersion of the survivors, marking the end of the Second Commonwealth. The coins depicting the triumphal march of the conqueror Titus through Rome bear the inscription *Judaea capta*, words that in some way are the continuing leitmotif of Jewish history through two thousand years of exile.

The Land of Israel, conquered many times since the dispersion and made the home of Arab peoples, nevertheless remained the centre of Jewish thought. Though in deepest exile, say amid the snows of Poland and Ukraine, a Jew could dream about walking over the hills of Galilee and standing at the ruins of the Temple. Prayers for this were said three times a day and on the Sabbath, the festivals, and the High Holy days.

But the Jewish experience takes place, as the philosopher Abraham Heschel reminds us, in space as well as in time. The geographic, political, economic, and social elements form contexts that shaped the evolution of communities in many countries and cultures in which Jews have lived for two thousand years. Countervailing the temporal dimension, moveover, the spatial element permits the continuation of the central elements of Jewish culture over centuries largely influenced by the local context in which Jews live. The constant interplay between culture and context presents the Jewish historian with an erratically moving target, an opportunity and a challenge to understand and describe to his readers the experience of this people both in space — in this case, Canada — and in time, with reference to the eternal co-ordinates of Judaism.

In the twelve chapters that follow, readers are offered a view of Canadian Jewish history that describes this encounter between continuity and change and takes up the story after 1920, where I left it in *Taking Root: The Origins of the Canadian Jewish Community*, a work published in 1992. Beginning with a portrait of the community's social and economic life in the interwar years, the story moves to a survey of Jewish immigration, with the First World War immigrants and their children encountering a nation recovering from war, a society driven by racial dualism, and an economy largely dependent on raw-materials exports in the flux of gyrating world markets.

One aspect of that encounter took place in that perennial Canadian hotbed of tension, Montreal. Here the generation-old issue of how Jews fit into the province's confessional school system arose once more and caused bitterness both within the Jewish community and among French-Canadian clerico-nationalists. The question of how Jews, who were defined as Protestants for educational purposes, should define themselves remained moot. But the debate, the resolution, and the aftermath had serious impact for the Jews of Montreal.

By the 1920s "the great Jewish *métier*," to borrow historian Moses Rischin's felicitous phrase, the clothing industry that is the subject of Chapter 4, had come into full flower, notably in Montreal, Toronto, and Winnipeg. Because of competition and pressures to lower costs, this frontier of enterprise was a well-known danger zone for both would-be manufacturers and their workers, some 30 percent of them Jewish. The resulting confrontations form an important chapter in the evolution of conflicting identities and goals within the Jewish community. The spirit of North American free-enterprise capitalism collided with the collectivist values of East European socialism and brotherhood within the Jewish world.

That socialist outlook, which many Jews shared to one degree or another — the subject of Chapter 5 — was largely coloured by their European backgrounds, where the battles for workers' rights, humanistic values, and democratic government were fought by socialists against the dark forces of reaction and antisemitism. And in the Canada of the 1920s and 1930s, amid recurring unemployment and massive social distress, it seemed that socialism had a future.

Antisemitism, the subject of Chapter 7, was present throughout the interwar period, just as it was elsewhere in the world, though its ugliness in Canada was exacerbated by the special situation of Quebec — French, Catholic, and introverted — where fascist-minded ultra-nationalists articulated an especially virulent form of racist Jew-hatred to add to the traditional religious anti-Jewish phobias.

Amid all these transformations, which were creating the circumstances for defining a Canadian Jewish identity, Canadian Zionists — the focus of Chapter 6 — were involved in the extraterritorial project of rebuilding the Jewish "national home" in Palestine. But the vast majority of Jews had no intention of personally participating in the Palestine project beyond occasional contributions of money. Instead, Zionism strengthened their identity as Jewish Canadians and provided an important vehicle for political expression and ethnic pride. This became even more clear during the Second World War, when, as Chapter 8 reveals, Jews participated honourably in Canada's military endeavour, but only at the same level as all other Canadians, despite widespread understanding that Europe's Jews were the special target of the Nazis. The Canadian environment had helped to transform exile into diaspora for most Jews, who were anxious to become as Canadian as local society would allow.

Zionism historically had deeper roots in Canada than in the United States, when measured by per capita financial contributions and volunteering for the Israel Defense Forces during the 1948–49 War of Independence. The rates of Aliyah, or migration to Israel, nevertheless were no higher then or later. The postwar era, the focus of Chapter 10, also demonstrates that Canadian Jews as a collective were seeking accommodation and integration into the mainstream and enjoying economic and social advancement at unprecedented levels. Antisemitism of the most malevolent pre-war forms virtually disappeared, and many of the old barriers against integration gradually fell away. Meanwhile, the community grew through renewed immigration, first of Holocaust survivors, then of Israelis, North Africans, and Russians, among others — all of them adding diversity while forming sub-communities within the larger collective. And at the same time, alongside the Holocaust the existence of Israel became recognized as a vital node of identity, a homeland whose survival, language, and culture became integrated into the Canadian Jewish mentality through schooling and visits.

The postwar migration of Jews, many of them survivors, and the transformations in the community after 1945 are the subject of Chapter 10. The attention paid to the Holocaust's tragedy, as Chapter 12 explains, in turn focused attention on allegations that hundreds, possibly thousands, of war criminals had found refuge in Canada after the Second World War. In the meantime, overall governance and fund-raising structures had changed out of all recognition in response to transforming communal needs.

Canada's Jews, numbering an estimated 360,000 persons near the end of the twentieth century, have entered the Canadian mainstream to a degree undreamed of in 1921, when this story begins, and constitute a much different community — if they are really still a single body — than they were. The interface between the eternal values of Judaism — Jewish culture, in other words — and Canadian context, its broadly conceived social space, when added to the Holocaust and Israel, has produced a much different community. The following pages attempt to examine how it got to where it is now.

Introduction

In the ramshackle Brantford synagogue of my youth, there was a point in the Yom Kippur *mussaf* (additional, or afternoon) service, during the prayer of Hineni ("Here I am, poor in worthy deeds"), when the cantor's voice would break and, as the *shaliach tsibbur* (the people's delegate), appointed to pray on their behalf, he was momentarily overcome by the majesty of the day. His strength gave way, tears welled up, and his prayer stopped while he choked back the emotion of knowing that the Lord's judgement was to be sealed by sundown and prayers to avert "the evil decree" were to be answered. The entire congregation was hushed, some of them also emotional, waiting for their delegate to continue.

At this moment, as perhaps at no other time during this annual Day of Awe, the Jewish people, then and now, confront eternity, history, and their souls while they stand emotionally naked, abject, repentant, and prayerful. This is, perhaps, Yom Kippur's defining few seconds, when the Jewish people again witness the binding of Isaac, the rescue from Egyptian slavery, the revelation at Sinai, the destruction of the Second Temple, the prophecies of Isaiah, the defence of Massada, the Bar Kochba Revolt, the dispersion, the compilation of the Talmud, the Inquisition, the Holocaust, the rebirth of Israel, the ingathering of the exiled, and other major landmarks of Jewish history.

Like the *shaliach tsibbur* on Yom Kippur, the historians of modern Jewry are often overcome by the enormity of their responsibilities. But the significance of the task and the imperative of continuing pushes them forward despite the acknowledgement of their own unimportance and the meagreness of their talent. Unlike the *shaliach tsibbur*, who is chosen to pray for forgiveness, the historians appoint themselves to interpret their people's history. They do not stand, fortunately, before the Lord to plead for mercy, to avert the decision of who shall live and who shall die in the coming year. Instead, they attempt, at the end of some four thousand years of history, to seek understanding and explain what happened and how.

Conversely, the *shaliach tsibbur*'s job may be easier than that of the historian because the Lord probably is much more merciful towards sinners than historians are towards the alleged transgressors who fall short in this demanding profession. So while I feel relieved that I do not have to plead on behalf of sinners, I realize the immensity of undertaking to examine the twentieth-century Jewish experience in Canada. It is an awesome task indeed for a mere historian, who like the *shaliach tsibbur* is, as the prayer goes, "poor in worthy deeds, [and] horribly frightened in thy presence," to tell this story with accuracy, balance, insight, and humanity.

Anyone who has tried to navigate in the sea of Canadian Jewish history must quickly develop a profound respect for the earlier explorers. Nearly sixty years ago, Louis Rosenberg published the modestly titled *Canada's Jews: A Social and Economic Study of the Jews in Canada*, published by the Canadian Jewish Congress in 1939, which, besides the invaluable data on Canadian Jews gleaned from the censuses of Canada to 1931, incorporated magisterial analyses of many of the Jewish community's principal historical themes. This book forms the basis even today of much of the work — including the attempt set forth in the pages that follow — that historians have essayed in examining the experience of the Jews of Canada in the twentieth century.

Rosenberg should have followed his pioneering account with a full-fledged historical analysis. But like so many members of the brilliant small cadre of Jewish Canadian intellectuals of those days, he had a more important agenda in the 1940s and 1950s and lacked the resources, time, and research funds needed for such work. Sadly, he was almost alone. Benjamin Gutl Sack, a professional journalist who wrote numerous historical articles for the *Keneder Adler*, in 1948 produced the first volume of history of Canadian Jewry, *Geschichte fun Yidn in Kanada: Fun Frantsoizishn Regim Biz Soif Ninestn Yahrhundert*. This richly detailed book, which covered Canadian Jewish history from the French regime to the 1880s, constituted a major landmark in the historiography of Canadian Jewry, a significant advance over previous attempts to tell the story of how his community evolved since the British conquest.

There were a few others working on the whole field of Jewish history who have provided such a fertile bank of ideas and historiographical landmarks, so many bright beacons of guidance and inspiration. Rabbi Stuart E. Rosenberg made an ambitious attempt to write such an overview in 1970. Throughout the years, David Rome, as head of the Jewish Public Library of Montreal (not just a library, but also a centre of Jewish cultural activity in Yiddish, English, and French) and as archivist at the Canadian Jewish Congress National Archives, encouraged numerous young scholars in this field. He also produced many volumes of commentary and documents in the Canadian Jewish Archives Series, a superb book on Hananiah Meir Caiserman, and several other works. He was followed a few years later by Erna Paris, whose *Jews: An Account of Their Experience in Canada* is a well-written, ambitious account of several important episodes illuminating many of the complexities and ambiguities in that history. Abraham Arnold's lively survey, graced by some of William Kurelek's paintings of rural and urban Jewish life, drew on a lifetime of active research in the field. Finally, Irving Abella's *A Coat of Many Colours* provided a masterful brief overview of the origins and transformation of the community since the first Jewish contact with Canada in the seventeenth century. All of these important works have lighted my own way towards an understanding of this period.

So have the studies by numerous, mostly younger, scholars whose recent books, theses, and papers on particular aspects, periods, or community organizations have made possible a far more nuanced and detailed comprehension of institutional and personal responses to a transforming context, as the endnotes to this book will show. With these new studies by sociologists, political scientists, and scholars of language and literature, Canadian Jewish historiography, while still in its formative stages, is already showing some of the sophistication that characterizes historical works on Jews in Britain and the United States.

Within these countries, Jewish historians have had almost a two-generation head start in assessing their pasts, in nations that, like Canada, evolved as English-language liberal democracies. Jewish culture was conveyed from Eastern Europe to all three parts of this North Atlantic triangle, Great Britain, the United States, and Canada, which already by 1920 had provided ample rewards to their Jews in conditions of domestic peace, political and religious freedom, and social and economic opportunity — conditions shaped by local tradition and circumstance. Thus, American Jewish historians Henry Feingold, who surveyed the period from 1920 to 1945, and Edward S. Shapiro, who studied the years from 1945 to 1980, broadly interpret the Jewish experience in the United States as a "Time for Searching" and a "Time for Healing," when Jewish life was shaped by the modernization of an increasingly powerful, centralized, rich, and self-conscious nation that was home to the largest Jewish community in the world. British Jewry, by contrast, was shaped within the context of a declining imperial power whose unitary government, emphatic nationalism, and mishandling of the Palestine mandate — as historian David Cesarani and others have pointed out in a series of superb studies — created tension, ambivalence, and fragmentation.

The Jewish experience is also one dimension of Canadian ethnic history, one community in a country that by 1920 embraced numerous others. Canada's characteristic of "limited identities" has allowed room for ethnic expression that is seen in some respects, especially recently, as legitimate and worthy in a nation without a pronounced single national personality. Jewish history in this context is but one voice in this Canadian multi-ethnic chorus, and the historian of Jews can, indeed must, be sensitive to contemporaneous transformations among, for example, the Italian, Ukrainian, and Mennonite communities, to name only three of those that have enjoyed significant historical investigation (by scholars like Franca Iacovetta, John Zucchi, Bruno Ramirez, Francis Swyripa, Lubomyr Luciuk, Orest Martynowych, and Royden Loewen). Helpful also are the brilliant synoptical analyses of ethnicity by the historian Robert Harney.[1] In one of his most penetrating analyses of Canadian multi-ethnicity, Harney observed that "ethnicity is more and less than a biological given. . . . It is processual. . . . Immigrants and their children negotiate their own identities."[2] Among other immigrant groups, Canada's Jews were between 1921 and the present in the process of negotiating who they were in a transforming and deeply challenging context.

As for historians of Canadian Jewry, their task is to evaluate the Jewish experience in a context of a nation that emerged from the First World War badly scarred by horrifying wartime losses, the breakdown of the old national political parties, and severely strained French-English relations. Meanwhile, the national dream of railways, immigration, and a western wheat boom conjointly fuelling economic growth that would make the twentieth century "the century of Canada," as Prime Minister Wilfrid Laurier had predicted in 1904, already lay in tatters. By the early 1920s, two of the three national railways had gone bankrupt and were being merged into one, the Dominion government was saddled with enormous wartime debts, and the western frontier's promise had petered out amid serious recession, farmer discontent, and declining immigration. Through the 1920s, under the leadership of William Lyon Mackenzie King, Canada sought a return to the political stability and growth of the pre-war era, only to be struck by the Great Depression, which, between 1929 and 1941, brought the nation's economy and its social system close to disaster. When King returned to power in 1935, after the five-year Conservative interlude under Richard Bedford Bennett, Canada was no better off. In some of the provinces, protest parties on the left and the right had emerged. Meanwhile, antisemitism, coupled with a general hatred of "foreigners," surfaced in especially ugly forms and resulted in a severe tightening of immigration.

The Second World War and the subsequent period of prosperity, though cyclical, transformed Canada. Sizeable European immigration resumed in the late 1940s and continued into the 1950s and 1960s, while in later decades Asian and Caribbean immigrants flowed in to what was becoming, literally and officially, an increasingly urbanized and multicultural nation. By the 1970s, however, regionalism and Quebec separatism had clearly emerged as the most serious challenges to the continuity of a federal union that had been erected only in 1867.

In the Jewish world, since 1920 the great Zionist experiment in Palestine had moved ahead under the guidance and with the financial support of Jews around the world, including those in Canada. But in Europe, it was clear by the early 1930s that a crisis was taking shape. Jews faced not just the normal religious and social antisemitism endemic in those societies — especially in Eastern Europe — but also a new, far more malevolent, racial variety spread by Nazis who were supported after 1933 by the resources of the German state. And farther away, in the Soviet Union, Jews faced lingering antisemitism, although at the same time enjoyed full equality as citizens and the official encouragement that the Soviet regime offered in the autonomous Jewish republic of Birobidjan, on the USSR's far eastern reaches.

Above all, the crisis produced by Nazi persecution in Germany, and the mass murder of six million Jews during the Second World War by the Nazis and their collaborators, destroyed one-third of the Jewish people and eliminated Eastern Europe from the Jewish familial, cultural, and social landscape. This Holocaust facilitated the emergence in 1948 of Israel, which slowly became a principal focus for Jewish identity and a refuge for Holocaust survivors, as well as North African and, later, Soviet Jews.

How did these contextual transformations affect Canada's Jews through the decades from 1921 until recent years? This tiny community of 125,516 persons, concentrated overwhelmingly in ethnic enclaves within major cities and composed of working- or lower-middle-class immigrants, already had behind it a history stretching back to the 1750s, when a few dozen Jewish traders had arrived in Canada and, in 1768, formed a congregation in Montreal. Thereafter, the community gradually expanded and took root in all of the British North American colonies that joined in Confederation on July 1, 1867, a union that within a few years grew into a transcontinental dominion fronting three oceans. When the sizeable Jewish migrations of the early 1900s entered this broad Canadian federation, the already established Jewish community was so overwhelmed that it needed substantial assistance from the philanthropist Baron Maurice de Hirsch to meet the challenge.

But not for long. While the Canadian Jewish Congress, which was brought into being in early 1919 after several years of effort, lasted only a year or two before going into limbo until it reappeared in 1934, it nevertheless symbolized a community that had already formed a distinctive character. In it, the East European immigrants served notice that they had arrived and would now share responsibility for defining the Jewish agenda through an organization that they insisted must become a genuine "parliament" of the whole national community of Jews.

How would Canadian Jews accommodate themselves to the national and regional contexts, both as Jews and as Canadians? Who, indeed, were Canada's Jews, and how did their ethnographic portrait change over the years? How would they fit their own "cultural baggage" with the Dominion's monumental national agenda, while adapting also to the special context of Quebec, where such a large proportion of them lived? What were the patterns of Jewish immigration and settlement after 1920 and how did the community, and Canadians generally, respond? What did Jews do for a living, where did they reside, and how did they fit into the economy, society, and polity of Canada? What were the issues around which the resulting intra-communal politics revolved? Even further, how did these elements change over time? And how did they respond to the war against Nazism and to the Holocaust? Numerous but vital questions such as these have shaped the narrative that follows.

This book attempts to trace the Jewish encounter with Canada and its other resident peoples from 1921 to the present day. It is a story both complex and fascinating, and it conveys a community in continuing transition within an ever-transforming nation. This book is an overview, not an encyclopedia, of Canadian Jewish history after 1920. It will not cover everything, nor will it be a who's who, listing the community's many luminaries. As a sequel to *Taking Root: The Origins of the Canadian Jewish Community*, this is a survey of that history after 1920. It will, no doubt, raise many questions among, I hope, its many readers. More research is needed, and I invite those who have additional information and different views on the subjects covered here — and on those not covered — to contribute to this fascinating, and largely unwritten, history of Canada's Jews. I offer this as a mere beginning.

List of Abbreviations in the Text

Amalgamated	Amalgamated Clothing Workers of America
AJCS	Allied Jewish Community Services, Montreal
CCIR	Central Committee for Interned Refugees
CIC	Canada Israel Committee
Congress	Canadian Jewish Congress
CPC	Communist Party of Canada
Hadassah	Hadassah-WIZO Organization of Canada
HIAS	Hebrew Immigrant Aid Society
ILGWU	International Ladies' Garment Workers' Union
IUNTW	Industrial Union of Needle Trades Workers
JCA	Jewish Colonization Association
JIAS	Jewish Immigrant Aid Society
JNF	Jewish National Fund
JOINT	American Jewish Joint Distribution Committee
KH	Keren Hayesod
KKL	Keren Kayemeth l'Yisrael
NBC	National Budgeting Conference
NCR	National Council for Refugees
RAF	Royal Air Force
RCAF	Royal Canadian Air Force
RCMP	Royal Canadian Mounted Police
RCN	Royal Canadian Navy
RNWMP	Royal North West Mounted Police

UJPO	United Jewish Peoples' Order
UJRA	United Jewish Refugee and War Relief Agencies
UJWF	United Jewish Welfare Fund, Toronto
WEC	War Efforts Committee, Canadian Jewish Congress
YMHA	Young Men's Hebrew Association
YWHA	Young Women's Hebrew Association
ZOC	Zionist Organization of Canada

CHAPTER

1

Jewish Geography of the 1920s and 1930s

The Jewish community in Canada absorbing the pre First World War immigrants and awaiting more during the 1920s and 1930s was one in transition, and in 1939 Louis Rosenberg, who directed the work of the Jewish Colonization Association (JCA) in Western Canada, gave readers of his superb book, *Canada's Jews: A Social and Economic Study of the Jews in Canada*, an excellent portrait of its evolution during these years.[1] His statistical evidence provided a highly detailed examination that surpassed any work then available on United States Jewry. Based on the Census of Canada returns for 1921 and 1931, it showed that the Dominion's Jewish geography had undergone significant changes since 1911. Overall, the Canadian Jewish population increased by 26 percent, from 125,197 in 1921 to 155,614 in 1931. Rosenberg's later surveys showed a mere 8.3 percent growth, to 168,585 in 1941. Compared with the total Canadian population between the world wars, Jews were more urbanized, more concentrated in lower-middle-class occupations, and better educated; divorce rates were higher, while fertility, death, and natural-increase rates were lower; and the Jewish population was younger.

The Jewish population was growing in major cities, especially Toronto, where it rose by 34.5 percent during the 1920s, exceeding Montreal's growth of 26.6 percent and Winnipeg's 19.0 percent.[2] The vast majority of Jewish residents in those cities were still concentrated in centretown wards: in Montreal's St. Louis and Laurier wards (where Jews were a majority), as well as in St. Michel and St. Jean Baptiste (where they were more than a third); in Toronto's Wards 4 and 5; and in Winnipeg's Main Street area, north of the

CPR yards. But suburbanization was under way as Toronto's Jews began moving into York township and Forest Hill; Montrealers into Outremont, Westmount, and Notre Dame de Grace; and Winnipegers north into newer areas of Ward 3.

Their numbers also increased in the smaller cities, such as Rouyn-Noranda, North Bay, Sudbury, Timmins, and Fort William, where resource-based industries created boom-town growth in the 1920s. In Cornwall, textile and paper factories had opened. St. Catharines, Oshawa, and Windsor, centres of automobile manufacturing, attracted rising numbers of Jewish businessmen and professionals.[3] And economic expansion created by Sarnia's petrochemical works, Hamilton's steel and numerous secondary manufacturers, and Kitchener's beer, rubber, and furniture plants, all gave rise to larger Jewish communities.

Although some towns flourished, others dwindled.[4] In the Maritimes, while the communities in Sydney, Moncton, and Fredericton grew, those in Saint John, Halifax, and Glace Bay declined. Out West, Jewish numbers were growing in Melville, Selkirk, Medicine Hat, Calgary, Edmonton, Regina, Saskatoon, Lethbridge, and Prince Albert. But those in small villages and towns, mostly in Saskatchewan, fell. Several towns in Quebec and Ontario (Kingston, Brantford, London, Sault Ste. Marie, Sherbrooke, Lachine, and Ste.-Agathe-des-Monts) showed decreases also, as did Victoria in British Columbia. Edmonton, Calgary, and Vancouver were all experiencing significant growth.[5] And as Rosenberg's volume emphasized, there was a wide dispersion of Jews in Prairie towns and villages, particularly in Saskatchewan, where Jewish populations disappeared in thirty-four places during the 1920s but turned up in sixty-four others.[6] In twelve Saskatchewan towns and villages, their numbers were significant, from 8.5 to 15 percent of the total,[7] even though life in small towns and villages was very difficult. "The majority of Jews living isolated in [them] must either cease to be Jewish except by accident of birth or must eventually leave for larger Jewish centres as soon as their children reach the age when they require Jewish education to supplement the education given in the public schools."[8] But apart from this dispersion and the general enlargement of western communities, Jewish settlement in eastern Canada was also growing, most noticeably in Ontario.[9]

Over 55 percent of Jews in 1931, in contrast to almost 51 percent of Canadians of all origins, were in what Rosenberg called the "productive age group," between twenty and fifty-nine "who are assumed to possess the full capacity to work."[10] Jews had the highest marriage rates of all Canadians over the age of fifteen; 41.33 percent were married, compared with 37.83 percent of "all origins," reflecting the fact that "Jews tended to immigrate as family units rather than as individuals."[11]

While they tended to have a higher propensity for marriage, this did not result in higher-than-average fertility rates. Between 1926 and 1936, the ten-year average Jewish birth rate was 14.2 (per 1,000), compared with 22.1 for "all origins,"[12] and the Jewish death rate was 5.5, compared with 10.3, making the Jewish rate of natural increase only two-thirds that of the national average.[13] Meanwhile, intermarriage rates were rising — but only slightly. Starting at 4.64 percent in 1926, they had increased to 5.5 percent in 1936. They were nearly twice as high for men as for women, although for virtually all other ethnic groups in Canada — the Chinese excepted — intermarriage rates were more than double.[14] Over time, then, with no new significant immigration, it would seem that Canada's Jewry would diminish in number.

Growing Jewish Urban Communities

Looking at the economic structure of Canadian Jewry, Rosenberg calculated that its gainfully employed constituted 47.54 percent of its population,[15] just marginally less than that of Canada as a whole. This was probably explained by the fact that Jews stayed in school longer than did most others.

As Jews moved out of the old inner-city areas into new suburbs, they built synagogues. In the early 1920s, Westmount's Jews erected two new structures, the Reformers' Temple Emanu-el on busy Sherbrooke Street and the Conservatives' Sha'ar Hashamayim (Gates of Heaven) on a quiet street a few blocks away. In the meantime, Toronto Reformers were completing their new Holy Blossom Temple on Bathurst Street. Whether of Romanesque and Moorish design, like Holy Blossom, or "modernistic," like most others, these substantial synagogues testified to the affluence, ambition, and self-confidence of their Jewish middle-class members. Some of these edifices included social and athletic facilities similar to those provided by nearby churches. There was no attempt at disguising Jewish identity, however. The structures could not be mistaken for churches. On the contrary, they often included domes, always prominently displayed the Star of David, and, usually, had large Hebrew lettering carved in stone over the entrance.

Not all the new synagogues bespoke such ambition, affluence, or architectural pretensions. Most were like Toronto's Rodfei Sholem's (Pursuers of Peace), a modest structure in the Kensington Market area, or the Agudath Israel Anshei Sepharade (Organization of Israel, Sephardic People), situated on Palmerston Avenue, both of them in the heart of the less affluent Jewish community, which was moving westward from the older centretown area of settlement.[16] Understated buildings were the norm in the smaller communities, too, although Windsor's Sha'ar Hashamayim (Gates of Heaven) congregation erected an impressive version of its Montreal namesake in 1931.[17] Some communities added a degree of decoration, such as Knesset Israel (Congregation of Israel), an unimposing structure in Toronto's Junction area that was adorned inside with depictions of scenes from the *Ethics of the Fathers*.[18] And if in some communities new structures were built, in others simple houses or former churches were con-

---

MORRIS "TWO-GUN" COHEN

At the time of Morris "Two-Gun" Cohen's death in 1970, he was a retired general in the Chinese army and the toast of Manchester, England. No one would have thought that the juvenile delinquent who arrived in Canada in 1905 would turn out so well. In that year, his Orthodox parents in London had banished the eighteen-year-old convicted pickpocket to Saskatchewan. They hoped the Great Plains and the untarnished optimism of North America would set their artful dodger straight. Cohen got to work on a farm outside of Whitewood. He planted crops, tended to the farm animals, and helped with the chores. And he also learned how to handle a pistol.

After a year on the farm, Cohen began wandering from Manitoba to British Columbia. He laboured in a brick yard, peddled questionable goods, and plied his trade as a con man, card sharp, and pimp. Not surprisingly, he regularly landed in police custody. If it wasn't for a twist of fate, Cohen would have been ignored by history.

Cohen was a portly man who loved Chinese food, and one evening, he walked into a Chinese-restaurant-cum-late-night-gambling-den in Saskatoon. There he stumbled into the middle of an armed robbery. Having boxed as a child, he easily clobbered the burglar. Such an act was unheard of; few white men ever came to the aid of Chinese men in early twentieth-century Canada. Cohen's actions immediately won him the respect of the Chinese community. His new Chinese friends spotted him wagering money and soon asked him to join Dr. Sun Yat-sen's political organization, the Guomindang. Cohen became a loyal member, learned of Sun's revolutionary teachings, and gave generously to various anti-Manchu funds.

Yet even with his political awakening, Cohen continued to drift. He eventually rambled to Edmonton, his arrival coinciding with the biggest land boom in the city's history. Real estate

verted for use. Whether grand or modest, the newer synagogues of the interwar years were testimony to their communities' commitment to Jewish continuity.

Jewish geography across Canada remained overwhelmingly urban. In nearly every city and town — as well as in many western villages — across the Dominion, there was a Jewish presence, if only a general store. In some, there

---

offered Cohen the ideal opportunity to combine his talents as a pickpocket, carnival talker, and gambler. In that city on the North Saskatchewan River, Cohen legally and lavishly lifted money from the pockets of unsuspecting rubes, making wads of cash unloading building lots, mines, and orchards.

When the real-estate bubble burst just prior to the start of the First World War, Cohen did what many recently unemployed men did: he enlisted. In Belgium, he and his comrades in the 8th Battalion of the Canadian Railway Troops built tracks to move troops and supplies to the front, and lived through some of the war's worst slaughter during the Battle of Passchendaele. After the Armistice, Cohen became heavily involved with the Great War Veterans' Association in Edmonton, acted as a political boss for the Chinese, and continued his advocacy for the rights of his Chinese brothers.

Life wasn't the same after the Great War. The Canadian real-estate market had not bounced back. Cohen was unsettled and wanted a change. So, in 1922, he headed to Shanghai, where his Guomindang contacts and fluency with a pistol secured him a job as a bodyguard to Dr. Sun. True to his nickname, Cohen always carried two pistols and earned a reputation as a tough customer, a man who would use his weapons to deadly effect at the slightest provocation. Following Sun's death in 1925, Cohen worked for a series of Chinese leaders. He was actively involved in the anti-Japanese war effort during the Second World War and was in Hong Kong when they conquered the colony.

With the start of the 1949 Chinese revolution, Cohen tried to re-establish his position in China. But there was no place for him in the new political pot. Even so, his time with Dr. Sun guaranteed him an extended twilight, during which he was always viewed as a friend of China and a loyal assistant to the father of that nation.

— *Daniel S. Levy*

was also a Jewish district, a group of stores constituting an ethnic sub-economy of delicatessens, bakeries, groceries, clothing stores, pawn shops, and institutions, which catered largely to a predominantly Jewish residential district close by. Such places were not "ghettos" in any sense; they were areas like Montreal's The Main, Toronto's Kensington Market, and Winnipeg's North End — areas where there was a large Jewish community and with it the opportunity to buy Jewish food, books, and religious items and attend Jewish religious, social, and political gatherings. Even a small city like Brantford, Ontario, had a tiny Jewish centrepoint near the old *shul* on Albion Street, with about a dozen Jewish families living within a four-block radius, close to Harris's grocery.[19] And in nearby Hamilton, the community centred on Cannon Street, with Boleslavsky's wonderful delicatessen serving as a favourite meeting place.

Such districts were not coterminous with all Jewish-owned businesses, especially retail stores or small workshops, which might be spread broadly across a city. These clothing stores, metal or upholstery workshops, and junk-yards were seldom oriented specifically to a Jewish clientele. Those businesses that were located in the "Jewish area," on the other hand, were specifically Jewish and were intended for a recognized and usually sizeable population. These areas were situated in close proximity to non-Jewish neighbourhoods like those populated by French Canadians and Ukrainians in The Main, Italians and Chinese near Spadina, and Ukrainians and Germans in the North End.

Even in Montreal's St. Louis and Laurier wards, where Jews were a majority, few streets or blocks were entirely Jewish; French-Canadian neighbours, stores, and churches were never far away. The same was true in the other cities. In Toronto, for example, while Harbord Collegiate was almost entirely Jewish and Central Tech largely so, the nearby Christie Pits baseball and football fields attracted a multi-ethnic presence.[20] In Winnipeg's St. John's Collegiate, Jews, while numerous, rubbed shoulders with the non-Jewish majority, which included pupils drawn from Ukrainian, Polish, and German backgrounds; together they shared the North End streets and parks. In all these major cities, then, life in Jewish districts was never largely distinct from that in non-Jewish neighbourhoods.

In Vancouver's small community, the immigrants who had settled first in the East End, and who had built a new synagogue in 1921, began moving towards the south and west very rapidly in the 1920s,[21] almost completely deserting the older area. A new Jewish community centre was built at 11th Avenue and Oak Street, reflecting the current economic improvement.[22] The shift in the city continued during the 1930s, although the old East End, now containing a substantial admixture of Asian and European residents, continued to serve as home to the stores selling Jewish foods.

JEWISH LIFE IN WINNIPEG

As the "Gateway to the West," Winnipeg had mushroomed in size during the great boom before the First World War.[23] The Jewish population had increased more than eightfold between 1901 and 1911, and by over 50 percent again to reach 14,837 in 1921.[24] It further grew to 17,435 in 1941. Thus, there was modest growth during the 1920s and 1930s, essentially mirroring the population changes in the city as a whole.[25] While almost 98 percent of all Jews remained within city limits, and mainly in Ward 3, they made a pronounced northward and eastward shift as they moved into newer and more commodious housing close to the older district and its community facilities.

Jews enjoyed a higher representation in Winnipeg's professional classes than they did in any other city in Canada at this time. This trend was accelerating. Although comprising only 7.5 percent of the population, they were 11.2 percent of its lawyers in 1931, and in 1941, 19.6 percent.[26] In these two census years, Jews were 11.5 and 18.3 percent of the doctors and 18.5 and 11.4 percent of that city's teachers. Meanwhile, Jews were a major force in commerce. By 1941, they made up more than a third of the city's retail merchants and more than two-thirds of its hawkers and peddlers. They were also overrepresented among skilled tradesmen like furriers, electricians, sheet-metal workers, tailors, and teamsters. Among women, on the other hand, the only professionals were teachers and nurses, and they were not overrepresented there. Others were retail merchants, sales people, bookkeepers and cashiers, and music teachers.

A high proportion of Winnipeg's Jews attended school. More than a third of all Jewish males had nine to twelve years of schooling, second only to the "Celto-Saxons" (Rosenberg's designation),[27] while women had even more schooling than their male counterparts. Among male Winnipegers having thirteen years or more of schooling, Jews led all other ethnic groups. At this level, however, Jewish women lagged behind the Celto-Saxons.[28]

The Winnipeg community then centred mostly in the North End, that broad area bisected by Main Street, in which thousands of Ukrainians, Poles, Germans, and others of European origin lived. Some describe the North End as an "unenclosed ghetto" where immigrants sought refuge and found some solace from what appeared to be a hostile and exclusionist environment.[29] The vibrancy of their cultural, educational, political, and social life made the North End a unique place and culturally rich, a veritable Jerusalem or Vilna, the latter a lively Lithuanian city of unparalleled Jewish intellectual life.

Winnipeg Jews never cease telling of the North End's special landscape, of restaurants, delicatessens, bakeries, barbershops, bookstores, photo studios, markets, synagogues, schools, and other monuments set in this Prairie metropolis of frigid winters and scorching summers. Jack Ludwig's story "Requiem for Bibul" recalls the flavour of its fruit peddlers in the smelly back alleys and run-down streets, horses, *shnorrers* (beggars), and rabbinical students, while Miriam Waddington's poems recount the sweetness of her youth amidst its special *Yiddishkeit*.[30]

The size of Jewish families was diminishing in the 1930s, but they were still larger than those of all other ethnic groups. In 1931, 41.6 percent of all Jewish families had three or more children, compared with 37.7 percent of East European, 27.2 percent of Scandinavian, and 24.8 percent of Celto-Saxon families. In 1936, the figures were 29.9, 28.6, 23.0, and 20.0 percent, respectively.[31] Both in 1931 and 1936, the proportion of Jewish families in Winnipeg without children was lower than that among any other ethnic group.

Housing patterns in Winnipeg were interesting, in that Jews stood behind East Europeans in the owner-occupant category in 1936: 42.1 percent as compared with 46.2 percent of all households.[32] Of all ethnic groups, Jewish households had the highest percentage, 56.5 percent, living in rented quarters as tenants or sub-tenants. This compared with 52.8, 67.6, and 61.6 percent among East Europeans, Scandinavians, and Celto-Saxons, respectively. Jews, therefore, were more likely than East Europeans to be renters, not owners, perhaps placing a higher premium on investment in business and education than in home ownership. In any case, they had larger accommodations, whether owned or rented; 62.1 percent of them lived in houses of four to seven rooms, compared with only 51.8 percent of households of all origins. Of Jewish owner-occupants, 52 percent lived in houses worth $3,000 to $8,000, compared with 43 percent of all owner-occupants.[33]

Winnipeg possessed twenty institutional buildings, including seven schools, eight synagogues, an old-people's home, a sick-benefit hall, a fraternal-lodge headquarters, a Zionist hall, and an orphanage.[34] Winnipegers also regarded Berel and Bertha Miller's bookstore at 816½ Main Street as an informal cultural home, especially for the newest immigrants.[35] Most of these institutions were clustered near Main Street above Aberdeen and thus served numerous organizations, including *landsmanshaften* (mutual-benefit organizations composed of people from the same town in Europe); free-loan, charitable, relief, and social-service societies; and many political and cultural associations.[36] Among the community's proudest achievements were its schools, which were monuments to their commitment both to continuity and to the variety of expressions of Jewish ethnicity in Winnipeg.[37]

The Winnipeg General Strike of May–June 1919, a confrontation between a united working class and city employers backed by a Dominion government determined to suppress what it believed was a challenge to legal authority, had left deep and lasting bitterness in both the city and the Jewish left-wing community. Among those Winnipeg ethnic communities blamed for the strike were several Jewish left-wing organizations. They were raided by Royal North West Mounted Police (RNWMP) officers. Desks were smashed, papers confiscated, the radical *Die Volk Stimme* (the People's Voice), a Winnipeg Yiddish weekly, was suppressed, as was its successor, *Die Naye Zeit* (the New Times). Jewish homes were likewise raided, and some Jews even feared arrest and deportation.[38] Hostility in the aftermath of the strike created anxiety and insecurity among Jews in this class-divided city[39] and affected Jewish political behaviour for many years. Several Jewish leftists were elected to municipal and provincial office. Abraham Heaps, one of the leaders of the strike, remained MP for Winnipeg North from 1925 until 1940, while Morris A. Gray served for many years as a provincial MLA.[40]

The strongest of Winnipeg's Jewish political organizations, though not necessarily the most numerous, were leftist. Those with a revolutionary outlook on world and Jewish problems established the Peretz School, which emphasized Yiddish language and literature, Jewish history, Hebrew, folk-dancing, and singing.[41] This orientation, which was emphatically socialist, secular, and nationalist, had widespread support. The school was housed in a large three-storey structure that also served a variety of social and cultural functions. Strong financial support was drawn from its members, especially its active *Mutter Farein* (Mothers' Club), which also provided women's educational programs. The mothers were also a significant political force within the system, helping to determine administrative and pedagogical policy for the school.[42] They established a kindergarten for pre-schoolers, and a full-day school.

Also on the left, the Arbeiter Ring (Workmen's Circle) operated a school with a program of instruction in Yiddish language and literature, Jewish and working-class history, current events, and singing. But doctrinal differences split its supporters, some of whom joined the Peretz School while the others, a majority, established the Liberty Temple School, which included evening seminars for adults and a syllabus with essentially the same subjects taught from a pronounced Marxist perspective.[43]

All of these institutions, as well as the synagogue congregational schools and the Talmud Torah, stressed traditional Judaism, Zionism, Hebrew, and Jewish history. Moreover, in an effort to reach the parents and the wider community, they all featured evening and Sunday extension courses, seminars for adults, and frequent lectures and conferences. In this city of varied ethnicities, the meaning of Jewish identity, not just locally, but worldwide in revolutionary USSR, in Palestine, and in North America, was debated.

Winnipeg also enjoyed a total of fifty-three Jewish *landsmanshaften*, free-loan, and sick-benefit societies.[44] The names, such as Chersoner Gubernia Landsmanshaft (People of Kherson Province) and Meziretcher Landsleit and Aid Society (People of Mezyretch), suggest the origins, transitions, and expectations of their immigrant members. There were separate societies for Jews from the provinces of Latvia, Podolia, Volhynia, and Bessarabia, as well as towns and cities like Kiev, Korets, Kremenets, Moghilev, Nikolayev, Pinsk, Pagreby, Propusk, Rowne, Vetka, Yedintsy, and Yekaterinaslav, all of them in Ukraine and Belarus. One other organization was simply called the Jewish Friends Lodge, still another the North End Hebrew Free Loan Association, while since 1924 the Achdus Free Loan Association functioned city-wide.[45] There were also three societies, the B'Not Dvorah, B'Not Sholem, and B'Not Zion (Daughters of Deborah, Peace, and Zion), that were specifically oriented to women, indicating a spirit of female independence and creativity in this male-dominated community.

Gatherings took place. Solemn marchers passed through the North End with Yiddish, Hebrew, and English banners to protest a pogrom, to mark anniversaries of old ones, and to celebrate on Balfour Day the promise of a Jewish national home in Palestine. These demonstrations marked a Jewish claim for recognition in urban public spaces, the Jewish equivalent of parades in honour of St. Patrick's Day, Orangeman's Day, and Robbie Burns Day — or, for the left, May Day.[46] Petitions were drawn up in favour of more liberal immigration to Canada. Executives were elected. Appeals for loans were heard, books carefully minuted meetings, and lists were kept of loans and repayments. These societies gave their members voices, assistance, advice, or comfort throughout the anxiety and hope of the Jewish immigrant experience. Through these associations, appeals were heard from the sick; from a distraught new widow seeking a loan to bury a husband; from desperate abandoned women and their children needing money for rent and food; from would-be small businessmen and -women wanting loans; or from lonely new immigrants asking to borrow enough for a *shifskart* (ship passage) to bring over a brother, sister, or parents.

Procedure was learned as well, though not so much from *Robert's Rules of Order* or the translations into Yiddish of parliamentary rules. In these chaotically democratic meetings, fraught with pressing needs, a new Jewish society was born. From this convocation of old East European communities there emerged a Winnipeg Jewry, schooled in communal governance and experienced in the practicalities of self-help.

Western Jewish Farm Colonies

As the western cities grew through the interwar years, the Jewish farm colonies that had been founded on the Prairies in the early 1900s began a slow decline. Louis Rosenberg, a University of Leeds economist who had taught school in the Lipton, Saskatchewan, colony from 1915 to 1919 and served as Jewish Colonization Association (JCA) director in the region from 1919 to 1940, attributed this to "the vagaries of drought, grasshoppers and world wheat prices."[47] Such an entirely reasonable explanation fitted in with the interwar context in which world wheat prices gyrated wildly and costly farm mechanization drove tens of thousands of bankrupt Western farmers off the land.[48] Rosenberg stated that the most serious decline in the number of Jewish farmers in 1931 came about because of drought conditions in Saskatchewan.[49] The same circumstances affected the settlements near Winnipeg, where Jewish farmers (at St. Anne, Gimli, Lorette, Transcona, Rosenfeld, Rosser, Bird's Hill, and West Kildonan), known to some local wags as the *milkhike Yidn* for their reliance on dairy operations, gradually succumbed to the Depression.[50]

In fact, as already noted, the number of people in the JCA farm colonies had been declining since the 1911 total of 1,316 persons. By 1921, there were 1,278, and in 1931 only 876.[51] The numbers on independent Jewish-owned farms had risen significantly, from 325 in 1911 to 1,290 in 1921 and 1,312 in 1931, but the heyday of the colonies was clearly gone. The total number of Jewish farmers fell from 405 in 1911 to 314 in 1921 and 191 in 1931.[52]

This decline probably was not entirely a result of "climatic and economic conditions," as Rosenberg stated, or of the lack of a sufficient institutional base to support Jewish community life.[53] The real problem was that Jewish farmers were seriously undercapitalized. The average value of a "Jewish farm" in Saskatchewan in 1911 was $3,086, compared with the average of $8,766 for all farms.[54] This enormous gap narrowed over the next ten years and disappeared by 1931, but even then, Jewish farmers grew significantly less wheat and oats than the average farmer, had less improved land per farm, and invested less money in implements. As late as 1931, one of every five Jewish farmers owned an automobile, and one in seven a tractor — compared with one of every two and one in every three non-Jewish farmers.[55] The ratios for combine ownership were even worse. Barring exceptions, such as the Hoffers at Sonnenfeld and "Uncle" Mike Usiskin at Edenbridge, Jews as a group had not succeeded at Western farming.

The JCA, which supported these farmers with loans, mortgages, advice, and grants, encountered serious discontent in 1930 among some of the Hirsch colony settlers because of a dispute over land titles and other matters.[56] Immigration department officials like F. C. Blair took note of these events, which coloured the department's very sceptical view of Jews as farmers.

Despite the vagaries of prices and the tyranny of fixed high costs, however, some Jewish farmers were succeeding and, overall, material conditions in the colonies in the 1920s had improved considerably. On a visit to the colonies in the early 1920s, Vladimir Grossman, a Montreal Yiddish journalist, observed prosperity:

> [T]he grain prices were very high, and a series of bumper-crops made for optimism and material welfare. . . . On the whole it was a period of work and growth. The younger generation was tingling with youthful vigor. New forces were evident on all sides. Almost all homesteads had grown beyond their original dimension. The 160 acres had been trebled, quadrupled and sometimes quintupled in area, and as is usual, the appetite of the farmers was whetted with the eating. They were convinced that the more land they had the better off they would be.[57]

He saw "splendid farm equipment, . . . expensive threshing machines and huge tractors . . . splendid horses . . . sleek cattle and yards full of chickens." At Edenbridge, farmers concentrated on growing wheat, and while Hirsch farms were being ravaged by an infestation of locusts, farmers there nevertheless were "looking forward to better times."[58]

Grossman shrewdly concluded, however, that the JCA had made a serious mistake, because the colonies were so "scattered and far flung." "Why such illogical and unintelligible planning? . . . " he asked. The distances between the settlements were so vast as to allow only the most infrequent contact. The farmers were "castaways." "Was no other plan available? Was it really impossible to build their colonies in some such way as to link them together, to create one large rural community and establish a contact between them? Was that planned or just hit and miss colonization?"[59] Despite these reservations, however, Grossman was optimistic. He wrote a book, *The Soil's Calling*, about what he saw and was so encouraged that he thought farming offered an opportunity for Jewish "young people with no future in the cities . . . [who] should be directed land-ward."[60]

Still, the existence was rough and demanding, especially during the lean years of the 1930s. No better insight can be gained than by reading Mike Usiskin's *Oksen Und Motoren* (translated as *Uncle Mike's Edenbridge*), about life on his colony north of Humbolt, in the Park Belt of the Saskatchewan north country. Written by a somewhat crusty old man who had toiled a lifetime on his farmstead, this memoir speaks of his love for the land, the freedom he found in clearing it, the joy of harvesting and helping neighbours — Jew and Gentile alike — and of the contentment of a simple life far from the corrupting city.[61] He recorded with delight the numerous social gatherings: dances, musicals, plays, pageants, and addresses by visiting speakers.[62]

Despite those rosy remembrances of simple pleasures amid constant toil, there were social problems at Edenbridge. Usiskin bitterly recalled that "though we had nearly everything we needed, one important thing was missing: unity."[63] The colonists never formed a coherent group, sharing the same origins, religious beliefs, or social outlook. Those like Usiskin who had hoped to create a co-operative way of life similar to some of the new Jewish settlements in Palestine were disappointed by these dissensions. "Our dreams were shattered," he lamented. The colony lived on nevertheless, buttressed by stalwarts like him who worked the land until they died.

Land of Hope, the memoirs of Israel Hoffer, a pioneer farmer in southern Saskatchewan near the colony of Sonnenfeld, tell a similar story of strife. Poverty, confusion, jealousy, and discontent with JCA's policies led to bitterness and, sometimes, to violence.[64] The hardships of life were too much for most people. "My parents were thirteen years in Hirsch farming . . . ," one daughter of colonists remembers. "They had a hard time . . . The last few years we were there the crops didn't yield so very good."[65] Lonely, poor, inexperienced, and uncertain of the future, Jewish farmers — like so many others during the Dirty Thirties — tended to give up and drift to the cities and towns. Many stuck it out at Sonnenfeld, however, while a few new colonists brought over by the JCA infused renewed life and helped for a few years to keep the colony going.[66]

With problems obviously showing up, Jewish officials were worried about the future of the colonies. L. Mallach, a writer for the *Keneder Adler*, travelled west in the summer of 1929 doing an on-the-spot survey of troubled Edenbridge. According to him, it was crucial that Jewish colonization succeed. "Unless we encourage more people to go on the land in Western Canada, there is a great danger that the doors of Canada will close entirely upon the Jews."[67] In his view, the JCA's practice of forcing settlers to whom it loaned money to sign over their farms until the loans were repaid — really only a form of mortgage — weakened the colonies. This undermined their self-respect and their desire to improve farms that, they assumed, no longer belonged to them.

Mallach had little use for the Jewish Colonization Association, an international organization centred in Paris, having observed its extensive efforts to establish Jewish colonies in Argentina, efforts that failed because of misguided policies. He thought the JCA insensitive and arrogant, alleging that its new Canadian director "has never so much as taken it upon himself nor did he think it advisable to go in person to [Edenbridge] so as to see things with his own eyes, to get a glimpse of the outlook of the colonists."[68] Consequently, the colonists were despondent. "Out of the eyes of every one of [them] despair stared me in the face," he wrote.[69] "Who is it that is going to reap the harvest of our toil?" they asked him. "I looked at their hands, so much like the plowed up fields and they looked to me not like skin and flesh but rather like fossilized rock, their faces were brown and burnt and their lips a froth-like blue."

Like their Ukrainian neighbours in the Park Belt area, Jewish farmers built their first homes and barns of specially selected logs that had been cut and dragged into place by horses or oxen. Moving from tent or lean-to to a cabin was a big step for a settler, and he usually required the help of several men, at least one of them experienced in this type of construction. Generally, these one-room log houses were not more than cabins, probably sixteen by twenty feet, with floors of pounded earth or of wooden slats.[70] One doorway and a window or two were cut out, the doors covered with slats and windows with greased newspapers. Roofs were made of shakes, shingles, or thatch and anchored down by poles and stones. A fireplace and chimney made of mud and straw was added along one wall while the spaces between the logs were filled (inside and out) with caulking made of clay, mud, moss, and animal hair to keep out the snow and cold, which came all too early. Like their Ukrainian neighbours, Jews often whitewashed the outside of the house. Barns were constructed on the same lines, and no farm was without a pit privy set at a discreet distance from the house.[71] A few years later, when sales of crops or JCA loans made farmers more prosperous, a "proper" house was built of sawn lumber. Such a home was likely a two-storey building of six or seven rooms, with a kitchen, a parlour, and a dining room downstairs and several bedrooms upstairs. It might even have an indoor bathroom!

In the towns and villages scattered across the Saskatchewan landscape, there were many Jewish storekeepers who knew enough Ukrainian and German to serve the immigrant farmers better than their Anglo-Saxon competitors, who probably knew none of these languages.[72] With its twenty to thirty Jewish families, Melville was typical, although larger than most of these towns. Here Jewish families — children especially — tried to balance their Canadian and Jewish identities. Ruth Bellan belonged to both Canadian Girls in Training (CGIT), which with Christian prayers caused her to wonder what she was doing there, and to Young Judaea, a Zionist organization that stressed Jewish identity and pride in the Zionist experiments in Palestine.[73] In Birch Hills, Gretna, Plum Coulee, Altona, and Grandview, the towns where her father opened one ill-fated store after another, Fredelle Bruser felt the angst of being a Jewish child, the only one in her town, who was denied the experience of Christmas in her Prairie community.[74]

Out in these small towns and villages, where most Jews survived on mutual support, Anne Werb remembered going from the hamlet of Richard, Saskatchewan, to a nearby village for the High Holy Days:

> I remember we went to the Leo Goldstein family in Hafford for Rosh Hashonah and Yom Kippur where other Jewish families from small towns were gathered. They had a minyan [the quorum of ten men traditionally required for congregational services]. Mrs. Goldstein was such a *berye* [an efficient housekeeper]. She used to feed us all. They used to make up beds in the store. We used to get kosher [ritually slaughtered] meat by train from Saskatoon. . . . My parents were very religious. I wouldn't dream of eating non-kosher meat. In North Battleford, they sometimes got kosher meat from Regina but mostly from Saskatoon. Also, in the wintertime they used to bring in a *shokhet* [ritual slaughterer]. He used to butcher and we used to freeze it.[75]

After moving to North Battleford, the Werbs enjoyed an active community life:

> Our community was famous for its hospitality. Jewish travelers who were supposed to have stopped over in Saskatoon used to come to North Battleford for the weekend [instead]. If we had a brit, bar mitzvah, or wedding we invited the community, including non-Jewish friends. We liked to celebrate.[76]

Jewish accounts of relationships with neighbours usually stress conviviality and co-operation.[77] Still, the stereotypes of Jews that persisted among some East European immigrants on the Prairies provided an underlay of antisemitism.[78]

Although failing, the Jewish farm settlements in Western Canada were unique in North America. While thousands of Jews lived on farms in the United States, an estimated one hundred thousand in 1930, all the surviving settlements by that time were close to the major eastern cities and even the most successful of them, at Woodbine, New Jersey, was struggling by the 1930s.[79] Though founded out on the western frontier, the Canadian experiment was in many ways more similar to the JCA's colonies on the Argentinian pampas. Both were intended to create a new Jew, a farmer who toiled like others and was committed to staying on the land, a veritable Jewish peasant. Before the Second World War, many assumed that this could be accomplished only in the West. Assessing the small Jewish farming community near Ste.-Sophie, north of Montreal, Mallach commented: "Jewish colonization, were it to be established in the East rather than in the West," would have no stability "because farming . . . is not the same as colonizing."[80] To him, farming meant "the production of farm articles," and colonizing implied permanence.

While this assumption might have been based on the success of some of the original settlers, such as Mike Usiskin and Israel Hoffer, it failed to recognize that idealism alone did not guarantee permanence. The inexorable market forces of profit and loss determined by soil, weather, technology, and prices; the changing values of family members, especially of children; the need for communal institutions which was difficult for only a few families to provide; and the pressure of an increasingly invasive materialistic and urban culture all combined to undermine and ultimately destroy the Jewish agricultural ideal in Western Canada.

After 1945, the JCA settled some Holocaust-survivor families on farms in the Niagara peninsula and southwestern Ontario. While some of them were

---

Ruins and Memories of the Hirsch Colony

Eli Mandel

near Hirsch a Jewish cemetery:
ann is taking pictures again
while I stand in the uncut grass
counting the graves: there are forty
I think
the Hebrew puzzles me
the wind moving the grass
over the still houses of the dead

from the road a muffled occasional
roar cars passing no one there
casts a glance at the stone trees
the unliving forest of Hebrew graves

in the picture I stand arms outstretched
as if waiting for someone
I am
in front of the gates you can see
the wind here   the grass
always bending the stone unmoved

rabbi berner's farm:
record your searching for the place
the years of childhood blown across
has scattered like the jews of Hirsch
wherever secondary highways lead
through renewed green fields roads
passing cattle sheds
his first wife
one son   friends   inhabit land lying
here or close to other townships
of the dead   he is alone
an island now
under warm rains and cedar

not even ruins here

From *Out of Place: Poems by Eli Mandel* (Don Mills: Musson Book Co., 1977).

successful, it was usually a one-generation phenomenon. As had been true of the West a generation earlier, most of the youth moved to the cities, where some of them treasured their memories of farm life — but at a safe distance. Nostalgia lingered, however. For many years, former residents of the Trochu colony in Alberta, now living in Los Angeles, formed their own club, met for dinner once a month, and reminisced about the old days.[81]

Rise of Toronto

In central Canada, Toronto's commerce and industry in the 1920s and 1930s began to rival that of Montreal. Its Jewish community approached Montreal's in size and wealth, increasing from 34,770 in 1921 to 46,751 in 1931 and 49,046 in 1941.[82] Although Montreal's Jewish population was almost one-quarter larger than Toronto's in 1921, the difference declined significantly over the next twenty years. Jews were the largest non-Anglo-Celtic ethnic group in the city.[83] Meanwhile, the Jewish population was gradually moving westward in the belt between Queen and Bloor streets, past University, Beverley, Spadina, and Bathurst Street towards Dovercourt.[84] One scholar found that "on many streets, such as Kensington Avenue, individual block[s] . . . which had been entirely non-Jewish were 80% or even 100% Jewish by 1931" and that 63 percent of Jewish families owned the premises they inhabited.[85] But this was by no means a Jewish ghetto. In the areas known as St. John Ward, the McCaul Street enclave, or Kensington Market, Jews had neighbours of Italian, Chinese, Polish, Ukrainian, and other origins.

Despite some segregation, self-imposed or otherwise, a degree of integration was taking place in the city's public schools. Immigrant parents were eager for their children, in the view of the historian Lynne Marks, to "become more Canadianized and thus better able to succeed in Canadian society . . . but only so long as it did not threaten their Jewishness."[86] Although they came from East European cultures in which women's roles set limits on their formal education in the 1920s, immigrants were anxious to send their daughters — not just their sons — to academic schools, like Harbord Collegiate. Parents believed that secular education — in Canada, open to women as well as men — was just as appropriate for their daughters as it was for others. It promised status, secular culture, and offered a route to Canadianization. In the process of migration, therefore, young women achieved degrees of both emancipation within the Jewish community and integration into Canadian society.

On average, Jewish children were doing well in Toronto's public schools, according to tests administered in 1926 to pupils at Ryerson Public School, where they comprised 80 percent of the student body.[87] Even though the language spoken at home usually was Yiddish, Jewish pupils not only had higher scores on IQ tests than Gentiles, but also excelled in "silent reading," arithmetic, and, in general, had "a greater percentage above the average," and surpassed Gentiles in the "superior" and "very superior" categories.[88] These results, the survey reported, accorded with those achieved in New York and California, although it was noted that at Ryerson, "while Jews are fairly representative of their race as such, the Gentiles are of a lower social order than

---

The Nineteen Thirties Are Over

Miriam Waddington

The nineteen thirties
are over; we survived
the depression, the Sacco-
Vanzetti of childhood
saw Tom Mooney smiling
at us from photographs,
put a rose on the grave
of Eugene Debs, listened
to our father's stories
of the Winnipeg strike and
joined the study groups
of the OBU always keeping
one eye on the revolution.

Later we played records
with thorn needles, Josh
White's Talking Union and
Prokofief's Lieutenant Kije,
shuddered at the sound of
bells and all those wolves
whirling past us in snow
on the corner of Portage
and Main, but in my mind
summer never ended on the
shores of Gimli where we
looked across to an Icelandic
paradise we could never see
the other side of; and I
dreamed of Mexico and shining
birds who beckoned to me
from the gold-braided lianas
of my own wonder.

These days I step out
from the frame of my wind-
battered house into Toronto
city; somewhere I still
celebrate sunlight, touch
the rose on the grave of
Eugene Debs but I walk
carefully in this land
of sooty snow; I pass the
rich houses and double
garages and I am not really
this middle-aged professor
but someone from
Winnipeg whose bones ache
with the broken revolutions
of Europe, and even now
I am standing on the heaving
ploughed-up field
of my father's old war.

From Gerri Sinclair and Morris Wolfe, eds., *The Spice Box: An Anthology of Jewish Canadian Writing* (Toronto: Lester & Orpen Dennys, 1981): 110.

those of most Gentile school districts, and hence are scarcely representative of the Gentile race."[89]

Most Jews had to scramble for a living while trying to adjust to new cultural realities. Allan Grossman, later a member of the Ontario Legislature and a cabinet minister, remembered the family tensions ensuing from these circumstances:

> As I look back at our family, it seems that the struggle for existence engaged our attention so much that we missed a great deal. There was a lot of bickering over such matters as who was paying what in the house and whether one was being treated better than another. There were seldom family outings except to the synagogue. Father must have been bitterly disappointed at the lack of zeal some of us showed for his strictly Orthodox faith. Perhaps this spiritual separation of immigrant parents from their children is part of the price of migration.[90]

Influenced by factors such as housing availability and opportunities for work in the Spadina district clothing factories, Jewish demography in Toronto was also in part dictated by legally enforceable restrictive covenants preventing them and other "undesirable" groups from buying property in certain areas of the city.[91] Nevertheless, some Jewish grocers, tailors, peddlers, salesmen, contractors, butchers, and junk dealers dabbled in real estate,[92] achieving modest upward mobility. Some itinerant peddlers of dry goods, for example, became small-scale storekeepers, proudly posing with their families for an opening-day portrait before the shop window.[93]

Immigrant Organizations in Toronto

In this community still largely composed of immigrants, the local *landsmanshaften*, fraternal orders, mutual-benefit and friendly societies functioned outside the established loop of "philanthropy," fund-raising campaigns, and boards of governors. With their welfare dimensions, provisions for burial, sickness or death benefits, familiarity, comfort, interest-free loans, friendly advice, and democratic character, the *landsmanshaften* possessed a *heymishe* (homelike) quality missing in the community-wide fund-raising campaigns. They provided also a "wraparound culture" of social and cultural activities that involved their members in regular, almost familial, association.

The Workmen's Circle and the Jewish National Workers' Alliance, both of them political organizations, also provided life insurance as well as sickness and death benefits.[94] By 1945, Toronto also had twenty-eight mutual-benefit societies, with memberships ranging from thirty-eight to 594, and Jewish lodges in the non-sectarian fraternal orders like the Knights of Pythias, the Ancient Order of Foresters, and the Independent Order of Odd Fellows. Formed to meet practical needs in the event of sickness or death, these associations grew from a total of 1,086 members in 1911 to 3,120 in 1921, 5,600 in 1931, 6,700 in 1941, and 9,500 in 1945.[95] Nearly half of all Jewish males between twenty and fifty-five years of age belonged.[96] The majority of members were wage earners, artisans, and salaried employees. For example, the Peretz Branch of the Jewish National Workers' Alliance had thirty-four wage earners and fifteen artisans among its sixty-eight members in 1941.[97] Of the United Jewish Peoples' Order (UJPO), a Communist organization, 441 members in 1936, or 68 percent, were wage earners, the vast majority of them needle workers. This radical left-wing group also included a few middle-class "bourgeois": thirty-four merchants and peddlers, nine doctors and lawyers, and three manufacturers.[98]

The names of most Toronto *landsmanshaften*, like those in Winnipeg, proclaimed their founders' origins. Most were named after towns in the Kielce area of southwestern Poland: Driltzer from Der Ilza; Stashiver from Stazow; Beizetchener from Beizetshin; Ozerover from Ozarow; Lagover from Lagow; Tzomerer from Sandomierz; Aptover from Opatow; Silipover from Slupca; Czenstochover from Czestochowa; Keltzer from Kielce; Lipsker from Lipsko; Ostrovtzer from Ostrowiec; Wierzbnicker from Wierzbnik; Iwansker from Iwanska; and Shedlower from Siedlce. There were the Warshaver from Warsaw, and a society of Jews from Romania.

While Polish Jews seemed to dominate here, other societies highlighted the presence of Jews from other places. The Husiatiner was made up of Galicians who followed the Husiatyn branch of Hassidism Society.[99] The Kiever group came from Ukraine, while the Minsker and the Mozirer derived from cities in Belarus.[100] Another society was named Anshei New York,[101] while yet another was grandly entitled Hebrew Men of England, both probably comprising East European Jews who lived for a few years in these places before moving to Toronto. For many, the borrowed prestige of the British Empire, whose benevolence towards Jews was evidenced by the Balfour Declaration and the League of Nations Mandate for Palestine, left a lasting impression.[102] New York was an equally important source of inspiration for North American Jews, as the names of a number of major Toronto Jewish business concerns testify.[103] Other societies were based on Jewish tradition, such as Chevra Mishnaith (Students of the Mishnah), or were given names like the Hebrew Friendly, Judaean Benevolent, Sons of Abraham, Tifereth Israel (Glory of Israel), Hebrew Sick Benefit, Beth Aaron, Agudath Achim (Club of Brothers), or, grandly, Pride of Israel. Other associations, those with less formal structures usually, were attached to the few Hassidic rabbis, like the distinguished Rabbi Yehudah Yudel Rosenberg (known as the Skaryszewer Ilui, the Genius of Skaryszew) who immigrated to Toronto in 1913 and six years later moved to Montreal, where he taught and wrote until his death in 1935.[104]

One thing that distinguished these Jewish societies from non-Jewish ones was their purchase and management of cemeteries — they owned 40 percent of all Jewish cemetery land — to keep their members' burial costs low.[105] Comparing Jewish and non-Jewish societies in Ontario, one study found that Jews had lower death and similar sickness rates, and roughly five to six times the hospitalization rates of non-Jews.[106] On average, Jews, however, paid at least twice as much in dues to their societies for these benefits and the support the societies gave to local Jewish philanthropies.[107] Of vital benefit to members were medical services, which were provided by long-term contracts, with doctors guaranteeing treatment to members and families in return for an annual per capita payment.[108] The societies paid out seven or eight times more than non-Jewish associations for medical attention.

Although the *landsmanshaften* might have provided small loans to their members, some Canadian cities, like many in the United States, had lending societies that served the entire community.[109] The 1918 annual statement of the Montreal Association's registry of applicants offers a valuable window on contemporary Jewish penny capitalism. Of 1,090 applicants, 31 were classified as ritual slaughterers, Hebrew teachers, or Jewish book sellers; 24 as merchants or manufacturers; 46 as peddlers (customer, jewellery, spectacles, dry goods, tea, coffee, etc.); 21 as shopowners (plumbing, blacksmith, tinsmith, upholstering, and cooperage); and 25 as agents. And there were many in more humble occupations: 16 farmers; 11 contractors (building, electrical, painting, carpentry); 38 custom tailors, tailor shopowners, or contractors; and 44 milk, bread, fruit or ginger-ale peddlers. There were owners of 47 shoe-repairing stores; 77 country, junk, rag, second-hand clothing, furniture, and fur peddlers; 54 small proprietors; 345 working men; and 239 store owners (jewellery, drug, clothing, dry goods, hardware, shoes, fruit, grocery, second-hand, butcher, bread, and barber shop).[110] While most of these loans were for business purposes, thirty-eight were for remittances to Europe and five "to marry off a daughter."

These free-loan societies reported considerable activity during the 1930s. Loans usually ran from fifteen to twenty-five dollars for four- to six-month periods; borrowers signed notes, which required one or two endorsers depending on the amount borrowed. Toronto's Association took no other forms of security, but Montreal's accepted jewellery and government bonds.[111] In the Depression year of 1932, with a capital of $53,849, the Montreal

Association loaned $105,227 to 960 borrowers (an average of $109.66), but reported that due dates for one-third of its loans had to be extended and that it was difficult to get endorsers. The situation in Toronto that year was similar. Virtually all of the $25,437 on loan to 653 borrowers was repaid, but more slowly than the year before. Then the situation worsened considerably. In 1937, it was reported that while the Association was offering "extensive delays to borrowers and their endorsers . . . the subscription list has become depleted in the last few years and several hundred members are needed now . . . to maintain . . . [this] sorely needed Jewish aristocracy of true service."[112]

By 1935, loans in Montreal rose 23.5 percent to $130,104, an average of $115.95, and in 1937 another 27.59 percent to $166,000, an average of $136.06. Toronto loans, meanwhile, rose from $24,775 in 1935 to $37,235 in 1937, an increase of 50.29 percent, and the average loan nearly doubled.[113] Despite mounting pressures during the difficult 1930s, however, reported losses were minuscule.[114] On the whole, then, borrowers paid back their loans, although during these hard years some required extensions.

Montreal: Language, Education, and Religion

Home to nearly one-half of Canada's Jews, Montreal* — the poet Abraham Moses Klein's beloved "City Metropole" — was also experiencing transformations: growth, migration, and integration. From 52,287 persons in 1921, the Jewish population reached 63,721 in 1941.[115] By the 1920s, virtually the entire city section from the waterfront north in a belt along St. Lawrence Boulevard ("the Main") to the lower reaches of Outremont constituted a huge, predominantly Jewish enclave of factories, shops, synagogues, and tightly packed housing. Although Jews lived in other districts, the fact that this "Jewish quarter" was at the geographical centre of the city and divided the French and the English sections of Montreal was symbolic of the precarious marginality of the Jewish presence to both communities.[116] The Jewish population in the suburbs of Outremont and Westmount (then separate municipalities) grew by nearly 60 percent each, while the city of Montreal's grew by 21.78 percent during these years. Clearly, the shifts out of the older areas of settlement along the St. Lawrence/Main axis to the western suburbs was well under way. Still, the vast bulk of the city's Jewish population lived on the eastern side of Mount Royal, though the movement there was northward and westward into the eastern fringes of Outremont.

---

* In the context outlined here, Montreal includes Greater Montreal and the municipalities of Outremont, Westmount, Verdun, and Lachine.

A similar shift to the westernmost suburb of Notre Dame de Grace and, to a minor extent, to Lachine on the western tip of the Island of Montreal was also in progress. This migration, especially of Canadian-born Jews, indicated the modest prosperity reached during the 1920s as families sought newer and more salubrious suburbs.[117] In the older areas and in parts of Outremont, the housing usually took the form of the traditional Montreal "plex" model. This included two to six apartments, some of them accessible only by winding outside stairways, which were a challenge in the best of weather conditions and often a serious problem during the city's ferocious snow and ice storms.[118]

Migration to "better" areas and suburbanization were accompanied by a growing integration into Montreal's anglophone and, to a much lesser degree, francophone cultures. A sociological survey of 512 Montreal Jewish families in 1938 showed that while in 9.4 percent of Jewish households French was spoken, English was used in all others, except for the 5.7 percent of households that relied solely on Yiddish.[119] In nearly 80 percent of homes, combinations of English and Yiddish; English and French; Yiddish, English, and French; English, Yiddish, and Hebrew; and other mixtures of languages including English were spoken. Yiddish was the sole language used in 13 percent of homes in the old area of settlement, but was negligible, except as a second language, among families in the suburbs. The same trend was evident in homes where both English and Yiddish were employed, although overall this combination was used in 59.6 percent of all Jewish homes in the survey. Thus, while English was the dominant language in Jewish Montreal, Yiddish remained strong, and French had attained only a minor presence.

The same survey showed English as the preferred language of newspaper and periodical readers, although in the older areas parents bought Yiddish dailies by a considerable margin, notably choosing those from New York over the local *Keneder Adler*.[120] But among children, even those in the old area, English publications far outranked Yiddish ones, while those in French and Hebrew ranked low. Grandparents in three areas, though diminishingly in the suburbs, preferred Yiddish reading material. Put another way, the Montreal English dailies, the Anglo-Jewish *Canadian Jewish Chronicle*, and English popular and educational weeklies all outranked Yiddish publications as the choice of readers in Montreal, even in the older areas, where some Yiddish was used in a majority of homes. The transition to English culture, obviously, was well under way. Without the antisemitism that barred even fuller Jewish integration into Montreal's anglophone society, such a transformation would probably have extended further.

Still, Montreal's Jews were not losing their ethnic identity, according to the survey's data on Jewish club or association membership; 44.3 percent of all parents belonged to a Jewish organization.[121] Children, however, preferred the recreational clubs like the Young Men's Hebrew Association (YMHA) and Young Women's Hebrew Association (YWHA), perhaps because others were not readily available. Jewish education was also of crucial importance. Canadian Jewish Congress surveys revealed that 82.28 percent of boys and 52.7 percent of girls had some formal Jewish education,[122] reflecting the stark reality that book learning for girls was considered of lesser importance (they were traditionally trained at home in the domestic arts); nearly half of all Jewish girls in Montreal had no formal Jewish education of even the most elementary kind.

However, the type of education children received was very uneven: 53.2 percent of them went to private schools, or *heders* (rooms), which operated after regular school hours and on Sundays and were run by freelance teachers. Here they received private tutoring, usually consisting of preparation for bar mitzvah, which normally ceased once the ceremony was over at age thirteen. Almost a third of Montreal Jewish children attended either Talmud Torah or the Peretz School, which provided a rounded program of Jewish history and culture. The Talmud Torah offered a program of traditional studies, while the Peretz School provided national and progressive education as well as considerable instruction in Yiddish.[123] Thus, Jewish associational life was healthy, but Jewish education appears to have had serious shortcomings.

As for synagogue attendance, figures in the 1938 survey showed that among males (women's attendance was not measured, probably because it was not considered mandatory by Orthodox Jews), 27.9 percent (in the suburbs only 17.6 percent) of grandfathers attended synagogue daily, in comparison with just 6.5 percent of fathers and 2.2 percent of sons.[124] Of course, the time available for daily synagogue attendance among the generations was different. Among fathers, however, 27.5 percent attended Sabbath services — though only 9.8 percent in the suburbs — while 34.5 percent of sons attended, with a remarkably high 43.1 percent in the suburbs, where new synagogues featured special Oneg Shabbat services on Friday nights.[125] On the three major holidays of Sukkot, Pesach, and Shavuot, 34.6 percent of fathers attended and 22.6 percent of sons, with slightly higher percentages in the suburbs. This data suggests that formal religious observance was high in Montreal among all three generations of Jewish males.

The survey's evidence on food-purchasing patterns adds to the impression of a religiously observant community. Almost 92 percent of all those questioned, even a surprisingly high 82.3 percent of the more acculturated Jews living in the suburbs, reported that they bought their meat in Jewish stores, in all likelihood kosher butcher shops. Fish and bread, too, were purchased in Jewish stores by 77.7 and 67.6 percent of those surveyed.[126] Loyalty to *kashrut* (the rules governing kosher food), then, was an important feature of Montreal

Jewish life. In all measures, including *kashrut*, synagogue attendance, education, and organizational affiliation, as well as in the speaking of a significant amount of Yiddish at home, Montreal Jewry remained by and large a traditional Jewish community. But as shown, while religious life thrived, education efforts did not reach nearly half of all girls and extended for most boys only until age thirteen.

Community Organization

Governance was a seriously divisive issue in all three cities. Strong efforts in Montreal, Toronto, and Winnipeg in the 1920s and 1930s to establish a *kehillah* (community) organization essentially for the supervision of *kashrut* were unsuccessful.[127] Moves to ensure a supply of kosher meat were highly contentious everywhere.[128] At issue was profit for the butchers, the *mashgichim* (inspectors), and the rabbis, who also sought the prestige of being the final authority in such important matters. To the Orthodox Jews, *kashrut* was a fundamental religious requirement, and for the many non-observant Jews, a matter of tradition and preference. However, the bitter and protracted disputations, lawsuits, and appeals for political intervention in Montreal, Toronto, and Winnipeg served only to confuse and, probably, disgust the observant, while amusing the sceptics. At the same time, the entire Jewish community was held up to potential ridicule for venting its religious disputes in public. Beyond this lay the significant fact that the internal unity of the community was fragile indeed. In the case of Toronto, there was serious acrimony between the older Jewish community, composed of Lithuanians, Russians, and Galicians, and the newly arrived Polish element.[129] Among many Jews struggling to make ends meet and those on the left, moreover, the issue of *kashrut* may not have been of paramount importance.[130]

Organized philanthropy in Montreal since 1863 had been dispensed by the Baron de Hirsch Society and a number of other loosely associated organizations. In 1916, the newly formed Federation of Jewish Philanthropies brought all of these groups under one fund-raising umbrella.[131] Allocations to the individual charities were determined by the federation's executive, composed mainly of the big givers. Similar organizations were established in Toronto the same year and, later, in Winnipeg and Hamilton.

While the federations had no legislative powers, they were able usually to influence community developments through the allocations process. Dominated by men of the established older community, they began to insist on "scientific philanthropy," which discouraged volunteerism and the more open-handed approach of old-fashioned spontaneous charity in favour of more formalized structures and professional social workers.[132]

The federations also assumed such new responsibilities as the provision of old-age homes in the three biggest cities and of Jewish hospitals in Montreal and Toronto, as well as social and recreational facilities for youth. All of these institutions required boards of management and, increasingly, professional staff. Thus, a small Jewish civil service was formed, and the donors who sustained the federations enjoyed even larger powers than ever.

Athletic facilities were another area of communal effort. In all three major cities, YMHA and YWHAs were formed to organize athletic teams and provide facilities for Jewish youth. Besides serving as outlets for youthful energy and competitiveness, and as places where Jewish youth could socialize, these organizations were yet another form of acculturation to North American society, in which athleticism and sportsmanship were highly admired. The YM/YWHA also offered a Jewish environment to their youth, who might not have felt welcome in other athletic venues like the YM/YWCA, which were pronouncedly Christian in character. Jewish teams competed in football, basketball, softball, and soccer in city and provincial leagues; the Winnipeg YMHA football team even won several city championships in the 1930s.[133] Making a statement in the venue of athleticism as Jews was important. Professional boxers like Toronto's Baby Yack and Sammy Luftspring and amateur wrestlers like the Oberlander brothers of Montreal often wore the Star of David as an assertion, a challenge to opponents, and an emotional rallying emblem for the Jewish spectators at these events. Sports, then, besides serving as a valuable activity in its own right, provided an additional vehicle for the assertion of Canadian Jewish identity.

Connections with kinfolk still in *der alter heim* (the old home) continued. Immigrants corresponded with their families in Europe, sending news, remittances, and photographs of their spouses and children (often standing proudly in front of a house or a new car), and in return received family and regional news, gossip, and publications. There was a continuing engagement with the "old country" families and places, which, to Jews now living in Canada, were remembered with considerable nostalgia. Such feelings were expressed in songs like "Belz," an enormously popular Yiddish theatre song "that expressed longing for hometowns in Eastern Europe."[134] While the song was about Belz, its nostalgia was probably typical of that of Jews from any place in that heartland of Jewish culture:

> Tell me, old man, tell me quickly because I want to know everything now: how does the little house look that once sparkled? Does the little tree I planted still bloom?

Belz, my little town, Belz
my little home where I spent my childhood years
Belz, my little town, Belz
in the poor little house where I laughed with all the children
Every shabes I'd run to read by the river
Belz, my little town, Belz
my little home where I had so many dreams.[135]

Many other Yiddish songs reflected these sentiments, such as "Bay dem Shtetle," which reminisces about the "little town . . . a little house with a green roof, and around the house many trees grow" and the days when "Father and Mother and Khanele and I . . . lived together there."[136] There were songs like "Warshe," about Warsaw,[137] and "Die Roumanish Kretchme" ("In a Romanian Inn").[138] There was "Galitsye" ("Galicia") and the all-time favourite, the show-stopping "Rumania, Rumania," whose, for those days, risqué lyrics recount the joys of life in a "wonderful land, where it was a pleasure to live, and to delight in the joys of wine, women, and camaraderie."[139] *"Ay, s'iz a mekhaye, beser ken nit zayn, ay, a fargenigin iz nor Rumenish veyn."*

Thus, recalling the old home in the old town by the old river in a life of simple pleasures was very much part of Canadian Jewish popular culture in the interwar years. In this landscape of memory, longing was mixed with pride in hometown distinctions and in luminaries such as distinguished rabbis. Not yet fully comfortable in their new home, many Jews still identified with *der alter heim* of vivid memory, making Eastern Europe a continuing part of their mental and cultural map.

Other popular songs, tunes, and ballads that circulated through the Jewish quarter on song sheets and phonograph records told of love, romance, marital problems, immigrant adjustment, wronged women, loving mothers, death, and financial embarrassment, as well as coarse and vulgar material about gamblers, prostitutes, criminals, and other low-life elements.[140] Poignantly soulful songs like "A Brivele der Mamen," about an immigrant's lonely mother in the old country, and "My Yidishe Momme," about neglect of filial piety towards an abandoned mother in the old neighbourhood,[141] were among the most popular songs. When itinerant actors and singers performed these soulful tunes and poignant dramas, there wasn't a dry eye in the house. Few, if any, of these songs were specifically Canadian in origin or content; along with the Yiddish theatre and, by the 1930s, Yiddish movies, they came north from the United States, usually from New York, whose Jewish community helped to set the cultural norms for Jews throughout North America in the interwar years.[142]

JEWISH COMMUNITIES IN ATLANTIC CANADA

In the east, where many Jewish immigrants had landed, most of Atlantic Canada's Jewish communities remained stable after the 1920s. Some, however, declined. Saint John, the largest, had grown from 642 persons in 1911 to 848 in 1921, but fell to 683 in 1931 and 569 in 1941.[143] Similarly, Halifax peaked and then declined, as did Yarmouth, Woodstock, Glace Bay, and New Glasgow, reflecting the general economic downturn in the region. But Sydney, with its busy steel mill, thrived during the 1930s, as did Moncton, a railway centre, and Fredericton, the New Brunswick provincial capital. These were small Jewish communities, the largest roughly the same size as that in Saskatoon, London, or Quebec City. Saint John before 1920 had boasted three synagogues, two of them catering to different social and economic groups (one to families from a particular village in Russia and the other to a group of Austrians, Germans, English, and "educated Russians.").[144] The third was a small chapel close to the business district.

This division was not atypical of some small-town Jewish communities. Immigrants from different parts of Eastern Europe followed varying practices in prayer, with their own special tunes, and had their own pronunciation of Hebrew and Yiddish, or what some scholars have called "the congregation's official liturgical rendition; the architecture of its sanctuary; the gestures, actions, dress and comportment of participants; role differentiation; any particular use made of the authorized prayer book; and many other things."[145]

It took time for these vital matters to be adjusted in the small communities. The most important decisions involved building a synagogue and the employment of a "rabbi" — who usually served as religious leader, teacher, *shokhet* (ritual slaughterer), and *mohel* (one who performs circumcision). In smaller cities, unlike major centres, Russian, Polish, Lithuanian, Galician, Romanian, German, and English Jews were forced to come together for the greater good and smooth over their differences, though such informal accords were never easy and dissension seldom far away. Mutterings against one group or another — "Polacks" and "Galicianer" for some reason were frequent targets, and "Roumanisher" were also somewhat suspect, while "Litvaks" and "Deutsher" were sometimes objects of amusement — were occasionally heard. Oddly, only "Russisher" seemed immune from such finger-pointing, snickering, suspicion, and disdain. In the big cities, on the other hand, such melding was not quite necessary, as there were enough, in Toronto, for example, Aptover, Lodzer, and Kiever among other *landsmanshaften* to pray together according to their own *minhagim* (customs).

The Halifax Jewish community was organized as the Baron de Hirsch Hebrew Benevolent Society in September 1890 — taking the name of the great Austrian Jewish benefactor of the day.[146] In 1894, a former Baptist church was converted for use as a synagogue. But, typically, dissension led to division, and another synagogue was formed a few years later. The first congregation's building was destroyed in the Halifax explosion of December 1917, and in 1920 a new structure was begun. By 1936, the rift was healed and the two congregations reunited, though tensions continued.[147] Like Saint John, Halifax played a special role by serving briefly as the host community for many of the Jewish immigrants who entered through the port, sometimes providing relief for the distressed and, during the 1930s, helping some families to settle on farms in rural Nova Scotia.[148] Meanwhile, congregations were also established in Moncton, Fredericton, Glace Bay, New Waterford, Sydney, and Yarmouth.

Jews settled in St. John's, Newfoundland (which entered Canada as the tenth province only in 1949), as early as the 1890s, formed a community in 1909, and in 1931 built a synagogue. Like most Jews in small-town Canada, they earned their living through petty trade, many of them having started as peddlers travelling through the colony's outports, where they sold goods to fishermen's families.

By 1921, there were an estimated fourteen Jewish families, including sixty-four individuals, living in St. John's, which had become the hub of Jewish life in the colony.[149] Israel Perlin, a former peddler who had settled there in the 1890s, operated a wholesale dry-goods store on Water Street and supplied itinerant Jews with goods and, no doubt, ample advice about prospects for business. The congregation's first endeavour was to purchase a cemetery plot. Various rabbis were hired, but none stayed for long. Meanwhile, the community grew and another started up in Corner Brook. Relationships between Jews and other Newfoundlanders were satisfactory. "There was no such thing [in Newfoundland] as segregation," one old-timer recalled. "I must say, [they were] very friendly. Never turned around and called you by any name as they did in some parts of Canada, when they say 'sheeny' or 'bloody Jew' or something. Never heard that. Never had any [bad] experience of any description, the greatest respect. We never heard it once mentioned, 'the Jew,' to us."[150]

As was the case in most small centres elsewhere in Canada, the problems of ensuring Jewish education and continuity in the younger generation influenced some settlers to leave the Maritimes once their children reached their late teens. Consequently, once vibrant communities tended to decline and, in some cases, flicker out altogether. Such was the fate of St. John's and Corner Brook, as of many other small Jewish centres across Canada, especially those in Northern Ontario.[151]

Community in Transition

The geography of the Canadian Jews showed a community accommodating to urban life in a nation struggling with serious economic and political problems, inter-regional tensions, and cultural and constitutional transformations.[152] All of these impinged on the Canadian Jewish community in various ways. Statistics proved that Jews were one of the most urbanized and best-educated groups in Canada; that on average they lived in better homes, lived longer, had fewer children, and were likelier to be married and found in middle-class occupations. The western Jewish farm colonies were still surviving in the 1920s, but with a diminishing population, a fact that was documented by government officials suspicious of petitions for further Jewish agricultural immigration.

Communal life in the large cities expressed itself in many forms of "limited identities." Yiddish publications, both secular and religious, thrived. The local press included Montreal's *Keneder Adler*, Toronto's *Yiddisher Zhurnal*, and Winnipeg's *Yiddishe Vort*, as well as association bulletins, weeklies like *Der Kamf* for the Communists, and periodicals for the Labour Zionists. And numerous pamphlets and books emerged, ranging from Rabbi Yudel Rosenberg's eloquent 1923 *A Brivele fun di Zisse Mamme Shabbes Malkese zu Ihr Zihn un Tekhter fun Idishn Folk* (A Letter from the Sweet Mother Sabbath Queen to her Sons and Daughters of the Jewish People),[153] which implored Canada's Jews to return to Sabbath observance lest they put off the coming of the Messiah, to more secular works. The latter included Nachman Shemen's 1939 *Tsvishn Kreig Un Friden* (Between War and Peace),[154] a wide-ranging analysis of world affairs. And poetry thrived too, notably in the small Montreal group that included Yacov Yitzchak Segal.[155]

Jewish culture possessed, as well, a consciousness of its historical roots in Canada. In 1926, Arthur D. Hart edited *The Jew in Canada: A Complete Record of Canadian Jewry from the Days of the French Regime to the Present Time*, overall a remarkable scholarly accomplishment that brought together significant articles on the community's history, current organizational structure, and leading citizens.[156] The search for a historical legitimacy included also *Looking Back a Century*, a work by Abraham Rhinewine, editor of the *Yiddisher Zhurnal*, published posthumously in 1932, the one-hundredth anniversary of Jewish political equality in Canada.[157]

Landsmanshaften and other organizations demonstrated that even in one city, many Jews maintained separate vehicles of identity that drew inspiration from a multiplicity of sources, such as regional origins, socialism, Zionism, and various religious affiliations. In the smaller communities, Jewishness was generally expressed less parochially and with greater sensitivity to the attitudes of non-Jews. In all, then, Canadian Jewry in the interwar years evidenced the growing complexity produced by the diversity of its people, their imported cultural baggage, and their accommodation to the Canadian urban and rural context. This was an important feature in a community, observers like Louis Rosenberg noted, that was not benefiting from the same level of immigration it had enjoyed earlier in the century. While much was changing, however, the question of communal enlargement and enrichment through immigration was experiencing special problems.

CHAPTER

2

Narrowing the Gates of Immigration, 1919–45

For eight years, Chaya Rivka Wolodarsky Forman, living in Rizshe, Ukraine, did not hear from her son, Joseph Wolodarsky, who had immigrated to Winnipeg in 1913.[1] When she finally received a letter from him in March 1921, she could hardly contain her joy.

> My Dear Loving son, Yosel Wolodarsky also to my Daughter-in-law as yet unknown to me! You should live and be well, my dear children! . . . Dear son, before I received your letter, Sarah-Malke's letter brought me news of your marriage. Mazel Tov, also the news that you have a daughter, mit Mazel. May she have a long and healthy life! I only hope that I will live to see all of you with my own eyes. Can you imagine, dear son, what I felt when I read this news? Suddenly, I have become so rich, a son, a daughter-in-law and a grandchild. Let us hope our luck has finally changed."[2]

Chaya Rivka finally arrived in Canada on July 1, 1922, to rejoin her family.

The most serious challenge facing the Canadian Jewish community in the 1920s was to make it possible for Chaya Rivka and so many other Jews to enter Canada. Postwar political and social problems affecting Jews in Eastern Europe, especially in Poland and the Soviet Union, were forcing them to immigrate to countries like Canada, which offered peace, freedom, and opportunity. Following the First World War, antisemitism was increasing in Poland, Romania, and Ukraine. At the same time, however, the Canadian Jewish community faced the early 1920s depression and other postwar readjustments, and its ability to aid in overseas relief efforts was limited.

Three major problems confronted the Canadian Jewish community in 1920 with respect to immigration. The first was the restrictive policy of the Dominion government, the second was the handling of newly arrived immigrants, and the third arose from the prevailing perceptions of Jews held by the Canadian public and by some important government officials.

Equally serious was the collapse of the young Canadian Jewish Congress. Considering the enthusiasm and energy that had inspired its founding in 1919, it is remarkable that by 1920 the organization was already moribund and a year later was dead. Hananiah Meir Caiserman, the Congress' general secretary, blamed a lack of funds, while Montreal businessmen Lyon Cohen and Mark Workman, the organization's chief elected officers, seemed to have lost enthusiasm for it.[3]

Money was certainly a serious problem for the Congress. In late March 1920, Caiserman sent a withering blast to A. B. "Archie" Bennett, secretary of the Ontario branch, for that group's failure to respond to a total of eight letters requesting payment of Ontario's two-thousand-dollar obligation to the national office in Montreal.[4] "Our Executive takes the point of view," he stated, "that not only should this amount have been remitted by you, but [other commitments should have been met also], if our budget arrangements made at the beginning of our activities meant anything at all." Caiserman then stated that Lyon Cohen refused to stand for a second term as president of the Congress because Ontario had appointed travel agent Harry Dworkin of Toronto to represent Canadian Jewry at the World Relief Conference. Perhaps Cohen thought that this honour should have been his. Clearly, there was serious tension between Montreal and Toronto, and once Cohen was out of the picture, efforts to work up enthusiasm for the Congress failed. A leaflet circulated in Toronto in March 1920 enjoined its Jews to register for Congress elections by pointing out that "[C]ongress organizations everywhere are the outcome of awakened Jewish pride, and the feeling that Jews can organize and look after their affairs through a representative body elected in a properly democratic manner."[5] But it was of little help. Neither was its Yiddish appeal, though it was more dramatic: "Help save the unfortunates in Poland and Ukraine."[6]

It seems ironic that the Congress should have died so quickly, since immigration, the important topic of the time, was so high on its agenda. Only a few weeks after the Congress' formation in March 1919, the national executive submitted a lengthy memorandum on proposed amendments to the immigration act to the Dominion government.[7] While this document questioned changes, such as a literacy test,[8] that were intended to severely curtail immigration, the main protest was against amendments that would exclude "men whose political past, as well as political thinking, is of such a nature as to cause very serious danger to the welfare of the country." The Congress was concerned with this because "it may unjustly affect the immigration of Jews into this country," and pointed out that "it is at best extremely difficult to ascertain the political past of any immigrant and there is great danger to giving to minor officials . . . a discretion which may be abused." It asserted that Jews have suffered oppression and "feel a natural resentment for the countries of their origin." Thus, it would be "unjust" to exclude people who, the Congress argued, "come to this country with no other desire than to be given an opportunity of earning an honest livelihood by honest work." It then asked "that special provision shall be made in this section for the Jewish people," or that officials be instructed to give Jews "special consideration."

Immigration Restrictions Begin

Jewish immigration in the 1920s was greatly threatened by the xenophobia that swept through Canada and the United States during and after the First World War. An earlier optimism for Canada's glowing future had encouraged governments and publicists to allow — even welcome — virtually any healthy white immigrants, who were expected to settle as farmers on the wheatlands of the Prairie provinces. Budding nativism had indeed been attacked in 1903 by none other than Clifford Sifton, then minister of Immigration, who favoured a liberal policy, although anti-immigrant sentiments were already rising, most notably in the West.[9] But the war losses, the fear of Bolshevism, and the hatred of enemy governments and peoples, together with the problems of reintegrating ex-soldiers into civilian life, a postwar economic downturn, and severe internal tensions, all combined to produce a new pessimism, tension, and bitterness in Canadian public life. Furthermore, the postwar breakdown of the national political parties, caused by deepening agrarian discontent centred in the Prairies and the continuing widespread resentment in Quebec over wartime conscription, created enormous uncertainty over the country's political future.[10]

In the wake of the 1919 Winnipeg General Strike and the accompanying "red scare," Ottawa moved decisively to plug certain "gaps" in the inflow of "undesirable" immigrants. Acting under the immigration law of 1910, which permitted the government to pass orders-in-council to regulate immigration, the Borden Cabinet started to enforce the 1908 provision for continuous journey, which required immigrants to enter Canada directly from their country of origin or citizenship "on a through ticket purchased in that country."[11] Other restrictions required immigrants to possess valid passports and $250 in landing money. This placed serious burdens on those, including Jews, who came from the war-ravaged lands of Eastern Europe and had taken refuge in other countries.

Mennonites, Hutterites, and Doukhobors were also affected by the postwar concerns over immigration, and it should be remembered that the immigration of blacks and Asians was severely limited. Faced with this hostile atmosphere and the threat of new restrictions on Jewish immigration in 1919 and 1920, Canadian Jewry responded by mandating the Congress to take up the issue with the highest levels of government. Strongly linked to their families and communities in the "old country," immigrants were vitally concerned with keeping Canada's doors open.

The representation of Jewish interests on immigration matters was of vital importance and it fell naturally to the only Jewish member of Parliament, Sam Jacobs, a Liberal who had sat for the Montreal riding of Cartier since the 1917 election.[12] In a speech to the House of Commons in June 1920, he lambasted the Conservative government's restrictive immigration policy for placing "stumbling blocks" in the way of "proper immigrants."[13] "We raise every kind of objection . . . we encourage only a certain class; [immigrants] must come from a certain district; they must be farmers and domestics." But, he continued, "there is no guarantee that the people we are bringing in are going to remain in the same avocation, for this is a land of opportunity and those who come to this country naturally expect to improve their lot, otherwise they would not leave their native land." In fact, there was a large turnover among all farmers on the Prairies, while population growth in western cities was higher than in the rural areas. Even by 1911, and later sped by war, a measurable drift was under way in Canada from farm to city. "We are aping the United States," Jacobs accused. However, while that nation of more than 110 million people could "pick and choose [its] immigrants," Canada was not in the same position. "[If] we blindly follow . . . the United States . . . we [will] be a land without people." Picking up on the favouritism shown to Nordics, the *Keneder Adler* even pointed out that some of them who claimed to be farmers were "not and never have been farmers."[14]

In April 1921, Caiserman complained to the immigration minister, saying, "Your department regards Jewish immigration as undesirable" because of "superficial knowledge of Jewish immigration to Canada."[15] He pointed to the fact that there were indeed Jewish farmers who had "proven to be a great success." His major argument was that if the government did not want Jewish immigration, it should say so. "I should then know that by working to aid Jewish immigrants . . . , I am working against the policy of our government, [even though] we had the right to expect that the Christian nations of the world would apply the great principles of Christianity in saving an innocent people from annihilation."[16]

Canadian immigration policy was changing in ways that adversely affected Jews, in particular, because the traditional preference for British subjects, Anglo-Saxons, North Europeans, and farmers was being enforced far more rigorously than ever before under the Immigration Act of 1919.[17] At the same time, "increasingly intractable immigration officials" were detaining and deporting Jewish immigrants at "the slightest provocation." Moreover, the "continuous journey" regulation adversely affected East European Jews because the shipping companies that reached Canadian ports did not operate in those countries. "It was therefore impossible for the east European Jewish migrant who did not possess a prepaid ticket to Canada to comply with this regulation."[18]

Regulations brought in by an order-in-council in 1921, which required immigrants to have valid passports from their countries of origin, complicated matters for many Polish and Russian Jews who came from the old Russian empire, now the Soviet Union. It was impossible for them to get passports unless they returned — a risk few would take. A requirement, introduced by another order-in-council in 1921, that all non-agricultural immigrants, such as Jews, possess $250 in landing money created further problems. This was replaced in 1922 by a stiff occupational test accompanying yet another order-in-council, which stipulated that Canadian, not British, consular officials examine all passports, a reasonable requirement, except that very few Canadian consular officials were posted anywhere near the East European Jewish migrants.[19]

The influx of Jews into Canada in the early 1920s was also affected by the severe restrictions placed on immigration into the United States by the Johnson Immigration Act of 1921 and its refinements in 1924. Under the act's provisions, strict quotas were allocated for specific ethnic groups, such as Jews, and the reunification of families was blocked.[20]

Canadian immigration laws were tightened still further in 1923 by Order-in-Council 183, which ranked immigrants according to the old racial preferences into "preferred," "non-preferred," and "special permit" classes. The last category included Jews, as well as Italians, Syrians, Bulgarians, Greeks, and Turks. They were subject to severe restrictions, which were refined over the next few years, notably limiting the family members who could be considered first-degree relatives. In practice, however, Jews were situated on the very lowest level of priority, along with blacks and Asians, who were effectively barred from entry.

Such exclusion did not escape the notice of those watchdogs of Jewish interests, the Yiddish newspapers, read so avidly by immigrants who, in many cases, were desperate to bring over members of their own families. Montreal's

Keneder Adler, for example, commented often on the discrimination against non-British and non-Nordics, observing mordantly in a November 1927 editorial that while Germans had been Canada's mortal enemies only ten years before, they were now among its preferred immigrants.[21] What motivated these policies was not always understood, though Jewish observers took appropriate note of events like the 1927 Synod of Anglican Bishops' meeting in Kingston, which voiced concern that an influx of Catholics, members of the Orthodox Church, and Jews would disrupt the make-up of Canadian society.[22]

In the 1920s, most of Canada's immigrant Jews came from Poland, the majority, judging from the names of Toronto *landsmanshaften*, from the Kielce region in the southwest. That area was still in an economic depression following the closure of industries that had depended on the Russian government; many Jews were thus immigrating to the Americas and to Palestine.[23] Because of the modernization of the Polish economy, moreover, Jewish artisans and petty traders were gradually becoming pauperized and there was severe social distress in the Jewish community.[24] Canada was far away, but as the old wisecrack put it: "from where?"

Certainly the Canadian community could not rely on Jewish steamship agents in Canada or abroad to deal satisfactorily with immigrants' problems. While some agents had the reputation of being scrupulously honest, others did not. But the existence of just one whose behaviour raised suspicions could do serious damage to the immigrants' interests and to the Jewish community generally. One such individual was Louis Gurofsky, a resident of Toronto. Since about 1907, he and his son had helped Jews living in Canada fill out forms to bring their relatives over from Europe. In 1920, he came under scrutiny by Department of Immigration officials because he claimed to be able to circumvent European barriers.[25] By that time, Gurofsky's firm had branches in Hamilton, Sudbury, and Montreal, and he was alleged to be taking bribes to get people into Canada.[26] He was also accused of swindling clients.[27]

The Department of Immigration received complaints about his operating procedures and became suspicious.[28] Frederick Charles Blair, a leading official in the Immigration Branch, branded him "an undesirable individual [who] . . . belongs to a gang of Trans-Atlantic swindlers and blackmailers [and] . . . is utterly unreliable."[29] An official at the British Consulate in Czernowitz, Romania, had evidence that "Gurofsky was arrested in Danzig for having taken hundreds of intending immigrants . . . helpless peasants and their own Jewish co-religionnaires . . . as far as Warsaw and abandon[ed] them there. . . ."[30] By August 1922, Gurofsky, now fully exposed, went out of business and was reported to have moved to Jerusalem.[31]

Despite swindlers like Gurofsky, others ran legitimate businesses. At least one major Toronto Jewish travel agency, that of Dorothy and Harry Dworkin, operated extensively in Poland in the early 1920s. On several occasions, the Dworkins travelled there to arrange the passage of immigrants whose Canadian relatives had prepaid their tickets. Many wives of husbands working in Canada anxiously awaited the tickets and money the Dworkins brought with them.[32] In April 1920, Harry Dworkin accompanied seventy-five Polish Jews who were *en route* to Canada from Warsaw to Antwerp.[33]

The Dworkins also conveyed back to Poland remittances from men who had left their wives and children behind while they got established in Canada. "I have loaned [a] lot of money, I hope they will pay," Harry wrote to Dorothy from Warsaw in March 1920. "I have [helped] out several [Zienice] customers, lent them money while they had moany [*sic*] of the Zienice checks, which

---

From South Africa to Canada — and Back, 1910–11

My father told me the following story: His mother was born Gertrude Gordon; his father was Isaac Heselson. Independently they had come as immigrants from Eastern Europe to Cape Town, South Africa, in approximately 1905–06. They had four children, my father being the second and the only son.

My grandmother Gertie had a sister, Rachel (Rae), who left South Africa and married Louis Vickar, a Canadian, and came to live "Out West." Louis was desperately trying to establish a Jewish community in Eden Bridge, and so he and his wife (Rae) persuaded Rae's sister, Gertie (my grandmother), to try living in Canada, hoping they would settle in Eden Bridge. Gertie packed up her then two children, a girl of three years, and my father, aged a year (he was born on January 4, 1910), and leaving her husband in Cape Town, travelled to Canada, where they spent a year.

My father recalled his mother's stories of a horrific winter, thigh deep in snow for many months, on a potato farm; outdoor toilets, bitter cold, and isolated because of the weather. Much as she enjoyed being reunited and close to her sister again, she couldn't wait to get back to sunny South Africa. So she left, went back to her husband, and never returned to Canada.

My father visited us in Canada on several occasions from 1970, when we settled in Kingston, until his death in 1993. Each time he was reminded of his mother's description of life in Canada in 1910–11, and would retell the story as he was told it.

— *Dr. Lynne Ginsburg*

they could not cash."[34] Dworkin did very well out of these currency transactions, as well as from travel services that included arranging for visas, steamship tickets, and the money that immigrants had to show to officials upon arrival. "I have loaned money to my passengers to come forward," he wrote in September 1920, "but every cent is good, and if the people [in Toronto] have paid you according to my cables, than [*sic*] we have doubled the *money all ready* [*sic*]. I also have a big stock in Russian and other money *we have got to get rich*."[35]

Efforts of Intervention

Sam Jacobs and various other Jewish "notables" approached the problem of immigration restrictions by undertaking *shtadlanut*. This centuries-old tradition of important Jews ("court Jews" in eighteenth-century Germany) representing Jewish interests before the secular powers to try to avert "an evil decree," such as expulsion, an extra "Jew tax," or other discriminatory legislation, was combined with new-style ethnic brokerage politics. In this spirit, they went to Ottawa and made the rounds of Cabinet ministers, influential MPs and senators, and department officials. Jacobs would, of course, make speeches in the House for the record, for their possible effect on public opinion, and less likely still (given the fact that he was a Liberal), for their influence on government policy, but men of his kind obviously knew that the way to try to get things done in Ottawa was to see people in their offices. Sometimes it worked.

To plead, even beg, that Jews be exempted from this or that regulation, and hint at possible political or other "benefits," was all part of traditional *shtadlanut*. The chances of success would be improved by employing all available resources, including using "notables" such as Lyon Cohen, the Montreal clothing manufacturer and president of the Canadian Jewish Congress. An even more important individual, however, was Lillian Freiman, the wife of Ottawa department store tycoon A. J. "Archie" Freiman, who had influence in government circles. She had persuaded Mrs. Arthur Meighen, the wife of the most powerful minister in the Borden Cabinet, to lend her official support to the Ukrainian orphans' project.[36] In the summer of 1919, the "Jewish representatives" succeeded in securing exemptions for Jews to a number of the postwar orders-in-council, most notably PC 1203, which prohibited the immigration of persons from former enemy countries (Austria, Germany, Bulgaria, and Turkey).[37] Jacobs and others appealed for the exemption of Jewish refugees from the Ukrainian pogroms, and for further exemptions from other restrictions. And in addition to Freiman's special appeal on behalf of Ukrainian orphans, she intervened on various other occasions later in the 1920s.

ORGANIZED RELIEF FOR REFUGEES IN EASTERN EUROPE

Immigration, though, was a divisive issue even in a strongly supportive community. This was highlighted in an unsigned memorandum (probably written by Caiserman) explaining the weakness of the Congress in 1920.[38] It asserted that organizing the gigantic protest meetings in major centres against the pogroms in Eastern Europe, and the necessary relief work associated with such programs, had exhausted the Congress' finances. In an effort to "reopen the immigration question so as to bring in the thousands of the Canadian dependents from European countries into Canada," especially from Ukraine, the Canadian Federation of Ukrainian Jews (the Ukrainian Verband), with the "close support of the local Jewish press," was ignoring the Congress. It was petitioning the Canadian government independently and preparing its own relief mission to Ukraine. Sensing that the Congress was in a weakened position, the Jewish Ukrainians were going it alone. They were creating confusion (especially in Winnipeg, where they were strongest) about unified Jewish allegiance to the Congress at the very time when it was conducting its 1920 registration.

But immigration was too big an issue to be handled by self-appointed fixers or a weak Congress. Thus, in 1920, the Jewish Immigrant Aid Society (JIAS) was formed by the Congress and other Jewish organizations. Led by Lyon Cohen and Sam Jacobs, JIAS became a major force through which the community could appeal to government. Measures to reduce immigration were being prepared through a new act, which contained provisions "to control, select, and if found necessary, reduce or entirely suspend immigration of elements deemed undesirable by allowing the Minister to regulate the inflow."[39]

JIAS was pressed by the associations (*verbands*) of Polish, Romanian, and Ukrainian Jews, which were desperately trying to rescue the thousands of refugees, many of them members of their own families. JIAS feared that the new act's provisions, which allowed the exclusion of a whole "race or nationality," might be used against Jews. While in this instance such a fear proved to be unfounded, JIAS did encounter mounting antisemitism among Immigration Branch officials. They were able to use their discretionary authority to curtail the immigration of Jews, who did not fit the established criterion that held that farmers were the model immigrants for Canada's agricultural frontier.[40]

JIAS also tried to "minimiz[e] the depredations of middlemen who charged exorbitant sums and were often unable to obtain the [immigration] permits they promised."[41] JIAS wanted to become the major address to which Jews wishing to sponsor immigrants would turn, and thus eliminate as much of the unseemly profiteering by ticket agents, influence peddlers, and lawyers as possible. This would not only lower costs considerably, but also streamline the process of dealing with officials who had the ultimate authority to issue permits.

From its headquarters in Montreal, JIAS quickly developed the knowledge of the legislation necessary to negotiate effectively with the Ottawa officials, who in turn preferred dealing with JIAS to dealing with the independent agents. In addition, branch offices of JIAS in Toronto and Winnipeg, as well as volunteers across the country, provided local support for landed immigrants and for the screening of prospective sponsors.[42] JIAS still competed somewhat with Canadian Jewish steamship agents in the sale of Polish and Russian remittance orders, for sending parcels overseas, and for arranging United States visa cases, and it tried to capture a "monopoly over permit applications."[43]

However important it was, JIAS nevertheless did not escape criticism inside the Jewish community. In Montreal, the *Keneder Adler* attacked the organization for not doing enough to encourage the immigration of Jewish farmers and for alleged improprieties.[44] These had been highlighted in the *Adler* in early 1927: a high-handed administration, excessive bureaucracy, exorbitant membership fees, and unfriendly employers.[45] The most damaging complaint against JIAS alleged favouritism in awarding permits.[46] Worse was to follow. In March, the *Adler* alleged that JIAS officials were in fact selling these permits and mismanaging the organization's funds.[47] Soon afterward, a gathering of concerned organizations heard that criminal charges of theft had been brought against two JIAS officials; it was recommended that the organization's structure be radically changed.

These contretemps and the continuing contest between JIAS and the travel agents illustrates that, as the historian Robert Harney has pointed out, migration was a complicated business in which some travel agents profited not only from the commerce in permits, steamship tickets, and remittances, but also while serving as notaries or translating documents, and even from real-estate transactions.[48] In the words of the historian Harold Troper, these travel agents were, in some ways, "the hub of the whole settlement process," at least until Jewish professionals emerged and JIAS became known and fully trusted as the appropriate address for immigration matters.

Meanwhile, in the wake of the Bolshevik Revolution and the ensuing civil war in Ukraine, widespread loss of life and destruction occurred among the Jewish communities in Eastern Europe. Hananiah Caiserman observed conditions firsthand during his 1920 tour of Eastern Europe, which he undertook to survey the destruction and to estimate how Canada's Jews could help the victims of mass murder, rape, and pillage.[49] These disasters produced tens of thousands of Jewish orphans, who roamed the Ukrainian countryside searching for food and shelter. In the summer of 1920, it was reported that there were some 137,000 of these Jewish children, many "practically living wild and semi-barbarous lives, . . . eating such edible wild roots and herbs as were left in a territory . . . sadly ravaged by war and post war excesses."[50] In late August 1920, some fifteen hundred Jews gathered in Saskatoon to propose their own response to the crisis; they unanimously favoured sending the orphans to Palestine, for which they offered strong financial support.[51]

Back east, a campaign led by Lillian Freiman also responded to this crisis. She was already deeply involved in helping Jewish immigrants, and on occasion went to Halifax to assist recent arrivals who were being threatened with deportation. One witness remembered that on one of these missions, "she put her motherly arms around the two or three closest to her [and] . . . kept repeating these words, 'Nisht vein, nisht vein' ['Don't cry, don't cry']. An overflowing heart more than made up for her imperfect Yiddish.[52] Alerted to the plight of the orphans in Ukraine, she rallied friends and associates across Canada to raise money for the Committee for the Relief of Ukrainian Orphans, which she had established to bring some of them over to Canada and to feed and clothe others.[53]

Exploiting her Ottawa contacts, Freiman negotiated an agreement with Blair of the Immigration Branch. He would allow up to two hundred of these orphans into Canada "on humanitarian grounds," as an experiment, with others allowable depending on the results.[54] For many, this campaign was personal. Mrs. S. Levine of Brantford, Ontario, wrote to Freiman, noting that her community had raised a thousand dollars,[55] and asked: "As I have a sister-in-law with three orphans in Warsaw, I would like you to bring them with the two hundred. Their father is dead and they are suffering terribly. Two children of that family have already died of hunger. When they come they will have a good home and will be well taken care of."

But despite efforts by Lillian Freiman and several other women — who served as the most active (but not usually the most recognized) members of groups forming to help immigrants[56] — as well as an apparently enthusiastic response to a special national gathering convened in Ottawa in early October 1920, the Canadian Jewish community could neither reach the campaign target nor find enough families willing to accept all of the orphans. Repeated appeals for money and for homes for the children brought in only meagre results — except in Western Canada, where communities outdid themselves in raising funds.[57]

In Montreal, contrary to expectations, the campaign was beset by apathy. The *Canadian Jewish Chronicle* complained bitterly that the communal leaders of Montreal "have established a reputation for 'passing the buck,' particularly in the matter of assuming the chairmanship of campaigns. One of the most popular games in this city is that of 'Chairman, Chairman, who'll be the Chairman?'"[58] Toronto was just as unenthusiastic, and the whole Jewish-Ukrainian relief effort faltered. What the *Chronicle* saw as an opportunity to "forge an unbreakable link between our Jewish people over here and our Jewish orphans over there — a link that will do much for the strengthening of our Judaism" was not taken up by the community at large.[59]

And while the *Chronicle* saw philanthropy as a positive phenomenon ("it has . . . done much to bring out the best in our people in the Western world"),[60] it was forced to conclude that the relief campaign was unsuccessful. Even appeals to history were of little avail: "The present is a crisis in Jewish history," the journal stated in late December 1920, "a crisis that is taking physical toll in Europe and spiritual toll in America. . . . The simple act of living in America," it continued, "engenders a moral and spiritual responsibility to equalize the toll of blood and tears that is being exacted from our people on the other side."[61] In April 1921, the *Chronicle* announced sadly that only "a very small proportion of Canadian Jewry is represented in the figures [of contributors]."[62]

Meanwhile, Harry Hershman and Dr. Joseph Leavitt of Montreal, along with William Farrar of Hamilton (a Christian who took a deep interest in Jewish religious and communal affairs), were dispatched as a team to Europe in February 1921. Operating in the Polish Ukraine with the support of the American Jewish Joint Distribution Committee, a United States Jewish relief organization, the Canadian group established itself in Rovno and began to select suitable candidates from the thousands of orphaned children in the area.

Hershman's letters from Poland tell of the numerous practical problems his team encountered. "It is almost impossible to do any work on account of the noise. You can imagine 90 kids or more running around the place," he complained in one letter to Lillian Freiman.[63] As he was making arrangements for transport, Dr. Leavitt, who was overwhelmed with medical inspections and the need to improve the children's nutrition, urgently wired Hershman: "INSIST FROM STEAMSHIP COMPANY THAT CHILDREN DO NOT IMMEDIATELY GO INTO QUARANTINE UNTIL I GET THERE AND SPEAK WITH LONDON OFFICE FIRST."[64] After appraising two orphan boys from the countryside, Hershman wrote to Leavitt: "Send along one suit of clothing size 28 . . . also send stockings and underwear for a boy of nine years the children are practically naked. I think I will have to take them to Rovno they have nothing in their home no beds, no food, no care but they are very nice boys."[65] Hershman's notes, written while searching for orphans in the countryside, are interesting: "June 16 p.m. Arrived Wyzwa at 7:45. Solomon S. OK Rather small for age. Obtained release; Herschel P. 12–13. To see again and decide. Parents died but aunt who was keeping him was killed."[66] Lillian Freiman, meanwhile, had gone to Antwerp, Belgium, where 146 chosen children were eventually assembled. On August 21, she brought the first group of 108 to Quebec; the others followed within a few weeks.[67]

By that time, the campaign in Canada was experiencing political and temporary financial problems. A group of dissidents had circulated letters inexplicably demanding that the selected orphans come only from the Soviet Ukraine.[68] This protest further soured fund-raising efforts, weakening the campaign. By early 1921, indifference prevailed, perhaps as a result of a severe business recession. Of the hundreds of Canadian Jews who at first had indicated a willingness to provide homes, only 149 valid applications arrived. This was well short of what was needed for the two hundred authorized children and barely enough for those who did reach Canada.[69] Certainly Freiman and her associates could take credit for mounting an important symbolic rescue effort. Aside from all her other work on behalf of Canadian Jewry, the image of this woman leading the children off the ship at Quebec after months of excitement made her the leading Canadian Jewish figure of her generation. While awaiting the ship that would take her and the children to Canada, she had presided over a moving Sabbath celebration. Hershman remembered that after he chanted the *kiddush* (blessing) over the wine, Freiman "carried the cup to each child to taste the *kiddush* [cup], and from her eyes flowed a stream of tears . . . but through the tears we could see her great *nachas* [joy] that she derived from this experience."[70]

While Freiman, according to historian Simon Belkin, had "put her heart and soul into the project," hoping to bring in more than 150 orphans, Harry Hershman's role was also unique.[71] Not only had he spent several gruelling months inspecting the children in Poland with Dr. Leavitt and William Farrar, but, after returning to Canada and up until his death in 1957, he constituted a one-man follow-up committee. Hershman sent the children clothing and presents for birthdays and bar mitzvahs; he attended their weddings and rejoiced in the births of their children. He also corresponded with many of them and their Canadian foster parents.

One foster parent reported to him: "Dear friend Mr. Hershman, if you saw Sarah now, you would not recognize her. She has grown, and is fat and healthy. She gets on good in school and I am proud of her. . . . I am sending you my Sarah's picture as a remembrance."[72] The correspondent informed him that "as Sarah told me she has left a sister in Russia, we would like to have her address so Sarah and her sister can correspond so they will not lose tract [*sic*] of each other." Hershman carefully answered all the letters he received. Some of his charges experienced difficulties and were a concern to him for many years; his files are a rich source on their adjustment to Canada, as well as a testament to the sustained devotion of one man, himself childless, to the Ukrainian orphans.

By the time they arrived, to be hailed by the *Chronicle* as "Canadian citizens of the future," concern for the orphans was overshadowed by the heartrending stories of other refugees still overseas, which continued to attract notice in Canada.[73] Monies left over from the orphan project were used to set up a soup kitchen for Jews in Ukraine.[74]

Jewish Intercession on Behalf of Detainees and Deportees

JIAS performed prodigious work on behalf of Jewish immigrants to Canada during the 1920s. Since the Congress no longer existed, JIAS worked alone. The situation for the newly arrived immigrants reaching Halifax, Saint John, and Quebec, however, was very precarious.[75] "That happy period when immigrants generally were welcome guests in Canada is gone . . . [and] each new arrival is looked upon with a thousand eyes and the stranger, the alien is sent back on the least pretext," wrote one observer in the *Chronicle* in June 1920.[76] Those Jews who failed to pass inspection or meet other requirements faced deportation.

The paper reported that in spite of Freiman's intercessions, a large number were sent back, while still other deportations were threatened. On July 2, 1920, the *Chronicle* reported that "only last Saturday, 350 Jewish immigrants landed in Quebec from the S.S. *Grampian* and were permitted to land only because of prompt intervention by several Quebec Jews. It is ridiculous to expect the small community of Quebec to undertake the whole burden for Canadian Jewry."[77] Later, the journal reminded readers that "the immigrant's present plight can only find its counterpart in our past or the past of our parents." Only a Jew can know the heart of a Jew. That is why the Jew is ready to take care of his own."[78]

During its first year, JIAS organized a headquarters in Montreal and branches across the country, selected personnel to acquaint themselves fully with Canadian immigration law and practice, met the ships to render legal and other assistance, established a structure to administer the whole effort, and raised money.[79] The chief operational task was dealing with the problems of the rising number of detainees, mainly at Quebec, Halifax, and Saint John.

Some immigrants allegedly were being handled with an astonishing lack of consideration, even inhumanity, by various immigration officials. At Saint John, in February 1921, JIAS complained that one official for many days had refused to allow the relatives of incoming immigrants to speak to their loved ones — some of whom they had not seen for as long as twelve years — until after they had been released from detention.[80] Officials, the allegation stated, had even refused to allow JIAS to send in kosher food. One little boy of eleven was so distraught at being separated from his family that he attempted to hang himself while in detention. He was cut down while still alive, quickly judged by officials to be insane, and immediately deported all alone back to Poland.[81]

JIAS representatives who tried to intervene on behalf of these and other Jewish detainees were, they claimed, met with delays, obfuscation, and contempt. Immigration officials, on the other hand, saw Jewish intercession as confusing and bothersome. E. J. O'Connell, an officer on the Quebec staff, reported to his superior in Ottawa that "for the last 6 weeks or 2 months, this office has been experiencing considerable difficulties and no end of extra work due principally to the activity of a number of local residents of the Hebrew persuation [*sic*], who in their enthusiasm to assist the Jewish Detentions, are causing a lot of friction and injury to the discipline in Detention Quarters, and unrest generally amongst all the detentions."[82] O'Connell complained that with "each trifle that occurs to a Jewish detention, let it be imaginary or otherwise, the supposed victim is ever anxious to request an investigation and every one of his countrymen detained with him is a willing witness to substantiate his storey [*sic*]." Without elaboration, he referred to the fact that "contraversy [*sic*] and evident bitterness that exists between the factions of Jewish residents in Quebec," was also making his work difficult.

The attempts to iron out difficulties with the Saint John officials began as early as December 1920.[83] Intercession was tried also by JCA officials, who were more experienced in immigration matters, and thus were somewhat calmer and more adroit in their approach.

Leon Rosenthal, a JCA administrator in Montreal in November 1920, wrote to the minister of Immigration on behalf of two hundred detainees — mostly young men aged twenty to twenty-eight — who had failed to comply with various regulations because of ignorance. Since these men could easily have been absorbed as labourers and farmers in the JCA's western farm colonies, and would have had that organization's guarantee of support, he pleaded that they be allowed to stay in Canada. Rosenthal ended his letter with an eloquent appeal "on purely humanitarian grounds," saying that "it would be a pity, a great pity, to condemn these 200 or more young men in the very bloom of their life. It would be unfair, and therefore unbritish, to adhere to the letter of the law without permitting a liberal interpretation thereof."[84]

During its first year of operations, JIAS attended to 1,788 cases of detention at the three major eastern ports. Of these, 1,306 persons were released, but 232 were deported, 2 died in detention, 226 "escaped," and 22 were further detained.[85]

Many of the detainees were entering Canada expecting to quickly move to the United States. According to Caiserman, "nearly 75% of all [Jewish] immigrants arriving to Canada through Quebec have as their destination United States of America."[86] United States regulations, however, required valid visas from an American consular officer in the country where the journey started.[87] Yet it was still difficult to stem the flow of such persons to Canada. JIAS blamed steamship agents in Europe, especially those of the White Star, Cunard, and Canadian Pacific lines, for misleading immigrants. They "give immigrants wrong addresses and tell them that when they get to Canada they will have no difficulties of [*sic*] proceeding to United States."[88]

The financial strain on JIAS as a result of this fraud was serious, and the human cost was worse. "Hundreds of immigrants," S. B. Haltrecht reported to New York's Hebrew Immigrant Aid Society (HIAS), the sister organization of JIAS, "are walking through the streets of Montreal, puzzled as to what they should do and we can give them no satisfactory advice."[89] Now nearly desperate to stop this influx, Caiserman wrote to the Danzig offices of HIAS, complaining about "criminal and irresponsible steamship agents," informing them of United States immigration laws that prohibited all but properly visaed immigrants from entering the U.S.,[90] and advising them to pass the information on to immigrants. He also requested the Danzig group to inform immigrants to Canada that they must fulfil the requirements of "continuous journey."

Sometimes JIAS officials in Montreal did not understand the difficulties experienced by the regional organizations. Occasionally Montreal received peppery communiqués asking it to mind its own business. In responding to a request for funds, a member of the Vancouver community who was engaged in immigration work there wrote:

> You are probably not aware of the problem in this work confronting the Jews of Vancouver. Apparently in your haste to organize your society in the East you have paid little attention to Vancouver. Do you know how much money was spent on this work and do you know the number of men who have been engaged in the handling of these affairs without one single dollar of remuneration?[91]

From the start, JIAS officials were aware that they required financial assistance from abroad. They secured a twenty-thousand-dollar subsidy from the

JCA and petitioned HIAS for information, advice, and money.[92] Caiserman wrote to the president of HIAS in October 1920 requesting "that your organization with its tremendous experience and larger means should share proportionally our burdens here."[93]

By early November 1920, JIAS was in a desperate financial state. "It is absolutely necessary," the general manager, Louis Lewis, wrote to the general manager of HIAS, "[for HIAS] to come to [our] assistance, as far as United States immigrants are concerned." John L. Bernstein replied that because "nearly all of the arrivals . . . to your country . . . are male immigrants who cannot enter the United States our Society cannot be of any help."[94] Bernstein advised the JIAS manager that the Canadian organization should provide for the arrivals out of its own funds, and hope that HIAS efforts to warn European Jews not to try to enter the United States via Canada were successful. Another appeal was sent to New York two weeks later, this one announcing the JIAS fund-raising campaign, regarding which the writer asserted, "we feel that you ought to render some aid . . . not financial but we do ask you to arrange for and to send us a capable speaker for our mass meeting."[95]

In 1921, Max Meyerson and Dr. B. Berkowitz of HIAS reported, after viewing the Canadian operation, that "we consider the work done by the Jewish Immigrant Aid Society of Canada has been splendid. Its officers and directors are heart and soul in their work and are very anxious to be of service to the unfortunate Jewish immigrants. . . ."[96] After estimating that the annual expenses of JIAS would be at least fifty thousand dollars, the two men concluded that its finances were so precarious that "unless HIAS comes to [its] rescue, the Jewish Immigrant Aid Society of Canada will be compelled to close its offices within the next thirty days." They thus recommended support of one thousand dollars a month.

Recognizing that "a very large number of [Jewish] immigrants . . . mostly young men of military age . . . who arrive in Canada are actually destined to relatives in the United States, and [that] it is our duty to help these immigrants just as we would be of assistance to them if they arrive at any American port," they urged that a HIAS official be sent to Canada to advise them on how to accomplish their goal.[97] The Americans observed that JIAS had been faced with a monumental job during its first year, especially in the spring and summer of 1921, when about 3,800 Jews had arrived in Canada. Many were detained "upon almost any conceivable ground," requiring the lodging of appeals against about five hundred deportation orders (some requiring three or four separate appeals), the placement of guarantees with shipping companies, the payment of the cost of feeding and sheltering detainees, and the posting of substantial bonds while their cases were under appeal.

The Jewish community was outraged by these detentions and deportations. Archie Freiman and the Montreal tobacco tycoon Sir Mortimer Davis utilized their political influence to pressure the Dominion government for relief from the enforcement of immigration regulations. "When advised yesterday that Jewish immigrants were released from detention[,] Freiman of Ottawa wired all Jewish Associations throughout Canada commending your action and urging all Jews to work for and support you next Tuesday," an organizer for the Conservative Party cabled Prime Minister Arthur Meighen in December 1921.[98]

But more of such interventions were needed to overcome the department's rigidity. "Department's action resented by Jews as unjust discrimination and serious breach of faith," the intervenor reported. "Respectfully submit that you instruct Minister to review these twenty cases immediately and arrange release. Please advise me by wier [*sic*] as to action taken. Am endeavouring to hold Freiman's good will," he concluded. Conservative candidates in constituencies with substantial Jewish populations lobbied Prime Minister Meighen to release detained immigrants.[99] A worried Charles C. Ballantyne, MP for the Montreal riding of St. Lawrence–St. George, complained to Meighen during the campaign that "My life here has been made almost unbearable by the requests . . . by prominent Jewish citizens . . . to use whatever influence I may possess with the Minister of Immigration to have some of these [detainees] admitted. I was given no peace night or day. . . ." Concerned about his chances for re-election in his riding, Ballantyne informed his national leader, "These Jewish citizens . . . will play an important part in my reelection, but in order to retain their enthusiasm and support it is up to me to demonstrate that I have been able to accomplish something for them. Unless I can do so I am afraid that I shall not get this large vote."[100]

Protests against deportations were mounted by the Jewish rank and file, as well. H. D. Rosenbloom, manager of the Toronto Joint Board of the Amalgamated Clothing Workers of America, cabled Meighen during the campaign on behalf of his three thousand members to "protest most vigorously against the wholesale deportations . . . and against restriction of immigration generally."[101] Meanwhile, individuals with influence on MPs tried their best to intervene, usually without success.

Once the Liberals returned to power in Ottawa after the general election of December 1921, the Jewish community widely hoped that the Dominion's immigration policy would improve. After all, that party had implemented an "open door" policy under Sir Wilfrid Laurier, and had not publicly repudiated statements made during the campaign by Jacobs and others favouring a more generous stance on immigration. That was, however, not a major issue in

Mackenzie King's successful campaign.[102] Indeed, the immigration question was a somewhat dangerous one, given the lengthy recession that was creating severe economic distress.

Under the circumstances, King was typically circumspect before the election. But once in power with a minority government, he and his Cabinet were vulnerable to strong pressures from within his party — and Sam Jacobs exploited the opportunity to force the immigration issue.[103] He was, in turn, under strong pressure from his Jewish constituents in Cartier. Their collective voice, the *Keneder Adler*, was closely attuned to the "downtown" Montreal Jews, many of them immigrants who hoped to bring their family members to Canada. The paper had instructed him after his election in 1917 to:

> Remember that you were not elected by the wealthy "Uptown" Jews but the common masses of the "Downtown" and with the help and influence of their Yiddish paper. Remember that the support of this paper was given to you readily and gratuitously with the sole aim that we should have a representative and spokesman in the parliament of Ottawa.[104]

To the downtown Jews this was a vital issue. Many hoped to be reunited soon with their families.

JEWISH PRESSURE ON IMMIGRATION POLICY, 1923-24

The most important JIAS interventions occurred in September 1923. At the urging of HIAS and the JCA, Sam Jacobs, Lyon Cohen, and several others persuaded James Robb, the minister of Immigration and Colonization, to allow one thousand Ukrainian Jewish refugees living in Romania to enter Canada.[105] Robb was new to this Cabinet post, and as MP for the Quebec riding of Chateauguay-Huntingdon, he was an associate of Jacobs in the Quebec Liberal caucus. He succumbed to pressure despite the build-up of resentment against Jews among some of his officials — F. C. Blair in particular[106] — and agreed to allow the refugees in at the rate of one hundred a week (later amended to three hundred a month). The department's deputy minister, William J. Black, favoured the plan and had helped to convince Robb.[107] All were aware that the minority Liberal government could not afford to alienate even the tiny Jewish community.

Discussion about Canada's role as a refuge for Jewish fugitives from the Soviet Union had begun in 1921, when the International Labour Organization made inquiries of Sir George Perley, the Canadian high commissioner in London, about Canada's willingness to take some of them.[108] When consulted, Blair pointed out that "the vast majority of these are no doubt Jews. . . . Nothing is more certain than that Canada is not in a position to offer any home to these people at the present time."[109] Blair had expressed his views on this matter to S. B. Haltrecht of the Montreal office of JIAS several weeks before. While he recognized that a great many Jews had been farmers in Eastern Europe, only "a very small proportion of those who have emigrated to Canada are engaged in that occupation in this country. . . . [T]he record of the [Jewish] Western colonies is not reassuring. . . . [Y]oung people have practically all left and gone to the cities. . . . [Land] brought under cultivation did not average ten acres per family. This does not look like real farming."[110]

The broad policy of limiting entry to genuine farmers was still being implemented. But with regard to Jewish refugees, J. A. Calder, Canadian minister of Immigration, was keenly aware of protests against repeating the generous pre-war policy of allowing "an influx of Continentals . . . [which] was larger than the country could afford."[111] In 1922, Lucien Wolf of the Board of Deputies of British Jews, possibly concerned with relieving pressure on his community, wrote to Perley, the Canadian high commissioner in London, with a proposal to send some of these refugee Jews to Canada.[112]

The matter rested until the summer of 1923, when it was raised by Philip Baker, a senior British government official. He had been contacted by Fridtjof Nansen, the League of Nations High Commissioner, who was negotiating with various governments to try to resettle these and other refugees from Russia.[113] Apparently aware of Canadian reluctance, Baker wrote to Mackenzie King somewhat apologetically: ". . . perhaps the Canadian government does not wish to receive Jews, [but] I believe that . . . they are very sober and hardworking people, and that the whole of their transportation and installation expenses would be met by the Jewish organizations which are helping them."[114] Three weeks later, King relayed the inquiry to Robb, his new minister of Immigration and Colonization, reminding him that he "may know [Baker] . . . personally. I shall be glad if you give this matter your attention."[115] In reply to Baker, King was non-committal, saying only that he was asking Robb "to bring the subject matter of your letter before our colleagues in Council at the next meeting of the Cabinet and a little later on to communicate with you direct."[116]

King's letter, however, constituted tacit approval for the idea, and Robb promptly referred the matter to his department officials. When it got to Blair in early September, he wrote to the deputy minister of Immigration to say that "it is manifestly impossible to open the door to the tens of thousands of these refugees. However, this view is not based on racial grounds, but on our inability to absorb them. . . . If the refugees were of the agricultural classes and had relations or friends on farms in Canada where they could find homes and employment, there would be no difficulty." Blair reminded him that the Canadian government already had spent $600,000 to bring in British immigrants that year and that funds could not be spent on aliens when "we have to be concerned with the fate of 12,000 British harvesters who may be unemployed."[117]

Aside from the assumption that Jews would fail as farmers, there also existed the belief that many, if not most, clamouring for admission to Canada would remigrate to the United States at the first opportunity. And this was undoubtedly true; the migration of Jews from Canada to the United States during the 1920s was substantial, although many other Canadians and immigrants also moved south.[118] This dim view of Jews was retailed by Blair, as well as by some shipping company officials, like Mr. McClure of the Cunard Line, who wrote: "There is the local Jew, the worst type in Siberia, who will take the opportunity of getting into Canada only to desert to the United States, or go into other Canadian cities and swell the ranks of the undesirables."[119] Such beliefs were prevalent during the interwar period and fitted in with an attitude that classed Canadians who migrated to the United States as "deserters."[120] Notwithstanding these criticisms, the prime minister's tacit consent to the refugee project and his directive to Robb provided the needed official approval.

The various difficulties in the transfer of this group, most of whom were unable to fulfil Canadian requirements for valid Russian passports, and the inability to arrange the transport of exactly one hundred persons week by week, were overcome through the intercessions of Jacobs and the Freimans. Moreover, leaders of several American Jewish relief organizations promised financial assistance to the Canadians if they could secure a more generous quota,[121] leading to pressure for its enlargement. Finally, Black and Robb agreed to allow in a maximum of five thousand Russian Jews stranded in Romania.[122]

Over the next year, these Jews were organized by officials into groups for despatch to Canada. Ships were hired to take them from the Romanian Black Sea port of Constanza to Quebec, Montreal, or Halifax. The project was enormously complicated and costly, and involved transportation, provisions for kosher food and medical assistance, and the maintenance of the immigrants until they could become self-supporting in Canada. Appeals for assistance from the Paris-based JCA and HIAS in New York brought in substantial subsidies. But even those sums, added to what could be raised in Canada, were not nearly enough. An unsigned letter (probably from Lyon Cohen) to the American Jewish activist Joseph Barondess, dated November

1924, after the last ship bearing refugees had arrived, blamed the lack of money for the failure to utilize the full quota.[123] "It is my belief that if American Jewry had listened to you and me in our appeals and had come forth early in the year with substantial assistance, the entire quota would have been conserved."[124] Canadian Jews could not raise the rest of the money needed, no doubt owing to the continuing economic recession.

Meanwhile, local volunteers did their best to cope. As the hosts at the major reception centre, the Jews of Halifax outdid themselves. In Toronto and Montreal, emergency committees rented rooms and arranged jobs. In Winnipeg, Harry Wilder served as chairman of the committee that was responsible for distributing the Ukrainian Jews to centres across the West. Several of the men were sent to work on farms, not always with great success.[125] "In some cases the individuals left for [the] West quite willingly," he reported, "[but] with others we had great difficulty. We had to use considerable pressure and met with strong opposition, while in one or two instances we were entirely [unsuccessful]. In these last instances . . . the committee was advised to positively refuse to give either food or shelter."[126]

Russian Jews aboard the S.S. *Madonna*, which reached Halifax from Constanza on August 30, 1924, were sent to Montreal, Toronto, and Winnipeg for dispersion across their respective regions, and Wilder was informed that "120 immigrants are expected to arrive in Winnipeg on . . . September 2nd on the Madonna Special."[127] In fact, 121 arrived. Fifty of them were to remain in Winnipeg, while the others were distributed as follows: Vancouver, 20; Edmonton, 17; Saskatoon, 12; Regina, 11; Calgary, 7; and Sibbald, 4. There is no record of his level of success in that endeavour.

The relief effort in the West was widespread, with people responding well. In November 1924, a Mrs. Margulies of Ebenezer, Saskatchewan, was sent a letter to "acknowledge receipt of six ducks and one turkey, which you have been good enough to contribute for the Refugees."[128] Mrs. Margulies had previously contributed ten dozen eggs, a sum of five dollars, and a parcel of clothes, including "4 middys, 1 jumper, 2 skirts, 2 dresses, 1 smol [*sic*] skirt, 1 towle [*sic*], 1 underskirt, 1 combination, 2 per slipers [*sic*], 2 p. shoes."[129] Although most of these refugees went to the cities, JIAS did succeed in distributing them across the country; 45 percent settled in the Maritimes and Quebec, 30 percent in Ontario, and 25 percent in the West.[130]

By the end of the project in November 1924, however, only 3,400 of the 5,000 permits had been used.[131] Efforts to allow the rest of the permits to be taken by refugee Russian Jews stranded in Constantinople or by relatives of Canadian Jews from other parts of Europe were refused,[132] as the new restrictionist-minded deputy minister of Immigration, William E. Egan, tightened the screws. The unused permits tantalized Jacobs and others, who were under pressure from Jews clamouring for permission to bring over members of their families. They pressed the government for a "quota" of three thousand Jews for 1925. It was granted, but that was the last of such arrangements.

Changes in Official Attitudes, 1925–26

Perhaps the extreme resistance by department officials to the petitions for allowing in Jewish refugees during the 1930s and 1940s stemmed from the pressures they had been subjected to in 1923 and 1924. In any case, by 1925 officials had stiffened their resolve against Jewish immigration, and by 1926 restrictionist bureaucrats determined to keep all non-British immigration to a minimum. Angry over concessions to Jewish pressures, they dominated the department. The sympathetic Robb had been replaced by other ministers, and antisemitic sentiment in Quebec was mounting. Ernest Lapointe led a group of sixty Quebec MPs, which comprised nearly half of Mackenzie King's Liberal caucus,[133] and from this point forward Lapointe's influence on the prime minister was paramount, especially on issues such as Jewish immigration. By 1925–26, the effectiveness of Jewish political influence and *shtadlanut* in the interwar years had terminated, and Jewish immigration to Canada slowed to a trickle. Blair was "determined never to be duped by Jews again."[134]

Nevertheless, the Canadian Jewish community was grateful for this large influx of Jewish immigrants. It was a feat that American Jewish organizations — facing even tighter restrictions — believed they could not accomplish. Jews in Saskatoon took the opportunity of the prime minister's appearance there in 1924 to express their "heartfelt thanks": "You, Sir, threw the doors of Canada open to [the refugees] . . . and told them to come in and take advantage of the innumerable opportunities that this country has to offer. . . . This kindness . . . that you have shown to our unfortunate coreligionists, the Jews of Canada will never forget and the Jews of the world will forever be grateful for."[135] It was the last major immigration of Jews into the country for more than twenty years.

In a letter written to future prime minister Richard B. Bennett in October 1925, however, Jacobs complained about the change in official attitude: "All our efforts during nearly a year have gone for naught. We were up against Egan and Black, a combination which was sufficient to break down the work over which we had toiled for so many months. Black — your former Party organizer — is preening himself on his success in outpointing us."[136] Deputy Minister of Immigration William Egan, while giving evidence before the House of Commons Select Standing Committee on Agriculture and

Colonization in 1928, reacted sharply when he was asked whether there were "any especially vigorous efforts on the part of certain people to get a large number of Jews admitted into the country." Egan replied, "There is a constant hammering from one end of Canada to the other. . . . I have been accused of introducing restrictive measures galore."[137] In 1930 and 1931 two new orders-in-council were issued. One permitted only immigrants with enough capital to buy and operate their own farms. The other barred all non-agricultural immigrants except those of British or American origin. While not totally ended, Jewish immigration — except by those who could qualify for "special permits" as first-degree family members — was effectively halted.

LEBN ZOL HERJOLFSON?

"*Lebn Zol Kolombus*" ("Long Live Columbus"), a popular song of the American Yiddish theatre of the interwar years, toasted Christopher Columbus — some of whose shipmates were Marranos, secret Jews — for his discovery of "*dem land dem nayen*" (the new land). It is not known whether the song was as popular on the Yiddish stage in Canada, and research has not yet uncovered a Canadian equivalent — say, "*A Lebn Af Dein Keppele Herjolfson*" ("A Blessing on Your Head, Bjarni Herjolfson"), to celebrate the Norse trader who landed in North America in 985, or a ditty in honour of the better-known Jacques Cartier. North of the forty-ninth parallel, Jews of that era, though mostly immigrants, probably had already absorbed the reticence then typical of Anglo-Canadian society (i.e., no national enthusiasm, please, we're Canucks). And yet, such a song could have been composed by a bold spirit to celebrate the intrepid Norseman who discovered North America or the Mariner of St. Malo, who touched down at Quebec in 1534, the first European — as far as we know — to do so, and in that sense, the founder of Canada. The words of the song praising Columbus ("No wars, no guns, no bloodshed; neither Czars nor tyrants") were as true of the Jewish experience in Canada as of that in the United States. No doubt, many Jews seeking entry to Canada understood, at least vaguely, the sameness between these two adjacent countries, even though those who stayed here after immigrating would soon appreciate some of the differences. And if they remained, as most did, instead of remigrating to the United States, they would have quickly realized the uniqueness of Canada in North America.

Lack of Support for Jewish Farming Colonies

Advocates of increased Jewish immigration hoped to expand the already existing Jewish farming colonies out West. But there was no support among immigration officials. As far back as 1921, F. C. Blair had been closely examining the Jewish colonies and had decided that their development did not warrant the special encouragement of more Jewish immigration.[138] After he became director in 1936, his surveillance increased and he commissioned a special report on the colonies.[139]

In authorizing this report, he was obviously preparing himself to respond to appeals for entry permits from Jews claiming status as farmers. He was determined to minimize Jewish immigration, and since he was familiar with the JCA's activities, he wanted an updated comprehensive assessment in order to refute any claims of success and thus refuse such applications. He directed his officers to provide statistical data on the areas under cultivation, as well as numbers of original families at the time of establishment or since placed in each colony, on those remaining, and on those who had acquired title to their lands. He asked about the extent of relief given in the past five or six years, and wanted information on "the young people still in the colonies, and some indication as to whether or not Jewish people have made, or are making, a success of land settlement in the several colonies."[140]

A field officer visited the six major Jewish colonies in March and April 1937, and reported at length on the basis of JCA files (readily shown to him by Louis Rosenberg in the JCA's Regina office), municipal and other records, as well as interviews with long-time non-Jewish neighbours, local bank managers, and the Jewish farmers themselves and their families (through an interpreter). He found that in the four most important colonies — Sonnenfeld, Hirsch, Lipton, and Edenbridge — "the Jewish people cannot be considered outstanding as a farming class. A few of them are good. The majority are average or slightly below."[141]

Some of the Jewish farmsteads had a downright unkempt appearance. Jews, he found, practised poor farming methods. He noted that "more active supervision should be given to . . . better farming practices. The control of weeds, the upkeep of buildings and the general appearance of the farm would go a long way towards creating a better impression both to local people and others." He pointed out, however, that "generally speaking the Jewish people get along very well with their various neighbours which are made up nearly of all nationalities and creeds." He also learned that instead of improving their farms, Jews put their spare cash into education: "One of the outstanding things noticed was the desire of the families to give their children the best education possible. To get money for this most everything else was let go."

The decline in two of the colonies was indeed serious: Lipton's population had fallen from 285 in 1910 to 71 in 1936, and Hirsch's from 162 to 66. Edenbridge and Sonnenfeld, however, had grown during those twenty-six years, though both were far from their 1930 peaks (227 for Sonnenfeld and 210 for Edenbridge). Nevertheless, acreage under cultivation in both colonies had increased more than twelvefold. Given the disastrous conditions in the rural Saskatchewan of the 1930s, these two colonies were more than surviving, and probably were doing far better than many communities in a province where the combined impact of soil erosion, pests, drought, and low world prices had nearly destroyed the wheat economy.[142] Jewish farmers were doing no worse under these circumstances than others, and quite possibly better than some.

Still, the report from the field inspector to the director of the Soldier Settlement Branch of the Department of Agriculture — to whom Blair had directed his questions — made no such comparison. Nor had Blair asked for it, possibly because he already knew the answer: Jews on average were likely no worse as farmers than anyone else. There were some very good, some poor, and many of more or less average quality — that is, the same as the general population.

Where Jews differed, apparently, was in the strong emphasis they gave to educating their children. As a result, their farmsteads were possibly more unkempt than those of their neighbours, and their agricultural practices less "scientific." But the emphasis on these points in the field inspector's reports, and even more so in the director's — without comparisons made with the general population — suggests that both men understood that Blair, who never kept his views secret, probably was looking for ammunition against Jewish immigration.

Blair's concerns about second-generation Jews staying on the land further revealed a strong bias. The director stated that "there has been a strong tendency on the part of [Jewish] adult sons and daughters to abandon farm life and engage in business or take some form of employment in the cities and towns, while not a few have entered the medical and legal professions."[143] This apparently was *ipso facto* evidence of a Jewish lack of aptitude for farming! He then went on to say that "the number who have deserted the farm ran from 25 to 50 percent, and it was frankly admitted that others still on the land were there merely because they were needed to assist their parents."[144]

Hence, 50 to 75 percent of sons and daughters were still on the land, surely not a low percentage. But some were there only because they wanted to help their parents. Why was this considered to be a lower level of motivation for staying on than any other? Again, did it differ significantly from patterns evident in the general Saskatchewan farming population? The director's report to Blair claimed so. "Truly, the picture is one which does not show up the Jewish farmer in a favourable light and cannot afford a great deal of satisfaction to those who have been behind the undertaking." However distorted, this was just what Blair wanted to read. Such government concerns were not lost on Jewish officials who, when possible, attempted to place immigrants on farms.[145] Vladimir Grossman's encouragement of Jewish farm settlement was motivated partly by the hope that it would help to obviate French-Canadian opposition to Jewish immigration. "Nor should the land be considered a mere alternative," he concluded. "It is the only way to a new Jewish life. . . . It is not a sacrifice but a great regenerative method by which we may gain security for the future."[146]

Restrictionist Immigration Policy, 1931-35

Immigration was a highly politicized question in Canada throughout the 1920s and 1930s. Prime Minister Mackenzie King, dedicated to national unity, was very sensitive to the contending arguments in the debate.[147] Powerful nativist sentiments against Asians and Eastern Europeans existed in Western Canada. There was also "widespread opposition to immigrants from southern Europe," while some French Canadians saw immigration as "a nefarious plot to reinforce the already preponderant majority."[148] Unions, too, were opposed to the importation of cheap immigrant labour, and Protestant groups and the Ku Klux Klan objected to an infusion of Roman Catholics.[149] Only railway companies and industry favoured a vigorous immigration policy, which would increase colonists and the labour pool.

The government's decision to accede to Blair's kind of attitudes kept Jews out.[150] Despite his protestations of sympathy for the Jews in Germany in the 1930s, along with his willingness to receive Jewish delegations and meet with the Jewish MPs (Samuel Jacobs, Abraham Heaps, and Samuel Spector), Prime Minister Mackenzie King was not prepared to overturn the established policy — inherited from the 1920s — of severely reducing Jewish immigration.[151]

Why? King was an extremely cautious politician. He knew that it was essential both for his government's survival and for national unity, precarious since the 1917 Conscription Crisis, to retain traditional Liberal support in Quebec. And while such support, marshalled by his able provincial lieutenants Ernest Lapointe and later Louis St. Laurent, did not depend only on a restrictionist, anti-Jewish, immigration policy, King nevertheless understood the risk in appearing to succumb to Jewish pressure to open Canada's gates to refugees.

Further pressures on the government to admit some Jewish refugees came from the Canadian National Committee on Refugees and Victims of Political Persecution (CNCR). Led by Senator Cairine Wilson and Constance Hayward, and backed by some sympathetic newspaper editorials in the wake of the *Kristallnacht* attacks on Jews in Germany in November 1938, this organization found no echo of Canadian public opinion in favour of refugee admissions.[152] Immigration was in bad odour with intellectuals such as the historian Arthur Lower, of Winnipeg's Wesley College. Through the 1920s and 1930s, he severely criticized the government's previously generous immigration policies. In his view, those policies had attracted many unsuitable immigrants. Worse yet, they created, in Lower's eyes, a situation in which Canada's Anglo-Saxon character and institutions were jeopardized because, like Gresham's law of bad coinage driving out good, "bad" immigrants drove "good" Canadians out of their own country.

Generally, the activities of the Jewish MPs or the CNCR were unable to move King and his government, although the CNCR (which believed Canadian public opinion was either isolationist or antisemitic) did save some lives and helped many of those few refugees who managed to gain entry.[153] It is interesting, though, that some of the German and Czech refugees who were admitted did indeed go into farming, like Samuel and Anne Sussel, who came to Canada in 1937 from Mainz. After spending four years in Edmonton with their two children, they bought a farm in 1941 near Chilliwack, British Columbia, and settled down there to run a small dairy herd, raise poultry, and grow raspberries.[154]

Thomas A. Crerar, one-time minister of Immigration, on four occasions in the late 1930s urged his Cabinet collegues to admit Jewish refugees. But each time he failed to persuade them and was forced to inform Jewish petitioners that the policy would not be changed.[155] In the final analysis, it was Prime Minister King, by no means an antisemite (though he was prey to then-current attitudes about Jews) and by his own account sympathetic to the plight of Jews in Germany, who determined that the immigration policy would stand. National unity required concession, conciliation, and compromise, and he had to meet the severe domestic problems of the 1930s.[156] The provision of refuge for Europe's threatened Jews was not perceived by the government to be in the national interest, despite the severe persecutions of the 1930s and the mass murder during the Second World War.

Restrictionism thus began to effect a drastic reduction in Jewish immigration to Canada. By 1931, it was less than one-fifth what it had been in 1930, only 649 compared with 3,421.[157] Figures rose somewhat over the next two years, then fell again in 1934. For the next twelve to thirteen years, despite desperate appeals from Jewish refugees and organizations, the government severely restricted Jewish entry into Canada on the theory that, as one official put it, "none is too many." Most of those who did manage to gain entry did so under the "permit system," which was characterized by a certain amount of influence-peddling.[158] When the Jewish refugee question emerged in acute form in 1938, King told his Cabinet that "the time has come when, as a Government, we would have to perform acts which were expressive of what we believe to be the conscience of the nation, and not what might be, at the moment, politically the most expedient." But because of opposition from Quebec members, King agreed that provincial governments should decide how many Jewish refugees they would admit.[159]

The provinces resented having to support unemployed immigrants on their relief rolls, and urged the Dominion government to "curtail the activities of the Department of Immigration," which they regarded as "over-zealous." Anxious to comply and still allow immigration of the "right sort" — that is, of farmers — King's government in 1927 had agreed to an arrangement whereby officials in the provincial governments, which were equally responsible for immigration, would "see that the [Dominion] regulations were even more restrictive than before."[160] In other words, the provinces were to have the key responsibility for immigration, and the premiers the deciding voice on their provinces' absorptive capacity. Such considerations would be decisive in determining how many immigrants would be admitted.[161] Because of anti-immigrant sentiments and, in the 1930s, severely depressed economic conditions, the provincial governments probably were as unsympathetic as Ottawa officials like Blair to Jewish immigration.

"Accidental" Immigrants

In 1940, Canada did receive some seventeen hundred "accidental" Jewish (or half-Jewish) immigrants. These German and Austrian refugees were rounded up in Britain in 1940 as aliens from enemy countries, and were shipped off to detention in Canada and other Commonwealth countries.[162] About a third were teenagers, among them rabbinical-school and university students, artisans, and professors.

After a week to ten days at sea in steerage — with the usual seasickness, salmonella poisoning, and food shortages — surrounded with barbed wire and machine guns, and on the same ships as Nazis and German prisoners of war, they disembarked in Canada amid tight security. Initially, camp conditions in the Eastern Townships were awful. Although officially categorized from the start of the war as "friendly enemy aliens" (class B) or "friendly aliens and refugees from Nazi oppression" (class C), the Jewish internees "were treated as if they were prisoners of war" or potential spies, even though Canadian authorities were informed by the British of their status.[163] On arrival in Canada, some internees were robbed by soldiers of all their valuables and were locked up — some in the same camps with Nazis and other war prisoners.

Canadian officials quickly separated the Jews from the prisoners of war. However, they initially enforced tight discipline, even making it difficult for Canadian Jewish Congress officials to visit. Two months after the internees' arrival, British authorities sent the Canadian government guidelines for their release. Some were to join auxiliary military units, participate in war work, or undertake further studies. The Canadian authorities balked, and the internees had to continue waiting in prison camps.[164] Some seven hundred of them were so disheartened that they accepted an offer to return to Britain, with the assurance that they could join the Pioneer Corps Auxiliaries, non-combat army labour battalions. Those remaining stayed on in the belief that, sooner or later, they would be released,[165] as some were in July 1941. An army officer in command of one of the camps warmly concurred:

> After nearly a year's experience with these people it is my opinion that this would be beneficial. They are highly temperamental and react very keenly to what they think are injustices and are very grateful for any favours given them.[166]

Those released went to the cities for further schooling or into war work. Others still in the camps readied themselves for civilian life. They studied English, general interest, and academic subjects in preparation for matriculation exams. "Generally life is very bearable," one of them wrote,[167] and the commissioner of the camps, Colonel Reginald Fordham, "was very sympathetic to the men under his care."[168] The guards — mostly French Canadians — were lenient and humane. The camp schools were run in co-operation with McGill University officials, and only four months after internment began, examinations were held.

At the same time, their lot was improved through the efforts of the Central Committee for Interned Refugees (CCIR), formed in 1941 by the National Council for Refugees (NCR) and the United Jewish Refugee and War Relief Agency (UJRA). Headed by Senator Cairine Wilson, the CCIR first laboured to have internees released and then arranged for jobs and support for them. The CCIR monitored their circumstances with concerned follow-up in the form of advice, support, board, and, sometimes, intervention with employers. Every petition was scrutinized by F. C. Blair, who "proved to be a formidable obstacle to the smooth and quick release of the interned refugees."[169] Every flaw in every file was of concern to Blair and was utilized as an excuse to deny release. "Blair . . . found the means to interpret the immigration regulations in their most restrictive sense." In early December 1943, the Canadian government issued an order-in-council (PC 9440) that closed the camps and freed the last of the internees. They were then free to find their way into Canadian life.[170]

The German and Austrian "accidental immigrants" of 1940 adjusted to Canadian life and the Jewish community in various ways. In some cases, however, there was a certain cultural dissonance. One of them reported:

> This was a funny thing, and I gave up after awhile to tell people. When I told people I came from Austria, they'd say "Oh, you're a landsmench of mine. You come from Galicia too" and I tell him no, I came from Vienna. "You come from Austria, so, you must come from the same part that I come from." So, after awhile, I say sure, I gave up. . . . I learned how to speak Yiddish. With my German background it wasn't too hard. I got along very nicely.

After their experiences, they were usually prepared for anything. Most of them adjusted well and developed considerable admiration for some aspects of Canadian norms, such as the absence of a stratified class system.

> What impressed me the most, coming to Canada, is the lack of the caste system. In Canada I learnt very soon that the only thing that counts was money, more or less, to determine your status. Another thing that I admired very much and that I was not used to from Europe was that Jewish people were workers here. . . . This impressed me very much in favour of this part of the world.

These "accidental immigrants," and the few thousand other Jews who had entered Canada during the Nazi era, were joined by many others when the war was over.

CHAPTER

3

The "Jewish Problem" in Montreal Schools in the 1920s

The Jewish community of Montreal faced special challenges because of the unique linguistic and cultural duality of the province of Quebec. Throughout the 1920s, its leading issue was the Jewish school question.[1] For many years, the Jewish community had demanded equal rights for Jewish pupils in the Protestant school system, which they could legally attend and were obligated to support through real-estate taxes. Eventually, some Jews started pressing for the right to establish a separate Jewish school system.

Montreal Jewry was torn apart by this issue, which involved not only two major factions within the community — those who wanted a separate Jewish school system and those who wanted equal rights within the Protestant system — but also the Protestant Board of School Commissioners, the government of Quebec, the Roman Catholic hierarchy, French-Canadian nationalist extremists, and the general public of the province. The Jewish school question elicited strong opinions on all sides. It went to the heart of other matters of central importance to many Quebeckers in the 1920s, such as the English/French and Protestant/Catholic balance of forces in the province and in the city of Montreal, and, to some, the undesirability of allowing non-Christians to obtain equality in the province. While comprising only 6.13 percent of the population of Greater Montreal in 1921, the city's Jews wielded greater influence than their numbers dictated. They were the third-largest ethnic community in the city, and were dominant in clothing manufacturing, the city's second most important industry. Living mostly in the St. Lawrence Boulevard north-south corridor, the strategically located dividing line between the English and the French sections of the city, Montreal's Jewish population constituted, geographically and culturally, a veritable "third solitude" in this city of historical tensions between English and French.

What the controversy bequeathed to the Jews of Quebec was a reaffirmation of their status as a double minority. In Quebec, the Catholic French saw themselves as an embattled minority threatened by North American materialism, world communism, and atheism. The Protestant English felt threatened by non-Christians who menaced the stability of their constitutionally guaranteed enclave in the midst of the majority Catholic/French culture. At the level of law, politics, and civil status, therefore, the Jews of Quebec were in an inferior position. There was no parallel to this situation anywhere in the United States or Western Europe, where, after 1919, virtually all countries established state school systems in which all citizens *de jure* enjoyed equal rights.

By 1920, the Jewish school question was one of the city's major public issues. A 1903 act of the Quebec legislature, following a court battle between the Jewish community and the Protestant school commissioners, had established the right of Jewish children to attend Protestant schools.[2] Jewish pupils became a prominent element, especially in certain inner-city areas, where they outnumbered the Protestants. Since then, the main issues had been Jewish representation on the Protestant board and employment of Jewish teachers. The Protestants maintained that because the Quebec educational system was a confessional one legally mandated to instruct pupils in the Christian religion, Jews could neither govern nor teach in their schools. Since most of the city's Jewish population was concentrated in a narrow corridor that produced a majority of children in several schools, the Protestants agreed to employ some Jewish teachers in those schools, although these teachers were nevertheless officially required as part of their duties to teach children the rudiments of the Protestant faith. The Protestants, however, firmly refused to accept Jews as members of their board. If the Jews did not like the existing arrangements, some Protestant spokesmen stated, they should seek to set up their own school system.

Easier said than done. There were two serious problems with this suggestion. The first was resistance to the very idea of a separate Jewish school system in a "Christian society," and the second difficulty — impossibility, really — was the lack of consensus among the city's Jews on the make-up of a Jewish school system. These two barriers to a satisfactory resolution challenged all of the involved parties, and periodically resulted in a flooding of the city's newspapers with long reports of numerous meetings held to stake out positions and explain them to an increasingly polarized Jewish community. The controversy also produced an angry and defensive Protestant school board. Expensive and lengthy court battles between Jews and Protestants went all the way to the Judicial Committee of the Privy Council in London, England. At numerous Jewish rallies, no eloquence was spared in enunciating the views of one party or another on this controversy. Montreal's Jewish communal politics were dominated by this issue throughout the decade because it crystallized the uncertainties of Jews living in a bilingual and bi-national province, and belonging to neither group. Moreover, the controversy became a vehicle for self-assertion in a community deeply fragmented by economic and social tensions.[3]

This question aroused strong feelings in the Catholic and Protestant communities as well. The Protestants were determined to retain full control over their school system and wanted compensation for the cost of teaching Jewish children. The Jewish community — as Reverend Canon Elson I. Rexford, a leading spokesman for the board, pointed out in a 1924 pamphlet entitled *Our Educational Problem: The Jewish Population and the Protestant Schools*[4] — had attempted since 1916 to force the Protestant board to accept one Jewish representative.[5] This was stoutly resisted because, as Rexford explained, "the main object of our public school system is the formation of Christian character."[6]

Like his associates, Rexford was not prepared to compromise. They informed the Jewish community's representatives that if Jews were not prepared to accept the status quo, the board would possibly "withdraw the Jewish children from the Protestant Schools";[7] in effect, evict them. There would be "no surrender" to the Jews, even to the proposed experiment to allow two Jews to sit on the board for ten years. The integrity of Christian education was at stake. "The Jewish population might rest assured," Rexford stated, "that the Protestant[s] . . . would never consent to hand over to Jewish administration and control [our] splendid educational system."[8] In fact, he contended, the presence of "a large number of Jewish children [in] our Protestant schools has seriously impaired the value of these schools as institutions for Protestant education and has led many Protestants to withdraw their children from these schools."[9] The possibility of an eventual Jewish majority in the Protestant schools, given the rate of increase during the previous twenty years, was worrisome indeed.[10]

To Reverend Rexford and the Protestant board, Jews were a most vexing problem. They had a large number of religious holidays, whose observance "seriously interferes with the working efficiency of the Protestant schools."[11] As for employing more Jewish teachers, Rexford stated that of the seventy Jewish women teachers already working, "many of them [were] from a foreign population [and] speak English imperfectly. . . . Moreover," he continued, "in mixed [Jewish-Protestant] classes it does not seem reasonable to place

Protestant children under [the] direction of these Jewish teachers."[12] In some of the centretown schools, where Jews were the majority, "it is most undesirable that [religious] instruction should be given to a few Protestant pupils in the presence of a large number of Jewish pupils who are simply listeners, and onlookers." As well, Jews made unconscionable demands such as "ask[ing] for special courses in the Hebrew language and literature under special teachers trained and appointed by themselves" — at the expense of the board, of course. Such cheek, Rexford implied, was more than the Protestants should have to bear!

Problematic as well for the Protestants was their belief that the Jewish community failed to pay its way. Although 13,954 Jewish children attended Montreal's Protestant schools in 1924, the proceeds from school taxes on Jewish-owned property ($368,794), according to Reverend Rexford's careful calculations, yielded less than half the annual cost of educating them ($837,240).[13] The Protestants who had to pay the difference felt financially pressed. In 1922, the Protestant board initiated a bill that required Jews to pay their school taxes to the province's "neutral panel" (an entity that received the school taxes levied on Quebec corporations and allocated these monies to the Protestant and Catholic school boards) and allow the Protestants to claim from it the full cost of accommodating Jewish children. This neat solution would allow the Protestants to lower their own school taxes by almost a third.

Owing to these persistent problems, the Protestants demanded the repeal of the 1903 act. Thus the constitutional rights wrongfully taken from them could be restored, and a bigger share of the "neutral panel" monies could be acquired to make up their losses on the Jews. And so, Jews, having created all these "problems," would remain in the Protestant schools, provided they did not cost the board any money and on condition that the 1903 act be repealed. Thus the board would be vested with power to deal with Jews as it saw fit, granting them "privileges," not "rights," in the schools. Clearly they would not have the same advantages as Protestants.

Jewish Integrationist Views

Ever mindful of the Jewish community's interests, the *Canadian Jewish Chronicle* countered the argument about financial losses by pointing out that the local "labelling of Jewish ratepayers seems to have been based on some mysterious plan. . . . [M]any a Jewish ratepayer has been set down either as Protestant or Catholic. . . ."[14] Others stated that Jews were undercounted. All Jewish Smiths and Millers were listed as Protestant, while Pascals were deemed Catholic. And some of the largest Jewish taxpayers were corporations whose taxes went to the "neutral panel."[15] But these rejoinders had no effect and the financial issue remained alive throughout the entire controversy.[16] Beleaguered and defensive, but tough-mindedly conscious of its unshakeable constitutional rights under the British North America Act of 1867, which confirmed the existence of two, Protestant and Catholic, confessional school systems in Quebec, the Protestant board and its community stood firm throughout the storm. It would countenance no Jewish representation, demurred at hiring more Jewish teachers, and demanded full compensation for its costs.

Within the Jewish community, there was little compromise between the two major and several minor factions that became involved, a fact duly noted by the Protestants. The government of Quebec and the Catholic church, to protect their interests, also became parties to this decade-long dispute. Many Jews living in upscale west-end districts represented by the Jewish Educational Committee favoured the continuation of the 1903 arrangement, with minor revisions, while many downtown (or east-end) Jews represented by the Jewish Community Council wanted to dissolve the existing compact and establish a separate Jewish panel.

Uptown Jews in fact were a much greater threat to Protestants like Rexford, who believed that those revisions would have severely altered the character of their schools. To the Jewish community, the refusal of the Protestant board to hire Jewish teachers, except for those who were to serve in the schools where Jewish pupils were predominant, was particularly humiliating.[17] This problem was highlighted by the *Keneder Adler* — a newspaper more attuned than the *Chronicle* to the concerns of the Jewish working class, whose upwardly mobile daughters, having qualified as teachers, were denied employment simply because they were Jews.[18] According to one *Chronicle* correspondent, there was a higher propensity among Jews than among Protestants in Montreal at this time to send children to high school (which required payment of high tuition fees), and more Jews than Protestants registered in them.[19]

The community's upper crust included not just some old wealth, but also patrician figures (like the tobacco tycoon Sir Mortimer Davis and Lyon Cohen and Mark Workman, well-off clothing manufacturers with wide-ranging industrial interests), while the outlying areas of Quebec included Montefiore Joseph, scion of one of Canada's first Jewish families. These families — which included many lateral branches touching even the illustrious Harts of Trois-Rivières, as well as some later additions from intermarried sons and daughters of the well-to-do immigrants of the 1880s and 1890s — constituted a plutocracy. It strongly influenced the community's internal affairs and — through lawyers Samuel Jacobs and Peter Bercovitch, MLA since 1916 for the St. Louis riding — had a voice in both Dominion and Quebec politics. It was a group that commanded a certain respect, indeed awe, even in the Bronfman family, which, with a substantial fortune made in the whisky business, settled in Montreal in 1924.[20] Led by Samuel, "Mr. Sam," as he was known, the Bronfmans amassed even greater wealth in subsequent years, while becoming involved in the highest levels of Montreal Jewish philanthropic activity, such as the campaign for the establishment of the Jewish General Hospital. For all the members of this class, and many other Montreal Jews who saw the school issue as a test of their eligibility for integration, the battle was a crucial one.

These uptowners had been led in many matters since the early 1900s by the venerable lawyer Maxwell Goldstein, K.C., who had conducted their battles for representation on the Protestant board and the hiring of Jewish teachers. By the early 1920s, even Goldstein's appeals that Jews be allowed to sit as "advisory" members of the Protestant board, to assist in solving questions on Jewish matters, were firmly rejected. The uptown Jewish Educational Committee believed that its integrationist position was the majority view of Montreal Jewry, and that Jews should not separate from the Protestant school system. Indeed, as far as they were concerned, "there is too much segregation already."[21] Jews constituted 90 to 100 percent of the students in twelve to fifteen of the large Protestant schools in the downtown area, Goldstein pointed out, and about 30 to 35 percent of the total student body in the entire Montreal Protestant system.

Although Goldstein, and probably most other integrationists, preferred a common school system for all denominations, he recognized this to be impossible in Quebec and conceded that the Protestant system "has been the most beneficial to the Jewish Community, and upon the whole has been fairly administered."[22] While ultimately seeking full equality, the integrationists nevertheless continued to press for representation. But in 1922, they were forced to mount vigorous opposition to the Protestant board's attempt to repeal the 1903 act and have the Quebec legislature pass a new law that would allocate Jewish school taxes to the "neutral panel" and allow Jews to attend either Protestant or Catholic schools. Goldstein saw the Protestant move as a serious threat to Jewish rights. He predicted the complete segregation of Jewish students in certain Protestant schools because they would be there only on sufferance, rather than as a right. His group was most dissatisfied with the interpretation of the 1903 compact, but under no circumstances would he accept the Protestant proposal to scrap it altogether and put the Jewish community out on the street, bereft of any rights.

The uptown faction was equally opposed to the separatist solution favoured by many downtown Jews. In October 1923, Rabbi Max J. Merritt of Reform's Temple Emanu-el,[23] a leading member of the Jewish Educational Committee, weighed into the debate with a strong denunciation of "short-sighted and illiberal factions" in both the Protestant and Jewish camps, especially the latter.[24] The establishment of a separate Jewish school system would be "a backward and deplorable step . . . a fatal blow [to] . . . the very heart of a genuine and all-inclusive national spirit which is as the very breath of life to this young commonwealth." He warned that "the ideal of a Canadian national unity will fade into mere nothingness [if] a group of Protestant extremists be permitted to join battle with a group of Jewish extremists to undermine secular and Canadian education."

Formerly at a pulpit in Evansville, Indiana, the Nebraska-born Merritt was unfamiliar with Quebec political and social realities, and with Montreal's Jewish cultural dynamics. A few months earlier, he was quoted as saying at a public meeting that "if our erratic, contentious, and short-sighted co-religionists of the East End [the downtowners] had had the wisdom to follow the wise, far-sighted, and statesman like guidance of our legislative representatives at Quebec . . . [and] the Jews of the West End, with their progressive, intelligent and truly Canadian vision," a good arrangement could be made with the Protestant board.[25] The *Chronicle* labelled these remarks "crude" and "tactless" and called on the rabbi for a categorical denial or explanation.[26] Understandably, Merritt did not respond.

But Merritt was not alone. Even the Conservative Sha'ar Hashamayim congregation, newly housed in an enormous edifice in Westmount, passed a resolution against a separate Jewish panel — despite an appeal by the congregation's president, the esteemed community leader and prominent clothing manufacturer Lyon Cohen, that it remain temporarily neutral.[27]

Cohen, in fact, favoured a compromise allowing a certain measure of Jewish cultural autonomy in the predominantly Jewish centretown Protestant schools.[28] But his was a rare voice in the west end, where the integrationist camp was strongest. Fearful of the long-term social and political results of ghettoization in a separate Jewish school system — which would also entail much higher educational taxes than they were paying under existing arrangements with the Protestants[29] — most west-end Jews were prepared to accept much less than the downtowners. They wanted to maintain the Jewish position under the 1903 act, not terminate it altogether. Public education in Jewish subjects was generally less important to them than political equality, and they could afford private Jewish education, regardless. They argued that the intermingling of children of all backgrounds at school would produce better citizens than segregation in parochial schools.

The nationalist position was also strongly supported by the Jewish Workers' Conference, which represented some ten thousand members of the clothing workers' unions, the Arbeiter Ring (Workmen's Circle), the National Workers' Alliance, and a number of left-wing cultural, youth, and consumers associations. Arguing for minority rights and for the protection of Jewish culture and tradition, they also made an interesting plea that a Jewish mentality is "distinguished from those of the English-Canadian and French-Canadian population insofar as they have different racial characteristics, customs, and habits, resulting from a somewhat varied environment and upbringing, all of which makes the task of their education abstrusive to the Protestant teachers. . ."[30]

Jewish Nationalist Views

The third party to the dispute were the downtown Jews, who were demanding the right to establish a separate Jewish school system, an earlier goal of some Jewish immigrant intellectuals. In 1912, the Montreal Poale Zion (Labour Zionists) had proposed that idea, and lengthy discussions transpired at the March 1919 meetings of the Canadian Jewish Congress.[31] Two major leaders of this cause in the 1920s were Hananiah Meir Caiserman and Louis Fitch, both of them well-known figures in Montreal Jewry.[32] They argued not only that Jewish pupils were subjected to various indignities in the Protestant schools, such as compulsory exposure to religious instruction in the New Testament (in spite of an understanding that Jews were exempt), but also that Jewish cultural interests were poorly served in that environment.[33] "The Protestant school implanted in the hearts of the Jewish children a Christian spirit . . . [and] the same Christian spirit has reached into many of our homes," Caiserman asserted.[34] "A generation of children is lost to Judaism at a time when the Jewish youth of . . . Canada is the greatest hope of Judaism."

Caiserman and other enthusiasts for a separate school system envisioned an opportunity to remedy what they viewed as the disastrously poor plight of Jewish education in Montreal, where fully two-thirds of the community's twelve thousand schoolchildren received no parochial education whatsoever! In their own schools, this trend towards ignorance and ultimate communal degeneration[35] could be reversed. William Nadler, executive secretary of the Jewish Community Council, expressed the view that "only by sending our children to school, where the teaching of Judaism will play a prominent role, can we give to this country, a good Jew and a good Canadian. Let us have Jewish separate schools, and we will contribute to Canada a finer and higher type of Canadian Jew . . . [able] to make the synthesis between Canadianism, Judaism and HUMANITY."[36] He hoped to set up about seven downtown Jewish schools, which would be supported by taxes and grants from the "neutral panel" on the same basis as the Protestant and Catholic systems.

A variation of this idea was advanced by Hirsch Wolofsky of the *Keneder Adler*, which throughout the entire controversy supported the nationalist position and frequently attacked the opposition for bringing "shame and ridicule" on the community.[37] These schools would be entrusted to a Jewish committee acting under the Protestant board, with instruction in Judaism to replace Christian religious teaching and Jewish teachers to be employed.[38] "This . . . plan would not affect the rights of the Reformed Jews in the West End," Wolofsky argued. "[It] would satisfy the nationalistic and orthodox Jews who supply 90 percent of the Jewish children in the local schools and would provide a basis for the institution of a system of separate schools in the event of this plan not working out successfully."

QUEBEC ROYAL COMMISSION ON EDUCATION

In 1924, this issue came before the Quebec provincial government, whose Liberal administration was headed by Premier Louis-Alexandre Taschereau, for his day a genuine progressive who abhorred racial and religious prejudice.[39] Tutored on this issue by Peter Bercovitch and Joseph Cohen, Liberal Jewish members of the provincial legislature for two downtown Montreal ridings, Taschereau was not indifferent to the outcome: he favoured an accommodation between moderate Protestants and Jews, but he would not countenance Protestant efforts to undermine Jewish rights. He insisted that Jewish children had the "same rights as Catholics and Protestants to receive education in schools which would not wound their religious sentiments."[40] In fact, he had openly supported the nomination of Bercovitch, an integrationist, over that of Louis Fitch, a separatist, as Liberal Party candidate in the riding of St. Louis during the election campaign of 1923.[41]

Seeking both enlightenment and respite, Taschereau in early 1924 struck a Royal Commission, composed of three Protestants, three Jews, and three Catholics, and chaired by the former premier, Sir Lomer Gouin, to look into the question. The Jewish members of this Committee of Nine, as it came to be known, were Michael Hirsch, Samuel Cohen, and Joseph Schubert. Hirsch and Cohen were uptowners and wealthy Montreal businessmen, the former a cigar manufacturer and the latter a mining engineer with extensive interests in Quebec asbestos and gold properties.[42] Schubert was a Montreal alderman, a socialist, a trade unionist, and a downtowner committed to the idea of a Jewish separate school system.[43]

Taschereau's admirable decision to appoint a commission of inquiry was marred, however, by his choice of its Jewish members. Major parts of the community were outraged. The *Chronicle* editorialized: "We cannot scare up even a breath of enthusiasm about the Jewish personnel of the School Commission."[44] While its Protestant and Catholic members were "giants," the Jews were mere "mice," no doubt recommended by Peter Bercovitch, whom Premier Taschereau consulted on the selection. Hirsch was already *parti pris*, having taken a strong stand for a renewed deal with the Protestants (i.e.,

---

TEACHING YIDDISH

J. I. Segal

The children from my neighborhood
all come to me to learn Yiddish:
I tell them not to open their books,
I want to look at them and read
their faces as if they were pages
in a book; I want to know and be known,
so this is how I talk to them
without ever saying a word.

Dear boys and girls, Yiddish sons
and daughters, I want to teach you
what you've come to study but first
I have to learn how to read you I
have to write you and describe you
as you are and I don't really want
to be your teacher but an older
brother; so what shall we do?

First I think I'll read a story
by Sholem Aleichem just to see how much
you know about Yiddish laughter.
If you can laugh with real Yiddish flavor
at one of Sholem Aleichem's stories
I won't need further proof;
you'll do well with chumish in Yiddish
and even with gemorah in Yiddish,
and with literature naturally —
in what but Yiddish?

From Gerri Sinclair and Morris Wolfe, eds., *The Spice Box: An Anthology of Jewish Canadian Writing* (Toronto: Lester & Orpen Dennys, 1981): 7.

returning to the 1903 accord), while Cohen — a newcomer to Montreal — had taken no part whatever in Jewish community affairs: "[W]e seek in vain for Mr. Cohen's name among the leading members in cultural, spiritual or even philanthropic, organizations. . . ." Even Schubert, the socialist and labour spokesman, "who may be said to be the only one who understands, and therefore 'represents,' a certain portion of that large majority of the Jewish community," was questionable because most Jews, the "traditionally orthodox both in . . . national and religious viewpoint," had no representative on the commission.

The Jewish Community Council, an essentially downtown organization led by lawyers Louis Fitch and Michael Garber, also protested.[45] In an open letter to Premier Taschereau, they claimed that Hirsch was already committed to continuing the status quo with the Protestants, while Cohen was not only an American (who was obviously unfamiliar with the local scene), but also "not . . . an enthusiastic supporter of Jewish religious and national education for the mass of Jewish children." Also, as a member of Temple Emanu-el, where the status quo–oriented Jewish Educational Committee was based, he was likely to be compromised. Arguing that "the School problem to Jews is essentially one of the preservation of national culture, language and those elements most dear to a self-respecting people," Fitch and Garber asserted that "the persons most fit to present these views, although recommended[,] have been ignored by the Government and its advisers."

Adding his voice to the contretemps over these appointments, Hananiah Meir Caiserman protested that Peter Bercovitch "does not appreciate the importance . . . the gravity of the school problem and its effect on Jewish life in this province."[46] The Jewish Community Council also protested to the premier that because Hirsch and Cohen both favoured the status quo, they would "give an undue advantage to the views of the Jewish Educational Committee" to the detriment of "the great majority of the Jewish people residing in the heart of the city [who] are Orthodox and desirous of procuring for their children some teaching for Jewish . . . cultural and religious lines."

Once the commission began its hearings, the bitterness between the Jews and Protestants surfaced. During one of its first sessions, the Protestant board spokesman Col. J. J. Creelman stated that aside from the financial question, the board considered Jewish holidays to be a serious problem, and that it was "impossib[le] [to] teach to Protestant children Protestantism in a Protestant way with Jewish teachers and in the presence of Jewish children."[47] For the downtown "nationalists," Louis Fitch retorted that this justified a separate Jewish school system: "The Protestants will be able to educate their children as good Canadians, at the same time not forgetting their ancient heritage."

Protestant spokesmen, however, were divided. Herbert Marler, MP for the

Montreal riding of St. Lawrence–St. George, criticized Creelman for intolerance and argued for a friendly solution on the grounds that "a large number of Protestants in this city are against the abrogation of the Act of 1903." Another prominent Montreal Protestant, W. D. Lighthall, supported Marler's views.[48] At the same time, Maxwell Goldstein proudly asserted: "If the Protestants are insistent that they don't want us, then we are too proud to stay with them, and we will get out and make our own separate schools." A former rabbi of Temple Emanu-el, Nathan Gordon, stated that "we [Jews] will not tolerate any humiliation. . . . if we cannot get along with the Protestants, then let us have a panel of our own." The *Chronicle* supported this position, while asserting that "we Jews have no desire to de-Christianize the Protestant schools, just as we are absolutely opposed to having our children Christianized in the Protestant schools."[49]

John Farthing, the Anglican bishop of Montreal, defended the superiority of Protestant Christian ethics and the letter of the law in the British North America Act. As he stated: "We have . . . a distinct civilization to maintain which is based upon the Christian teaching . . . and if we should in our schools weaken that influence . . . we undermine the very civilization that is built upon that foundation."[50] Notwithstanding, then, the demurral of a few of its liberal members, the Jewish community could expect little from the Protestant Board of School Commissioners. The *Chronicle* observed: "It is . . . infantile to expect . . . that should we succeed in keeping our children in the Protestant schools in spite of the aggressive attitude of the Protestant Commissioners. . . . [T]hey will be regarded as . . . aliens to be segregated from the rest of the herd."[51]

All the while, the Montreal Jewish community was alive with intense debate.[52] Appearing before the three Jewish commissioners were spokesmen for various positions on the issue — and several individuals eager for a chance to make a speech. The newspaperman Israel Rabinowitz observed these meetings and took the opportunity to poke fun in his columns for the *Adler* at some of the pompous personages, including Rabbi Joseph Corcos of the Spanish and Portuguese synagogue and other uptown dignitaries, who spoke at these meetings.[53] But there was pathos too. Miss Pass, a recently graduated teacher from McGill's Macdonald College, stated that many Jewish women teachers could not get jobs in the Protestant schools. These meetings also provided opportunities for the rhetorical settling of old scores. Hirsch Wolofsky ridiculed the "assimilationist" Jews. Because their children had to endure the indignity of being segregated into Jewish-only classes within the Protestant schools (on the grounds that Jewish holy days interrupted the studies of the non-Jewish pupils), they were ready to demand separate schools. "It has been the fate of our race," Wolofsky stated, "that those Jews who stand on the threshold between Judaism and Christianity will, when they realize that anti-Semitism does not spare them, either return to Judaism or else cross over the threshold altogether and pass over to the Christian fold."[54]

The Judgement of the Commission

When the Royal Commission's report was made public in early 1925, its Protestant and Jewish members divided along predictable lines. The three Protestant members insisted on the unconstitutionality of the 1903 act and on keeping complete control of their schools regardless of the Jewish presence in them. "The question of Jewish holidays, Jewish teachers and of segregation are questions of administration," they stated, "and as such must remain subject to the discretion and control of the Protestant Board." But they did recommend concession and conciliation. "Such questions should be approached, considered and dealt with by all those interested in the spirit of equity, fairness and toleration."[55]

This was not good enough for the *Chronicle*. "Once we admit that the idea of segregating Jewish children as if they were lepers or the breeders of contamination is purely an impersonal matter of administration, we admit that there [are no] Jewish school problems," it commented. "Once we say that it is all right for a Jewish girl to make all the sacrifices necessary for obtaining a teacher's diploma, . . . but that her chances for obtaining a position are nil . . . then we do admit that there is no Jewish School Question, and we can stop worrying about it here and now."[56]

Two of the Jewish commissioners, Hirsch and Cohen, reported that there was no need for a separate Jewish school panel, "providing there is no discrimination against Jews and other non-Protestants and non-Catholics," a point, the *Chronicle* asserted, that was meaningless in view of the Protestant board's renewed discriminatory practices. It recommended that the provincial government establish a Montreal financial school commission to have full control over finances for all non-Catholic education in the Protestant schools, so that "there would be no discrimination . . . by the board or by principals or teachers, and that segregation because of religion, race, or creed be illegal."

In a minority report, Schubert recommended that a Jewish committee be set up by the Protestant board to administer those schools with overwhelming Jewish enrolment, and that religious instruction be carried out after hours. Common to all three Jewish commissioners, however, was an insistence that, as Hirsch and Cohen put it, "[those in] the Jewish community . . . have to extricate themselves and their children from the humiliating position in which they have been, and are being[,] placed."[57] Believing that the time was ripe, Hirsch Wolofsky invited all classes in the Jewish community to unite behind a demand for Jewish separate schools.[58] He noted that "different factions in the community were never closer to an understanding than they are at present." He called for a conference chaired by Lyon Cohen and Samuel Jacobs to prepare a presentation to the provincial government.

Premier Taschereau, who had hoped for a compromise, was now faced with a problem. At the urgings of Jewish representatives, he referred the act of 1903 to the Quebec Court of Appeal for an advisory opinion. "Are we to force [Jewish children] to go to Christian schools where they may be taught things repugnant to them?" he asked in the Legislative Assembly. "Are we to leave these 13,000 children without education? Are we to say that the Jews have no status whatever in Quebec, that they are, in the words of one of the judges, outcasts? Is that the meaning of the British North America Act? . . . [I]t is necessary that the Jews should be able to determine their position. They have asked for this legislation so that they may go to the Supreme Court and the Privy Council, and we are permitting it. They had to find out what are their rights. . . ."[59]

In the advisory opinion handed down in March 1925, the court found the 1903 act *ultra vires* on the grounds that it violated Article 93 of the British North America Act, which guaranteed Christian schools in Quebec.[60] Consequently, the court held, Jews could not be appointed to the Protestant board as either active or advisory members, and had no right to teaching positions. And most menacingly for the Jewish community's uptown faction, the court ruled that the Protestant board had only "as a matter of grace" to allow Jews to attend their schools. Jews, therefore, had no legal right to attend Protestant schools.

Moreover, the court found that the Quebec legislature did not have the power to establish separate schools for Jews or other non-Protestants or non-Catholics, such as Greek Orthodox. This judgement was appealed to the Supreme Court of Canada, which not only upheld the Quebec court, but also found further complications in the act of 1903.[61] Equally disturbing was the court's finding that while the Jewish population of Montreal had the "privilege" of attending either Protestant or Catholic schools at its option, this applied only to the city of Montreal as it existed at Confederation in 1867. This right, therefore, did not necessarily apply to Jews in sections of the city that were annexed later, and definitely was not available to the substantial numbers who lived in municipalities like Westmount, Outremont, and Lachine.[62]

The school question continued to be an issue in the May 1927 election, in which Taschereau's Liberal government was challenged by Camillien Houde's Conservatives. On the strength of his espousal of the "nationalist" cause, Louis Fitch opposed the well-ensconced Liberal incumbent, Peter Bercovitch, in the heavily Jewish St. Louis riding, which he had represented since 1916.[63] Fitch hoped to exploit the resentment many downtowners felt towards Bercovitch, who opposed a separate Jewish school system, believing that "a significant degree of integration with the Anglo-Protestant community held the key to progress for the Jewish population."[64]

Despite his championing of a separate Jewish system, and the support of both the *Keneder Adler* and the *Chronicle*, Fitch lost. Elections are rarely won on only one issue. Many downtowners probably were more interested in supporting a member of the Legislative Assembly from the governing party than in supporting educational separatism (which some of them may not have favoured) and Houde's attacks on Taschereau's liberal views.[65] The *Chronicle*, meanwhile, voiced the frustrations of a beleaguered Jewish community: "The Protestant Commissioners can, if they choose, compel attendance on Jewish holidays. They can ignore the prohibitions of the conscience clause. Whether they will do so, as a matter of policy, is another question. It is sufficiently significant that it is within their power to do so."

The contest was not over, however. The Supreme Court of Canada overturned the Quebec court's decision by finding that it was within the power of the Quebec legislature to establish a third school panel, one for Jews. This judgement was upheld by the Judicial Committee of the Privy Council, which in 1928 concurred that the Quebec legislature was indeed empowered under the British North America Act to establish a separate Jewish school system in Montreal.

Ongoing Infighting within the Jewish Community

Responsibility for ameliorating the Jewish school question now rested with the Quebec provincial government. But there was an equal onus on the Jewish community to inform the Taschereau government that a Jewish school panel was indeed what it wanted. However, the divisions between the uptown "integrationists" and the downtown "nationalists" had probably worsened. In his presentation to the Law Lords, Sir John Simon, counsel representing the uptown interests, stated that "the Jewish population, speaking generally, was very poor and made hardly any contribution to the local taxes and were not in a position to establish their own schools."[66]

The *Chronicle* saw in this aside and other presentations by uptown lawyers at the London hearings suggestions that Jews who felt entitled to their own schools were "ludicrous" and "misguided." It was a dangerous kind of Jewish antisemitism that "would have left the Jewish population without a single means of escape from an intolerable position, where they would have had no educational status except as may have been granted them by Protestant tolerance, and one lacking any sanction other than the good will of the latter."[67] A broad Jewish communal understanding of the Privy Council's judgement was now needed. If exploited effectively, it provided an opportunity either for concessions to allow the teaching of Jewish subjects in Protestant schools or for establishing a separate, publicly funded Jewish school system. The question of the hour was this: Could the community realize the potential of the opportunity now presented to them and come together in common cause?

Hirsch Wolofsky demanded the formation of a united Jewish committee to confer with the Protestant board and then with the government, "so that when the next session of the legislature arrives we will at least be informed on the question and demand what is possible, just and within our powers."[68]

Intracommunal discussion abated for about a year while some parleys with the Protestant board, initiated by Provincial Secretary Athanase David, were undertaken by Jewish representatives. Peter Bercovitch, in his capacity as MLA, was apparently consulted by David.[69] Bercovitch stated that although "there appears to have been a difference of opinion between the understanding which the committee had of the procedure they were to follow and my understanding thereof, I am, however, convinced the committee at all times acted in entire good faith in their negotiations with the Protestant Board." The negotiations resulted in a bitter exchange of letters between Samuel Cohen (who had changed his name to Livingston) and Michael Hirsch.[70] Communal unity on this issue was nowhere in sight.

By January 1929, the downtown "nationalists" were up in arms over these negotiations. "We are now faced with a bitter struggle," Louis Fitch thundered at a late January mass meeting, "with those of our own people who would teach Protestant culture to Jewish children — a fight against the assimilators, a civil war, a war between brothers." The Maccabees who combated the nefarious influences of Hellenized Jews in ancient Israel, he stated, were engaged in no more momentous battles. The argumentation for a separate Jewish school system was becoming sharper. One speaker suggested that it would help Jews "develop a culture centre in Quebec which would be unique," a kind of centre of Jewish cultural creativity, possibly similar to Warsaw, Odessa, or New York.[71] But the major point was that compromise between the two Jewish factions now seemed unattainable.[72]

Negotiations between Jewish and Protestant board representatives failed at this stage possibly because of deep dissension within the Jewish community. Then, in late March, the Quebec legislature passed a bill to allow the allotment of a portion of the neutral panel's proceeds to be used for the education of mainly Jews and about one thousand Greek Catholics who attended the Montreal Protestant schools.[73] In supporting the legislation, Premier Taschereau again indicated his preference for a Protestant–Jewish accommodation. "There are some Jews who ask for a separate panel," he said in the assembly. "I do not think it to be desirable. A third panel would mean perhaps a lesser Canadian spirit." In Quebec, he continued, "we have the greatest respect for minorities. French-Canadians in other provinces have suffered too much to be willing to sanction religious intolerance where they are in a majority."[74] Experienced politician that he was, Taschereau's strategy was clearly to strengthen the negotiating position of the Jewish community *vis-à-vis* the Protestants in order to bring about an arrangement acceptable to the majority on both sides.

Further talks between Jewish and Protestant representatives followed, much to the annoyance of the Jewish "nationalists" (or "separatists," as they now sometimes called themselves).[75] Efforts by Bercovitch and Cohen to get Jewish representation on the Protestant committee of the Council of Public Instruction failed, despite the eloquent minority appeal of a McGill botany professor, Carrie Derrick, who felt that Jews should not be subjected to taxation without representation.[76] Bercovitch, however, continued searching for a solution, reiterating that if the Protestants would not co-operate, he would be "the first to ask for our own schools, despite the fact that I am opposed to separate schools."[77]

This was precisely what the "nationalists," with the support of the *Chronicle* and the *Keneder Adler*, had been demanding for years; that is, to leave the Protestants alone. Their attitude continued to be "They don't want us and we don't, or shouldn't, want them. Let us set up our own school system at long last and build a real Jewish culture in Montreal." By January 1930, the now-frustrated Bercovitch, true to his word, prepared the bill that provided for the establishment of a five-person separate Jewish school board empowered to set up Jewish schools on the same taxation basis as the Catholic and Protestant ones. The Jewish board was also enabled "to enter into arrangements with any other board of school commissioners or school trustees" for the education of Jewish children.[78]

This was an obvious opening for those like Bercovitch who still hoped for a last-minute deal with the reluctant Protestants, who, in the *Chronicle*'s words, "are prepared to face [a Jewish withdrawal] with equanimity."[79] Because the David Bill (named after its sponsor, Provincial Secretary Athanase David) only enabled legislation, it would take time — a year at least — and much further detailed work before a Jewish school system in Montreal could be functioning. In the interim, Jewish children — who according to the Privy Council's judgement had no rights — would have to attend Protestant schools.[80]

As well as expressing concern over appointments to the new Jewish school board, some doubted the government's will to follow through. Writing to the premier in later March, Hananiah Meir Caiserman pointed out that the bill needed amendments giving the Jewish school commission the same powers as the Protestant and Catholic committees of the Council of Public Instruction, which controlled education in the province of Quebec. This empowerment was potentially important, especially when the Catholic hierarchy insisted that, in the *Chronicle*'s words, "it is the duty of the State to prevent teaching the child anything that may be considered anti-Christian or subversive to the social order."[81] If this principle was accepted, Judaism could not be taught because it would be regarded as anti-Christian. The latitude needed in teaching history and social science might also run afoul of the prohibition on propagating revolutionary doctrine. If Jewish schools were ever established, the *Chronicle* stated soothingly, "nothing will ever be taught . . . to bring into contempt the teachings of Christianity . . . nor is there any possibility of Jewish public schools being employed for the propagation of revolutionary ideas."[82]

But this was all theoretical because of the composition of the board. Besides Livingston, it included Rabbi Herman Abramowitz of Sha'ar Hashamayim synagogue; Nathan Gordon, former rabbi of Temple Emanu-el; A. Z. Cohen, activist for the United Talmud Torahs; Edgar Berliner, a wealthy businessman; Max Wiseman, a prominent local obstetrician; and Michael Garber, "an out and out separatist." Thoroughly outraged by these appointments, the *Chronicle* thundered that they had "been chosen for the purpose not of undertaking to create a system of Jewish schools, but primarily [to] negotiate an honourable treaty with the Protestant School Board."[83]

The Jewish school board asked for four "privileges" from the Protestants: the addition of Jewish history and Hebrew language and literature to the curriculum, positions for Jewish teachers in classes where Jewish children predominate, official recognition of Jewish holidays, and the termination of involuntary segregation of Jewish children. Moreover, they sought an end to "the many instances of petty insults offered to Jewish children by teachers."[84]

Defeat, however, seemed guaranteed. By the end of 1930, the opposition of the Roman Catholic hierarchy, the rise of the antisemitic press, wavering by the Taschereau government, and the divisions within the Jewish community led most of the Jewish commissioners towards a compromise solution.[85]

In early December, a contract was made with the Protestant board of Montreal and Outremont. It included the acceptance of Jewish children as a right and the ending of segregation. But Jews, in turn, had to accept compulsory Christian devotional exercises, loss of credit for holidays, and discrimination against hiring Jewish teachers.[86] This was the will of the majority, the *Chronicle* conceded bitterly, and "those who seek to foster Jewish education amongst the masses and to arrest the forces of national and religious disintegration must seek other means to achieve their purpose."[87] There were at this point no such arrangements, however, with the Protestant boards of Westmount, Verdun, and Lachine, where there were considerable Jewish populations.

THE CATHOLIC CHURCH RESPONDS

The fourth major party to the dispute was the Catholic church. It began to formulate its response to the Privy Council decision and the possibility of a separate Jewish panel by consulting with the Catholic committee of the Quebec Council of Public Instruction. While the provisions of a bill to permit such a panel were under discussion in March 1930, Monseigneur Georges Gauthier, co-adjutor archbishop of Montreal, published an open letter in *L'Action Catholique* to warn Premier Taschereau of "the most serious consequences" of this bill, which would apply to the whole province and "would not fail to get us into trouble wherever one finds a group of Jews."[88] His major, and probably justified, concern, however, was that "the favour granted to Jews today will perhaps be demanded tomorrow, under the same pretexts, by other religious denominations or even by anti-religious sects."[89]

In an emotional address at St. Joseph's Oratory in March 1930, Gauthier condemned the premier for extending the Jews "an entirely unwarranted sympathy" that would "overturn an educational system which is for us [French Canadians] a safeguard and a security."[90] At the same time, Jules Dorion in *L'Action Catholique* criticized the government for recognizing Quebec Jews "as a distinct NATIONALITY, as considerable as the English or the French nationality of the province." Dorion stressed that "the Jewish children cannot nor must not be considered as being anything but English-speaking or French-speaking Canadians."[91] Raymond-Marie Cardinal Rouleau, archbishop of Quebec, publicly warned that while the church had no objection to Jews getting the same educational privileges as Catholics and Protestants, there was serious danger of the 1930 bill leading to the creation of a religiously neutral school system in Quebec.[92]

Other Catholic spokesmen held more extreme views. Abbé Antonio Huot, author of a 1914 tract on Jewish ritual murder, editor of *Semaine réligieuse de Québec*, and author of numerous anti-Masonic and antisemitic writings,[93] strongly opposed a separate, publicly supported Jewish school system in editorials for *L'Action Catholique* in mid-May 1926. He demanded that the provincial legislature protect "the interests of Christianity in the public schools of our province."[94] It would be a sad day for French Canadians, he said, to see Jews, "the last immigrants to our country," endowed with rights that "have been refused to our French-Canadian compatriots in Manitoba" — where, in 1890, Roman Catholic schools were abolished.[95] If the existing arrangement was not satisfactory to the Jews, they were free to educate their children at their own expense in private schools, or, possibly, to negotiate with the Protestants for the establishment of distinct schools where the religious instruction would be suitable for Jewish children.

In the editorial columns of *Le Soleil*, the daily French newspaper in Quebec City, there was deep concern for the preservation of the province's Christian character and reminders that Jews were guests, not equal members, of Canadian society.[96] In early February 1926, *Le Soleil* informed its readers that "being immigrants, and sons of immigrants, [Jews] have no special rights."[97] "We owe nothing to the Jews," *Le Soleil* stated two days later, and concluded that "moreover, as we are a Christian country, a Christian nation and not a neutral, unbelieving and materialistic one, to claim for non-Christians the best one can get indicates a strange broadness of outlook, an absence of judicial principles, a notorious inconsistency."[98]

One year before, Jules Dorion had written in *L'Action Catholique* that the stumbling-block of neutral or common schools could be avoided if Jews were given their own separate school system.[99] This was a far more liberal position than that taken by Huot and the Catholic hierarchy after the Privy Council's decision in 1928. The churchmen were opposed to allowing Jews to sit on the Council of Public Instruction (the general supervisory body responsible for education in the province), on the grounds that this would undermine the Christian character of that body.[100] Cardinal Rouleau wrote to Premier Taschereau on February 28, 1930, a few weeks after the bill passed the legislature, to express his concerns and keep the pressure on. He was joined in this campaign by Monseigneur Gauthier, as well as Monseigneur Georges Courchesne, bishop of Rimouski; Alfred-Odillen Comtois, auxiliary bishop of Trois-Rivières; Monseigneur Joseph-Simon-Herman Brunault of Nicolet; Monseigneur François-Xavier Ross, bishop of Gaspé; and Monseigneur Fabien-Zoël Decelles, bishop of Saint-Hyacinthe. They maintained that while Jews should have their own schools, they would not accept the principle of Jewish membership on the council.

These high-level episcopal attacks on the implications of a Jewish school system were clearly of such importance during the controversy that Premier Taschereau felt it necessary to consult these religious authorities while the bill was being drafted.[101] Implementation of the bill was delayed because of the divisions among representatives of the Jewish community, some of whom were privately negotiating with the Protestant board for a return to the 1903 accord. Taschereau's government saw an opportunity to extract itself from the imbroglio and induce a compromise, which they had always favoured, between Jews and Protestants. The government repealed the David Bill, and passed a new act — which had the prior approval of Cardinal Rouleau and Monseigneur Gauthier — to establish instead a board of Jewish school commissioners for Montreal, whose sole purpose was to negotiate a new deal with the Protestant board.

By this time, however, Catholic opposition to Jewish claims and to the perceived threat of neutral schools had aroused some virulent antisemitism. Camillien Houde, leader of the Conservative opposition in the Quebec Legislative Assembly, had been a supporter of the David Bill, but now, as a candidate in the Montreal mayoralty race, he thundered: "If the Jews are not happy, they can leave."[102] At the same time, an editorialist in *L'Action Catholique* commented, "We must never forget [. . .] that the Jews readily put up with neutral schools, divorce and in general, every anti-Christian law."

Meanwhile, Adrian Arcand, leader of the nascent Quebec Fascists and editor of *Le Goglu* — a Montreal weekly newspaper dedicated to publishing antisemitic articles and cartoons, and inspired by the German-Nazi organ *Der Stürmer* — exploited the controversy. In April 1930, he asserted "[that] every religious or racial denomination other than the bilingual Christian denomination does not have any right to be recognized by our parliaments and our courts."[103] Other expressions of antisemitism in Quebec were mounting during the early 1930s.[104] The historian David Rome contends that "The imagery of the Jews conveyed so successfully in the campaign about the school question became deeply rooted in the thinking and in the articulation of that nationalistic church-led portion of French Canada."[105]

Montreal's Divided Jewish Community

The crisis was resolved by an agreement between Jewish representatives and the Protestant school board. It nevertheless resulted in bitter, long-lasting communal divisions. The "nationalists" lamented a lost opportunity to establish a separate Jewish school system — with the enormous cultural opportunities it was believed to hold out — and the "integrationists" regretted their failure to secure significant concessions within the system they were compelled now to support. The failure of the "nationalists'" attempt to found their own tax-supported school system is also important for the pattern it did *not* establish for Montreal Jews. It forced them to seek further integration into the city's unyielding Anglo-Saxon culture, perhaps weakening their own Jewish culture while at the same time emphasizing their precarious marginal status to both the English and the French communities.

Catholic French Canada was now thoroughly aroused to a perceived "Jewish menace." "There is no doubt," the historian Cornelius Jaenen observed, "that increasing anti-Semitic feeling and organization, the exclusion of Jewish refugees, the enforcement of Sunday observance legislation and the school question were all linked in some way to each other and were part of a socio-cultural phenomenon."[106] The Protestants of Montreal, meanwhile, still in full control of their schools, were again saddled with a large Jewish minority and all of the same "problems" they had long resented.

This protracted controversy left Montreal Jewry divided and threatened by a virulent form of antisemitism that was sparked in part by the controversy itself. In the face of this threat there were appeals for the establishment of a Jewish Vigilance Committee, as the *Chronicle* saw it, "to protect the good name of Jewry" in Montreal, where "we have been made the object of libellous attacks by certain vigilant tabloids."[107] As a small minority, Jews had no choice but to accept a public humiliation. That the humiliation had come in a country that saw itself as part of the British Empire — in which, as John Farthing, the son of the Anglican bishop of Montreal, aptly put it, "freedom wears a crown" — could well have made Jews apprehensive, defensive, and cynical. It was a bitter irony that, largely as a result of divisiveness in the Jewish community and the lopsided compromise with the Protestants, Jews were officially relegated to second-class status in the very province that in 1832 had led the entire British Empire in extending them equal rights.[108] Continuing attacks on Jews in the antisemitic Quebec press and the removal in 1936 of the Jewish exemption to the Quebec Sunday Observance Act (designed to protect workers against undue exploitation) increased their uncertainty.

This affair was a lesson in Canadian constitutional wrangling over education that went far beyond Quebec. Schooling had always been a battleground for contending religious and linguistic interests, even before Confederation. The New Brunswick school dispute of the 1870s, the Manitoba school question in the 1890s, and the Ontario bilingual schools dispute in the 1910s, along with other bitter controversies since then, indicate that conflict over the role of church and state in education have been major issues of Canadian history.[109] Lengthy court battles were fought by some of the best legal talents, and governments fell or were elected on the issue. This history, probably known, most likely would have provided little comfort in 1931 to the Jewish contestants in the battle they had just lost so completely and humiliatingly. But solace could have been taken from the continuing existence of the parochial schools, those privately funded institutions that provided a source for cultural strength, the preservation of Yiddish, the cultivation of Hebrew, and the basis of a growing sense of a distinctive Canadian Jewish identity.

At one point in the struggle, the *Chronicle* commented ironically on some unwelcome advice to Montreal Jewry that had appeared in one of the New York Yiddish dailies and concerned the injection of "Jewish nationalism" into the 1927 Quebec provincial election campaign. "It is futile for [the New York papers] to remind us that we are not living in Poland or Roumania," the editorial stated, "and that it is wrong to inject Jewish nationalism into the elections of a free country. If [Canada] is a free country, as the *Jewish Morning Journal* implies, it is precisely because its constitutional basis is the recognition of more than one national entity within its framework."[110] The editorialist showed a clear understanding of the differences between two neighbouring, but highly distinctive, Jewish social and political contexts.

Perhaps the best statement of Canadian Jewish awareness of its unique situation, and of its distinctiveness from the American Jewish context, was yet another comment in the *Chronicle* late in the school controversy: "The British Imperial policy derives its strength on the principle of the preservation of every individual culture within its realm."[111]

From the Montreal Jewish school controversy many Canadian Jews came to understand not only that Canada was different from the United States, but also that Quebec was possibly a bell-wether for the entire country. The *Chronicle*'s editorial expressing regret over the Quebec appeal court's decision had observed that

> the school question has . . . developed into the larger issue of the rights of Jewish citizens not only of this Province, but of the whole dominion. Hence the answer of the Privy Council . . . will have a far-reaching effect upon the whole body of constitutional rights of the Jews of Canada. For if the Privy Council should decide that the Canadian Constitution made no provision for the Jewish inhabitants of Canada . . . it would mean that Jews have no educational rights in any Province of the Dominion. And if the Protestants in the other Provinces should feel inclined to follow the example of the Protestants of Quebec, there would be no constitutional bar to prevent them from doing so.[112]

The year 1931, then, was an ominous one for the Jews of Montreal. The Depression was entering a desperate phase. And in Germany, the Nazi Party under Adolf Hitler had made enormous gains in the elections for the German Reichstag in September 1930. For Quebec Jewry, the decade opened in abject defeat, deep disunity, and serious menace abroad.

CHAPTER

4

"Rag Trade": The Clothing Industry in Flux

Profound philosophical differences over schools echoed even deeper divisions between Jewish employers and workers in the burgeoning clothing industry. This industry created both an economic frontier for Jewish entrepreneurs and a factory for the Jewish working class, which formed a large component of the industry's labour force in Montreal, Toronto, and Winnipeg. Both the leadership and the rank-and-file membership of the major clothing-trade unions were predominantly Jewish.[1] As well, Jews became some of the largest manufacturers in the apparel trades.

After the First World War, of greatest significance was the enormous increase in the manufacture of dresses and other women's ready-to-wear items. This became the dominant segment of the womenswear sector, which previously was restricted mostly to the production of mantles, coats, and suits. Known colloquially among its Jewish practitioners as the *shmata* business, or the rag trade, it took on a personality of its own and attracted many daring (or foolish) entrepreneurs. The trade had rapidly increased during the war, when the market for inexpensive cotton smocks, housedresses, and shirtwaists increased, thus drawing large numbers into the factories. During the 1920s and 1930s, an even larger market emerged for inexpensive but stylish dresses for the growing numbers of women working in offices, banks, and stores.[2] For its workers, however, the dress industry created some of the worst labour conditions in Canada.

Dress manufacturing was a risky business, a gambler's industry in which only the very few shrewdest or luckiest survived. Owing to rapidly changing whims of style, some manufacturers were left with unsaleable racks of garments and others with "runners" for which demand was practically insatiable — until consumer preferences changed, sometimes suddenly. In the 1920s, it was said in the trade that to last for as long as ten years was a miracle. The bonanza mentality was also encouraged by the industry's relatively easy entry. As in most branches of clothing manufacturing, start-up costs — estimated at $1,500 to $2,000 — were relatively low, machines easily rented, inexpensive accommodation leased, and cheap labour readily hired. With increasing urbanization, changing tastes in clothing, and the expansion of the retail sector following the First World War, markets were not only growing, but also becoming more accessible. Major department stores like Eaton's, Morgan's, Simpson's, the Hudson's Bay Company, and a number of smaller chains were expanding their branch stores and order offices. Meanwhile, independent storekeepers were proliferating. In 1921, there were some 104,000 independent stores in Canada. Twenty years later, there were 128,000.[3] Specialized dress shops were springing up everywhere — a high percentage of them Jewish-owned — featuring frocks in the latest styles and fabrics at modest prices. This form of enterprise was favoured by many Jews because of its low capital threshold and its folklore of rich rewards. From the old country many Jews brought a familiarity with clothing manufacturing and textiles.

Jewish leadership in this industry reflects an interesting aspect of their economic and social history. Jews had an overwhelmingly urban background and were uniquely oriented to the clothing trades. In Europe, considerable numbers were associated with clothing as tailors.[4] Settling in urban centres also led to employment in this industry, which was seasonal, low-paying, non-unionized, and unskilled.

While diversifying, clothing production was also spreading. In addition to the principal centres of Montreal and Toronto, Hamilton remained a secondary production centre for men's clothing, as did Ottawa and London in central Canada and Winnipeg, Edmonton, and Vancouver out West. After 1920, fur-processing and womenswear manufacturing developed in Winnipeg, while entrepreneurs in Edmonton and Vancouver produced clothing for the local market.

Significant also was the efflorescence in Montreal and Toronto of the Jewish-dominated trade unions, including the Amalgamated Clothing Workers of America (Amalgamated); the International Ladies' Garment Workers' Union (ILGWU); the United Hat, Cap and Millinery Workers International Union; and the Industrial Union of Needle Trade Workers (IUNTW), an affiliate of the Workers' Unity League. Several features of this development are noteworthy. These unions, as Ruth Frager's *Sweatshop Strife* demonstrates, were not concerned only with shop-floor struggles; their battles for better material conditions were linked to "a broader social vision." For many of their members, these unions and the battles for improved conditions were "an intrinsic part of the class struggle that would one day bring about a socialist society."[5] Such views, however, led in different political directions, creating severe tensions. And while such transcendent socialist values were present among many leaders and rank-and-file Jewish unionists, the struggle to make a living while working in such a volatile industry blunted much of the idealism. Most union leaders, in any event, concentrated on basic issues like the dispersion of the clothing factories, the improvement of wages and working conditions, and the establishment of union shops. Their goal was industrial stability, not revolution.

All of the unions, except for the National Clothing Workers of Canada, an affiliate of the All-Canadian Congress of Labour and the IUNTW (a branch of the Workers' Unity League, which was in turn a wing of the Communist Party of Canada), were branches of internationals based in New York. Most of the strikes conducted by both the ILGWU and the Amalgamated were directed by organizers sent from the New York headquarters, which sought to establish industry-wide standards across North America. Moreover, there was severe tension between the ILGWU, the Amalgamated, and the IUNTW during the late 1920s and early 1930s. The battle nearly wrecked the ILGWU and substantially weakened the Amalgamated, and reflected the volatile conditions prevailing in the needle industry. The ILGWU also faced a series of daunting problems in Quebec, where employer resistance was particularly strong and political opposition prevalent. In Quebec there was also reticence among French Canadians, who were pressured to join the accommodationist Catholic syndicates instead, thus weakening the ILGWU's general effectiveness until the late 1930s.

Jewish Manufacturers and Contractors

The new dress-manufacturing business has been described as "a trade for nervous men,"[6] — or perhaps one in which a stable person endeavouring to be a manufacturer would likely become nervous. Traditionally, women's cloak and suit manufacturers operated much as their counterparts in the menswear industry.[7] Some of them established factories encompassing all stages of production for higher-quality goods and were able to maintain essential quality control this way. Large-scale manufacturers like Toronto's John Northway produced ready-to-wear coats, mantles, suits, and skirts, while others manufactured girdles and other undergarments. Northway sold his own product in a thriving chain of retail outlets in western Ontario, a vertically integrated operation that foreshadowed many others.[8] Some did only the cutting in their own factories and let the sewing out to contractors, while others used contractors for all operations, even the cutting, and took delivery of finished goods ready for shipment to their customers. Still other large-scale retailers, such as Eaton's, manufactured goods in their own factories in Toronto.[9]

Contractors were the marginal men, neither manufacturers nor workers. Often they were both. They usually possessed skill and experience as tailors, designers, or cutters, but lacked capital or commercial connections in the retail sector — or perhaps even an adequate command of English. Most of them were Jews.[10] Operating on the margins of the industry, they offered manufacturers a cheaper means of production. Contractors cut costs to the bone by operating in low-rent lofts, garrets, or the workers' own homes. In the worst of these shops, investigations reported crowding, poor ventilation, lack of sanitation, low wages, long hours, and the widespread use of child labour.[11] Competing with each other for contracts, the operators of these businesses were under constant pressure to drive costs down still further. In such circumstances, the most ruthless contractors tended to push the more humane and scrupulous ones out of the business.

Marginality did not prevent some from prospering and ultimately becoming manufacturers in their own right. They produced garments for sale to their own customers from the remnants (known in the trade as cabbage) of the cloth given them by manufacturers or, if their credit with textile wholesalers or banks was good enough, entirely from their own goods. As in the menswear trade, the existence by the early 1900s of a substantial number of Montreal and Toronto Jewish-owned manufacturing firms in the women's cloak-and-suit industry was evidence of upward mobility from the precarious margins of contracting.

Dress manufacturing by the 1920s revealed a continuity of the industry's worst problems, particularly the exploitation, or "sweating," of workers.[12] These issues had been addressed and partially resolved by the collective agreements in menswear after the bitter and bloody strikes in 1917. Most of these accords, though, had broken down by the early 1920s, owing to postwar readjustment. Employers then reduced wages, reestablished piece-work, and evaded unions altogether by moving their plants to outlying centres, operations that the unions called runaway shops. One Montreal men's clothing firm reacted to "unbearable" union demands by simply moving its production to Joliette.[13] While this battle was fought throughout the 1920s without a clear victory for either side, the majority of strikes and lockouts were short. Most contractors were eventually brought into line, even though the number of runaway shops was considerable.[14]

Dress manufacturing, unlike the production of menswear, was not only relatively new, but also characterized by a bonanza mentality. The hope for quick and large profits, combined with a relatively low capital threshold, attracted many entrepreneurs. The choice of an attractive style in the right fabrics and the most popular colours had to be made months in advance, but could be affected by radical changes during one season. Competition was so intense and the market so unpredictable and ungovernable that it approached what economists call perfect competition, a market with so many producers that no single firm can affect the price.

The predatory buying practices of the major Canadian department stores, described so graphically in the evidence given before the 1934 Royal Commission on Price Spreads and Mass Buying, helped turn the dress industry into a jungle where only those able to carry out the most ruthless cost-cutting measures survived. Wages provided the most obvious opportunity to cut costs. Even though charges of racketeering, corruption, loan-sharking, fraud, hijacking, sabotage, and other forms of criminality — all of which characterized the New York industry — did not arise in Canada, the trade was bedevilled by assorted kinds of intensely vicious, if not exactly criminal, conditions, including style piracy, unfair returns, predatory price-cutting, unethical practices by large buyers, and unconscionable labour exploitation.[15]

These actions were particularly true of Quebec, where wages were traditionally lower than in Ontario and where a population influx from rural areas created a huge pool of unskilled, cheap labour. The negative attitude of the Roman Catholic Church towards the international unions for a long time prohibited the effective organization of the French-Canadian workforce. The Catholic syndicates were organized in opposition to the "internationals" and what the church perceived to be excessively leftist ideologies.

Dress Manufacturers Establish Themselves

One highly successful dress manufacturer was Abraham Sommer of Montreal. Born in 1878 in Lodz, Poland's textile manufacturing centre, he immigrated to the United States, where he worked in the women's apparel trades. After moving to Montreal in 1901, Sommer established the Queen Dress and Waist Company. During the 1920s, he and his brother Charles built it into one of the leading firms in the business.[16] He eventually constructed the Sommer Building, which was one of the major centres of the industry in the downtown Montreal garment district.

Sommer also became an important figure in the local Jewish community by joining many of its leading social and charitable groups. His career was in some respects typical of dress manufacturers, many of whom began as salesmen rather than as tailors or contractors. With their retail experience — including a good sense of style — they would partner with an experienced cutter or designer and set up their own business.[17] If successful, they might invest in real estate like Sommer, developing buildings designed to accommodate the many and often transitory small-scale manufacturers. Some became importers of goods from New York or Paris.[18] Most supported trade associations that were organized to regulate the industry. Sommer and Abraham Gittelson, another major Montreal women's-apparel manufacturer, organized the Ladies' Garment Manufacturers' Association of Canada[19] to protect the interests of the manufacturers in labour matters.

The major Toronto dress manufacturers of the 1920s and 1930s were mostly pre-1914 immigrants with experience as salesmen, cutters, or designers, and were willing to take the dangerous leap to producing their own goods. Abraham Posluns founded Superior Cloak in 1916 and produced goods for the "carriage trade." Another was Charles Draimin, who, like Posluns, was a small-scale manufacturer until the 1920s, when his firm burgeoned. Elias Pullan specialized in the manufacture of suits and coats. Many others lasted in the business for varying lengths of time,[20] depending on their ability to cope with the volatile conditions.

In Winnipeg, several manufacturers set up businesses to exploit the growing western market for ready-to-wear goods. Morris Haid, arriving in Canada from his native Austria in 1893, established the Western Shirt and Overall company around 1900.[21] Haid and his partner, Harry Steinberg, prospered.[22] Benjamin Jacob, with partner John Crowley, founded a highly successful women's coat-and-suit manufacturing business during the 1920s, employing more than two hundred workers even in the depressed early 1930s.[23] A number of Winnipeg Jews were active in the local fur-processing business.

By this time, in Montreal, Toronto, and Winnipeg, the large downtown buildings erected by successful manufacturers housed increasing numbers of small dress factories. Producers located their offices, cutting rooms, and, often, factories in these buildings because they were close to their buyers, who either worked in the local large department stores or were out-of-town retailers staying in nearby hotels during buying expeditions. These new buildings towered as high as twelve or fourteen storeys — large for the time. During the early 1900s, the Blumenthal, Wilder, Jacobs, Sommer, and Mayor buildings, as well as other ungainly structures, ringed Montreal's Bleury–Ste. Catherine intersection, Phillips Square, Peel Street, and led up St. Lawrence Boulevard ("the Main") to Sherbrooke. In Toronto, such edifices stretched along Adelaide and King streets, west of University, and up Spadina Avenue from King Street to College Street. Winnipeg's garment centre arose after 1920 in the area northwest of the Main-Portage intersection. In all three cities each building accommodated dozens of shops and as many as two or three hundred workers.

Working Conditions and the Advent of the Unions

Even as some of these entrepreneurs thrived, the conditions of the workers worsened. The piece-work system of payment bred severe competition among workers, as well as among the manufacturers and contractors. In 1925, a Jewish immigrant worker in a Montreal dress factory complained:

> You can never do enough for the boss. Every half hour the boss counts the number of dresses on our chairs. I am a finisher, and sometimes I feel like doing something desperate when I see the girls rushing the lives out of themselves, each to do more dresses than the others.[24]

Because of the volatility of the clothing industry, unions of that era had a hard time surviving. In Montreal, problems abounded. French-Canadian workers, mostly women, were difficult to organize, and disruptions to the cloak-and-suit trade during the First World War had seriously affected membership and caused organizational problems.[25] By 1920, the ILGWU, with nearly twenty years' experience in Canada, was still struggling to improve working conditions in Montreal and Toronto.[26] A series of North America–wide strikes in 1918 and 1919 had forced employers to sign collective agreements with the union, but serious structural problems were still prevalent.[27]

The 1920s brought more uncertainties. The severe economic recession of 1920–22, the rise of dress manufacturing, and a well-managed open-shop campaign among manufacturers placed the ILGWU on the defensive. Piece-work was reintroduced by Toronto manufacturers, hours were increased, and conditions generally allowed to deteriorate as new firms ignored the union-employer agreements reached only a few years before. Many new firms remained non-unionized.[28]

Montreal conditions were worse. In January 1925, their womenswear industry was racked by a general strike over wages, hours, and working conditions that dragged on for months.[29] Although the ILGWU locals had a large combined membership of 1,500 to 1,600 workers, the strike affected a total of 6,000.[30] A month later, the Toronto ILGWU joined in.

The leader and strike spokesman for the Montreal clothing unions was Joseph Schubert, a long-time city alderman and leading leftist. His presence was symbolic of Jewish leadership in the clothing-trade unions throughout North America. Jews were generally the second- or third-largest ethnic group in the Canadian clothing trades throughout the 1920s. At Montreal union meetings, separate organizers spoke in Yiddish, Italian, and French, and the three city locals were based on these three ethnic divisions.[31]

Even though Jews were not a majority of the workforce — except perhaps in men's clothing — Jews like Schubert were usually selected to head the joint boards of both women's and men's industry locals because virtually the entire

---

YUDICA:
YIDDISH POETESS OF SPADINA'S CLOTHING FACTORIES

Yehudit "Yudica" Zik was born in 1896 in Gorzsd, Lithuania. After a peripatetic childhood and youth that took her to England, East Prussia, Russia, Sweden, and Finland, she separated from her husband and came to Canada in 1929 with her three-year-old son, Gerald. She was by then an accomplished and well-recognized poetess whose work appeared in the left-wing Yiddish press and in many anthologies. After a very brief sojourn in Montreal, she moved to Toronto. There she toiled in various garment factories on Spadina and at Tip Top Tailors on the Lakeshore. Around 1960 she moved to New York, where she died in 1987. Perhaps her most evocative Canadian poem is "Spadina," with its garment-worker's plight, here translated from the Yiddish by Adam Fuerstenberg:

Thinly fragile is dawn's early air.
Spadina, street of stores and factories.
Lies under a web of gray
And dreams the dream of workers' fortunes.

Individual steps on echoing sidewalks
Merge with hundreds of steps together.
A sound that comes from laneways and streets.
A sound of toilers, of hands occupied.

Spadina, the street of the Labour Lyceum.
With stairs and chambers for labouring men.
With their own judges, with laws that are just —
Only unity is missing among the worker masses.

leadership of the New York–based international was Jewish. Some of them likely had experience in the European clothing trade and a strong commitment to left-wing ideology. A certain degree of ethnic solidarity may also have helped. Moreover, it was probably assumed that Jews were best qualified to represent the union in negotiations with employers who were mainly Jews.

The presence of so many Jews in an increasingly militant workforce sometimes attracted adverse publicity. During the 1925 strike in Montreal, Schubert felt it necessary to stress that contrary to rumours intended to discredit the strikers, they were not entirely Jewish.[32] In fact, he said, as if to prove the legitimacy of the strike, there were four hundred French Canadians among the sixteen hundred picketers. The prominence of Jews among both the rank and file and the leadership was also an issue in the ILGWU strike, which began in Toronto in early February of that year. One leading Jewish Toronto manufacturer, who represented fourteen producers employing 65 percent of the womenswear workers, alleged that the union was attempting to oust Christian workers from the shops.[33] Replying for the union, Mary McNab

---

How many dreams are buried in the walls
Of the massive bricked in shops —
Of the young, who gave up their schooling,
Fortune and future to find in work?

Spadina, the street of worker struggles —
I give you in example my personal fate:
My child, which I leave in gray morning.
Hungry, abandoned, in rooms among strangers.

My sorrow, wandering without direction through ruined worlds.
Through horrible sufferings of peoples bleeding
To the clanging of wheels, machines and irons.
You soak in my tears and my youth.

Spadina, the street of stores and factories.
Of people who wait and pine for work —
The day that'll unite us all
Will be the golden key to freedom.

See Adam Fuerstenberg, "Yudica: Poet of Spadina's Sweatshops," *Canadian Woman Studies* 16, no. 4 (1996): 107–11, 109.

noted, "it was rather laughable to have a Jew manufacturer claim defence of Gentile girls." Tim Buck, an official with the Communist Party of Canada, claimed that police were "selectively harassing Christian pickets while leaving the Jews alone," presumably acting on orders from the manufacturers to foment ethnic conflict.[34]

While manufacturers deplored charges of preferential hiring of Jews, they did concede that "the needle industry was largely in Jewish hands."[35] Thus the Jewish presence was perceived as dominant, and was clearly evident in the leadership of the unions. All the chairmen of the Toronto, Montreal, and Winnipeg joint-boards of the ILGWU; the United Hat, Cap and Millinery Workers' International Union; the International Fur Workers; and the Amalgamated were Jews, while only the few union locals established for other ethnic groups were headed by non-Jews.

The Montreal and Toronto strikes of 1925 were the spearhead of the ILGWU's drive for recognition, better sanitary conditions, an end to piece-work, and an industry-wide forty-four-hour week. Most firms, especially the larger ones, chose to settle quickly; in early February, twenty-seven manufacturers employing seven hundred workers signed contracts with the ILGWU.[36] By early March, only six of the 115 shops that had been struck first were still holding out.[37] They too gave up and signed.

For the next few years, the 1925 agreements were observed and the industry was free of major disputes. But in 1928, the ILGWU was beset by competition from a rival union, the Industrial Union of Needle Trade Workers (IUNTW). They not only attracted members from ILGWU locals, but also mounted left-wing attacks that diverted energies from the main tasks. Employers benefited from this friction, and the spirit of the 1925 collective agreements disappeared amid bitterness and tension.

Meanwhile, the Jewish presence in the Montreal clothing workforce was rising. By 1931, there were more than 6,300 Jews working in all its branches, from a total Jewish population of 57,997. Louis Rosenberg pointed out that nearly three-quarters of all gainfully employed Montreal Jews worked in the industry; they constituted 35 percent of its workers, while more than 53 percent were French Canadian.[38] In the women's-clothing sector, Jews, half of them women, constituted 32 percent of all workers. French Canadians were nearly 60 percent of its workforce, and of that number nearly 92 percent were women. The vast majority of them were also young.

By 1930, reports of desperately competitive Montreal dress manufacturers operating their plants seven days a week united the ILGWU, the newly organized Catholic syndicates, and various other unions. They hoped to force these firms into reducing their hours and to create opportunities for some two hundred unemployed cloak-makers and four hundred dressmakers. The unions targeted Sunday work[39] and the sweatshops. Some of these shops were dangerous fire-traps where workers were so badly exploited that many overexerted themselves to earn a livelihood.[40] Manufacturers capitulated soon after it became clear that some fifteen hundred members of the ILGWU were ready to strike at seventy firms for a forty-two-hour week and wage increases.[41] These conflicts were settled by an agreement and the establishment of a grievance board, which was headed by Rabbi Harry Stern of Temple Emanu-el and comprised three representatives each from labour and management.[42] The presence of a rabbi from an "uptown" temple as board chairman is an interesting reflection of Stern's commitment to social action and of the progressive thought prevalent among Reform rabbis of that era.

This agreement, though, failed to stop manufacturers from reducing labour costs by allowing year-long contracts to lapse so they could hire new workers at lower wages. Both the union and the manufacturers also faced the problem that the new non-organized firms were able to undercut those that were organized. There were frequent strikes in the Montreal and Toronto dress industry as the ILGWU tried frantically to organize workers in these new firms and force them to accept its conditions. While most disputes were resolved quickly, many firms avoided a settlement by contracting out or leaving town.

In 1933, Gustave Francq, chairman of the Quebec Women's Minimum Wage Board, reported that "owing to disrupted conditions in the clothing trade, many firms are not operating but letting their manufacturing out to subcontractors, who are in many cases 'fly by night' factory owners."[43] Meanwhile, unemployment among unionized workers increased. Department of Labour statistics showed that by December 1931, 59.7 percent of unionized garment workers were unemployed.[44] While this picture improved in the ensuing months, there was still an average of more than 20 percent out of work during the busy months from July to September. By December 1932, unemployment in the industry was back up to almost 50 percent.[45] And there it stayed.

Transformations in the 1930s

Faced with deteriorating conditions, workers were economically distressed. This situation put increased pressure on local charities. Applications for relief grew substantially in Canada during the 1930s, and Jewish agencies in Montreal, Toronto, and Winnipeg were also paying much more than ever before to the unemployed.[46] From Montreal's Baron de Hirsch Institute, social workers and home visitors reported widespread economic distress in the city's

Jewish community, as well as a significant increase in social and medical problems. For many of Montreal's working-class Jews, living standards had substantially deteriorated from levels reached in the late 1920s, and the institute's annual reports for the 1930s included case histories indicating serious problems. By early 1931, distress among working-class Jews was so severe that the publishers of the *Keneder Adler* and the *Canadian Jewish Chronicle* started a special campaign to raise five thousand dollars "to be used as an emergency [loan] fund for our unemployed. . . ." The *Chronicle* reported that "the degree of unemployment in the Jewish community is very large. Thousands of family breadwinners are working either not at all, or only on part time, and earning mere pittances."[47]

In October 1931, in anticipation of a hard winter "with a large number of persons unable to find employment and the demands for charity even greater," fifteen Montreal labour organizations established the Peoples' Kitchen to distribute soup, meat, and tea to Jewish unemployed.[48] Women and children also showed up at the Kitchen, leading a reporter for the *Chronicle* to comment: "Even two or three days a week in a dress, millinery or cloak shop would be welcomed these days by the Jewish unemployed girl."[49]

In Montreal, the Jewish People's Restaurant for the Unemployed gave out ten thousand meals to the needy in 1931,[50] and in the first four months of 1932, gave another thirty thousand meals. The Federation of Jewish Philanthropies was hard-pressed to keep up with the need.[51] Throughout the early 1930s, the "cry of the poor . . . the sick, the aged and the orphan" was voiced frequently,[52] and the Federation of Montreal Jewish Charities ran advertisements in the *Chronicle* appealing to employers to hire Jewish workers.[53]

Unemployment was not the only problem; even those with jobs could not make ends meet. Although physical conditions in clothing factories were more comfortable and safer than in the lofts or country workshops, wages in the dress industry were abysmally low. Commenting on conditions generally prevailing in the needle trades during this era, the Royal Commission on Price Spreads reported in 1935 that

> aside from extreme variations in wages, the industry was afflicted by oppressively long hours, and violations of laws governing employment conditions, hours, and wages especially in the dress trade.[54]

Existing labour legislation could not restrain employers from exploiting workers. Quebec's labour code was probably as enlightened as that of any other industrialized province, such as Ontario. Provisions were made for factory inspections in an 1884 statute, and later laws provided for the maintenance of sanitary conditions, minimum wages, hours of labour, and other standards.[55] But in much of the needle industry these regulations were not systematically enforced; inspections were rare and incomplete, and in rural areas the legislation was entirely ignored. Thus while the minimum wages set for women operators in the dress industry ranged from $7.00 to $12.50 a week under Quebec law, employers rarely paid that amount. If they did, they forced their employees to work extremely long hours for it.[56] When he arrived in Montreal from Chicago during the winter of 1934 to organize dressmakers' locals for the ILGWU, Bernard Shane found girls earning between $5 and $10 a week. But the price spreads commission heard harrowing stories of even lower wages and longer hours in some of the shops outside Montreal, where a few employers were engaging in fraud to reduce wages.

By the 1930s, the overwhelming majority of workers in the Montreal dress industry were women. Many of them were girls as young as ten who were enduring low wages and extremely poor shop conditions. Thousands of these operatives, known as *midinettes*, (a contraction of the French words *midi* and *dinette*, meaning "short lunch"), thronged the streets and squares of the factories and nearby commercial districts at midday as they came down from the large buildings.

Seasonal employment created intensely busy periods of several weeks, followed by very long stretches of inactivity in which many, especially the unskilled, were laid off. During a busy period, a worker might earn a living wage in return for up to eighty or more hours of labour. But in slack periods, they would earn very much less — or nothing at all. Testimony by people involved at all levels of the industry to the price spreads commission indicated that, at best, a needle worker got forty weeks of work annually. Between jobs they either "lived off their fat" or took other employment. The statistics for seasonal unemployment during the 1920s show that in April, May, and June, almost one-third of all them were out of work, while in some years unemployment ran as high as 60 percent.[57]

Adding to the uncertainty of employment was the general volatility of the industry. Between 1916 and 1928, the average annual failure rate in dress manufacturing was 18.62 percent; during the mid-twenties, the failure rates approached 30 percent.[58] Despite such risks, by 1934 there were at least 693 manufacturers of women's apparel in Canada, almost double the number in 1924. Between 1922 and 1930, statistics for the Quebec women's clothing industry — numbers of employees, wages paid, and value of production — more than doubled.[59]

Testifying before the price spreads commission in January 1935, J. P. Levee, of the National Associated Women's Wear Bureau, reported that between 1932 and 1934, 232 new firms entered the industry.[60] At the same time, however, the gross value of production fell to about two-thirds of what it was in 1929, resulting in more firms chasing fewer sales. Many manufacturers were entering the field just as others were leaving, possibly because of a failure to make ends meet. It was, perhaps, in this kind of volatile environment that one dress manufacturer asked another, "How's business?" to which his interlocutor replied, "How's business? Business is so bad that even the customers who don't intend to pay aren't buying."

Meanwhile, the labour market was seriously disrupted. Workers were suddenly put out on the streets as owners closed their shops, often without paying past-due wages.[61] More companies were starting up and the number of employees was increasing, yet total salaries and wages were falling drastically.

Working conditions were often hot, crowded, dank, and unsanitary, especially among the contractors, who generally economized by crunching their workers into cheap and unsafe quarters.[62] Some subcontracted work to others, often women who worked at home. The virtual self-exploitation that ensued was responsible for the worst of the sweatshops. As the price spreads commission heard from its witnesses, this situation was difficult to investigate, because the shops frequently moved from place to place.[63] Leah Roback, then the educational director of the ILGWU in Montreal, recalled that conditions in most dress shops were "vile."[64] Even those in the big buildings (named after owners like Jacobs and Wilder) were known as cockroach shops. In many of these, she noted the sordidness of bosses favouring workers "who were willing to give [them] the very fine intimate favours."

By 1931, rising poverty levels resulted in an increase in marital breakdowns.[65] A number of the free-loan syndicates, which "include in their membership several thousand families of workmen or petty tradesmen," were likewise in danger of foundering.[66] The Montreal Federation of Jewish Charities admitted to being "caught in the vicious circle of a condition of affairs which makes the maximum demands . . . [when] revenues are likely to be at their very lowest ebb." Its president, the businessman Allan Bronfman, expressed concern that the federation "will find itself in serious difficulties."[67]

Editorials in the *Chronicle* favourably noted the scheme of the American Jewish Agricultural Society to resettle underemployed workers as part-time farmers on the outskirts of the cities. "The back-to-the-land movement on the part of our people serves many functions," ran one such editorial. "It not only tends toward a solution of the economic problems of surplusage and unemployment, but it also removes from our midst the ever-present and ever-unjust accusation that we are by psychology and habit a race of middlemen, a race of parasitic *luftmenschen*."[68]

The situation in Toronto during the Depression was similar, and its Federation of Jewish Philanthropies faced mounting pleas for help from the unemployed.[69] The ineligibility of some families for municipal assistance and a widespread belief among Jews that it was a disgrace to apply for public charity put even heavier pressure on the resources of the Toronto federation.[70]

Trade Union Activity

Trade unions reacted to the poor conditions of workers in a variety of ways. At its meeting in November 1933, the Federation of Catholic Workers of Canada passed a resolution favouring a change in the Lord's Day Act that would forbid storekeepers from opening on Sundays. This practice had presumably developed to allow religious Jews to observe their sabbath on Saturday.[71] The *Ligue du dimanche*, a watchdog group, alleged that some Jewish-owned factories — under the guise of liberality to their employees — were operating seven days a week whether employees were Jews or not. To correct these alleged abuses, the provincial government amended the Lord's Day Act to prevent all Sunday work, creating a considerable hardship for Sabbath-observing Jews. Of course, the *Ligue* (which had originated in Trois-Rivières to protect workers against exploitation) did not target only Jews. In the highly religious atmosphere of Quebec in the 1930s, its activities reflected an understandable religious orthodoxy and a humane concern for workers' welfare. The same atmosphere, however, made the *Ligue* seem, to Jews, antisemitic.

The most significant effort to improve these conditions was the drive to unionize all workers.[72] A series of strikes in 1934 and 1935 forced major women's apparel companies into line.[73] The organization of an international union such as the ILGWU or the Amalgamated in Quebec not only aroused the opposition of the church and the rivalry of the Catholic syndicates, but also stimulated antisemitism. Recalling her attitude to the organizing efforts of Shane and other leaders of allegedly communist or socialist international unions, one of the *midinettes* remembered that "*Ils me semble bien amiables; mais ils était juifs comme les patrons et je ne comprenais pas en ce tempes-là qu'ils puisse être de notre côté.*"[74]

These suspicions were overcome partly through the efforts of Claude Jodoin, later enlisted by Shane to act as a bridge to the French-Canadian workers, and Rose Pesotta, a Russian-born, Jewish anarchist, feminist, and seasoned veteran in organizing women workers in the United States.[75] While these victories for the ILGWU in Montreal indicated a growing degree of trust and respect by French Canadians for the Jewish workers and the union organizers, Jews and French Canadians remained members of separate locals, as was the case with the Amalgamated in Montreal's men's-clothing industry.

But close communications between the locals in each industry were maintained by a governing council called a joint board.

The Catholic syndicates organized unions that competed with the ILGWU. Encouraged by the Quebec provincial government and some Roman Catholic clerics who were fearful of the detrimental influence on French Canadians of international unions like the ILGWU, syndicate representatives opened negotiations with Montreal dress manufacturers in April and May 1934. These talks were accompanied by an attack on the ILGWU by Quebec's premier, Louis-Alexandre Taschereau, who accused its members of communism.[76]

Leah Roback

Born in Montreal to a traditional Jewish family in 1903, Leah Roback spent her early years in Beauport and was educated in Quebec City. She studied at the Université de Grenoble, in France, and returned in 1927 to New York, where she became involved in leftist movements. She lived in Berlin for several years in the early 1930s.

Roback returned to Montreal in 1932 to take a job as program director of the Young Women's Hebrew Association (YWHA). She joined the Communist Party and lived for awhile in the Soviet Union, returning to Montreal in 1935, just in time to campaign for Fred Rose, who was running for the CPC (Communist Party of Canada) in Cartier in that year's general election. A year later, Roback, who was fluent in French as well as Yiddish, was recruited by the ILGWU to help organize the four thousand women toiling in the "cockroach shops," making women's ready-to-wear clothes. Besides poor pay, filthy working conditions, and long hours, women often had to endure widespread sexual harassment and exploitation by foremen and shopowners. Roback was highly effective as an organizer, earning enormous respect from francophone and Jewish women workers, and she helped win the strike of 1937, after which the ILGWU became firmly established in the Montreal dress factories.

See Allen Gotheil, *Les Juifs progessistes au Quebéc* (Montreal: Éditions par Ailleurs, 1988), 67–103; Ghila Bénesty-Sroka, "Entrevue avec Léa Roback, une femme engagée dans de justes causes: Une mémoire contemporaine, *Canadian Woman Studies* 16, no. 4 (1996): 81–85; and Irving Abella and David Millar, eds., *The Canadian Worker in the Twentieth Century* (Toronto: Oxford University Press, 1978): 198–203.

Despite the presence of the ILGWU and the syndicates, the main opposition to the terrible working conditions was mounted in 1934 by the Communist IUNTW.[77] Led by J. A. Guilbeault and Leah Roback, some four thousand dressmakers went out on strike and closed down 125 shops in an effort to organize their fellow workers and to ensure a forty-four-hour week with a minimum weekly wage of $12.50 and various benefits.[78] Strikebreakers provoked serious violence in the Ste. Catherine Street and Phillips Square clothing sector. While some employers signed on, the majority of the large owners held out, and the strike failed partly because of the ILGWU's opposition to the IUNTW, reflecting the bitter rivalries between the Social Democratic and Communist left.

DIVISIONS WITHIN THE JEWISH COMMUNITY

During the strike, Charles Sommer, the triumphant head of the Montreal Dress Manufacturers' Guild, continued discussions with syndicate representatives, exposing the deep social and economic fissures within the Jewish community. In a March 1934 feature article, provocatively entitled "A Disgraceful Climax in a Paralyzed Industry," the *Chronicle* had castigated him and other Jewish employers for "engaging in a dispute with unionized Jewish wage earners . . . [and] fleeing from . . . Montreal, taking their shops with them to the small country towns."[79] This trend had become "epidemic in character," the intention being to lower the Jewish "wage standard to that of their 'village' [French-Canadian] competitors." The manufacturers all along believed "that the quicker they dispensed with their Jewish employees, the less danger there would be for all organized unions [because] the natural trend for the Jewish worker is to be associated with a union."[80]

The *Chronicle*, then edited by Rabbi Charles Bender of the prestigious Spanish and Portuguese congregation She'erith Israel (Remnant of Israel), offered a sympathetic assessment of the competing French Canadians.[81] In contrast to the Jewish workers, they were ". . . sons and daughters of the farmers in the area . . . willing to work for a pittance. As little as they earned, it was pin money and savings." Now these French-Canadian workers "are no longer farmer's sons, but members of the proletariat . . . now nursing bitterness in their hearts towards their employers, who are exploiting them, and the 'juif' is mentally accused by the employees for all their personal difficulties." Some Jewish employers in the villages were accused of ignoring women's minimum-wage laws. The *Chronicle* cited a report in *La Presse*, alleging that one manufacturer in Joliette "was . . . labelling pay envelopes of the women workers with a greater amount than is actually to be found when the envelope is opened."[82] Here was an opening for antisemites ". . . because so many non-Jews would like to hold up this type of manufacturer as the symbol of Jewish morals in business."

So while Jewish unemployed clothing workers "walk the streets in an endless search for work because in the name of justice and humanity, they sought to organize the worker, and better the lot of every employee, Jew or non-Jew, in the clothing industry, the Jewish populace in general will be held responsible for a situation that the Jewish workmen sought to avoid, and because of which they were punished with unemployment and starvation." A letter to the *Canadian Jewish Review* commented that the dubious business ethics of some manufacturers were "a disgrace to the Jewish community at large and not worthy of the name of Jew."[83] And in his weekly *Review* column, Rabbi Harry Stern expressed "a great deal of sadness . . . that among those alleged guilty of underpaying their help are listed the names of Jewish citizens. . . . The Jew who fails to deal ethically with his fellow man stands especially condemned. . . . [T]he laborer must be given his just desserts."[84]

In late June, the *Chronicle*, concerned with protecting Jewish jobs, attacked both the Catholic unions and the Jewish employers for signing "sweetheart contracts."[85] "The Jewish needle trade [is] confronted by [a] serious situation" because if the Catholic unions controlled the clothing industry, Jewish labour would not be hired. "The purpose of this article is to warn the Jewish needle workers of the ambitions of the Catholic unions, and to place them on guard against a situation that may become another 'Notre Dame Hospital incident' [a reference to the strike by Catholic interns against the hiring of a Jewish doctor]. . . . [I]f they gain control over the 'needle trade,' and if a strike should occur, it will not be for higher wages or shorter hours, but for the same reason as led to the strike of the interns."

In pursuit of profits, the *Chronicle* asked, how many employers would resist reputed offers of no strikes or stoppages and the probability of lower wages? After Premier Taschereau publicly attacked the international unions as "American agitators," the writer Israel Medresh warned Jewish workers to be on their guard. In January 1935, the *Chronicle* published a statement by Joseph Schlossberg, the international head of the Amalgamated, attacking the discrimination practised by Jewish employers against Jewish employees.[86]

The behaviour of some Jewish manufacturers during the 1934 strike in Montreal was extremely provocative. According to one reliable Jewish witness, "they hired gangsters to beat up the union organizers and . . . workers on the picket line. . . . Quite a number of . . . the gangsters . . . were Jewish boys, from . . . the Main in Montreal."[87] The most militant strikers, according to this account, were Jewish women, who unsuccessfully battled the employers' goon squads.

Because of their militancy, Jewish women were increasingly refused jobs in the dress shops. Desperate for work, some of them tried to disguise themselves by speaking French and wearing crosses around their necks.[88] Vicious class warfare had broken out in a community that was also under attack from without. In fact, some employers fostered antisemitism among the French-Canadian workers. This tactic, though, appeared to backfire, as many of the latter showed stubborn solidarity with the Jewish strikers.[89] A temporary agreement was reached, but the continuing flirtation of Sommer and other dress manufacturers with the Catholic syndicates and their discrimination against fellow Jews was becoming a public scandal.[90]

Strikes

The newly re-established Canadian Jewish Congress was aware of the plight of Jewish workers caught between the upper and nether millstones of Catholic syndicate antagonism and Jewish employers' hostility. Executive-director Hananiah Meir Caiserman (who had led workers successfully in the 1917 menswear strike) was deeply concerned over the industry's troubles. He criticized Canadian Jewry for not fighting discrimination against Jewish employees, and suggested that this issue should be placed on the agenda of the Congress.[91] Particular concerns were the worsening plight of the Jewish unemployed and complaints of discrimination against Jewish workers in the Montreal dress industry by the local Manufacturers Protective Association.[92] The same complaints arose in Toronto, where unemployed Jewish clothing workers organized the Alle Far Einem (All for One) society and a Women's Consumers League for mutual assistance.[93]

Caiserman even appealed to Archie Freiman, the department-store magnate and president of the Zionist Organization of Canada (ZOC), to use his influence to settle a strike at one factory and protect the jobs of forty-five workers.[94] In March 1935, the Arbeiter Ring (Workmen's Circle) in Hamilton wrote to Caiserman complaining of "prominent industrialists who are prepared to sell the poor for a few cents' profit. They discriminate against Jewish workers no less cruelly than do the official anti-Semites."[95]

Caiserman was convinced that this discrimination was widespread.[96] However, all efforts at mediation failed. At the Congress' Dominion Council meeting in December 1936, it was reported that 270 Jewish workers were fired when a major Jewish-owned clothing factory was shut down and moved from Montreal to Sherbrooke.[97] And one ILGWU official confided that the Jewish employers' collaboration with the Catholic syndicates in the leather trades, some of whose leaders were activists in the antisemitic Achat Chez

Nous movement, "will result in the slow elimination . . . of Jewish workers in these shops."[98]

In June 1936, Louis Rosenberg pointed out that as Jewish employers moved their shops out of Montreal, or employed contractors who did the same, the ensuing unemployment forced workers, a very large segment of the community, to seek relief from the communal welfare agencies that were directly dependent upon the Federation of Jewish Philanthropies. It was an indictment and rebuke of the industry's Jewish manufacturers. The runaway shop, Rosenberg noted, was "not only a demoralizing factor in industry generally, but strikes at the very basis of 30% of Canada's Jewish population, and further restricts the possibilities of Jewish employment." He went on to say, "Those who sow the wind of [seeking] increased profits by encouraging the flight of contractors' shops in search of cheaper operating costs, not only reap the whirlwind of increased Jewish unemployment and increased Federation budgets in the larger cities, but are pulling down about the ears of the entire Canadian Jewish population, that economic, cultural and educational life which has been built up by the Jewish pioneers of the past sixty years or more."[99] Because three-quarters of Montreal's "gainfully employed" Jews were clothing workers, Rosenberg's message was clear. The Jewish employers' continuing flirtation with the Catholic syndicates would endanger the livelihoods of thousands of households.[100]

Some rabbis urged the factory owners to show greater compassion for their Jewish workers. With remarkable courage, Rabbi Stern appealed directly to Charles Sommer, one of his own congregants at Temple Emanu-el, "not to throw them out onto the street."[101] Attacking what he called Jewish antisemites, Rabbi Bender condemned employers "who barricade [the] door against Jewish help . . . [and] make a specialty of engaging non-Jewish labour although the same work could be carried out as efficiently and as ably by Jewish hands."[102]

But conditions were not improving, despite government investigations, the 1934 Royal Commission hearings and report, and widespread publicity. As late as 1937, observers noted that the industry still suffered from overproduction and unhealthy competition.[103] As manufacturers' profit margins fell, they boosted output to keep their businesses afloat. Surplus production was being "dumped" in cities across Canada. Meanwhile, labour was still severely exploited. Some manufacturers were evading Quebec's minimum wage laws through the use of "cunning schemes . . . and we often read in the daily papers of manufacturers brought to court on charges laid by inspectors from the Minimum Wage Commission." One of the offenders convicted under these laws had been fined in March 1934 for paying one girl $2.70 for a week's work of forty-eight hours.[104]

Meanwhile, the battle for control of the workforce between the ILGWU and the Catholic syndicates continued. In January 1937, the *Chronicle* warned of "Fascism in the needle trades," arguing that the same French Canadians who fostered the Achat Chez Nous campaign had "given birth on the fertile soil of this province with its bursting bag of Jew-baiting tricks . . . [to a] Fascist union. . . ."[105] Promising to ensure "no communism, no radicalism, no red-ism . . . the idea is to inveigle the Jewish manufacturers into recognizing the Fascist union as the one most compatible with employers' interests."

The outlook was bleak, unless Jewish employers would "not be bamboozled." The community faced "another link in that devilish chain [with] which destructive forces are continually trying to encircle us." In April, the *Chronicle* warned that if Jewish employers signed on with the Catholic syndicates, whose slogan was No Foreigners [international unions] Should Interfere in Quebec Affairs, they could themselves be in trouble. The paper hinted darkly at "certain powers, other than those of employers and employees [who] are behind this latest effort to throw the industry into turmoil. The ILGWU will be the first to go. Who knows, maybe the Montreal Dress Manufacturers Guild will be next."[106]

The Roman Catholic Church's appeal to French-Canadian workers to support the Catholic union outraged the *Chronicle*: "[What] we have here was [the] first taste of the padlock law against Communism with its elastic interpretation."[107] Even worse was that Jewish manufacturers "were boycotting Jewish labour." The church was trying to convince French-Canadian workers — then about 80 percent of the dress-trade workers — to join Catholic unions despite the fact that, according to the *Chronicle*, "about sixty percent of this number are all in favour of the [ILGWU]."[108] "The reprehensible feature about the present situation," the *Chronicle* continued, "is the attitude of the Jewish grandees of the dress industry. Many of them have done all in their power to boycott Jewish labour. With one hand they deprive the Jews of their earning capabilities, and with the other hand they support charitable institutions to dole out relief to these people." There could be "a boomerang of unpleasant consequences," it predicted.

Meanwhile, the *Keneder Adler* also condemned the manufacturers "for raising a racial issue and creating an anti-Jewish worker movement."[109] One manufacturer, who also deplored the guild's encouragement of antisemitism, voiced his dissent: "The bringing in of the religious issue in a conflict between capital and labour in a trade which lies mostly in the hands of Jewish manufacturers is terrible for the whole Jewish folk."[110]

By the spring of 1937, the Montreal dress industry was in the midst of another strike, the most momentous of all. The ILGWU was determined to stabilize the chaotic situation and reverse the disastrous defeat of the dressmakers in the 1934 debacle. The union knew that instability in Montreal could affect Toronto dress manufacturers, who might also be tempted to relocate to low-wage Quebec towns, saving about 40 percent of the labour costs.[111] Officials in the New York union headquarters worried about wider destabilizing effects, as some American manufacturers were moving across the border.[112] At an October 1936 conference on the Canadian situation, ILGWU representatives resolved to establish "uniform industrial standards" across the industry in Ontario and Quebec.[113] To help the Montrealers, the New York ILGWU headquarters in early 1937 sent them Rose Pesotta, one of its best organizers. She surveyed the scene and decided, as she put it in her autobiography, *Bread upon the Waters*, "the dressmakers needed a woman's approach."[114] Indeed they did. Women canvassers went house to house to recruit members. Social gatherings were organized and a radio broadcast made. The union headquarters were improved with a re-equipped library and kitchen, while a stage, piano, radio, and phonograph were added. A celebration of Ste. Catherine's Day, the holiday for "old maids," drew a huge crowd of dressmakers. The organizing drive became an enormous success.

But it also attracted notice from the opposition. When seven workers at one factory were fired for union activity in January, the plant was quickly struck. The owner capitulated, and as the news spread that the ILGWU was serious, its headquarters were inundated by appeals from other workers for strikes in their shops too. In early April, the union decided to shut down the entire Montreal dress industry to force employers to sign contracts with them rather than the opposing Catholic syndicate.[115] Within days, more than five thousand workers had struck in one hundred factories and enthusiasm ran high. Improvising on a French march, the *midinettes*, in company with Jewish women, composed and chanted their own song out on the picket lines. An English translation would read:

With the union
We are working
Against the bosses.
We will win.

For the International
Is our ideal.
Mr. Trepanier
With the workers
Is tireless.

We will win.
Miss Pesotta
Of trouble she can make a lot o'
But she smiles a charming ha-ha
Amidst the brouhaha.[116]

La Nation referred to the strike as a plot by *"la juiverie internationale,"* and *Le Devoir* pointed to *"profiles sémitiques"* on the picket lines.[117] But the *midinettes* and their allies stuck to their guns.

Although half the dress manufacturers still favoured the Catholic union,[118] by mid-June they were forced to accept the ILGWU — the so-called Jewish union — because it demonstrated that it could shut down the entire Montreal dress industry with the support of the vast majority of workers, notably the brave *midinettes* who conducted an intensive campaign to bring their sisters into line.

Ultimately, most workers focused, not on the union's ethnic composition or its leadership, but on their material well-being. *Midinette* Aldea Guillemette recalled that "when the midinettes of Montreal rejected ugly appeals to religious and racial prejudice . . . they built . . . a union so powerful that not even the combined efforts of politicians and unscrupulous bosses could destroy it . . . because our purposes [were] the same, whether Catholic or Jew, French-Canadian or Italian."[119]

The rejection by most of the *midinettes* of antisemitism possesses a rather special eloquence. On the other hand, the exploitation of this hatred by some Jewish employers (and advanced by some parish priests in Sunday sermons and *Le Devoir*, which called Shane *"un Judeo-Américain"*)[120] for their own economic advantage is a noteworthy reflection of the industry's volatility and the precarious solidarity of Canadian Jewry. The irony was that while Congress, in an effort to preserve workers' jobs and community solidarity, was fighting antisemitism, some dress manufacturers were spreading it. Highlighting yet another problem, Rabbi Stern used his column in the *Canadian Jewish Review* to ask, "Are there not many even today despite minimum wage laws who keep the pay of their employees down to the lowest notch? And are not these often the persons who head [Jewish] charity lists?"[121]

The strike highlighted acute intra-communal tensions even though the contract that was won provided for benefits, wage increases, and grievance machinery.[122] This deep animosity was further reflected in a letter that year from F. White, the secretary-treasurer of the Montreal Joint Board of the Amalgamated, to Allan Bronfman, the president of the Jewish General Hospital. White protested the appointment of Henry Weinfeld, a key legal adviser to the dress manufacturers, to the hospital's campaign council. "Mr. Weinfeld's role in the recent silk dress industrial conflict amounted to an attempt to eliminate gradually every single Jewish worker from the industry. . . ."[123]

These strikes showed, among other things, that space and culture were not necessarily definitive aspects of Jewish identity — even in Montreal, where historians have stressed ethnic solitudes, not only French and English, but also Jewish. Clearly, the factory floor was what defined one form of identity, that of workers seeking improvement in working conditions, without regard for ethnicity and religion in the Quebec of that era. Culture, therefore, must yield to space, at least in this context, as the determinative factor for Jewish clothing workers in the 1930s.

Equally important was this existence of serious class conflict in the clothing industry. Jewish manufacturers — themselves in many cases former workers — and their associations were in bitter battle against Jewish workers and their unions. In the community, this was the most contentious issue because, at root, money was at stake, through the livelihoods of the workers and the profits (and livelihoods, too) of the manufacturers. It was a conflict of the values of North American free enterprise, the profit motive, and entrepreneurial derring-do versus the spirit of East European left-wing *chavershaft*, utopianism, and beliefs in the dignity of labour. But the industry also became an arena of conflict for Jews and French Canadians, who constituted the majority of the clothing workforce. The exploitation of workers by bosses had an ethnic face. Just as important, however, the unions provided bridges between the cultures, avenues of co-operation between Jews and French Canadians in a deeply divided Quebec. It was not only "the great Jewish métier," to borrow the historian Moses Rischin's felicitous phrase, it was the central feature of Montreal's Jewish economic and social existence for the interwar years and beyond. By 1940, virtually all women's-apparel factories in the Montreal region had signed contracts with the ILGWU, which by the 1950s had established major health and welfare benefits for its members.

Organizing Toronto

In Toronto as well, the womenswear sector was in flux. In response to attempts by the Communist IUNTW to organize the dressmakers, and in the aftermath of a disastrous strike in early February 1931, the rival ILGWU (for some years firmly established among the city's cloak-makers) set up a dressmakers' local and called a general strike in late February 1931 to demonstrate that it could bring the manufacturers into line.[124] But this strike also failed, as employers refused to further increase the wage differentials between themselves and the

Montreal manufacturers. "We are willing to come to terms," the employers stated, "if they [the ILGWU] will organize Montreal at the same time."[125]

This was not happening and, following the ILGWU's 1931 defeat, Toronto was chaotic. The lower Spadina Avenue dress centre was the scene of several strikes and demonstrations over barely sufficient wages, especially those of the women workers, who vastly outnumbered men.[126] Employees at Delight Dress Workers, who were affiliated with the IUNTW, struck in May 1932 but failed to win any concessions. This action petered out, but not before violence erupted on the picket line, leading to the arrest of one woman.[127] Another IUNTW-initiated strike in March 1934, at Title Dress, also resulted in failure.[128] In the meantime, several bitter strikes in cloak-and-suit shops, called by the ILGWU, created continuing tension on Spadina; in January and February 1934, some two thousand Toronto cloak-makers paralyzed that sector by striking until manufacturers settled.[129]

The real watershed in the Toronto womenswear industry was the protracted strike at Superior Cloak, which was called by the ILGWU in July 1934. It lasted for forty-nine days.[130] The owner, Samuel Posluns, determined to break the union's power over his firm, locked out his two hundred workers and, under a newly formed company, Popular Cloak, moved his production to Guelph, where he employed local non-union workers.[131]

Former employees from Toronto drove to Guelph and picketed the Popular Cloak plant. Violence erupted and arrests of numerous strikers followed. Posluns was charged by police with firing a revolver at one of them, and several strikebreakers (who had moved to Guelph from Toronto) were taken to hospital with serious head injuries after a bloody mêlée of stone-throwing, fisticuffs, and clubbing. Police had to call in the local fire department to help control the fighting. Sam Kraisman, an organizer for the ILGWU, alleged he was threatened by members of the employer's goon squad bearing knives and lead pipes. In the aftermath of the affray, a magistrate ordered picketers Joe Zlotnick and Gael Goldenberg (described as "foreigners"), both up on charges of causing a disturbance, to "get out of town immediately and stay out."[132]

Meanwhile, the ILGWU called a general strike at all Toronto cloak factories to enforce industry-wide standards of improved wages, hours, and working conditions. Kraisman alleged that "bootlegging [union shopwork done by non-union labour], contracting and subcontracting . . . in the cloak trade bedroom and sweatshops . . . is carried on under the most vicious conditions," while some firms were avoiding minimum-wage laws by withholding (and never paying) 10 percent of workers' earnings on various pretexts.[133] Most companies settled within days.

Posluns remained adamant, however, and the Guelph strike continued ever more violently. A riot outside the plant in late August ensued after nearly one thousand persons gathered to protest his obduracy; one of Posluns's cars and a police vehicle were destroyed, and tear gas was used to disperse the crowd. The attempts of the Guelph Retail Merchants' Association to mediate a settlement failed and, after the violent confrontations, police reinforcements were called in from nearby towns. Truckloads of union supporters also arrived, and the mounting tension prompted Guelph Mayor R. B. Robson to call for "martial law." It was rumoured that he also asked Minister of Labour Arthur W. Roebuck to send in the Ontario Provincial Police, armed with bayonets and machine guns. Conferences involving union, management, the Ontario ministry of Labour, Kraisman, and David Dubinsky from ILGWU's New York headquarters finally settled the conflict in September. Posluns signed an agreement with the union providing for an increase of wages and the return of production to Toronto. Popular Cloak remained in Guelph, but the following June, after a brief strike, Posluns signed an accord with the ILGWU bringing his subsidiary into line with the other firms in the trade.[134] With this agreement, which complemented a settlement made in the Toronto dress industry earlier that year after a short but violent strike, the major Toronto womenswear conflicts of the 1930s came to an end.

Meanwhile, the Jewish component of the Winnipeg clothing workforce was increasing. By 1931, of nearly two thousand workers employed in the industry, more than a quarter were Jews. Ten years later, they were a third of all Winnipeg needle workers and were instrumental in drives to organize unions.[135] Sam Herbst successfully brought women's-apparel workers into the ILGWU and fought several bitter strikes to create a very strong union, which achieved recognition and material benefits throughout that city's women's-apparel trade.[136]

Men's Apparel

As these struggles continued, other sectors of the apparel industry were similarly affected. Men's clothing, for example, was readjusting after the First World War. The conversion of the industry from uniform to suit production took place during the 1920–23 recession. New manufacturers, some formerly contractors, prepared to challenge older firms.[137] They could produce good-quality, ready-to-wear suits at modest prices, having learned techniques during the war for more precise standard sizing and mass production.

David Dunkelman's Toronto firm, Tip Top Tailors, was one of the most successful of these newer companies producing and marketing medium-priced men's ready-to-wear suits and coats.[138] After starting his suit business in 1910 with an initial investment of $1,500, Dunkelman quickly expanded. By the 1920s, he was operating on an immense scale. In 1930, he built a huge new factory to produce tens of thousands of suits and coats for sale in his own retail outlets located in cities across Canada. Tip Top Tailors was by then one of the nation's biggest men's-clothing manufacturers and retailers,[139] and it forced some older, less competitive firms to go out of business.

Sam Rubin in Montreal was another entrepreneur in men's ready-to-wear. He started out in 1920 and quickly prospered. By the early 1930s, his factory occupied twenty thousand square feet on the top floor of a Bleury Street building and did $1,000,000 in annual business, producing twenty-five hundred garments a week. By this time, employing what was by now a standard tactic, Rubin had moved part of his production to the village of Ste.-Rose. He claimed, nevertheless, that his entire workforce was unionized, and that 75 percent of his three hundred employees were Jewish.[140]

Some menswear manufacturers pressured by competition became convinced that reducing labour costs would solve their problems. The availability of non-unionized labour and willing contractors tempted many of them to try escaping from the agreements they had signed with the Amalgamated during the First World War. These accords, which provided for union recognition, a forty-four-hour week, weekly wages, and improved sanitary conditions, had established relative stability in the industry from 1917 to the early 1920s. When Montreal firms began reducing wages by about 15 percent following similar wage reductions in Winnipeg, Sault Ste. Marie, London, Hamilton, and Toronto,[141] strikes immediately broke out. In Montreal, twelve hundred workers struck against wage reductions, a lengthened work week, the re-introduction of piece-work, and the open shop.[142] More labour disputes occurred the following year, most of them in Montreal. Throughout the 1920s, repeated strikes and lockouts created chaos in the industry.

As well, owners increasingly resorted to contractors and moved their production to nearby towns. By the early 1920s, Fashion Craft had moved to Ste.-Rose, the Elkin Company to Victoriaville, Rubin Brothers to St.-Hyacinthe, and Crown Pant to Cornwall. The union fought these "runaway shops" by trying to organize French-Canadian workers in these towns.[143] At the same time, they struggled to maintain standards in previously unionized shops and to organize workers in contractors' shops. Similar problems were experienced in the Toronto menswear trade, where the union demanded the same conditions as in Montreal.

On the educational front, the union organized a series of study programs in its Amalgamated Active Workers' School. There were twice-weekly classes in English and public speaking, weekly discussion groups on issues and forms of organization regarding labour problems, and a series of lectures by university professors on modern history, labour conditions, science and civilization, and education.[144] Other unions, like the United Hat, Cap and Millinery Workers' Union, organized similar programs.[145]

Equilibrium in the men's-apparel industry was re-established in 1925 by agreements between the union and the manufacturers.[146] The union felt restored and confident about the future,[147] but its sense of ease was misplaced. By the 1930s, the men's trades were again in disarray. The rivalry of Communist and Catholic unions in Montreal, lay-offs, and the rising trend towards the use of contractors and "runaway shops" greatly weakened the union.[148] The effects of the Depression were especially damaging in all locations. Union membership dropped significantly, while unemployment increased and wage levels fell. In a full-scale study of the industry in Montreal and Toronto in 1934, a McGill law professor, Frank Scott, and Harry Cassidy, a University of Toronto professor of social work, found widespread distress among workers. Short hours, frequent lay-offs, seasonal unemployment, and deteriorating working conditions prevailed, while some unionized shops were attempting to evade their agreements by farming out work to contractors or moving their factories out of town.[149]

These findings were reinforced by Cassidy's evidence to the 1934 price spreads commission. Conditions were so bad, he testified, that "a great majority of [workers] in the industry are now close to or below the border line of abject poverty."[150] Workers had been on half-time since 1931; many families were on relief, while others needed two or more wage earners to keep them going. Although employees' conditions were better in the unionized factories, some non-unionized workers were earning as little as four dollars for a sixty-hour week,[151] while "one young girl received $2 for 55 hours work before the [1933] strike." There were rumours that in some Quebec home workshops, conditions were even worse.[152] In the industry generally, Cassidy testified, "in both Ontario and Quebec, there has been an appalling degradation of labour standards during the depression. In both provinces labour in the men's clothing industry has been exploited and sweated. . . . The suits we are wearing to-day," he told the commissioners, "many of them, have been made in sweat shops, under disgraceful conditions."[153]

The wide variations in shop conditions and pay depended, Cassidy stressed, on factory location, union affiliation, and the employer's humanity. In general, conditions were better in Toronto than in Montreal, in unionized rather than in non-unionized shops, and in larger rather than in smaller factories.[154] But the insidious and destructive processes — especially severe in depressed economic conditions — of open competition in the industry drove manufacturers to cut costs any way they could. Even employers "who have endeavoured to maintain fair conditions for labour have been severely affected by the competition of employers who have not been maintaining fair conditions."[155] Thus a vicious downward spiral existed, with bad labour conditions driving out the good in an effort to meet rivalry in this open market. As Cassidy observed: "[T]he burden of cutthroat competition . . . has fallen more heavily upon the firms that have endeavoured to maintain fair conditions of work and wages and that have avoided sharp competitive practices. We were informed that firms of this sort had quite definitely lost business to lower standard concerns."[156]

The worst offenders were the large department and chain stores, which relentlessly exploited the chaos, especially among the small, marginal firms whose "uneconomically low prices eagerly sought by mass-buyers endanger the solvency of more reputable and stable establishments and contribute to the general disorganization of the industry."[157] They forced manufacturers starving for business to drastically cut prices, offer generous inducements, accept large numbers of returns, and tolerate repeated contract violations. So advantageous was this method of procuring merchandise that some large stores discontinued manufacturing goods in their own factories. They were the real titans of the apparel trades, indirectly deciding which firms would live or die — who by sudden bankruptcy, who by slow strangulation, who by labour strife, and who by despair. There seemed no way out of these appalling circumstances in which both employers and employed were being relentlessly ground down.

To address these problems, the Ontario and Quebec governments passed legislation attempting to control this chaos. Quebec's Collective Labour Agreements Extension Act of 1934 provided a framework in which agreements were established and made obligatory throughout the entire clothing sector.[158] A year later, Ontario brought in the Industrial Standards Act, which provided similar machinery for the resolution of disputes.

These were also years of serious political turmoil for many unionists. In the late 1920s, leftists affiliated with the Communist-led Workers' Unity League attempted to win control of some locals of the Amalgamated. In Montreal, the contest between these leftists and the majority, who were called rightists by the *Keneder Adler*, was sometimes bitter and violent.[159] Peace was eventually restored, but the differences simmered for years. The United Clothing Workers, an affiliate of the All-Canadian Congress of Labour, briefly drew off some of the Amalgamated's members. A general strike forced employers, some of whom had exploited the labour tension by lengthening hours and moving their production out of town, to accept the union shop and a 20 percent wage hike.[160] By the end of the decade there was a degree of stability, however, with only some minor disruptions.[161]

*

By the late 1930s, the Canadian clothing industry had undergone some important transformations that directly affected the Jewish community. The Jewish component of the labour force was significant and ever-increasing, while their influence in the apparel unions was very strong. Meanwhile, the industry grew more specialized, with Montreal becoming the major centre of both the men's fine-suit trade and low-priced dress production, a dynamic new sector that mushroomed in importance despite its essential instability.

Thus, paradoxically, the evolution of the clothing industry in the interwar era provided both important opportunities and bitter tensions to Canadian Jewry. On the one hand, a new but risky frontier of entrepreneurial activity opened up, attracting penny capitalists. The dress trade thus acted as a bonanza — almost a "next year country" — in which the hope of a big payoff in the near future enticed would-be manufacturers. Many of these so-called nervous men were ground down by the business and eventually extinguished. On the other hand, the labour sector was seriously disrupted by the actions of manufacturers trying to raise or even maintain slim profit margins. Insofar as the large numbers of Jewish workers were concerned, these conditions not only worsened their lives materially, but also embittered them towards Jewish capitalists.

Tensions between these two opposing forces were reflected in other sectors of Jewish life in all three metropolitan centres. The well-to-do clothing manufacturer who served as a Jewish community leader and philanthropist was an object of disapproval among both Jewish and French-Canadian workers. Clearly, for many Jews, class consciousness conflicted with, and sometimes overrode, ethnic identity.[162] Thus, while the clothing industry provided "a zone of emergence" for Jewish business activity that was daring, creative, flexible, and tough, it also created a launching pad for workers' militancy and a forum for the reconfirmation of the class-consciousness that many Jewish workers had brought with them from the old country.

CHAPTER

5

"The Earth Shall Rise on New Foundations": The Jewish Left in the Interwar Years

The Bolshevik Revolution of October 1917 changed political life in countries around the world. In the Canadian context, some saw communism as the fulfilment of their Jewishness. "I never had a conflict about being a Jew and a Communist," reflected the long-time Canadian activist Joshua Gershman. "I became a Communist because I am a Jew."[1] Many Jews, used to watching for the appearance of the Messiah, the redeemer of mankind, were drawn to communism. That ideology promised a new age of peace, freedom, and equality and, as its sayings went, a society "from each according to his ability, to each according to his needs," a message that carried with it "the prophetic ring of the coming of the Messiah."[2] Jewish youth, dismayed at the seeming rapaciousness of worldwide imperialism, brutal antisemitism, and a viciously exploitative international capitalist system, joined with others of all races and nationalities in rallying around the red flag and the stirring "Internationale," the anthem of the Communist movement. Some were ready to dedicate their very lives to this inspiring cause. They studied the works of early socialists like Karl Marx, Vladimir Ilyich Lenin, and Leon Trotsky, the brilliant Jewish ideologue who combined military genius with rousing oratory. At countless meetings, legal or clandestine, throughout the world, they stood with clenched fists raised in salute to sing these words:

Arise, ye pris'ners of starvation!
Arise, ye wretched of the earth,
For justice thunders condemnation,
A better world's in birth.[3]

In labour temples, union halls, and community buildings throughout Canada in the 1920s and 1930s, the Communist ideal was spread by publications and the fiery speeches of intellectuals and visitors from the Soviet Union, many of whom devoted their lives to delivering their message to the curious, the revolution-minded, the unemployed, or the disaffected. They were secular missionaries, traversing the country and preaching that the better world "in birth" was theirs to create and enjoy. Their mission was to overthrow capitalism, replacing it with a new social and economic order. "By no means all communists . . . in those days were Jews, but I think it a fact that it was the Jews who provided the passion," wrote Hugh MacLennan of Montreal in the 1930s. "Who could blame them? For they knew, while the French and English blocs did not, exactly what Hitler was preparing for all of us."[4]

A number of Jews, along with Finns and Ukrainians, had been active before the First World War in the Socialist Party of Canada and the Social Democratic Party.[5] Jewish-dominated trade unions like the ILGWU and the Amalgamated were believed by the Royal North West Mounted Police (RNWMP) to have connections with the radical One Big Union. This dreaded union was thought to have fomented the Winnipeg General Strike of May 1919.[6] One Jew in particular, Louis Kon (alias Koniatski, Kohn, or Cohn), was described in police files as "a rabid Socialist and Bolshevist . . . very active during the first week of the strike, in spreading Bolsheviki propaganda among the foreign element of the East Kildonan district. . . . That Kon is in close connection with the Strike Leaders now on trial for Seditious conspiracy is shown by the fact that during the strike the different leaders were constantly in communication with Kon on the telephone."[7]

A later report stated that "he is very intimate with [strike leaders] R. B. Russell, Rev. Ivens, Alderman [A. A.] Heaps and [blank] and W. A. Pritchard. He does not do much public speaking and prefers to work 'inside.'"[8] There is some evidence that this ascription of an important "backroom" role to Kon was part of a wider attempt by the RNWMP to implicate Jews. On May 27, 1919, at the height of the strike, one officer reported that:

> The Jewish element of Winnipeg are taking a very active interest in the strike, even those who have nothing in common with the labor movement are devoting their time in an endeavour to augment this movement.[9]

Another RNWMP officer reported that "Two brothers named Oshenski (Jews) were agitating for the [postal workers] to remain on strike, one of them stating in my presence that 'They were not going to swallow the "Crap" handed out by the speakers.'"[10]

Jewish orphans from Ukainian pogroms in Rovno pose with Dr. Joseph Leavitt (far left) and Harry Hershman (far right) in 1921. Some of these children may have been among those brought to Canada by Leavitt, Hershman, William Farrar, and Lillian Freiman.

CANADIAN JEWISH CONGRESS NATIONAL ARCHIVES, MONTREAL

Ottawa department store magnate Archibald J. Freiman was president of the Zionist Organization of Canada from 1921 until his death in 1944.

CANADIAN JEWISH CONGRESS NATIONAL ARCHIVES, MONTREAL

Lillian Freiman seems never to have rested from strenuous efforts on behalf of Jewish immigrants to Canada, the building of the Jewish national home in Palestine, and the causes of Canadian Hadassah-WIZO.

CANADIAN JEWISH CONGRESS NATIONAL ARCHIVES, MONTREAL

Second annual picnic of the Borchov Branch, no. 124, of the Farband (Labour Zionists) in Toronto, c. 1920–21.

ONTARIO JEWISH ARCHIVES

Jewish farmers harvesting their wheat at Sonnenfeld, Saskatchewan, 1925.

NATIONAL ARCHIVES OF CANADA PA201332

Badges worn on ceremonial occasions, such as funerals, by members of benevolent societies, including Toronto Zion Benevolent Association and the Ostrovtzer Independent Mutual Benefit Society.

ONTARIO JEWISH ARCHIVES

The Jewish quarter in Toronto produced numerous baseball teams in the interwar years named for a street, playground, or school. Not much is known about this team, the D'Arcys, which probably included members of other ethnic groups besides Jews.

ONTARIO JEWISH ARCHIVES

Jewish steerage passengers bound for Canada on deck of Cunard liner, 1926.

ONTARIO JEWISH ARCHIVES

Like Miller's bookstore in Winnipeg, Hyman's Book and Art Shop on Toronto's Spadina Avenue was a favourite meeting place for many Jewish intellectuals. Benzion Hyman, an electrical engineering graduate of the University of Toronto, poses proudly in 1925.

ONTARIO JEWISH ARCHIVES

Dedication of the new synagogue, Kirkland Lake, Ontario, September 1, 1929. Rabbi Rabin is carrying the Torah.

NATIONAL ARCHIVES OF CANADA PA103552

NON-NEGOTIABLE NON-TRANSFERABLE

No. 19 $11.00

Founders and Charter Members of

Founded October 11th 1931

Calgary, Alberta

The Polish-Jewish Family Loan Association

This is to Certify that Max Switzer Jr of the City of Calgary, in the Province of Alberta, has made contributions to the Society for the year ending December 31st, A.D. 1932, to the total amount of $ Eleven 00/100 Dollars

Dated at the City of Calgary, in the Province of Alberta, this 30th day of July A.D., 1936

PRESIDENT SECRETARY

Certificate for Max Switzer, Jr., for donation to Polish Jewish Family Loan Association, Calgary, Alberta, December 1932. The photograph shows the founders and charter members.

GLENBOW MUSEUM AND ARCHIVES

Samuel Bronfman speaking to the delegates at the fourth plenary session of the Canadian Jewish Congress in 1939, where he was elected president. Bronfman remained in office until 1962, having directed the organization through its most crucial challenges.

CANADIAN JEWISH CONGRESS NATIONAL ARCHIVES, MONTREAL

Delegates to the plenary session of the Canadian Jewish Congress in Toronto, 1939.

CANADIAN JEWISH CONGRESS NATIONAL ARCHIVES, MONTREAL

One month later, Courtland Starnes, the RNWMP's senior officer in Manitoba and a man who believed that the strike marked the start of class war in Canada, observed that the country's welfare hinged on "keeping away from Jewish Capitalists or Labor men."[11] Meanwhile, an organization called the Jewish Labour League was named as one of eighteen groups spreading sedition on the Prairies.[12] Other Jewish radical groups of the early 1920s, including the Jewish Socialist Party of Toronto and the Jewish Socialist Democratic Party of Canada, were equally active.[13] The former organization was especially busy in October 1920, publicizing Russian communism and hosting the Winnipeg revolutionary Moses Almazoff, who had been victimized in the aftermath of the 1919 General Strike. He called for the organization of "a strong protection army with a dictatorship and discipline."[14] But the RCMP (as the RNWMP was renamed earlier that year) was not worried. In November it reported that of the approximately five thousand Jewish workers in Toronto, only about fifty had joined this group.[15] Although the RCMP mounted special watch and maintained spies in ethnic communities they suspected of harbouring communists, they felt they need have little concern about links between Jews and communism.[16] This report from an officer viewing the situation in Edmonton was probably typical: "I have never received any information that the Jewish element of this district had any serious revolutionary aims. . . . [They] appear to be a quiet, law abiding people."[17]

While comprising only a small minority of the whole community, Jewish Communists fervently supported what they believed was a brilliant new socialist experiment being created in the Soviet Union. A few Canadian Jews, Ukrainians, and Russians even moved there.[18]

Jewish Communists in the 1920s

One very active Jewish leader of the movement in Canada was Maurice Spector, a Ukrainian-born University of Toronto graduate and Osgoode Hall law student.[19] By 1920, he was well-versed in Marxist theory, a member of the Young Socialist League, and a regular contributor to socialist newspapers. An activist on campus, Spector also edited the *Varsity*[20] and taught classes at the Ontario Labour College. In early 1918, as *Varsity* acting editor, Spector criticized the war and the Allies' role in it, allegedly violating wartime censorship laws. He was removed from the paper and threatened with expulsion.[21] In 1921, Spector, a committed Communist, was the principal member of the three-person committee that drafted the first program of the Communist Party of Canada (CPC).[22] He also authored "The Constituent Convention of the Workers' Party of Canada," a lengthy report on the CPC convention in February 1922.[23]

Although reportedly not an inspiring speaker, Spector was one of the movement's chief spokesmen even before the CPC was founded in 1921. He was recognized as one of its leading minds, a man who "combined a knowledge of Russia with enough intellectual curiosity to probe beneath the surface of Comintern and Soviet politics."[24] Spector, editor of *The Worker* from 1922 to 1928,[25] toured Canada during the early 1920s, calling for disciplined work in the labour unions, agitation in election campaigns and in Parliament, mass demonstrations, organization of the unemployed, and participation in the everyday struggles of the working class.[26]

During these tours, Spector sometimes spoke at meetings of the Young Jewish Socialist Club and the Young Communist League, which, according to the RCMP, were "90 percent . . . Jewish".[27] On one occasion, he was reported to have told his Jewish listeners: "I know that the young Jewish fellows who are arriving in this country from Poland are real revolutionaries, and we need such young people in this country to help us educate the Jewish workers, who have been slaving in this country for years."[28] He urged them to "join your trade unions and work inside; form little groups in the unions and see if any of the officials are trying to give you away to your Boss. If so, get rid of them and put in a more active revolutionist."

He warned his listeners that "the Union Officials in this country and America are bought by the Capitalists. It is up to you when you join such a union to look out for such traitors." He even believed "that the Army and Navy would help the Canadian worker to overthrow the present system."[29] An advocate of world revolution, he urged one Young Communist League audience to "never let Canadianization in the interests of Capitalism get hold of you."[30]

Advocating Canadian independence from Britain, Spector proclaimed that the Canadian bourgeoisie "must be pushed forward to more aggressive action against British imperialism,"[31] with the support of the Canadian working class and the CPC. Besides editing *The Worker*, Spector served the party as its chairman, which allowed him to attend the Third Congress of the Communist International in 1923 in Moscow. He subsequently spent some months in Germany observing the revolutionary situation there.[32] Spector influenced the CPC not to condemn Trotsky despite events in the USSR,[33] and he even attacked the Communist Party of the Soviet Union on some of its major policies and practices. This caused considerable debate among members and was seen as evidence of Spector's plan to split the CPC.[34] Several years later, after attending the Sixth Congress in Moscow and continuing to espouse Trotsky's views, notably the critique of Stalin, he was expelled from the CPC in 1928.[35] Undaunted, however, he continued to voice his opinions.

In his academic life, Spector resumed his legal studies.[36] In 1929, he formed an active but ill-fated Trotskyist organization and maintained a lively correspondence with the American Trotskyists Max Shachtman and James P. Cannon.[37] Spector also contributed articles to their weekly, *The Militant*. His Toronto group was beset by serious factionalism, and in October 1932, Spector informed Shachtman that "the reorganization we carried through has relieved us of the narrow, stifling ghetto element which is given to stewing in its own juice." He slipped illegally into the United States in 1936 to further his cause.[38] Eventually, though, this too failed, and Spector ended up as an employee of a Labour Zionist organization in New York.

Within the CPC itself two Jewish women, Annie Buller and Becky Buhay, rose to leadership positions.[39] By the First World War, both were active in the Montreal socialist movement and had formed a close friendship. They attended the Rand School of Social Science in New York and returned to play roles in the CPC throughout the 1920s and 1930s, Buller as organizer (with Bella Hall Gauld) of the Montreal Labour College and the business manager of *The Worker*, and Buhay as an activist in the needle trades and the secretary of the Canadian Labour Defence League.[40] Both as well had partners in the movement. Buller married a party activist, Harry Guralnick, and had a son, while Buhay lived with Tom Ewen and his four children. Buller was arrested for her provocative role in the bloody Estevan, Saskatchewan, coalminers' strike in 1931 and was sentenced to a year in jail. Buoyed by their unbreakable faith in the cause and steeled by adversity, including the antisemitism directed at them, Buhay and Buller, in the historian Joan Sangster's words, "occupied strategic positions" and "commanded [a] lasting mythology" in the party throughout the interwar years.[41]

Buhay's brother, Mike Buhay, was also a strong activist. An ardent advocate of the general strike, he spoke often at gatherings of the Montreal branch of the One Big Union and to Jewish Communists while serving as the business agent of the Montreal locals of the Amalgamated.[42] Sometimes using the alias William Morris, he was described by the RCMP in 1923 as "a well educated man and a very good propagandist of the Bolsheviki. . . ." He ran for the party in the 1944 Quebec provincial election in the Montreal riding of St.-Louis. During the campaign, he spoke out against race discrimination and Fascism in Quebec — he cited the recent burning of a Quebec City synagogue as evidence — and held open-air political meetings in the lanes of the city's notorious slums.[43]

The CPC established a special section, the Jewish National Bureau, which employed a series of organizers and in 1926 began publishing the monthly Yiddish periodical *Der Kamf* (the Struggle). The "Official Organ of the Jewish

Propaganda Committee Communist Party of Canada," *Der Kamf* (which was regularly scrutinized by the RCMP) became a semi-weekly in October 1934[44] and, with other publications, was distributed at workers' mass meetings.[45] A Jewish Proletarian Authors' Circle was formed in Montreal and Winnipeg, providing Marxist writers with a formal venue to air their views on proletarian literature.

In Toronto, the Yiddisher Arbeiter Froyen Farein (Jewish Women's Labour League) was founded in 1923.[46] This association of Jewish working-class women, most of them housewives, organized a children's camp, canvassed for Communist candidates, and raised money for *Der Kamf* and for ICOR, the Association for Jewish Colonization in the Soviet Union.[47] Moreover, they worked for the party's electoral campaigns and strike activity, and they were an essential feature of their movement's culture of radicalist education and social protest.[48] In 1924 and 1933, the women of the Farein helped to organize kosher-meat boycotts to try to bring down its exorbitant costs for working-class families. While the Farein did not make gender equality an issue, the Jewish Communist movement provided a modest forum for the expression of women's aspirations, as well as offering a vehicle for the "political mobilization of women for the class struggle."[49]

Activity in the 1930s

Uncertainties and fluctuations of the 1920s gave way to total economic collapse and widespread distress in 1929 and 1930. By the early 1930s, Canada saw lines of men waiting for food outside soup kitchens. Abandoned Prairie farmhouses stood half-buried in wind-blown topsoil. Bedraggled families posed for photographs in front of horse-drawn cars dubbed Bennett buggies in honour of a prime minister who seemed indifferent to their suffering. These and other images in movies, in photographs, and in the memories of those who survived the Great Depression are engraved in Canada's national consciousness more deeply perhaps than any other. It was not just the widespread hunger or unemployment that made this decade so painful; much worse was the loss of hope that ordinary people held for the future. Many despaired for any survival of an economic system in a country, so rich in resources, that failed to provide even the basics of life for so many of its citizens.

By 1933, 27 percent of the labour force was unemployed. One in five Canadians, some two million people, was totally dependent on relief.[50] Out of this great economic disaster, which was possibly worse in Canada than in any other industrialized country, emerged new beliefs in the state's responsibility for the welfare of its citizens.[51] The misery continued while federal, provincial, and municipal governments grappled with these problems and tried to devise appropriate responses.

There were few answers, at least among the prime ministers of the decade. First was Richard Bedford Bennett (1930–35), a wealthy Calgary lawyer known on the left as Iron Heel; then came William Lyon Mackenzie King (1935–47), whose chief anti-Depression policies seemed to be a mixture of obfuscation, evasion, and delay. To those on the left, only the Co-operative Commonwealth Federation (CCF) and the Communist Party of Canada faced the problems of the Depression squarely. Both of them proposed a radical restructuring of the Canadian economy. But neither party elected enough members to the House of Commons or provincial legislatures to form governments. The seven feisty members of the CCF who were in the House after 1935, though, believed that they helped to move the King government slowly towards economic and social reform.

While many young Jews were drawn to the radical and moderate left during the 1930s, it was not strictly from a desire to reform or overturn capitalism. Opposition to the growth of Fascism and Nazism were also important to the Young Communist League (YCL), which included many Jews.[52] The RCMP even took note of the fact that at the almost all-Jewish Baron Byng school in Montreal, the YCL's influence was "particularly strong. . . ."[53] They mounted a sharp watch for Jews and usually tried to calculate their numbers at Communist youth gatherings, such as one held by the Canadian Student Assembly in 1940, where the "amount of Jews, . . . mostly from the West and McGill, was remarkable."[54]

The RCMP were under no illusions that Jews dominated the CPC, however. They recognized that Finns comprised the largest ethnic component of the party, whose membership fluctuated between 2,500 and 5,000 (usually hovering around 3,000). Ukrainians were the second most numerous group, Jews the third.[55] According to secret RCMP estimates, Jews made up less than 10 percent of the CPC's membership. In 1931, the Mounties counted some 400 Jews, 3,000 Finns, 800 Ukrainians, and 200 Anglo-Canadians in the CPC.[56] Together these four ethnic groups made up 90 to 95 percent of the party's members.

Since 1924, the party also conducted a vigorous campaign among Canadian Jews to support ICOR (Yiddishe Kolonizatsye Organizatsye in Rusland), the Association for Jewish Colonization in the Soviet Union, which was establishing Jewish farm colonies in Ukraine, Crimea, and, in 1934, Birobidjan,[57] a 14,000 square mile region in the Soviet far east. Much of this propaganda and fund-raising took place in the West because it was assumed that Jewish farmers were likelier to agree to live in this new frontier, or support the project with donations, than those in the cities.[58] Intended to thwart the Zionist endeavour in Palestine, ICOR also mounted vigorous propaganda campaigns in the 1930s to combat ethnic nationalism and link Jewish identity to the class struggle.[59]

In early December 1931, Professor Charles Kuntz of California spoke at the Edmonton Arbeiter Ring Hall about his recent trip to Birobidjan. He informed his listeners that all was not well. The Soviet government, he said, had exploited the Jewish settlers, giving them very small pieces of land and "very poor housing accommodation." Kuntz pleaded for help, saying that "it was up to all the Jews in the rest of the world to support the Jews in Russia, who were being mistreated by Soviet officials."[60] A Canadian section of ICOR was organized in March 1931 and began publishing a newsletter, *Kanader Icor*. Chapters were established in seventeen cities across Canada.[61] A group of its members attended Moscow's November 1934 celebrations honouring the revolution.[62]

In 1935, Harry Guralnick spoke on behalf of ICOR in Saskatoon, Edenbridge, Melfort, and other Jewish communities, where he compared conditions for Jews in the Soviet Union and North America.[63] Guralnick painted a picture of Jewish national autonomy in the Soviet Union. There, some 3.5 million Jews, previously engaged in non-productive activity, were able to participate in industry and agriculture in flourishing Birobidjan, resource rich in coal, gold, iron, forests, and fertile land. Under Soviet benevolence, Jews could become a true nation in their own autonomous republic.[64] But a vigilant RCMP reporter noted that "not much interest is manifest in this particular move among the Jews in the Edenbridge or Gronlid districts."[65] While one RCMP informant believed that most Edenbridge Jews "are supporters and have [a] sympathetic view with the ICOR movement," others were sceptical.

Undercover RCMP officers maintained regular surveillance of Jewish communities in Western Canada. Some of their reports make interesting reading. "The Saskatoon [ICOR] organization was not strong," wrote one informant, because "the Jews of this city lacked the true proletarian outlook. They all considered themselves capitalists and potentially at least wealthy. In a word, they were possessed of a strong bourjoisie [*sic*] psychology."[66] The RCMP believed that ICOR had active branches in nearly every important centre in Canada. However, there is little evidence of significant activity outside the West.[67]

At a meeting of Jewish Communists in Edmonton on October 21, 1934, approximately eighty people heard Guralnick proclaim that in Birobidjan, Jewish workers were "building socialism," and that the Soviet system would eventually "spread all over the world.[68] But according to RCMP observers, even this audience was not particularly receptive. Guralnick was interrupted several times and the audience "took very little interest in the speech." The Edmonton commissioner of customs informed his superior that "almost all of the membership of the 'ICOR' Committee in Edmonton are of the lower class of Jew, small storekeepers and peddlers of a class who, while at the present time do not actually associate themselves with Communism, would in a second jump to which ever way they think would suit their purposes. . . . It is of note," he continued, "that as far as we can gather none of the wealthy Jews seem to associate themselves with this committee."[69]

The CPC supported Jewish settlement in Palestine, but favoured "the solidarity of the Jewish and Arab toiling masses. . . . There is room . . . for both peoples, and . . . a basis for their cooperation."[70] In 1937, several months after the outbreak of the Arab Revolt in Palestine, Jewish CPC members supported efforts to create Jewish–Arab amity and joined Montreal leaders of the Labour Zionists, the ILGWU, the Amalgamated, and the Workmen's Circle at a mass meeting to promote Jewish–Arab cooperation "as an antidote against the poison of chauvinist propaganda."[71]

Emma Goldman, the renowned Socialist leader, spent considerable time in Canada in 1926 and 1927. A vociferous opponent of Soviet communism, Goldman lectured frequently in Yiddish (of a highly Germanized form called Daitshmerish, which was in common use in the early twentieth century by platform speakers) and English to appreciative audiences in Montreal and Toronto on topics like "The Present Crisis in Russia."[72] She also campaigned for funds for political prisoners there, lectured on modern drama, and became involved in a public controversy over free speech and planned parenthood.[73] During her stay, she was visited by family and friends (including her lover, Leon Melamed) and established considerable, though brief, contact with Canadian revolutionaries.

Goldman enjoyed the radical scene in Toronto. "The comrades in [Toronto] are an exceptional bunch of people," she wrote to a New York friend in February 1927. "In all the years I do not remember having met with so much genuineness, so much sweet hospitality, such fine spirit."[74] Goldman soon moved on to Winnipeg, where she received an equally enthusiastic reception, but by the spring of 1927 she had grown tired of the Canadian radicals. She nevertheless stayed on for another year, lecturing on a wide variety of political, social, and literary topics.[75] She returned to Canada in December 1933, staying only as long as necessary to secure a visa to enter the United States. By this time, her intellectual concerns had shifted to the threats of European Fascism and Nazism. She returned to Canada several times in the late 1930s, lecturing to well-attended meetings in Toronto and Winnipeg. She died in Toronto in May 1940, while on a speaking tour.

These mavericks aside, most Canadian Jewish Communists in the 1930s adhered strongly to the Comintern's policies on capitalism and world peace. Along with the professional revolutionary Joshua Gershman, who led the radical labour movement in the needle trades and the IUNTW, Fred Rose (Rosenberg), a Polish-born Montreal electrician, was very active in CPC circles. Shortly after he entered the country from Poland in 1924, Rose joined the Young Communist League (YCL). He became its national secretary in 1929, attended a course of instruction in Russia in 1930, and served on its international executive committee.[76] Monitored closely by the RCMP, Rose was convicted in 1931 of sedition under Section 98 of the Criminal Code and served a year in Montreal's Bordeaux jail. Upon his release, he served on the CPC's secret Central Control Commission.[77]

Rose's real talents lay in political propaganda. In 1939, he published a well-documented pamphlet alleging that big companies in the Sudbury area employed professional investigators to ferret out union sympathizers among their workers. Those accused were then fired.[78] That same year, he reacted to the British and French sell-out of Czechoslovakia with another pamphlet: *Stop Hitler! The Nazis Have Struck Again!* He noted that "the truth is that the second world imperialist war to redivide the world has been on for two years: in Spain, China, Ethiopia, Austria and now Czechoslovakia!" He then asked, "Who will be next?"[79] His most famous pamphlet was *Hitler's Fifth Column in Quebec*. Published in 1942, it was a damning indictment of clerico-fascism in the province[80] and caused such a furore that Montreal's future mayor, Jean Drapeau, then a member of the Bloc Populaire Canadien, sued Rose for libel. The action dragged on for years and was settled out of court only in February 1946.[81] During the 1930s, Rose ran for office unsuccessfully both provincially and federally in Montreal ridings. Finally, in August 1943, he won Montreal-Cartier in a by-election, and successfully defended his seat in 1945.[82]

Rose was a powerful and effective campaigner. During the 1943 contest, he strongly attacked Fascism, employing the endorsement of Fina Nelson, whose son Willie had been killed in action while serving with the RAF in 1940. "Fred Rose fought the crime of Munich that made Hitler strong," Nelson said. As for Rose's opponents, she said: "Where were the others then? Where was the voice of Mr. [Lazarus] Phillips and Mr. [David] Lewis then? Fred Rose . . . is the kind of man into whose hands my hero son would have been glad to trust the world and its affairs when once this war is finished."[83]

Rose also exploited the fact that his riding had some of the worst slums in Montreal. He published a large handout containing photographs of dirty and hungry-looking children, crowded and dilapidated housing, cluttered backyards, unpaved lanes, abandoned stores, and homes filled with bedraggled children and pregnant women staring vacantly into space.[84] Once elected, he regularly communicated with his constituents through pamphlets containing some of his numerous speeches in Parliament, including *Fred Rose in Parliament* (a fifty-page Yiddish translation of his speeches on domestic and foreign policy issues), *Le Masque tombé*, and *La Menace du chaos: Le Complot Tory contre le Canada* (on Fascism in Quebec).[85]

Although popular in the Cartier riding, Rose was in serious trouble with the law. He had been arrested in September 1942 on charges of subversive activities as a member of the CPC. (The CPC was outlawed in 1940 and renamed itself the Labour Progressive Party in 1942.) He confessed to all of the charges, promised not to participate in party activities, and was released a few weeks later.[86] However, Rose was soon engaged in serious espionage activities on behalf of the Soviet Union, and he was arrested shortly after the revelations of the Soviet embassy clerk Igor Gouzenko were made in September 1945. The court found Rose guilty of espionage and sentenced him to six years' imprisonment.[87] He was released in 1951 and spent the remainder of his life in Poland.

At least six other Jews, of a total of twenty-six individuals, were named in the Royal Commission investigations based on the Gouzenko documents.[88] One of them was Sam Carr (Schmil Kogan). Born in Ukraine, he arrived in Canada in 1924. Carr worked as a harvester and a labourer in Saskatchewan, joined the Young Communist League in Montreal, and became one of its organizers. In 1931, four years after moving to Toronto and joining the CPC,[89] he became its organizing secretary and was soon up on charges laid under Section 98. The charges stuck, and he was sentenced to ten years' imprisonment; but he was released in 1935, just in time to become one of the main activists of the On-to-Ottawa March of the unemployed.[90]

Carr then helped to recruit Canadian volunteers to fight for the Republicans in Spain. He also edited the CPC's *Clarion* from 1938 to 1940, subsequently went "underground," and resurfaced in September 1942. The RCMP arrested him on a variety of charges, but let him go a few weeks later on condition that he cease all party activities.[91] Like Rose, however, Carr also worked for Soviet intelligence. Both men, in fact, were agents of the NKVD (the precursor of the KGB) for years, reporting on the CPC, various political matters, and, on rare occasions, providing information on Canadian political, military, and diplomatic matters.[92] Active in the Soviet military intelligence network (GRU) since 1942, Rose and Carr successfully helped the Russians recruit a wide network of subagents in Ottawa, Toronto, and Montreal. Their spying continued until the Gouzenko revelations brought on the Royal Commission inquiry, which resulted in their prosecution and imprisonment.[93]

The Jewish Communists were profoundly concerned about the rise of Fascism, especially after the Nazis came to power in Germany in 1933. One scholar contends that at this time, "anti-fascist politics became dominant in the Jewish Communist movement."[94] In this context, terms such as *Zionist fascists* and *Zionist Hitlerites*, which were routinely levelled against the pro-Zionist Jewish bourgeoisie, were dropped, as were calls for the Communists to try winning over Jewish workers who belonged to Zionist groups.[95] Such efforts by the Communists backfired, however. An anti-Nazi conference in December 1935, attended by all factions of the Jewish left, quickly descended into chaos as the Poale-Zion (Labour Zionists) charged the Communists with attacking them and the Palestine Mandate authorities. The Communists retorted that these charges were spurious, rightist-inspired attempts to frustrate the formation of a United Jewish workers' anti-Nazi front.[96] These efforts were not helped by charges from Communist spokesmen like Sam Carr, who asserted that Zionism was "inspired by . . . fascists."[97] Jewish Communists continued their anti-Nazi campaign through the Canadian League against War and Fascism. But because of their simultaneous attacks on Zionism and their charges that community activists such as Peter Bercovitch were "fascists" who were not doing enough to combat antisemitism, they failed utterly to attract either the Jewish masses or the community's leaders.[98] The bitterness between the Communists and the rest of the Jewish community emerged in especially strong form during provincial and federal election campaigns in constituencies like Cartier in Montreal, where Fred Rose ran against the incumbent Bercovitch in the 1936 provincial contest.[99]

No friends of capitalism, the Jewish Communists did not hesitate to publicly attack Jewish capitalists and try to embarrass them in the community. Lyon Cohen, a prominent Montreal activist and well-to-do men's-clothing manufacturer, was the owner of the Cuthbert Company, a large brass foundry that workers struck in July 1937. Cohen refused to negotiate.[100] The local Communist Party Trade Union Commission tried to organize a concurrent strike at Cohen's clothing factory and threatened to distribute Yiddish leaflets and hold public protest meetings in the Jewish district to try to force Cohen to the bargaining table.

Epithets of "social Fascism" flung at the Canadian Jewish Congress ceased by the mid-1930s. The Communists then directed their energies to creating a Jewish united front against the real Fascist menace in Europe.[101] In July 1935, *Der Kamf* even found Zionist socialists to be acceptable allies in the battle against Fascism.[102] While the Congress viewed such efforts with scepticism, the Canadian Communists persisted in trying to build a broad Jewish–anti-Fascist coalition. Yet after the German–Soviet non-aggression pact was signed in August 1939, many somewhat embarrassed Jewish Communists temporarily dropped their popular-front efforts, while still continuing to condemn Fascism.[103] Gershman, perhaps a maverick on this issue, believed that the Soviet Union had no alternative but to sign the agreement.[104]

The infamous pact created what the RCMP labelled "confusion among communists," and it resulted in significant disaffection among many Jewish comrades.[105] In October 1939, the RCMP reported that "a great number of erstwhile members, mostly of the Jewish faith, have left the ranks, disclaiming the 'good intentions' of Russia in its fight against the Jew-baiting Nazis."[106] But while Jewish rank-and-file support was falling off, most leaders remained loyal to the party.[107] Despite strong anti-Communist attacks, their candidates in the Winnipeg municipal elections of 1940 did relatively well in the Jewish polls. Joseph B. Salsberg, an activist in the United Hat, Cap and Millinery Workers Union during the 1920s and 1930s and a member of the Toronto city council since 1938,[108] was beaten in Toronto's Ward Four partly because of a decline in Jewish support.[109] He entered provincial politics in 1943 and, aided by the fact that the Soviet Union was by then an ally, was elected to the Ontario legislature from Spadina, a largely Jewish riding. Another Communist, Joe Zuken, served for many years on Winnipeg's city council.[110]

The United Jewish People's Order

No other Jewish leftist organization attracted more attention from the RCMP than the United Jewish Peoples' Order (UJPO). Although it had branches in major cities throughout Canada in the mid-1940s, it was principally centred in Montreal, Toronto, and Winnipeg.[111] The UJPO was formed in 1945 by an amalgamation of the Labour League of Toronto, the Jewish Aid Society of Montreal, and a group known as the Jewish Fraternal Order of Winnipeg.[112] These groups were in part composed of defectors or expellees from the Arbeiter Ring who objected to that organization's anti-communism and wished to support the CPC.[113]

The principal actor in the establishment of the UJPO was Joshua Gershman, who also served as national Jewish organizer of the Labour Progressive Party.[114] By 1946, the UJPO had established branches in Hamilton, Windsor, Calgary, and Vancouver, and had set up a new camp near Winnipeg (to add to those near Montreal and Toronto), as well as a summer seminary for young leaders. The organization also sponsored choirs, lectures, and concert tours. In fact, the long-lived and enormously popular Toronto Jewish Folk Choir became an institution on the Toronto cultural scene.[115] Throughout the UJPO youth activity was strongly supported, and by 1947 the organization had a youth wing numbering five hundred members. Gershman, Salsberg, and Rose were frequent speakers at youth meetings on cultural and social themes, and often discussed "new institution[s] for the welfare of the Jewish masses."[116]

While its agenda was progressive in the very broadest sense, the UJPO's principal concerns were Jewish issues based on the belief that the Jewish Communist movement was in some ways distinctive or independent,[117] accepting implicitly the premise that "Jews did constitute a nation."[118] At its 1945 founding convention in Montreal, the organization condemned the revival of antisemitism in Quebec ". . . as if nothing would have happened in the last 6–7 years."[119] Speakers attacked the anti-Jewish policies of McGill University, and condemned British imperialism in Palestine and India; the ganging up by the United States and Britain against the Soviet Union; the return of Fascism in Germany, Italy, and Greece; and so-called red-baiting in North America.[120]

While not outspokenly anti-Zionist, the UJPO objected to what it regarded as the excessively Zionist character of the Canadian Jewish Congress prior to the Second World War. In January 1938, Gershman had lamented that the Congress was not "a convention of the Jewish masses."[121] After the war, however, the UJPO, now an active component of the Congress, strongly favoured Jewish immigration to Palestine and the building of the Yishuv (settlement) there.

In late April 1948, on the eve of the Israeli war of independence, the *Vochenblatt* called upon Canadian Jews to mount "a more mighty struggle against every sign of compromise [by the U.S. and Britain] . . . to destroy and bury the decision of the UN to establish a Jewish state. . . . Not a single Jew must stay outside of this struggle! As Canadian citizens and as Jews we must not allow the Zionist leaders to be satisfied with a quiet and weak request to the Government [of Canada]. What is necessary is a complete mobilization of all for a demonstrative and active struggle."[122]

Although the UJPO enjoyed considerable support, the actual size of its membership is not known. The RCMP estimated that crowds of "some eight hundred persons of Jewish racial origin" would turn out to hear its speakers.[123] Similar sized crowds attended banquets and other occasions, where, the RCMP noted, a comradely spirit prevailed. Indeed, the "constant usage of the term 'comrade' whenever the participants addressed one another" was also noted by the RCMP, with some concern.[124]

RCMP scrutiny of the UJPO included very careful review of the *Vochenblatt*, which was translated by an unnamed person denoted only as "MHA." On one occasion, the election of a UJPO member to the executive of the Ostrovtzer Aid Society in Toronto led an officer to comment that "this would seem to indicate how the Communists are penetrating the Jewish landsmanshaften with the ultimate object of turning them into the tools for their policies."[125]

The RCMP also noted with concern the organization's success in gaining representation in the Canadian Jewish Congress at its Sixth Plenary Session in 1945. A statement presented by the so-called Leftist Jewish Movement was signed by various members of the Labour Progressive Party, including Fred Rose, then a member of the Congress' Dominion Council.[126] It called on the Congress to combat antisemitism, to request the softening of immigration laws, to assist Jewish immigrants to Canada and other countries, to help in "the upbuilding" of Palestine, and to provide "moral support and sympathy" for the Jews in the Soviet Union. Although these ideas were hardly radical — they were mainstream Canadian Jewish Congress goals — an RCMP report noted worriedly that

> Thus the picture becomes more clear, that of a nationally organized Jewish Order under complete Communist domination with ties growing ever closer and stronger with the International Workers' Order, I.W.O., in whose steps they are following move by move with the ultimate object of gaining a stranglehold on Jewery [*sic*] throughout Canada in an effort to control and direct their activities along Communist lines.[127]

Another contemporary RCMP report ascribed even darker purposes to the UJPO. It stated that "[E]ach move [is] an attempt to infiltrate into the Canadian Jewish Congress with the ultimate object of splitting that organization or gaining a controlling hand."[128] The UJPO in fact had no influence on the Congress, then firmly controlled by the Montreal whisky tycoon Samuel Bronfman and its executive director, the lawyer Saul Hayes. Like most Canadian Jews, these two men were not in the slightest way sympathetic to the CPC.

The UJPO's multifarious activities involved charitable as well as cultural efforts and included a fund-raising campaign to help build orphanages in Poland and one to settle Jewish orphans in the Soviet Union.[129] Education was also of great importance to the UJPO. By 1945, it supported two afternoon schools in Montreal, both named after the radical theoretician Morris Winchevsky. Several hundred students attended these educational programs. It also sponsored several children's summer camps founded by the Arbeiter Ring in the 1930s, such as Nitgedeiget (Don't Worry), which was also attended by French-Canadian children.[130] Other camps included Kindervelt (Children's World), established near Toronto in 1925, and Naivelt (New World), which since the late 1930s conducted a systematic educational program on the working-class struggles and the rising threat of Fascism.[131] A "Spanish Week" was observed there in the summer of 1937, in support of that beleaguered republic's government. The Soviet theme was prominent at Kindervelt, which was dominated by a huge statue of a man and woman clenching a hammer and sickle in their hands.

Despite these substantial efforts, however, the UJPO had little success in recruiting a second generation to the movement in the 1940s. First, socialism was eroded because few Canadian-born children of radical socialists became workers.[132] Second, the use of Yiddish diminished as the children chose instead to speak English. Thus the ideas contained in the writings of Winchevsky and other Jewish Communist theoreticians were no longer easily accessible. And last, the Second World War and its ensuing prosperity made Communism — especially the repressive Stalinist variety — seem at worst repugnant and at best irrelevant. The UJPO, like most other Jewish left-wing organizations, was a one-generation phenomenon. It spoke to issues that had little relevance to a generation schooled in North American values and avid for its rewards — and carried its message in a language that, to most, was far less important than English.

The Non-Communist Jewish Left

The Communists, however, were by no means the only significant Jewish leftists in the interwar and immediate postwar years, and it would be a serious mistake to ignore the intense political and cultural life of the non-Communist Jewish socialists, who, collectively, were far more numerous. Certainly, the socialist platform was much closer to the community's mainstream Zionist ethos, and many socialists were active members of the Canadian Jewish Congress, which sought to serve as a non-ideological representative body, or parliament, for all Jewish organizations and communities across the Dominion. If one were to construct a very rough chart of the Canadian Jewish left, it would look something like the one on the following page.

Several points require explanation. The first is that while these organizations had defined identities that conformed to ideological beliefs, their affiliations developed in different ways. The split between left (*linke*) and right (*rechte*) Labour Zionists developed much more sharply in Toronto than anywhere else in Canada because of deep ideological differences there over whether Hebrew or Yiddish was to be taught in the Nationale Radicale Schule (the National Radical School), which held classes in the afternoons and on Sundays for children.[133] The left group in Toronto, though Marxist, was staunchly anti-Communist and, in fact, led the fight against Communist influence in the Toronto clothing-industry unions in the 1930s.

<table>
<tr><th colspan="4">Jewish Left in Canada</th></tr>
<tr><th colspan="2">Poale Zion (Labour Zionists)</th><th>Arbeiter Ring (Workmen's Circle)</th><th>United Jewish People's Order</th></tr>
<tr><td>Right (rechte) Generally known as Labour Zionists. Farband Sick-Benefit Yiddishists and Hebraists.</td><td>Left (linke) Marxists. Followers of Ber Borochov. Known as Achdut-Avoda-Poale Zion. Published Proletarishe Gedank (Workers' Thought; and Unzer Vegg (Our Way) Independent Arbeiter Ring Sick-Benefit Yiddishists.</td><td>Bundists. Included territorialist and anarchist wings in some cities. Arbeiter Ring Sick-Benefit Yiddishists.</td><td>Communists. Anti-Zionists until 1948.</td></tr>
</table>

The UJPO on the far left sometimes attempted to mask its thoroughgoing Communist affiliation, despite its strict adherence to the Kremlin's policies and pronouncements. The Arbeiter Ring (Workmen's Circle) was a fraternal order with socialist ideas and programs that were dedicated to the promotion of progressive Yiddish culture.[134] Because the Arbeiter Ring members were influenced by East European Bundist ideas, which emphasized Jewish cultural autonomy in the Diaspora and were therefore non-Zionist, some wags called them "Zionists with sea sickness." Some of its members were inclined to be more radical politically in smaller offshoot or affiliated wings, or in anarchist or territorialist groups in some cities. (Territorialists favoured a non-Zionist Jewish homeland.)

The left Poale Zion (sometimes known as Achdut-Avoda-Poale Zion) were followers of Ber Borochov, a Zionist socialist theorist who tried to mobilize the Jewish proletariat to the Zionist national revival.[135] The organization's main publications, *Proletarishe Gedank* (Workers' Thought) and *Unzer Vegg* (Our Way), had a lot of Toronto content. Its sick-benefit offshoot was known as the independent Arbeiter Ring (not be confused with the Arbeiter Ring).

The Labour Zionists organized fund-raising campaigns to aid workers' causes through the General Federation of Labour in Palestine. In 1938 a new umbrella organization, the Labour Zionist Movement of Canada, unified and strengthened these efforts.[136]

There were other differences — some doctrinal, others personal — within these groups in Winnipeg and Montreal, and the future historian of the Jewish left has a fascinating, yet arduous, task. What needs full examination, besides the ideologies particular to these groups, are the political and social expressions of these manifestations of secular Judaism.

The Jewish labour movement covered the full spectrum of ideas, ranging from Soviet communism to Zionist socialism, but all celebrated the liberation of the common people from the shackles of oppression. All organizations trumpeted this goal in their publications, manifestos, and speeches with an almost religious zeal, and no occasion suited them better than May Day, the international workers' holiday. In Toronto, as Ben Lappin recalled in a touching memoir, May first was alive with preparations for the annual Jewish workers' march in honour of this festival.[137] Union locals marched in formation next to the Labour Lyceum, while the left and right Poale Zion and Arbeiter Ring organizations gathered separately on a nearby street. Fraternal orders, youth groups, schools, and sports clubs also came together to parade. And then, with gaudy banners in Yiddish, English, or Hebrew proclaiming the rights of working men and women on high, they set off in formation up Spadina to Bloor towards Christie Pits, where they would hear lengthy and flowery Yiddish speeches and proclamations on *chalutziut* in Palestine and the strength of united Jewish labour. Meanwhile, the Communists conducted their own march towards Queen's Park, where they denounced capitalism and the brutal oppression of workers, under the scrutiny of secret RCMP informers and the steely watchfulness of mounted Toronto policemen, members of Chief (General) Dennis Draper's so-called Red Squad, who were ready to wade into the crowd with truncheons flailing at the slightest provocation.

These ideas influenced many Jews as the Depression hit even deeper into the souls of Canadians. In the CCF, David Lewis, who became national secretary in 1936, was well-versed in British Labour Party thought. "My brand of socialism," remembered Lewis, a Rhodes scholar from a Bundist family background that stressed Yiddish culture and socialism,[138] "was of the rather harsh medicine variety, the only cure for an increasingly sick system. It was of working-class origin and [had] nothing but contempt for 'hypocritical bourgeois morality.' It was hard-nosed, derived from Marxism of the revisionist kind, and concentrated more on strategies to smash the capitalist system than on programs to build a more humane one." But at McGill, he learned to temper these views under the influence of young professors associated with the League for Social Reconstruction who stressed "the need for positive programs."[139]

Lewis, a Polish-born agnostic Jew, contributed enormously to making the CCF a party of democratic socialism similar to the British Labour Party. He combined the qualities of leadership, the penetrating mind of "an intellectual deeply committed to matters of definition and policy," and a brilliant capacity to organize.[140] He did not, however, attempt to follow the British model slavishly, and understood the special problems of the Canadian economy. Unlike Britain, Canada depended heavily on exports of raw commodities and was thus seriously exposed to the vagaries of international markets. Lewis stressed the need for democratic planning to keep control of the sick Canadian economy.[141]

Despite his radical socialist origins and his early willingness as CCF national secretary to co-operate somewhat with other working-class parties, Lewis was strongly anti-Communist.[142] He became aggravated by some of their "slick [electoral] manoeuvre[s]" and their control over the committees to aid Spanish democracy during the Spanish Civil War.[143] Lewis, allied with the Anglo-Protestant ex-clergyman and CCF leader James Shaver Woodsworth, was a major builder of the democratic socialist party. Many of his efforts in these years were spent in establishing links with the Canadian labour movement, which he recognized "was necessarily engaged on the economic front against the same forces which the party faced on the political front."[144] Here he developed even stronger suspicions of, and antipathies towards, the Communists. He struggled through the late 1930s to keep them from interfering with the CCF's efforts to win union support.[145]

Canada's Jews and the Spanish Civil War

The Spanish Civil War crystallized the political issues that were at stake for many Canadian radicals in the 1930s. The democratically elected Republican government in Spain was attacked in 1936 by powerful Fascist forces led by Gen. Francisco Franco, who was well-supported by military advisers and air and ground forces from Nazi Germany and Fascist Italy. The Spanish Republicans, on the other hand, were boycotted by the Western democracies and were only weakly supported by the Soviet Union. To offset this imbalance, thousands of Communists and other radicals from Europe and North America volunteered to serve in the International Brigades, which formed to fight in defence of Spanish democracy.

Among these forces was a Canadian contingent, the Mackenzie-Papineau Battalion, that comprised some twelve hundred men, including thirty-eight Canadian and thirteen American Jews.[146] This was a substantially smaller contribution, in relation to the Jewish populations of the two countries, than was made by the American Lincoln Battalion, of which 371 persons, or 21 to 30 percent of the volunteers, were Jews.[147] All Canadians who fought there were in violation of the Foreign Enlistment Act, which was specifically designed to prevent Canadians from serving in the Spanish conflict. While most used their own names, some assumed aliases as part of their "underground" journeys to Spain. For example, Muni Erlick signed up as Jack Taylor, Paul Skup as Paul Scott, Matthew Kowalski as Jack Steele, and Alan Herman-Yermanov as Ted Allan.[148]

Sympathy for the Spanish Republicans went far beyond Communist and Socialist ranks. One senior External Affairs official, Lester Pearson, was pro-

---

Maurice Constant

Born into a well-to-do Toronto family on July 1, 1914, one of five children, Maurice Constant struck out on his own into the world of ideas at an early age. He rejected religion, refusing to go through bar-mitzvah training. He read widely in the classics of world literature, philosophy, and psychology in his teenage years while attending Jarvis Collegiate. He entered the honours science program at the University of Toronto in 1935, taking a special interest in the life sciences and, extracurricularly, in the Canadian Officer Training Corps, wrestling, judo, fencing, and basketball. Restless at university, he affiliated himself with the left-wing Zionist youth movement Hashomer Hatzair and was swept away by the radical views of André Malraux, who spoke at Hart House in March 1937. Shortly thereafter, he left Toronto for New York, where he made contact with the Communist movement. Hoping to report for the *Toronto Star* on the fight against Franco's Fascist insurgency in Spain, he returned to Toronto, where he joined a group of Canadian volunteers who went via Halifax, Liverpool, Le Havre, Paris, Toulouse, and Perpignon over the Pyrenees to Figures and Barcelona. Once there, he decided to join the International Brigades as an infantry officer. He served both as adjutant of the intelligence section and as commander of the reconnaissance platoon of the 15th International Brigade. He fought at Brunete, on the Aragon front, at Fuentes de Ebro, and at Caspe, where he was wounded. He was eventually evacuated to Barcelona, where he was later mustered out and sent back to Canada.

Interview with Maurice Constant, 13 Aug. 1996. See also Victor Howard, with Mac Reynolds, *The Mackenzie-Papineau Battalion: The Canadian Contingent in the Spanish Civil War* (Ottawa: Carleton University Press, 1986).

Republican and — despite Canada's formal neutrality — even facilitated at least one Canadian's transfer to Spain to join the fight.[149] In 1938, the CCF adopted a motion favouring the Republicans at its national convention.[150] One of the party's leading intellectuals — Frank R. Scott of McGill University's faculty of law — infuriated and sickened by the refusal of the Western powers to assist Spain's elected Republican government, headed the Montreal Committee for Medical Aid to Spain.[151] Many other Canadians, both left and centre, shared these views. Meanwhile, the conservative Catholic community, especially in French Canada, vehemently opposed the Republicans and actively supported the Fascist insurgents.

In the wider Jewish community, there were some expressions of sympathy for the Spanish Republican cause. In 1937, Rabbi Stern published a letter from a Mac-Pap volunteer, Samuel Abramson, in his weekly column in the *Canadian Jewish Review*, but he prefaced it with the caution that

> we are not so sure about all the issues involved in the fratricide war raging in Spain. . . . We know there are those who look upon General Franco as ineffable. Then there are the uncompromising "left wingers" who are convinced that Barcelona's conduct is perfect and that by all means, fair or foul, the Loyalists are justified in uprooting the vested interests in Iberia.[152]

Marc Chagalle, who had received some letters from Canadian Jewish boys in Spain, offered a more sympathetic view in the June 1937 issue of Toronto's *Jewish Standard*: "[P]owerful interests inside and outside of Spain, seeing their profits threatened because of the election of the democratic People's Front Government, declared war on the Government of the Spanish People. These interests started the war."[153] Chagalle argued that "if the letters that the Jewish boys write are any indication of the spirit and discipline of the loyalists, then we may rest assured that Fascism will be defeated in Spain." *Der Kamf* informed its readers of the Spanish situation throughout the conflict and published a lengthy article on some of the Canadian Jewish volunteers after their return in 1939. It featured interviews with Izzy Goldberg, Isaac Shatz, Sydney Cohen, and Victor Himmelfarb.[154]

While only 25 percent of the volunteers for the Spanish Republicans were Canadian-born, 65 percent of the Jewish volunteers had been born in Canada.[155] Moreover, with one lawyer, two doctors, two pharmacists, a social worker, and a male nurse among them, the Jews had a higher level of education and skill than the average Canadian. Their ranks also included a number of working-class types, however, such as an aviation mechanic, a fur cutter, a miner/prospector, two students, a musician, a warehouseman, two painters, two salesmen, two clothing workers, a driver, two seamen, and a barber. Eight of the Jewish volunteers (including the writer Ted Allan) served in non-combat roles, as medics and journalists, for example. Only seven, four of whom were veterans of the Canadian Expeditionary Force in the First World War, had previous military training. Of those whose fate is known, twenty left Spain alive, and seventeen returned to Canada or the United States. Two were prisoners of war, eight were wounded in action (some more than once), six were killed in action, and one was declared missing.

Most Jewish volunteers had belonged to the YCL and the CPC or the Communist Party in the United States or Spain. Commitment to the cause was generally strong. "Being of Jewish origin, my hatred for fascism was so great as to compel me to leave a good home and fight these bastards,"[156] wrote Isaac Shatz of Toronto in the questionnaire that all volunteers were asked to complete upon arrival in Spain. Some of the Jewish volunteers had colourful backgrounds. Muni Erlick was a Ukrainian born in 1906. He joined the YCL in Paris in 1924, moved to Romania in 1925, then immigrated to the United States in 1926 and lived briefly in Detroit. In 1927 he moved to Montreal, where he joined the CPC and managed the party's Jewish weekly. Erlick also served as the national secretary of the Jewish Bureau of the CPC and worked in various other party capacities until he shipped off to Spain in 1937.[157] Following his return to Canada, he joined the Canadian Army in November 1942, served in the Armoured Corps, and was killed in action in France in August 1944.[158]

Bert "Yank" Levy was born in Hamilton in 1897 and grew up in Cleveland. He served in the merchant navy and joined the Jewish Legion[159] in 1918, serving as a machine-gunner. He went to Mexico in 1920–21, did some gun-running to Nicaragua in 1926, and spent six years in a United States jail for armed robbery. He joined the International Brigades in 1937, becoming an officer in the machine-gun company of the British battalion. Captured at the Battle of Jarama, he spent six months in one of Franco's prisons. Upon his release in 1940, he travelled to Britain and became a lecturer to the British Home Guard on guerrilla warfare, which was also the subject of a work he wrote for United States Army's *Infantry Journal*. The article was published as "Guerrilla Warfare" in 1942[160] and in its day served as the standard text on the subject.[161]

Sam Abramson, a Zionist activist, went to Spain in June 1937 and served as an ambulance driver. In a series of letters to Hananiah Caiserman at the Canadian Jewish Congress, Abramson described the military situation in Spain, appealed for Canadian Jewish support of medical assistance to the

A. M. KLEIN ON SAM ABRAMSON

Sam Abramson's efforts in Spain did not go unnoticed in the Montreal Jewish community. In the June 1938 issue of the *Canadian Forum*, A. M. Klein, then editor of the *Chronicle*, published a moving tribute to his boyhood friend.

To One Gone to the Wars
For S.H.A.

Unworthiest crony of my grammar days,
Expectorator in learning's cuspidor,
Forsaking the scholar's for the gamin's ways,
The gates of knowledge for the cubicular door.

How you have shamed me, me the nobler talker,
The polisher of phrases, stainer of verbs,
Who daily for a price serve hind and hawker,
Earning my Sabbath meat, my daily herbs.

'Tis you who do confound the lupine jaw
And stand protective of my days and works,
As in the street-fight you maintain the law
And I in an armchair weigh and measure Marx.

Alas, that fettered and bound by virtues long
since rusty,
I must, for spouse and son,
Withhold, as is befitting any prison trusty,
My personal succour and my uniformed aid,
And from the barracks watch the barricade —
Offering you, meek sacrifice, unvaliant gift,
My non-liturgic prayer:
For that your aim be sure,
Your bullet swift,
Unperilous your air, your trenches dry,
Your courage untainted by defeat,
Your courage high.

From *Canadian Life and Letters 1920–70: Selections from the Canadian Forum* (Toronto: University of Toronto Press, 1972).

Republican government, conveyed greetings (including regards from Emma Goldman), and stated his commitment to the battle against Fascism. "I have been doing all I can to get people back home to start a Jewish Committee for Medical Aid to Spain," he wrote in March 1938.[162] "We must all contribute to the defeat of fascism," he continued. "Will you give them your help[?]"

Two months later, Abramson urged Caiserman, who was battling Fascism in Canada through the Congress, to "treat the fascists like what they are, and when you strike, strike hard. . . . Fascism is more than an academic problem to you these days. Don't give way an inch for if you do you'll get no thanks from the enemy."[163] Abramson even had some cogent advice for the Congress' attempts, in a 1938 pamphlet entitled *Facts about the Jews*, to soft peddle the existence of Jewish Communists in Canada. "I can't say I was pleased with the general tone of the pamphlet." Condemning its virtual apology for J. B. Salsberg, Abramson countered angrily: "Isn't he a damn good civic representative? Should we [not] rather apologize for a Peter Bercovitch who voted for the Padlock law?"[164]

Following the disbanding of the International Brigades in Barcelona in October 1938, Abramson's heart was bursting:

> Barcelona gave us a big farewell yesterday. It was simply magnificent, almost beyond words. Hundreds of thousands of people turned out, the streets were strewn with flowers, women kissed us as we marched along, everybody was quite overcome with emotion. . . . I hope to be home about the end of the year, and back to work. There's plenty to be done. Our fight is not yet over. Spain must not become another fascist victim. . . . Salud y Victoria.[165]

A week later he expressed his anguish over leaving Spain, whose "fine people" he had come to love, and proclaimed his determinaton to continue his work for democracy there. "If Fascism triumphs here," he observed prophetically, "then there will be a great offensive on the few countries still holding out. No Pasaran."[166]

Jews and Communism: Some Comparisons

In both Great Britain and the United States, many Jews were strongly attracted to the Communist Party. In the United States, it was estimated that 15 percent of the party membership was Jewish during the 1920s.[167] In Britain, Jews accounted for 35 to 40 percent of party membership during the Depression. But actual numerical support at election time was low. Of some

800,000 Jewish votes cast in the 1930 congressional elections in New York State, only 50,000 went to Communist candidates. Their appeal was essentially to the youth and the intellectuals, who saw in communism the fulfilment of their reformist or revolutionary hopes. Yet the strongest attraction for Jews was the Communist Party's uncompromising opposition to antisemitism and Nazism — at least until the Hitler/Stalin pact of 1939.[168] "The Communist party," notes the historian Henry Feingold, "shrewdly exploited the panic many Jews felt as antisemitic spokesmen echoed the Nazi line," one of whose mainstays was "based on an imagined link between Jews and communism."[169] Thus while most American Jews were overwhelmingly drawn to the Democratic Party, a significant minority supported the Communists.

Much the same was true in Britain. There Jews largely supported Labour, although a significant minority were Communists, some for idealistic reasons and others because the party supported non-Zionist socialism "in confrontation with the British Union of Fascists [BUF]."[170] In fact, Communist phalanxes of dockworkers joined with Jewish streetfighters in stopping the Oswald Mosley–led BUF parade through the Jewish area of Stepney, in London, on October 4, 1936. The so-called Battle of Cable Street effectively ended such marches in Britain. Similar Communist muscle in defence of the Jews was employed in Manchester.[171]

Nevertheless, the appeal of communism was not numerically significant, although the historian David Cesarani suggests that "large numbers of young Jews associated themselves with the party and a generation of gifted Jewish East End writers aligned themselves with the party and celebrated it in their novels of East End Jewish life."[172] Jewish involvement in the British Communist Party is also attributable to a growing "preoccupation with the threat from German-inspired Fascism" in the 1930s, a concern that no doubt affected Canadian and American Jews as well.[173] But in Canada in 1943, Jews constituted only a tenth of CPC membership and of pro-Communist voters. In 1945, Jewish supporters numbered no more than five thousand, the equivalent of about 1.5 percent of the Jewish electorate.[174]

In French Canada, and in the mind of Abbé Lionel Groulx, Jews were Judeo-Bolshevists. On occasion — such as during rallies on behalf of the Spanish Republicans in 1937 — Université de Montréal students paraded through Montreal's main streets chanting, *"À bas, à bas, à bas les Communistes. À bas les juifs!"*[175] To them, Jews were the purveyors of the modernization that threatened the very survival of French Canadians in America. Indeed, domestic fascism seemed a greater threat than it was in either the United States or Britain, and as a result, Communism was possibly stronger among Canadian Jews. (This is suggested by the election in 1943 of two Communists from primarily Jewish constituencies — Joseph B. Salsberg to the Ontario legislature and Fred Rose to the House of Commons.) Some French-Canadian nationalists of that era even admired the politics of Salazar and Mussolini. In fact, support for Fascism was often publicly manifested in Montreal, where nearly half of all Canada's Jews lived, providing one strong reason why communism, the mortal enemy of fascism, had such an appeal in sectors of the Jewish community. Comparisons are difficult across such widely differing contexts, but communism seems to have registered a greater degree of electoral success in Canada than in the Jewish communities of the United States or Great Britain principally because Canadian Jewry was more strongly galvanized by communism for domestic reasons.

Certainly, the general public blamed Jews for much of the Communist agitation in Canada, especially in Quebec, where the Taschereau government tended "to blame Communist activity on Jewish radicals."[176] When questioned in connection with the Gouzenko allegations in 1945, Gordon Lunan was asked, "How could someone with your [British] background and education get mixed up with people like this — he read off some names — Rosenberg, Kogan, Gerson, Mazerall [*sic*]. The Z in Mazerall's name was evidently enough to reclassify him from Gentile to outcast Jew."[177]

Recalled Lunan, "A sizeable section of the movement . . . was essentially [a] middle class Jewish association of well-informed, culture-oriented, free-thinking people who did not or would not fit into conventional Montreal society. . . . For many, the odour of persecution and pogroms was still in their nostrils."[178]

The association of communism with Jews contributed to antisemitic sentiment throughout the world. In Britain, "the belief that the October Revolution was a 'Jewish plot' gained currency even in sections of the 'respectable' press."[179] As the historian Sharman Kadish observed, "The charge of 'Jewish Bolshevism,' gave more mileage to antisemitism [in Britain] in the years after the First World War."[180] This held true in Canada and the United States too, even though Communism attracted only a tiny minority of Jews. Antisemitism, of course, did push some Jews to the CPC, the one party that was outspoken in its rejection of all forms of race hatred and discrimination. But yet another political movement, Zionism, had always held an important place in Canadian Jewish hearts, and in the interwar years it became even stronger.

CHAPTER

6

"Not Complex or Sophisticated": Cheque-book Zionism between the Wars

Messianic dreams were not confined to the far left. Modern political Zionism, the ideal of creating a Jewish "national home" in Palestine, had sunk deep roots among Canada's Jews since Theodor Herzl established the movement in 1897.[1] Having grown and flourished before and during the First World War, Zionism in Canada changed significantly in the interwar era as the Jewish community continued to diversify. In the Zionist Organization of Canada (ZOC) and the Hadassah-WIZO Organization of Canada (Hadassah), both of them non-ideological groups affiliated with the World Zionist Organization, younger men and women had already assumed leadership roles. At the same time, Labour Zionism was gaining considerable strength among Jewish socialists, members of the working class, and others who supported the collectivist values and projects of the Palestine labour movement.

Although its headquarters were located in Montreal, the ZOC had as its president through the 1920s and 1930s A. J. Freiman, an Ottawa department store owner[2] with a baronial mansion in the city and an imposing country estate at Meech Lake in the nearby Gatineau Hills. A tall, heavy-set man of direct speech and open countenance, genial personality, and generous purse, Freiman, generally known as Archie, was an excellent choice for president of the country's oldest and most prestigious national Zionist organization. He made friends easily, entertained heartily, and watched over the ZOC with unswerving commitment to the cause. During his twenty years in the chair these qualities were tested often. He and his wife, Lillian, who headed the powerful national women's Zionist organization, Hadassah, gave themselves unstintingly to the movement.

The Freimans enjoyed the confidence of Zionists in both Toronto and Montreal and across the country. But because Archie lived in Ottawa and was unable to attend to affairs on a daily basis, and because the organization was growing and becoming more complex, the Montreal headquarters needed more personnel. To aid Leon Goldman, the ZOC executive director in Montreal, Rabbi Judah L. Zlotnick was hired in 1921 to organize Jewish National Fund (JNF) activities for land reclamation in Palestine. With an impressive record as an organizer, fund-raiser, educator, and intellectual in his native Poland and in the United States, Zlotnick soon replaced Goldman as executive director.[3] Freiman also relied heavily on regional lieutenants, such as Louis Fitch and Michael Garber of Montreal, Moses Gelber of Toronto, and Harry Wilder of Winnipeg.

Fitch and Garber were both McGill graduates and practising lawyers. They shared a lower-middle-class background and had by 1920 become prominent in Montreal. Fitch was well-known because of his position on the Montreal Jewish school question and his closeness to the "downtown" Jews who favoured a separate Jewish system.[4] As a Conservative, he was atypical in the community, which generally supported the Liberal Party. He ran unsuccessfully several times for a seat in the Quebec legislature. Serving on the ZOC's executive in various capacities throughout the 1920s, he and Garber together were Freiman's leading Montreal lieutenants. Fitch was interested in both international and domestic politics, and gave valuable advice to Freiman on these matters.

From Winnipeg, Harry Wilder served in various capacities on the ZOC national executive.[5] He was the proprietor of the Israelite Press, which published an English-language weekly and a Yiddish daily (*Yiddishe Vort*) that circulated in the strongly Zionist Prairie Jewish communities. Wilder did not always agree with ZOC policies or support Freiman's leadership. In a candid letter to Chaim Weizmann, head of the World Zionist Organization, in January 1932, Wilder suggested that Freiman "be relieved of his [ZOC] leadership. . . . The height to which we Canadian Zionists have raised him — (and where his money kept him) — made him somewhat dizzy. The ascent was somewhat too rapid for him. He mistook the smoke of incense which we burned at his shrine (in a spirit of jubilation, not adoration) for real clouds, above which he was soaring. I am not speaking from rancour because, personally, I like Archie . . ."[6]

Montreal and Toronto were the largest centres of Zionist activity, but the movement thrived in the smaller cities as well. There and in the Maritimes devoted followers ran the local campaigns, attended the national and regional conventions, sold the fifty-cent *shekels* that denoted official membership in the ZOC, and emptied the JNF blue boxes. On a per capita basis, Jews in the non-metropolitan centres were Zionism's strongest backers. In 1923–24, 60 percent of the contributors to Keren Hayesod, the Palestine Foundation Fund dedicated to building an infrastructure of Jewish settlements in Palestine, came from the 35 percent of the Jewish population living outside Montreal and Toronto. Most came from the West, where Zionism took on an especially fervent and independent spirit.[7] *Shekel* sales, a rough indicator of participation in the ZOC, suggest that membership was inversely proportionate to the total number of Jews living in each place. In centres outside of Montreal, Toronto, and Winnipeg, an overwhelming majority of Jews bought the *shekel*, while in the metropolitan cities only a tiny fraction did.

Even though the ZOC was the only truly national Jewish body from 1920 until 1934, when the Canadian Jewish Congress (defunct since 1920) was re-established, it was clearly not representative of all segments of Jewish political opinion or social classes. Besides the ZOC, many Jews were drawn to labour and religious organizations within the Zionist movement, such as Poale Zion and Mizrachi. Indeed, many immigrants, especially those living in the large cities, were not Zionists at all. While the ZOC remained stoutly independent of its American counterpart, strong links were forged between Canadian and American members of Poale Zion and Mizrachi, especially in their youth movements.[8]

The Canadian Zionist Perspective

The Balfour Declaration of November 2, 1917, while eliciting emotional support from many Zionist and non-Zionist Canadian Jews, raised an important question: Was Palestine the national home for all Jews or just a refuge for the persecuted? Because so few had moved to Palestine, most Canadian Zionists obviously believed the latter. But a national home under British sponsorship meant perhaps that the refuge would be larger, stronger, and more secure. And with British support, the dream would be realized much sooner. Thus, while Canadian Zionism retained its well-established philanthropic emphasis at home, its contributions to Jewish settlement in Palestine intensified, encouraged by the prestigious backing of Great Britain and the League of Nations.

Just as it was the dominant Zionist activity in other Western countries, fund-raising was central to the ZOC's activities, as was clearly indicated at their 1924 biennial convention[9] in Toronto. At the opening session, the chairman, Moses Gelber, welcomed Chaim Weizmann with the assurance that he was "amongst warm and loyal friends and supporters," and that Canadians realized "the great task you have before you but we are confident that you will be successful in your work." Gelber continued that "Canadian Jews and American Jews would raise the necessary funds to rebuild."[10] This was to be achieved by a division of labour in which the world movement set general policy, the *halutzim* (pioneers) and others in Palestine performed the actual physical labour, and North American Jewry helped supply the necessary financial resources, uniting all Jews in a common endeavour.[11]

This assertion of Jewish peoplehood[12] was clearly affirmed, judging by the success of Canadian Zionism over more than thirty years.[13] Zionism continued because it suited an immigrant population that was groping for an identity as both Jews and Canadians in a country that was still British and had a vibrant and sizeable French-Catholic minority. Many Canadian Jews were drawn to Zionism because it provided a workable definition of a new Jewishness, one no longer solely religious, and also emphasized historical continuity and a promising future.

The movement enjoyed the approval of Canadian politicians. In fact, the Federation of Zionist Societies of Canada, which preceded the ZOC, had received regular goodwill messages from prime ministers and other politicians.[14] Canada's governments, both Conservative and Liberal, would go no further, however, and politely deflected ZOC efforts to influence British authorities on Palestine mandate matters. Prime Minister Mackenzie King appeared only occasionally at the ZOC's biennial conventions, but usually sent Cabinet ministers or supportive telegrams. Reporting to Chaim Weizmann on King's address to the 1922 gathering, Freiman exulted, "he gave us all an inspiring message, speaking in a most glowing way of the accomplishments of Jewry generally and particularly praising the great ideal which lies at the bottom of all our work."[15] Canadian Zionists seemed to be grateful for this pretense of support. It made them feel they belonged to a world movement that enjoyed wide approval. Moreover, even nominal support from Canadian politicians legitimized Zionism as a form of Canadian Jewish identity. To a community overwhelmingly composed of immigrants, such prestigious endorsement was valued very highly.

Despite the relatively small size of their community, Canadians since 1917 had raised huge sums for the Jewish settlements in Palestine, collectively known as the Yishuv, through the Helping Hand and Restoration funds. Because Palestine was administered by Turkey, an enemy country, these monies were sent through American organizations. The success of those campaigns was attributable both to the prosperity of wartime and to the Jews' deep commitment to the Zionist enterprise.

Canadian Jewry was on a fund-raising roll right after the war. Lillian Freiman campaigned strenuously throughout Canada and was largely responsible for the funds' successes.[16] Clothing, food, and money were collected and dispatched through the International Red Cross. The Restoration Fund, launched in 1919, set an unprecedented goal of $250,000, an enormous sum considering that Canadian Jewry, under the newly organized Canadian Jewish Congress, was also sending aid to Jews recovering from the war in Eastern Europe.

The wartime experience helped to crystallize several features of Canadian Zionism. The most important was the reaffirmation of their independence from the American Zionists and from the world headquarters' heavy-handed direction.[17] In late 1919, Leon Goldman expressed to Shmarya Levin his indignation that American Zionists had not informed him of Canadian contributions to the funds and of *shekel* purchases: "You can easily imagine the hindrance which is caused to our efforts when we appeal for funds without being able to produce public recognition of funds already remitted."[18]

Goldman and other ZOC officers also took pains to remind world leaders of the limitations of Canadian goodwill. In 1919, he informed Levin that contradictory communications from Jerusalem were making it difficult to get "wholehearted support in Canada."[19] He also demanded that the London Zionist office notify him of recent discussions of the Actions Committee (the executive of the World Zionist Organization), "so as to enable us . . . to discuss intelligently the workings of our Organization, when we are dealing with our branches and affiliations in this Country. . . ."[20] After receiving letters from London dunning the ZOC for money in December 1919, he replied that fund-raising efforts in Canada were Canada's private business. "Canada's Jewish community [has] its limitations[,] and its material wealth . . . cannot be compared in any degree with that of our brethren in the United States of America."[21] Goldman also explained that Canadians were fully aware of conditions in Eastern Europe and resented being badgered for money. They would do their best. And that would be that.[22]

While his objections were usually acknowledged, follow-up reminders were sometimes needed. As a result, some Zionist officials touring Canada did not appreciate Canadian assertions of independence.[23] But throughout the 1920s and 1930s, Goldman and his successors at ZOC headquarters in Montreal bluntly told officials of the Zionist movement that shrill demands for more funds, however badly needed, were simply unacceptable. Fluctuating Canadian economic conditions and serious problems directing fund-raising campaigns over Canada's vast spaces made it impossible for quotas to be successfully imposed.

Zionist fund-raisers from abroad recognized the distinctiveness of Canadian Jewry. Although tiny in comparison with the United States community, the Canadian Jewish community seemed an oasis in the American Zionist desert. One visitor in 1927 commented that he felt "a completely different atmosphere, more friendliness, more intimacy . . . [in] Winnipeg and Edmonton [than in the United States]," while another observed that "in Potage-la-Prairie [*sic*], every Jew knows he is Jewish and in what way. . . ."[24] Vladimir Jabotinsky, head of the Zionist Revisionists, however, was apathetic towards Canada, and after a visit in 1924 "it was coupled in his mind with Manchuria,"[25] although on a later visit he was more favourably impressed.

Canada was all the more fertile ground because Zionism had received the imprimatur of Great Britain. Still legally and, for many, emotionally Canada's mother country, Great Britain was also the principal benefactor of the Jewish people because it was the facilitator of their national homeland. Such circumstances created a near-perfect environment for Zionists because, in sharp contrast to the cause in the United States, no problem of alleged dual loyalty arose.

In his opening address to the 1924 ZOC convention, Freiman waxed rhapsodic on this "joint enterprise between the British people and the Jewish people," emphasizing the benefits of a Jewish homeland to the British Empire.[26] Loyalty to Zionism, to the British Empire, and to Canada was an attractive "package deal" for Canadian Jews, with no apparent drawbacks.

Schooled for a mere fund-raising role within the Zionist movement by Clarence de Sola, who had founded the Federation of Zionist Societies of Canada in 1899, the ZOC retained its subservient posture throughout the 1920s and 1930s. Not only did this conform to tradition, but it also suited Canadian Jews: as financial "foot soldiers" in the Zionist "army," their obligations were essentially limited to writing cheques. And though they were badly in need of money to implement practical work in Palestine, the Zionist "generals" in Jerusalem and London never explicitly asked Canadian Jewry for a stronger commitment than that.

An implicit bargain — one that has lasted to this day — was struck: Canadian Jewry's role in Zionism was to provide cash. Freiman put it equally clearly: Canadians would raise the money and the Jews of Palestine would build the homeland.[27] World circumstances after the First World War had thrust North American Jews into a new and more important role in the Zionist cause, but Weizmann and his organization still directed the movement. For the most part, Freiman and his associates discussed financial and organizational matters and spent virtually no time examining ideas, education theories, world politics, or the general philosophy of the Zionist enterprise.

Chaim Weizmann understood the relationship. In a letter in 1923, he pointed out that in contrast to British Jewry's political utility in the Zionist cause, "it is quite another matter . . . with the Jews of America who are anxious to cooperate. . . . [They] are not complex or sophisticated, and they are ready to take a great share in the raising of funds. . . . Now the only way to deal with these people is with absolute candour, and . . . simplicity."[28] While these observations reflected a growing rift between himself and some Zionists in the United States, Weizmann's patronizing attitude towards "America's" other Jews, the Canadians, was essentially the same, though with one minor difference: he decreed that Canada could serve, on occasion, as a back-door link to Britain.

Weizmann, in fact, was not above using Canadian Zionists as channels for petty espionage. In late 1922, he asked Freiman to gather "interesting information with regard to Lord Beaverbrook's antecedents, which might, in certain circumstances, be of great value."[29] Irritated by the anti-Zionist tirades in Beaverbrook's *Daily Express*, Weizmann wondered whether "some of the leading Canadian Zionists . . . could not . . . intimate to Lord Beaverbrook that as Canadian Jews, they have watched the malevolent campaign which he is conducting with amazement and indignation." Loyal to his chief, Freiman did his best to comply.[30]

Weizmann also tried to exploit Canada's imperial connection to Britain. In 1928, he urgently requested that Freiman arrange a meeting between the president of the Zionist Organization of America, Louis Lipsky, and the British colonial secretary, Lord Amery.[31] In September 1936, he cabled Freiman requesting that he entreat Mackenzie King and Governor-General Lord Tweedsmuir to protest British policy restricting Jewish immigration to Palestine. "I spent over two hours with [King] at his summer residence. While it was obvious that he was extremely sympathetic towards our cause, for political reasons his hands were tied," Freiman reported.[32] On another occasion, Freiman briefly outlined "the present political crisis in Zionism" and asked King to "use his influence on our behalf."[33] Nothing came of these overtures.

While generous financial help was given, such philanthropy sometimes stood in the way of a deeper and more positive Zionist experience, one not encouraged by the movement's leaders, that might have stimulated a cultural renaissance. Thus Canadian Zionism had few cultural dimensions, except within Poale Zion, Mizrachi, and the youth movements. Perhaps the Russian- and Polish-born Jews, who by the 1920s comprised most of Canadian Jewry, needed little of this cultural stimulation. Many had brought with them enough for their own lifetimes. Consequently, Zionism in Canada produced only a handful of intellectuals able to energize the movement or challenge the predetermined direction and leadership of the ZOC.

Zionist Women's Organizations

The women who were responsible for the success of the First World War campaigns were drawn largely from the Hadassah-WIZO Organization of Canada (Hadassah).[34] In centres large and small, Hadassah women worked fervently for several specific Palestine causes, such as the Girls' Domestic and Agricultural Science School at Nahalal, a nurses' training school in Jerusalem, a convalescent home, and a tubercular hospital.[35] They held raffles, bazaars, teas, and tag days to raise money. Through not only their practical work for Palestine, but also their dedication to Jewish women and children, they nurtured the Zionist cause and infused it with a sense of immediate and pressing concern. Their efforts brought together thousands of members across Canada to work assiduously to help their sisters in Palestine.

Hadassah was a women's organization that was dedicated to helping women in a Zionist world that was overwhelmingly dominated by males. Like women in the Canadian Ukrainian community, who were awakening to similar national impulses, Canadian Jewish women recognized that Zionism provided an opportunity to identify a specific female agenda — women's education and health and child care — within the movement for Jewish national revival.[36]

If Zionism in Canada ever had a vanguard, it was the women of Hadassah. This was especially true in Western Canada.[37] At the 1924 ZOC convention, a Western delegate reported that

> in . . . Winnipeg — and in many cities through the West — . . . [t]he women are almost frantically active. When it is considered that the two [Winnipeg] chapters, . . . have some 600 members, embracing all classes and sections of our population, the wealthiest as well as the poorest; that they meet with religious regularity; that they display a degree of enthusiasm and devotion heretofore unsuspected and unhoped for — I believe that, slow as might be our progress, small as might be our present achievements, the future is bright and certain, because the "mothers in Israel" have that future in their keeping.[38]

Lillian Freiman emphasized that Hadassah was a women's movement. In the spirit of the "new womanhood" that was current among gender-conscious Canadian women, she always referred to its members as "sisters," to their efforts as "our hands joined in true sisterly love and endeavour," and to the collectivity as "our Jewish womanhood."

In her opening statement to the 1924 Hadassah convention, she linked Hadassah and other female expressions of Zionism to a broad embodiment of women's consciousness. "The flame," she said, "that has swept through the ranks of our womankind and sent them rallying round the standard of Zionism, is the same flame that has raised women the world over to the heights of martyrdom and of heroic achievement."[39] She quoted Theodor Herzl's statement: "When the women will be with us, then will our cause indeed be won."

Rank-and-file members of Hadassah in chapters across the country felt these bonds of sisterhood and saw themselves essentially as exponents of a new Jewish woman's identity.[40] Their dual role was to rebuild their national home in Palestine and to "promote the health and welfare of women and children" there. With the slogan The Healing of the Daughter of My People as its emblem, Hadassah devoted itself both to fund-raising for women's health, educational, and social welfare projects and to elevating women's consciousness in Canada and Palestine. As well, beginning in the early 1920s, Hadassah supported the girls' agricultural school at Nahalal.[41]

In the late 1930s, reacting to the male leaders' hesitation in bringing Jewish children from Germany and Austria to Palestine, Hadassah women formed their very own rescue organization, called Youth Aliyah. Toronto's *Hadassah Reporter Magazine* complained in January 1939 that "some infection must be drying up the channels of pity in Jewish life when Jewish fathers who could, with the stroke of a pen[,] lift a child from hopelessness to happiness have failed to do so."[42]

On their own and together with sister groups elsewhere in the free world, these women aggressively raised money to save and support tens of thousands of children who were otherwise doomed to die in Europe between 1939 and 1945. Founded in the United States in 1935 by Henrietta Szold, Youth Aliyah moved thousands of children to Palestine during the 1930s and 1940s. As mothers themselves, the organization's members knew the cause was indeed urgent. Canadian Hadassah responded to Szold's appeals with Herculean efforts. In fact, Youth Aliyah became the major focus of Canadian Hadassah, as more facilities were needed to receive thousands of these children. By 1938, three thousand were arriving annually in Palestine, and in subsequent years numbers increased substantially.[43]

Youth Aliyah and numerous other specific women's and children's health projects funded in part by Canadian Hadassah became models of dedication and efficiency. Because most Hadassah women were middle class, they were far more financially able than their working-class sisters to engage in fund-raising campaigns and to maintain the extensive educational program outlined in the organization's publications. They also shared the broader "ideals of womanhood," by which all women had to struggle for equal citizenship with men. In October 1939, the *Hadassah Reporter Magazine* observed:

> Both as women and as Jews we have had a long and hard struggle for equal rights as citizens. If this hard won position is not to be lost, we must assume with seriousness and sincerity our responsibilities as Jews and as citizens.[44]

Labour Zionist women mobilized for their own causes. Pioneer Women, a group formed in Toronto by Florence Manson in 1925 as a branch of an American organization, had an explicitly feminist and socialist-Zionist agenda. It attracted mostly young, secularist, working-class Jewish females, often recent immigrants, who, because they were poor and "green," felt uncomfortable with what they perceived as a middle-class, English-speaking Hadassah.[45] Many were attracted to the collectivist outlook of the movement, which also "provided its first generation of members and many of their daughters with an important social outlet and source for the learning and development of numerous skills."[46] Often also members of unions, or strongly sympathetic to the unionist cause, these women embraced this philosophy of Labour Zionism. One member wrote:

> We are socialists . . . not only in Palestine. We seek a life of social justice and equality, of creative living not only in Palestine, but in every land where human beings are conscious of society.[47]

But they also wanted to assert themselves as women. As one founding member put it: "The women wanted to break away from the men because the men didn't think that the women had any brains. They were prejudiced against women."[48] With a cultural program in Yiddish that included classes on literature, history, Yiddish and Hebrew folk-songs, Zionism, politics, medicine, children, and education, the Pioneer Women's movement successfully launched itself in Canada.[49] The organization grew by advancing "the creative activities of the working woman and working mother" and by promising that "with the awakening of the will to create our own national life, there will come to the fore a tangible expression of the power and force of women."[50] Four more Pioneer Women groups were formed in Toronto in the 1930s, and in 1939 its first English-speaking club emerged, made up principally of daughters of the founders and graduates of the *Farband* (Labour Zionist) *Folk Schule* and Young Poale Zion.[51] For many years, Pioneer Women was the most accessible organization for many immigrants, a place where they found both a role for themselves as socialists and a comradely, family-like atmosphere.

Zionist Youth Organizations

Zionist enthusiasm flourished in Young Judaea, the youth branch of the ZOC. Despite having the example of its founder, Bernard (Dov) Joseph, who immigrated to Palestine in the early 1920s, the organization never officially espoused Aliyah (emigration) as a goal for its members. Rather, it remained essentially what the ZOC hoped it would be: an educational force among Jewish youth, used "to instil in the young a loyalty to the Jewish people and its glorious traditions; to inculcate a devotion to the Jewish homeland in Palestine and an appreciation of the Zionist aim and willingness to serve in the cause for the reestablishment of the Jewish Nation on its own soil." Zionism, then, was seen as an educational vehicle "to bring our Jewish youth under the influence of Jewish ideals and to improve them with sentiments of love and loyalty to all that is characteristically Jewish."[52]

Some Judaeans, with the enthusiasm and certainty of youth, believed Zionism required a deeper commitment. Phillip Joseph (brother of Bernard), when made president in 1924, told the ZOC convention that "we haven't the money to contribute, and I do not know that we could raise it, but we have human lives to contribute, and these we have contributed. In the City of Montreal there were seventeen Young Judaeans, and they are already in Palestine, living there and," he added for emphasis, "not coming back." This was the ultimate commitment of all — Aliyah to Palestine. "There are others in Montreal who may leave within three months," he continued. "I do not know their value in dollars and cents, but to me they are worth more than dollars and cents, because you can't buy them."[53] Phillip Joseph went to Palestine, like his brother Dov, to serve as an example to other Young Judaeans.

But to the ZOC leadership, Young Judaea's primary functions remained education and fund-raising. Joseph thus found it necessary to defend his organization on those grounds alone. "We are looking after the young," he exulted at the convention. "[I]t is a good investment . . . [because] the Young Judaeans are the future Canadian Jews . . . good Canadian Zionists in future." Therefore, more money would be collected. "Look what Young Judaea has done, what you have collected from them for Keren Hayesod. . . . Therefore I say give us $10,000 and we will give you $20,000." This was the one statement that earned Joseph the applause of the delegates.[54]

Abraham M. Klein, editor of Young Judaea's 1931 yearbook, searched for the middle ground. He carefully defined Young Judaeans as "Canadian Jewish Youth consciously aware of [their] Jewishness . . . concerned with that difficulty, which was proved to be the *pons asinorum* of twenty centuries, but which now for the first time seems to be nearing a definite solution: the ubiquitous

Jewish Problem."[55] Concerning Aliyah, he presciently recognized that "due to the favorable economic conditions, and the mentality of Jewish Youth, a *Chalutz* movement in America is so obviously futile that it needs no proof."

Even so, Klein believed that Palestine's culture could be brought to Canada: "[T]he purpose of Young Judaea is thus an attempt to overlap, through education, the several thousand miles which separate us from Palestine."[56] Canada's Jewish youth had "a curved ghetto spine." Young Judaeans must become "spiritual *chalutzim*" in Canada and create an appropriate environment for nurturing "a race consciousness . . . [to] be born out of a nation's will-to-live. . . . We must be the masters of our own fate!" He concluded, "Jewish life, as at present constituted, with its barrenness, and emptiness, its utter meaninglessness, its haphazard activity, stands as an imperious challenge to Canadian Jewish Youth."

By the mid-1920s, Young Judaea clubs had sprung up all over Canada; a national organization had been established in 1919 and a full-time director hired in 1924. Though it faced competition from more idealistic organizations connected to worldwide *chalutz* movements, which strongly emphasized Aliyah, the very lack of a clear-cut ideology beyond a benevolent attitude towards Zionism lessened demands on its members and therefore gave it broad appeal. Most Jewish youth could identify with its stance and caused their parents little concern that its Zionist program would encourage Aliyah.

The weekly educational program consisted of lectures and discussions of Jewish history and current events, as well as "readings from Jewish literature, the singing of national and traditional melodies, the celebration of Jewish festivals, dramatic presentations and debates" and some athletic events. But one early handbook distributed to group leaders advised that the teaching of Jewish history "must be made *to illustrate present day tendencies in Jewish life* . . . and must be made to give the clearest conception of the inherent instability and the tragic waste of Golus' [exile's] life. . . . "[57] Largely financed by the ZOC, Young Judaea mirrored its characteristics, including the national organizational superstructure, the biennial conventions, the regional conferences, the transnational social contact, and the aura of middle-class benevolence.

Fund-raising soon became a leading preoccupation of the clubs, most notably with Jewish National Fund (JNF) collection boxes. This excessive emphasis, however, soon gave rise to serious reservations. In 1927, Lionel M. Gelber of Toronto warned that if Young Judaea's principal educational role was to continue, it must not "deflect its energies into the channels of practical Zionism. . . . Young Judaea must not lose sight of its main purpose."[58]

Louis Rasminsky, the Young Judaea president in 1927 and a future governor of the Bank of Canada, echoed Gelber's concerns. To him, the organization's role was to rescue an entire generation of Jewish youth from widespread indifference towards and ignorance of Jewish culture and history. "It is tragic," he wrote, "that precisely at this time the Jewish youth should . . . cease to be interested in its Jewish heritage and cut itself entirely adrift from any form of constructive Jewish life." At a time when the detrimental forces of "neglect by parents, the American environment, the overwhelming spirit of the age — the weakening of all Jewish traditional bonds in North America" were impacting on Jewish youth, fund-raising should not deflect the organization from its very reason for being: education.[59]

In Toronto and southwestern Ontario, these ideas were translated into intensive activity, with Young Judaeans raising money to buy books on Jewish history, culture, and religion for their libraries. By 1927 Toronto leaders had organized thirty-three clubs, with some 650 members across the city. Hamilton, Brantford, Kitchener, London, and other cities across the province also had active groups. The organization flourished in Montreal, and throughout the Maritimes, Young Judaea clubs became the single most important tie among Jewish youth in the region. Clubs in Winnipeg, Edmonton, Calgary, and Vancouver, as well as those in a number of smaller cities, prospered, contributing in a major way to the perpetuation of Zionism in Canada. Young Judaea's impact on the youth of the smaller centres, who had little opportunity for Jewish expression, was profound.

Other youth associations proliferated in the 1920s and 1930s, to reawaken a Jewish consciousness. The most prominent were Hashomer Hatzair (Young Guard), Hechalutz Hatzair (Young Pioneers), Zeire Zion (Young Zion), Young Mizrachi, and Gordonia (followers of the early pioneer A. D. Gordon).[60] In concert with their sister groups in Palestine, these organizations emphasized their own particular brand of Zionist ideology.[61]

Hashomer Hatzair stands out in this respect. It espoused a Marxist ideology (which seemed at variance with its dedication to Zionism), rigid discipline, and a personal commitment to building a collectivist society in Palestine. Organized in Montreal in 1923, Hashomer Hatzair advertised itself as "the Jewish Youth for the Jewish Nation . . . defenders of the National Home . . . a bulwark against assimilation. . . . Hashomer wants your souls."[62] Its program proclaimed that "the building up of Palestine is . . . imposed on our youth of the present." Rebelling against capitalism and materialism, the members, who called themselves *shomrim* (guards), were committed to Aliyah and saw themselves as the vanguard of a Jewish national renaissance, and as militant socialists living lives of selfless idealism and collectively rebuilding the land with their own sweat and blood.

The Montreal group was the strongest in North America. In 1931, it supplied five of the six *shomrim*, most of them women, going to Palestine. They were the first from the North American movement who were among those who founded Kibbutz Ein Hashofet.[63] A few years later, they were joined by nine other Montreal *shomrim*; they also toiled in the fields, constructing their new community and living in tents for years. "We wanted to be pioneers. We wanted to build a country," the early settler Celia Cohen recalled. "It seemed then — and even now in memory — a nobler ideal than the desire to 'make it' in America," another *shomer* remembered.[64] Propelled by Zionist and socialist zeal, Hashomer Hatzair also established groups in Toronto, Winnipeg, Hamilton, and Ottawa during the 1930s.[65] In ensuing years, the movement sent hundreds of *shomrim* from Canada. The majority of them were women, perhaps because women — unlike their male counterparts, who had stronger career concerns — were better able to retain the integrity of Zionism's quasi-religious vision. This was in part because it offered them, as women, an equal opportunity to build a new egalitarian society with men.[66] Their example stood as both a reminder and a reproach to cheque-book Zionists. Their songs evoked a romantic declaration of their zeal to make the world anew:

In our homeland Eretz Yisrael
We would struggle but we wouldn't fail.
Here we'd live forever more
Here we'd flower as ne'er before.
We had come to build our kibbutz
Every one a farbrenter chalutz.[67]

Some of them, however, defeated by the Spartan conditions and extreme dangers, eventually returned home in disappointment.

Youth organizations committed to other ideologies also emerged, among them Betar (an acronym for Brith Trumpeldor, named in memory of Joseph Trumpeldor, who fell in defence of Tel Hai in 1921). This movement, which spread throughout Central and Western Europe during the 1920s under the inspiration of the brilliant intellectual and soldier Vladimir Jabotinsky, emphasized Jewish pride and military training, and intended to transform "the Jew of the Diaspora into a fighter."[68] Habonim (the builders), a youth branch of Poale Zion, established groups in Montreal, Toronto, and Winnipeg, where it became a thriving and influential organization that stressed Aliyah and *chalutziut* (kibbutz).[69]

The Keren Hayesod Campaigns

Zionist fund-raising peaked in the 1920s. At the same time, however, aid towards the reconstruction of Eastern European Jewry society and for many projects in Canada involved enormous financial commitments and competed with the Zionist endeavours. While Canadian Jews gave generously during the late 1920s, this picture was to change considerably in the Depression of the 1930s.

Canadian Zionists, based on several successful campaigns, believed themselves to be ahead per capita of their American cousins. Just after the Keren Hayesod was launched in 1921 to finance and co-ordinate the Jewish settlement in Palestine, Shmarya Levin, its chief spokesman in North America, visited Canada to help plan a vigorous national campaign.[70] He persuaded the ZOC to raise a million dollars with an appeal to "Jews of Canada to rally to the glorious cause of laying the foundation of a true Jewish homeland in Palestine."[71] In the United States, however, the Zionist Organization of America (ZOA) sharply objected to the Keren Hayesod's mandate.[72] ZOA president and United States Supreme Court Justice Louis D. Brandeis, who viewed Zionism as a progressive movement for American Jewry, objected to what he believed was the inefficient management of the Keren Hayesod. Because Canadian leadership was less critical, these reservations found no echo in Canada. Also unlike the United States, Zionism had no organized opposition in Canada. However, certain prominent Canadian Jews were not supportive and occasionally launched public attacks against features of Zionist philosophy.

One such strong opponent was Maurice Eisendrath, an American who had been rabbi of Toronto's Holy Blossom Temple since 1929 and was a prominent activist in the Canadian peace movement.[73] Like many Reform rabbis of his era, Eisendrath believed that Zionism weakened Jewish integration into Canadian life. His anti-Zionist sermons, public speeches, and articles in the *Canadian Jewish Review* asserted that Zionists were like "our oppressors [who wish] to incarcerate us once more! . . . [T]he anti-Semite and the extreme and fanatical Jewish nationalist have much in common."[74]

He later compared young Zionists with "storm troopers or Komsomols" and asserted that "Jewish nationalism [was] . . . as dangerous to the essential spirit of the Jew as Fascism, Communism and Hitlerism are to the essence of Christianity." Eisendrath's anti-Zionism caused a serious furore within his congregation.[75] Others were also outraged by such messages. The Ontario Hadassah leader, Rose Dunkelman, decided to publish her own weekly newspaper, the *Jewish Standard*, to counter the *Review*, and hired Meyer Weisgal from New York to edit it.[76] Weisgal threw himself into the work with enthusiasm.

He battled not only against Eisendrath in print and in weekly debates at Holy Blossom, but also against the Revisionists (opponents of Chaim Weizmann's policies), who were gaining strength in the late 1920s.

There were also persistent attacks on Zionism by Jewish Communists, who used terminology such as "Jewish fascists" and "Zionist fascists" to describe both members of the ZOC and Jewish socialists who were critical of the Soviet Union in the 1920s.[77] Such language was intended to deepen the association of Zionism with the Jewish bourgeoisie, as well as condemn rabbis whose class interests opposed those of the Jewish workers. As an editorial in *Der Kamf* stated in October 1929:

> In the Jewish milieux, we see a united front of the *yarmulka* (skull cap) with the Zionist and with the yellow "socialist." They hold their class interests under one roof. . . . The revolutionary worker rips the masks off both the parasitic rabbi and the laborite, and in their nakedness they lock hands against the only workers' republic where the workers are tearing off their earthly and heavenly chains. The rabbi and laborite and the Zionist decide on a fascist front against the conscious workers.[78]

Sometimes Communists also linked Zionism together with British imperialism in opposing the Palestinian Arab national liberation movement. Instead, the Jewish Communists supported "a homeland" and settlement in the Soviet Union, in Birobidjan, to end the curse of Jewish homelessness.[79] However, such anti-Zionist attacks ceased during the mid-1930s. At that time, the Communists devoted their energies to fighting Fascism through the Popular Front, in which, they believed, all Jewish factions should stand united.

Aliyah

Such critiques of Zionism had little effect on rank-and-file ZOC and Hadassah members. The vast majority happily supported a movement that did not promote Aliyah. Only a few Canadian Jews immigrated to Palestine between the world wars; the most famous of them was Bernard (Dov) Joseph, who had become a prominent Jerusalem lawyer and rising star in the inner councils of the Jewish Agency. A few less-renowned individuals had gone up to Palestine. Some had bought small farms with the help of the Keren Kayemeth (Jewish National Fund) in Jerusalem. "My thoughts frequently turn Eastward," wrote Dr. M. S. Rady from Winnipeg to the Keren Kayemeth's Menachem Ussishkin in 1929, "wondering whether some day I will be able to emigrate there, and participate in the actual upbuilding of our Home Land. . . .

Some day when I decide to take this step, I would like to feel that I am the owner of a small section of land, on which there is already a house where I could immediately go and live. . . . There in Palestine, you are enjoying the fairest of weather and bathing in the happy rays of the Eastern Sun."[80] Thus a Jew living in the midst of Canada's own Eden dreamed of a rural arcadia in a promised land he barely knew.

Personally, however, the ZOC executive director, Rabbi Judah Zlotnick, thought many Canadian Jews should move to Palestine. After a visit in the summer of 1931, he wrote, "it is time, I believe, for all lovers of Zion to come into closer contact with our country, or at least bring their children and their families closer to Eretz Israel [the land of Israel]."[81] He called on Canadian Jews to settle on orange farms in the Emek Hepher (an extensive area of Palestine that was purchased in 1927), both to build the national home and to secure their own financial position and that of their families."[82] Only a very determined few followed Zlotnick's example, as the hardships of life in Palestine were extremely daunting. In any event, the ZOC did little to encourage such enthusiasm. When several Montreal members of Hashomer Hatzair petitioned the ZOC to support their Aliyah in 1931, the sceptical National Council appointed a special committee "to see that they are of the right and proper type."[83]

Whether they went as pioneers on the kibbutzim, as small farmers or as urban dwellers, there was only a trickle of Canadian immigrants to Palestine through the thirties and early forties. Most were members of Hashomer Hatzair who underwent a year of agricultural instruction on *hachshara* (special training farms) in the United States. But the ZOC took little notice; as late as January 1936, it did not know how many Canadians were on these farms.[84]

Molly Lyons Bar-David

Next to Bernard (Dov) Joseph, the most famous Canadian to immigrate to Palestine in the interwar period was Molly Lyons Bar-David. Born in 1910 in Rosthern, Saskatchewan, where her father owned a farm and a store, she settled in Palestine in 1936. She wrote regular columns on daily life for American Hadassah magazines, the *Jerusalem Post*, and the *Winnipeg Free Press*, which earned her a wide readership. She returned to Canada for speaking tours for Canadian Hadassah-WIZO. Her 1953 book *My Promised Land* includes a superb memoir of a young girl reaching maturity in the small Saskatchewan towns where her family had lived.

Even Hechalutz, the organizational arm that trained thousands of Diaspora youth for agricultural life in Palestine,[85] did not establish a branch in Canada, probably realizing that the recruitment would be negligible. And the ZOC remained so focused on fund-raising that Aliyah was not an issue.

However, the ZOC did support some individuals, like Max Adilman of Saskatoon, who had moved to Palestine. "The fact that Adilman is settling [there] will have not only a moral effect on Canadian Jewry in general," Zlotnick wrote to Menachem Ussishkin, the JNF head in Jerusalem, but he believed it would also have a positive influence on some well-to-do Western Canadian Jews who might be persuaded to settle in Palestine.[86] Aside from Adilman and a few others,[87] the major Canadian investor in Palestine was Asher Pierce of Montreal.[88] He believed that Canadian Jews — and those from other Western countries — should bring their Western ideas and capital to help build the economy of the Yishuv.[89] In 1927, he established the Gan Chayim Corporation to develop orange plantations on the Sharon plain, and also built a house on his own estate, which he called Tel Asher (Asher's Hill). Pierce was also involved in other development projects.[90] Similar investments by Canadian Jews signalled a continuing financial interest well before the Second World War and foreshadowed their considerable investment after Israel's establishment in 1948.[91]

While still not publicly encouraging, the ZOC was helpful to those contemplating Aliyah. Indeed, more Canadian Jews might have moved to Palestine but for the mandate government's restrictions on entry, especially during the late 1930s, when only a limited number of "certificates" were issued. In April 1936, a ZOC official, Rabbi Jesse Schwartz, wrote to the immigration department of the Jewish Agency asserting that "Canada is entitled to a certain amount of consideration and we would ask you to do everything possible to give us the skilled labour certificate referred to."[92] In view of the German refugee crisis, however, Canada's claims were given short shrift. The year before, Schwartz had tried to get two or three certificates for young women intending to make Aliyah.[93] Seventeen-year-old Ben Dunkelman, understanding Zionism to mean Aliyah, moved to a kibbutz in 1931 and again in 1935, but eventually gave in to his parents' urgent requests and returned to Toronto.[94] Though ardent Zionists, Rose and David Dunkelman obviously believed that Canadian Jews should contribute money, not their lives or their children, to the enterprise.

Cheque-book Zionism

The first Keren Hayesod campaign was launched in May 1921 with considerable fanfare. While on a tour of the United States, Chaim Weizmann, together with Shmarya Levin, a powerful Yiddish orator who appealed greatly to immigrants, also visited several Canadian cities. Weizmann's memoirs provide a revealing account of his impressions:

> . . . a big donor would often make his contribution to the fund conditional on my accepting an invitation to lunch or dine at his house. Then I would have to face a large family gathering — three of our generations — talk, answer questions, listen to appeals and opinions, and watch my replies carefully, lest I inadvertently scare off a touchy prospect. I would sit through a lengthy meal and after it meet a select group of local celebrities; and again listen and answer till all hours of the night. Generally, I felt that I had fully earned that five thousand dollars.[95]

However harrowing it was for Weizmann, his visit was a triumph for the Zionist cause in Canada. Wherever he went, masses of Jews congregated, moved by his message. Yet even he could not breathe life into a campaign that faltered in the recession of the early 1920s. Only one-fifth of the million-dollar target was raised, and local campaign chairmen reported that economic conditions prevented further collections. Archie Freiman wrote Weizmann of his disappointment at being unable to collect on pledges because of the downturn in business.[96]

Zionist officials in London were not sympathetic, however. "The position in Palestine is exceedingly critical," wrote one in November 1922, "and for a country like Canada to discontinue its regular remittances for months at a time is a very bad sign."[97] Long used to such reprimands, Leon Goldman dispatched a peppery reply. Attacking what he called London's "dunning methods," he objected strenuously to excessive expectations and warned that if they continued, Canadian Zionists could well become completely discouraged.[98] His message to London was to back off. Conditions in Canada were so critical that many Jews were reduced "to a condition of receiving, instead of giving." After waiting some months to assess this disaster, the ZOC leaders, under heavy pressure from Keren Hayesod officials in London, reluctantly agreed to mount a follow-up campaign. It began in early 1923 with a tour led by Colonel A. H. Patterson. As commander of the Zion Mule Corps at Gallipoli and, later, a battalion of the Jewish Legion, he was a hero to many Jews.

The Patterson tour was a success, especially in the West. Reporting from Winnipeg in February 1923, an official who was accompanying him wrote: "If the big Jewish communities of Eastern Canada would contribute on the same proportion, the result would be an extraordinary one."[99] The same enthusiasm seemed evident in Toronto a few weeks later, and officials were encouraged.[100]

Still, by the end of April, only about $175,000 had been raised, mainly because Montreal results were poor. The economic situation was so bad, an official reported, that "the rich are keeping aloof from . . . Jewish affairs. Even the local charitable institutions suffer very much. . . . In Zionist affairs one notices a mighty wave of pessimism and depression . . . general apathy and indifference."[101] So serious was the fall-off in Zionist and charitable giving in Montreal that Rabbi Herman Abramowitz of Sha'ar Hashamayim synagogue publicly attacked the city's Jewish plutocrats (many of them members of his own congregation) for their general lack of generosity to local charities, as well as to the Keren Hayesod.[102] And while every other Jewish centre contributed well, despite a depressed economy, Montreal's leaders were, as Rabbi Abramowitz put it, like King Saul hiding in their tents, afraid to fight in defence of Israel. By late April, the campaign there was still a disaster.[103]

Weak leadership in Montreal not only bedevilled most campaigns throughout the 1920s, but also, given the city's importance and size, affected the rest of the country. Montreal was so short of canvassers that Lillian Freiman came down from Ottawa to help out, but results rose only slightly, from disgraceful to merely poor. Even Louis Fitch and Michael Garber were unable to bring Montreal Zionists to life. Possibly, the ideological, class, and economic differences in that community affected the Zionist climate there.

Keren Hayesod's campaign in 1924 was no better, leading to an exchange of increasingly acrimonious letters between London officials and Leon Goldman.[104] This tension, which lasted for the remainder of the decade, was compounded by an unseemly jurisdictional dispute between the Keren Hayesod and the JNF for Canadian contributions. An arrangement had been worked out in London headquarters whereby the former was to accept only donations over twenty-five dollars, while all lesser contributions went to the JNF. Canadian practice violated this agreement, and the ensuing debate between Leon Goldman and London officials rapidly became abrasive.[105] London also complained that the Canadian organization's operating expenses were too high.[106]

Behind all of this controversy was the mounting impression among world Zionist leaders that Canadian Jews were underachieving. In early January 1924, Weizmann assessed the Canadian situation for the London directors of Keren Hayesod. "Canada could raise for the Keren Hayesod much more than it has done; although trade is not flourishing they could certainly make a much better effort." With quite astonishing hauteur and lack of understanding of current economic conditions, he claimed that Canadian Jews "get their money in fairly easily," and asserted that "they could easily raise double if the three leading spirits of Canadian Zionism, Freiman, Levin, and Fitch[,] would apply themselves to the task. If Archie Freiman goes to Winnipeg he can raise double what Winnipeg gives now and it would be nothing but a pleasant trip for him. The same is applicable to any other city.[107]

Weizmann's optimistic expectations were shared by touring Keren Hayesod and JNF officials. David Rebelsky visited a number of Canadian cities on behalf of the Zeire Zion, a moderate socialist-labour movement, and reported to London in March 1925, "I think like you that even under the present conditions, it is possible to obtain larger sums in Canada."[108] The weak point, he asserted, was the lack of a maximum effort in the major centres of Montreal, Toronto, and Winnipeg, where 120,000 of the country's 130,000 Jews lived. He calculated that as a result, the smaller places were contributing twenty-five times the amount raised per capita in the three largest centres. They needed better organization to tap the potential and handle the funds.

Equally important, in Rebelsky's view, was that Zionist propaganda had been neglected, leaving local organizations weak and directionless. But while emphasizing the need for better management, he stressed that "the human material of Jews is better here than in any other country," a compliment to the high level of Jewish culture in Canada.

Jewish National Fund Activities

With the growth of the Canadian Keren Hayesod activities, however problematic they were, the earlier prominence of the Jewish National Fund was eclipsed. By 1921, its Canadian receipts had fallen to only one-seventh of the 1918 figures.[109] The ensuing recession made it difficult for these small, scattered communities to meet their million-dollar commitment to the Keren Hayesod and also support the JNF. Leon Goldman explained to JNF officials that in this situation, he had backed away from a campaign, "owing to the destitute conditions of the poorer classes."[110]

Rabbi Zlotnick a few years later, however, was successful in his work for the JNF, greatly increasing its receipts and exploiting its use as a Zionist educational tool. But like Leon Goldman, he was forced to rebuke the head office, which seemed to feel that its knowledge of Canada — and the money-raising potential of its Jewish community — was better than that of the Canadians themselves.[111] Undeterred by such reprimands, officials objected that Canadian

Zionists had belittled the JNF.[112] In February 1924, Goldman was forced, once again, to send a tart reply:

> You must leave the running of affairs in this Dominion, to the discretion of the Zionist Organization here and rely on its judgement as dependable . . . instead of the repeated — and unwelcome officious rebuke and faultfinding . . . [and] over-frequent campaigning.[113]

Unconvinced, the JNF replied from Jerusalem that "we cannot for a moment accept the view that Canadian conditions are so different that, alone of fifty-one countries, it must be allowed to carry on its JNF work independent of the Head Office."[114]

Until the 1920s, the JNF had collected modest sums from the sale of stamps and tree certificates, registrations in the JNF Golden Book, and contributions to the blue boxes in many Jewish homes. Rabbi Zlotnick, however, pitched appeals to the wealthy for large donations.[115] He increased the emphasis on hundred-dollar Golden Book subscriptions and on contributions to the Land Fund during a special High Holidays appeal in 1924 and 1925.[116] In both, a modest increase was noted.[117]

However, the blue boxes to collect money for land purchase remained the most popular and successful JNF activity.[118] The idea of buying land and planting trees in Palestine had both a practical and a sacred appeal. As well, it was an excellent device with which to explain Zionist ideals to the community, especially to children. Supported by Hadassah and Young Judaea, the boxes were placed all over the country; Zlotnick reported that the number of centres using them increased from twenty-six in 1923 to forty-two in 1925, and that the income from them increased threefold.

Enthusiasm was especially strong out West. In Winnipeg by the mid-1920s, a voluntary "amusement tax" was levied on all Jewish dances, theatre performances, bridge parties, and other gatherings.[119] Blue boxes were circulated at weddings and bar mitzvahs, and were placed in nearly five thousand homes and four hundred businesses. Zionist educational material, mostly about pioneering in Palestine, was distributed, some of it written especially for Western Canadians. Dozens of small towns and villages with Jewish populations were canvassed.[120] "A Penny a Day Will Drive the Golus [Exile] Away" was one of the slogans printed on cards and circulars distributed across the Prairies.[121] In Winnipeg, teenagers initiated monthly collections and raised large amounts of money.[122] So successful were these campaigns that suggestions were made that the Canadian JNF office be moved to Winnipeg. Eastern Zionists, however, were not amused.[123]

Despite this general growth in JNF revenues, officials in Jerusalem continued to chastise Canadian Zionists.[124] The headquarters still set quotas and made invidious comparisons (Canada was usually compared with South Africa, which sent much higher per capita contributions) in an unrelenting barrage of letters containing special instructions urging Canadians to do their duty.[125]

Under this mounting pressure, JNF activities in Canada, like Keren Hayesod and virtually all of the other good works of the Zionists, became focused almost purely on fund-raising. With the return of prosperity in Canada after 1925, Canadian remittances for the JNF began to rise again. By 1927, they surpassed $50,000 per year and seemed still to be increasing, with Winnipeg producing half of the total blue-box collections for the whole country.[126]

Encouraged by this improvement, Jerusalem officials campaigned to have Canada raise a million dollars to buy land at Emek Hepher, on the Sharon plain north of Tel Aviv. JNF officials were anxious to acquire this large tract of uninhabited sand and swamp when it became available in the mid-1920s. When the Freimans arrived in Palestine on a brief visit in the spring of 1927,

---

SONG OF THE EMEK

Now rest has come unto the weary,
And repose to him who toils.
Now the night lies pale upon
The rich fields of Esdraelon.
Dew below, moonlight over all,
From Bet Alfa to Nahalal.

Ah, ah, the day has gone.
Silence in Esdraelon.
Sleep, O valley, glorious land,
We are the watchmen at your hand.

The sea of ripening corn is swaying,
The sheepbells tinkle from afar,
This is my land I stand upon,
This is the valley Esdraelon.
Bless you, land, and fare you well,
From Bet Alfa to Nahalal.

From Ruth Rubin, *A Treasury of Jewish Folksong* (New York: Schocken Books, 1950), 199.

Menachem Ussishkin, head of the JNF, received their promise of help. On their return to Canada, the Freimans lobbied other Zionists at the July JNF convention. Ussishkin himself even appeared and, with an emotional speech, was successful. Canadian Zionists committed themselves to raising a million dollars over the next seven years.[127]

Though this commitment did not seem inappropriate for this modestly prosperous community, by late 1929 it had become an intolerable burden. While $300,000 had already been sent, most of these monies were bank loans to the ZOC advanced against future revenue from drives that were faltering now. Faced with commitments of $100,000 annually for seven years, the ZOC was in serious financial trouble. A 1928 United Palestine Appeal campaign brought in a mere $230,000 in pledges. Of this, the JNF would get only two-fifths.

By the spring of 1929, Ussishkin was desperately begging the Canadians to honour their Emek Hepher commitment.[128] Some money was sent, but the Canadians, so deeply in debt to the banks, were "finding [it] difficult to pay up, on account of the present depressing financial times." Zlotnick wrote pointedly to Ussishkin that "your continual urging us to make remittances is of no avail, and only serves to strain the relations existing between your office and our Zionists."[129]

The financial situation in Canada made it impossible to approach the banks for more loans. Zlotnick wrote, "[O]ur collections have been very poor."[130] A year later, with the JNF still owing money on its bank loans and now $200,000 in arrears on its commitment, Archie Freiman informed Ussishkin: "It is absolutely useless to talk about borrowing $100,000. There is not a bank in Canada that would advance us this amount at the present time, and even if we could get it, we have no moral right to accept it until we are more certain as to the results we will achieve in the near future."[131] The tension and bitterness between the financially strapped Canadians and the insistent Jerusalem officials continued until 1937 when, at last, the final payment was made.

Mizrachi and Revisionists

Unity was rare in Zionist ranks. Mizrachi, the religious Zionist organization that emerged in Canada in the interwar years,[132] became an occasional annoyance during the ZOC's fund-raising campaigns. Not satisfied with the allocations by the ZOC, Mizrachi's Canadian supporters in 1920 demanded "that a certain percentage of the total amount collected [in Canada] should go to the Mizrachi Fund, Keren Eretz Israel."[133] Still unsatisfied, in 1928, Mizrachi inaugurated its own campaign just when the JNF and Keren

Hayesod were kicking off theirs. The *Keneder Adler* observed that this was an inopportune time "to institute a further campaign for Zionist purposes," and that "this would certainly prejudice the interests of the Keren Hayesod." Worse still was that the Mizrachi leaders allegedly "made a violent attack on the Haluzim, the builders of Palestine," pointing out that they ate *trayf* (unkosher food) and violated the Sabbath.[134]

Mizrachi's appeal was strong, given the belief, as expressed by one community leader, "that the majority of Canadian Jewry are eager to see Palestine rebuilt in the spirit of Jewish traditions and along religious lines."[135] Zlotnick, himself an Orthodox rabbi, believed that "the greatest majority of Canadian Jewry are favoring the orthodox mode of life."[136] Mizrachi's independent fund-raising campaign continued for some years, eliciting bitter comment in the Canadian Jewish press, as well as continuing resistance from the ZOC.[137] But the ZOC wanted Mizrachi support for the Emek Hepher project, and advised Jerusalem, "It is our opinion that it would be most judicious and beneficial to our cause that as many as possible of the religiously inclined element should be settled there."[138] Noted Zlotnick, "This is especially important from the point of view of propaganda in Canada. . . . [S]uch a Mizrachi settlement should be organized at the earliest possible moment." But the tension between the ZOC and Mizrachi over fund-raising persisted. In 1940, their representative in Canada tried to inaugurate a separate campaign on the eve of a nationwide drive for the United Palestine Appeal, which combined Keren Hayesod with other projects. "Discipline in the Zionist ranks was not to be expected from Mizrachi," one Montreal ZOC leader complained.[139]

Revisionists — followers of Vladimir Jabotinsky's Zionist-Revisionist breakaway from the World Zionist Organization — began organizing in Canada in 1926, during Jabotinsky's North American tour.[140] While the turnout to his lectures was small, a few fervent supporters were recruited.[141] During a tour of Canada in 1935, however, he received a somewhat warmer reception and some favourable comment in the Canadian Jewish press. The Toronto *Hebrew Journal* stated that Jabotinsky "deserves to be heard with all due respect," while the *Keneder Adler* regarded his criticisms of Weizmann as "salutary and necessary." The *Chronicle* argued that "we should re-study the many important issues that the Revisionists have raised and decide for ourselves whether our present policy is the best one, the one most likely to succeed."[142] By 1931, a national conference of Revisionists was planned.[143]

One 1932 Revisionist complaint to the ZOC about the inadequacy of its efforts was answered patiently by Archie Freiman. "I should imagine if you find our . . . activities in Canada inadequate, if you feel that we are actually dead, and having the cause at heart, there is no reason why you should not make an effort to the things that your conscience dictates to you in the light with which you are blessed, rather than to ask me to do the work who may not see eye to eye with you."[144]

Revisionist clubs were active in Toronto, Montreal, and, oddly, in the small communities of Newcastle, New Brunswick, and New Waterford, Nova Scotia. In March 1932, a monthly bulletin, *Tel Hai*, began publication to distribute news and program guidelines, including instructions that "it is necessary to participate in the general Zionist work [such] as National Fund [JNF] . . . and Keren Hayesod. . . ."[145]

Canadian Zionist leaders seemed little interested in seeing Palestine. Archie Freiman visited only once. Few of the other major figures bothered to do so at all. Hirsch Wolofsky and Hananiah Caiserman went there on tour in the 1920s. Mordecai and Hiram Weidman of Winnipeg visited in 1923 and published a fascinating memoir of their trip.[146] And there were other occasional Canadian visitors, such as Rabbi Harry Stern of Temple Emanu-el in Montreal, who escorted a student study group in 1929.[147]

Perhaps most indicative of Canadians' subservient role in the Zionist cause was their poor participation at World Zionist congresses. These international gatherings of Zionist leaders and intelligentsia were a kind of world parliament of the Jewish people. Freiman appeared only once, although in 1929 he made an effort to send a "real delegation" of ten persons.[148] The few Canadians who did attend were in Europe primarily on other business or on holiday.[149] Thus Canada had little input in these discussions; their delegates spoke only perfunctorily, reporting on their activities. The exception was Hananiah Caiserman, who, on the one occasion when he represented Canada, spoke with his characteristic emotional eloquence.

Zionist "Culture" in Canada

The emphasis on fund-raising was rarely questioned openly, although Hananiah Caiserman shrewdly observed the discomfort felt by many Zionists. After an extensive educational tour of Western Canada during the autumn of 1925, he reported to the ZOC national executive that "in the whole West . . . nearly the whole correspondence which they receive is referring to the collection of funds. . . . Speakers who come to them are not coming to impart Zionist information . . . but just to appeal for funds." He warned that unless Zionists got substantial assistance for cultural programming, the movement would falter and the ZOC decline.[150]

Caiserman observed that Young Judaea's successful programs were eliciting great interest. This cultural endeavour was essential, he said, "in order that they are equipped to persuade the inhabitants of their communities to give liberally towards Zionist funds."[151] He embarked on a strenuous campaign, giving a total of 103 lectures during his western tour on topics related to his trip to Palestine. He addressed groups of Hadassah, university students, Zionist societies, Young Judaea, B'nai Brith, and Talmud Torah classes, as well as non-Jewish groups and churches.

But it was difficult to break what had become a hardened pattern. Even appeals for more cultural content from Jerusalem officials of the JNF were met with responses that were strangely unsympathetic. One of them thanked Caiserman for giving him "a clearer insight into prevailing conditions in Canada," but then mused about "the significant fact that the Funds for carrying on the campaign for Irish independence came very largely from the savings of Irish domestic servants in America," obviously suggesting that Canadian Jews draw inspiration from that experience.[152]

While he accepted Caiserman's assertion that Canada had suffered an "economic decline," this official insisted "that had we a stronger and more extensive organization [in Canada,] Palestine would not have suffered to the extent that it has done at the hand of Canadian Jewry." As to the need for education, he stressed that "educational activity should [not] be set up as [an] alternative to practical work. I am convinced that the two can and must go together. . . . We must eliminate the idea that cultural work is something opposed to collecting. . . . I think it would be an error if Young Judaea were to ignore this aspect of Jewish junior activity, because of exclusive concentration on the educational side of the movement."[153] These patronizing attitudes towards Canada prevailed throughout the interwar period.

Even the German and Austrian Jewish refugee question of the late 1930s did not deflect Canadian Zionists from their belief that Zionism came ahead of "the emergency settlement of Jewish refugees now being deprived of livelihood and freedom."[154] Officials of the ZOC, Poale Zion, and Mizrachi, meeting on July 10, 1938, unanimously rejected a proposal from the Canadian Jewish Committee for Refugees that they co-operate in a joint fund-raising campaign with the United Palestine Appeal. While pledging support for "any practical proposals that offer a chance of salvation for our stricken brethren," the Zionists asserted that "Jewish settlement in Palestine belongs in a different category. . . . Zionism strives to establish a Home for the Jewish people and not a refuge. . . . [T]he task of the Zionist movement involves more than the settlement of refugees."

Freiman had been encouraged to take this position by Weizmann, who in July 1934 wrote that "during my recent visit to Palestine I had every opportunity of seeing at first hand the work that is being done there for the reestablishment of German refugees, and I came back more than ever convinced that it is only in Palestine that this work has any prospect of permanency. It would be a tragedy if this work were to be held up for lack of funds."[155]

On the left, however, the much smaller Poale Zion pursued a very different philosophy and lifestyle. Their program had more educational content than that of the ZOC. The ephemeral Mizrachi organization, meanwhile, tried to advance the cause of Torah in Zion. These and a few similar organizations, which existed in a relatively small number of the larger Jewish centres, held strong beliefs in a specific philosophy, and pursued programs that focused on self-improvement and on Zion's redemption.[156] But though vibrant and dedicated, they were comparatively small and received less coverage than the ZOC in the newspapers of the time.

Although much of the ZOC's leadership was drawn from Montreal, Toronto, and Winnipeg, the organization also drew considerable strength from smaller communities across the country. This was reflected in its membership statistics and in the composition of the national executive, which was headed by Archie Freiman. As an exceptionally generous donor to Jewish causes, Freiman was typical of the leaders and many, perhaps most, of the rank-and-file ZOC members in the smaller cities. While the metropolitan centres contained an occupationally diverse Jewish population,[157] the Jews of the small cities were concentrated overwhelmingly in commerce, many of them as small shopkeepers. These small-town Jews, selling clothing, shoes, and hardware in their stores along the main streets and collecting scrap metal in their junkyards, were an important component of Canadian Jewish life.

Whatever their trade, they were decidedly middle class in occupation, self-image, and aspiration, and they seem to have been inclined to identify with their leaders, who were usually highly successful businessmen. Zionism — which stressed the redemption of Palestine by having Jewish pioneers rebuild, replant, and defend it — provided Canadian Jews with the responsibility to support financially those lofty purposes. From its founder, Clarence de Sola, through Archie Freiman to Samuel Zacks, who took over in 1944, there was a succession of businessmen at the helm of the Zionist movement in Canada.

The fundamental character of Zionism in Canada changed little during the 1920s and 1930s. This era ended, as it began, with almost obsessive fundraising. And yet, within the movement a diversity of expression and alternative affiliation was now possible. There were youth wings that attracted growing numbers and where many, for the first time, studied Jewish culture. Indeed, involvement in the Zionist movement was growing considerably. Certainly Canadian Jewry's financial commitment to it was immense; its leaders undertook important obligations from the end of the First World War until the acceptance of the staggering million-dollar Emek Hepher project in 1927. With these burdens, the pace of campaigning increased, the size of the organizational professional staff grew, and the number and amount of donations rose.

Of utmost importance during these years was the provision, through the ZOC and Hadassah, of a unifying framework for the community. Their biennial conventions and the more frequent regional gatherings provided the only national and regional forums for the expression of common attitudes and aspirations, as well as for the establishment of a Canadian Jewish personality. Consequently, without any seriously competing organizations, their leaders had a considerable legitimacy, inflating their importance and establishing the identity of Canadian Jewry. Zionism, nevertheless, was largely an invented identity that was inherently extraterritorial in its primary goals. In the meanwhile, there were serious clouds on the world Jewry horizon to which Zionism was not an adequate response.

CHAPTER

7

Antisemitism from the Twenties to the Forties

Antisemitism emerged in virulent forms in the interwar years. The weekly *Canadian Jewish Chronicle*, since 1914 the principal English-language Jewish newspaper in Eastern Canada, reported on antisemitic happenings around the world and, along with other Jewish periodicals, also had plenty of local nastiness to fill their pages. In the 1920s, the *Chronicle* took notice of the antisemitism (which it termed "racial sadism") found in *La Croix*, a religious Catholic weekly. Yet after a few years of concerned reaction to *La Croix*'s antisemitic fulminations, the *Chronicle*'s editors decided that "the nature of its comments is so distinctly psychopathic that it really cannot bias any of its readers unless they are similarly degenerate and depraved. . . . [F]or the future we are inclined to believe that it ought to be ignored."[1]

La Croix continued its attacks on Jews until ceasing publication in 1936. Meanwhile, the *Chronicle* covered antisemitism in the United States, Europe, and Canada, where insults, allegations that foreigners were "taking over," "No Dogs or Jews Allowed" signboards, exclusion, and misrepresentations (sometimes joking) of Jewish religious and social practices were common fare. The paper made a special point of responding to the worst examples that appeared in the Quebec English and French press.[2]

But more vicious forms of prejudice were emerging, imitating antisemitism in Europe. The spread of the fraudulent pamphlet, *Protocols of the Elders of Zion*, which falsely alleged a world Jewish conspiracy, and the occasional reprinting of excerpts from it in otherwise respectable newspapers like the *Quebec Chronicle*, were noted and condemned, usually to good effect.[3] The recantation of Henry Ford, antisemitism's chief North American evangelist of the early 1920s, may have reduced the flow somewhat, but the *Protocols'* poisonous lies continued to be influential and worrisome to the Canadian Jewish community.

In French-speaking Quebec, the most serious antisemitic accusations held the Jews responsible for the Russian Revolution and the spread of international communism. Articles stridently alleging these untruths frequently appeared in *La Semaine Commerciale*, *L'Action Catholique*, and *L'Action Française*, as well as, in milder form, in English dailies like the *Montreal Star*.[4]

In a major editorial in November 1920, the *Chronicle* argued that antisemitism was the fault of the "Gentile environment," which "has created the modern Jew."[5] The paper was prepared to concede "the truth of some of the accusations levelled against the Jews[,] and it is certainly stretching a point far to concede this, [but] there still remains no foundation for anger or hostility, because there can be no blame where there was no alternative. . . . The Ghetto developed the Ghetto Jew."

Such arguments, however conciliatory, had no measurable effect, especially in Quebec, where economic factors encouraged the rise of antisemitism. French-Canadian owners of small businesses, corner grocery stores in particular, felt threatened by competition from Jewish retailers, wholesalers, and mass marketers, a fear that gave rise to a boycott movement in the early 1920s.[6] The movement, activated by a Montreal priest, advised French Canadians to boycott Jewish businesses and buy at home: "*Achat chez nous.*"

By early 1924, *La Croix* was calling for a boycott of Jewish businesses "to get rid of them either by elimination or by annihilation."[7] A few months earlier, it had published excerpts from the *Protocols*, along with an editorial announcing that "these documents are undoubtedly of Jewish origin. . . . It is a well-known fact that immigrant stations in the United States are filled with Jewish inspectors whose chief business it seems to be the insult and injury of incoming people other than Jews."[8]

Such concern about "Jewish control" emerged occasionally in Montreal's English-speaking community as well. In August 1921, one of its members alleged that the redrawing of municipal-ward boundaries would give Jews four rather than two representatives — and thus control of city council![9] An effort by Jewish community leaders to have *La Croix* denied mailing privileges was defeated on the grounds that in the view of one official, "its antisemitism is not . . . of such a character as to disclose an intent, or to have a direct tendency, to excite His Majesty's subjects to a violation of the laws or to offend public order."[10]

The "Achat Chez Nous" campaign was growing strong. Writing in *L'Actualité économique* of June 1926, Henri Leroux expressed alarm at what he saw as new business trends. "Canadian retailers in Montreal, one could say, must fight against only one foreign race: the Jews," he wrote.[11]

Why did Leroux see the Jews as a more serious menace than all other ethnic competitors? It was because they dominated or tried to "take over the retail business by any means." Jews were by nature commercial, Leroux continued, operating small grocery stores throughout Montreal and staying open day and night. With capital thus amassed, they entered clothing manufacturing. As both manufacturers and retailers, they drove French Canadians out of business. Jews also invaded the shoe, fur, meat, and fruit trades, employing French Canadians as their front men. In fact, Leroux asserted, Jews were successful because of their "lack of sincerity and honesty." They bought bankrupt stock and goods of poor quality, then sold them for lower prices. They cheated on weights and measures. They even saved by cutting expenses, including personal living expenses, and employing their families at home.

But French Canadians were retaliating, Leroux rejoiced, by advertising, just like the Jews, and "by studying their ways of doing business, and by behaving honestly, by selling new items at reasonable prices. . . . [T]here is still enough

---

Abbé Groulx on the "Achat Chez Nous" Campaign in 1933

> Antisemitism, not only is it not a Christian solution; it is a negative and silly solution. To solve the Jewish problem, it would be sufficient for French Canadians to recover their common sense. There is no need for extraordinary legislative machinery, no need for violence of any kind. We would not even give our people this order: "Do not buy from the Jews!" We would simply tell French Canadian customers: "Do as everyone else does, do as every ethnic group does: *"Buy at home!"* [. . .] And there, that is about all we would say. And that, by some miracle, our order was understood and followed and, in six months, a year, the Jewish problem would be solved, not only in Montreal but from one end of the province to the other. Only the Jewish influence able to survive on its own would remain. The rest would have been cleared off, inevitably dispersed, to find its existence in occupations other than business.

Abbé Lionel Groulx (pseud. J. Brassier), "Pour q'on vive," *L'Action Nationale* 1 (April 1933): 243; quoted in Jean-Pierre Gaboury, *Le Nationalisme de Lionel Groulx: Aspects idéologique* (Ottawa: Éditions de l'Université d'Ottawa, 1970), 35.

time for Canadians to wake up."[12] In discussing other threats, such as department stores like Eaton's, Dupuis Frères, Dominion, and Piggly-Wiggly, Leroux avoided ethnic attacks entirely. About his fellow French Canadians, he wrote:

> We are shocked to see how our small retailers lack practical sense, an ability to adapt to circumstances. Is it due to their education? their background? their race? One must rather attribute it to their lack of initiative, to their inclination for routine. We say to ourselves: my people succeeded this way in the past, why not me?[13]

In an issue of *Le Détaillant* (the Retailer) in May 1927, J. E. Sansregret, vice-president of the Retail Merchants Association of Canada, pointed out that in a survey of the Montreal suburb of Saint-Henri, 79.13 percent of all stores were French-Canadian owned, a figure roughly equal to their percentage of the population.[14] Still, the presence of Jews was vexatious: "[W]e notice that to dress the brother, the father, the husband, there is not one English, not one French Canadian, but 8 Jews are there to wait on you. There you go!"

It was not enough, he pronounced, for French Canadians to keep their former position; "[rather,] we must develop more, increase gains recently realized, with the risk of regressing." French Canadians go into unprofitable lines and "we give to our fellow citizens of Hebrew origin the making of the supposedly profitable cloth." And while French Canadians resisted hiring bilingual personnel in their stores, Jews had no hesitation, thus attracting a large and diverse clientele.[15]

Are we masters in our own house? Sansregret wondered. Hardly. A French Canadian must understand his duty, "which is to buy from his fellow countryman." If he was to boycott the Jewish stores for six months, at least half of them would close up "and the business which puts all goods into circulation would be handed back to us and everyone would be better off." (Except the Jews, of course.) This was a question of the very survival of French Canada, Sansregret stated. "Today, the issue of nationalism has become an economic issue."[16] The vilification of the Jews was also included in Dupuis Frères' in-house publication, *Le Duprex*, which went chiefly to employees. In its February 1927 issue, it condemned French Canadians who purchased "vile Jewish bric a brac."[17]

Jewish stores were sometimes boycotted in Western Canada. In Winnipeg, the Retail Merchants Association's attempts in 1921–22 to regulate Sunday shopping resulted in conflict with Jewish retailers and some expression of antisemitism. Similar conflicts arose in Toronto.[18] The nationally organized Retail Merchants Association had a pronounced nativist ideology,[19] but only in Quebec did this result in a campaign aimed almost exclusively at Jews.

Consequently, some Jews suffered considerable hardship. One general-store owner, Aron Grosser of Nicolet, Quebec, who boasted in April 1924 that "my relations with my neighbours have always been of the very friendliest," was told by a hostile townsman that "it was the duty of good Christians . . . to drive all the Jews out of the country."[20] His "friendly" neighbours showed him a copy of *La Croix* that informed its readers all about the Jews. "My store is practically boycotted," he wrote. "The people won't come to buy. They only come in to ask me what would I do if my store was plundered or burnt down or if I was driven out of the country. Wherever I go, I hear them talking about Jews or I see them showing each other the paper."

This "Achat Chez Nous" campaign continued into the 1930s. In the St. Denis area of Montreal, the local St.-Jean Baptiste Society also launched a "Save the Corner Store" campaign, stating:

> Just so long as we neglect our merchants, our corner grocer, to give our money to foreigners, our race will play a secondary role in commerce and our patriotism will be reduced to empty words which do no good to anybody if not to those who have interest in keeping us down.

Antisemitism in Quebec in the 1920s and 1930s

Much of this antisemitism was generated by writings in *L'Action Catholique*. Its wide clerical readership made it an especially influential newspaper in the province. As the historian Richard Jones demonstrates, it contributed a powerful message to the priests who read it and spread the word to their parishioners.[21] Antisemitism was not incidental to the paper's editorial writers. In numerous articles on many subjects, they conveyed the persistent message that Jews and Judaism were a dire menace, not just to Catholic Quebec, but also to the civilized world.[22]

Then even more extreme writings appeared. "Jews," wrote Abbé E. V. Lavergne in 1922, "as a race, are our enemies. Their goal is to destroy Christianity, but in order to achieve this goal, it was necessary to shed floods of blood."[23] Thus images of Jews attacking and killing Christians were employed to depict Jews as inhuman creatures who communed with the devil.[24] In league with the Freemasons and the Bolsheviks, J. Albert Foissy wrote, the Jews wished to "reverse the established social order"[25] and establish Bolshevism, which is "an episode of the battle involving fanatical Jews who, by the paths of international anarchy, pursue only the ruin of Christian and civilized nations."[26]

Just as the *Protocols* had forecasted, the Jews were determined to dominate the world. If the world press failed to expose this threat, it was of course because Jews also controlled that medium.[27] *L'Action Catholique* stated that even the League of Nations was composed mainly of and manipulated by Jews.[28] Thus they secured the League's mandate for Britain to establish a Jewish national home in Palestine, which Abbé Arsène-Louis-Phillipe Nadeau saw as "a real challenge for all of Christianity" because the Jews "would be able to erect factories or dumping grounds on Sacred Lands . . . if they would not go as far as erect temples of debauchery."[29]

Equally as bad, in the eyes of *L'Action Catholique*'s writers, was the Jewish domination of Poland, where three million "parasites eat away at its exhausted body." These "Yid traitors, thieves, spies, crooks, howling Bolshevists, Hun-loving arrogants who go as far as insulting Polish emblems [are] full of hate, so much so that they attack Polish soldiers who have strayed, by mistake, into the ghetto districts."[30] In the United States, Jews possessed an "extraordinary power" in the press, the arts, the theatre, opera, jazz, and fashion, where morals were corrupted and decadence fostered.

In exposing these nefarious Jews, *L'Action Catholique* saw itself as protecting Christian interests. In fact, Abbé Lavergne said he wished Jews well, so long as they did not "block the path, and by the exploitation of bad passions throw our people in hell, those we wish to meet in Eternal Bliss."[31] And when persecutions of Jews commenced in Germany, *L'Action Catholique* extended both Christian charity and blame towards the victims. Thus writers like Jules Dorion complimented Hitler for giving Jews a little "pull on the ears."[32] In general, though, they condemned the means but not the end — suppression of the world's "undesirables," the Jews.

At this same time, Jeune-Canada arose. A small group of young French-Canadian intellectuals inspired by right-wing clerics and nationalists, Jeune Canada was led by the student activist André Laurendeau, who mounted an antisemitic public rally at Montreal's Gésu Hall in April 1933.[33] Staged to rebuke French-Canadian politicians who had attended a mass meeting held by the Montreal Jewish community to protest German Nazism, the Jeune-Canada rally denounced Jews who "represent . . . the dream of Messianic mission [in which] Israelites aspire to dominate the world."[34]

Jeune-Canada's leading spokesmen led the attack. Pierre Dagenais condemned "the Jew [who] professes a spirit of proletariat internationalism," while Pierre Dansereau announced that "the Jewish element . . . represents in Canada a power stronger than the voice of the blood."[35] Another speaker alleged that "150,000 Jews in Canada own a quarter of the Dominion's wealth and the 80,000 Jews in Montreal control two hundred million dollars worth of industry and commerce."[36] Stung by criticisms from Senator Raoul Dandurand, who condemned "the most cruel attack I've ever heard of," and by Jewish reaction, which called Jeune-Canada members "disciples of German Naziism,"[37] Laurendeau replied with still more antisemitic attacks alleging that Quebec's Jews threatened the province's "linguistic balance" and were carriers of both international communism and exploitative capitalism.[38]

In May 1933, Jeune-Canada launched a newspaper, *Le Patriote*, which, the *Chronicle* reported, was initiated "with the usual . . . anti Jewish fulminations, and proves itself a worthy successor to the *Goglu*."[39] That paper, published by Joseph Ménard, an associate of Adrian Arcand's, had alleged that Jews murdered the Lindbergh baby for ritual purposes.[40] A month later it announced that Jews were responsible for the downfall of the Roman Catholic Church in Spain, and that they "have gobbled up the treasures of the Russian church."[41] In August, *Le Patriot* alleged to its readers that Sir Herbert Samuel, a prominent British Jew then visiting Vancouver, "has been sent by the Elders of Zion to open up the gates of Canada to hundreds of thousands of German Jews."[42]

Dabbling also in theories of racial superiority, Jeune-Canada declared that while French Canadians could become "a superior race," the Jew was "like a necessary canker for Christianity, and confirms the incompatibility between Israelites and Christians."[43] Such verbiage, in all likelihood borrowed from Lionel Groulx or his intellectual mentors in France, inspired Laurendeau to proclaim:

> Jews . . . represent a wild and dangerous dream that we must suppress at all cost: messianism. The Israelites aspire [to] . . . the day when their race will dominate the world. They do not come from one nation, but they come from every country; everywhere the power is communicated by money, they run the politics. . . . [44]

Quebec's Jews felt besieged in the 1930s. While present throughout Canada, antisemitism seemed most pervasive in *la belle province*. Apart from the press, it also surfaced in other public forums. In 1931, for example, aldermen in Montreal's Villeray Ward considered blocking off a Jewish cemetery in the north end with new streets to prevent its expansion. They also objected to a proposal to build a new Jewish hospital there.[45] That same year, Abbé Edouard Lavergne proclaimed, in radio broadcasts and in *L'Action Catholique*, his racist theories about a Jewish plot to corrupt good Christian morals, theories, he said, that were confirmed by the *Protocols of the Elders of Zion*.[46] In September 1931 two Montreal aldermen led an attack on immigrants "whom certain groups are endeavouring to bring to Canada [and who] are mostly Communists and propagandists of anti-Christian ideas."[47] Jewish meetings were interrupted by "Fascist mobs . . . with the battlecry of anticommunism and pro-clericalism . . . with the police . . . looking on benignly and — who knows — maybe indulgently."[48]

J. A. Chalifoux, the leader of a brown-shirted Fascist group, appealed to Premier Taschereau and proclaimed, "we will fight the Jews on behalf of the merchants of Montreal."[49] At a meeting in St.-Jérome in August 1933, Chalifoux and his followers threatened that "they will tell [the Jews] to go to Palestine and if they refuse they will kill them." He also threatened to lynch a local Jew.[50] The city of Montreal, recognizing that many Jews were not yet naturalized, limited the street sale of newspapers, largely a Jewish trade, to "British subjects" of at least five years.[51] City officials also penalized Jews for opening bakeries and delicatessens on Sunday.[52]

Response of the Canadian Jewish Congress

The Canadian Jewish Congress, dormant since 1920, was revived in 1934, principally because of this emergence of antisemitism. It was not just that among contemporary opinion-makers, "the Jew simply did not fit into their concept of Canada."[53] Nazi-style uniformed "storm troopers" also rallied and marched in several cities. Jews were denied professional, residential, and economic opportunities. Occasional antisemitic violence erupted. And enough open antisemitism was expressed in newspapers, political forums, the courts, and everyday life to convince Canadian Jews that they had to react defensively and diplomatically to these hate-mongers.[54]

Unlike other ethnic groups that were also suffering from discrimination, Jews had some means, through the Congress, their three MPs, and several prominent individuals, to mitigate prejudice. Yet what distinguished Canadian antisemitism from other racism was that it was part of a worldwide phenomenon. As part of an international campaign, political parties in France and Germany included Jew-hatred in their ideology and electoral platforms. The Roman Catholic Church officially conveyed suspicion and contempt. In the United States, Henry Ford's daily newspaper, the *Dearborn Independent*, was filled with fulminations against the "international Jew." A pamphlet of the same title was circulated nationally in the millions, translated into several languages, and distributed throughout Europe.[55]

In North America, groups such as the Ku Klux Klan promoted antisemitism, and during the late 1930s the Michigan-based hate-monger and Roman Catholic priest Father Charles Coughlin broadcast virulent Jew-baiting messages from his headquarters. English Canada was influenced by the United States as well as by Britain. Emulating Hitler's brown-shirts and Britain's black-shirts, swastika clubs sprang up in Ontario during the 1930s. Meanwhile, branches of the Ku Klux Klan operated in Western Canada, principally Saskatchewan. More genteel antisemitism was also in evidence. Universities limited Jewish admissions, especially into medical and dentistry programs, and restrictive covenants prevented Jews from living in certain urban areas.[56] Bans existed on Jews at many resorts and private clubs. Such restrictions elicited numerous jokes. One of them poses a Jew seeking admission to an exclusive Toronto club only to be rejected as "pushy" by a member who proudly announces that one of his ancestors signed Magna Carta. "Is that so?", replies the Jew. "One of mine signed the Ten Commandments." Many other jokes also deftly punctured antisemitic stereotypes, but all to little avail. Jew-baiting remained a popular Canadian past-time.

In Quebec, dedicated antisemitic weeklies such as *Le Goglu*, *Le Miroir*, and *Le Chameau*, which regularly featured cartoons caricaturing Jews as low, vile, and filthy, were circulated by Adrian Arcand and his associates. Arcand's blue-shirts, modelled on its Italian Fascist and German Nazi counterparts, marched and organized. From his position at the Université de Montréal, Abbé Lionel Groulx published denunciations of Jewish materialism, communism, and capitalism. At the respected and influential newspaper *Le Devoir*, the editor, Georges Pelletier, regularly published antisemitic pieces, as did the editors of the monthly periodical *L'Action Française*. Students at the Université de Montréal demonstrated against "Judeo-Bolshevism." The interns at four Montreal francophone hospitals went on strike in 1934 to protest the hiring of a Jewish intern at Notre Dame. As if these problems were not enough, Quebec Jews also had little help from the Anglo-Protestant community, which considered them, officially, second-class citizens in elementary and secondary education. At McGill, meanwhile, Jews had serious problems gaining entry on the same basis as other Quebeckers. All of these unpleasant and menacing elements put the Jewish community on notice that, with respect to antisemitism, *"la province de Québec n'est pas une province comme les autres."*

As a reaction to these threats, the Congress embarked on a program to educate Canadians about Jews and to enlist help from the Christian community in these anti-defamation efforts. Sam Jacobs, the MP for Cartier, persuaded Henri Bourassa to support this campaign by strongly condemning antisemitism in two speeches in the House of Commons in the spring of 1934.[57] Similar lobbying with a leading Quebec liberal, Olivar Asselin, also bore fruit, while discussions with Bourassa and Father Paré of the Palestre National resulted in a meeting with high Catholic authorities and three lectures by Bourassa condemning antisemitism.[58]

In responding also to Hitler's persecution of Jews in Germany, the Congress adopted an aggressive policy of boycotting German goods entering Canada, and continued this campaign through the 1930s. In 1935 and 1936, it tried also to prevent Canadian participation in the 1936 summer Olympic Games in Berlin. The Congress received backing from the Trades and Labour Congress of Canada, which supported a Germany boycott, called for the non-participation of Canadians at the Berlin games, and sent "representations to the dominion Government . . . to break off diplomatic relations with the Hitler Government until such time as this Government ceases their persecution of the organized working class of Germany, and to express abhorrence for the regime which has overthrown civil and religious freedom." The Congress wrote to labour representatives throughout the country, urging them to form boycott committees "which should make it a daily duty to visit friendly organizations. . . . And use any platform which will denounce Naziism and propagate the boycott."[59]

The Congress' boycott committee received numerous letters from businessmen promising to shun German goods. Reitman's stores wrote in May 1934, "We assure you that we feel the same towards Germany as you . . . do and under the circumstances, we have ceased to do business in Germany."[60] General Secretary Hananiah Caiserman also tried to get Canadian manufacturers onside by warning them of the German practice of dumping goods in the Canadian market.[61] He conducted a vigorous campaign against German coal and German-made gloves, which were fraudulently labelled Made in Holland.

The responses to these efforts were mixed, even in the Jewish community. In one of his follow-up letters, S. D. Cohen, boycott committee chairman, cautioned that "we have learned that quite a number of Jewish merchants are continuing to buy and sell German merchandise. We express the sincere trust that *you are not one of them*."[62] In a communiqué to eleven hundred wholesalers and retailers, the boycott committee asked recipients to state, "in writing, that you are ready to cooperate wholeheartedly with the Boycott, which every decent Jew in the world is compelled to conduct against Nazi Germany."[63] The Congress even urged Canadian importers of German military braid to join the boycott. Although Canadian trade with Germany actually rose during the 1930s, by 1939 it had declined relative to Canada's total trade, and the fall in imports of German textiles, a sector in which Jews were especially prominent, was significant.[64]

The Congress also reacted strongly to Canadian antisemitism. But this was like trying to wrestle an octopus. Often the Congress was in only an advisory role, as in the case of Alderman Max Siegler of Montreal. Siegler was the object of a virulent campaign against his nomination for deputy mayor led by Le Club Ouvrier Maisonneuve, which protested that "it is a shame to see that our French Canadian aldermen could not find anything else but a Jew as deputy mayor . . . [and] that we must humble ourselves before the Jews. . . ."[65]

Besides protesting to politicans, the Congress tried to organize communities to educate their compatriots. In 1937, it began distributing literature explaining the dangers of Nazism, the falsehood of claims such as those in the *Protocols of the Elders of Zion*, and the need for vigilance against antisemitism at home.[66] Up to twenty different pieces of information were sent to public schools, theological colleges, universities, school boards, mechanics' institutes, provincial legislatures, and law schools throughout Canada.[67] All proved of little avail. Antisemitism continued to rise. In September 1938, the Congress' eastern division was warning that "Fascist and Nazi organizations in Canada are plotting to obtain political control of this province [Quebec] and to destroy the Jewish people."[68] Pointing to the assistance given to this "Fascist machine" by a powerful press, as well as "an avalanche of Nazi literature" emanating from "French Canadian political, religious and economic groups," the Congress asserted that "these have during the last few years created an anti-Jewish atmosphere which is especially dangerous during elections."

Literature circulated by the Congress in Quebec and the Maritime provinces stressed that "the rising tide of anti-Semitism throughout the world is having its repercussions in Quebec, [where] the National Social Christian Party, led by Adrian Arcand, already boasts of having 15,000 members . . . [and] uniformed 'legions' hold weekly parades. . . . Scurrilous and malicious propaganda continues to pour out and poison the minds of innocent people."[69] Photographs showing Canadian Fascists at a "council of war" and ones depicting saluting Montreal Fascists bore the captions "Fascists hope to rule Canada in 1940," "It may happen here!" and "Fascist legions are preparing to march in the streets of Montreal in the Spring of this year."

The fact that some of these emotional statements were followed by appeals for funds to support the Congress' anti-defamation work suggests scaremongering, but there was genuine widespread fear in Eastern Canada of the Fascist menace. Pamphlets circulated bearing titles such as *Canada under the Heel of the Jew*, *Why We Should Oppose the Jew*, *The Grave Diggers of Russia* (showing a face with exaggerated "Jewish features"), *Politiciens et juifs*, *Fascisme ou socialisme*, and *National social chrétien*. Ideas derived from Hitler's *Der Stürmer* were widely distributed, as were such French slogans as "Jews are the enemies of God and of all mankind. St-Paul"; "The enemy of the JEW and of Communism is FASCISM!"; "Fascism is the powerful weapon of the true Christian"; "The JEWISH rat gets richer with smuggling, drug trafficking and the white slave trade."[70] Antisemitic hate-mongering was serious.

Much of the counter-propaganda was conducted by the Committee on Jewish-Gentile Relations, a Toronto-based group headed by Dr. Claris E. Silcox of the United Church of Canada and Rabbi Maurice N. Eisendrath of

Holy Blossom Temple.[71] The committee boasted fifty permanent members drawn from the major Christian and Jewish organizations, and was mainly devoted to distributing literature such as Dr. James Parks's *The Challenge of Anti-Semitism to Democracy*. It also distributed exposés of Father Charles Coughlin, the inventor of hate radio in Detroit.[72]

Coughlin apparently had some supporters in Canada, and his broadcasts had an audience here.[73] A 1932 survey of radio-listening preferences in London, Ontario (where people were likely to tune in to American stations), revealed that his program, considered to be "religious" in content, was well-known.[74] By 1938, his diatribes against Jews had grown increasingly virulent.[75]

German Nazi antisemitism influenced some Canadians, especially in the Mennonite community, even though groups like Deutscher Bund Canada and the National Socialist Party (the NSDAP) had very few members — only eight-eight in 1937.[76] The distribution of antisemitic propaganda among Germans living in Canada was undertaken by the Nazis in the 1930s on a significant scale.[77] In early 1935, Hans Seelheim, one of two German consuls in Canada, delivered a talk to the Women's Conservative Club of Winnipeg about "Jewish flesh merchants." They, along with drug dealers, he said, "are all Jews and the same goes for most boot-leggers."[78] The consul went on to Vancouver, where he delivered another antisemitic broadside to the Lions Club, drawing a vigorous protest from the local branch of the Congress.[79] Such messages were also spread among German Canadians.[80]

In Ontario, the Jews' response to antisemitism was weak initially, which was understandable given their minority status and immigrant make-up. But it grew stronger as the community learned better methods of coping. In 1932, E. Frederick Singer, a Jewish Conservative MLA for the St. Andrew riding in Toronto, introduced a bill to amend the Ontario Insurance Act. It would prohibit the common practice of insurance companies of discriminating against minorities by charging higher premiums and providing inferior coverage.[81] Meanwhile, at the urging of Toronto Jewish community leaders, the municipal council prohibited discrimination in leases for the rental of city-owned land.

The Congress also lobbied against antisemitic signs — such as those at various resorts that allegedly read, "No Dogs or Jews Allowed" — as well as discrimination in employment and housing. Such efforts were generally not successful. During the Second World War, even while Canada suffered serious shortages of manpower in vital industries, discriminatory hiring continued. However, the Joint Public Relations Committee of Congress and B'nai Brith did succeed, with the National Selective Service, in stopping such practices, and in 1944 they encouraged the government of George Drew to pass the Racial Discrimination Bill, which outlawed some racist practices in Ontario.[82]

The Congress' 1938 claim that its "moral authority is recognized by our Federal, Provincial and Municipal Governments" was probably justified.[83] Through its public-relations efforts, it had established a unique relationship not only with governments, but also with the press, public bodies, churches, and labour. The Congress had also developed such moral authority in the Jewish community that it had "done away with the deplorable conditions which prevailed . . . when any private individual spoke in the name of Canadian Jewry. Today only one organization speaks for and represents Canadian Jewry in an emergency, and that organization is the Canadian Jewish Congress."

That view was not uncontested, and the Congress warned against unnamed "left labour organizations in Montreal [that] interfere with the authority of the Congress by duplicating activities, which will result in more harm than good." However, the only serious rival for national pre-eminence, the ZOC, had effectively yielded its role to the Congress. The Congress, by 1939, had lasted for more than five difficult years. It seriously needed new leadership and stronger financial backing to deliver on its agenda of combating antisemitism and to push the Dominion government harder on the issue of admitting more refugee Jews to Canada.[84] Through the efforts of some Labour Zionists, the Montreal whisky tycoon Samuel Bronfman was persuaded to accept the presidency, a post he filled with dedication for the next twenty-two years.[85]

Bronfman was very much his own man. Though he brought his enormous energy and financial resources to bear on Congress affairs, he also stressed the patriotism of Canadian Jewry and the need for public spiritedness to "gain the respect of [its] fellow citizens — the non-Jewish citizens" (as he told Congress delegates shortly after his elevation to the presidency).[86] With this attitude, Bronfman was not influenced by those who would press for a more favourable immigration policy. He therefore, in the view of historian Michael Marrus, "sounded a particularly patriotic note while ignoring the burning Jewish concerns of the hour."[87]

Antisemitism in Quebec Worsens

Meanwhile, Abbé Lionel Groulx continued his sustained attacks on Quebec's Jews. As a highly influential intellectual and teacher of Quebec history, he was bound to affect his students at the Université de Montréal and readers of his voluminous writings. Some of these were published in *Le Devoir*, which was read by francophone opinion-makers, "the clergy, the university community, civil servants, and the liberal professions."[88]

Groulx was heavily influenced by the French racist nationalism of *L'Action Française*, a Paris-based movement. Its major philosophers, Charles Maurras,

Maurice Barrès, and Gustav Le Bon, espoused extremist ideas of exclusivist racial purity, right-wing nationalism, and violent anti-liberalism.[89] Ever since 1919, when he wrote *La Naissance d'une race* to glorify the racial purity of the French-Canadian folk, Groulx was obsessed with the extreme racialism which emphasized "socio-psychological characteristics [that] are transmitted through the blood" and the "degeneration" that comes from racial mixing.[90] In his novel, *L'Appel de la race* (1922), he emphasized the drawbacks arising from an English/French marriage. To him, the fusion of soul, blood, and soil were the true source of the race. Groulx's numerous writings emphasized "the biological transmission of psychological characteristics," ideas current among Fascist and integral nationalist groups throughout Europe.[91] Through his lectures, the pages of *L'Action Nationale*, and various historical works, Groulx's clerico-fascist, racist, and antisemitic ideas became the intellectual inspiration for Laurendeau's Jeune-Canada movement and for the writers of *Le Devoir*, including its editor, Georges Pelletier.

The McGill sociologist Everett C. Hughes observed in his seminal 1943 study of French Canada that antisemitism was a minor and symbolic aspect of French-Canadian nationalism in the 1920s and 1930s. It was, he said, a reflection of "the more bitter attacks which the French Canadians would like to make upon the English or perhaps even upon some of their own leaders and institutions."

However, the historian Esther Delisle emphasizes that it was the "primary focus" of Quebec nationalism.[92] The Jew, identified in the mind of Groulx as the very essence of all that is despicable in religion, politics, and morals, was also racially inferior and, in Groulx's words, characterized by "a fatal, invasive illness, one that no cordon sanitaire can artificially arrest."[93] To be sure, Groulx, Pelletier, and other antisemites were a minority among Quebec intellectuals and in the nationalist camp itself, where newspapers like *Le Jour*, *Le Canada*, and *L'Autorité* and figures like Olivar Asselin and Henri Bourassa condemned antisemitism.[94] When interns at Montreal's francophone hospitals struck against the presence of Dr. Samuel Rabinovitch at Notre Dame Hospital in June 1934, Edmond Turcotte denounced them in *Le Canada*:

> The revolt of Notre-Dame's interns and of their colleagues at Miséricorde, Hôtel-Dieu and Sainte-Justine is an issue of serious reflection for citizens whose straight and strong reason refuses to surrender before the crowd. The vile and mocking press and the spiritual and swarmy little runts that fused it together carry a terrible responsibility in this type of morbidity that the still sane and lucid minds dreadfully see the centres of legitimate defense of the National French Canadian organism being conquered.[95]

Olivar Asselin, the editor of *L'Ordre*, in which he published an attack in March 1934 on Hitlerism and French-Canadian antisemitism, also denounced the strike: "The strike of the French Canadian interns could have only been motivated by racial hatred."[96] This seems to have been the extent of editorial condemnation of antisemitism by French-Canadian journalists and intellectuals. However, the historian Pierre Anctil points out:

> . . . as suggested by the CJC [Canadian Jewish Congress], Quebeckers as prestigious as Henri Bourassa and Olivar Asselin, each in his sphere of activity, publicly sided against antisemitic cliques, and several lesser-known individuals at the time see themselves fed with reflections and are weighted down by documents proposing mutual tolerance.[97]

It is not clear what this activity against antisemitism amounted to within French Canada. While the province's most widely circulated newspapers, *La Presse*, *Le Soleil*, and *La Patrie*, were free of its poison, the antisemitism of Groulx and others still had enormous effect. One editorialist even averred that Jewish claims to public rights could bring "violent reprisals." Marcel Hamel, the editor of *La Nation*, stated:

> Communism, a Jewish invention, would thus become the most enormous lie to brutalize the working class and worsen the economic illnesses suffered by a world which waits for the future King of Israel to enthrone himself on top of a pyramid of corpses.[98]

In the pantheon of perceived Jewish subversion of French Canada, there was also capitalism, liberalism, the cinema, violence, vulgarity, and filth. Jews, according to articles appearing in *Le Devoir* during the 1930s, were "aliens, circumcised, criminals, mentally ill, trash of nations, Tartars infected with Semitism, malodorous — they smell of garlic, live in lice-ridden ghettos, have greasy hair and pot bellies, big crooked noses, and they are dirty."[99]

Jews were also the subject of verbal attacks by prominent French-Canadian politicians. The Hon. Arthur Sauvé, postmaster general for Canada in R. B. Bennett's Conservative government from 1930 to 1935, collaborated with a group that was affixing antisemitic stickers to letters. He also "launched a tirade against the projected attempt to get an undesirable element . . . which is hostile to the French Canadian people, to the French language and to their religion" into Canada.[100]

J. E. Grégoire, mayor of Quebec City, professor of economics, and key lieutenant to Maurice Duplessis, leader of the Union Nationale, praised the antisemitic newspaper *Le Patriote* before a crowd of twenty thousand in Montreal in July 1936.[101] Paul Gouin, leader of Action Libérale Nationale — a movement strongly influenced by Bourassa, Groulx, and *L'Action Française* — allowed his journal, *La Province*, "to wander into incoherent excursi on the Jewish problem in such manner as to leave no doubt of the implications which this Fascist ideology holds for the Jews."[102]

When the Union Nationale won the 1936 provincial election, the *Chronicle* called upon Premier Duplessis to disavow the antisemitic views of "a few *Judenfressers* such as our old friend Saluste Lavery."[103] In March 1936 while bemoaning the fate of Quebec farmers, the MLA Laurent Barré announced — without any evidence — that some New York Jews had taken over a large milk concern in Montreal.[104] Premier Duplessis saw fit to publicly link the Jewish MLA Peter Bercovitch, a Liberal, with the Communists, branding him their "echo in the Legislature."[105]

Open violence against Jews was mounting. Premier Duplessis's public targetting of Communists as enemies of Quebec society occasionally encouraged street violence against Jews. "The affinity between the two," the *Chronicle* commented, "has been drummed into their heads so persistently by certain elements that an anti-Communist riot immediately becomes an anti-Jewish riot."[106]

This proclivity, coupled with negligible assistance from the Montreal police force, led to occasional Jewish self-protection. Street terrorism in the guise of popular anti-communism by Université de Montréal students was becoming a problem in October 1936, especially when the scholar-thugs received official approval and police protection.[107] Police also failed to protect Jews during an antisemitic riot in Ste.-Adèle in mid-August 1937.[108] Houses occupied by Jews had their windows broken and two houses were torched. This came two years after a violent incident in Val David, in which the synagogue and its Torah scrolls were destroyed and swastikas smeared on the walls.[109] A Jewish summer colony in Ste.-Rose had to be abandoned, and the Val Morin synagogue was also daubed with swastikas.[110]

Such trends influenced political behaviour, with Jews overwhelmingly supporting Liberal candidates in provincial elections, largely because of Taschereau's accommodationist stance towards the Jewish community. There were also widespread fears of Maurice Duplessis's reactionary Union Nationale policies, as well as of the presence of antisemitic elements within his party.[111] Solidarity with the Liberals faltered briefly when Jewish voters backed Louis Fitch in a 1938 by-election; he narrowly won for the Union Nationale.[112] But it was ethnic politics pure and simple — "Jews were willing to abandon the Liberal party in order to have a Jewish political representative" from the governing party.[113] A year later, however, Jewish voters returned to the Liberal

Party and elected Maurice Hartt, mainly to protest the premier's anti-war stance and because of fears of antisemitism among some of Duplessis's nationalist supporters.

The most virulent expressions of Quebec antisemitism were to be found in three small-circulation weekly newspapers, *Le Goglu*, *Le Miroir*, and *Le Chameau*. They were largely devoted to disseminating lies, cartoons, innuendo, and accusations against Jews. They included not just the standard shibboleths of Judeo-Bolshevism, but also, in Abraham M. Klein's words, "all the Judaeophobic lampoons of the Dark Ages. . . . They filled their papers with slander as headline, garbled quotation as footnote, and forgery as space-filler."[114]

Klein, editor of the *Chronicle*, called for a strong and immediate Jewish response to these lies. "The situation is serious; it merits drastic action . . . the battle is in our hands, and the law courts are open," he wrote in a July 1931 *Chronicle* editorial urging Jews libelled in these papers to "take immediate action, if not in their own interests, then in the interest of the Jewish community in which they play a prominent part."[115]

Quebec antisemitism was hardly muted by the onset of the Second World War. In an October 1939 editorial in *Le Quartier Latin*, the Université de Montréal student newspaper, Jean Drapeau, a law student and the future mayor of Montreal, stated that Jews

> [are] transforming the main business artery of our city . . . into a filthy carnival where rotten meat sits stacked beside stale crusts of bread, and where the sidewalks too often serve as garbage pails for decomposing fruits and vegetables; . . . by bestowing on our metropolis repulsive neighbourhoods we cannot pass through without our stomachs turning; . . . [and by] ruining French-Canadian business by disloyal competition, based on immoral if not openly dishonest tactics.[116]

In 1942, the anti-conscriptionists in Montreal, many of them veteran ultranationalists and active antisemites, vented their anti-Jewish venom physically. The Congress press officer, David Rome, reported that there were several clashes in the streets.[117]

The Quebec City Synagogue Affair

Quebec City, the quiet and sleepy provincial capital, produced it own special incident. There, a tiny Jewish community of about one hundred families encountered the first attempt made in Canada to pass municipal legislation specifically against Jews. In 1932, the community purchased a property on

Learmonth Avenue in the west end. They wished to build on it a synagogue to replace the old one, which was located in the former Jewish area of town. City authorities approved their plans to build a structure that would fit in with the architectural style of the neighbourhood,[110] but because of protests by a small group, the city council passed a bylaw preventing the erection of new buildings other than private dwellings or stores. However, several schools and hospitals were subsequently built on the same street. The Jewish community acquiesced with barely a whimper.

In 1941, it tried again. After carefully consulting the mayor and the city's legal officials, it purchased a property on Crémazie Street and obtained a building permit. But again local opposition arose, and the proposed synagogue became an issue in the municipal elections of 1942, with one candidate promising to prevent its construction. Although this person was defeated by a large majority, the city council still passed a bylaw prohibiting the building of a synagogue in that district.

The city also announced that it would expropriate the property (which had been for sale for ten years before being purchased by the Jewish community) in order to extend an adjacent park. In a debate in city council, certain aldermen indicated their intention to expropriate for parks and playgrounds any other land that the Jews might buy for a synagogue. One even suggested a resolution forbidding synagogues within city limits.[119] "Are the councillors of Quebec City aware of the fact that a war is being fought for the four freedoms?" the *Chronicle*'s editor, Abraham M. Klein, asked. "Or does Quebec fight for only three of them?"

Klein could not resist having a bit of fun with this situation:

> We do not know whether the Municipal Council of the good City of Quebec has yet seen fit to pass a resolution of gratitude to its Jewish community for being instrumental, if only indirectly, in contributing towards the scenic embellishment of that fair metropolis, but certainly such a resolution has long been overdue. . . . No other group of citizens . . . has recently done more towards the increasing of parks and playgrounds than the Jewish community . . . in its futile quest for a site for its synagogue.[120]

The Jewish community, now thoroughly intimidated, offered to turn the property over to the city in return for a building permit anywhere in Quebec suitable to the community. The city refused this offer and, by a narrow majority, passed an expropriation bylaw. The entire Jewish community of the province was now on the alert and so were some of its leading public figures.

Premier Adélard Godbout appealed several times for tolerance. Montreal's Jean-Marie-Rodrigue Cardinal Villeneuve and Abbé Joseph-Thomas-Arthur Maheux of Quebec pleaded in the same vein. The Jewish community, building permit in hand, decided to go ahead with construction while at the same time contesting the expropriation bylaw in court. In late May 1944, the new edifice was completed. It was a modest one-storey building that included a downstairs community hall, a kitchen, and classrooms.

On the eve of its dedication and opening, on May 25, the building was set afire and severely damaged. The arsonists were never found. The outrageous act was condemned in the press, with the *Montreal Star* saying the incident had a "Nazi odour." Reverend Dr. Claris E. Silcox, director of the Canadian Council of Christians and Jews, stated that "the act of vandalism . . . is the logical sequence of the 'achat-chez-nous' movement, . . . the bitter anti-Semitic propaganda before the war and the un-Christian petitions circulated by French Canadian organizations against allowing any Jewish refugees into Canada."

However, not a word of disapproval was heard from the provincial government or the clergy. From the editor's desk at the *Chronicle*, Abraham M. Klein asserted that the "dubious honour — the burning of synagogues — which hitherto characterized only Nazi cities is now shared by the capital of our province."[121] Attorney General Léon Casgrain uttered the lame *non sequitur* that "this Province is one where freedom of worship exists in its complete form," but everyone else was silent.[122] The synagogue was repaired and used for many years, but the municipal council's use of legal means to deprive Jews of their basic civil rights left a lingering after-taste. As Caiserman put it, "Never before in the history of our country had [the] right to erect a house of worship for the citizens of the Jewish faith. . . been so openly or so unashamedly suppressed or challenged."[123]

Antisemitism in the Universities

Jews also experienced growing discrimination at some Canadian universities in the 1930s. This was especially serious at McGill, the only English-language university in Montreal, which attracted the city's Jewish youth. R. A. MacKay, McGill's dean of arts (and later a distinguished External Affairs official and Rowell-Sirois commissioner), acted on the view that "the simple obvious truth is that the Jewish people are of no use to us in this country,"[124] and that "as a race of men their traditions and practices do not fit in with a high civilization in a very new country." He convinced the university's administration to limit Jewish enrolment in his faculty to 20 percent and to require Jews to have high-school averages of 75 percent (in contrast to averages of 60 percent for Gentiles).

Other McGill faculties followed suit, and by 1939 the Jewish presence had declined to about 12 percent in arts and medicine and 15 percent in law.

At the University of Toronto medical school, by contrast, the percentage of Jewish students rose rapidly after 1920; by 1930, Jews constituted more than one-quarter of its undergraduates.[125] The rising number of Jews attending the university in the 1920s and early 1930s became an issue among both its senior officials and the general public, who wrote letters to complain about it.[126] One of them referred to the "Hebrew problem" and started to keep a yearly record of Jewish enrolments.

Prejudice existed not only at McGill and Toronto. When a group of Jewish students began to congregate regularly in an undergraduate common room at Queen's University in the early 1930s, a sign appeared that read: "We gave you Palestine; now give us back this lounge."[127] In reaction to the increasing numbers of Jews entering the University of Manitoba medical school in the early 1930s, the faculty imposed in 1936 a severe quota on Jews and others such as Ukrainians, Poles and other East Europeans, Mennonites, Italians, and women, regardless of academic standing.[128] After a group of students, who were supported by some members of the faculty, informed the university's governors of these facts, the practice was stopped. Nevertheless, by 1944, the

---

SONNETS SEMITIC

A. M. Klein

Now we will suffer loss of memory;
We will forget the tongue our mothers knew;
We will munch ham, and guzzle milk thereto,
And this on hallowed fast-days, purposely . . .
Abe will elude his base-nativity.
The kike will be a phantom; we will rue
Our bearded ancestry, my nasal cue,
And like the Gentiles we will strive to be.
Our recompense — emancipation-day.
We will have friend where once we had a foe.
Impugning epithets will glance astray.
To Gentile parties we will proudly go;
And Christians, anecdoting us, will say:
*"Mr. and Mrs. Klein — the Jews, you know . . ."**

From Gerri Sinclair and Morris Wolfe, eds., *The Spice Box: An Anthology of Jewish Canadian Writing* (Toronto: Lester & Orpen Dennys, 1981): 7.

number of Jewish students had fallen drastically, from twenty-eight to nine in the first-year class.[129] At the same university, it was equally difficult for Jews to enter engineering.[130] As an undergraduate at Manitoba in the late 1930s, Ernest Sirluck felt that "Nazi and Fascist successes in Europe and the growth of similar movements closer to home brought out latent hostility among Gentiles and made Jews more worried and defensive."[131]

Interning, the vital training of medical-school graduates in hospitals, however, was so restricted for Jews and other non-preferred immigrant stock that access to the major hospitals, such as the Toronto General Hospital (TGH), was nearly impossible.[132] Jewish graduates of the University of Toronto's physiotherapy program were also not allowed to do their clinical training at the TGH.[133] Discrimination against Jewish doctors and patients in Montreal's hospitals was so serious that the community felt compelled in the late 1920s to build its own hospital.[134] Most Jewish and other minority medical graduates from Canadian universities were forced to go to the United States for their internships. Many of them stayed there.

Universities also harboured other forms of discrimination. Jews and other "non-preferreds" were denied membership in fraternities and sororities,[135] and those Jews who had accidentally been recruited were suddenly dropped from the rolls. Such practices were ignored by university administrations. Both Ernest Sirluck and Albert Rose, students at the University of Manitoba and University of Toronto in the late 1930s, found antagonism to Jews and Judaism.[136]

The McMaster University student newspaper, the *Silhouette*, in a January 1936 commentary on antisemitic legislation in Nazi Germany, advised caution: "We, on this side of the Atlantic, probably do not fully realize or understand the conditions existing in Europe." While Jews have little influence in business or the professions in North America, it continued, "in Europe the situation is different and this difference must naturally alter opinion on the subject." The article was entitled "The Case for Germany."[137]

University teaching positions were scarce during the Depression, and Jewish applicants had an especially tough time, but a German Jewish refugee scholar, the meteorologist Bernhard Haurwitz, was accepted by the University of Toronto for a Carnegie fellowship leading towards a permanent position.[138] Leopold Infeld, a distinguished scientist from Poland, was hired at the University of Toronto in 1938.[139] During the Second World War, one or two Jewish mathematicians and scientists were employed at other Canadian universities,[140] and were among the approximately twenty Jewish refugee scholars who had been on the staffs of Canadian universities since the 1930s.[141] But there was strong resistance at McGill to the hiring of German Jewish refugee scholars.[142]

Jews found it impossible to secure positions in medical research and teaching at the University of Toronto, "an institution permeated with genteel antisemitism." Here the discoverer of insulin, Frederick Banting, had openly expressed his anti-Jewish bias.[143] By the 1930s, however, a changed Banting had "shed his antisemitism" and publicly supported aid to Jewish refugees and a liberal Canadian immigration policy.[144]

Meanwhile, promising Jewish Canadian scholars could not get university appointments. Lionel Gelber, Rhodes Scholar, political scientist, and future adviser on foreign affairs to Prime Minister John Diefenbaker, "did not get the permanent position for which he was amply qualified" at the University of Toronto, even though he was supported by the influential historian and political thinker Frank Underhill.[145] Leon Edel, who would eventually write a five-volume biography of Henry James, also could not get a post, while the future chief justice of the Supreme Court, Bora Laskin, got a lectureship in the law faculty only after making "an extraordinary declaration of loyalty." He joined Jacob Finkelman, who had been there since the early 1930s.[146]

Queen's University was somewhat more liberal than either McGill or Toronto. By 1938, the medical scientist Benjamin Kropp and the mathematician Israel Halperin were on the faculty. But an issue arose in 1943 because Jewish enrolment had jumped from forty-five to 127 students since 1938 and had doubled over the previous year.[147] The following year, Jews constituted 15.1 percent of arts enrolments and 13.4 percent of those in medicine, leading Principal Robert C. Wallace to express the concern that restrictions on Jews at McGill were "send[ing] the less competent Jewish students to Queen's."[148] Antisemitic views were voiced at a board of trustees meeting and the question was referred to a committee, which recommended raising admission standards all around to solve the "problem of Jewish students".[149]

McGill and the University of Toronto would not admit German Jewish refugees as students, but Queen's also took a decidedly more liberal attitude in this, allowing in a few, including Alfred Bader and Kurt Rothschild. Remembering his reception at Queen's, Bader wrote: "[T]he principal, the registrar and the professors treated me with care and respect; one family, that of Professor Norman and Grace Miller, treated me with love. . . . Norman was not one of my teachers, but he and his family treated me most kindly. . . . I have no idea why I was invited there so often."[150] In August 1942, Carleton W. Stanley, president of Dalhousie University, tried to enroll three Austrian Jewish refugees in the medical school but was stymied by the faculty, most of them downtown practitioners.[151]

Nevertheless, neither Queen's nor the other universities were hotbeds of antisemitism. Despite restrictions, they were generally forums of integration for many Jewish students. Contacts made in sports, clubs, residences, and classes led, in some instances, to lasting friendships, and even business relationships, between Jews and non-Jews. As well, universities provided a generation of Jewish students with the benefits of higher education, a familiarity with the best of Western culture, a sense of accomplishment at the highest levels of learning, and an entrée, albeit sometimes a problematic one, to the professional class. As well, the universities fostered secularization among the first-generation Jews, who mastered skills and confidence that, later, enabled them to become leaders in the Jewish community and to take a slowly increasing part in Canadian public affairs during and after the Second World War.

Antisemitism across Canada

Other forms of antisemitism were also current. The Ku Klux Klan surfaced briefly in Canada in the 1920s. Although more of a threat to Catholics than to Jews, it carried powerful antisemitic messages warning of Jewish domination in industry, corruption, plots against Christianity, and vice.[152] With the expected appearance of the Klan in Montreal, the Jewish community was warned of "trouble in the future on account of the large proportion of Hebrews [here]," although nothing came of the scare.[153] The Klan's greatest Canadian success was achieved in Saskatchewan in the late 1920s, but it never struck deep roots among farmers.[154]

Other manifestations of antisemitism abounded, some of them relatively minor. In June 1937, the Toronto Tennis League refused an application for membership from the Hudson Tennis Club, which was Jewish.[155] Meanwhile, the local St. Andrew's Golf Club, which had been founded with Jewish support, barred Jews with a sign that read Gentiles Only.[156] Antisemitic materials were circulated, some directed against specific individuals, like Archie Freiman, who sued an Ottawa policeman for an antisemitic libel.[157]

Antisemitism was present in Western Canada as well. Efforts to get support for elevating the long-time Liberal MP Sam Jacobs to the Cabinet in 1925 went nowhere.[158] When the Alberta Social Credit Party swept into power in 1935, it carried with it a considerable background of virulent antisemitism inherited from its British intellectual father, Maj. Clifford H. Douglas.[159] In his writings, Major Douglas employed the imagery of the *Protocols of the Elders of Zion* to depict high finance as part of a Jewish conspiracy to control the world.[160] The Social Credit Party was intended to free society from the grip of these international Jewish financiers and establish a monetary system based on true values. Douglas's antisemitism, one scholar recently found, combined traditional Christian antisemitism with modern varieties of Jew-hatred, "which desired to keep Jews as a marginalized group not worthy of equal political, economic, or social treatment."[161] When William "Bible Bill" Aberhart became Alberta's premier, the province did not have an antisemitic tradition any stronger than that which prevailed generally among Western farmers, who disliked banks and had absorbed a Prairie populism that vaguely associated the institutions with Eastern Jews.[162]

This mild antisemitic strain was infected by Douglasite virulence against the Jews. "Antisemitism emerged among some Social Crediters . . . [because], for many Albertans, Douglas provided the key to unlock the mysteries of what had gone wrong with the world economic system."[163] But Aberhart, who "could have turned anti-Semitism into a dangerous political dogma," was highly ambivalent about Jews. On the one hand, he publicly denounced antisemitism, partly because his brand of Christian fundamentalism generally "predisposed him towards a positive view of Jews" and partly because he had a special fondness for them. On the other hand, he believed that there was a tie between certain Jews and a world banking conspiracy.[164] Thus in the very statements in which he condemned antisemitism, he "included comments that sounded implicitly antisemitic."[165]

Some Alberta Social Creditors were outspokenly prejudiced against Jews. John Blackmore, MP for Lethbridge from 1935 to 1958 and the first house leader of the Social Credit group in the House of Commons,[166] and Norman Jaques, MP for Westaskiwin from 1935 to 1949, were virulent antisemites. The party's national organ, the *Canadian Social Creditor*, was rife with antisemitic sentiments. Within the provincial administration, a Cabinet minister and a key official openly espoused Douglas's views.[167] In Quebec, meanwhile, the Social Credit publication *Vers demain* printed similar antisemitic diatribes.[168] Other party organs continued to publish considerable amounts of such material during the Second World War. It was not until 1948 that Ernest Manning, who had succeeded Aberhart as provincial leader and premier, publicly rejected Douglas's antisemitism and ousted the extremists; they, nevertheless, continued to propagate their views and influence some people.[169]

Antisemitism among Minorities

Antisemitism flourished among some other minorities. In Winkler, Manitoba, a mainly German-speaking Mennonite farming community, antisemitism deeply affected Ernest and Robert Sirluck, who were born and raised in the town. On his first day at school, Ernest was told by fellow pupils that he "was a dirty Jew who had killed Christ."[170] "Nor did things change a great deal as

I was growing up," he recalled. "There was always someone willing to defend Christianity, and indeed racial purity, by hitting a smaller Jew, and since I was more lightly built and less developed by hard physical labour than these sturdy Mennonites and Lutherans, most of these encounters ended with my taking more and harder blows than I was able to give. . . ."

His brother, however, took up body-building, bested the most aggressive school bully, and was never picked on again. In the 1930s, as sympathy for German Nazism flourished in Winkler, Ernest acquired a handgun as a complement to his rifle and engaged in target practice in full view of his neighbours, some of whom subscribed to German Nazi publications like *Der Stürmer* and *Volkischer Beobachter*. One Lutheran family posted the newest issues in their windows fronting the town's main street.[171] "Everyone in town knew that I had two guns, liked using them, and usually hit what I aimed at," Sirluck reflected.[172] Nevertheless, after *Kristallnacht*, on November 9, 1938, antisemitism grew "more virulent and menacing."[173] When Britain was attacked by the Luftwaffe in mid-August 1940, "many in Winkler said that the British had brought it on themselves by their stubbornness. . . ."[174]

Antisemitism was present in the Ukrainian community as well. A teacher for several years in rural Saskatchewan recalled:

> Dark sinister tales throw up shadows of a hideous past. The terrible old story of the ritual murder of young Christians by the Jews at Passover is an oft-repeated legend . . . told to him by a small Ruthenian [Ukrainian] child — the capture by the Jews of a Christian child, the fattening of the child on sweetmeats, the murder by placing her in a barrel with nails and rolling the barrel, the drinking of the blood to secure the strength to dominate Christians for ever. . . .[175]

Jewish-owned stores predominated in the 230 towns located within the Ukrainian block settlements on the Prairies. One or two Jewish general stores could be found in half to two-thirds of the towns in the Ukrainian areas of rural Manitoba and Yorkton, Saskatchewan.[176] There were also Jewish-owned stores throughout Winnipeg's North End, where Jews lived among Ukrainians and other ethnic minorities. In this area, Jewish merchants, who often offered lower prices than their competitors, were patronized by many Ukrainians "out of habit." Despite their conspicuous presence, Jews sometimes were portrayed by the intelligentsia of the Ukrainian movement and by their competitors as "intruders." Jews were "accused of using false weights and measures, selling inferior merchandise at inflated prices, writing bogus cheques, and demoralizing settlers by selling alcoholic beverages, operating hotels with beverage rooms, distributing free beer to attract new customers, and criticizing Ukrainian reading clubs and co-operative stores."[177]

In 1912–13, boycotts were organized against the Jews, who, according to the weekly newspaper, *Ukrainsky holos*, "have been clinging to our national organism since time immemorial, gnawing and destroying it like maggots in their capacity of tavernkeepers, village usurers and agents of political demoralization during elections."[178] Jews usually were depicted in pageants and plays as ridiculous and contemptible figures and "audiences were . . . left with the simplistic impression that heartless Jews, devoid of all human qualities, were somehow singularly to blame for the Ukrainian peasantry's desperate condition."[179] They were condemned by some religious leaders as progenitors of socialism.[180] An Edmonton Ukrainian-language newspaper, *Klych* (the Call), edited by Anthony Hlynka, the Social Credit MP for Vegreville, was noted by the Congress to be antisemitic and "filled with traditional Ukrainian antipathies to Jews."[181]

However, in a community as diverse as the Ukrainian one, there was no single image of the Jews. The *Ukrainian Canadian*, a newspaper published in Winnipeg that represented the interests of working people, was inconsistent in its attitude towards Jews.[182] A sampling of its editorials and news reports in the 1920s reveals no overt antisemitism. On the contrary, one article concerning a meeting of Western Canadian Jewish teachers was very positive, concluding that "There is more than a little that we Ukrainians could learn from these Jewish 'teacher patriots.'"[183]

Moreover, frequent reports from Ukraine favourably mentioned Jews fighting alongside Ukrainians against the Poles in Galicia and depicted Jews as fellow sufferers under Polish domination. On the other hand, once Bolshevism became firmly rooted in Eastern Ukraine, Jews were seen as collaborators against the Ukrainians, although occasionally this link was applied only to "some Jews." Reports of Soviet persecutions of Jews, meanwhile, were often sympathetic to the Jews. The effect of all this coverage on readers is impossible to measure, of course, but letters to the editor reflect little antisemitism.

Patriotic and nationalistic Polish community newspapers reacted strongly to Jewish charges of Polish antisemitism and pogroms, as well as to Ukrainian allegations of brutality towards their countrymen in Galicia.[184] But while Ukrainian claims for cultural autonomy in Poland were viewed as legitimate, Jewish demands for the same were rejected and Jews in Poland viewed "as a non-Polish element," guilty of "disloyal conduct and criminal behaviour."[185] The journalistic stance protected Polish national honour against Jewish complaints of mistreatment, which were published in the international press. The Polish-Canadian newspapers did not, however, applaud the antisemitic policies of Poland's governments after the death of Marshal Jozef Pilsudski in 1935 and even expressed strong sympathy for the plight of Jews in Germany, speaking of "Jewish martyrdom" after *Kristallnacht*.[186]

However, one scholar found that "numerous brief references throughout the period reveal that the editors' anti-Jewish attitudes had not changed." These antisemitic feelings were often suppressed, as their "public posture was modified to fit the realities of Canadian life." They feared that expressions of overt antisemitism might prejudice the Canadian anglophone establishment against Polish Canadians.

The Riot at Christie Pits, August 1933

A community of about forty-five thousand people in a city of more than half a million, Jews constituted Toronto's largest ethnic minority after the Irish Roman Catholics. Italians lived in the same neighbourhoods — some, indeed, in the same houses — as the Jews in "the Ward," an area just north of city hall, or in the crowded west end, south of Bloor Street and east of Christie Street. Polish, Ukrainian, Irish Catholic, and other ethnic communities lived there too, amid the overwhelming majority of Protestants of British origin.

Baseball teams met frequently for tense, hard-fought games at a west-end park called Christie Pits. Jewish and Italian players dominated several teams and earned reputations for toughness and excellence in both hardball and softball contests. But far from paving the way to a brotherhood of sportsmen, these games often degenerated into epithets, insults, and fisticuffs. Jewish amateur and professional boxers Nat and Max Kadin, Sammy Luftspring, Davy and "Baby" Yack, "Spinney" Weinreb, "Panco" Bergstein, and many others received much the same treatment.

In mid-August 1933, Jews fought a bloody four-hour battle against a group of antisemitic Anglo toughs.[187] Hundreds of Jewish youths, assisted by a small number of Italians and Ukrainians, battled the Pit Gang, a crew with a long tradition of harassing minorities in Toronto's lower west end.

After a baseball game held earlier that evening between local Jewish and church teams, the Pit Gang had unfurled a large banner bearing a swastika to well-orchestrated shouts of "Hail Hitler." Jewish players and spectators had tried to tear the banner down. Within minutes, axe handles, lead pipes, chains, and other weapons were wielded with terrible effect by both sides.

Hurriedly summoned from pool halls, smoke shops, delicatessens, street corners, club rooms, an assortment of drinking and gambling establishments, and front verandas, Jews in the district raced to join the fight. It took repeated charges by mounted police, motorcycle squads, and a substantial force of constables swinging nightsticks to separate the Jews from the Pit Gang. Reinforcements for both sides kept pouring in from surrounding neighbourhoods.

Serious trouble was brewing that summer in Toronto. In the city's east end, populated overwhelmingly by Anglo-Celtic Protestants, the area known as the Beaches had also become extremely tense. Members of recently formed swastika clubs sported Nazi badges and shirts and hurled insults and punches at Jews and other minorities who had gone there to escape the city's heat. A huge Nazi banner with the slogan Hail Hitler in large block letters was painted on the side of one of the beach clubhouses one day and an organized force of about fifty Jewish youths suddenly turned up to do something about it. The Toronto police intervened, and the mayor, several aldermen, police, and Jewish community notables urged both sides to remain calm. But tension continued to mount. As the swastika clubs flourished, more ugly antisemitic incidents occurred. Jewish resentment smouldered because of these humiliations, and was compounded by daily reports in Toronto's newspapers of the persecution of German Jews by Hitler's Nazis.

When Toronto Jews reacted to these provocations, they were responding not only to the specific recent humiliations they had suffered, but also to the whole climate of antisemitism prevalent in the city. They and their Italian and Ukrainian allies — who experienced many of the same insults and indignities as the Jews — delivered a message to the Anglo-Celtic tough guys that they would not forget. Certainly, Toronto's Jews would long remember the so-called Battle of Christie Pits. The following year, the newly organized Ontario region of the Congress wrote to the presidents of several Toronto Jewish organizations, advising that

> to prevent a recurrence of last year's regrettable incidents, . . . it is essential that Jewish organizations of the Community do not hold large gatherings in any portions of the City where such a gathering is liable to arouse the animosity of certain classes of the Non-Jewish population.[188]

They were soon to experience much deeper concerns.

The Darkening Clouds

Canadian Jewry had begun to worry about the worsening state of Jews in Central and Eastern Europe. In Germany, by 1935, Hitler had begun the process of identifying and excluding them from German society, while other forms of persecution were taking place in the streets. In Poland, Marshal Pilsudski's death that same year unleashed antisemitic forces that severely worsened the lot of that country's Jews. Meanwhile, in Hungary and Romania, antisemitic political parties seriously contended for power.

All the while, through newspapers and personal letters, the alarming news of deteriorating conditions in Europe arrived in Canada. European relatives pleaded, with mounting desperation, to their families in North America for help in entering Canada. Urgent appeals were likewise made to government officials, to the Congress, and to MPs.

As the historians Irving Abella and Harold Troper have shown,[189] Canada's gates were all but locked to Jewish immigration. Not only was Canada experiencing a severe economic depression, but Prime Minister William Lyon Mackenzie King was also prey to antisemitic bogeys.

In fact, Canada's virtual exclusion of Jews was due primarily to the prevalence of antisemitism, particularly in French Canada, where some priests, politicians, and intellectuals actively opposed Jewish immigration. Petitions circulated by the St.-Jean Baptiste Society drew tens of thousands of signatures. King's Quebec lieutenant, Ernest Lapointe, "took a hard line with respect to refugees," convincing King that to do otherwise would strengthen the Quebec nationalists and weaken the Liberal Party in Quebec.[190] As well, in Alberta Social Creditors like MP Norman Jaques issued statements attacking the prospect of Jewish refugee immigration.[191]

Most Canadian intellectuals and opinion-makers said little in favour of accepting Jewish refugees. As already noted, the influential historian Arthur Lower, of Winnipeg's United College, was an outspoken opponent of immigration. Other intellectuals, such as Frank Underhill and Frank Scott on the left, apparently kept silent on this issue, while the social policy activist Charlotte Whitton let her anti-foreigner views be known.

In the meantime, Jewish leaders lobbied unsuccessfully in Ottawa — although "some prominent Jews were given special immigration permits to be distributed to a fortunate few in the community."[192] Reflecting many years later on his own valiant efforts to secure more entry permits, the Congress' Saul Hayes said:

> when the survivors blame the Jewish communities of the free world for not having tried to force the hands of the Roosevelts, Churchills, MacKenzie [*sic*] Kings, etc., they're probably right. Actually I don't think we could possibly have even if we had marched on Ottawa every hour on the hour. But we can't have an easy conscience because we didn't try to the extent that we should have. We were too damned polite about it.[193]

Coping with opinion-makers opposed to Jewish immigration was one problem; facing like-minded persons in power was another. Frederick Charles Blair, director of the Immigration Branch of the Dominion government's department of Agriculture, was adamantly opposed to Jewish immigration. Operating on the theory that "none is too many," Blair scrutinized all applications for entry and determined to keep Jews out. He was aided in this by many other officials, including Vincent Massey, Canadian high commissioner in London, and by widespread public opinion in favour of a closed-door immigration policy. "Canadians preferred almost anyone — including Germans — to Jews."[194]

However, a small group of Canadian churchmen — Anglicans, United churchmen, Presbyterians, Baptists, and Quakers — gathered in response to Rev. Claris E. Silcox's call for action in early 1936 and came out publicly for "a reasonable number of selected refugees."[195] This hedged appeal, which, oddly enough, did not specifically mention Jews, was only one of many denunciations of Nazism from churches — the Anglican and United churches were the most active — and from clergymen like Silcox and Tommy Shields of Toronto's Jarvis Street Baptist Church. A convention of Quebec and Ontario Baptists in June 1939 resolved that:

> Whereas there is still needed, on a vast scale, amelioration of the lot of the refugees, whether Jewish or Gentile, in Europe . . . this Baptist Convention do[es] urge upon proper governmental authorities the desirability of admitting to Canada carefully selected individuals or groups of refugees. . . .[196]

In 1943, the Baptist intellectual Watson Kirkconnell decried the mass murder of Jews in Europe in a moving poem inspired by Isaiah and entitled "The Agony of Israel":

> *Bow your heads, all ye nations*
> *And humble yourselves, all ye peoples*
> *In the presence of sorrow unspeakable*
> *At the sight of anguish beyond measure;*
> *For the sons of Israel are slaughtered all the day long*
> *And the daughters of Jerusalem are violated and slain*
> *And the synagogue is burned in fire*
> *And the place of the congregation is utterly destroyed.*[197]

Despite his literary eloquence, Kirkconnell did not call for the admission of refugees. Neither did Rev. Ernest M. Howse, of the United Church, when he delivered his stirring address "I speak for the Jew" in October 1942 at the Winnipeg Civic Auditorium:

> So I speak for the Jews. But I speak for someone not different from myself. When I read the dark and bloody record of what, in these very days, just beyond a curve of this good earth, is happening in Nazi lands, I think not of Jews and Jewesses; I think of men, women, and children, of young lovers and little babies, of homes and families. And when I plead for the Jew I plead for my own family and yours, and all the families of mankind.[198]

What is notable is that, however fragmented, weak and inadequate, there was a Canadian Christian witness to the worsening plight of European Jews in the 1930s and 1940s.

Antisemitism: A Perspective

All of these nasty incidents must be contextualized in the bleakness of the times, the bitterness of the Depression, and the prevalence of worldwide antisemitism — not to mention the open hatred expressed towards other minorities in Canada. In England, Oswald Mosley's uniformed Fascist phalanxes marched through the Jewish areas of London's east end as if to bait the Jews into an open fight — which, eventually, they did. In the United States, a variety of militant forces were outspokenly antisemitic, and the German-American Bund for a time even mounted pro-Nazi rallies in New York City, in the very face of the largest Jewish community in the world.

Thus one could argue that it could have been worse in Canada. Did antisemitism severely intrude on the daily lives of the vast majority of Canadian Jews, and was it the single most important factor impeding their progress and mobility in business, the professions, or on the shop floor? Antisemitism was undoubtedly present, but in the 1930s so were massive unemployment, a poor economic outlook, an absence of cash, poverty, malnutrition, anger, restlessness, and a general resentment towards foreigners. In fact, Jews were only one of many groups experiencing hatred and, sometimes, violence. It is significant, too, that those pillars of the Canadian establishment, the chartered banks, did not discriminate against small-scale clothing manufacturers — the vast majority of them Jewish — in the interwar period, although Jews would not be hired to serve the banks' customers.[199] Even the antisemitism present in French Canada was essentially rhetorical and, although extremely unpleasant, may not have disturbed the everyday lives of most Jews, who continued to live amid French

Canadians in generally "correct" relationships and often genuine neighbourliness.[200] So the material conditions of Canadian Jews may not have been significantly affected by antisemitism, but in the context of the 1930s, when European antisemitism, previously also essentially rhetorical, turned into severe persecution, Canadian Jews were understandably apprehensive.

CHAPTER

8

Canada's Jews at War

To interpret the impact of the 1940s on Canada's Jews, it is essential to study their involvement in the Second World War.[1] Such an examination is crucial not just to give a sense of the numbers involved, but also because an analysis of the recruitment to service in the army, navy, and air force helps to understand Jewish society in Canada at this stage.

How did the Congress and the community respond to the war in 1939 and its various stages until 1945? How did the war impact on the people and how did they react to it? What percentage of Jews of military age joined or were conscripted into the armed forces? What branches did they serve in? How well did Jews perform in the services? How were they treated as Jews and what were their perceptions of antisemitism? Did they fight the war to settle an ethnic score with the German Nazis or as loyal Canadians? What efforts did they and the Congress make to establish an environment that facilitated Jewish cultural identity among servicemen, and how successful were they? These and other questions must be asked by historians seeking to understand the Canadian Jewish experience in the 1940s.

THE CANADIAN JEWISH CONGRESS AND THE NATIONAL WAR EFFORT

The Congress, since 1939 firmly presided over by Samuel Bronfman, monitored all aspects of the Canadian war effort for several important reasons. The first of these was public relations. The Congress wanted Canadians to know that Jews were doing their full share for the country, contrary to the perception that their contribution during the First World War was inadequate.[2] Bronfman was strongly patriotic and insisted that Canada's Jews, united in the Congress, get fully behind the war effort from the very beginning.[3]

The Congress' second major reason for watching the conflict so closely was the nature of the war. This was a fight against Nazism, a party already trying to clear Germany of Jews and one dedicated to the same end in the rest of Europe. The Congress viewed this threat and Canadian antisemitism in particular as major concerns. Third, the Congress recognized — in part because of the First World War experience — that Jewish soldiers required an active support system to help them deal with religious, social, and even dietary needs. Much of this was channelled through Jewish military chaplains, all of them rabbis, working with the Congress to reach Jewish service personnel.[4]

The Congress formed the National War Efforts Committee (WEC) in late 1940 to "stimulate . . . and guide . . . the contribution to the national war effort by Canadians of the Jewish faith, to develop new functional activities [and] to keep an accurate record of contributions made by the Jewish community and its individuals to all phases of war effort, so that this record would be available during and after the . . . war."[5] Military recruitment centres were opened across the country, and Bronfman paid particular attention to the figures of Jewish enlistments, directing WEC to do all it could to encourage Jews to join the colours.[6]

Until mid-summer 1942, the WEC concentrated on mobilizing the community behind the national war effort while organizing a co-ordinated program of service to Jewish personnel scattered in camps throughout Canada.[7] Once there were more Jewish enlistments in the armed forces — part of a general trend that year — and considerable numbers of Jewish men were stationed near major cities, the WEC sent out field workers to organize hospitality, recreation, and entertainment for them. This plan was never fully implemented, and it fell to the local communities and Jewish military chaplains to provide much of this outreach.[8]

Jewishness and Volunteering to Fight Nazism

Even though there was widespread information available about the mass murder of Jews in Europe by late 1942, those reports were not universally believed, even by Jews. The allegation that North American Jews failed to respond appropriately during the Holocaust looms large. The American historian Henry Feingold attributes this inaction largely to the fact that American Jewry lacked unity, and therefore did not successfully convince President Roosevelt to actively save European Jewry.[9]

Given the widespread newspaper coverage of the systematic harassment of Jews in Germany during the 1930s, one might assume that all eligible Jewish males in the free world would have rushed to enlist immediately at the outbreak of war. After Hitler's accession to power in 1933, this persecution was given generous and detailed coverage in the mass media, especially in the *Toronto Star*,[10] whose Berlin correspondent, Pierre Van Paassen, sent back daily reports on the Nazi revolution. These reports were often given front-page coverage.[11] The Yiddish press also reported these events, as did English-language newspapers like the popular *Canadian Jewish Chronicle*. Did this knowledge of events — not to mention the antisemitism current in Romania and, after 1935, in Poland — stimulate massive Jewish recruitment to the armed forces after Canada entered the Second World War on September 10, 1939? Is it reasonable to expect that all Jewish males of military age should have rushed to join the colours to fight the persecutors of their people? The historian Jack Granatstein believes that "the sons of Eastern European Jewish immigrants should have had a special urgency; . . . they ought to have enlisted in what was unquestionably a just and necessary war, especially for Jews."[12] Whether it is reasonable to expect Jews to have volunteered *en masse* for such units in a war against Nazism remains a question that only the soldiers themselves — and those eligible Jewish men who, along with many others, avoided military service altogether — can answer.

At a distance of fifty years, some Jewish veterans reflected on their own reasons for volunteering. "As a Jew, you had to go," veteran Aaron Palmer recalled. Barney Danson remembered that "the evil of Nazism existed and we had to be in it, as Jews and as Canadians." Edwin Goodman also believed that he had a special responsibility to fight Nazism. On the other hand, Robert Rothschild, a regular army officer in 1939, did not feel an especially strong motivation because of his Jewishness. He did get that feeling after the war had started, however, and was proud of his four male cousins, who enlisted and fought in combat units. "I felt better about them," he remembered. Barney Danson felt some anger at the thought of the Jewish boys who did not join up. "I don't know how they could live with themselves. How could any [such] Jew look himself in the mirror?"

Ernest Sirluck joined the Canadian Officers Training Corps and sought a combat posting because "Jews had a special stake in this particular war and in the defeat of Nazism."[13] He believed that "[Jewish] behaviour in this war would profoundly affect their status in the future, that any effort to avoid military service or get into its low risk branches . . . would be closely monitored and unfavourably interpreted by a suspicious and often hostile population, among whom the antisemites had said from the beginning that the war was being fought for the sake of the Jews." Sirluck later turned down a safe berth because "as a Jew I should be in the dangerous shooting part of the war,"[14] especially after his brother, Robert, was killed in action while serving with the RCAF. Seventeen-year-old Martin Roher tried to enlist in 1941, immediately after his older brother was killed in an RCAF training accident just before he was to have received his wings. Rejected for flight training, Roher joined as a physical-training instructor and was employed giving swimming lessons to commando troops.[15]

Many had no doubt about what to do. Ben Dunkelman, an ardent Zionist, did not hesitate in 1939. "My mind was made up," he said. "I wanted to get into the war. . . . [I]t was quite clear to me that, as a loyal Canadian, it was my duty to volunteer to fight. Besides, as a Jew I had a special score to settle with Hitler. . . . [T]he anti-Semitic persecutions raging in Germany and the other countries dominated by the Nazis had made it clear that these men were the implacable foes of my people."[16] Harold Rubin "began to picture [his] loved ones being subjected to . . . horrible atrocities . . . [and] found it difficult to get to sleep, even after an exhausting day at work."[17] He joined up a few days after the outbreak of war.

Monty Berger, the son of Montreal's Rabbi Julius Berger, had an "acute consciousness" of why the war had to be fought. He tried to join the RCAF in May 1940 as aircrew, was rejected on medical grounds, and served as an intelligence officer with an RCAF Spitfire wing.[18] "Not unlike other Jews in Canada," he recalled, "I had heard of cousins and relatives who had disappeared, or were killed in the nightmarish world that descended on Europe's Jewish population in the late 1930s. . . . [M]y identity as a Jew ran deep. I felt fully the sense of frustration seeing Hitler and the Nazis go unchecked."[19]

Willie Nelson, who had joined the RAF in 1936 and was awarded the Distinguished Flying Cross in 1940 (the first Canadian Jew to be decorated), wrote home just before he was killed in action:

> . . . the Nazi regime must be crushed, and I thank God that I shall be able to help crush the regime that persecuted the Jews. . . . I have never had such a desire to live as I do now; nevertheless, my feelings are so strong, that the personal element doesn't mean a thing . . . and if I leave while flying . . . it is the way I want. . . . I am happy in the thought of helping to crush Hitler.[20]

Judging, however, from some memoirs, there were those with little concern for the fate of European Jews and no strong enthusiasm for fighting Nazism. A young Toronto Conservative politician and insurance agent, Allan

Grossman, thirty years old in 1940, offered to join the army if he could get a special berth with a political crony. When that did not work, he joined the reserves.[21] Irving Layton, twenty-eight years old in 1940, idealist, intellectual, and poet, applied to join the medical corps at the outbreak of war but was turned down. He subsequently joined the Canadian Officers Training Corps, washed out in 1943, and decided to sit out the rest of the war.[22]

One intellectually precocious, nineteen-year-old Mount Allison University student, Nathan Cohen — who later became one of Canada's most important drama critics — wrote in May 1942 that "Hitler and Mussolini precipitated no war, they are the products of our own sloth and shame."[23] David Lewis, thirty-one years old in 1940, was national secretary of the CCF when war broke out. He felt no compulsion to object to his party's commitment to pacifism during the late 1930s. "No one had any doubts," he recalled, "that war with Hitler was almost certain, yet we could not bring ourselves to support expenditures to improve Canada's preparedness."[24] His memoirs reflect no personal struggle over the question of enlistment in spite of his Polish birth. Lawrence Freiman, who was thirty, decided to enlist at the outbreak of the war but was dissuaded by his father's serious illness and the ensuing family responsibilities.[25] "It was one thing for a dental graduate to accept a commission in the medical corps," Mordecai Richler recalled, "something else again for a boy to chuck law school for the infantry."[26]

From its beginnings in 1940, the WEC actively encouraged Jews to enlist, "the primary duty of citizenship in the crisis which our country is now facing."[27] Information on enlistment was widely distributed through speeches, pamphlets, and offices manned by Jewish First World War veterans. Special registration bureaus were opened on Spadina Avenue in Toronto and in the Jewish district of Montreal.

While important, these patriotic efforts, at least according to H. M. Myerson (who oversaw recruiting in Central Canada in 1940 and 1941), were peripheral matters. The Canadian Jewish war effort, he reported to the Congress, "will be gauged in terms of able-bodied young men who have risked their all."[28] Several obstacles to the recruitment of young Jews had already surfaced, including general indifference and apathy ("indolence of mind, . . . desire to follow line of least resistance, . . . having a good time, . . . absence of pride in one's self, [or] in group [and] national life.") Parents, Myerson found, were reluctant to encourage or even permit their sons to join up, while young men feared they would not be able to get along with Gentiles. And the old Jewish hostility towards the military in general was still present. What to do? Myerson urged the Congress to mobilize the entire Jewish community to promote military service by popularizing the idea in the Jewish press, making direct approaches to eligible young men, and giving appeals at meetings of all Jewish organizations, especially youth groups. He urged all the Congress top brass to get behind this recruitment campaign.

In 1942, the WEC launched a large-scale drive "to awaken . . . [the] realization of the gravity of our country's need and the necessity of making every possible sacrifice to enable all able-bodied Jewish Canadians to take their places in the ranks of Canada's fighting forces." Rabbi David Monson of Toronto went out on recruiting drives using the argument that Jews would be affected by this war more than others: "If Hitler wins, Christians will be slaves. Jews will be committed to death."[29] Monson encouraged men who had already signed up to bring in their friends and relations. He went to Toronto's Brunswick Avenue YMHA and to youth clubs, where he got a mixed reaction; some joined up right away, others said they would ask their families. The Jews he addressed during these recruiting drives, he believed, knew what Hitler stood for and were influenced by parents who in many cases had relations still living in Europe. Some parents reproached him, but he replied that service in the Canadian armed forces was necessary to ensure Jewish survival. Other Jewish recruiters did the same.

Strong support for a vigorous war effort also came from the far left — especially following the German attack on the USSR on June 21, 1941. Jewish Communists then redeployed the rhetoric of the Popular Front, which had been suspended since August 1939, the period of the German-Russian non-aggression pact. They issued calls for "a second front now" to smash Nazi Germany. The Communists discouraged strikes and pressed for increased war productivity and for funds for Soviet medical relief. Above all, they appealed for unity among Jews, "the first victims of fascism wherever it appears."[30] Marches and rallies were held, such as the one at Maple Leaf Gardens in September 1943 for Shlomo Michoels, the head of the Soviet Jewish Anti-Fascist Committee, and Itzik Feffer, a distinguished Yiddish poet.[31] Attended by Jews of all political persuasions, this meeting reiterated the Communists' support for a war against Fascism, and for the gargantuan effort conducted by the Soviet Union against Nazi Germany's eastern front. With the elections of Joseph B. Salsberg to the Ontario legislature in August 1943 and of Fred Rose a few days later to the House of Commons, the war effort was a major theme in their speeches everywhere.

Jewish Recruitment to the Armed Forces

According to the records of the War Efforts Committee, 16,441 Jewish men and 279 women served in the Canadian armed services during the Second

World War, and 163 Canadian Jews served in other Allied armed forces.[32] Jewish women constituted 0.55 percent of all Canadian women who joined navy, army, air force, and women's nursing units.[33] This was substantially lower than the percentage of Jewish women in the Canadian population in 1941 (1.46 percent by religion). However, because of strong patriarchal values, families tended to be highly conservative and likely resistant to the enlistment of their daughters. One Jewish woman, Rose Goodman of the RCAF, was killed in a training accident in February 1943.

Only 39.1 percent of Jewish men of military age (eighteen to forty-five) were taken into the Canadian armed forces, as compared with 41.4 percent of all Canadian men.[34] This included volunteers and conscripts drafted under the National Resources Mobilization Act of 1940.[35] Of the 16,441 Jewish men enrolled, 3,479 (or 21.2 percent) were NRMA men, or "Zombies" (draftees who refused to sign up for overseas service).[36] Although Jews constituted 1.46 percent of Canada's total population, they were 2.2 percent of its Zombies. Interestingly, Jews apparently had a lower level of service in the combat arms than the general population. The death rate of all personnel in the Canadian armed forces during the Second World War was 4.08 percent (42,042 of the total intake of 1,029,510 men[37]). Using the same calculation for the Jewish community, the death rate was 2.61 percent (429 deaths among 16,441 men). This was 62.25 percent of the national average, lower by more than one-third.

If Jews were less numerous in combat units, as these numbers suggest, it was probably because they tended to have a higher level of education than the general population. Of all Jewish students in Montreal Protestant schools in 1937, 25.46 percent attended high school, compared with 16.16 percent of all origins.[38] In Canadian universities, 58.97 percent of Jewish students were enrolled in professional schools (primarily medicine, law, pharmacy, and dentistry), compared with 45.94 percent of people of all origins.[39] In 1935–36 Jews constituted 14.18 percent of all medical students in Canadian universities, 9.05 of law students, 17.30 of dentistry students, 14.83 of pharmacy students, and 13.48 of architecture students.[40] Thus, on recruitment, many Jews could have been assigned to units that required higher levels of education, such as desk jobs and duties in rear-echelon units, where casualty rates were insignificant.[41] Under the army's personnel selection policy, by contrast, men with the least education ordinarily were sent to infantry units, where casualties were highest. Jews presumably could have volunteered for service at the front with the infantry, armour, engineers, and artillery, with the RCN, or with RCAF aircrew. The lower than average death rate suggests that the majority did not do so.

Some Jews seem to have had difficulties getting into specific regiments as officers, even if they were qualified. After waiting to be posted to a combat role, Ernest Sirluck and a colleague applied to a regimental camp where the commander, unaware of his religious affiliation, said to him, "You're just the kind of officers we want, not like those pesky Jews who keep trying to get in."[42] In the early stages of the war, regimental commanders apparently could bar Jews and other "undesirables" from entering their units as junior officers. Sirluck, however, accepted an invitation to join the Royal Regiment of Canada.

Because Jewish conscripts had suffered severe persecution in the armies of the Eastern European countries — from which virtually all of Canada's Jews had originated — they traditionally tended to avoid military service. Some families even maimed their young boys to keep them out of uniform.[43] Though circumstances in Canada were very different, this fear of the military probably still continued in many Jewish families. Sirluck believed that there was much antisemitism in the armed forces, and when he enlisted in the COTC, he wrote "none" for religion, fearing that if captured by Germans, "it wouldn't be pleasant to have 'Jew' on my name tag."[44] Possibly many other Jews did the same. Sirluck could have had O.D. (for "other denominations") on his identification discs like other Jews.

Though schooled in a strong pro-British environment, many Jews, like Canadians of other ethnic origins, may not have felt a deep enough personal loyalty to the British Empire to volunteer. Those on the far left would have regarded the war as imperialistic, at least until Germany attacked Russia on June 21, 1941. Early on, even Canadian Jews from Eastern Europe did not believe that the Germans — who in the First World War had behaved decently towards them — were capable of mass murder.

Jews had served in the Canadian Expeditionary Force in the First World War, a few earning distinction for bravery in battle. However, neither this nor the service of several hundred in the Jewish Legion (recruited by the British government to help liberate Palestine from the Turks in 1917) constituted a Canadian Jewish military tradition. It is perhaps not surprising, therefore, that the Jewish inclination to enlist did not exceed that of most other groups of Canadians. After the widespread revelations of the mass murders of Jews in late 1942, they could reasonably have been expected to enlist, but available data does not reveal recruitment patterns at that point.

Perhaps Jews should have wanted to join armies in their adopted countries to express gratitude for having full civil rights, which most of Canada's Jews — except those in Quebec — enjoyed.[45] It might even be argued that Jews who believed Canada to be antisemitic should have been motivated to join in order to strengthen claims for full acceptance.

Non-Jewish perceptions of Jewish recruitment varied. In September 1940, the *Winnipeg Free Press* slammed those who were alleging that "no Jews are joining the army, navy, or air force" as a "Goebbels gang" of baseless liars.[46] Canadians should know, the editorial continued, that at a recent Canadian Jewish Congress meeting, Jews declared "they were ready to dedicate their lives and all they possess to the cause of victory."[47] An RCMP report from Regina in December 1940 stated that "despite anti-semitism in Saskatchewan, instigated by Nazi agents, Jews continue to enlist. . . . [T]he military authorities in Ottawa know full well, Jewish-Canadians are enlisting away out of proportion to their quota of the population."[48] The report continued:

> The Jewish community as such has subscribed generously, away out of proportion, not because they consider it a "Jewish" war, but because they understand the clear cut policy of decency versus brute force much better than people who take their freedom too much for granted. . . .[49]

Another RCMP report, of July 1941, stated that out of the fifteen Jewish families in Kamsack, Saskatchewan, thirteen men had volunteered for active service overseas, with the Altman family contributing all five of their grown-up sons.[50]

The Congress was very sensitive to the continuing allegations that the Jewish community was shirking its military duty. Since 1940, it compiled data on the names, addresses, regimental numbers, and next of kin of Jewish servicemen. This enabled them to refute such charges. When, in the spring of 1943, Toronto alderman Leslie Saunders — a leading Orangeman and first-class bigot — publicly alleged "that the Jews of this country are not doing their duty in this war," the Congress replied that there were "well over 10,000 [Jewish] men and women in the service forces of Canada."[51] Saunders, on the basis of what he said were "official Government figures," insisted that Jews constituted only 0.6 percent of the "active forces" (by which he would have meant "general service" volunteers in the army, as well as RCAF and RCN personnel).

At this point in the war, the Congress claimed there were 4,677 Jews in the army, 4,009 in the RCAF, and 206 in the RCN, for a total of 8,892 Jewish personnel. This figure did not include what the Congress called draftees or others who might have missed its count, nor what it believed was a large number of Jewish men who did not attest to being Jews, "fearing the treatment that would be meted out to them by Nazis in the event of their being captured as prisoners."

On behalf of the Congress, A. B. "Archie" Bennett of Toronto challenged Saunders's assertions, stating that he was prepared to show the Congress' records to anyone prepared to tell the truth. While conceding that Saunders's figures could be true for the army in the early stages of the war, Bennett stated that they were outdated by July 23, 1942. February 1942 data "showed the Jews forming 1.7 percent of the RCAF." But a report published in 1943 by the Congress press officer, David Rome, stated that "the problem of enlistments declined in importance as conscription was more generally put into effect,"[52] suggesting that Jews, unlike most other Canadians, had less of a propensity to volunteer for military service. This has now been confirmed.[53]

The Congress' figures show that over the course of the war, Jews constituted 1.44 percent of the army, 2.61 percent of the RCAF, and 0.60 percent of the navy.[54] Thus only the Jewish contribution to the RCAF was larger than the Jewish percentage of the Canadian population (1.5 percent in 1941). In all, Jews constituted 1.6 percent of the total intake of personnel into the Canadian armed forces.

It is not clear why Jews preferred the RCAF. It did have higher educational standards than the army, more glamour, less spit and polish, and earlier involvement in the fight against Nazism. As for the low number of Jewish volunteers for the RCN, the perceptions of snobbery and some early antisemitism could have deterred all but the most ardent sailors from volunteering for the "senior service."

The Congress continued to encourage Jewish enlistments through pamphlets, advertisements, and by a widely distributed series of illustrated booklets about Jewish war heroes. In 1940, the Congress published a large-format leaflet entitled *They Answered Hitler's Challenge*, which showed photographs of some 120 Jewish men serving in the forces and offered regrets that it could not publish hundreds more.[55] Its western division distributed a lengthy questionnaire to communities to gather information on contributions to all manner of war work.[56]

In mid-July 1941,the Congress' officials summoned community leaders to a conference in Montreal to discuss ways of increasing enlistments. Caiserman urged that "an intensive and enthusiastic recruiting drive" be undertaken immediately.[57]

> Jewish parents must explain to their sons that Jews were never, in their long and tragic history, in such jeopardy as they are now. . . . Jewish youth of military age must set an example of patriotism by enlisting in great numbers for active service. They must do so voluntarily and must not wait to be conscripted. . . . Enlist NOW. Enlist for ACTIVE SERVICE. ENLIST, IF YOU ARE A JEW.

Typical of these appeals was a candidly worded leaflet in Yiddish whose motto was *"Siz a koved tsu kemfen unter der britisher fon kegn undzer soynim"* ("It is an honour to fight under the British flag against our enemies").[58] Addressed to *"brider und shvester"* ("brother and sister"), the leaflet continued:

> What must be our stand both as Canadian citizens and as Jews?. . . Jewish fathers and mothers! Encourage your children to join the Army! It is for you and for them an honour to fight for freedom, for Canada, for our people. . . . Jews! Take a rifle and sword in hand and go into battle for [your] country and people![59]

The results of these recruiting efforts are not clear. The memoirs of several rabbis and other Jewish communal leaders include no mention of this and, indeed, very little about the war itself.[60]

The Congress also urged Jews to vote "yes" in the plebiscite that was held in April 1942 to free the Dominion government from its pledge not to conscript men for overseas duty. "Canadian Jewry will most certainly vote Yes," Abraham M. Klein prophesied in a *Chronicle* editorial.[61] "A war against a ruthless foe cannot be fought with restrictive measures, and . . . with one hand tied behind one's back. Against totalitarian aggression, the only answer is total resistance!" Hitler's persecution of Jews was also mentioned, but Klein's justification for a "yes" vote was the government's need for a "full and unrestricted mandate in the prosecution of the war . . . and in that decision Canadian Jewry must play the part which both its Canadianism and its Judaism demand."[62] The call was heeded. Cartier — a densely Jewish area of Montreal — was one of Quebec's nine "yes" ridings.[63]

By mid-1942, reports were appearing in several Canadian newspapers about the mass murder of Jews in Europe. On June 16, the *Globe and Mail* published a front-page headline announcing that Lithuanian police had massacred sixty thousand Jews in Vilna. Two weeks later, the *Toronto Daily Star* published a story of another thirty thousand Jews being slaughtered in that country.[64] Soon reports were appearing regularly in the Canadian press, and by 1943 the destruction of the Jews of Europe was indisputable.

Absence of Serious Antisemitism

Antisemitism within the ranks was not a significant problem. Ex-servicemen, when interviewed fifty years later, testify that manifestations of antisemitism, even casual remarks, were rare among the troops and officers during training and in wartime combat.[65] Reports of such incidents were extremely unusual.

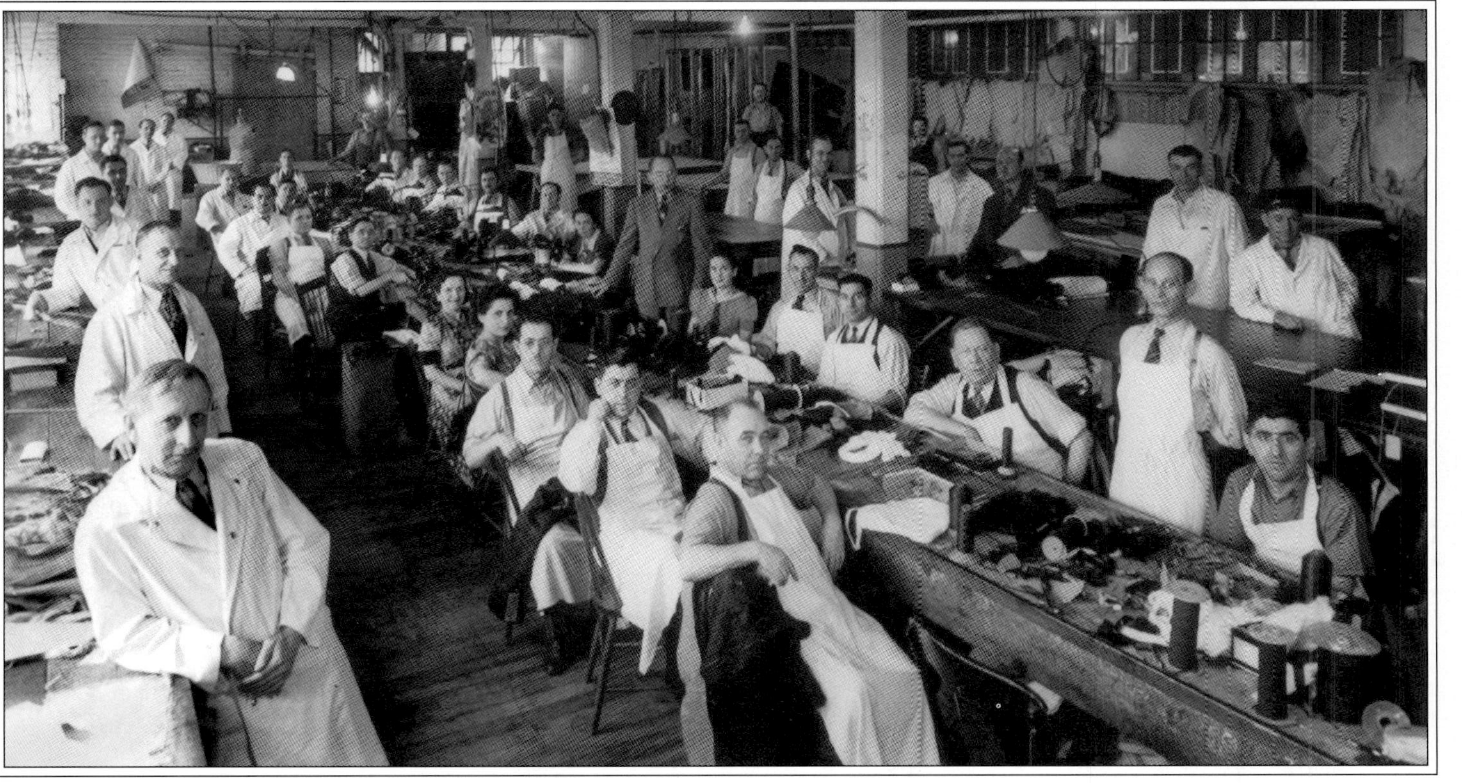

Workshop of the Atlantic Fur Company, Toronto, in the 1940s.

ONTARIO JEWISH ARCHIVES

Le Goglu depicts an innocent and unsuspecting French-Canadian girl at the mercy of a lustful Jewish storekeeper. "Le nombre de Montréalaises qui se plaignent des insultes des marchands juifs est incalculable." In this and many other cartoons, Jews have enormous mouths and noses, very thick lips, bushy eyebrows, and outlandish hair styles.

LE GOGLU, MAY 30, 1930

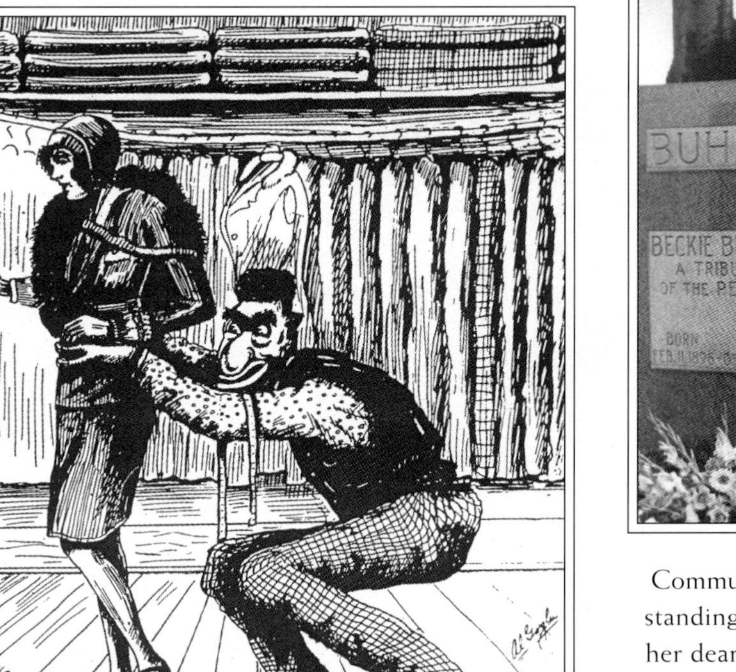

Communist activist Annie Buller standing beside the gravestone of her dear friend and sister activist, Becky Buhay, "a tribune of the people."

NATIONAL ARCHIVES OF CANADA

PA202170

ALWAYS BUY GENTILE!

BOYCOTT THE JEWS!

THE CANADIAN NATIONALIST

THE LIGHT OF TRUTH

SERVIAM

"Speak the truth and bend the bow"

Vol. 2, No. 2. | February, 1938. | Price 5 Cents

FREEMASONRY IS JEWISH!

SOME STARTLING INFORMATION FROM FREEMASONIC BOOKS

The Canadian Nationalist Party has taken a firm stand against Freemasonry because it is a subversive organisation controlled in its high degrees by unscrupulous Jews who are using it as a "Gentile front", in accordance with their plan for the subjugation of the world, as laid down in "The Protocols of the Learned Elders of Zion."

Protocol No. 4 reads:—

"Gentile Masonry blindly serves as a screen for us and our objects. . . . "

Protocol No. 11 reads:—

"For what purpose then have we invented this whole policy and insinuated it into the minds of the goys without giving them any chance to examine its underlying meaning? For what indeed if not in order to odtain in a roundabout way what is for our scattered tribe unattainable by the direct road. It is this which has served as the basis for **our organisation of secret Masonry** which is not known to, and aims which are not even so much as suspectd by,

THE SNAKE CHARMER!

The Canadian Nationalist, a Nazi publication issued in Winnipeg, featured many cartoons and headlines linking Jews to Masonry and Communism. This one was published in February 1938.

ONTARIO JEWISH ARCHIVES

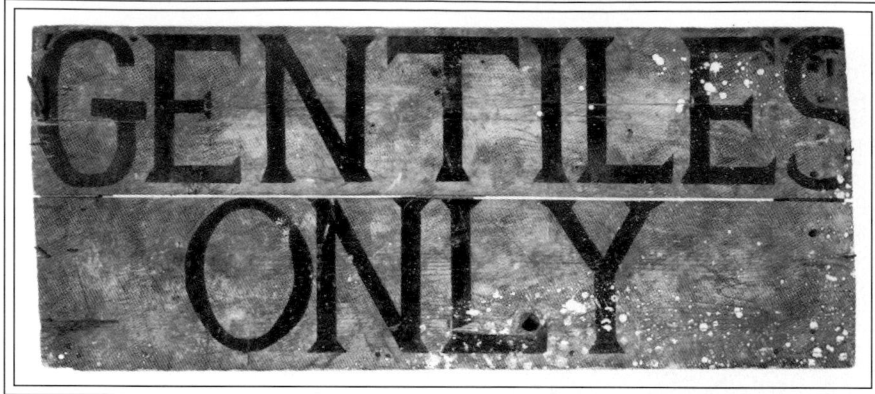

This sign, which was found near a resort northeast of Toronto, was typical of those posted at many places, before they became illegal.

ONTARIO JEWISH ARCHIVES

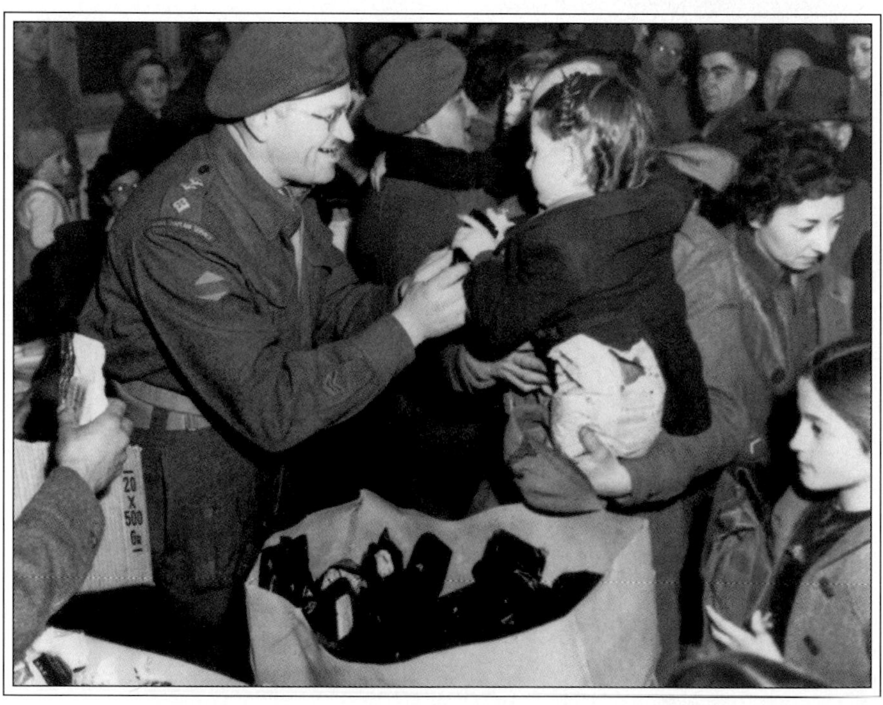

H/Captain Rabbi Samuel Cass, Canadian Army Jewish chaplain, and Canadian Jewish soldiers distributing gift bags to children at a Chanukah party in Antwerp, Belgium, December 6, 1944.

NATIONAL ARCHIVES OF CANADA PA202174

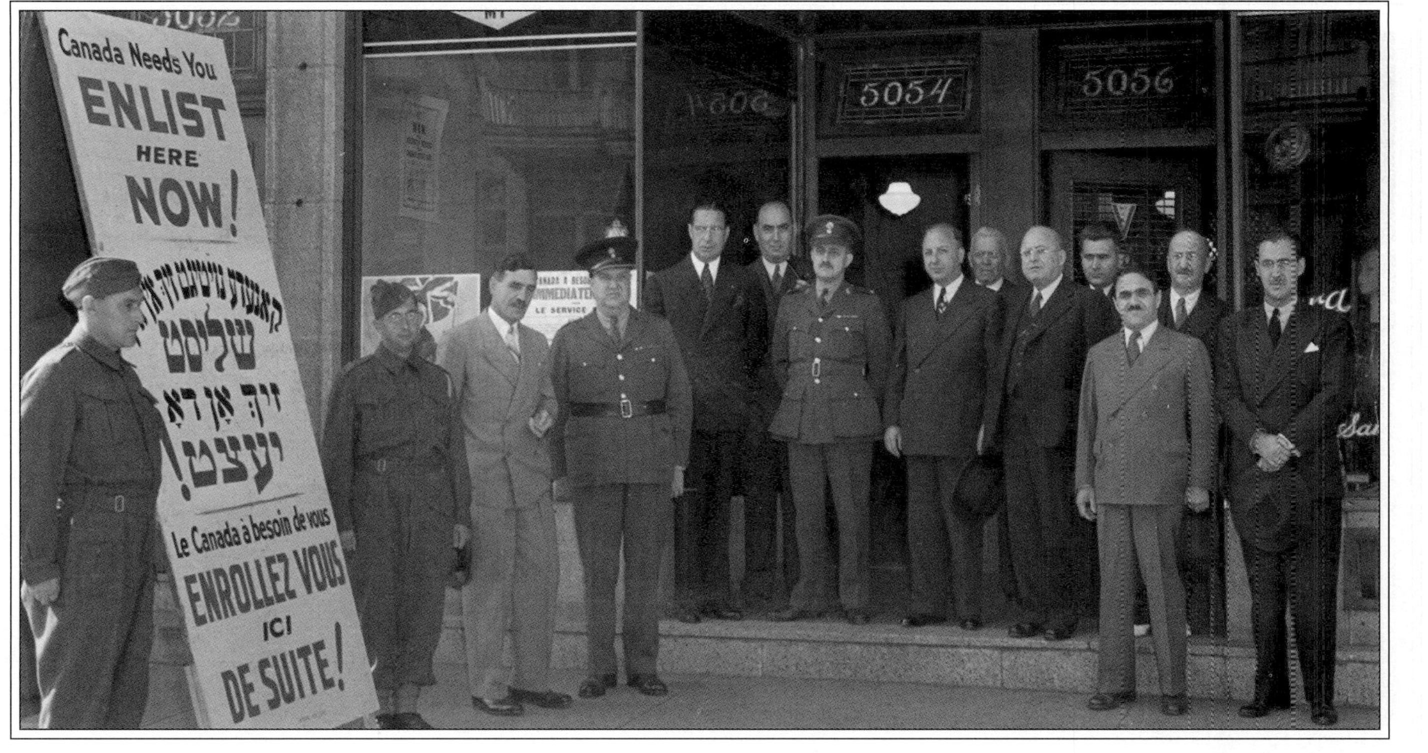

A recruiting office, opened in 1940 by the Canadian Jewish Congress on St. Lawrence Boulevard, in the heart of Montreal's Jewish quarter.

CANADIAN JEWISH CONGRESS NATIONAL ARCHIVES, MONTREAL

To encourage joining the armed forces, the Canadian Jewish Congress published a number of these biographies in its "Jewish War Heroes" series in 1944. This one on Willie Nelson was the third in the series.

CANADIAN JEWISH NATIONAL ARCHIVES, MONTREAL

Hananiah Meir Caiserman (middle) and Sam Lipshitz (right) of the *Toronto Hebrew Journal*, about to leave Montreal to visit Poland, 1945. Canadian Jewish Congress official David Rome stands on left.

CANADIAN JEWISH CONGRESS NATIONAL ARCHIVES, MONTREAL

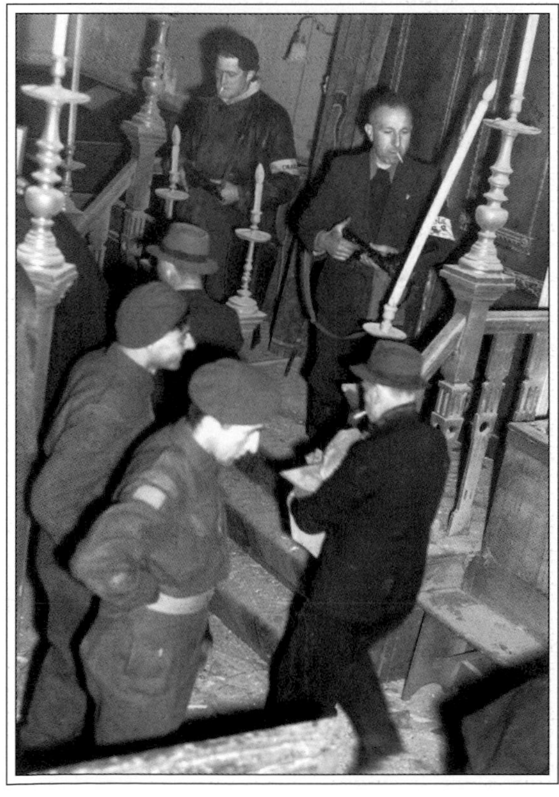

One of three photos taken by Canadian Army photographer Lieutenant G. B. Gilroy, who captioned them: "Collaborators and members of Dutch S.S. cleaning and repairing desecrated synagogue under supervision of Jewish members of 1st Canadian Division, Nijkirk, Netherlands, April 30, 1945." Armed members of Dutch resistance stand guard.

NATIONAL ARCHIVES OF CANADA PA116329

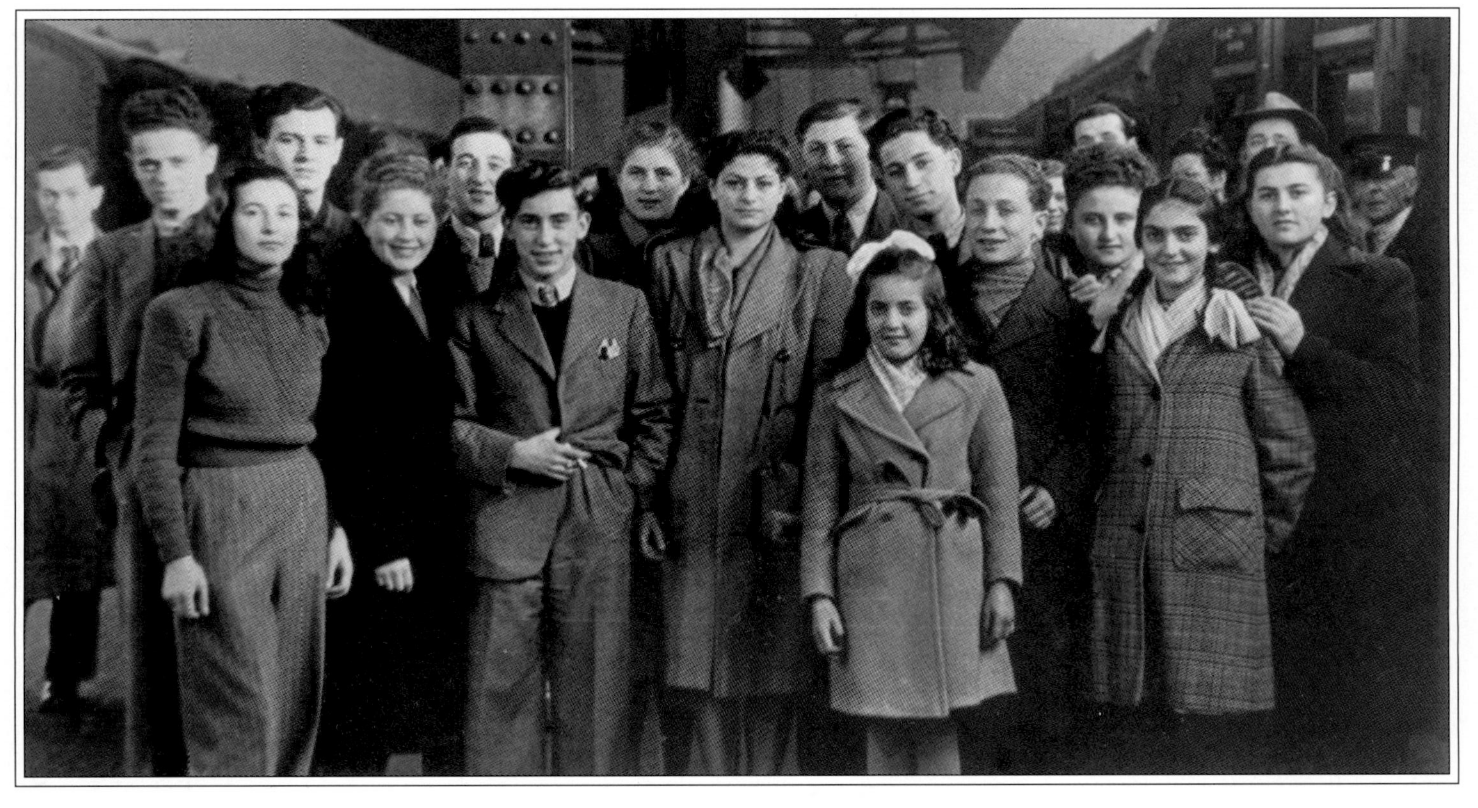

A group of Jewish war orphans at a London railway station before departure for Canada, September 1947.

CANADIAN JEWISH CONGRESS NATIONAL ARCHIVES, MONTREAL

A. M. Babb, the Saint John rabbi and unofficial chaplain to Jewish personnel stationed in southern New Brunswick, reported in June 1941 that six Jewish soldiers in the Dufferin and Haldimand Rifles, an NRMA unit composed of "Zombies," alleged that they had been subjected to humiliating treatment. Babb requested guidance "for the sake of Jewish lads that will eventually come to the Regiment," and five of the soldiers requested transfers to other units.[66] A young private in the 6th Light Anti-Aircraft Regiment complained to the army's chief rabbi, Gershon Levi, that his sergeant loaded him up with petty duties with the remark "Let the Jew do it."[67] Harold Rubin, a sergeant in the Governor General's Foot Guards, recalled "being subjected to a lot of embarrassment by some provocative Jew baiters," but as a six-footer weighing 190 pounds, he found that "after a few bouts with boxing gloves on, I gained the respect that was unobtainable in any other way."[68]

In letters from Jewish servicemen to their chaplains, there are very few indications of antisemitism. In fact, there was much evidence of harmony and camaraderie, like those expressed by a naval rating on the HMCS *Unicorn* (the navy's shore establishment at Saskatoon), who wrote that he was lonely because "at present I am the only Jewish boy on the *Unicorn*. . . . However, I can truly say that I have never met a finer bunch of men and officers than those serving with me."[69] Robert Rothschild, a Royal Military College graduate of 1936 and a regular force officer in the Royal Canadian Horse Artillery who later served as the key staff officer to Lieutenant General Guy Simonds,[70] stated that "throughout my military career, I never experienced a semblance of discrimination," though during the war he once overheard a fellow officer refer to another Jewish officer as "that Jewboy," for which the offender later apologized profusely to Rothschild.[71] A corporal serving with 4 C.I.B. Company, Royal Canadian Army Service Corps, wrote to Rabbi Samuel Cass to say that in his unit, "we [Jews] get along very well with our French Canadian camrades [sic]," and he wondered "why can it not be so on civvy street?" The answer, he said, was "we [must] not pretend to be better than they are . . . [and] show them our good points, rather than allow them to think of us as scoundrels. . . ."[72]

Edwin Goodman, who served through the war as an officer in the Fort Garry Horse, remembered that one Jewish trooper from Winnipeg punched out a sergeant who had called him a "fucking Jew" (and was sentenced by a court martial to twenty-eight days in cells for the offence).[73] Major Goodman, an attack-minded squadron commander, overheard one of his sergeants say "that fucking Jew will get us all killed if he keeps on this way." Goodman let it pass. In 1939 Goodman had tried to join the RCN's officer-training program, but the recruiting officer at its Toronto shore establishment, the HMCS *York*, asked him, "By the way, are you Jewish?" When he answered "yes," the officer stated: "I doubt that anyone who is Jewish will be an officer in this man's navy."[74] Ephraim Diamond, an RCN engineering officer, once overheard some of his fellow officers laughing about "a funny Jew." They quickly changed the subject when his presence was noted.[75]

Ben Dunkelman applied to join the RCN in 1939 and was told that their officer quotas were full. He waited to be called, but was told by a Jewish friend that "the navy would not accept Jewish officers."[76] As the "senior service," the RCN was somewhat precious in its attitude towards aspiring officer candidates for much of the Second World War. Barney Danson, a junior officer in the Queen's Own Rifles, remembered overhearing remarks that "the Jews are running the country." Rabbi Monson remembered being told by Jewish servicemen of antisemitism in the ranks of the Canadian army, especially remarks about Jews being the cause of the war. Still, such comments were relatively rare.

Some racial stereotyping, if not outright antisemitism, emerged nevertheless. Sam Finkelstein, an RCAF flight lieutenant attached to an RAF Pathfinder squadron in 1943, was asked by an English officer, Ray Hawken, to join him as navigator/bomb aimer in his Mosquito bomber. "Why do you want me?"

MITCHELL STERLIN

Born in Montreal in 1922, Mitchell Sterlin attended Shaarei Tzeddek (Gates of Righteousness) Synagogue, West Hill High School, and McGill University, where he studied biochemistry. He enlisted in the Canadian Officers Training Corps in 1939 and was commissioned in 1942. Sterlin was remembered affectionately by a fellow officer as "highly intelligent, but stocky, overweight and poorly coordinated."

He joined the Royal Canadian Regiment ("the Regiment"), trained in Britain, and landed in Italy in September 1943. On the eighth and ninth of December, near Ortona, having failed to receive the order to withdraw in the face of "very determined German counter-attack," he commanded 16 Platoon, D Company, in the defence of a strong point that was memorialized as Sterlin Castle in the records of the Regiment.

"Only 16 Platoon stood in the path of the enemy advance and it gave the Regiment one of its finest hours," an official regimental history states. A survivor of the battle said, "Lieutenant asked Finkelstein. "You're Jewish, aren't you?" replied Hawken. "Yeah, but so what?" said Finkelstein. "Well, all Jews are smart, and I want a smart navigator."[77] After further discussion, Finkelstein agreed. He and Hawken flew fifty missions together (twenty more than the stipulated amount), without getting a scratch, and became lifelong friends. Barney Danson remembered that in his regiment, the Queen's Own Rifles, commanding officers "often tried to push you into areas of perceived Jewish expertise. I recall at one time they wanted me to take over the running of the men's canteen. On another occasion they wanted me to become part of the group assessing individual capabilities, called Army Examiners."[78]

Some antisemitism was observed by non-Jewish soldiers. At a stand-easy before landing in Sicily in July 1943, Captain Ian Hodson of the Royal Canadian Regiment, which had several Jewish officers, was told by three of his subalterns, "You've got to get rid of [name withheld]." "Why?" said Hodson. "Because he's a Jew," they answered. "Listen," said Hodson, ending the informality, "if I ever hear that stuff again, you'll be on your way back home so damn fast your head will spin."[79] At the subsequent battle of Ortona in December, Lieutenants David Bindman and Mitchell Sterlin, both of them Jews, gave distinguished service before being killed in action.

Sterlin was everywhere, organizing the defence, looking after the wounded, the expenditure of ammunition." It was only a lack of sufficient ammunition to continue the fight that forced a withdrawal, though not before Sterlin's platoon killed numerous Germans.

Sterlin survived the battle but was killed in a fire fight at the Ortona crossroads nine days later. He is buried in the Moro River Cemetery near Ortona. Some Kingston veterans of the Regiment commissioned a painting, *The Defense of Sterlin Castle*, to commemorate the gallant action by Sterlin and his platoon. Immediately after that battle, he was nominated for the Military Cross, but once dead could not qualify. He was awarded instead a posthumous Mentioned in Dispatches and is remembered as a hero in the annals of the Regiment.

From J. T. B. Quayle, *In Action: A Personal Account of the Italian and Netherlands Campaigns in WW II* (Abbotsford, B.C.: Blue Stone Publishers, 1997); and David Rome, ed., *Canadian Jews in World War II, Part 1: Decorations* (Montreal: Canadian Jewish Congress, 1947): 80.

The Chaplains and Jewish Culture in the Armed Forces

All military personnel had to fill out a religious attestation on their enlistment forms. This created a moral problem for many Jews, who were fearful of both antisemitism in the army and mistreatment if they should be captured by German forces.[80] In the beginning, then, many Jews did not indicate their Jewishness, and some of those who did wanted "J," signifying Jew, or "H," for Hebrew, removed from their identification discs. It was soon decided that discs worn by Jewish personnel would carry the initials "O.D.," to signify "other denominations."

The WEC's correspondence indicates that, when possible, unit commanders co-operated with Jewish chaplains in allowing leaves for the High Holy Days or Passover. On many bases, Jewish personnel held services during Sunday Church Parade. None of the Jewish chaplains complained of official barriers to the performance of their duties. Chaplain David Monson, who asked for air transportation to visit a Jewish soldier stationed at a remote northern base, remembers an exchange with a senior officer: "You want to go all that way for just one Jew?" "Sir," Monson replied, "if there were more than one, I wouldn't ask." The request was granted.[81]

The chief Jewish chaplain of the Canadian army was Gershon Levi.[82] He was appointed in March 1941 and served until the end of the war. Under him there were Rabbis Samuel Cass, Isaac Rose, E. F. Mandelcorn, H. Gevantman, and David Monson, who served for various periods. Jews in the RCAF were ministered to by Rabbis David Eisen, Julius Berger, and Wilfrid Gordon. Like all chaplains, these rabbis were given honorary military rank. In addition, there were a number of part-time Jewish chaplains, usually rabbis of small communities like Saint John, who were called upon to visit personnel on nearby bases or to arrange regular religious services, burials, home visits, and social events. There was no Jewish chaplain in the Royal Canadian Navy, though Rabbi Abraham Greenspan in Halifax served some of its Jewish personnel on occasion.

Levi and his associates tried to reach as many Jewish servicemen as possible. In 1941 thousands of copies of a prayer book, prepared for Jewish members of His Majesty's Forces by Joseph H. Hertz, Chief Rabbi of the British Empire, were distributed. They also sent out *A Book of Jewish Thoughts* and a Jewish calendar showing festival dates, sabbath candle-lighting times, and other observances. These publications were small enough to fit easily into the servicemen's battledress pockets. The prayer book contained English and Hebrew versions of some daily, sabbath, and festival prayers extracted from the Orthodox *siddur* (prayer book), as well as a group of special prayers for the sick and wounded, for the dying, for those going into battle, and for those going overseas.[83] The prayers employed both the supplicant's Jewishness and his patriotism. The "Prayer for Men on Active Service" appealed to "God of the spirits of all flesh . . . [to] endow us with courage and steadfastness loyal to do our duty as true Israelites to King and Country, and to take our full share in this War for Freedom and Righteousness."[84] *A Book of Jewish Thoughts* included some inspirational passages from the Bible, the Mishna, the Talmud, and some modern Jewish religious writing. Jews in the RCAF also received a book of psalms specially printed in Canada for this purpose.

These books were popular among Jewish personnel. Although wide distribution was attempted, many servicemen who were missed wrote to Levi asking for copies. Later, many expressed their appreciation. Ordinary Seaman Abe Halpern, serving on the HMCS *Bytown* (the navy's shore establishment in Ottawa), stated that "the Prayer Book will be little used, [though] a Book of Jewish Thoughts and the Calendar will be of some value to me. . . . So far as religion is concerned, I am an agnostic."[85]

To other servicemen, it meant a lot to have these books. Their Jewish identity and self-understanding were reinforced. Halpern, after declaring his agnosticism, stated:

> But so long as there exists a "Jewish Problem"; so long as Jews are ridiculed, hated and discriminated against; so long as Jews are not given a country for themselves, in which they may prove their ability to build and create; so long as Jews remain disunited and tricked into complacency by our so-called tolerant democracies; so long as conditions exist which breed antisemitism — I am a Jew.

Ordinary Seaman Louis Roter, serving aboard the HMCS *Orillia*, thanked Levi: ". . . it is very nice of you for thinking of us Jewish boy's [*sic*] in the fighting forces."[86] Herbert Vineberg, of the RCAF, expressed his appreciation thus: "when I received the siddur [Prayer Book] . . . [I did] not [feel] a religious glow or even the sparkling of a dead or dormant religious philosophy. It was just a comfortable pick-up that indicates that my people do not forget their soldiers. I'd never have believed it."[87]

In letters received by Levi in 1942, some Jews expressed thanks because the books reinforced their faltering sense of Jewishness. S. S. Berlin, a Royal Canadian Navy Volunteer Reserve lieutenant then stationed at navy headquarters in Ottawa, wrote, "I was actually thrilled with the receipt of this gift. . . . [T]his little [prayer] book is bound to provide the "lift" without which it sometimes becomes so difficult to carry on."[88]

Others needed more. Pilot Officer John Marcus, posted to a night fighter squadron as a radio observer, wrote a long letter to Levi from "somewhere in England" stating: "Before I left Montreal I called you, but I also would have liked to have seen you, had a chat with you and asked you for your blessing. . . ."[89]

Levi and Cass even received requests from Protestant chaplains for the prayer book and the *Book of Jewish Thoughts*. In the absence of a Jewish chaplain, the Protestants were officially responsible for Jewish personnel.[90] Levi routinely left a supply of the prayer books with Protestant chaplains for distribution.[91] Some also wanted them for their own interest.[92] One chaplain wrote to Levi, "As Protestant Padre here I have given out the booklet to the best of my ability and will be pleased to continue doing so."[93] Sometimes requests came from other non-Jews.[94] Occasionally, the base education officer or the commanding officer's adjutant would see to the distribution.[95] Hon. Flight Lieutenant David J. Lane, part-time Presbyterian Protestant chaplain at RCAF base No. 12 Elementary Flying Training School, and at No. 31 Air Navigation School near Goderich, Ontario, wrote to Levi in March 1942 that he had not only "distributed these three [Prayer] books to the boys of the Jewish faith, [but also] called them together and spoke about getting together and reading the service with each other, and also promised them any help I was able to give them."[96]

Hospitality and Making Contact

Because they were living in barracks, eating army food, training to fight, and subject to tough discipline, recruits were grateful for sanctuary in a Jewish home, with friendly faces — and familiar food![97] The Halifax community, judging from the testimony of many servicemen and the records of its Servicemen's Centre, was exceptionally hospitable to the Jewish boys. One airman wrote Levi "to tell you of the wonderful way in which the Jewish people of Halifax treated me along with many other Jewish servicemen. . . . Mrs. Finberg, along with her wonderful husband, treated many of us like her own children so it was no wonder she was 'Mom' to us. It was swell to have a good Jewish meal for a change. . . ."[98] Ordinary Seaman Jack Bernstein echoed the same sentiment: "The Jewish people of Halifax, led by the eminent Rabbi Greenspoon [Abraham Greenspan], are very hospitable to all the servicemen, and are doing all they possibly can, to make us feel at home."[99] The Halifax Jewish community, especially its women's organizations, responded generously to the needs of Jewish personnel who trained at nearby bases or had a layover there on their way to Britain. In February 1940, the Hebrew Community Council of Halifax was established for the war effort and the local Jewish women ensured that Jewish service personnel were invited to their homes for High Holy Day meals. They helped organize and staff the heavily used hostel for them, cooking kosher meals for hundreds of soldiers at a time.[100]

Other communities were just as accommodating. From St. John's, Newfoundland, an RCAF serviceman named Monson reported to Levi in March 1942 that he had "met most of the Jewish families here and they are like all Newfoundlanders exceptionally hospitable. Mrs. Sheffman, about whom I am sure you have heard, has been very nice to me and [I] will be spending at least one Seder night at her home."[101] Naval rating Bernard M. Saipe wrote from St. John's that the local synagogue "is indeed the meeting place for the boys in the various services that are stationed here and though the Jewish community is small they have certainly opened their hearts to us."[102] Jacob Feldman, a trainee on an airframe mechanic's course at an RCAF station near St. Thomas, Ontario, wrote to Levi in February 1942: "I think you would be happy to know that the Jewish families in London, Ontario, have been treating the Jewish boys in uniform very decent and we really appreciate their hospitality."[103]

There was an apparent comfort factor in being with other Jews and in keeping rough track of them. Warrant Officer Sarah Lacle reported to Levi in November 1941 that "Flt./Lieut. Durbin has left Paulson and is at Lethbridge. I would have been only too pleased to convey your regards, I also found him to be very nice."[104] There are numerous references in the letters of thanks to Levi to the fact that the correspondent knows of other Jews on his base who had not received books and would like to, of Jewish servicemen posted elsewhere, and of Jewish friends and kinfolk elsewhere in the services.[105]

Max Greenberg, on an RCAF station, wrote in April 1942: "I believe that all the Jewish boys on this station have received the Prayer Book. If I hear of any new fellows that have not received one, I will ask them to write you."[106] "I am at present home on embarkation leave," M. Charton wrote. "I shall be only too glad to have any Jewish members of the Armed Forces not in receipt of this book write."[107] Levi, therefore, was at the centre of a vast Canada-wide network of information on what might be called Jewish military geography. He clearly utilized these sources to reach as many Jews as he could — and not just to ensure that they received the books, but also to encourage them to attend services, to urge them to observe Passover and the High Holy Days, and to try to arrange family visits to nearby Jewish communities.

Interviews with ex-servicemen confirm that Jews often avidly sought out other Jews, especially relatives and home-town boys. Barney Danson looked out for his boyhood friend Fred Harris, also with the Queen's Own Rifles, until Harris was killed on D-Day. Aaron Palmer, a sergeant on the headquarters ordnance staff of the Third Canadian Division, recalled his joy in meeting another Jewish soldier from his home town of Kingston just by accident at a depot in France. "Wasn't that something!" he exclaimed.[108]

Overseas

After Jewish servicemen reached bases in Britain, chaplains followed. Levi and Cass went over in 1943, and Rose and Monson in 1944. Overseas, they lacked the support system that was so available in Canada, but Jewish Canadians were being warmly welcomed by British Jews. In March 1942, Pilot Officer John Marcus wrote to Levi thanking him for the prayer book. He already had been given one by an English rabbi-chaplain named Marcovitch: "He had organized a club at his synagogue of which you no doubt have already heard about from other members of the RCAF overseas. The Jewish women and girls come to entertain us and a jolly time is had. There are games and dancing, also refreshment."[109]

In fact, Marcus had taken the initiative: "I enquired a few days ago where I could find him from some Jewish people I went out of my way to meet, and they also told me that there are about 12 or more Canadian Jewish soldiers stationed near here, and I shall try to get to meet them." The warm reception he got from one family embarrassed him. Some host families with marriage-age daughters especially welcomed single Canadian and American Jewish servicemen.[110] Barney Danson met his future wife at the home of one of these hospitable British Jews.[111]

By late 1942, some Jews, most likely cognizant of the confirmed reports of mass murders in Eastern Europe, fought with extra fervour. Sam Finkelstein remembered having a special feeling when he released bombs over German targets. Occasionally, much to his pilot's horror, Finkelstein would break radio silence, shout curses in German, and quickly switch off. Barney Danson remembered that as a Jew, he felt pressure to perform better, but he did not think he had to have special courage. When he was wounded, he thought, Oh, hell, I let the guys down. Edwin Goodman, however, had mixed feelings: "I knew that they [Germans] had killed my co-religionists and friends, but when I got the papers and personal effects of some of the Germans we killed, I felt compassion." Morris Lazarus, who served in the Italian campaign with the Canada–U.S. Special Service Force, an elite parachute unit, wanted to get at the enemy and volunteered for all the combat he could get.[112]

Moe Usher, an RCAF wireless operator/gunner who flew on bombing missions from an RAF base in Northern Scotland, wrote to one of his brothers in Montreal: "If . . . my being over here helps to let youngsters like Danny [a nephew] soil their hands without fear of shadows overhead — it will be well worth fighting for. . . . I have often thought of the contrast between the kids over here and back home," he continued. "It is not very pleasant and the thought of my family going thru the suffering endured by civilians here makes me thank God you are all so far away."[113] Cognizant of his short odds of surviving much longer, he sent money to a brother in Montreal to buy a watch for his girlfriend, Shirley. Moe and his crewmates were killed soon afterwards, when their plane went down while they were returning from a mission in late March 1942.

Some Jewish servicemen took considerable pride in the fact they were doing well. RCAF Corporal Fitterman, in training near Brantford, wrote proudly to Levi in August 1941:

> [You would be proud of] *our* men in the service . . . it will please you to learn that at present we have 18 and their record is beyond reproach. . . . [It is] truly a good example to others, that whatever we do, we do well. Last week we had "wings parade." The two Jewish pupils, Sgt. Pilot Markus (Toronto) and Gasco (Montreal) finished very close to the "top" and [were] posted for overseas duty, and these lads should be heard from, real fighting spirit and born leaders."[114]

Chaplains overseas kept in touch with some of the families of the wounded, the missing, and the prisoners of war. One mother with two sons in the army fighting in Italy wrote to Capt. Isaac Rose, Jewish chaplain to the Canadian forces in Italy, in September 1944:

> I'm very anxious to hear which one you've seen as my youngest son was wounded while in action on Sept. 3rd & we just received the telegram . . . I do understand that you are very busy but I am a mother & very anxious to know exactly how he is & your letter came at an opportune moment so if its Johny Levine, 5th Can. Infantry R.C.A.S.C. [Royal Canadian Army Service Corps] you've seen I wonder if you'd look in at the one in the Hospital for me. He's 0-191 SPR Lawrence Levine, 3rd Arm'd Reconnaissance Reg't. Governor General's Horse Guards. "God" bless you for the good work your [*sic*] doing. . . .[115]

A sister wrote regarding Pvt. Max Dankner: "We received a telegram notifying us that he was severely wounded other than that we have not received word. . . ."[116] A brother wrote regarding Pvt. William Klein, of the Irish Regiment of Canada, "I received a telegram last week stating William was

FLIGHT-LIEUTENANT SYDNEY S. SHULEMSON, DSO, DFC

Sydney Shulemson was born in Montreal in October 1915. He attended B'nai Jacob (Sons of Jacob) Synagogue, the Jewish People's School, Bialik, Commercial High School, Baron Byng, and McGill University. He enlisted in the RCAF in 1941. He received his wings and commission at Aylmer, Ontario, in July 1942, and trained in reconnaissance at Summerside before embarking for Britain in September. He was attached to various fighter squadrons and flew numerous sorties.

In February 1944, he was awarded the Distinguished Service Order for his participation in an attack on enemy shipping, an almost unique honour for an officer of his low rank. The citation read as follows:

This officer has completed numerous sorties, including several successful attacks on shipping. He is a skilful, courageous, and determined leader, whose example has inspired all. In January, 1944, he participated in an attack on a convoy consisting of enemy merchant vessels and four armed ships. In the face of considerable anti-aircraft fire, the attack was well pressed home, and a medium-sized merchant vessel and two smaller merchantmen were hit and set on fire; hits were also obtained on two of the escort ships, one of them appearing to blow up. As course was set for home, one member of the formation was attacked by a fighter and sustained damage. Flying Officer Shulemson immediately turned and joined the fight. By skilful and daring tactics he drew away the attacker, thus enabling his comrade to fly clear. Some 18 minutes later the enemy aircraft was forced to terminate the engagement and Flying Officer Shulemson flew on to base and landed safely in spite of a burst tire on one of the landing wheels. Throughout the sortie this officer displayed inspiring leadership, great skill and courage.

A year later, while flying with the Buffalo Beaufighter Squadron, Shulemson won the Distinguished Flying Cross for displaying similar courage under fire. For a junior officer, earning the DFC *and* the DSO was recognition second only to the Victoria Cross.

David Rome, ed., *Canadian Jews in World War II, Part 1: Decorations* (Montreal: Canadian Jewish Congress, 1947): 1–2.

wounded in action on Aug. 31. As yet I have not received any information as to the extent of his wounds. . . . [M]y dad does not know about it, nor do I intend to let him know until Bill is quite well, and on his way home."[117]

A mother wrote:

> My son has been wounded. The extent of the injury is as yet unknown and I'm terribly anxious. Please Sir, try to visit him as soon as possible as he is all alone and I am very concerned as to details. . . . I am a widow . . . and my three sons are in the Service, two being overseas. Gabriel is my youngest so please do your utmost to cheer him up and pray for my young son.[118]

Mrs. S. Bach, of Hamilton, wrote at length concerning her son, Dave: ". . . my heart goes out to him, what would I not give to get a glimpse of his dear face, also my oldest son who is in Ireland some where. . . . Yes Sir we are very proud of our dear sons, as they are some of the very best, never think of themselves, but who they left behind."[119] She continued:

> I must tell you Sir that we are very Orthodox Jew. . . my Hubby also Sons never ate *trafe* [nonkosher food] until the Boys went to the Army and Air Force, and the both boys and their Dad davened [prayed] untill [*sic*] they went into the Army, my Husband does yet; and I keep a very *froom* [religiously observant] House, you see my Grand Father on my Dear Mothers side was Rove [distinguished rabbi] . . . and I like to keep it up . . . and my Dave writes to me that when he will please God come home safe and well he will begin where he left off. . . .

From Owen Sound, Mary Nidelman wrote to Rabbi David Eisen in July 1942 concerning her son, Bernard, "our beloved and only son . . . who has been reported missing in air operations overseas."[120] She continued, "We still cling to the hope that we may yet hear favourable news in the near future, but if that is not to be, we will bear up, and be proud that our son was bravely helping his country." Mary Lozdon wrote to Cass about the loss of her husband, Morris Lozdon, who was with the Royal Regiment of Canada and whose body was never found after the Dieppe raid in August 1942: "[U]ntil I hear further I shall keep on praying to God, as do our three little children. . . . To lose such a man is more than any one can bear, & especially as young as he was, he was just 31 yrs & had ten hard lean years of marriage but we took it on the chin, & now this."[121]

The chaplains also visited Jewish personnel on their bases and kept up an astonishingly active correspondence with many of them. In the process, of course, they received complaints and requests for support for compassionate leave, and provided moral support in cases of family problems back home. News of sickness, business reversals, delinquent children, and marriage breakdown were reported to the chaplains, who did their best to comfort the servicemen and limit the damage to their morale.

Cass also had to deal with "matters involving extra-marital sex relationships of married men and the personal indulgences of non-married men and women . . . very often leading to complicated and difficult situations. . . ."[122] One can only guess what he could say to the trooper serving with the 28 Armoured Regiment, who received this letter (known in the forces as a "Dear John") from his Toronto fiancée:

> I am very sorry to have to say this, but it happened so, that I met a fellow and I find he is the one for me. Don't think that I was going out all this time with other fellows, though I met this fellow and I feel sure of myself in fact I know he is the one. Do you want me to send back the ring to you, if so let me know. It's up to yourself. I'm terribly sorry if this is going to hurt you, but it's better that it happened now then later. I'm sure you understand. . . .[123]

Or to this guardsman serving with the 21 Armoured Regiment, Governor General's Foot Guards, who reported to Cass that he had heard that his English wife "wasn't behaving herself and . . . refused to even treat me as a husband."[124] Other soldiers' letters were, no doubt, much easier to deal with. A private serving with 4 Canadian Infantry Brigade, Royal Canadian Electrical and Mechanical Engineers, informed Cass that he planned to get married while on leave and wanted to know "the dates when weddings are permitted according our law during . . . April and May . . . in case my leave should occur during the forbidden days [the period between Passover and Shavuot] for Chupes [weddings]."[125]

Religious Services

The chaplains made great efforts to arrange services for Jewish soldiers at the military bases on the high holidays of Rosh Hashana and Yom Kippur. At camps in British Columbia in August 1942, Cass tried to respond to entreaties from Pvt. Philip Levine of the Brockville Rifles (also an NRMA unit composed of "Zombies"), who informed Cass that "At yesterday's Jewish Church Parade in which the three regiments were present in force, a thorough discussion was held with a view to holding Rosh Hashana and Yom Kippur services here in

Prince George. There is a keen desire by the greatest majority of the men concerned to hold these services."[126] A cantor was needed, even though "among us there are a few who could help out under the direction of a qualified reader, and these incidentally are the men who have been conducting our weekly service." Levine had been searching for local Jewish religious resources and had found that "there is a Jewish resident in town who has a 'sefer torah' and a 'shofer' which he has offered to us." He stressed to Cass "that there is the will of over 100 Jewish men to consider in this project and it is therefore deserving of your most earnest consideration."

Unable to locate a rabbi to conduct the services, Cass wired the Protestant chaplain, Captain Brandt, at the Prince George military camp, pleading, "I must, therefore, ask of you that you supervise the arrangements for these services and encourage the men to take various parts of the service, which I am sure they can do." He added:

> I know that you will do everything within your power as a Chaplain to make the men feel that they can carry on under their own power and experience the sacred traditions of their religion while carrying out the highest duty that they owe to their country and mankind. . . . I am sending you religious messages in the nature of sermonettes. . . . May I invite you personally to add to these services by giving them a message of your own."[127]

Despite Brandt's misgivings — probably because of his unfamiliarity with the Jewish faith — he, apparently, did as he was asked.[128]

A similar problem arose at the RCAF station at Prince Rupert, where, as Cass was informed by Flying Officer O. Fleishman, there were some twenty Jewish boys[129] but no one capable of conducting the services. Cass wired him saying that he was sending twenty-five sets of "the Adler Mahzor" and a suggested outline for the various services by express, as well as some "religious messages . . . which may be read by yourself or someone you appoint." He instructed Fleishman:

> [I]n conducting the services, I would urge you to allocate different parts to several men so that everyone will have an opportunity to participate in them. . . . Although these arrangements may seem to be a very hasty makeshift, it is really not so. We cannot expect in the course of our duties in wartime to carry on as usual, and they will really experience all the more the sacredness of our High Holidays through their personal efforts on their behalf.

He wired also to Pvt. A. Rosner of the Winnipeg Grenadiers, then stationed at Terrace, that Fleishman would be holding services at Prince Rupert. Cass urged that if he and other Jews there could not attend, "your men will carry on under your own power, and will experience the sacredness of the traditions of the High Holidays all the more intensely because you have put forth every effort in personal participation."[130]

It was obviously difficult for the chaplains and the WEC to monitor all the bases on which Jewish servicemen were located. Sometimes nearby communities took the initiative. In March 1943, Archie Dover, a member of Cornwall, Ontario's Beth-El congregation, informed the Congress that there were twenty-five Jewish soldiers at the local training centre:

> We are only too happy to take care of them in our synagogue, and have a service for them, but we are wondering if there would be some way of appointing our local Shochet [ritual slaughterer] to be an assistant Chaplain and have him conduct services at the Training Centre on Sundays for the Jewish boys.[131]

Cass discovered that "there are fifteen boys from Toronto and several of them insisted that they attend Synagogue Parade only, [but] I don't believe it is wise to have Mr. Levine [Cornwall's *shokhet*] conduct service in the Camp with such a small number. . . if the boys still insist [on] attending Synagogue on Sunday."[132]

Gershon Levi organized weekly services wherever possible. In February 1942, he informed commanding officers of the RCAF stations in the Trenton area that "arrangements have been made for the conduct, at the synagogue in Belleville, of Religious Services each week for RCAF personnel of the Jewish faith stationed at Mountain View, Belleville and Trenton. The services begin at 1100 hours, and last for 30 minutes." He requested posting of notices and transportation for personnel attending.[133]

The Jewish chaplains, like others, had to bury the dead, see that graves were marked with the Star of David, and write to bereaved families. Gershon Levi was especially concerned that all Jews be identified. "Charlet is definitely Jewish," he wrote to Cass in January 1945, "whatever the burial return may say, [but] Sgt. Kaughman does not appear in my records, nor in those of Congress, and does not look as if it should."[134] Levi designed two different temporary Star of David markers made of boards and sticks for Jewish soldiers' graves.

Reuben Slonim, rabbi at Toronto's Beth Hamedrash Hagadol (McCaul Street Shul), conducted services every Sunday at the British Commonwealth

Air Training station at St. Thomas for about one hundred Jews. With the help of one of his "parishioners," Sam Brownstein, and the *shul*'s women's auxiliary, he provided elaborate Passover seder fare for the boys, including matzoh ball soup, gefilte fish, roast chicken, carrot tzimmes, prune compote, nuts, and sweets.[135] On his Sunday visits, in company with Brownstein, Slonim brought salamis, pickles, corned beef, baked beans, "and all the other marvellous kosher ambrosia from the Spadina Avenue delicatessens. . . . Nothing was too good for them: *foile verenikes, kamish broit,* knishes filled with potato or kasha, almond rolls and honey cake, pepper fish with plenty of sugar, according to the recipe of the Jews of Lodz and Warsaw."[136]

Parcels from home or from the many Jewish support groups were most welcome, especially if they contained food with a *yiddish tam* (that special Jewish flavour). Jewish veterans' eyes light up, even after fifty years, at the thought of food. Barney Danson and Edwin Goodman relished receiving *vurst*, which had to be specially packed in parafin wax. To this day, Danson remembers regretfully having to throw away one *vurst* that he wrongly thought had gone bad. (It had just matured, he later realized.) In a letter to his mother in December 1944, Aaron Palmer wrote: "Just received Aunt Hendah's parcel and the Voorsht that Aunt Leah sent. Everything came in fine condition."[137] To another donor, he wrote: "Received your lovely parcel. . . . Boy what a treat. All those fancy nuts, peanut brittle and chocolates."[138] Harold Rubin, along with another Ottawa Jewish soldier, went on a kosher delicatessen "crawl" one night in Leeds. "We couldn't help comparing these English establishments to Barney Weiss's delicatessen on Rideau Street," he remembered.[139]

One non-Jewish observer witnessed Jewish families visiting their servicemen at a camp north of Toronto just before the soldiers' departure:[140]

> Every mother and grandmother had a huge food parcel for a son or grandson. . . . I have never seen such a feast in all my life. There was every kind of Jewish delicacy you can name. . . . Today I still remember the feeling of wonder and humility that hit me as I stood at that gate in front of those Jewish parents.

Passover seders celebrating the Exodus from Egypt required elaborate arrangements. In early April 1944, Cass wrote to the commanding officer of the base at Debert, Nova Scotia, requesting "adequate provisions for personnel of Jewish faith to celebrate the Feast of Passover in Debert Camp." He also wrote with elaborate instructions to the messing officer for the preparation of matzoh meal balls, *charoseth*, sponge cake, matzoh meal pancakes, matzoh fry, and matzos with scrambled eggs.[141] He asked "that Ordnance supply this mess with new dishes and cutlery, that have not been used before, as also pots, pans, etc. for preparing meals. In addition to the usual setting at table, wine goblets will be needed. . . ." Prepared gefilte fish and smoked meat were sent by the WEC. For Passover observances in 1945, some 800 pounds of matzohs and 553 pounds of smoked meat were sent for Jewish servicemen in Canada.[142]

Cass, recognizing the importance of Passover seders, took pains to organize these celebrations in the most difficult of circumstances:

> [Rabbi] Cass told me that as Passover in 1945 was about to begin, troops of the First Canadian Army were poised to cross the Rhine. Needless to say, all the troops — and especially the Jews — were apprehensive and jittery about entering Germany. Cass contacted General Crerar directly and stressed the importance of providing a seder and Crerar, bless his heart, immediately contacted CMHQ in London and the necessary food was flown over from London. Cass said it did wonders for the morale of the Jewish troops.[143]

"I shall always remember," Cass wrote in his war diary, "the Passover Sedorim in the only structure left standing at Cleve where our men were marshalled to cross the Rhine and storm the east bank, taking matzohs and provisions with them from the Seder tables. . . ."[144]

Jewish Service Personnel and Holocaust Survivors

Most service personnel were not likely to have access to information on the wider war and the disasters that had befallen European Jewry. In one book issued in 1944 for educational purposes, *The Battle of Brains: Canadian Citizenship and the Issues of the War*, soldiers were informed that small children were made to read *Der Stürmer*, "which is full of abuse against Jews," and that "a systematic cultivation of a hatred of Jews has helped considerably to unite the German nation."[145] By the time this work was published, most of Europe's Jews had been destroyed; but the book's readers were informed only that in the concentration camps, "no Jews are accepted as sick; they could only be 'well' or 'dead.'"[146]

By late 1944, however, when the Canadian forces moved into Holland, Jewish servicemen began providing assistance to Holocaust survivors in various locations. In December 1944, about five hundred children evacuated to Britain from German concentration camps were given food, chocolates, and toys at Chanukah parties, and supplies were sent to children still at Belsen.[147] Cass also reported to the principal chaplain (Protestant) that Chaplains

Gevantman and Rose, then stationed in Holland, "were very active in making the . . . Jewish festival a happy one for Jewish children. . . . Through the Jewish Coordination Committee in Amsterdam, sweets were distributed to upwards of 3,000 children in the country."[148] Jewish communities in Amersfoort, Apeldoorn, Nijmegen, and Amsterdam were also given assistance, and "troops were notified of all these functions and attended at the locality nearest their Units." Thirteen days after the town of Nijkerk was liberated by forces of Canada's 1st Division on April 17, 1945, Jewish soldiers happily observed armed members of the Dutch resistance supervising the clean-up of a local synagogue by captured local Nazi collaborators and SS men.[149]

For the fifteen weeks immediately following the end of hostilities, Cass and Rose ran courses each week on Jewish history, religion, and culture for thirty men still in Holland.[150] Between August and November 1945, Cass, Gevantman, and Rose gave lectures that were intended "to help the soldier refresh his knowledge of Judaism and . . . to discuss the application of the ideals of Jewish religion and culture to the soldier's re-establishment in civil life." Those who took these courses visited Jewish families in Amsterdam and toured its Jewish hospital, which housed many concentration camp survivors. Course discussions focused on antisemitism, Zionism, Holocaust survivors, and the postwar condition of Jews in Holland. Many highly appreciative letters were received from servicemen. One wrote that through this contact "with Jewish men and women who witnessed and survived the Nazi bestiality, . . . I have learned the meaning of life. . . ."[151]

For some Jewish service personnel, their Holocaust consciousness emerged when they searched for relatives in Eastern Europe at the end of the war. Pvt. J. Chackowitz, who had not heard from his parents or any other family members in his Polish home town of Kosow-Telaki since 1940, applied to Cass for compassionate leave to try to find them.[152] In June 1945, Guardsman Julius Gosevitz wrote asking for Rose's help in getting information from the International Red Cross about his wife's family in Brest-Litovsk.[153] Pvt. W. Liebovitz requested permission to spend leave with an aunt and uncle living in Paris.[154] A private serving in the Toronto Scottish Regiment in Holland asked Cass for help in locating a Jewish couple whose last known address was in Antwerp: "The request was made in a letter received from an aunt in Toronto, that I do what I can to discover the fate of Mrs. Weiss and her children. . . ."[155] If successful in their applications, these soldiers would have learned all too well what happened to the Jews of Poland and France. But they were only a few, and the majority of servicemen returned to Canada, very likely still unaware of the true dimensions of the Holocaust.

Some Jews serving with the Canadian army in Holland only saw firsthand what the Holocaust had wrought in that country. Only a day after Westerbork concentration camp was liberated by Canadian troops on April 12, 1945, Rabbi Cass was walking through it talking to as many of its surviving inmates as he could, and then conducting an emotional religious service.[156] A gunner serving with 13 Field Regiment, Royal Canadian Artillery, reported to Cass that when he was in Gorredojt, Friesland, he visited a synagogue: "Sir the windows were broken but the ash was still up and there are five sefer torah in it . . . and the Torahs are on the floor it is a shame to leave them like that."[157] A British Army gunner, serving with the 125 L.A.A. Regiment, Royal Artillery, reported that on seeing the "disgusting mess" inside the synagogue in Nijmegen, he "was shocked and filled with a deeper hatred of Naziism."[158] But when amid this devastation he saw the wall inscription *Da Lifne Mi Ata Omed* (Know Before Whom You Are Standing), he sensed that "there still prevailed a spirit of holiness in this atmosphere."

Writing to the Congress' officials in January 1945, Cass reported on the Chanukah celebrations he had organized in several liberated Belgian and Dutch towns: "Parties were arranged for hundreds of children . . . and for adults too, for whom this was the first celebration in years." In what must have been a most moving re-enactment of the first Chanukah, which marked the rededication of the Jerusalem Temple defiled by the ancient Greeks, Cass and scores of Jewish soldiers and civilians "met in Synagogues which had been stripped and vandalized and rededicated them through the kindling of Hanukah lights." He described how they "met within front line areas under shell fire that seemed to burst just when an Amen was indicated in the Service." Enthusiasm for these efforts ran high among Jewish soldiers. "I am proud to say that our men contributed thousands of chocolate bars, bags of candy, and other delicacies as Channukah gifts to the children."

Not content with organizing such celebrations, however, Cass stressed that rebuilding the Jewish communities in Holland required both physical and spiritual resources. With no rabbis, teachers, or *shokhets*, "the reorganization of religious and communal life is a task for generations." Cass urged the Congress to help fill the needs of thousands of children who were hidden during the war and were now looking in vain for their parents.[159]

Like many Jewish chaplains in Allied armies, Cass stayed on for almost another year in Holland and Germany, doing his best to help Jewish survivors.[160] His diary records his continuing encounters: a visit in early December 1945 to Bergen-Belsen, where, he observed among the youthful Jewish inmates, "Palestine is magic not only to their physical surroundings but to their entire spirit. It offers hope, pride, labor, creativity, a future, even in the depressing and dismal atmosphere of life in a military barracks."[161]

Cass received many letters of gratitude. This one, from a sergeant in the First Canadian Army, Royal Canadian Electrical and Mechanical Engineers, who was about to leave for home, is worth quoting at length:

> I particularly remember your inspiring reconsecration of the little synagoge in Voghel, and your sermon last May in Almelo. I must confess that I was beginning to be discouraged and disappointed in our fellow Jews who had survived the horrors of the occupation. Your sermon showed me that I was wrong and led me to approach my fellow Jews with greatest sympathy and greatest understanding. As suggested in your bulletin, I have signed over my parcels to you. . . .[162]

Service and Citizenship

With support from the WEC, chaplains also tried to make life easier for the families of Jewish service personnel. In July 1943, Cass wrote to the Montreal YMHA requesting a reduction in camp fees for children of servicemen. "Please understand these families are not under normal circumstances, recipients of charity, nor do they wish to accept any now," he wrote.[163] The chaplains and the WEC kept a list of the eighty-four Canadian Jewish prisoners of war, forty-four of whom were RCAF personnel.[164]

The chaplain-soldier relationship provides insight into the level of Jewish education in the servicemen's communities and families. Many of these sons of immigrants, born in the late 1910s or early 1920s, apparently had relatively little Jewish education. Cass sadly noted "an abyss of misinformation and of ignorance" about Judaism among the Jewish soldiers he encountered.[165] Whether they were typical of their generation is probably impossible to know. But since they did constitute nearly 40 percent of the men aged eighteen to forty-five, these soldiers were a good representative sample of the Canadian Jewish community's "culture" in the interwar years. Many required chaplains or other Jews to translate the Yiddish letters they received from relatives.[166] Perhaps the war changed some of them. Many of those Jews who enlisted already possessed, or later developed, a very strong sense that they were fighting for the Jewish people. One example of this attitude was that about 240 Canadian volunteers — including a number of non-Jews — followed Ben Dunkelman and joined the Israel Defense Force in 1948 to defend the new Jewish state. This was the second-highest per capita enlistment outside of Israel itself, surpassed only by the contribution of South African Jews.[167]

The Second World War military experience occurred inside some emphatically Canadian institutions: the army, the RCAF, and the RCN. Sabbath

observances took place on Sundays, not on the Jewish sabbath. Food was not kosher, except probably on Passover, when it was specially brought in (or possibly some mess officers attempted to follow Cass's elaborate instructions for preparing kosher food).[168] Services were of limited duration and, from a rigorous religious perspective, probably unsatisfying. Jewish servicemen and -women were thrown together, most of them probably for the first time in their lives, with non-Jews. Both would have seen each other in situations of mutual dependency. "On the whole," Cass reflected, "relationships between Jew and non-Jew were of an excellent and wholesome character of comrades in arms." Most Jews made "splendid adjustments to their non-Jewish buddies, considering the fact that many of them, particularly the large numbers enlisted from . . . Montreal and Toronto, enjoyed only Jewish social relationshps before enlistment." He went on to say, "Prejudices very often melted away in the flames of battle and fast friendships were formed between Jew and non-Jew."[169]

In a sense, then, the services constituted a school for a type of Canadianization that went far beyond what most Jews had received previously. The soldiers willy-nilly, and probably unwittingly, absorbed the Canadian "culture" of their military context. It might well be that the decline in antisemitism in Canada after 1945 was as much an outcome of this enforced togetherness and camaraderie as it was a reaction to the horrors of the Holocaust and an offshoot of the prosperity that North America was enjoying. At the same time, for many Jews, service in the forces heightened their awareness of Judaism and deepened their identification with the Jewish people. The efforts of the Jewish chaplains, the soldiers' own war experiences, and a growing understanding of the evil intent of Nazism sharpened their dual identity.

At war's end, the troop ships brought the soldiers home to their loved ones. Some veterans, especially those who had seen combat, wandered confusedly like Benny, the protagonist in one of Mordecai Richler's short stories, unable to adjust to civilian life and deeply unsettled for many years.[170] The vast majority, however, got on with their lives. But that is another story.

CHAPTER

9

The Struggle for Israel, 1943-52

The Holocaust of European Jewry, which intensified in June 1941, accelerated the activity of Canadian Zionists. More determined than ever to build a secure Jewish homeland in Palestine, they redoubled their fund-raising efforts. In addition to these greater financial obligations, Canadian Zionists also vigorously popularized the movement, organizing diverse activities.

Following the death of Archie Freiman, a presidium composed of Samuel Zacks of Toronto and Michael Garber and Samuel Schwisberg of Montreal was established in 1944 to run the Zionist Organization of Canada. Toronto-Montreal tensions had by then been somewhat reduced, but the division of leadership between these two centres had so limited the organization's effectiveness that it was beginning to suffer severely by 1943.

Of the three presidents, Zacks was dominant. A forty-year-old wealthy Toronto stockbroker, he had for several years been involved in Jewish war-refugee work and Zionist activity in the Toronto area.[1] He enjoyed a reputation as a dedicated and hardworking individual, and he applied to his Zionist work the drive, initiative, and shrewdness that had earned him a fortune in Canadian mining promotions and great respect from a wide circle of friends.

Along with his organizational ability, Sam Zacks had a winning way with people. Outgoing, friendly, and diplomatic, Zacks was above all a doer, and he saw, in the building of a Jewish homeland in Palestine, an immense outlet for the energies of Canadian Jewry. An avid fund-raiser, Zacks sometimes mixed his Zionism with business; in 1944 he promised one individual that he would double his money on a share purchase if he would increase his contribution to the ZOC.[2] Zacks was an essentially practical and pragmatic person who understood the necessity of drawing as many people as possible — even non-Jewish Canadians — into the cause. Perhaps the keys to his success, however, were his open mind and the broad, conciliatory, and liberal approach he used to secure support for the entire movement.

While the Canadian Jewish community was being canvassed for more and more money for relief efforts in Europe, the Zionist campaigns for Palestine became more insistent through the United Palestine Appeal. Labour, religious, and Revisionist organizations, however, conducted their own campaigns. By 1943, there were also some city welfare funds, which attempted to co-ordinate fund-raising in some fifteen or twenty communities and allocate the monies to local and international causes, including Palestine. In this somewhat complex and, occasionally, confusing scene, the ZOC often felt frustrated.

Zacks spoke of these problems to Chaim Weizmann, who, in a separate endeavour, had been appealing to Canadian Jews throughout the war for support of the Sieff Institute, a research centre in Rehovoth, Palestine, that Weizmann headed.[3] In responding to a letter from Weizmann on this subject in January 1943, Zacks showed his exasperation. "One of our main difficulties, in Canada," he explained, "as far as the Zionist movement is concerned has been the plethora of Campaigns. . . . In view of the fact that there is only a handful of workers, it places a heavy burden on the small group and the best results are not obtained." He tried to make Weizmann aware that "this country would be capable of much greater effort if things were not so chaotic and there was a greater coordination in the fund raising program."[4] Weizmann, with a remarkable lack of understanding, continued to push his own private cause, demanding that the Canadians raise $150,000 to build a laboratory.[5]

Zacks favoured a comprehensive Zionist fund-raising campaign, which he believed would raise more money and also allow for independent rescue programs for European Jewry. In 1943 he calculated that American Jewry contributed between fifty cents and one dollar per capita, but Canadian Jews gave approximately five dollars. He believed this was because American Zionists had abandoned their separate campaigns. If they had run their own appeals, Zacks wrote to one associate, Sam Drache, "Zionism would have been many times more powerful there. Then they probably would have risen to the occasion and taken courageous steps to rescue European Jewry, instead of sleeping complacently, drugged by the opium of philanthropic appeals."[6]

Zacks also understood the need to do more than just canvass for cheques. To the Halifax activist Sam Jacobson, Zacks wrote: "We should realize that fundraising is secondary to the other important work that faces us in the present crisis."[7] "My feeling is that we are making too much of a fuss about fundraising to-day," he wrote to Drache in Winnipeg in early December 1943. "Other work seems to be so much more important. I am losing patience with all the internal squabbles regarding fundraising." He thought that this bickering over allocations could be ended by holding a referendum and letting all subscribers to Zionist funds decide the matter.

The ZOC, co-operating with other Zionist organizations in the United Zionist Council, attempted to influence the media and several politicians through a co-ordinated public-relations campaign.[8] Its major target was the British government, which many Zionists felt had betrayed its Palestine mandate with the 1938 White Paper that severely limited Jewish immigration and land purchases. London had steadfastly refused to modify this policy, even while millions of European Jews were being systematically exterminated.[9]

Public relations became the most important aspect of Zionist activity. The urgent push to move Holocaust survivors to Palestine required an end to these British restrictions. Within the Canadian Jewish community, this struggle against Britain became increasingly popular. Anti-Zionism was rare.[10] In fact, membership in the ZOC increased considerably, and some young Jews displayed a growing enthusiasm for emigration (Aliyah) and agricultural pioneering (*chalutziut*). Thus during this dramatic period between 1943 and 1952, Canadian Zionists experienced the most intensive activity in their fifty-year history.

Before 1943, attempts to stimulate pro-Zionist sentiments had been limited. Politicians were sometimes invited to Zionist conventions, and the Canadian press had been broadly supportive of the idea of a Jewish national home in Palestine.[11] But the sharp attack that Canadian Zionists mounted just after the British White Paper was published was so brief and unco-ordinated that it attracted only passing attention in the nation's newspapers and resulted in little public debate.

The Zionists Mobilize

When news of the mass murder of Jews by the Nazis began reaching the West in the summer of 1942, a mood of impatience and bitterness gripped North American Jewry. At a rally of Jews in New York's Madison Square Garden in March 1943, Chaim Weizmann proclaimed that two million Jews had already been murdered and that "the world can no longer plead that the ghastly facts are unknown or unconfirmed."[12] Canadian Zionist figures joined the protests and, like Sam Zacks, participated in efforts to save as many Jews as possible through rescue. Access to Palestine had to be improved, which meant either the suspension or the withdrawal of the White Paper. Canadian Jewry was unable to exert strong influence on the British government on this issue, but the Zionists assumed that pressure from the government of Canada or from major segments of the Canadian public might make a difference. With this in mind, the public-relations committee of the United Zionist Council formed a separate organization.

The keystone in the campaign was the Canadian Palestine Committee (referred to by Zionists as the Committee). The Christian Council for Palestine, established at the same time to recruit clergymen to the Zionist cause, proved only a modest success. Established in the summer of 1943 under the direction of Henry F. Janes, a Toronto public-relations consultant who was later replaced by Herbert Mowat, the committee was nominally headed by Sir Ellsworth Flavelle, a prominent Canadian businessman. (All three of these men were non-Jews.) The Committee first tried a direct approach at the highest political level. In December, Archie Freiman (still the ZOC's president) asked Prime Minister Mackenzie King to press the British government to lift the White Paper's immigration restrictions.[13]

The Committee approached King on the White Paper again in March 1944. A large delegation of Jewish and non-Jewish members of the Committee met with King in Ottawa to acquaint him with the issues relating to Canada and the Palestine question.[14] They argued that as the friendship between the United States and Britain had been strained over Palestine, "Canada has a grave responsibility in any matter involving British-American relations, not merely as an interpreter between the two partners, but as an interpreter who is a partner in disputes under discussion. Further, Canada has a vital interest in all matters of policy which might be termed British."

The committee also reminded King that in the postwar years, when "multitudes of uprooted people . . . would be knocking on the doors of all countries, . . . a generous measure of this uprooted humanity could be taken care of in a country geographically convenient for the purpose if the doors of Palestine were left open to Jewish immigration."[15] In the end, King promised to support this view at an upcoming meeting of the Commonwealth prime ministers. But he would not challenge the White Paper. Committee delegations met with King and officials of the department of External Affairs periodically thereafter to present position papers on the Palestine issue.[16]

But King's advisers at External Affairs counselled him to demur on the grounds that this would be detrimental to eventual Jewish-Arab rapprochement in Palestine, and King refused Freiman's appeal. Zacks's efforts to persuade King also proved unsuccessful. In the words of the historian David Bercuson, "Canada . . . stood snugly aloof" from the Palestine question, "and no amount of Zionist public relations could change this fact."[17]

There was no discernible shift in the policies of the Canadian government concerning Palestine.[18] But some newspapers began to publish sympathetic editorials and, more important, to give extensive coverage of anti–White Paper protests and Committee meetings.[19]

ISRAELIS

Irving Layton

It is themselves they trust and no one else;
Their fighter planes that screech across the sky,
Real, visible as the glorious sun;
Riflesmoke, gunshine, and rumble of tanks.

Man is a fanged wolf, without compassion
or ruth: Assyrians, Medes, Greeks, Romans,
And devout pagans in Spain and Russia
— Allah's children, most merciful of all.

Where is the almighty if murder thrives?
He's dead as mutton and they buried him
Decades ago, covered him with their own
Limp bodies in Belsen and Babi Yar.

Let the strong compose hymns and canticles,
Live with the Lord's radiance in their hard skulls
Or make known his great benevolences;
Stare at the heavens and feel glorified

Or humbled and awestruck buckle their knees:
They are done with him now and forever.
Without a whimper from him they returned,
A sign like an open hand in the sky.

A pillar of fire: Their flesh made it;
It burned briefly and died — you all know where.
Now in their own blood they temper the steel,
God being dead and their enemies not.

From Gerri Sinclair and Morris Wofle, eds., *The Spice Box: An Anthology of Jewish Canadian Writing* (Toronto: Lester & Orpen Dennys, 1981): 191.

Frustrated at this level, the Committee engaged in pro-Zionist activity by sending out literature, news releases, and speakers to inform non-Jewish Canadians across the country. Janes saw this activity not as publicity, but as goodwill, and he reported to the ZOC in early January 1944 that "in his campaign, he touches on anti-semitism, [Jewish] achievements in Palestine, the White Paper and the plight of the Jewish people, the fact that the Arabs deserve no consideration because of their attitude in this war, whereas the Jews have suffered on one hand and served on the other."[20]

The Western group of the Committee was exceptionally vigorous, and it quickly established contacts in the major Prairie cities.[21] A Winnipeg lawyer, Irwin Dorfman, John Dower of Edmonton, and Jacob M. Goldenberg of Saskatoon became its most active members. Dorfman advised Zacks that a co-ordinated campaign to achieve their main objective "of seeing the [Palestine question] brought up in Parliament" should be started immediately. "Merely having the unorganized sympathy of a number of liberal minded non-Jews," he explained, "will get us nowhere."[22] He recommended a series of separate committees, one each for members of Parliament, the clergy, newspaper or radio persons, labour leaders, and major businessmen — all "building up goodwill and public opinion until such time as the Parliamentary Committee is prepared to bring the matter up in Parliament."[23]

The Westerners organized widespread distribution of pamphlets such as *His Terrible Swift Sword* by Dr. Norman MacLean — a former moderator of the Church of Scotland — as well as other write-ups that presented the Zionist case to non-Jewish local committee members, the press, business leaders, the clergy, and political figures. They also sent out speakers who were effective at awakening Christian sympathies for Zionism. A large number of prominent Canadian public figures, including politicians, labour leaders, and university faculty members, were influenced.

Rabbi Harry Stern of Montreal's Temple Emanu-el was one of the most active emissaries in the 1943–44 campaign — and was thought to be "the best asset we have." Janes, himself an expert on public relations, wrote of Stern, "his understanding of public relations is not equalled by any man I've met in a long time."[24]

Not only did Stern undertake several speaking tours, but he was also instrumental in setting up the Christian Council for Palestine, through which the Zionists hoped to influence Canadian clergy.[25] The Council was organized in early 1944 by Janes,[26] who prepared a list of nearly eight thousand Protestant and Roman Catholic clergymen to whom pro-Zionist material was sent. This mailing included reviews of Pierre Van Paassen's *Forgotten Ally* — a book that detailed the contributions of Palestine Jews to British military efforts in the North African campaign — though any anti-British sentiments were carefully removed.[27] Groups of pro-Zionist clergymen of all Christian denominations sprang up in Montreal and Toronto, as well as in a number of other centres. They disseminated information about Zionist achievements in Palestine, the Balfour Declaration, British immigration restrictions, and Jewish suffering in Europe.

By June 1944, the executive director of all these pro-Palestine committees was Herbert Mowat, an effective spokesman and a highly efficient organizer. His speeches, like the one broadcast on June 5, 1944, over CHNS, a Halifax radio station, related some of the known facts of the Holocaust and discussed the need for a safe Jewish homeland where a million more refugees could be accommodated. The absorptive capacity of Palestine, which was greatly increased by Jewish agricultural innovations, was stressed, while British immigration restrictions were condemned as contrary to "the humanitarian needs of our day."[28]

As a result of these efforts, the roster of supporters increased and, by July 1944, included sixteen MPs and many other prominent Canadians. By October 1945, the list included sixty-four MPs, twelve senators, various MLAs, and a handful of professors.[29] Mowat, a highly accomplished speaker, addressed meetings of the Lions, Rotary, and Kiwanis clubs, ministerial associations, and labour temples, and made radio broadcasts all across Ontario and the Prairies during the autumn of 1944. Although he usually included local Jewish communities in his tours, his main objective was to win the support of Christians for the moral, historical, and humanitarian Jewish claims for a national homeland in Palestine.

The Committee also lobbied newspaper publishers and editors for their support of Zionism. In November 1943, Zacks told a Winnipeg associate that Joseph Atkinson, publisher of the *Toronto Star*, was "our main sponsor."[30] In fact, after having spent many hours with various Ontario newspaper editors, Zacks reported a great deal of positive feedback:

> We have been promised tremendous support from the Toronto Daily Star, the Evening Telegram, the Globe & Mail, Saturday Night and MacLean's [*sic*] Magazine. I have given them great material and you can expect real action. I have contacted leaders throughout the Province and am getting back some beautiful editorials. The Hamilton Spectator, Kitchener News Record, London Free Press, etc., have published outstanding articles.

Some of these efforts failed, however. In the aftermath of the assassination of Lord Moyne, the former British high commissioner for Palestine, in Cairo in November 1944 by Jewish terrorists, *La Liberté et le patriote* of Winnipeg commented:

> the Congress Bulletin, organ of the Jewish minority in Canada, has made a fuss, as we recall, of the alleged persecution which the Jews of Quebec have to suffer. It freely accused French Canadians of persecuting the Hebrew minority. It swamped the newspapers of the country to spread these falsehoods. What will it say of the actions of the Jews of Palestine?[31]

Responses to Pressures

The Committee usually found that the media responded favourably, if less than enthusiastically, to the Zionist case, while the White Paper often got a non-committal response. Still, most editorial writers refrained from criticizing Britain. The reproaches from those newspapers that did criticize were, at best, qualified, at least during the Second World War. After May 1945, editorialists saw less justification for excluding refugees from Palestine, but outright condemnation in the Canadian press of British policy was still rare, probably because of isolationism and a lingering colonial attitude. Some newspapers even occasionally criticized the United States for "interfering" with Britain's mandate for Palestine.[32] Thus the Committee refrained from being too stridently anti-British, and also distanced itself from the terrorist acts of Jewish extremists in Palestine.

J. M. Goldenberg of Saskatoon argued that Canadian Zionists should:

> guard against excessive criticism of Britain . . . because I believe there exists in Canada such a strong pro-British attitude, that it will not tolerate violent British criticism. I believe that violent anti-British criticism will align a large section of the public against us. It is not a case where large sections of the population like us less, but I think, they like Britain more, and they would not hesitate to sacrifice us, if they thought it served Britain's interest best.[33]

While Revisionists were distributing stickers reading "We will buy no English goods or services as long as England bars the Jews from Palestine," for its part, the ZOC followed a more cautious course.[34] Following the assassination of Lord Moyne in November 1944, Mowat wired Zacks that "it would be a fatal error from the point of view of public relations to issue any statement that could be interpreted as a reply to Churchill," who condemned the killing as an interference with the war effort. "My recommendation," he continued, "is for the Canadian Zionist Organization to send a strongly worded resolution to the Jewish Agency in Jerusalem advising an all-out effort to eradicate these terrorists in Palestine." He again warned that Zionists should be concerned about "the bar of non-Jewish public opinion."[35]

But Zacks believed that British policy was partly responsible for the rise of Jewish terrorism, and he informed Mowat that "all of us were a little taken aback and could not understand . . . how you could arrive at such a point of view." Prime Minister Winston Churchill "seems to be falling prey to the British Colonial officials' policy [of] fighting a rear-guard action to offset the growing feeling in the U.S. . . . in favour of Jewish commonwealth. . . ." Although Zacks rejected the terrorists' methods, he also resented charges from some British officials that the terrorists were impeding the war effort, allegations that reflected badly on Jews generally. "The least [the British] could have done," Zacks wrote, "was to recognize the great contribution in this war by the Jews, which is greater than that of any other people."[36]

In response, Mowat assured him that his telegram was for private consumption only. "*In public*," he said, he endeavoured to present Jews as a "people of peace":

> Jews have traditionally accepted violence and offered none; they maintained a fine dignity in the face of unbridled Arab violence in the pre-war period and suffered much. It is possible that the present situation may be traced to the injustice of that period which caused many Jews great suffering and has unbalanced members who have gone berserk. [Jews] are united in this endeavour and in the effort to dispose of their own members [who] are creating difficulties.[37]

Thus Mowat, in his presentation to non-Jewish Canadians, attempted to exploit the traditional image of the Jew as passive victim and juxtapose it against that of the new Jew as progressive pioneer farmer in Palestine.

He remained vigilant on this aspect of Zionist public relations. In early 1947, Mowat reported that while in Calgary, he "was informed that the flogging of the British officers in Palestine [by the Irgun Zvai Leumi (National Military Organization), the military wing of the Zionist Revisionists, in retaliation for the caning of several of their members in prison] had caused a greater deterioration of the Jewish cause in [Calgary] public opinion than all other factors combined in the last year. . . . At the bar of public opinion the cause of Zionism in Palestine touched an all time low." The event had made a "malignant impression" on the minds of Calgarians.[38]

Public Relations after the Second World War

After 1945, editorial writers generally were sympathetic to the Jewish "victims of Hitlerism" and the partitioning of Palestine into Jewish and Arab states.[39] But there was also much sympathy for Britain. The Toronto *Telegram* stated, in October 1946, that while Zionists were putting pressure on Britain to admit Jews to Palestine, "no Jew on this continent has asked for the admission of Jews here, which proves the political rather than the humanitarian nature of the Zionist movement."[40] (In fact, the Congress had tried to get some Holocaust survivors admitted to Canada.) As well, President Truman's efforts on behalf of this cause had attracted widespread opposition in the Canadian press and some sympathy for Britain.[41]

Generally, the press was favourable to the idea of Jewish emigration from Europe to Palestine after 1945, in large part, apparently, because Canadians were not keen on Jews coming to Canada.[42] A poll conducted by the Canadian Institute of Public Opinion in early 1946 found that 49 percent of those polled favoured free Jewish access to Palestine; a few months later, the institute found that 49 percent of those polled regarded Jews as the second least desirable immigrants to Canada (Japanese were first on the list). But the Irgun and Lehi (Stern Gang) anti-British Terror campaign, which started with the bombing of the King David Hotel on July 22, 1946, "almost completely derailed the Zionist campaign for public support in Canada."[43] Further harm was done, especially to the Zionist relationship with the government, when it was discovered that the *Haganah*, one of the ships used to run illegal Jewish immigrants to Palestine, was a former Royal Canadian Navy corvette sold as surplus by the War Assets Corporation "to Jewish interests in New York."[44] These factors, and the prevailing government inclination not to get involved in the "Palestine mess," meant the Zionist public-relations campaign had only limited success to this point.

Although Zacks understood the complex roots of Jewish terrorism, he and the ZOC actively condemned both it and the efforts by the American League for a Free Palestine (organized by the American novelist and playwright Ben Hecht) to form branches of the Irgun. In addition to finding terrorism morally repugnant, Zacks was concerned about the possibility of a serious public-relations backlash. During January to March 1947, he noted that the media had given considerable coverage to Jewish terrorism and its backers in the United States and Canada.

> [The] point of view [of] the overwhelming majority of Jews and Zionists who do not belong to and do not help [those] groups should be made known. . . . The United Zionist Council of Canada . . . wishes to reit-

> erate its stand against these small dissident groups. . . . The flamboyant, bitter, anti-British . . . campaign builds nothing and destroys much. . . . We regard these people as irresponsible sensationalists and believe that they do not represent Jewish opinion anywhere.

He appealed to "the press and radio [to] contribute to the struggle against political irresponsibility by accurate and balanced presentation of the news and widely considered comment."[45] Mowat observed that he was "put on the defensive attempting to explain what is called Jewish terror. . . . It is my technique to attack the other side . . . but it is a trying procedure in the teeth of the destructionist violent activities of the Irgun, which all regard as blatantly criminal."[46]

In a letter to M. M. Harrison at the *Windsor Daily Star*, Harry Rosenthal of London complained that a column that referred to an advertisement of the American League for a Free Palestine "can stir up a considerable amount of hatred against Canadian Jews who are in no way responsible for what Mr. Hecht does, and who in no way agree with his statements." He urged Harrison to "at least . . . [point out] that the ad admits it does not represent Jewish opinion. . . . All Jewry, American and Canadian and Palestinian, for that matter, are opposed to terrorist tactics."[47]

Canadian Zionists and the Jewish Brigade

After 1944, when the Jewish Brigade — a specially formed, Palestine-raised infantry unit of the British Eighth Army — went into action in Italy, the Zionists challenged the image of the typical ghetto Jew with the picture of the Palestinian Jew fighting on the side of Britain and the Western democracies. This was also the theme of Pierre Van Paassen's book, *The Forgotten Ally*.

Before the brigade even got to Italy, however, Canadian Zionists were drawn into discussions about the very creation of the unit, which the British government had announced it would form in August 1942.[48] In late September 1943, the ZOC executive asked the Jewish Agency in Jerusalem if it should seek permission from the British government for Canadian Jews to join these formations. On October 4, 1943, Jesse Schwartz wired Zacks that the agency "suggest[ed] you obtain consent [from] your government before we take action here."[49] A year later, when the brigade was actually being mobilized, Schwartz informed Zacks that "they are not keen in the United States about pressing the matter of having American boys in the Brigade," which would include a token force of only fifty to one hundred British Jews among the thousands of Jews from Palestine and the "stateless Jews."[50] "In view of all this," he continued, "I personally feel that we should not press the matter in this country." ZOC officers Michael Garber, Sam Schwisberg, and Harry Batshaw, however, believed "it would be a desirable thing to get a token number of Canadian Jewish boys to volunteer for the Brigade," and they urged Zacks to "clear the matter with the Public Relations Committee of Congress in Toronto, while they would do the same in Montreal."[51]

By the middle of November, however, Garber and Schwisberg advised "that we should not enter into any discussions even among ourselves regarding Canadian participation in the Jewish Brigade until we see what happens in Parliament on Nov. 22nd. It's a very delicate situation."[52] Zacks, meanwhile, informed Schwisberg that "I have been getting inquiries almost every day from Jewish soldiers in the Canadian army asking if they would be allowed to join the Jewish Brigade. . . ."[53] But he and Schwisberg were concerned about a possible adverse reaction in Canada, even though, as Schwisberg confided to Zacks, "it goes without saying that thousands of our boys would rather wear the Jewish uniform."[54] Zacks apparently made no reply to this astonishing assertion, and the matter was dropped.

Education and the Ideal of *Chalutziut*

The campaigns also likely helped to galvanize the Jews of Canada into action, while at the same time providing many who were ignorant or unpersuaded with information about the Zionist cause. One Halifax Zionist, Sam Jacobson, commented to Zacks in May 1944 that the "Jewish masses are as much strangers to Zionism as non-Jews."[55]

Oriented almost exclusively to fund-raising activities, with the encouragement of world Zionist leadership, the ZOC had never placed a priority on the education of these Jewish masses. But Zacks and some other officers regarded education as Zionism's "main work" and gave it as much encouragement as they could. Zacks favoured establishing a publishing company to disseminate books, magazines, records, and music, and to arrange concert and lecture tours.[56] He had, in this, the support of Zionists like Sam Jacobson, with whom he corresponded often about the direction of the movement. Jacobson saw Zionism as a "mass humanitarian liberal movement, with the courage to arouse sympathy among Jew and non-Jew. . . . A movement that will be alive and growing; with a future, and not a narrow philanthropic movement using pussy-foot methods. . . . I believe [in] a strong [and] aggressive cultural program. . . ."[57]

By the early 1940s, the fire of idealism began to motivate small groups of Canadian Jewish teenagers to consider *chalutziut* in Palestine in a kibbutz, tilling the land and shouldering a rifle. The image of the rough-hewn pioneer living a simple, frugal, communal-farming life on the ancient soil became a symbol of the renewal of both land and people. It did not matter to these young people that this life was dangerous and difficult, both physically and psychologically, or that their parents likely would object strenuously to their leaving. Films, songs, dances, and visitors from Palestine all told them that any difficulties could be overcome, and that the sweet joy of Zion's redemption would compensate for any pain or loss.

The *chalutz* ideal grew among some segments of the youth of Montreal, Toronto, and Winnipeg. By the spring of 1941, it was reported that five hundred members of various youth movements were committed to Aliyah and thirty *chalutzim* were prepared to leave for Palestine at the first opportunity. Many of them already had one or two years' agricultural training in the United States.[58] "The Canadian Chalutzim are burning in their zeal to go to Palestine and participate in its defense at the present moment," one writer claimed, and barriers to entering the United States during the war made "a training farm for Canadian Chalutzim . . . the demand of the hour."

The activist Shalom Stern saw that because Canadian Jewry was part of the Jewish "historical process," it must "recognize the fact that it is free to act in the interest of the Jewish masses . . . for the purpose of salvaging the wreckage of Jewish life. It can also partake in the creation of the new living already preponderant on the soil of Palestine."[59] But Stern also emphasized that "we are undoubtedly . . . an integral part, of that particular cycle of history which embraces Jewry. In that sense Canadian Jewry must consider the Palestinian struggle a manifestation of our own battle."

In 1944 the Hashomer Hatzair organization in Canada established a *hachshara* (training) farm near Prescott, Ontario, where about a dozen young people prepared for life on a kibbutz.[60] Although Joseph Israeli, the American Jewish Agency representative in New York, was aware of the difficulties in attracting North American Jewish youth to *chalutz* life, he optimistically estimated that perhaps as many as one thousand would move to Palestine at the end of the war.[61] The Canadians from the Prescott farm would be part of this vanguard of pioneers. Badly in need of financial support, the group requested assistance from Zacks — the socialist youth asking the arch-capitalist for help in establishing a workers' commonwealth in Palestine.[62]

His good friend Meyer Weisgal urged Zacks to do his best for them. "The work the Hashomer Hatzair is doing, whether we agree with their ideology or not, is most important and deserves the support of the Zionist movement everywhere. They are the ones who are doing the real work in preparing young men and women for Palestine. I wished the General Zionists would make

Chalutziut [settlement of kibbutzim] part of their program and enlarge the scope of their work."[63] Zacks not only helped the *hachshara*, but also visited it and warmly encouraged the young people in their endeavour.

While some members of Hashomer Hatzair, and of other youth movements like the Labour Zionist Habonim, made Aliyah and settled on kibbutzim, the agricultural life on Israel's embattled frontiers did not suit them all.[64] Indeed, some recruits to such radical movements may not have had the loftiest of ideals. Mordecai Richler, for one, recalled:

> The truth is, I hadn't joined Habonim . . . because of an overwhelming commitment to Zionism. I had done it to spite my [religious] grandfather. . . . There was another consideration. I longed to meet girls who could stay out after ten o'clock at night. And according to the disapproving gossip I heard in the Young Israel Synagogue, the girls in the movement, especially those who were allowed to sleep over at our Camp Kvutza, where there was no adult supervision, practised "free love."[65]

Some of the *chalutzim* eventually moved to the city or returned to Canada, often greatly disillusioned but seldom regretful at having given their sweat and blood for the realization of the dream.

In the early 1940s, local Zionist groups began experimenting with various summer camps. Finally, in 1943, Camp Kadimah (Forward) was opened at Port Mouton, Nova Scotia, for forty-seven campers drawn mostly from Halifax.[66] By the time it moved three years later to a larger site, the camp had become a vibrant centre for Young Judaea activity and a strong social bond for Jewish youth across the Maritimes.[67]

Around the same time, Camp Hagshama (Connection) was formed near Perth, Ontario; it was joined in 1948 by Camp Shalom (Peace) near Gravenhurst, Ontario, and Camp Hatikvah (Hope) near Oyawa, British Columbia. Other organizations established their own camps, a veritable network of institutions intended by the elders to perpetuate their form of Zionist attitudes while offering youth healthy outdoor activity away from the summer heat for a few weeks. But idealism was in the air and many of Young Judaea's teenage leaders were swept away.

It was heady, intoxicating almost, for teenagers belonging to Zionist movements to mature within its rich atmosphere of socialism and worldly culture. "You realized," remembered the Hashomer Hatzair veteran Mesh Butovsky (who went on Aliyah in the early 1950s), "that you were the vanguard of the Jewish people, transforming them through *chalutziut* to productive working class people. . . . The movement was our whole existence: In its relentless intensive atmosphere we were preparing for our new life in Palestine."[68]

Turmoil in Young Judaea

With these influences, a greater zeal began to spread through the ranks of Young Judaea. By 1944, in fact, the enthusiasm for *chalutziut* reached such proportions that it precipitated a major confrontation with the ZOC, which regarded Young Judaea as its youth wing and provided funds for its activities. The trouble started in Winnipeg. Its large Jewish population, always active in Zionist life, had, for its size, probably the most impressive record of achievement of any community in Canada. Over the years, a small number of its people had gone to live in Palestine, among them Norman Shiffer, the director of Winnipeg's successful JNF campaigns of the 1920s. Soon the Young Judaea organization in Winnipeg began to develop a somewhat more radical tinge than its sister groups elsewhere.

By the early 1940s, this radicalism had been strengthened and co-ordinated by a small group of students at the University of Manitoba — some of them allegedly affiliated with the Labour Zionist youth group Habonim.[69] Intense, articulate, and totally committed to the goal of inculcating real purpose and direction into what they regarded as a bourgeois organization, the Winnipeg idealists were determined to make *chalutziut* the core of Young Judaea's program. After gradually winning over the youth group's leadership and converting its members to the new goal, the radicals were opposed by the local Jewish establishment and Young Judaea was officially banned from the city's Zionist centre. This nasty dispute soon came to the attention of the executive board of the ZOC, which in early 1944 decided to stop the spread of these "dangerous" ideas.

Meanwhile, the national council of Young Judaea tried to prevent the zealots from manipulating the organization by barring members of other Zionist groups from becoming officers.[70] The threat of a left-wing takeover was considered to be very serious. Moreover, the ZOC leadership was distressed because some Judaeans in both Toronto and Winnipeg were engaging in "outside political action without prior consultation with and approval of the local Public Relations Committee." One ZOC executive member was even in favour of ousting any "persons who have definite political leanings . . . [because] Young Judaea should be an educational movement."[71] In order to secure all the necessary information about these activities, the ZOC appointed a special youth commission, headed by Saul Chait of Montreal, to investigate.

When he reported back several months later, Chait stated that the condition of Young Judaea was "unsatisfactory."[72] The youth organization was weak in Montreal, where a small group was trying to gain control by disseminating ideas that were opposed to those of general Zionist youth education in Canada. Chait found them to be "exceedingly aggressive and militant, and are using Young Judaea as a platform and forum for the propagation of their special political and economic viewpoints."

On his recommendation, the youth commission was empowered to remove those "causing friction" from the organization and to undertake "a vast program of educational work and membership expansion among Canadian Jewish youth." The commission was also authorized to employ the *Judaean*, the organization's influential monthly magazine, as a vehicle for this message. But this program aroused resistance from both the young zealots and some of the old guard. John Devor, a former Young Judaea activist who was serving in the RCAF, wrote to Sam Zacks in 1944 objecting to the youth commission's "turning Young Judaea into . . . another YMHA or A.Z.A. [young B'nai B'rith]."[73]

The youth commission quickly began expelling "radical" elements, especially in the West. A year later, the purge had become so severe that even the conservative Nathan Shuster, president of national Young Judaea, complained to Zacks about "just how serious is the damage which the Youth Commission has done."[74] But Zacks, who felt that Young Judaea should have non-ideological appeal among Canadian Jewish youth, refused to weaken the commission's powers.[75] He was also, no doubt, subject to pressures from parents who were fully prepared to write cheques but did not want their own children to go on Aliyah and thus were worried by the radical trends within the organization.

Since its appointment, the commission had attempted to give the *Judaean* wider appeal and had sponsored national arts and crafts and oratory contests. It also tried to "reach as many Canadian Jewish youth as possible" by appointing more leaders, distributing programs, and organizing adult groups to assist the Young Judaeans in various ways.[76]

Young Judaea's rank and file objected to this interference. At their annual convention in September 1945, they demanded that the ZOC "revise the set-up and personnel of the Zionist Youth Commission . . . [and make it] clearly understood that this Commission should act only as an advisory body and at no time [infringe] upon the constitution of Canadian Young Judaea."[77] Led by a contingent of Western insurgents, the convention of 1945 affirmed the ideals of *chalutziut*.

The tension with the parent organization continued. At the ZOC convention in January 1946, strong condemnation of these radical tendencies was again voiced and the youth commission was praised for its watchfulness. The newly elected president of Young Judaea, Max Bookman of Ottawa, suggested that senior Zionists act as club leaders and that the president of Young Judaea be given membership on the ZOC's executive board.[78] A pro-*chalutziut* element secured the passage of a resolution favourable to their ideals, however, much to the embarrassment of the national executive.[79]

And still the controversy continued. On Young Judaea's thirtieth anniversary in 1946, the national convention was held in Ottawa and several strong pro-*chalutziut* resolutions were adopted. These met with the resounding approval of the rank and file, which elected a new executive headed by Lionel Druker of Halifax, a Second World War veteran who was soon to join the fledgling Israel Defense Force. Opposition to these resolutions from the parent organization was swift. "Many of us have grave doubts," wrote S. Hart Green to Sam Zacks in April, "as to whether [we] should be parties to training young Canadians to go to Palestine, unless under very exceptional circumstances. I trust, therefore, that no action on the recommendation . . . [will be taken]."[80]

When the ZOC's Young Judaea Committee, a monitoring body, addressed the issue in May 1947, it recommended that a special group known as Plugat Aliyah be formed for all Young Judaeans contemplating immigration to Israel.[81] But Plugat Aliyah was allowed to disseminate only information "which shall be of a nature as to conform to the policy of the ZOC and which shall be disseminated with the knowledge and approval of the ZOC." Young Judaea was allowed "to help by supplying information to all those . . . who are interested in *chalutziut* and Aliyah without intentionally inculcating Aliyah in the program of the movement."[82]

This issue was never fully put to rest in Young Judaea. In fact, the question of whether the organization should attempt to instil those values continued to arise at official gatherings and at the movement's summer camps for many years. While Zacks was obviously sympathetic to *chalutziut*, he tended to favour a form of personal involvement he called Chalutz Capital, an apparently self-contradictory combination of leftist idealism and private entrepreneurship. At the ZOC's 1950 convention, he stated, "It is not enough for Zionists to give money to Israel or to go there as tourists. Today, Israel, to become self-sufficient, needs Chalutz Capital, needs investments. . . . The more that goes into investments, the more self-sufficient Israel will become and the less dependent upon charitable gifts."[83] He accepted *chalutziut* for those desiring that collectivist pioneering rural life, but he favoured private investment and the urban settlement of Canadian Jews, who were "needed for their vitality and their Western World skills . . . [and] would provide a needed counterweight in the population of Israel to the large numbers of broken and handicapped graduates of the concentration camps and of Hitler's shattering terror." Aliyah, in his view, need not be permanent. He thought that "even if persons of special skills go only for five years, they can make a contribution of the highest value."

These were progressive views, but Zacks practised what he preached by making substantial investments in Israel and encouraging others to do the same. Privately he was very cautious, however, and he harboured considerable reservations about Israel's investment climate. "The price level in Israel is too high," he wrote to Harry Batshaw in June 1949. "Until such time as the economy is put in order, I feel it would be better if we went slowly. People are discouraged and are turning against Israel because of its economic set-up. I feel that the approach should be a very selective one and only to ardent Zionists."[84]

At the same time, some Zionist leaders wanted to send senior Young Judaeans to Palestine for advanced training. In 1945 the youth department of the World Zionist Organization began dispatching youth leaders from abroad for a year's course of study and kibbutz labour. The first contingent was drawn from South Africa, but officials of the Jewish Agency in Jerusalem wanted international participation. Dov Joseph, the founder of Canadian Young Judaea, repeatedly urged his former organization to send representatives. He and his colleagues at the Jewish Agency informed Rabbi Jesse Schwartz that "we attach the greatest importance to this scheme. We believe that in the course of this year it will be possible to teach the students to speak, read and write Hebrew fluently and to secure a real understanding of life in this country. There can be no doubt that this will enable them to be of the greatest help to the furtherance of Zionism . . . on their return."[85]

The youth commission recommended that the ZOC shoulder the entire cost of sending a Young Judaean, but at its August 19, 1946, meeting, the ZOC executive board decided "to leave the matter in abeyance in view of the fact that at the present time there is no Judaean eligible for the suggested scholarship."[86] The Judaeans, however, eager to participate, unsuccessfully pressed the ZOC for funds. In 1947 they decided to raise money themselves to send three leaders to the Jerusalem course. Still the ZOC objected. Though Zacks was agreeable and funds were eventually allocated in 1949, Young Judaeans did not join the scheme until 1951.[87]

Zionist Outreach

While local Zionist activities, especially in the smaller centres, tended to originate with youth and Canadian Hadassah-WIZO groups, some ZOC members were cognizant of the need to provide a stronger network of men's organizations. In most cities outside the large metropolitan centres, there were no organized men's groups. The men were simply "organized" by a few local activists during the annual United Palestine Appeal campaign. At a general meeting, financial pledges were made in response to an outside speaker's appeal for funds. The organizers would follow through by collecting the pledged amounts and forwarding them to headquarters. A similar burst of activity took place every few years on the eve of the World Zionist congresses. Efforts were made to sell the *shekel*, a symbol of membership in one of the Zionist organizations, in order to broaden the base of support for the political parties with which these Canadian groups were affiliated.

The ZOC was in the best position to establish local men's associations because of its non-ideological stance and its considerable fund-raising strength. Also, most Jews in the non-metropolitan areas were already affiliated with the ZOC as contributors or *shekel* holders. There were few members of the Labour or religious Zionist organizations in these communities, not because of a lack of interest, but because establishing one broadly based organization proved easier.[88] Nevertheless, even the ZOC found it difficult to begin locals of its men's group, the Zionist Order of Habonim, in the smaller communities.

Always a pragmatist, Zacks realized that Habonim clubs — with their somewhat intensive cultural program — would not be suitable everywhere, so he favoured establishing autonomous Zionist societies, ones with a "provision for Zionist content," in every community in Ontario, where he felt the movement was weakest.[89] "We have had many speakers, spasmodically and without plan, go into the towns, in the past few years, but with no attempt to follow up or organize along Zionist lines."

Most of Canada's Jews could participate only vicariously in the struggle for Israel's existence. But still the joy of involvement, especially among Zionist youth movement members, was one of the high points of their lives. Mordecai Richler recalled the scene in the St. Urbain street area when the United Nations General Assembly voted, on November 29, 1947, to partition Palestine and allow the establishment of a Jewish state:

> In our neighborhood, people charged out into the streets to embrace. . . . Men and women who hadn't been to a synagogue since last Yom Kippur surprised themselves, turning up to offer prayers of gratitude and then toss back glasses of schnapps with slices of schmaltz herring. Horns were honked. Photographs of Chaim Weizmann or Ben Gurion, torn from back issues of *Life* or *Look*, were pasted up in bay windows. Blue-and-white Star of David flags flapped in the wind on some balconies.

> Many wept as they sang "Hatikvah," the Zionist anthem. . . . We gathered at the [Habonim] house on Jeanne Mance Street, linked arms, and trooped downtown singing "Am Yisrael Hai" ("The People of Israel Lives") and then danced the hora in the middle of St. Catherine Street, just outside the Forum, bringing traffic to a halt.[90]

Similar though more modest celebrations occurred elsewhere. In Brantford an impromptu party was called, bottles of schnapps produced, and traditional food proffered. Rabbi Gedaliah Felder solemnly pronounced the traditional blessing (*Shehecheyanu*) that marked major events in the Jewish calendar to honour this day, which foreshadowed the Jewish state. Toasts were drunk, embraces exchanged, and tears flowed.

Canadian Volunteers for Israel's Defence

The security of the Yishuv was seriously threatened on the eve of the British departure from Palestine in the spring of 1948. At the urging of Ben Dunkelman and other Jewish war veterans, the ZOC co-operated by recruiting Canadian volunteers for Israel's defence and by sending over certain "materials" — in fact, munitions and arms.[91] Zacks, frustrated by the ZOC's administrative and financial problems, also pushed for action: "I personally would like to see things proceed at a faster tempo because I feel it is the only way results can be obtained."[92]

Leon Crestohl of Montreal, head of the United Zionist Purchasing Commission (which was assembling vital materials for the Yishuv) and later a Liberal MP for Montreal-Cartier, was another Zionist who actively supported recruitment.[93] RCMP informers who attended a mid-March 1948 meeting of the Montreal Jewish youth council, reported:

> *Leon* CRESTOHL then spoke very forcibly about 20 minutes on the emergency facing Jewry, claiming it to be the greatest the Jewish people had yet faced; he berated those who thought that it was not their concern. . . . He strongly urged all Jewish youth to give full support to this Appeal, then remarked "I do not urge you to go to Palestine and fight, as I do not know the legality of such urging, however you all know what you should do."[94]

As a result of such encouragement, and some direct recruitment campaigns, fifty-three Canadians, including fifteen non-Jewish flyers, were recruited to the Israeli air force during the War of Independence.[95] Six of these men, two of them non-Jews, were killed. In the army's ground forces, 232 Canadian volunteers, all but a few of them veterans of the Canadian armed forces, joined up.[96] Lionel Drucker served with distinction in the armoured corps and Ben Dunkelman as a senior officer in an infantry battalion. Some were put together with volunteers from other English-speaking countries in the so-called Anglo-Saxon Battalion (the 72nd) of the Israel Defense Force Seventh Brigade. Others were assigned to the so-called Canadian Platoon, which comprised about half of 2 Company of the Haganah's Givati Brigade.[97]

Not all the Canadian volunteers were happy with their assignments in the IDF. Hymie Klein of Vegreville, Alberta, who, possibly, wanted to be in a Hebrew-speaking formation, complained of being "railroaded" and "tricked" into an English-speaking unit, but he realized that "Eretz is not to blame. . . .

Reuben "Red" Schiff

Reuben "Red" Schiff was one of the Israel Defense Force's first casualties from Toronto. The only son of a hardworking family, Red left his home to join the Canadian army at age seventeen and was honourably discharged in 1945 after being wounded in Germany. In 1947 he was a volunteer sailor on the *Geulah*, a forty-five-year-old former U.S. navy ship, when it brought 1,388 Holocaust survivors to the shores of Eretz Israel in defiance of the British blockade. Schiff and a *Geulah* shipmate, a U.S. army veteran named Louis Ball, were interned in Cyprus for several weeks, but finally got to Haifa in late November 1947. Having become close friends, the two men joined Kibbutz Mayan Baruch. They later enlisted in the Palmach's famous Negev Brigade, whose members were known as the Beasts of the Negev, and took part in all its battles until both were felled just two days apart.

Described in IDF Yizkor records as a "cool and collected fighter who knew no fear," Reuben Schiff was killed on July 11, 1948, near the village of Abu J'Ab while looking for Ball after he failed to return from a battle for the nearby Iraq el Sueidan police fortress. Red was first buried at Kibbutz Ruhama, then on May 16, 1950, was re-interred in Tel Aviv's Nachlat Yitzhak military cemetery.

— *Eddy Kaplansky*

See also Joseph N. Hochstein and Murray S. Greenfield, *The Jews' Secret Fleet* (Jerusalem: Gefen Publishing, 1988), 181–82.

We must give it a chance."[98] In general, however, the volunteers were happy serving the Jewish people in this way. They risked, and in some cases gave, their lives — a sacrifice far more substantial, obviously, than even the most generous donation made by the cheque-book Zionists back in Canada.

Leadership Training in Israel

The experiences of the Young Judaeans who attended the one-year Machon (Institute) program in the early 1950s were probably typical of those of the few young Canadians who went to Israel as leadership trainees from the various youth movements. Their observations of the country at that crucial time in its history, when it was absorbing so many immigrants of diverse cultures, capture the contrasts and collisions that necessarily accompanied the ingathering of Holocaust survivors and Jews from Arab lands.

The Young Judaea leader Ben-Zion Shapiro of Toronto wrote home twice a week — a good son — reporting on what he observed of Israeli social and cultural life. What seems to have made the deepest impressions on him was the intense commitment by the kibbutzniks to their way of life. But the underside of Israel also struck him: the thriving black market, the shortages of food and other essentials, the *protektsia* (influence-peddling), and the Spartan conditions of the established settlers (which, next to the awful circumstances of the new arrivals, seemed almost luxurious).

Above all, however, there was the joy of Jerusalem, even though it was divided between Israel and Jordan, which controlled most holy sites, including the Western Wall. "We never tire," he wrote shortly after arriving in September 1951, "of walking through the streets to see all the different quarters and the different costumes and appearances, as well as to hear the babel of languages spoken."[99] And the smells of Jerusalem, wafting from the bushes and trees scattered through the city, added an aroma found nowhere else. The changing colour of the city's stonework as the sun moved from midday to dusk and then sank into the coastal plain made an indelible impression. And encounters with Israelis brought on discussions, not always polite, about the importance of the state to Jewish survival. "We . . . bemoan the fact that there is no sign of Liberal Judaism [here]," Shapiro wrote early on in his stay, and then commented on the quaintness of the religious Jews in Jerusalem's Mea Shearim quarter, many of them Hasidim. "Most Israelis find it quite hard to understand the attitude of people, who refuse to accept their view that all Jews should move to Israel," he wrote after a few weeks in the country. "They give the Jewry of America up as bound to assimilate before long, and gradually disappear, or be subjected to the same end as German Jewry."[100]

Louis Greenspan, who entered the same program in 1952, reflected many years later that on leaving his native Halifax for Israel (on a boat full of American Jews), he was entering fully into the Jewish world, the "one which is rained on by history."[101] Israel baldly presented him and the other Canadian Machon-niks with challenges and perplexities which required him to confront his Jewishness in a self-dialogue that lasted, in his case, the entire year — and, for some, nearly a lifetime. What did it mean, he mused, to be a Jew in the time of Israel's rebirth? While pondering this nearly impenetrable mystery, he encountered, for the first time, the bewildering conflict of right- and left-wing Zionism — and the many permutations in between. There was also the exposure to modern literature, which was discussed at night by university students, and the encounters with the brilliant Zionist intellectuals who taught courses in history, geography, sociology, religion — and, of course, Hebrew. In the Jerusalem of the early 1950s, there were also resonances of Central and East European secular culture: films, music, and lectures. At the same time, the students witnessed weekly the piety of the Hasidim enjoying their sabbath, soaring away in song and dance from the earthly Jerusalem to "the Jerusalem above." This, above all, was what Israel offered: a new view of Jewishness. "In Canada," Greenspan reflected, "we had achieved what the Enlightenment promised. We were Jews at home and women and men in the streets. Here in Israel the streets were Jewish."

This idealism was catching. For some of the youth, camp life provided forums for other types of discovery than those offered by the close proximity of both sexes. After a summer of intensive indoctrination from an Israeli *shaliach* (delegate), during Camp Biluim's first season in 1951, fifteen of its teenage leadership trainees solemnly resolved to form a *garin* (seed group) to prepare to build Young Judaea's first kibbutz.[102] There was a certain irony in this teenage earnestness, coming as it did through the efforts of Israeli educators who, in some cases, had themselves abandoned the collective life they were encouraging the youth to embrace. A few members of the *garin* did make Aliyah, but they all eventually returned home, defeated by the demanding realities of Israeli life and the special circumstances of collective living.

An Overview

Canadian Zionism in this period reached a level of intense activity that was never to be equalled. Long-established fund-raising programs were joined by a new interest in local political activity and a serious concern with *chalutziut*. In these respects, it might be said that the movement had matured. The vigorous political work undertaken by the Canadian Palestine Committee matched in intensity that of its American counterpart, though it probably had less effect on Canadian public opinion because of Canada's quasi-British identity. Nevertheless, many minds were either changed or strongly influenced, and though perhaps not critical in the formation of Canada's policy on Palestine between 1945 and 1948, the publicity drives and lobbying efforts undertaken by the Zionists can only have helped the cause.

The public-relations campaign had a series of goals. Initially, it attacked the British White Paper. Then it began to focus on Palestine partition and the full recognition of Israel by Canada. Finally, the campaign pushed for Israel's acceptance into the United Nations. Thus between 1943 and 1948, the work of the Canadian lobby — mainly, but not exclusively, through the Canada-Palestine Committee — was uninterrupted.

This serious activity served also to further unite the Canadian Jewish community. Virtually all the pro-Zionist segments — except for the Revisionists, who favoured the use of other methods — supported the work of the Canada-Palestine Committee. Indeed, the Canadian Jewish Congress, which embraced virtually the entirety of Jewry, endorsed the committee's work from the beginning. This unity had been building for at least a decade.

Even non-Zionists could support the establishment of a Jewish refuge in Palestine. The Holocaust not only changed the course of modern Jewish history, but also reduced the intellectual options open to those concerned with the ongoing "Jewish question." Indeed, the very nature of the question was suddenly altered forever. From 1945 onward, Zionism moved slowly towards a position of legitimacy within the Jewish world.

Thus, by 1948, Zionism had become, by *force majeure*, as close to being the universal credo of Canadian Jewry as any belief could. To be sure, the battle for its acceptance had never been as difficult as it was in the United States. Indeed, significant organized Jewish opposition to Zionism had never materialized in Canada, owing to a combination of interesting historical circumstances that, in some respects, sharply distinguished Canadian and American Jewry. There were many non-Zionists and some anti-Zionists in the community, of course, but apart from sporadic and ambivalent attacks on Zionism by the Jewish Communists, no Jewish group set itself up in sustained opposition to Zionism. This is not to say, however, that the Canadian Zionist spirit was necessarily more intensive or profound than the American one.

Was Canadian Zionism at this time essentially just a philanthropic activity intended for Jews already in the land of Israel? The evidence is mixed, but this description is not really sufficient. For Canadian Jews, Zionism in the 1940s and early 1950s carried immense meaning, especially within the context of the Holocaust. Zionism kept many Jews closer to their roots than they might have been otherwise. It perpetuated and deepened their sense of unity and common purpose with Jews around the world, while at the same time offering hope for survival and for national reconstruction. Like Zionists everywhere, Canadians believed themselves to be working under pressure, against dark forces that were destroying the Jewry of Europe and threatening their survival in Palestine. Resources were needed to rescue, to defend, and to build.

In the disorder of the wartime era, the Jews of the free world were the only ones in a position to provide resources. Canadian Jews accepted increasingly heavy financial responsibilities and put immense energy into urgent fund-raising appeals in the belief that they also serve who write and gather cheques. To such people, the youthful enthusiasm for political ideologies and dubious settlement schemes was, at best, an unrealistic distraction from what they thought had to be the main goal of all Canadian Jewry: sending help.

Canadian Zionists not only gave financial support, they also believed themselves to be an integral and vital part of Zionist labours. The fact that they themselves were not smuggling Jewish refugees illegally into Palestine, not building new settlements, not fighting off marauders was less important than that they felt at one with their brother and sister Jews who *were* performing these heroic acts.

The Future of Zionism in Canada

The support for Zionism in Canada did not end in 1948 when Israel was established. Indeed, the movement became much stronger from that point on because a growing number of Canada's Jews were Israel-centred. Ironically, though, success in establishing the state had, in some senses, lessened the urgency and the power of the Canadian Zionist work; Israel became the possession of all Jews, Zionist and non-Zionist alike.

By the early 1950s, the ZOC — and indeed all Zionist organizations — was becoming a less significant vehicle for Canadian Jewish engagement in the affairs of Israel. In part, this was a result of the growing strength of community fund-raising activities through the new federations of Jewish charities, which decided how much to allocate to Israel and to other causes. Zacks lamented this transformation in a letter to Batshaw in December 1951.[103] But he also observed that

> there seems to be an awful lot of confusion. Many who do not want the ZOC to be political have succeeded in diluting it to such an extent that it is gradually losing its strength and vigor. There are also many

> who feel that it is no longer a general Zionist body. . . . It is painful to watch the disintegration.

Having lost its fund-raising muscle to the United Israel Appeal (except in some small communities), the ZOC began to fade into insignificance. What emerged in place of it and its brother Zionist organizations — with the exception of those which, like Canadian Hadassah-WIZO, maintained fund-raising autonomy — was a new and much broader Canadian Jewish partnership with the state of Israel and its people.

CHAPTER

10

Postwar Adjustments, 1945–60

"There ought to be a monument to each and every one of them," commented Phillip Stuchen, a Canadian who spent nineteen months between 1945 and 1947 at displaced persons' (DP) camps in Landsberg and Heidelberg assisting Holocaust survivors. Stuchen was one of several Canadian Jews who worked for the United Nations Relief and Rescue Agency (UNRRA) and the American Jewish Joint Distribution Committee (the Joint). After a five-week orientation course in New York, he arrived in Germany in the summer of 1945. There he joined the health and welfare effort, which was seriously hampered by shortages of supplies.[1]

Stuchen was impressed by the courage and determination of the survivors he met in the camps. Writing for the autumn 1947 issue of *Queen's Quarterly*, he described the strenuous efforts made by former concentration camp inmates to rebuild their lives by learning trades, producing goods for themselves and the occupation forces in Germany, and administering the displaced persons' camps. That this "saving remnant" would be useful immigrants for Canada he had no doubt:

> They will see the results of their own efforts. Their daily toil will mean clothes and shoes for their newly found wives and rapidly increasing families. The mass employment scheme will quicken the morale of these deserving people. And finally, it will leave a people well equipped with a trade or profession for that day when their emigration to Palestine, to the United States, to Australia, to Canada or elsewhere will take place.

It may well happen, indeed, that a machine operator trained at Lampertheim or a tailor employed at Camp Landsberg will eventually find his way to Montreal or Toronto or Winnipeg.[2]

Hananiah Meir Caiserman, dispatched by the Congress in 1946 to report on the condition of Jews in Poland and help Canadians locate surviving members of their families, observed that "all is dust and desolation."[3] When he met some survivors in the ruins of Bialystok, Caiserman wrote: "The twenty-five people (men and women) who had supper with us, each had a number

---

Mommy, Why Did You Leave Me?

Ibolya Grossman

I was only four years old when I saw you last.
But your kind and lovely face
Is still in front of my eyes.
You said many times how much you loved me
Then why? Why did you leave me?

We had many lovely times together
You took me in the park to play
You read my favourite books to me every day
And you said that you always,
Always wanted me close to you.
You held me tight and kissed me
Then why? Why did you leave me?

It's been three years already
I'm a big girl by now, over seven
But every night when I close my eyes
And before I go to sleep I still think of you Mommy
Why? Why did you leave me?

I'm in a children's home now
With many other orphaned children
And I have friends and nannies I like.
But one day I was told that evil men had killed you
Because there was a war.
But what did you do? What was your sin Mommy?
Why? Why did you have to leave me?

burned on their arm while in the concentration camps. Each has a story of horror and slow death both physical and moral and one continues to wonder, 'How could they stand it? How?'"[4] Appealing to Canadian Jews to send relief to Polish Jewry, he commented: "I was not prepared to understand the real meaning of finding 65,000 Jews from 3 1/4 million who lived there before the war. Under the circumstances, I did not expect to find their loyalty as Jews unimpaired."

In another communiqué, Caiserman reported a conversation with Yechiel Leben, a nine-year-old boy living at a children's home in a town near Warsaw. "'My father and mother were both burned alive. I only have my little brother, David, one year old, at the same children's home,' he said. He also has an uncle, Zigmund Leben, in Lodz, Poland. He knows he has another uncle named Leben who lives in Canada or in the United States. 'Find him for me,' he actually cried and I cried with him."[5] Especially moved by the plight of children who "had escaped annihilation [and] wandered about the forests and fields of Poland, often dying friendless and without finding the peace of a

---

You should have told those evil men
That you had a little girl at home,
You should have told those bad people
To leave you alone.
If you loved me and you had told them about me . . .
Then why? Why did you have to leave me?

I believed you when you said you loved me.
I loved you too, I still do.
But I wish somebody would tell me
Why? Oh why did you have to leave me?

Ibolya Grossman, originally from Hungary, survived the Holocaust in the Budapest ghetto. She now resides in Toronto. After the Second World War, Grossman worked as a nanny in a Jewish orphanage in Budapest. There she met a little girl whose parents were killed by the Nazis in 1944. This poem is from that child's point of view. Grossman received an award from the Jewish Book Committee of Toronto for her work in Holocaust literature.

From *Outlook* 35, no. 3 (1997): 18.

grave,"[6] Caiserman adopted one of these orphans and urged Canadian Jewry to open their homes to others whom the Congress was sponsoring.

When he arrived back in Canada with 1,500 letters and messages from survivors to their families, Caiserman was so emotionally overwrought that he was forced to rest for several days in Halifax before proceeding to Montreal. There he was disappointed by the initial response to the project of bringing Holocaust orphans like Yechiel Leben to Canada, a response that, he commented, "does not reflect honour on Montreal Jewry."[7] And he was outraged by the callous disregard of the Joint's appeal for assistance in placing Jewish women and girls whom the Canadian government was prepared to admit as domestics. Jewish housewives did not want them. "I cannot believe that Jewish women would discriminate against Jewish girls and thereby deny them Canadian entry," he thundered.

> Jews of Canada as elsewhere are living through the greatest crisis in our history. Each Jew must be aware of this and must draw conclusions of personal responsibility. Is there a greater humanitarian deed than the rescue from D.P. Camps of as many Jews as possible? . . . How could there be a prejudice? . . . It is a shameful prejudice against our own sisters. It is a matter of Jewish honour.

In the meantime, public attitudes remained strongly antisemitic, notwithstanding the newsreels showing horrific scenes from the Belsen and Dachau concentration camps. In an October 1946 Gallup poll that asked respondents to list nationalities they would like to keep out of Canada, Jews were deemed the second least desirable immigrants. The Japanese were considered the most undesirable.[8]

The attitude of some Canadian officials was as bad or worse. In a letter from the Canadian high commission in London, one official wrote of the "black marketing, dirty living habits and general slovenliness" of the Jewish Holocaust survivors in the German DP camps.[9] Nevertheless, Canada's virtually exclusionist immigration policy softened in 1948, when the government recognized the need for an increased labour supply in a more buoyant economy and also gave in to "irresistible pressure from her U.N. Allies." Substantial numbers of Jews began arriving, starting with the 1,116 war orphans sponsored by the Congress.[10] In Prien, Germany, Ethel Ostry (a Winnipeg native and a social worker with experience in Manitoba, Toronto, Montreal, and Palestine) handled the job of organizing the orphan children whom the Canadian government had allowed to enter the country.[11]

Enormous communal resources were mobilized by a committee headed by

Samuel Bronfman, who took a special interest in this project. Reception centres were set up and foster homes arranged in communities from Glace Bay to Vancouver.[12] That same year, 1948, 1,800 Jews arrived under the so-called Tailor's Project, which arranged for experienced workers in the men's-clothing industry to be admitted under the auspices of a committee representing the Congress, industry, labour unions, and JIAS. In all, Canadian Jewry spent nearly three million dollars on the reception, resettlement, and rehabilitation of approximately 11,000 Jewish displaced persons and some 4,000 to 7,000 other survivors who entered Canada between 1946 and 1951.[13]

One scholar points out that Canadian officials, chiefly those of the Congress and JIAS, were much more vigorous than their American counterparts in lobbying to receive Holocaust survivors. "Congress' post-war activities were overwhelmingly concerned with bringing survivors into Canada, whereas in 1943 American Jewish organizations had already designated Palestine as the post-war haven for surviving Jews of Europe."[14] Using its pre-existing network in the clothing industry, Canadian Jewry got governmental permission to recruit skilled garment workers, "an example of the ethnic chain forging new links."[15] From her key position in the German DP camps, Lottie Levinson, a former executive-secretary of the Canadian Jewish Congress of British Columbia, worked on the assumption that survivors would prefer to immigrate to Canada rather than to Palestine and deplored "the fallacy of too much nationalism" among them.[16]

Although overwhelmingly drawn from Eastern Europe like earlier Jewish immigrants, these migrants were different. They had experienced the Holocaust. Most were of Polish origin, and had endured the destruction of both family and home; they'd persevered through years of fear, hiding, and hunger, and had survived loss of childhood, values, and hope. The difficulty of their adjustment to Canadian life was observed by one Toronto social worker, Ben Lappin, who pointed out that the Canadian emphasis on "positive ends [such] as the achievement of social and economic independence . . . [evoked] bitter memories and suspicions among the orphaned children," who might have expected a deeper understanding of their precarious mental state at that time.[17] Many Jewish professionals reported difficulties with the lay community, whose goodwill often surpassed their understanding of the need for a certain detachment in handling these cases.[18] Although orphans and other immigrants benefited from the concern and support of the community, their difficulties in adjusting often prevented a meeting of minds.

Some of these survivors had intended to go to Palestine, but were forced by the delays in getting permits and by the conditions in the DP camps to go to Canada instead. One remembered:

> We lived in what had been a bathroom, in the barracks. The walls were mouldy. We lived there two years. I was sick — I lost a baby. One day my husband came home and said, "Come on, we're going to Canada." "Wait a minute," I said, "that's not in the plan." "Look at you," he said, "we can't live like this. At least in Canada we can live." So he was chosen to come as a tailor, and we came.[19]

Some immigrants, offended by what they perceived to be "negative reactions and attitudes," withdrew from the community. After a serious disagreement with a local union activist, one survivor realized "that this person knew nothing about the . . . Holocaust . . . [and I] pledged never to discuss my experiences again with a non-survivor."[20] Other survivors developed a resentment towards the established Jewish community. One commented, "Maybe they were going around with the guilt they could not work out with themselves that they left us over there. They didn't put up here a big fuss."[21]

In Hamilton, where the community hosted twenty-five orphans and several other survivors, inexperience in handling such cases and the "problems of personality difficulties stemming from their concentration camp and other war-time experiences," sometimes led to serious difficulties.[22] Even though their language training, clothing, loans, housing, recreation, and medical needs were provided for, the immigrants found they had difficulty making themselves understood to community workers. For a variety of reasons, some did not feel comfortable at the Jewish Community Centre,[23] where, as one of them put it, people were greeted coldly with "'Hello, how are you,' and that's all."[24] And the social workers had their own complaints. One observed that the immigrants "have adopted the 'I have suffered and you owe me' concept."[25] In fact, many immigrants felt alienated from North American Jews, were haunted by horrible memories, longed for lost loved ones, were fearful of anti-semitism, and in a few cases, were morally corrupted by their wartime experiences. The vast majority of them soon settled into jobs, families, and homes, but others just drifted.

The ease of the survivors' adjustment seemed to have depended on the social norms in the Jewish community where they settled. On the basis of extensive quantitative comparisons, Jean Gerber found that in Vancouver's small Jewish community of about 3,100 persons, "the fluid nature of the receiving . . . Jewish society allowed survivors easy access to institutions and economic mobility."[26] And because survivors came from so many national and educational backgrounds, they easily "integrated into existing patterns already established by the host Jewish group," moving into the same neighbourhoods, occupational networks, and institutions. They strengthened the Vancouver Jewish community, contributing money, participating in its governance, and bringing "a unique perspective on recent Jewish history, both in the realm of ideas and in . . . teaching and documenting the Holocaust."[27]

In some cases, the new arrivals started off as labourers. One recalled working on a CPR construction crew near Penticton, British Columbia:

> There was [*sic*] nine Jewish boys in that railroad gang, so the Jewish community of Vancouver got permission, and they brought them down for Pesach and they had a seder for them and [one of us] decided when his contract expired that he's going to come to Vancouver and settle. Being a tailor by profession it was very easy for him to get a job here.[28]

Even though she wanted to be with other Jews, one female survivor, at least initially, found it difficult to join the High Holiday services in the Vancouver synagogue:

> When I went to the synagogue here and I looked down and I've seen all the families, all of a sudden it was such a shock to me, I couldn't take it. I felt that we had nobody, that I'm a piece of sand somewhere on an island, like [I had] no past. And I went out. I said, "Am I jealous? No, I'm happy for the people," but I couldn't take it. Then I said, "I have to deal with it." I bought some records of the famous *Chazzanim*, I took a few friends who didn't go to the holidays, and we would sit at home and listen. I couldn't face it for a long time.[29]

By 1970, however, the vast majority of immigrant Jews had prospered and were employed alongside the native-born Jews, even occupying a higher percentage of the professional class.[30]

In Montreal, on the other hand, many survivors clubbed together in their own *landsmanshaft*, bonding in anguish, memory, and hope. A member of the Czenstochover Society reflected:

> We were very close, very, very close. . . . We used to tell stories. Do you remember this? As I said before, familiarity [with the past] is a very, very touching thing, which you can't buy for money. And we enjoyed it immensely, all through the years. . . .[31]

Another observed:

> I feel the closest to the people who came from the Zamosc roots. . . . It was very important for me, very important. Among these people, it was possible to reminisce about my home. This was a constant theme of our conversations. We used to remind ourselves of all the different things in our old home. This enriched my life very much.

A woman survivor who was crying at a Holocaust memorial service in 1949 was told by a Canadian-born Jew to stop. "Enough is enough. . . . No more crying and no more talking about what happened. This is a new country and a new life."[32] But among themselves, survivors felt free to reminisce: "Amongst our group, if we felt like talking about something, we could. We were listening to each other's stories, and it was just fine." These small outfits, dedicated to mutual aid, support for Israel, and Holocaust commemoration, thrived, helping survivors to adapt. Many married, started businesses, had children, and established homes. Some lapsed into a lifelong depression that affected even their children and grandchildren. Most felt the significant distance between themselves and the established Jewish community open up again over the proper response to the re-emergence of pro-Nazi organizations in the early 1960s.[33]

But their very presence in the communities also contributed, in the words of Jean Gerber, to "the emerging ideology of post-war North American Judaism, . . . [which] sought to explain the Holocaust and the rise of the state of Israel as interconnected events."[34] In a wider sense, the survivors, as "eye-witnesses to the Holocaust, influenced the direction of community thinking about the nature and meaning of Jewish life. . . . They did this not only by appealing to a shared distant past, but by presenting a Judaism in which survivor and native-born could share a sense of history as well as a destiny."[35]

Though survivors formed the majority of postwar Jewish immigrants (some 30,000 to 35,000 of them and their children had come by 1956),[36] many other Jews were also arriving, including substantial numbers from the United States and the British Isles. There were also rapidly growing numbers from Israel, especially during the early 1950s, when Israelis comprised the largest single component.[37] Three-quarters of the Israeli immigrants had moved to the homeland after the Second World War; only 11 percent were born in that country. By 1963, nearly 11,739 Israelis had reached Canada and many more were to follow.[38] By that time, the five thousand Hungarians who had arrived in 1956 and 1957 had been absorbed, with large Congress assistance, and a substantial inflow was coming from Morocco, Egypt, and Tunisia.[39] Meanwhile, the beginnings of what was to become a significant South African migration were already in evidence.

Ebb and Flow of Quebec Antisemitism

Life for Jews in Canada became easier after 1945. The nastiest forms of antisemitism virtually disappeared from view, especially in Quebec. Human-rights and antidiscrimination legislation allowed for easier social and economic mobility, and general postwar Canadian prosperity facilitated an enormous expansion of the Jewish community's institutions. The struggle for Israel mobilized Jews behind the Zionist banner as never before, providing them with a sense of purpose that combined the urgent rescue of Jews at risk with the idea of national revival in the ancient homeland. There were antisemitic incidents, to be sure, some of them very serious. Graves were desecrated, anti-Jewish literature was circulated, poisonous remarks were made by public figures, restrictive covenants prevented Jews from living in certain areas, and Jews still were barred from many resorts and private clubs. But all of these episodes were minor compared with the antisemitism current in Canada in the 1930s.

The change was particularly evident in Quebec.[40] David Rome, the Canadian Jewish Congress press officer who closely monitored the local scene, had reported in 1942 that "the vigorous anti-conscription campaign in Quebec took a violently anti-Jewish form and was marked by several clashes in the streets of Montreal." He observed the following year that only the Quebec City synagogue issue marred an otherwise quiet provincial scene.[41] There was an upsurge of antisemitism in 1944, with the burning of the newly finished synagogue in Quebec City and the emergence of the "Jewish issue" in the August provincial elections. But matters were generally improving in the province. In 1945 Rome recorded only the damaging of several tombstones in a Montreal cemetery, while noting that Father Stéphane Valiquette had published an article in the influential Jesuit publication *Relations* that was sympathetic to the plight of Jews who, in his view, were in an inferior position in the Protestant school system.[42] "There has been a diminution of anti-Jewish agitation. . . in the province of Quebec . . . and there have even emerged the beginnings of intergroup activity with the participation of the dominant Catholic Church."

The community still felt oppressed by the Anglo-Protestants, who insisted that Jews had no rights in the Protestant school system. In 1945 the Protestant school board of the city of Outremont — where Montreal's Jewish population was beginning to move — refused to renew the agreement allowing Jewish children to attend their schools. Premier Maurice Duplessis personally tried to persuade the Protestants to reconsider, but the issue took time to be resolved,[43] leaving the Jewish community sorely agitated. A few years later, similar problems arose in the suburb of Hampstead, which was experiencing a substantial Jewish influx. In this case, too, the Union Nationale provincial government attempted to moderate the position of the Protestant board towards the Jewish presence.

Changes in Quebeckers' Attitudes to Jews

Despite these isolated incidents, something astonishing was taking place in Quebec. In Rome's words, it was "the remarkable rapprochement between the Jewish community and the French-Canadian Catholic majority."[44] When Laurent Barré, the provincial minister of agriculture, made some antisemitic comments in the Legislative Assembly, he was publicly condemned by Mgr. Henri Jeannotte, a member of a special committee put together by Montreal's archbishop, Joseph Charbonneau, to deal with questions related to Jews. Jeannotte's statement met with approval in the French-language press. "For the first time in the history of this province the Church condemned a public figure for his anti-Semitism," Rome exulted. Meanwhile, the committee began a systematic and widely noticed education campaign directed against antisemitism. It also played a key role in quashing the re-emergence of *Le Goglu*, the vicious antisemitic rag of the 1930s.[45] A Catholic youth publication that included antisemitic attacks was condemned, withdrawn, and reprinted with the offending passages excised. Archbishop Charbonneau even pressed *Le Devoir*, where antisemitic articles, so common in the 1930s, had completely disappeared, to employ younger, more progressive, and more humanistic editors. In a November 1952 issue of *Le Devoir*, none other than André Laurendeau, the leader of Jeune-Canada's antisemitic campaign of the 1930s, published a scathing critique of Senator Joseph McCarthy's antisemitic attacks:

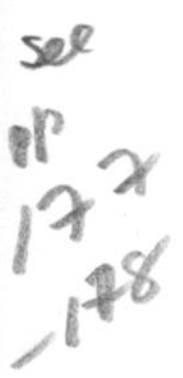

> After the assassination of six million Jews under Hitler's reign, one must not have a too delicate stomach to swallow these fanatical denunciations without heaving. Such antisemitism is so stupid that it turned us into philosemites. . . .[46]

What explained this shift from what Rome called "longstanding prejudice" to "remarkable rapprochement"? Rome believed that French Canadians, who long had resisted close contact with members of different religions and races, finally had begun meeting with other groups "to deal with common problems and to bring Canadians of various faiths together." He pointed to the Council of Christians and Jews and the Quebec Federation of Youth as venues for the "sympathetic appreciation of the intellectual and communal life of the Jewish and other groups in the country."

This rapprochement was also apparent in the welcoming reception given works by the Quebec Jewish poet Abraham Moses Klein and the painters Norman Leibovitch and Louis Muhlstock in French-language periodicals. Several Montreal Catholic groups even initiated lectures by clerics on Jewish topics. In 1949 Rabbi Chaim Denburg was appointed a lecturer in medieval studies at the Université de Montréal, the first Jew to join the faculty of a Catholic university in Canada. While Rome recognized that "anti-Jewish prejudice was [not] destroyed in the province," he believed "it [had] distinctly lost the influence and the respectability which it once enjoyed."[47]

Journalist Betty Sigler observed that the medical school at the Université de Montréal, unlike McGill, had no Jewish quota and that Dominican and Jesuit priests were actively trying to dispel French-Canadian prejudice against Jews. "French Canadians," she stressed, "are no more anti-semitic than their English compatriots and a greater frankness often makes them easier for many Jews to get along with than the more circumspect British."[48]

Much was happening in Quebec to change traditional views. French Canada, as the sociologist Everett Hughes explained in his 1943 scholarly study, was still "in transition," under the powerful influence of massive industrialization wrought largely by American investment throughout the province.[49] The battering-ram of capitalism was destroying the old way of life, and the Second World War had accelerated the transformation from an essentially rural province to an increasingly urban, industrial society, which in turn brought a growing degree of secularization.[50]

Some elements of the church became infused with ideas such as those espoused by Father Georges-Henri Lévesque, a Dominican priest-academic deeply committed to democratic norms and liberal values in transforming Quebec and who established the School of Social Sciences at Laval University in 1938.[51] The relationship of church and state and the definition of Quebec's very personality were undergoing significant revision. "From 1945 on," Pierre Elliott Trudeau observed, "a series of events and movements had combined to relegate the traditional concepts of authority in Quebec to the scrap-heap."[52] Trudeau himself was one of a small group of French-Canadian intellectuals with a new openness to ideas that rendered Quebec less isolated and inward-looking. He was among those who led the 1949 Asbestos strike, which symbolized the end of the old Quebec and the dawning of the new. André Laurendeau and others began to meet French-speaking Jewish intellectuals and re-evaluate, and even repent, the antisemitism of their youth.

By the late 1940s, the Quebec Catholic church was no longer as monolithic, parochial, and nationalistic as it had been between the wars. The church was beginning to shift its discourse to focus on more universalistic values. This was seen in the emergence in Montreal of a more liberal clergy, many of whom were attempting to enter into dialogue with non-Catholics. After the war, the Vatican also stressed to Quebec clergy the importance of the European refugee crisis and the necessity of bringing an end to the traditional anti-immigration attitude in the province.

As Rome shrewdly noted, however, antisemitism had by no means disappeared in Quebec. Canon Lionel Groulx, for one, did not change his views about Jews after the war. In 1954, when asked for his opinion on "the Jewish problem," he replied that while "Christian kindness forbids us all forms of antisemitism, . . . history and daily observations have only shown us [Judaism's] revolutionary tendency." And because of the Jewish passion for money, he contended, one finds Jews at the bottom of "every shady affair, of every pornographic enterprise: books, movies, plays, etc." That's why, Groulx continued, Jews are prepared to sacrifice in business and the professions "all moral scruples."[53] *L'Action Catholique* continued to publish articles demonizing Jews — just as it had in the 1930s.[54]

The idea of the mythical Jew as enemy of French Catholic communal purity continued to find public expression, moreover; the Custos report on the Asbestos strike of 1949 blamed the event on "Judeobolshevists."[55] In the late 1940s, an affair involving Comte Jacques Dugé de Bernonville, who had been convicted and condemned to death by a French court for war crimes during the Vichy regime, indicated that, for a few at least, Fascism was alive and well in "la belle province."[56] This collaborator was illegally brought to Quebec and protected by local pro-Fascist sympathizers, including the prominent historian Robert Rumilly. One provincial politician, René Chaloult, delivered a strong antisemitic statement in the National Assembly in defence of Bernonville, and Montreal mayor Camillien Houde led the campaign to prevent his deportation. Accusations surfaced that as many as twenty more French war criminals were hiding out in Montreal.[57]

Meanwhile, several prominent Québécois citizens wrote to Prime Minister Louis St. Laurent, one describing de Bernonville as the victim of "a well-organized plot by the Left which breathes hatred and dissension against those who would grant him shelter."[58] Church officials described the count as an "excellent citizen" and "a Christian gentleman," and the St.-Jean Baptiste Society formed defence committees in Montreal, Quebec, and Trois-Rivières. While the controversy raged, and unbeknownst to the public, the Dominion government passed a special order-in-council that allowed five other former Vichyites who were under sentence of death or being sought by French courts to remain permanently in Canada, despite the fact that they had entered this country illegally.[59]

Overall, however, the old clerico-fascism and its associated "moral crusades" were out of favour, even among most of its former adherents.[60] Although Adrian Arcand surfaced again in the mid-1950s to fulminate against Jews in his monthly journal, *L'Unité national*, he had little influence and soon disappeared from view. Undoubtedly, antisemitism was still present in Quebec and the rest of Canada, but the Holocaust and the postwar Nuremberg trials made public displays less respectable.

At this time, the Jewish community began to pro-actively reach out to francophone clerical and intellectual leaders.[61] Led by Saul Hayes and David Rome, Quebec Jewry reactivated their public-relations committee and established the Cercle Juif de la Langue Française to demonstrate to French Canadians that Jews were not "on the side of the English" in Quebec. In fact, a segment of Montreal Jewish intellectuals was genuinely interested in French culture and in establishing a dialogue in French with like-minded Québécois.

In 1954 Naim Kattan, a francophone Jewish immigrant from Iraq and a distinguished author, was employed by the Congress to direct the Cercle Juif's activities and edit its *Bulletin*. Kattan established good relationships with several leading francophone journalists, including André Laurendeau and Jean-Marc Leger of *Le Devoir*, Roger Duhamel of *La Patrie*, and René Lévesque of the CBC.[62] Their response was warm, but they cautioned that the Quebec Jewish community should cease presenting "an English façade, [and] airs of unilingual English-Canadians," as Conrad Langlois of *La Patrie* put it.[63] While the efforts mounted by the Congress could not entirely rid the Jewish community of its English "façade," they did provide a highly useful meeting ground for some Montreal intellectuals from two of Quebec's three solitudes.

Still, manifestations of antisemitism persisted. As late as 1965, the Quebec liberal thinker Claude Ryan expressed the view that if French Canadians and Jews were to achieve a full rapprochement, "a certain updating of the Jewish religion might be in order."[64] When faced with Jewish concerns about the course of French-Canadian nationalism, Ryan also reacted strongly, believing that the Jews put the questions to him

> in a rather aggressive tone, as if they were entitled to get firm assurance from a humble person like myself. . . . The only thing I can tell them . . . is that to the extent that they associate with the search that is going on . . . in the French Canadian mind, . . . there is a greater chance that this search will end up in a happy way. But to the extent that they keep putting questions as if they were standing in an outside position, the dangers are extremely great that this might explode in their faces.[65]

Jews must change, Ryan contended, to overcome the old antisemitic attitudes "still very much alive in the minds of most French Canadians." Among other things, Ryan asserted, many Québécois believe that the Jew "will do practically anything in order to make a fast dollar"; that he has "the reputation of paying low salaries and being not too scrupulous about working conditions"; that Jews in general "are extremely important in the making of financial decisions" in Canada; that Jewish notaries "have tended to specialize in practices that leave much to be desired"; that "Jews will support one another to death"; that "Jews killed Jesus Christ"; and that "Jews do not care for morality."

Meanwhile, Jews were accorded an unprecedented degree of recognition by Québécois. Dr. Victor Goldbloom was appointed to the Cabinet in the Liberal government of Jean Lesage in the 1960s. At around the same time, Jewish parochial schools were accorded recognition and generous financial assistance by the government, and the semi-independence of the Jewish social-welfare network in Montreal was also upheld.[66] Jews were even appointed to teaching posts in francophone universities. At the same time, however, Quebec's Jews still felt that they were walking a tightrope. The separatist upsurge in the 1960s, the language legislation of the 1970s, the October Crisis, and statements by some sovereigntists made Quebec Jews nervous and uncertain of their future. Many Jews, especially the young ones who were concerned that Québécois nationalist policies might hamper their career choices, began to leave the province.

Antisemitism outside Quebec

Antisemitism survived elsewhere in Canada, too. The Social Credit movement in Alberta (and in Quebec), for example, continued to harbour antisemites who made their views public on the platform and in print.[67] Alberta-based members of the Canadian Jewish Congress monitored the situation closely and regularly urged Montreal headquarters to institute countermeasures. By the late 1940s, however, antisemitism had become such an embarrassment to the Socred national organization that it repudiated those factions and "dissociate[d] itself from the racial and religious intolerance which they are propagating."[68] Even so, these elements continued to put out antisemitic literature on a regular basis; *The Canadian Intelligence Service* (edited for many years by Ron Gostick) was one such periodical. Occasionally, pamphlets like *Plans of the Synagogue of Satan* by Colonel F. H. M. Colville, a British Columbia Socred member, appeared, but these were always repudiated by the movement's leaders.

Prejudice persisted in other forms. Restrictive covenants, for example, were contracts that prevented the sale of properties to Jews and other "undesirables."

In one Ontario case, Bernard Wolfe of London agreed to purchase a summer cottage at nearby Beach O' Pines resort, but he was prevented from taking possession by such a covenant, which barred sales to persons of "Jewish, Hebrew, Semitic, Negro or colored race or blood."[69]

The Ontario Court of Appeal upheld a lower court decision declaring the covenant valid, but the Supreme Court of Canada overturned it in November 1950. Meanwhile, the Ontario legislature passed a bill voiding all covenants restricting the sale or ownership of land for reasons of race or creed.[70] Although these actions lifted the prohibition on residence, the Congress and B'nai Brith still battled against racial, ethnic, and gender discrimination in the work world and the schools. In the wake of the Beach O' Pines decision, the Ontario government discouraged summer resorts from advertising that their clientele was "restricted" or "selected." It became increasingly difficult for haters to discriminate, and utterly impossible to restrict Jews from living in certain areas.

Ontario, which enacted the Racial Discrimination Act in 1944 and the Fair Employment Practices Act in 1951, led all levels of government in passing comprehensive bills to outlaw discrimination and the dissemination of hate literature. Joseph Salsberg, Rabbi Abraham Feinberg, various labour leaders, the Canadian Jewish Congress, Jewish activists in the Ontario Progressive Conservative Party, and the Canadian Jewish press were all leading advocates for human-rights legislation.

The Congress official Ben Kayfetz recalled, "When I was first employed by CJC in April 1947, the chairman of the Joint Public Relations Committee said my first priority was to plan and work towards the enactment of a Fair Employment law. It came much sooner than we expected, in 1951."[71] The act received support from an increasingly sympathetic public,[72] many of whom had their opinions about the Jewish minority in Canada changed by the Holocaust.[73] Ontario premier Leslie Frost took a special interest in this body of legislation, even though some of his constituents saw this bill as an infringement of their rights. One old friend of Frost's complained, "I do not want a coon or Jew squatting beside me."[74]

Unfortunately, neither legislation nor embarrassment prevented continuing antisemitism at the universities. The admission of Jews to some medical schools was still severely restricted. McGill, for example, limited Jewish admissions to a rigid 10 percent until the 1960s and the University of Toronto required Jews to have higher marks than other applicants. Most Jewish U. of T. graduates had to leave the city for the necessary year of internship because, with a few exceptions, Toronto's hospitals would not accept them, regardless of their academic standing. It was also still difficult for qualified Jewish doctors to acquire admitting privileges at these hospitals. When Mount Sinai Hospital was completed in the late 1950s, its status as a teaching hospital for the University of Toronto was delayed until 1962.[75] Such discrimination forced the Toronto and Montreal Jewish communities to continue to support their own hospitals. Indeed, hospital building campaigns were the focus of their largest fund-raising efforts; roughly 25 percent of all monies raised for capital projects in the 1950s and 1960s went to hospitals.

Undoubtedly, the continuing concern about the persistence of antisemitism in postwar Canada influenced the Congress' submission to the 1949 Royal Commission on National Development in the Arts, Letters and Sciences (known as the Massey Commission). Congress argued that Canada's national cultural institutions (such as the National Library, the Public Archives, the National Gallery, the National Museum, the National Film Board, and the Canadian Broadcasting Corporation)[76] should "search for the formula which will vouchsafe the creation of a vibrant and meaningful Canadianism."[77] Speaking on behalf of the Congress, Saul Hayes insisted that if these bodies made Canadians aware of the contribution to the nation of the country's many different ethnic groups, Canadian democracy would be strengthened and "the best of national characteristics of the people who inhabit Canada, through the catalysis of conditions here, [would] emerge as a distinctive element of North American civilization."

This was an argument, in short, for multiculturalism.[78] But Hayes was forced to recognize that the theory had flaws. Should literature and artistic expression be rewarded along ethnic lines? "Are you going to limit the form of those works?" Professor Hilda Neatby of the University of Saskatchewan asked. "[Do] you . . . want to offer special incentives to the people to express themselves along particular ethnical lines?"[79] Asserting that "you cannot look at the Canadian scene without being aware of the existence of groups," she appropriately suggested that "general encouragement" of literature and the arts would be just as effective. In the end, Hayes's arguments did not move the commission to recommend multiculturalism in Canadian arts and letters. But his brief, which anticipated by a generation the multicultural policies implemented in the 1970s, was an attempt to address the new ethnic reality of Canada, and to prove that all forms of racism could be reduced through new approaches to the question of Canadian identity.

Moving into the Suburbs and Modernity

A new-found freedom of mobility and less overt antisemitism allowed Jews, like all Canadians who were now better off, to leave the old, crowded districts of the urban centres and move into newer housing in the city suburbs. In

Montreal the biggest movement was up from Outremont over the mountain into Côte-des-Neiges, Notre Dame de Grace, and the western suburbs of Saint-Laurent, Côte St-Luc, Chomedy, and Dollard-des-Ormeaux. In Toronto the main Jewish migration pushed up Bathurst Street, past St. Clair, Eglinton, and Lawrence.

In Winnipeg, Jews moved out of the old north end into adjacent West Kildonan and southward into River Heights.[80] They built synagogues, schools, and social facilities, replacing virtually all of the previously existing institutional network. In Vancouver they moved from the east-end immigrant quarter to the newer, lower-middle-class, west-side neighbourhoods, leaving behind the synagogues and kosher food shops that were later replaced by newer and more elaborate structures.[81] Although the vast majority of these families were by no means affluent, they were able to afford the down payments, modest under National Housing Act provisions, for these new bungalows and split-level homes.

The old Jewish neighbourhoods, meanwhile, certainly did not disappear. Many of the older generation of immigrants — now joined by Holocaust survivors — stayed on. Emotionally attached to their old synagogues and comfortable in their houses, they continued to walk the familiar streets and frequent the customary stores. Perhaps they looked with understanding and sympathy at the recently arrived Italian, Greek, and Portuguese immigrants now buying houses and shops in what was once a Jewish neighbourhood.[82] And of course, not all Jews were financially able to move "uptown" in the 1940s and 1950s. For years, the inner-city neighbourhoods retained some Jewish families and the old hang-outs. The corner of College and Spadina in Toronto continued to draw people whose nicknames (Big Norm, Stok, Shacki, Feets, Applejack, Babe, Joe the Ball, Dapper, Dizzy, Jackriv, Fat Sam, Schvitzie, Gijik, Bagels, Baby, Piggie, Pork Chops, Oogie, and Butterballs) suggested the street smarts, derring-do, and postwar hipness of the Jewish would-be "wise guys."[83]

Some more affluent Toronto Jews moved away from the areas of first or second settlement to swanky Forest Hill, but collided with its well-established Anglo-Saxon Protestants and a small and smug pre-war Jewish group. The results, as reported in the 1956 sociological study *Crestwood Heights*, were interesting. Many of the new arrivals shed their "old-fashioned" ways — abandoning Orthodox religious observances, for example — and adopted upper-middle-class norms, while some of the long-settled Christians enrolled their children in private schools so they could avoid contact with Jewish students.[84] Both the Gentiles and the older Jewish settlers tended to regard the newcomers as "vulgar, ostentatious, ignorant, and detrimental to the community."[85] Christian parents did not want their children to be at schools where

Jews were the majority, even though teaching standards were higher in Forest Hill than in almost any other Toronto neighbourhood. Private schools, one Christian parent believed, were necessary for her children "to get the social graces." At Forest Hill Collegiate, on the other hand, she thought her children would "learn materialistic values . . . mainly because of the insecurity of the Jews which has driven them to make a materialistic display of their position and wealth."[86]

With prosperity growing across Canada between 1945 and 1952, more than $31 million was spent on Jewish community buildings (including $11.5 million on hospitals, $8 million on synagogues, $5.24 million on YMHAs and community centres, and $4.18 million on schools).[87] New and expanded health and recreation facilities consumed more than half of the community's financial expenditures, while religious and educational institutions accounted for more than one-third. Social-welfare programs and general community administration took up the remainder.

Synagogues were springing up in the suburbs, and old *shuls* in many smaller communities were being replaced by new edifices that sometimes included community centres and athletic facilities. Typical of the latter were the Jewish centres in Halifax; Brantford, Ontario; and Saskatoon.[88] A plot of land was purchased near the houses of the community's observant Jews, building and finance committees were struck, and a contractor engaged. Once the new building was completed (often after stormy meetings where members, now "experts," hotly debated plans for the new structure), the congregation took its leave of the old *shul* with prayer and rejoicing.

In Brantford the procession was led by children bearing the Union Jack and the Star of David; they preceded several elders carrying Torah scrolls and a newly acquired edition of the Talmud. Next came an aged but energetic violinist, who led the congregants from the old *shul* to the new one as he lovingly played Yiddish tunes. Although the distance was only a hundred metres, symbolically it was one more major step away from the *shtetl* towards modernity.

In the bigger cities, many downtown congregations were re-established in new synagogues by members who had moved to the suburbs. In some cases, these new structures were built by amalgamations of two or three congregations that could not have afforded them individually. Other synagogues were built for entirely new congregations emerging on the city's outskirts. One, the Conservative Beth Am (House of the People) congregation, which was formed in 1954 by a group of working- and lower-middle-class Jews living in northwest Toronto, saw its fortunes fluctuate as Jewish geography changed.[89] It first assembled for services in a tent, then in a house, next in its own hall, and later, in a newly erected sanctuary. As Jewish numbers grew, Beth Am developed a large school, which flourished in the late 1950s and 1960s. However, a migration farther into the suburbs reduced membership in the 1970s, and the school's enrolment also declined sharply. By the mid-1970s, the congregation's long-range future was viewed as "tenuous,"[90] and in 1976 it amalgamated with another congregation.

Meanwhile, most of the old downtown synagogues were converted to churches or community halls for the new immigrants to the area. Only a few synagogues remained in use by the people unwilling or unable to move; others were kept going for the weekday convenience of businessmen whose stores or offices were located nearby.

Virtually abandoned, too, were the Jewish labour halls. In Toronto the Labour Lyceum on Spadina, once home to the needle-trade unions and other left-wing organizations, and the major forum for debate for a generation of working men and women, struggled on with a rapidly diminishing and greying Jewish proletariat. By the mid-1950s, its May Day observances, once attended by hundreds of marchers proudly displaying their solidarity with workers

---

Rabbi (Rav) Gedaliah Felder

Polish-born Gedaliah Felder, an outstanding Talmud scholar and the rabbi of congregation Shomrei Shabbos, became the dean of Toronto's rabbinical community soon after he moved there from Brantford in about 1950. His weekly Talmud class attracted a large following, and he earned wide respect around the world for his distinguished published work, including the four-volume *Yesodei Yeshurun* (a compendium of laws relating to prayer, the synagogue, and the sabbath), *Nachlat Tzvi* (a survey of rabbinic literature relating to adoptions and conversions), and *Sheilath Yeshurun* (responses on contemporary issues). Rabbi Felder's scholarly distinction even attracted interest from outside the Jewish community.

Perhaps just as important was his *menschlichkeit*. He welcomed everyone who came to seek his counsel with a warm smile, and the hospitality of his home was boundless. After leaving yeshivah studies in Toronto, Rabbi Felder served the Jewish communities of Sarnia, Belleville, and Brantford. Every Shabbat afternoon, he conducted a wonderful class for post–bar mitzvah boys on Pirkei Avoth and the Baba Metziah section of the Talmud. All the while, his wife served the students delicious cakes with tea and his two little sons got into endless mischief.

everywhere, drew only a handful of the faithful. A story was read, labour songs were played, and a Yiddish speaker bitterly attacked the youth who had betrayed the movement and regarded their radical parents as "simple-minded papas and blintz-frying mamas who cannot begin to fathom the *Weltschmerz* of our fine-cut intellectual offspring."[91]

Such mordant views of ungrateful, non-comprehending, indeed self-absorbed youth, while understandable, were simplistic. As the postwar Jewish geography changed, so did the community's ideals. The confusion and despair that gripped the Jewish radical left during trials of the Moscow doctors accused of plotting against the Soviet state and the treason charges against Rudolf Slansky in Czechoslovakia in the early 1950s — both clear evidence of anti-semitism in Soviet-dominated Eastern Europe — destroyed the last vestiges of Communism's credibility for many Jews. Kruschev's revelations of Stalin's crimes at the 20th All-Union Party Congress in 1956 was the final straw. All that remained were a few cultural expressions of the movement's one-time fervour — the Toronto Jewish Folk Choir, for example, performed to full houses for years to come — and memories of the heyday of the Jewish left.[92]

The Realm of the Jewish Woman

Some evidence of the type of Jewish family values that were current after the war can be found in a widely distributed cookbook and festival guide called *A Treasure for My Daughter*, published by a Montreal Canadian Hadassah-WIZO chapter in 1950.[93] This "handbook for the Jewish Home" contains menus and recipes and explains the festivals and rituals through a conversation between a fictional mother and her daughter, Hadassah, who is soon to marry her sweetheart, David. It vividly depicts the 1950s assumption that the Jewish wife's basic role was to establish and maintain the Jewishness of home life by following *kashrut* and culinary tradition. "Woman is to be the helpmate of man, socially, spiritually and physically," Mother explains at one point, as if to underline the subservience expected. Regarding *nidah* (the period of separation between a husband and wife during the menstrual cycle), the mother adds that "through the guidance in these vital matters which our laws afford, Jewish men have been taught respect for womanhood, moral discipline and ethical culture."[94] The daughter, portrayed as essentially ignorant of these matters and completely submissive to her family's wishes, asks questions about such fundamentals as betrothal and marriage, *mezuzah*, *kashrut*, sabbath, festivals, holidays, circumcision, *pidyon ha-ben*, bar mitzvah, and mourning — all the major events in the Jewish life cycle.

This book, and others like it, depicted the subservient and dependent role of the Jewish wife in the 1950s. Although poorly educated in religious traditions, she was, however, responsible for the domestic observances of the holidays, including the laborious preparation of special foods. Assumed to be a "housewife," her responsibilities outside the domestic realm included an active role in Canadian Hadassah-WIZO, the premier Jewish women's Zionist organization. Such volunteer groups were viewed as adjuncts to the main Jewish communal structure, which seldom allowed women into their higher councils.

These women became the "matriarchs of Jewish suburbia," fulfilling their roles both at home and in their cultural organizations and synagogues. The writer Erna Paris, who grew up in Toronto's gilded ghetto of Forest Hill, remembered it like this:

> Our lives in the forties and fifties were insular and "unreal." . . . We knew almost nothing beyond the Village, the downtown department stores where we'd sometimes wander on Saturday afternoons and charge clothes to our father's accounts, and the bits of northern Ontario where we summered. . . . My friends were inordinately interested in clothes, encouraged by their mothers, who were grooming them as poised and beautiful Jewish Princesses (it must be said) from an early age.[95]

Erna Paris and most of her contemporaries might have fitted neatly into this role, but their younger sisters and, later, daughters were less likely to follow suit. For one thing, more young Jewish women were pursuing higher education and entering the professions. By 1971, nearly 21 percent of all Jewish working women were professionals, compared with 4.4 percent in 1931.[96] Over the same period, the percentage of working Jewish women in blue-collar occupations fell from 33 percent to less than 6 percent. And increasing numbers of women who formerly had been housewives entered the workforce, while still continuing to be homemakers.[97]

But the status of women in the workforce was far from equal to that of men, largely because "they enter later, often less prepared, and are often underpaid and overworked with their two jobs of paid work and homemaking."[98] For most working women, therefore, entry into the workforce was not necessarily a liberating experience, and their responsibilities at home were not shared or reduced. A growing discontent raised the level of women's consciousness and led to the feminism that was to emerge in the 1970s and to flourish in the 1980s and 1990s.

Jewish Demographics, 1946–60

These transformations were also reflected in shifting Jewish occupational patterns. The professional classes accounted for 5.62 percent of the gainfully employed in 1941 and 8.57 percent in 1951.[99] The percentage of Jews in commerce trade held steady, but in manufacturing it dropped almost 10 percent. By 1961 the percentage of Jews in professional occupations had risen to 13.59, while the number working in manufacturing had fallen dramatically.[100] The Jewish community also had twice as many university-educated members as any other ethnic group.[101]

According to the 1961 census, Jewish males had the highest average income in Canada ($7,426, compared with $4,414 for all Canadians).[102] This, perhaps, had much to do with the fact that 98.8 percent of Jews lived in cities, and Jews were the most highly urbanized of all Canadians.[103]

A more important factor, however, was the Jewish proclivity for self-employment, a preference explained partly by job discrimination, which on a fairly serious scale still persisted.[104] Many Jews, anticipating anti-Jewish bias in fields like engineering and teaching, chose business or the professions instead. Consequently, 42 percent of all Jewish males were self-employed, a rate nearly three times higher than that for any other ethnic group in Canada.[105] This meant that Jews were more likely than the general population to remain in the labour force after age sixty-five, though they also entered it later because of a tendency to remain in school longer.[106]

The face of Canadian Jewry was changing, and its numbers were growing. The Jewish population rose from only 168,585 in 1941 to 204,836 in 1951 and 254,368 in 1961. It was registering its most significant growth rates in Alberta and British Columbia, even though the vast majority of immigrants moved to Montreal and Toronto.[107]

Edmonton, Calgary, and Vancouver showed the highest urban growth rates between 1951 and 1961, Winnipeg one of the lowest.[108] Its age profile and intermarriage rates were equally low. In 1931 Jews made up a larger percentage of Winnipeg's fifteen- to forty-nine-year-olds than Canadians of all other origins, but in 1941 this cohort had shifted to ages twenty to fifty-nine, and in 1951 to ages twenty-five to sixty-four.[109]

In 1931, 19.71 percent of all Canadian Jews were between five and fourteen, but only 14.4 and 14.27 percent were in that age group in 1941 and 1951. "By 1951 average Jewish family size was the smallest of any among the eight largest ethnic groups in Canada," Louis Rosenberg observed in his 1955 report on Canada in the *American Jewish Year Book*.

As family size plummeted, marriages between Jews and non-Jews rose. They had skyrocketed from 4.9 percent in 1926 to 12.4 percent in 1944, declined to 10.4 percent in 1946, and risen again to 12 percent in 1953.[110] Intermarriage rates continued their inexorable rise in the late 1950s and early 1960s. By 1963, they reached 18.5 percent, and had doubled in the Atlantic provinces, British Columbia, Saskatchewan, and Alberta.[111]

Regarded as a growing challenge to Jewish survival, intermarriage attracted considerable attention from community leaders who viewed it as a very serious threat.[112] "A high rate of intermarriage weakens the norm of Jew marrying Jew and thus makes marriage to Gentiles more acceptable in the future," wrote one scholar.[113] Intermarriage rates rose even more rapidly in the 1960s, however, as postwar Baby Boomers came of age and a high percentage of them attended university.

The solutions to this problem were not readily apparent. Greater educational efforts and "consciousness-raising" among the young were viewed as necessary measures by some, while the sociologist Morton Weinfeld suggested in 1981 that "an open door policy [towards converts], in which every potential Jew counts, may do justice to both the diverse nature of Canadian Jewry and the need to minimize the population loss."[114] To add to the demographic conundrum, studies of the reproductivity of Canada's Jews in the early 1940s concluded that birth rates were so low that, barring changes to fertility or immigration levels, the community would ultimately die out.[115]

Between 1946 and 1960, Canada received some 46,000 Jewish immigrants, a figure equal to 27.3 percent of the 1941 total Jewish population of 168,585.[116] This constituted a far higher level of postwar Jewish immigration than in the United States.[117] It has been estimated that by 1990, Holocaust survivors comprised about 8 percent of the U.S. Jewish community; in Canada they accounted for between 30 and 40 percent of the total Jewish population by the same date.[118]

Religious Life

In some respects, the face of Canadian Jewry was unchanged since its pre-war days. A survey taken in 1960 showed that established synagogue affiliations had not fundamentally altered since 1935. For example, 140 congregations out of 152 were Orthodox in 1935 (92.11 percent), and 174 out of 206 were of that affiliation in 1960 (84.47 percent).[119] The number of Conservative congregations had grown from 9 to 25 and Reform from 3 to 7.

Although before the war the majority of Orthodox rabbis serving Canadian congregations had been European-born and trained, by 1960 virtually all of them were graduates of seminaries located in the United States, with a few from the four small yeshivot in Montreal and Toronto. Conservative congregations continued to draw their rabbis from the Jewish Theological Seminary in New York and the Reform from Hebrew Union College in Cincinnati.

Membership levels in Conservative and Reform congregations had grown enormously and their new synagogues and temples usually were large structures accommodating hundreds of people. In contrast, most Orthodox congregations were much smaller, some unable even to afford their own rabbis.[120] In general, Louis Rosenberg noted, "The rise in synagogue building and membership appeared to be motivated by a desire to 'belong' rather than [by] strong religious conviction. . . . With the exception of the ultra-Orthodox, postwar active participation in Jewish religious life appeared to be limited to *bar mitzvah* and *kaddish* observance and synagogue attendance on Rosh Hashana and Yom Kippur. . . ."[121]

Traditional Judaism nevertheless experienced a revival in postwar Canada. Once drawn only from a portion of the immigrant population, the Orthodox community soon had growing numbers of synagogues. They still enjoyed relatively little of the public renown and social consciousness that was characteristic of rabbis in the much smaller Reform movement, however.

The Orthodox revival began in the autumn of 1941, when thirty-seven rabbinical students of the Lubavitch Hasidic movement arrived from Shanghai.[122] Refugees of the Lubavitch Yeshiva near Warsaw, these newcomers galvanized their nearly defunct community in Canada and served as forerunners for the Satmar, Belz, Klausenberg, and Tash Hasidim, whose communities formed in or near Montreal. Together they added a new vibrancy to Orthodoxy in Montreal. The Lubavitchers, who actively reached out to the rest of the Jewish community, most notably in the universities, also had a significant influence far beyond their own confines.

The Hasidim and other Orthodox immigrants who reached Canada in the postwar period had an especially important impact on religious education through the yeshivot they established soon after arrival. By 1955, there were three Montreal yeshivot training young men in Torah studies. Some of their graduates were the first Canadian-trained rabbis to serve in congregations.[123]

As well, a greater number of Canadians were pursuing advanced religious training in the United States. Between 1946 and 1955, twenty-three Canadian students graduated from American rabbinical seminaries and forty-eight were still in training.[124] These rabbis brought fervour and learning to their congregations, and an ability to relate well to young people. The Orthodox congregations, meanwhile, created more religious day-schools, offering instruction from kindergarten through high school. Jewish subjects were taught in Hebrew and Yiddish, secular subjects in English. Their constituency was drawn from the large infusion of ultra-Orthodox Jews, who accounted for about one-third of the 46,000 Jewish immigrants who had arrived in Canada between 1946 and 1960.[125]

Post-War Relief Work and Fund-Raising

Thanks mostly to increased immigration levels, Canadian Jewry did not falter, either in numbers or in spirit. Their philanthropic efforts were especially strong, and the community carried out enormous fund-raising campaigns for both domestic needs and overseas projects. The greatest of these provided assistance to European Jews, who required massive aid. Canadian agencies operated mainly through the powerful American Jewish Joint Distribution Committee, to which the United Jewish Refugee Agency (UJRA) had contributed $350,000 in 1941 and 1942.[126]

In the spring of 1943, Canada sent another $100,000, along with shipments of food, blankets, and soap, to Russia, and provided subsidies to other aid programs.[127] Huge relief shipments were also sent to Jews in Poland, France, Palestine, England, and Iran. In 1945 expenditures on these efforts reached one million dollars. The Congress employed Lottie Levinson, Ethel Ostry, and Phillip Stuchen to work in Europe with the United Nations Relief and Rescue Agency (UNRRA) and the American Jewish Joint Distribution Committee.[128] The Congress also marshalled the resources of various other organizations to help re-establish contact between Canadian Jews and their surviving family members in Europe and worked to facilitate good relationships between Jewish organizations and the UNRRA, efforts that were vitally important to advancing the welfare of Holocaust survivors.

Fund-raising through the UJRA, which received money from intensive campaigning that reached out to every Jew in the Dominion, brought in $1.5 million in 1946. Virtually all synagogues made the Kol Nidrei appeal before the prayers ushering in Yom Kippur, when it was hard to ignore such a request. In addition, clothing and other supplies were collected and shipped to Yugoslavia, Poland, France, and Belgium, while several Torah scrolls were also dispatched. In 1947 one million pounds of kosher meat were sent to Eastern Europe, Italy, Germany, and France. European relief needs began to decline in the 1950s, but Canadian commitments to Israel had grown enormously.

Although assisting Holocaust victims in Europe was a conditioned response to tragedy, aid to the Jews of Palestine, known as the Yishuv, arose from millennia of hope. Both activities were deemed necessary, but one was inspired by a sense of closure while the other was evoked by the Messianic hope of return to the ancient homeland and national revival.

This is not to say that the Holocaust and the rebirth of Israel were unrelated events, but the response of the Jewish world to each was inspired by different emotions. Consequently, by the early 1950s, fund-raising campaigns for the Yishuv had assumed primacy over all else. In 1952 alone, of the $7.7 million raised for local and overseas needs, $3.8 million was allocated to Zionist endeavours. Another $1.3 million was provided for overseas and refugee aid, as well as all local Canadian social needs.[129] At the same time, State of Israel bonds were being sold in Canada.

Increasing numbers of Canadian Jews — proud of the military and economic successes of Israel, and curious about the country and its people — went there as tourists. Although often taken aback by the forthright, assertive behaviour shown to them by Israelis, Jewish tourists could take pride in having contributed a great deal to Israel. On a trip there in 1962, Mordecai Richler mused that

> these people, clearly dejected because not flowers but scorn was thrown in their path in Israel, had, it suddenly occurred to me, done more real good than I ever had. Tiresome, vulgar, rude they might be, but the flawed reality of Israel was testimony to their generosity. Evidence of their achievement was everywhere. Hospitals, factories, forests, libraries, schools, mostly paid for out of tin boxes in corner groceries as well as big donations pledged in the heady atmosphere of the country clubs.[130]

Fund-raising campaigns were marked by considerable emotion, feelings usually heightened when eyewitnesses visited the European displaced persons' camps or viewed the success of the Yishuv. Less noticeable perhaps was the development of more skilled fund-raising campaigns in the bigger communities by business and professional groups who targeted their own members for donations. Increasingly, too, professional fund-raisers, many of them from the United States, were employed to manage the campaigns, while the federations who oversaw these efforts (such as the United Jewish Welfare Fund in Toronto and the Combined Jewish Appeal in Montreal) had the responsibility of distributing the monies among a variety of local institutions and organizations.[131]

Raising funds for Israeli and local requirements became a major preoccupation of Canadian Jewry in the 1950s, and one that necessitated continuing consultation between organizations. In 1951, the Congress, the ZOC, the Canadian Council of Jewish Welfare Funds, and B'nai Brith formed the National Conference for Israel and Jewish Rehabilitation to mobilize Canadian Jewry to meet rising demands more effectively. The United Jewish Appeal combined fund-raising activities for all overseas needs and for local and national Jewish social services in one united drive.[132] Though most organizations co-operated, these increasingly efficient combined appeals were never able to bring all fund-raising efforts in the community under their administrative control.

The Canadian Jewish Congress Continues

The one enduring umbrella organization during these years was the Canadian Jewish Congress. Presided over through the 1950s and up to 1962 by Samuel Bronfman, and administered by a civil service headed by the executive director, Saul Hayes, the Congress had an authority unequalled by the American Jewish Congress. The Congress in Canada had several strengths. First, it was headquartered in Montreal, the country's premier metropolis and the home to about 40 percent of Canada's Jews. Second, Samuel Bronfman's powerful personal involvement helped to give both focus and prestige. Above all, unlike its American counterpart, Canada's Congress effectively embraced Jewish organizations of all political and social stripes in the country. This kind of catholicity, which derived from the dedication of officers like Hananiah Caiserman, was not equalled anywhere else in the world and made of the Congress a true parliament of Canadian Jewry.

In the 1940s and 1950s, its gatherings were momentous events, and not just because of the pomp and ceremony so beloved by its elected leaders. The Congress' meetings informed Canada's Jews about crucial elements in their lives: the fate of less fortunate brothers and sisters around the world; the future of the state of Israel; and issues surrounding immigration, antisemitism, community relations, social changes, and education. Moreover, the Congress served as a forum for debate and a school for training new leaders. What also helped to strengthen its authority was the work of its brilliant director of research, Louis Rosenberg, whose numerous statistical reports, community studies, detailed investigations of the Jewish presence in Montreal schools, and historical documents in the Congress archives provided convincing evidence of the organization's sense of historical continuity and its commitment to addressing issues of vital concern to Canada's Jews.[133]

CHAPTER

11

Jewish Ethnicity in a Multicultural Canada, 1960–80

When Herb Gray, member of Parliament for Essex West in Ontario, was appointed minister without portfolio in Prime Minister Trudeau's Cabinet in October 1969, he was the first Jew ever to reach that position in Canada.[1] He was not, though, the first to be considered for the federal Cabinet. David Croll was widely believed to have come close after he was elected in the Spadina riding in 1945, but was ultimately rejected, it was thought, because he was a Jew.[2] Others, such as Jack Austin, Robert Kaplan, and Barney Danson, followed Gray into the Trudeau Cabinet. By the late 1960s, a good number of Jews had been federal MPs, and many more had served as MLAs and provincial Cabinet ministers and on municipal councils as mayors and aldermen.

Although Gray's elevation to the Cabinet was the acme of political achievement, short of being elected prime minister, he was only one of many Jews who were "making it" in Canadian public life. Pierre Trudeau's determination to create opportunities in federal politics for all able Canadians allowed Jews and other minorities to enter doors that were once tightly shut. By the late 1960s, some Jews were highly placed in the country's judiciary and civil service (the prestigious governorship of the Bank of Canada, for example, was held by Louis Rasminsky), and Jewish prominence in the professions was already noteworthy.

Moving towards Integration

The rapid growth in appointments of Jews to university faculties was especially remarkable. After increasing slowly during the 1950s, Jewish appointments soared as universities expanded in the 1960s and 1970s. Faculty members were in short supply, and thus more Jews and other minorities were recruited. Society's disapproval of open expressions of racial and religious prejudice — not to mention new laws that mandated fair-employment practices — also helped to open doors. In 1961 there were 132 Jewish men and 19 women on university faculties; by 1971 those numbers had increased to 1,280 men and 225 women.[3]

At Queen's University, despite a tiny Jewish student enrolment, the number of Jewish faculty members rose rapidly during the 1960s, from about five to approximately thirty-five. At the University of Toronto, the increases were even greater. In the faculties of law, medicine, psychology, and sociology, Jews were a high percentage of the total faculty, but there were fewer of them in modern languages, classics, and history, and fewer still in engineering.

This acceptance of Jews extended even to the senior levels of university administration. The University of Toronto philosopher Emil Fackenheim and the law professors Bora Laskin of Toronto and Maxwell Cohen of McGill were notable not only on their respective faculties but also in Canadian Jewry generally, through their participation in community affairs. Fackenheim, besides his eminence in Hegel and German philosophy, wrote profound works on the Holocaust and modern Judaism.[4]

Both within and outside the universities, scholarship on Jewish subjects was emerging for the first time through the writings of such academics as the historian Michael Marrus of Toronto and the literary scholar Ruth Wisse of McGill. It would not be long before courses in Jewish studies were introduced in some departments, providing a kind of legitimacy that had previously been confined to rabbinical academies.[5]

By the 1960s, a number of Jewish business tycoons had emerged to take their places alongside the fabulously wealthy Bronfman family. Sam Steinberg of Montreal parlayed a modest grocery store that was established by his mother in 1917 on St. Lawrence Boulevard into a chain of supermarkets across western Quebec. He then successfully branched out into real estate, department stores, restaurants, and sugar refining to create a multi-billion-dollar empire before his death in 1978.[6] Steinberg's achievement was based on a combination of careful attention to detail and the unusual (for the time) understanding that to attract a large clientele in Quebec, it was essential to operate his businesses in French and to recruit able francophones for positions in his stores.[7] By 1960, he had sixty stores in Montreal and thirty-two others across the rest of Quebec, even in distant Cap-de-la-Madeleine and Baie-Comeau.[8]

Real estate was an even more lucrative frontier of enterprise, and by the 1960s, Jewish firms were major players in the development of housing, industrial buildings, and inner-city skyscrapers across the country. In Calgary and Vancouver, the Belzberg family was prominent. In Toronto, numerous Jewish-owned companies — Principal Investments, Cadillac-Fairview, and Olympia and York were among the leaders — helped to rebuild much of the downtown, while also constructing suburban developments.

The most dynamic of such real-estate firms was the Reichmann family's Olympia and York, which skyrocketed to astonishing success in the 1960s by developing small industrial buildings and housing estates principally in Toronto and Montreal.[9] The family, led by brothers Albert, Paul, and Ralph, went on to erect major buildings in Toronto's burgeoning downtown financial core, with its *tour de force* being First Canadian Place, the headquarters of the Bank of Montreal.

By the mid-1970s, the Reichmanns — who were also major benefactors of Jewish religious institutions and generous donors to clinics and hospitals sponsored by other religious denominations — with perfect timing, made hugely lucrative purchases in Manhattan "just as the . . . property market began to pivot from bust to a boom of epic proportions."[10] Other enormously profitable New York real-estate deals followed, and the whole venture was capped by the World Financial Center, a skyscraper dramatically situated near Battery Park, overlooking the Statue of Liberty at the entrance to New York harbour. After acquiring major shares of Gulf Canada and Abitibi-Price, the Reichmanns ventured into a major British development at Canary Wharf in London's Docklands area, a project that came to interim completion a few years later. These and many other transactions over the years turned the Reichmanns into billionaires.

Jewish Education

While transforming itself in these respects, the community was also adjusting to new social realities outside its fences. The long-standing search by the Montreal Jewish community for equality in the Protestant school system finally was successful. Various Protestant organizations, in hearings before the 1960 Quebec Royal Commission of Inquiry on Education, recommended that Jews be granted representation on the board.[11] In August 1962, Claude Ryan, a leading Quebec intellectual and later the editor of *Le Devoir*, urged the provincial government to legislate this change on the grounds that

> in granting complete school equality to the Jews, who already bear heavy sacrifices to maintain their culture, we will show the entire country the true roots from which spring our attachment to our own cultural treasure. . . . We will prove that what we ask for ourselves we also want for others. . . .

The following year, Jews began to sit on Protestant school boards.

Meanwhile, the provincial government had begun to pay tuition grants to parents of children in the Jewish day-schools.[12] Across Canada, these schools were multiplying. By the early 1960s, there were no fewer than thirty schools offering twelve to twenty-five hours per week of instruction in Jewish subjects in addition to the secular curriculum. Montreal had 13, Toronto 8, Winnipeg 5, Calgary 2, and Edmonton, Ottawa, Vancouver, and Hamilton one each.[13] There were 8,348 children in these schools, following programs that varied according to the religious and political orientation of their supporters. Some were yeshivot, which emphasized the study of sacred texts, while the modern schools offered courses in Hebrew language and literature, and Jewish history, religion, and customs. Schools with a left-wing orientation also offered Yiddish. In addition, there were some 14,500 pupils attending congregational afternoon schools, which offered about ten hours a week of instruction in basic Hebrew language and Jewish religion. Sunday schools, usually in Reform congregations, offered three hours of instruction by part-time teachers each week. Overall, about forty thousand elementary schoolchildren were enrolled, but this represented only half to two-thirds of all Jewish children in the major cities.[14]

However, the Jewish educational system was already severely strained. A shortage of qualified teachers was one problem, even though teachers' seminaries had been in operation in Montreal since 1946 and in Toronto since 1953. An equally vexing difficulty was that the financial resources were insufficient to pay adequate teachers' salaries and finance expansion, forcing teachers to leave the profession and saddling families with high tuition fees. Moreover, Dr. Joseph Klinghofer, the Congress officer who was supervising education in the smaller Ontario communities, noted "a drop in enrolment of post–bar mitzvah age, and little interest in Jewish studies among university students and adults."[15] Jewish education in Canada was not in a healthy condition. Although this situation worried the Congress and other observers, it was unclear whether the Jewish community was willing, or able, to undertake serious remedial action. Beyond that lay the question of whether even a significant strengthening of Jewish education would arrest the trend towards assimilation and the inexorably rising intermarriage rates.

NEVER AGAIN: THE CAMPAIGN FOR SOVIET JEWRY

Besides harbouring a growing concern for the well-being of the citizens of Israel, which was registered in mounting contributions to the United Jewish Appeal, Canadian Jewry was now deeply worried about the welfare of Jews in the Soviet Union. The Soviet government's campaign against Zionism was viewed as a "euphemism for antisemitism" and as part of attempts to suppress Jewish cultural and religious expression, which had been revived in the Soviet Union following the Six Day War in 1967. Protests went into high gear across Canada in 1968. Speakers addressed public gatherings, and demonstrations took place on university campuses, on city squares, and in front of the Soviet embassy and its consulates.[16] At the urging of numerous synagogues and organizations, many Jews included a special prayer for Soviet Jewry in their Passover seders.

After meeting with a Congress delegation in the fall of 1970, Prime Minister Trudeau promised to do his best during a forthcoming visit to the Soviet Union to persuade its government to "allow Jews cultural freedom and permit some emigration to Israel."[17] Meanwhile, the Students for Soviet Jewry held a torchlight procession in downtown Toronto and a large teach-in was held at McGill to denounce what Saul Hayes of the Canadian Jewish Congress called "the Soviet denial of rights to Jews which are granted to other religious and ethnic minorities."[18]

At a Montreal gathering in November, Rabbi Gunther Plaut condemned "outright antisemitism by government plan" in the Soviet Union. Perhaps recalling the alleged silence of Canadian churches during the 1930s and 1940s, he demanded to know:

> Where are the churches, where is the voice of organized Christian religion? Why are they silent? Why do they not help us mount a universal campaign to expose this latest example of cultural and religious genocide? They can speak on so many issues and do so most forcefully. Why not here and now?[19]

Answers from the churches were weak.

The campaign for Soviet Jewry accelerated in 1971. When eleven Soviet Jews who hijacked a Russian airliner were convicted in Leningrad (two were sentenced to death while the others were given very heavy prison sentences), the Congress called for mass demonstrations. In their thousands, Jews in Montreal, Toronto, Winnipeg, Vancouver, Edmonton, and Halifax complied by marching through the streets with placards proclaiming their indignation. The community, moved by a growing consciousness of the Holocaust —

especially in the wake of the trial of Adolf Eichmann in Jerusalem — and of the threat to Israel posed by continuing Arab hostilities, responded with an emotive slogan: Never Again.[20]

Some eight thousand Jews assembled on Parliament Hill in Ottawa to demand justice for Soviet Jewry, while Minister for External Affairs Mitchell Sharp told a Congress delegation that the government of Canada had expressed concern. Even though he served as MP for the largely Jewish Toronto constituency of Eglinton, and acceded to some Jewish pressure to officially protest the Soviet mistreatment, Sharp nevertheless usually resisted. In his view, quiet diplomacy was better: "Sometimes a public protest by the Canadian government made it more difficult for the Canadian ambassador to be successful . . . on behalf of those who were being mistreated."[21]

When Premier Alexei Kosygin paid a state visit to Canada in October 1971, Canadian Jews staged a massive peaceful demonstration demanding that Soviet Jews be given full rights to cultural expression and freedom to immigrate to Israel.[22] A group of sixty rabbis prayed in front of the Soviet embassy and on Parliament Hill while heading a mass demonstration of thousands.

Similar rallies were held in Vancouver, and at Toronto's Science Centre some twelve thousand Jews protested again.[23] This campaign continued through the 1970s. Similar efforts in the United States and Europe kept the public informed of growing worldwide Jewish solidarity against official antisemitism. The Jewish community also pressured free-world governments like Canada's to force the Soviets to change their Jewish policy.

And they did. In 1971 Jewish emigration levels from the USSR were nearly three times the totals for 1968 to 1970. In 1972 immigration to Israel and North America more than doubled again, and it continued at high levels through the rest of the 1970s.[24] At the same time, Canadian Jewry was affirming not only that Jews were morally responsible for each other — *kol yisrael arevim zeh bazeh*[25] — but also that, in the post-Holocaust era, Jewish ethnic identity possessed new pride, assertiveness, commitment, and daring. A campaign to liberate the Jews of Syria from a horrifically oppressive regime, however, was not as successful. Tactics used on behalf of the Soviet Jews were redeployed, but the Syrian government was "impervious to protest" and the campaign lagged for years.[26]

Some Soviet Jews used Israel as a temporary refuge, leaving for Western countries as soon as possible. Others, instead of immigrating to Israel, chose Canada. Their adaptation to the Jewish community was difficult. A study of about two thousand Soviet immigrants in Toronto conducted during the late 1970s found that they expected to be offered secure jobs that were roughly equivalent to their former occupations, far exceeding what JIAS or any other local agencies could offer. These immigrants, the study found, believed that Jews in Western countries could provide them with full support, indeed special treatment.[27] Frustration and bitterness emerged when these expectations were not met.

Most Soviets, contrary to the assumptions of many Canadian Jews, did not arrive with a passion to identify with other Jews. They immigrated instead in the belief that they could enjoy better economic and educational opportunities. They also had "a great desire to retain certain aspects of their Russian-Soviet cultural heritage, primarily the Russian language."[28] Moreover, these generally highly educated people, who saw themselves as at least the equals of Canadian Jews, rejected "the status traditionally accorded to immigrants by the Jewish community." Thus some time was required for both groups to adjust to each other's attitudes and expectations. Assertions of solidarity were one thing; reality was another.

We Are One: Solidarity with Israel

Canadian Jewish ethnic identity encompassed an increasingly strong association with Israel during the 1960s and 1970s. Always a Zionist community, Canada's Jewry became deeply involved in pro-Israel activities during the Middle East crisis of 1967 and the subsequent Six Day War. The first response to the news in May of Egypt's attempt to block shipping to Eilat, Israel's southernmost port, was more fund-raising. A special nationwide campaign raised more than $25 million, and local committees canvassed as never before.

It was a highly emotional time, when Israel's very life seemed to be threatened. The country's victory in the Six Day War increased its popularity among Canadian Jews, just as it elicited awe and admiration from the Canadian public and press.

Israel thus became an overriding focus for a majority of Canadian Jews. Previously, judging from post–Second World War statistics on funding priorities, much more was spent on building synagogues, community centres, and hospitals in Canada than on aid to Israel. With this threat to Israel's existence in 1967, however, the emphasis changed and the community became "Zionized" to an extent that must have surprised and pleased old-time Zionists.

While the crisis in the Middle East mounted, North America's Jews — brought to a new level of Holocaust awareness by the Eichmann trial in Israel a few years earlier — eagerly followed events in the press and on television. Emotions ran high, owing to a new and widespread awareness of Israel's apparently precarious circumstances. Spontaneous fund-raising campaigns took place, and some volunteers flew over to fill civilian jobs vacated when workers who were reserve soldiers were called up to serve with the Israel Defense Force.

Meanwhile, a group of Canadian Catholic and Protestant clergymen, profoundly conscious of historical precedents, wrote to the Soviet premier, Alexei Kosygin, who had supplied enormous amounts of weaponry to Egypt, and stated:

> Once before in this century the leader of a nation proclaimed the aim of destroying the Jews. The world did not believe him. The world stood by. Again the leader of a nation has proclaimed the aim of destroying Jews — this time the State of Israel. Let us not believe that the unbelievable cannot happen again. This time let us not stand by. The undersigned speak as Christians who remember with anguish the Nazi holocaust and are filled with deep apprehension about the survival of the State of Israel.[29]

Blood banks were set up, and material and medical supplies were collected by the Federated Zionist Organization of Canada, the Congress, and B'nai Brith. The Canada-Israel Committee (CIC) was also mobilized to solicit wider backing for Israel among all Canadians. Several terrorist attacks in 1972 and the Yom Kippur War of October 1973 renewed concern among Jews, who again demonstrated solidarity with Israel by large-scale fund-raising initiatives and attendance at mass demonstrations in major cities. This outpouring of material aid to Israel has continued to this day.

On a trip to Israel years later, the writer Mordecai Richler observed evidence of this generosity. He noted that "just about every park, library, synagogue, operating theatre, yeshiva, or gym is tagged in celebration of one family or another."[30] Rich Diaspora Jews, he stated, "are expected to endow university chairs, and in return clothing manufacturers, real-estate mavens, and stock market gaons are flattered with honorary degrees and photo-ops with the prime minister. No issue of the *Jerusalem Post* is complete without its obligatory photograph of a middle-aged American or Canadian couple beaming in front of their gift: a bloodmobile, Talmud study room, tennis school, or intensive care ambulance."[31]

However, support for Israel did not end with material aid. Public-relations initiatives and pro-Israel lobbying gained increasing importance among community leaders, who worried about Israel's image in the media after her military successes and her occupation of the West Bank, Sinai, the Golan Heights, and the entire city of Jerusalem. The CIC, which was composed of representatives of the Congress, B'nai Brith, and the Canadian Zionist

Federation (whose long-serving guiding spirit was Rabbi Gunther Plaut of Toronto's Holy Blossom Temple), tried to respond to the mounting criticisms of Israel. The CIC also dealt with the media's misrepresentations of Zionism and Judaism, as well as charges made by some members of the Canadian Arab community and several anti-Zionist Christian clergymen that Zionism was "political Nazism."[32]

One group of distinguished Christian clergymen in Toronto, who opposed such distortions, stated that "Israel [was] the visible and tangible manifestation of both Jewish survival and Jewish security. . . . It is profoundly wrong to oppose Israel because of its Jewish foundations and to seek to dismantle its Jewish character as the anti-Zionists invariably desire."[33] Generally, however, such unqualified backing was absent from statements made by religious groups on Israeli/Arab relations. Despite the fact that the 1973 war was initiated by Egypt and Syria, there were no statements condemning those countries from the churches or the government of Canada.

At a special session of the House of Commons, External Affairs Minister Mitchell Sharp carefully stated that most Canadians preferred a balanced approach to restoring peace to the Middle East, but that Egypt and Syria had violated the 1967 cease-fire lines. "It may be neither appropriate nor possible," he said, "for Canada to maintain a perfect sense of balance in the present crisis."[34]

Sharp walked a fine line between an increasingly assertive Jewish community and a public that wanted him to maintain an even-handed policy. Canada's support for United Nations Resolution 242, which called on Israel to withdraw from territories occupied in the Six Day War, was the keystone of this neutral position. "It was my view and the view of my departmental officials," Sharp reflected many years later, "that this difference will be resolved if and when Israel and its Arab neighbours (as Israel and Egypt were able to do eventually) get together to negotiate peace treaties."[35]

Although they called for lasting peace in the Middle East and the right of Israel to exist within secure borders, the government of Canada and most of the non-Jewish community maintained a neutral stance on the Arab/Israeli conflict after 1967. Polls showed that in the late 1970s, the Canadian public was massively disinterested in these issues, though three-quarters of the 30 percent who did have an opinion supported Israel.[36]

The Trudeau government did bow to pressure from Jewish groups to cancel the Fifth United Nations Congress on the Prevention of Crime and the Treatment of Offenders, which was scheduled to take place in Toronto in September 1975, because the PLO had been granted observer status. But the government did not block the May 1976 UN Habitat Conference, which PLO representatives attended. Meanwhile, the secretary of state for External Affairs, Allan MacEachen, wanted to weaken connections between Canada and Israel and make contact with PLO "moderates."[37] At an October 1975 meeting between MacEachen and the CIC, called to discuss Canada's abstention on the UN vote inviting PLO participation in the debate on the Palestinian issue, Jewish representatives received only a polite hearing. "Canada," the minister informed them, "was not prepared to prejudge the PLO issue."[38]

Clearly the government was unmoved by the CIC's lobbying efforts, which up to that point had been deliberately and wisely low key, as Rabbi Plaut put it, so as not to "antagonize the government." While Canada's policy of keeping up good relations with both Israel and the Palestinians made the CIC uneasy, Rabbi Plaut continued to employ a cautious approach. "We cannot afford to throw our strength into a battle with our own government on the issue of the PLO," he told his colleagues when the question of trying to block PLO representation at the 1976 Vancouver Habitat conference came up.[39] Because the Canadian government and its people had the right to form opinions and policies on the Middle East that did not accord with those of Israel or of those Canadian Jews who uncritically supported Israel's policies, Plaut's restraint was entirely appropriate.

The Dispute with Reverend A. C. Forrest

Criticisms of Israel's militancy spread in the 1970s. On university campuses, strongly pro-Arab literature was circulated, and meetings and numerous demonstrations condemning Israel were held. Increasing numbers of radio and television broadcasts showed such an anti-Israel slant that both the Congress and the Zionist Federation of Canada felt it necessary to combat them vigorously.[40] In the late 1960s, a worrisome spate of articles written by Reverend Alfred C. Forrest began appearing in the United Church *Observer*. In them, Israel was severely taken to task for its policies towards Palestinian refugees. Forrest was not the only leading United churchman to be so critical. Deeply upset by Israel's capture and occupation of the whole of Jerusalem in the Six Day War, Ernest M. Howse, a former United Church moderator, attacked the Jewish phrase "next year in Jerusalem" as insincere and Israel's desire to hold on to the city as motivated solely by economic considerations.[41]

But it was Forrest, with his widely read critiques of Israel appearing in the editorial columns of the *Observer*, who worried Zionists the most. As the official publication of Canada's largest Protestant denomination, the *Observer* reached approximately 300,000 homes and was obviously an important voice.[42] Forrest, perpetuating a view of the Zionist movement evident in the the *Observer* since

1948, held Israel to blame for the Arab refugee crisis. At the same time, he stoutly resisted dubious attempts to link criticisms of Israel with Christian indifference to the fate of the Jews of Europe during the Holocaust.[43] Letters by Jewish luminaries to the *Observer*, as well as meetings they initiated with leaders of the church, did nothing to change the paper's strong pro-Arab slant.

To M. J. Nurenberger, the editor of the *Canadian Jewish News* and not the most temperate editorialist himself,[44] Forrest was "the symbol of anti-Israelism in this country. . . . The most dangerous enemy of Israel because he is subtle and articulate."[45] After a ten-month Middle East tour in 1968, Forrest published *The Unholy Land*, which included a description of Israel as "a racist and aggressive state" that further enraged the Jewish community. In subsequent articles, he drew infuriated replies from members of the Jewish community when he opposed Soviet Jewish immigration to Israel "on the grounds that it was part of a sinister Zionist plot to expel the Palestinians," and when he insisted that Christians did much to stop Hitler's murder of Jews.[46] Counter-allegations of Zionist attempts to manipulate the news followed.

In December 1969, Forrest's exhortations to Canadian Christian clergymen to oppose Israeli government–subsidized "study tours" to Israel as nothing more than "propaganda, . . . anti-Arab cliches turned out by the P.R. experts in Tel Aviv," increased tensions.[47] Nurenberger excoriated Forrest, whom he said knew "that any dissemination of hatred against the Jewish state is aimed indirectly at the Jewish people as well," a charge that inappropriately put Forrest on the same level as Soviet antisemites.[48] A few months later, Nurenberger held him up as an "apostle of neo-antisemitism" and a disseminator "of distrust and mutual suspicion among Jews and Christians in Canada."[49]

Thus the Jewish community, viewing Forrest's critiques as antisemitism, felt embattled in its support for Israel. Meanwhile, Forrest, who also felt besieged, continued, as Rabbi Gunther Plaut put it, "on a one-way mission and no one could deter him."[50] When, in the November 1971 issue of the *Observer*, Forrest implied that the Second World War was fought to save the Jews, he had passed into unreason. This outrageous comment angered even some members of the United Church, although delegates to its twenty-fifth general council gave him a standing ovation and protested against government of Canada loans to Israel.

It was only after the election of Bruce McLeod as United Church moderator and the murder of the Israeli athletes at the Munich Olympic Games in 1972 that Forrest's influence faded. Nevertheless, the seven-year contretemps severely damaged relations between the Jewish community and the United Church.[51] In his searching and balanced account of the conflict, which he labelled a "family quarrel," Rabbi Reuben Slonim pleaded for understanding on both sides. "Only the most fervent partisan of the United Church or the Jewish community would maintain that all the right is on one side and all the wrong on the other."[52]

Political Pressures on Behalf of Israel

The Jewish community, led by the CIC, had only marginal influence on the Canadian government's Middle East policy.[53] For example, they failed to persuade the government to thwart the Arab boycott of Israel and of Jews working for Canadian companies that dealt with Arab countries.[54] The Trudeau government did not consider the boycott a priority matter, and the federal Cabinet — bowing to business interests — was unwilling to pass anti-boycott legislation.[55] In December 1977, the ministers of both Trade and External Affairs explained to the House of Commons that although the government opposed the Arab boycott, it would not agree to publish a list of the Canadian firms that had been asked to take part.[56] The CIC did succeed in getting the government of Ontario to pass anti-boycott legislation in 1978.[57]

The CIC also failed in a bid to persuade the Trudeau government to move the Canadian embassy in Israel from Tel Aviv to Jerusalem, an act that would signify Canada's approval of Jerusalem as the country's capital. Trudeau, who represented a heavily Jewish riding, had resisted pressure from Israel's prime minister, Menahem Begin, in November 1978. However, Trudeau's chief rival, Conservative Party leader Joe Clark, was anxious to please the Jewish community, and hoped to win two or three key constituencies in the 1979 election campaign.[58] Despite warnings from his officials, he pledged to make the move.

Immediately after winning the election, Clark seemed intent on keeping his promise. When he took office, however, he finally bowed to enormous counterpressures from Arab governments, Canadian churches, Cabinet ministers, and government advisers (not to mention unofficial and indirect "cautions" from British officials), and rescinded his promise.[59] When he was re-elected in 1980, Trudeau, who was resentful of the Jewish community's lobbying for Israel on the Arab boycott, decided to chart a new course for Canada's Middle East policy. He was decidedly more open to the idea, as expressed by External Affairs Minister Mark MacGuigan, that in 1982 "the legitimate rights and concerns of the Palestinians have to be realized."[60]

In a similar situation, Canada refused to soften its official criticism of Israel's invasion of Lebanon in 1982, even though the CIC tried hard to modify it. Broadly speaking, moreover, the media's response to Arab/Israeli issues was not favourable to Jewish positions, with the exception of occasional editorials in the *Globe and Mail*. In fact, opposition to Israel's policies accelerated sharply during the Gaza and West Bank disturbances, which started in December 1987.

By 1982, even some sectors of the Jewish community publicly opposed the Lebanon incursion, and the CIC was no longer the "universally acknowledged . . . principal spokesman for Canadian Jewry on Israel-related questions."[61] The unquestioning support of Israel by Canada's Jews began to be challenged by small but vocal groups who criticized the invasion and the shelling of Beirut and condemned the alleged complicity of Israel in the Sabra and Shattila massacres by Christian militiamen. Still, Canadian and American Jewry had little success in influencing their countries' foreign policies in the Arab/Israeli dispute in the 1970s and 1980s.[62]

While "the unconditional support of the organized Jewish community for Israel" was unshakeable, its followers were not entirely blind, deaf, and dumb. Even so, there was a general belief that Israel could do no wrong, that Diaspora Jews had no right to criticize because they did not share Israel's real tax and security burdens, and that internal criticism only strengthened Israel's enemies and antisemites everywhere — and this belief served to keep the Canadian Jewish community quiet about, if not subservient to Israel on, Middle East issues.[63]

The most dramatic manifestation of community defensiveness regarding Israel occurred in 1988, when fifteen Jews and fifteen Arabs participated in a government-sponsored seminar — a Jewish-Palestinian dialogue — on the Middle East at Château Montebello.[64] Critics of the seminar objected that the Jewish participants had been "selected in a manner that produced greater support for the idea of a Palestinian state than existed in the community." This exercise in Arab-Jewish dialogue was so controversial, in fact, that plans for holding a second seminar were shelved. Such a move succeeded only in angering those who believed in the necessity of such discussions to achieve peace in the Middle East, however.

Dissenting opinions also arose over Israeli policy on certain domestic issues, such as the emergence of liberal Judaism and the "Who is a Jew?" debate of the 1980s. Reacting strongly to questions surrounding the legitimacy of Reform and Conservative synagogues and their rabbis in Israel, the Canadian Reform movement established Kadima (Forward), a Zionist organization that was to support Reform Judaism in Israel, and launched a highly successful membership drive during the High Holy Days of 1977.[65] Kadima joined the Canadian Zionist Federation and sought representation at the World Zionist Congress so it could articulate its position at the highest levels.

Both the Reform and Conservative movements were also reacting to the emergence of Israeli ultra-Orthodox antagonisms in Toronto, where, they asserted, relationships between those three branches of Judaism were deteriorating.[66] Rabbi Herbert Feder of Toronto's Conservative Beth Tikvah congregation complained that "Orthodoxy has been . . . boycotting meaningful dialogue with the Conservative and Reform movements to such an extent that we no longer meet. There is . . . no arena in which individual rabbinic spokesmen talk as human beings. And that's a disgrace." In response to criticisms from an Orthodox source of Kadima's effort to gain official status, Rabbi Plaut commented: "If they [Orthodox Jews] are willing to dissolve Mizrachi [the religious Zionist organization], then we will dissolve Kadima." He predicted that "if Israel adopts a restrictive interpretation of what constitutes proper religious practice, that will bring about alienation in the Diaspora."[67]

Increasingly, Israel had become a central feature of Canadian Jewish identity. It was a source of pride because of its many economic and military achievements; it replaced pre-1939 Eastern Europe as the source for a new Jewish culture; and it served as a focal point for enormous fund-raising and organizational activities, which were motivated by the ongoing need to rescue Jews and rebuild the ancient homeland. Perhaps a sense that they might not have done enough to help save their brethren during the Holocaust was one factor pushing Canadian Jews to make these efforts.

Influenced by a climate of multiculturalism that was officially encouraged by the Trudeau government after 1972, Canadian Jews found their ethnic identity increasingly shaped by Israeli paradigms and rhythms: the gathering of the persecuted, Independence Day, the pulse of Tel Aviv and Jerusalem, and Israeli music. When modern Hebrew was given stronger emphasis in Jewish schools across the country, Israel entered the very souls of many Canadian Jews. What the historian Jack Wertheimer notes as the indelible impression that "Israeli outlooks and practices" have made on the institutional life of Jews in the United States is no less true north of the forty-ninth parallel: "Most synagogue-going Jews pronounce their prayers in Israeli Hebrew, listen and sing along to Israeli liturgical compositions, and wear and use religious articles imported from the Jewish state."[68] Jewish schools focus heavily on Israeli culture, employ Israeli teachers, and send their students to spend a year of study in Israel. Through them, and American and Canadian yeshivah students, Israel has a "radiating effect" on the whole community. "I cannot explain," the McGill literary scholar Ruth Wisse reflected, "the joy of Jerusalem in our lives. Many of us around the [Passover seder] table have lived in Israel, plan to live in Israel, want to live in Israel, or believe they ought to live in Israel, though we could not separate out these impulses or even account for all of them."[69]

Notwithstanding the growth of this Israel-centredness and the rising financial contributions to Israel, higher per capita than anywhere except South Africa, few Canadian Jews were prepared to go there on Aliyah. Comfortable in their newly tolerant multicultural climate, Canadian Jews, in fact, have the second-lowest Aliyah rate in the free world.[70] Many Jews probably echo the sentiments of Mordecai Richler, who, after a 1992 trip, wrote:

> all at once, I . . . was fed up with the tensions that have long been Israel's daily bread. . . . I was raised to proffer apologies because my ostensibly boring country was so short of history, but now, after five weeks in a land choked by the clinging vines of its past, a victim of its contrary mythologies, I considered the watery soup of my Canadian provenance a blessing.[71]

There was also some growing discomfort with the policies of Israel's Likud government. Led since the 1977 election by Prime Minister Menahem Begin, Likud was viewed by many as excessively stringent and resistant to legitimate Palestinian claims.

It was somewhat paradoxical that while support for Israel rose among Canadian Jews, backing for the Zionist organizations such as the ZOC waned. Zionism had become such an integral aspect of Jewish identity that formal affiliations were no longer deemed necessary. More important, the organizations were no longer the primary fund-raisers, because the financial power had shifted to the federations of charities campaigning under the United Jewish Appeal. Monies were allocated to both local and overseas causes, including Israel, except in a number of small communities, which, having few welfare needs, sent all their proceeds to Israel. The days when Zionist organizations ran their own separate national campaigns, therefore, had largely disappeared, except in a few isolated cases.

Even the left-wing organizations, with their deep commitment to collectivist principles, experienced declining popularity. Their founding members aged and were not followed into the organizations by their sons and daughters, who shunned formal membership with groups whose socialist goals had little meaning for them. By 1970, the recently formed Federated Zionist Organization of Canada, which included all Zionist groups, was itself embroiled in a bitter dispute about the number of representatives allowed to its constituent parts.[72] Such petty bickering marked the nadir of these once-proud organizations, whose day had passed.[73] In fact, Israel was now so important to Canadian Jewry that no one organization could embrace all the features of its centrality.

Israel had come to be much more than a fund-raising project, especially to a generation of Jewish youth that, in the rebellious 1960s, had little patience for formal structures, banquets with their gowned and dinner-jacketed participants, and the shallowness of cheque-book Zionism. In rising numbers, these Jews were going to Israel to study, travel, and absorb the atmosphere. In 1969 Keren Hatarbut, the Canadian Association for Hebrew Education and Culture, undertook to send 250 Jewish boys and girls for summer sojourns on Israel kibbutzim to encourage them to go on Aliyah.[71] Synagogues were even more active, especially in sending youth over to Israel for summer programs meant to increase their Jewish consciousness. Meanwhile, tourism soared, and El Al's airliners carried hundreds of Canadians on its twice-weekly flights from Montreal and, later, Toronto to Israel.

The Arts

Expressions of Jewish identity took on cultural dimensions as well. Canadian Jews by the 1970s were being informed of their history in the republication of B. G. Sack's *The Jews in Canada*; a major two-volume illustrated survey by Rabbi Stuart E. Rosenberg; the publications issued by the Congress' national archives and written and edited by David Rome; the *Canadian Jewish Historical Society Journal*; and the activities of numerous local historians, who collected and stored documents, taped interviews, and wrote histories of their communities.

Their identity was also being expressed artistically, especially in literature. From the late 1930s to the early 1950s, Abraham M. Klein's poetry on Jewish themes embodied the culture of *Yiddishkeit*: the Talmud, festival observances, and the transforming rhythms and contexts of both the old *shtetl* and the new urban ghetto.[75] Klein's poetry after 1939 was profoundly influenced by the agony of the European Jews. His *Hitleriad* of 1942 and, perhaps most graphically, his 1951 *Second Scroll* — a powerful story of the search for a survivor — were the first English-language literary responses to the Holocaust by a Canadian Jew. In the glosses for *The Second Scroll*, his major opus, Klein reached deep into that parochial well to evoke memories and images of "ghetto streets where a Jewboy dreamed pavement into pleasant Bible-land," and praised God, who "hast condescended to bestow upon history a shadow of the shadows of Thy radiance." Klein was followed by the poets Irving Layton, Leonard Cohen, and Eli Mandel, who in the 1970s articulated both a response to and an awe of the Holocaust. After these poets burst on the scene, in the phrase of the literary scholar Michael Greenstein, "words [were] in exile."[76]

In the 1960s and 1970s, such evocations were largely absent from Canadian Jewish literature, although Miriam Waddington's poetry contained echoes of the secular Yiddish culture she absorbed through her Winnipeg Peretz School education, and Jack Ludwig's stories reflected the struggles and the poignancy of living in that city's North End melting pot.

Adele Wiseman's *Sacrifice*, Mordecai Richler's *Apprenticeship of Duddy Kravitz*, and the poetry of Irving Layton and Leonard Cohen shone as major literary achievements of that era. Wiseman explored the familiar anguish of intergenerational relationships, Richler the seldom-examined underside of Jewish economic upward mobility — he also displayed, in *St. Urbain's Horseman*, a deep sensitivity to the Holocaust[77] — Layton the ebullient awe of life and sexuality, and Cohen "love's solitary survivor."[78] Through their work, these first-generation Canadians often analysed the period of their lives spent growing up in Montreal and Winnipeg during the 1940s.[79] Perhaps because it lacked those cities' internal tensions and ethnic diversity, Toronto did not produce Jewish literary figures of equal stature. Even though Waddington and Wiseman lived in Toronto for many years, their work continued to reflect their early Winnipeg experiences.

MELECH RAVITCH

In the late summer of 1976, one of the Jewish community's bright cultural lights was extinguished. The beloved and distinguished Yiddish poet, Melech Ravitch, died in Montreal.

Ravitch had enjoyed a celebrated career in 1920s Poland, where as a member of Di Khaliastre ("the Gang") he was a major figure in Warsaw's Yiddish literary circle. After wandering across the world visiting Jewish communities, Ravitch settled in Montreal, where he joined an already distinguished group of Yiddish poets and writers. The group included J. I. Segal, Shalem Shtern, Rokhl Korn, and Mordecai Husid, as well as other intellectuals like David Rome, and was centred at the Yiddish Folks Bibliotek. "He was among the most highly regarded cultural personalities of world Jewry," David Rome wrote in a moving obituary.

One of Ravitch's best poems, which evokes his typically elegiac spirit, is his "Tropic Nightmare in Singapore," where he revisits his birthplace:

Over seven continents, seven seas,
On fire-wind wings, dreams soar,
And in these soaring dreams
I am a child once more

These literary landmarks not only evoked a past now becoming almost mythological. They marked the entry of Jews as major figures in Canada's literary canon, with their images, characterizations, and language now part of the national cultural landscape. Their popularity attested to a growing general interest in reading the works of those who were sensitive to the peculiarities and particularities of the Jewish experience. These writings seemed to recognize that the Canadian context had placed distinctive boundaries on and provided opportunities for the Jewish culture imported from Europe, and that the discovery of their past would help readers understand their identity as both Jews and Canadians. And the works of these poets and novelists attracted wide audiences in the non-Jewish community as well, where these writers became highly regarded voices of Canadian ethnic diversity.

Critiques of the Congress

Because of their new-found confidence, younger members of the community began to question the leadership of the Canadian Jewish Congress. On the question of aid to Soviet Jewry in the 1960s, Congress leaders had allegedly

---

Momma says, "You really believe —
I can read it clear in your face —
That the world out there is something more
Than our little marketplace

Well, out through the window go
Your continents, if you please,
And into the kitchen pail
*I pour your seven seas.**

(Translated by Robert Friend)

With Ravitch's death, the little group of Montreal Yiddish writers was severely diminished. After the passing of Rokhl Korn and Sholem Shtern a few years later, the light of Yiddish literature in Canada had nearly flickered out.

---

* See David Rome, "Melech Ravitch: Dean of Yiddish Poetry," *Canadian Jewish Outlook* (Sept.–Oct. 1976): 10; Goldie Morgentaler, "Melech Ravitch," *Pakn-Treger* (fall 1997): 74–75; Irving Howe, Ruth R. Wisse, and Khone Shmeruk, eds., *The Penguin Book of Modern Yiddish Verse* (New York: Viking, 1987): 301.

been "lethargic, often passive." But of greater concern to some of these young Jews was the Congress' opposition to government aid to denominational schools on the grounds that religious instruction did not belong in publicly funded schools. The Congress, conscious of a difference of opinion among the rank and file, had reluctantly acquiesced to having a course in world religions taught in Ontario high schools but had opposed aid to denominational schools — even Jewish ones — in Quebec and Alberta.[80] Such a position was no longer acceptable to many Jews. A new group, called the Ontario Committee for Government Aid to Jewish Day Schools, was formed in 1971 to lobby the provincial government. Although it was part of a growing grass-roots movement, the committee failed to make any significant headway. Nevertheless, it persisted until a 1996 decision of the Supreme Court of Canada effectively blocked all denominational claims for financial support.

Criticisms of the Congress went beyond school questions alone. Indeed, the fundamental character of the organization was at issue. Rather than serving as an effective "Jewish parliament," the Congress had become more of "an antidefamation, civic-defense type of organization," according to Rabbi Stuart Rosenberg, and it failed to keep abreast of the times. Its national religious affairs committee could not resolve disagreements among Reform, Conservative, and Orthodox Jews on a variety of issues.

Local welfare organizations, moreover, objected to the Congress' assumption that it was the "official" Jewish voice. In arguing that "the problems facing us are serious [and] a different community is emerging," the organization's detractors highlighted several features of the changing community profile: most Jews were Canadian-born, a high proportion was under thirty-five, the number of university graduates was much higher than in previous generations, the foreign-born included many Holocaust survivors, and there were now many Jews from Arab countries.[81]

A more fundamental transformation, the critics alleged, was that religion, which had been a "stabilizing influence" on most of the pre-1940 Jewish population, "is significant by its very absence or by the markedly changed role of religion in the life of the ostensibly committed individuals."[82] This transformation was attributable to advancing cynicism, profound social changes, and "a new, vigorous, and healthy diaspora Jewish posture and meaning." Posture and meaning were not just euphemisms for disdain for the past, but were new assertions of confidence, even intemperate bravado.

Thus the future of the Congress seemed shaky. Rabbi Rosenberg noted that in the United States, after the First World War, the American Jewish Congress lost credibility with that community's increasingly diverse constituents. In his view, Canadian Jewry, now much more complex than it had been before the

Second World War, had perhaps also outgrown the need for the Congress. "Could Congress," he wondered, "still retain its role in a larger, better educated, more ideologically diverse, and thus more complex Jewish community? Indeed, in an age of so-called participatory democracy, could, or should, any single group purport to speak for all Jews? Even in Canada?"[83]

Quebec Separatism and the Montreal Jewish Community

Quebec's separatist movement was potentially the greatest external challenge Canadian Jewry faced in this period. Though the Parti Québécois was not antisemitic, there was a perception that separation included a significant threat to the Jewish community. Except for a substantial francophone element from North Africa, Jews were overwhelmingly English-speaking. Though the Royal Commission on Bilingualism and Biculturalism reported that bilingualism was higher among Quebec's Jews than in the anglophone community as a whole, separatism seemed dangerous. At the end of an illuminating review of the situation in 1972, Rabbi Rosenberg concluded that for Quebec Jewry, "the road ahead is uncertain, fearful, even fraught with unknowable dangers."[84]

Basing his analysis largely on the Jewish experience in Europe, where Jews were a minority in territories converting into national states, Rosenberg saw two problems emerging in Quebec. One arose from the emphasis the separatists placed on the pre-eminence of the French language. Legislation limiting parents' rights to choose the language of instruction for their children had been passed by the Union Nationale government in 1969. Although it was not a threat to the French-speaking segment of the Jewish community, this law upset the traditional rights of English-speaking Jews and other non-francophones, and also seriously endangered the continuity of the English language in Quebec. The second problem was the separatist belief in *étatisme*, the view that the state was supreme, a poor portent for Jewish survival.

Such pessimism, which was shared by many in the Jewish community, was understandable given the emotional circumstances of these years. This feeling was not lessened by the attitude of Quebec's most prominent nationalist, René Lévesque, who told a Toronto audience in December 1971:

> I know that eighty to ninety percent of the Jews of Quebec are nervous about the effects of separatism. I know that history shows that a rise of nationalism means Jews get it in the neck. But what can I do about it? I can't change your history. But I know that anti-Semitism is not a significant French-Canadian characteristic. The more serious

problem for the Jews is that Jews in Quebec are closely related to the English community. If they choose to put in with them, what can I do?[85]

Still, there was no clear evidence of antisemitism in the Parti Québécois. Statements made by the Front de Libération du Québec (FLQ), which was responsible for the bombings of the 1960s and the October Crisis of 1970, however, contained some antisemitic references. Such sentiments can hardly have inspired Jewish confidence in their future in a separate Quebec. While most Quebec separatists of the 1970s did not openly espouse antisemitism, some avowed and suspected antisemites among them attracted the notice of non-Jewish observers. The journalist Peter Desbarats noted that "Jews in Quebec . . . have a right to be concerned about nationalist developments in Quebec which would assume a chauvinist character and would create a tolerance for discrimination against non-French groups. There are two kinds of Jews in Quebec: the optimists who teach their children French and the pessimists who teach them Hebrew."[86]

Some of the new antisemitism in Quebec was masked by anti-Israel rhetoric. The 1970 kidnapping and murder of Quebec's minister of Labour and Immigration, Pierre Laporte, for example, reportedly was preceded by an unsuccessful FLQ attempt to kidnap the Israeli trade attaché in Montreal.[87] In the separatist monthly *Ici Québec*, one writer called Zionism "the cancer of the world" and alleged that Israelis injected mercury into oranges.[88] In 1973 the president of the Montreal council of the Confederation of National Trade Unions (CNTU) stated, before the Federation of Canadian Arab Societies, that

> the Jewish population of Quebec enjoys more privileges than any other minority in the world. We don't want them to poison the air of this country any further. Israel is now committing the same barbaric crimes against others that were committed against her in her previous history. We are sick and tired of being called antisemites.[89]

A few years later, Yvan Charbonneau, head of the Quebec French Catholic teachers' union, returning from a meeting of the International Association Against Racial Intolerance, stated that "it was incumbent on Quebec teachers to instill anti-Zionist sentiments in the minds of their pupils." These remarks were vigorously repudiated by the archbishop of Montreal, Mgr. Paul Grégoire.[90] On the eve of the Parti Québécois victory in the 1976 provincial election, Charles Bronfman, in remarks to Jewish community leaders, was quoted as saying that the party was "a bunch of bastards who are trying to kill us."[91] He also allegedly threatened to pull his family's enormous capital out of the province.[92]

In the Jewish community, memories of pre-war antisemitism ran deep. The concept of francophone Jews serving as a bridge to French Quebeckers could not have encouraged the English-language Jewish community, especially in light of reports of very high rates of intermarriage between French-speaking Jews and non-Jews. The Parti Québécois victory therefore produced considerable anxiety in the Jewish community over what its future might be in a separate state.

In an article published in *Commentary* six months after the election, two McGill professors, Ruth Wisse and Irwin Cotler, wrote that Quebec's Jews had entered into a state of almost continuous caucus, "in anxious discussion about their future under a government promising to aggressively pursue separation from the rest of Canada."[93] While in the past "Quebec's climate of candid ethnicity had made Montreal . . . hospitable to groups (like the Jews) that could readily maintain their distinctiveness," the authors argued that the situation had changed.

Although they sympathized with the strong French-Canadian desire for cultural distinctiveness, Wisse and Cotler asserted that "Jews fear the inevitable fallout of these nationalistic impulses and oppose their repressive dimensions." Even though the Parti Québécois was committed to both democracy and fair treatment of minorities, the McGill professors charged that there were already signals of authoritarianism and insensitivity — including the coercive features of Bill 101, which institutionalized the French language. Even more worrisome were some signs of racism and the fact that a labour leader's expressions of sympathy with the Palestinian cause suggested antisemitism was not repudiated by the French-Canadian elite.

According to some Quebec intellectuals, however, Wisse and Cotler misrepresented the true nature of the Parti Québécois' nationalist program — as well as erroneously depicting a previous lack of "hospitality" towards minorities on the part of French Quebeckers.[94] Michel Laferrière, rebutting Wisse and Cotler in *Commentary*, asserted that if Jews had become increasingly bilingual, it was only "because they had to . . . [since] most of their income derived from the French Canadians, for Jews were often small shopkeepers and small landlords . . . [and were] often perceived as direct exploiters." Thus, he wrote, French-Canadian antisemitism was similar to black antisemitism in the United States; it was merely an opposition to "Jewish exploitation." And Laferrière rejected as outright defamation the suggestion that the Quebec nationalist song "The Future Belongs to Us," which was sung at Parti Québécois rallies, resembled a Nazi song from the movie *Cabaret*. The intention behind Bill 101, he continued, was to make French the only official language in Quebec, "and corresponds to the legislation and practices of other provinces, which have made English the only language of social life, *de facto* or *de jure*."

Another commentator observed that Jews prospered in Montreal, where, instead of seeking contacts with French Canadians, they had aligned themselves with the dominant anglophones. Thus Jews regarded English as their only "cultural gateway to Jewish self-expression."[95] The Wisse-Cotler insistence that the French-Canadian elite should repudiate statements from radical leftists was also unacceptable. "If Mrs. Wisse and Mr. Cotler already hear Nazi boots on the sidewalks of Montreal, that is really their personal problem," the commentator asserted, then claimed that they could not cite a single antisemitic action by the new government against Jews in Quebec.

Irwin Cotler surely had it right in recognizing that the use of French "as the *lingua franca* of Quebec society," had become "a [Jewish] communal imperative — indeed a moral imperative."[96] But if Quebec nationalism was exclusive rather than inclusive, and Jewish nationalism was becoming increasingly transnational and "concerned with the indivisibility of Jewish peoplehood," he observed, these Jewish and French-Canadian solitudes "are likely to mis-read, if not misinterpret, each other's symbolic language."[97]

Although this was not quite a *dialogue des sourds*, clearly the two sides of this debate were miles apart. Jews, perhaps, did not fully comprehend the Québécois nationalists' sense of precarious marginality in a province whose economy was still dominated by non-francophones and a continent whose major language was English. Jews were unable, the scholar Pierre Anctil observed, "to understand the language, the context, where the nationalists were coming from."[98] At the same time, the nationalists did not fully grasp Jewish fears of authoritarian nationalism with racist undertones. Both sides felt threatened and both were assertive and emotional. Little understanding was possible in such an atmosphere.

Antisemitism would not completely die in Quebec — or elsewhere in Canada. It would reappear at moments of crisis, such as during the provincial referendum votes in 1980 and 1995. But the public expression of Jew-hatred was increasingly marginalized. Indeed, the community of Quebec, bolstered by a significant influx of francophone Jews from North Africa, enjoyed a certain rapprochement with Québécois from the Quiet Revolution onward.

At the same time, the perception of Jews by some French Canadians had changed significantly by the 1960s. Antisemitism in Quebec was certainly waning and, as Naim Kattan observed, "Relations between the two communities are only just beginning to be established on the social and human levels."

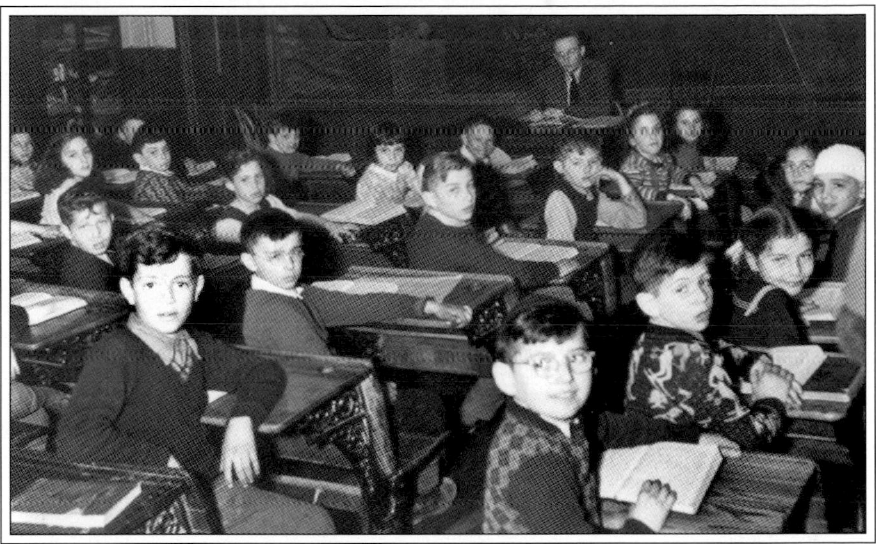

This class in the Ottawa Talmud Torah on Rideau Street (probably early or late 1930s) takes a break from studying.

NATIONAL ARCHIVES OF CANADA PA105086

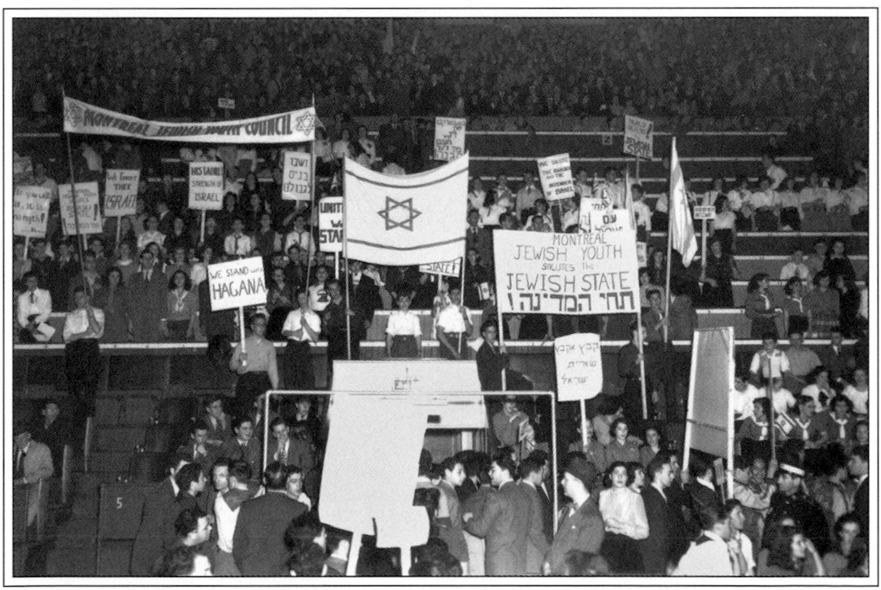

Jewish rally at the Montreal Forum to celebrate the founding of the state of Israel, May 16, 1948.

GAZETTE, MONTREAL; NATIONAL ARCHIVES OF CANADA PA116478

Canadian Jewish Congress official Benjamin Robinson receives a torah scroll from one of the war orphans in 1947. The scroll cover was made in one of the Displaced Persons camps.

CANADIAN JEWISH CONGRESS NATIONAL ARCHIVES, MONTREAL

Poet Abraham M. Klein addressing a farewell gathering for Rabbi Aron Horowitz in Montreal, 1949.

FEDERAL PHOTOS, MONTREAL; NATIONAL ARCHIVES OF CANADA PA202171

Front of the Sanctuary of Toronto's Beth Tzedec Synagogue (Conservative), one of North America's largest. This synagogue was built in the mid-1950s after the merger of two former downtown congregations.

ONTARIO JEWISH ARCHIVES

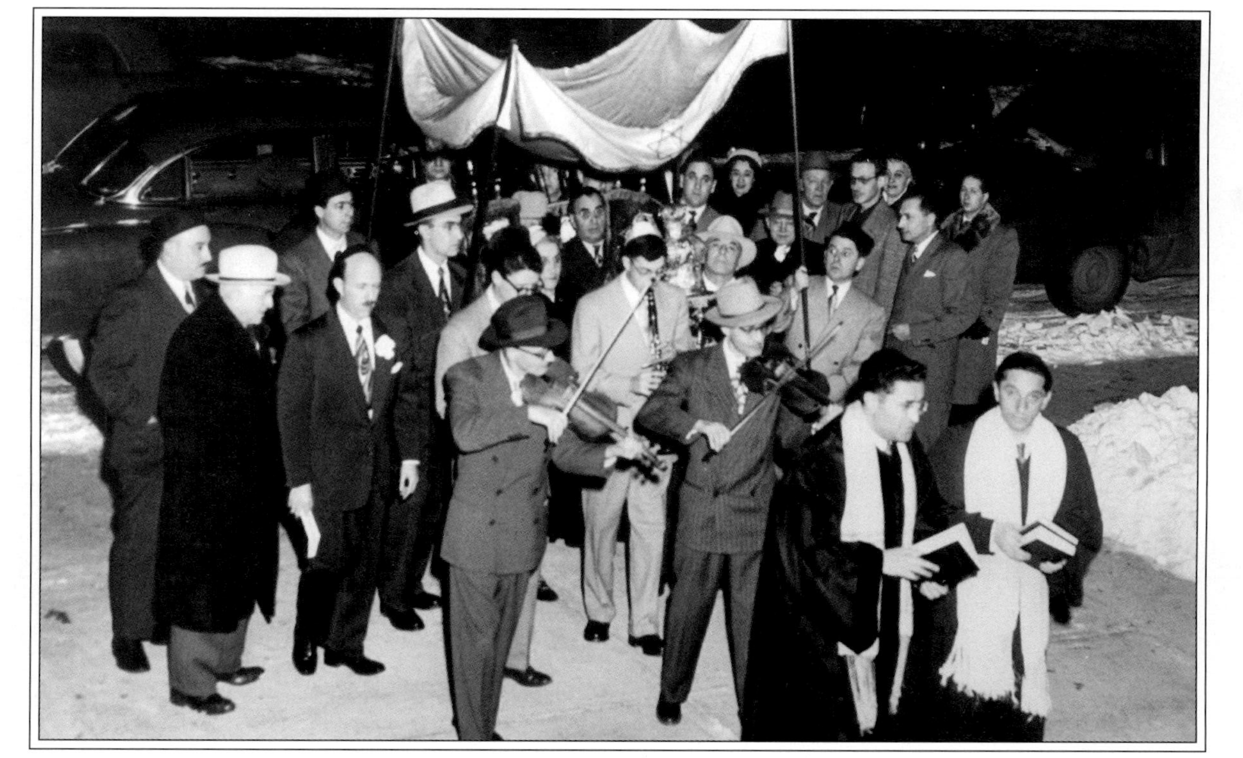

Captioned "Conducting honoured guest into synagogue," this photograph shows a procession, led by Rabbi Eliezer Ebner and Cantor Morris Goldblum, for the dedication of a new torah scroll at Congregation Beth Israel in Calgary, Alberta, 1951.

GLENBOW MUSEUM AND ARCHIVES

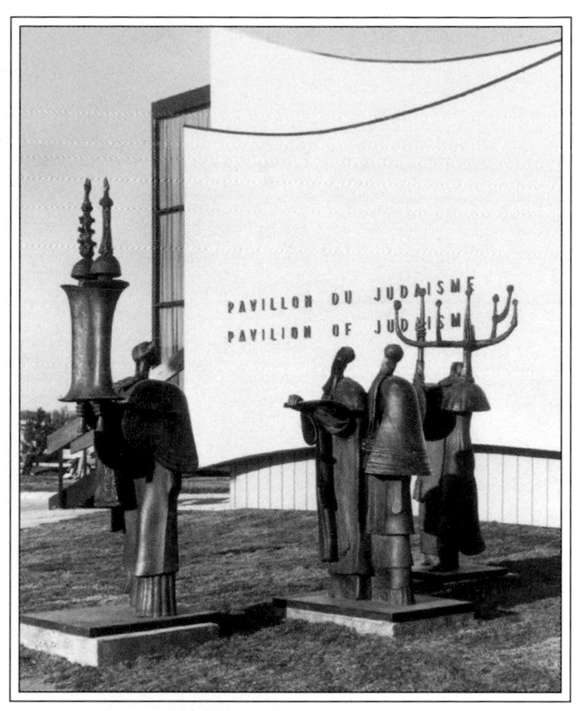

"The Procession," by Ethel Weinberg at Pavilion of Judaism at Expo '67 in Montreal. One figure holds torah aloft; others represent religious figures. Menorah in background.

NATIONAL ARCHIVES OF CANADA PA186313

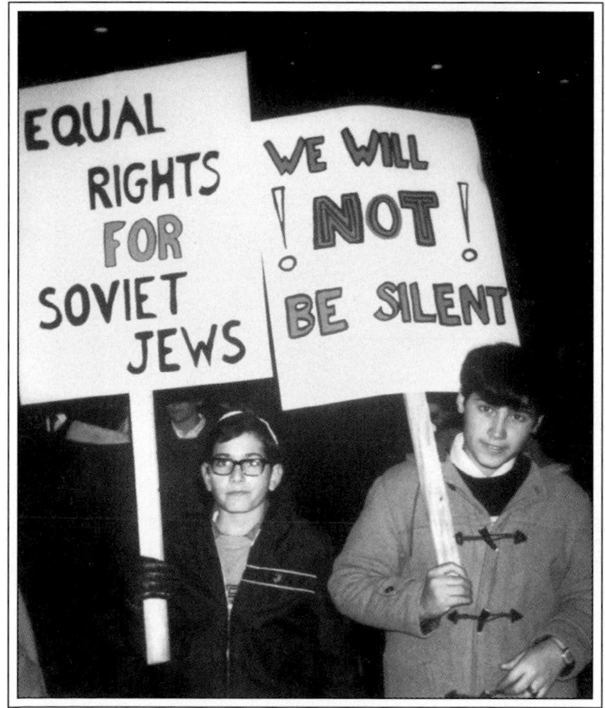

At the first of many rallies on Simchat Torah (Rejoicing with the Torah), Toronto Jewish youth show their solidarity with the Jews of the Soviet Union, 1967.

ONTARIO JEWISH ARCHIVES

Thirtieth anniversary celebrations to commemorate the founding of Israel, Montreal Forum, May 11, 1978.

ALAN R. LEISHMAN; NATIONAL ARCHIVES OF CANADA PA201334

Chanukah menorah and holiday greetings sign from Chabad Lubavitch on the grounds of the Ontario Legislature, Toronto, December 1997.

STEVEN L. TULCHINSKY

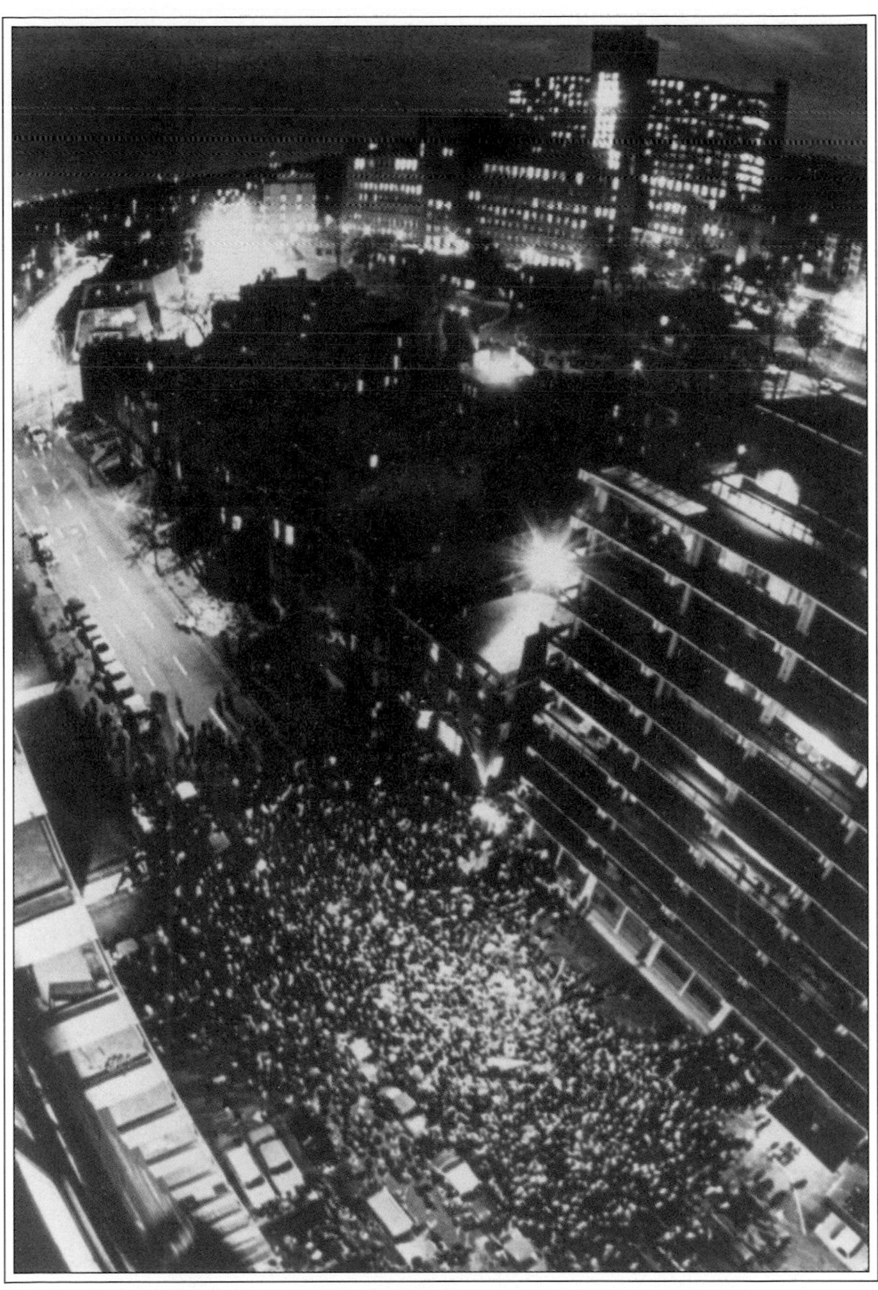

Masses of Montreal Jews march for Soviet Jewry on Simchat Torah, October 1973, en route to the Soviet Consulate.

CANADIAN JEWISH CONGRESS NATIONAL ARCHIVES, MONTREAL

The family of Haim Ben Haim from Morocco arrives at Montreal's Dorval airport in the early 1960s to add to Canada's growing Sephardic community.

CANADIAN JEWISH CONGRESS NATIONAL ARCHIVES, MONTREAL

Jews even began to appear — perhaps for the first time — as sympathetic figures in French-Canadian novels of the 1960s.[99] Finally, to French-Canadian writers like Yves Thériault, "the Jew is no longer . . . far-away . . . but [is] the neighbour, someone nearer, the Jew who lives on the next street."[100] At last, the Jew was someone with whom it was possible to empathize, whose "Jewish music, . . . soul and . . . spirit" Thériault might appreciate. The Jewish experience as a minority group, Kattan suggested, was seen almost as a model or symbol of the French-Canadian predicament, and served "as an example, an encouragement, a confirmation." Although most of these literary interpretations depicted the Jew only from the outside, never penetrating his soul, the generally favourable representation in literature was a watershed in French-Canadian attitudes towards the Jewish stranger.

Jewish perceptions of French Canada's distinctive personality were often decidedly sympathetic. The Royal Commission on Bilingualism and Biculturalism was a major forum for public debate on the future of Canada in the early 1960s. It held hearings across the country on the state of relations between English and French Canadians, while still recognizing the contributions made by other ethnic groups.[101] A submission from the Jewish Labour Committee (which represented trade unions with predominantly Jewish membership) expressed "deep respect for the very survival of French-Canadian culture in an overwhelmingly Anglo-Saxon surrounding."[102] The committee asserted that rapprochement between the English and the French was essential for Canada's national survival, and that French and English must continue to be Canada's only official languages.[103] Although it rejected official multilingualism, the committee argued that governments should support every ethnic group's right to assert its cultural distinctiveness.

In the long run, fears of Québécois nationalism generally proved to be ill-founded. The Parti Québécois' record towards the Jewish community belied the concerns of Rabbi Rosenberg and others about an *étatist* denial of communal rights. In fact, the provincial government increased financial support for Jewish denominational schools and cultural projects.

Nevertheless, Jews, like other anglophones in Quebec, are worried. After the passage of a far-reaching law in 1977, language became the overriding issue for non-French minorities. This law required that people moving to Quebec send their children to French schools, a stipulation that effectively discouraged all but francophones from moving to the province.[104] While a 1984 Supreme Court decision guaranteed the right to an English education to persons from other parts of Canada, the children of immigrants from abroad were still required to attend French schools. This was emblematic of the Quebec government's determination to advance the French language *à outrance*.

In 1990 the Quebec National Assembly passed Bill 178 in an effort to regulate the size and placement of store signs in languages other than French. To enforce the law, "language police" were hired to inspect business premises and fine offenders. Quite apart from the costs associated with enforcing the legislation, the Draconian nature of the law raised serious questions about the survival of civil rights for non-francophones in Quebec. If their language rights could be removed, what else might be threatened?

This law caused deep concern among both Jews and anglophones, many of whom failed to recognize that it was vigorously denounced in both *L'Actualité* and *Le Devoir*, the nationalistic and prestigious French daily.[105] The Jewish community was especially affected by the need to bilingually label kosher food products. Although this was done routinely on goods packaged in Canada, those from the United States, which carried English-only labels, violated the law. Efforts were made to have these items exempted, but as late as 1996 the issue occasionally cropped up, usually to the embarrassment of both the Jewish community and, apparently, the government of Quebec.[106]

Les Juifs Francophones

Montreal's Jewish community diversified further during the 1960s, with the arrival of French-speaking immigrants from Morocco and smaller numbers of Spanish speakers from Tunisia, Algeria, Egypt, Lebanon, and Syria. Some francophone Jews originated from Ashkenazim in Central or Eastern Europe, where French was the language of the elite.[107] Largely because they spoke French and had absorbed the culture of metropolitan France in the schools of the Alliance Israélite Universelle (Alliance), these immigrants were attracted to Montreal.[108]

Because they were more comfortable among themselves, these newcomers formed L'Association Sépharde Francophone, an umbrella organization of the francophone chapters of B'nai Brith, Hadassah, and other associations.[109] "Francophone" was subsequently dropped from this organization's title and it was renamed the Communanté Sépharade du Québec, both in recognition of the other languages spoken by some of its members, including Judeo-Spanish (spoken by some Turkish Jews) and English (spoken by some Sephardim), and to emphasize its location in Quebec.

While these Jews wanted to maintain their unique identity as both French-speakers and Sephardim, they faced the problem of being a double minority. As Jews in a predominantly Christian province and francophones in a largely English-speaking community, they were in danger of losing one or, possibly, both features of their identity. In 1972 Rabbi Stuart Rosenberg observed that the francophone Jew "has a choice of identifying either with the existing Anglophone Jewish community and probably losing his unique French-Sephardi cultural heritage, or with a non-Jewish Francophone community and thus probably losing his Jewish religious connections."[110]

The shortage of Jewish French-language services and institutions, especially schools, was problematic. Because of the confessional educational system, there were no French-language elementary schools for non-Catholics. Consequently, French-speaking Jewish children were forced to attend the Protestant English-language schools. Thus until their language skills improved, they were placed in lower classes. A small number of Sephardi children did attend French-language Hebrew day-schools, which were associated for a few years with the Catholic school boards.[111]

This situation presented a challenge, the *Canadian Jewish News* editorialized in December 1963, for both the Jewish community of Canada and the government of Quebec:

> the problem is to find a solution which would prevent the estrangement of these youngsters. For the government of Quebec, the problem is to see that these French-speaking North Africans, among whom many have contributed in the past to the spiritual grandeur of France, are not lost to Canadian French culture.[112]

A special Sephardic day-school was opened with broad communal support in 1968. "The assistance which the Ashkenazis [of Montreal] are giving us in terms of money," the school's principal commented, "[has] amazed me. . . . This spirit of 'Kol Yisrael chaverim' is a heartwarming thing and will do much to cement the ties of brotherhood and friendship between the two sections of our people."[113]

As their numbers grew, the Sephardim formed their own synagogues, fourteen of them by 1979; these were supervised by the Rabbinat Sépharade du Québec. Even so, strong religious and family ties were not enough to stop the acculturation of young francophone Jews. A 1972 study of intermarriage in Montreal revealed that 50 percent of North African Jews were marrying non-Jews.[114]

Eventually, two francophone Jewish day-schools were established in Montreal — École Maimonide and École Sépharade — and French-language classes in the anglophone Jewish day-schools were expanded with strong financial incentives from the Quebec government. During the 1980s, the Sephardic presence was also becoming evident in Toronto, although the Ontario Sephardic Federation, in alliance with the Communanté Sépharade du

Québec, was concerned because "community organizations were not doing enough to integrate the Sephardim fully."[115] In Montreal, meanwhile, the Sephardim, previously focused on their own communal needs, "began to make their presence felt in broader community settings," forcing major Jewish organizations to use French and include more Sephardic representation.[116]

In spite of these breakthroughs, the Sephardim often felt hostility, fear, and resentment emanate from the existing Montreal Jewish community. New immigrants (once called greenhorns) had always encountered the patronizing attitude of some of the earlier arrivals, and the Sephardim were no exception. But as both French-speakers and North Africans, they were viewed sceptically by Montreal Jewry for wanting to maintain a separate identity. Even then, "separatism [was] an explosive political subject in Quebec."[117] A 1972 survey demonstrated that the Sephardim believed deep divisions existed between themselves and the anglophone Jewish majority in Montreal. The survey reported that the Sephardim considered certain groups to be more accommodating than others, starting with other francophone Jews, and followed by French Canadians, other North Africans, and Muslims. Canadian Jews were a distant fifth.[118] Some 20 percent of respondents expressed an outright dislike of the Ashkenazim.

The Sephardim resented the disparaging remarks made about their Arabic, and allegedly primitive, origins by persons they perceived to be former residents of spindly one-room shacks in East European *shtetls*. Many Sephardim were proud of their roots and of the enlightened aspects of the Arabic culture of North Africa. As devotees of metropolitan French secular culture, they were resentful of being regarded as a threat by the rest of Montreal Jewry. Their École Maimonide was ignored by the local association for Jewish day-schools and received only minimal financial support from the Allied Jewish Community Services (AJCS). When other early requests for community assistance were rejected, Sephardic resentments towards Montreal Jewry mounted.

Occasionally, community responses to this discrimination were warmly sympathetic. Having surveyed these complaints, the *Canadian Jewish News* observed in early 1972 that "the grievances reported must be dealt with in earnest for they concern fundamental issues."[119] It called for Jewish employers to provide on-the-job training to upgrade the skills of these immigrants and urged Jewish agencies to recruit francophone personnel to meet the Sephardi community's needs. The following year, the sociologist Jean-Claude Lasry commented that Montreal Jewry, "as a whole, was beginning to recognize the needs of Sephardim."[120] To overcome a general lack of understanding among most Jews, JIAS official Dr. Joseph Kage called for a wide-ranging program of education on Sephardic culture.[121] In 1979, at a meeting in Montreal of the

General Assembly of Allied Jewish Federations, the AJCS responded to complaints of discrimination. They recommended ten major steps to strengthen Sephardi culture and proclaimed that "Sephardi survival represents an important and urgent problem and a priority in the Jewish world."[122]

Despite the genuine efforts mounted during the 1980s to accommodate and integrate them, many Sephardim in Montreal maintained their isolation and their distinctive identity.[123] Settled mostly in the Côte-des-Neiges area and in the suburbs of Saint-Laurent, Laval, Côte St-Luc, and Dollard-des-Ormeaux, they attempted to navigate the turbulent waters of Montreal Jewish social politics and *la milieu Québécoise* without compromising, and if possible strengthening, their identity. Their adherence to French led to an increased socialization with francophone Quebeckers, to the formation of synagogues with Sephardic rituals, to the retention of strong family ties, and to strong associational links. Apart from being shaped by local context, their identity was formulated also by poignant memories of the Maghreb: its French colonialism, Arab nationalism, and Jewish communal and family life. At the same time, the socialization of their kinfolk in Israel and France strengthened tendencies towards secularization and political assertiveness.

To Monsieur Chevalier's House

Sholem Shtern

To greet the sleigh
the wooden gate is opened wide.
Burly Monsieur Chevalier stands beside his greystone house
and beaming broadly says:
"Honored guests, members of an old
and venerable tribe,
step across my humble threshold!
I'm sure you're thirsty
for a cup of fragrant coffee,
or a glass of sweet hot tea.
My wife will never make you wait —
the scrambled eggs
are ready for you on the plate.
Bowls of sour cream, fresh butter, cheese —
Man, just open up your mouth and eat!"

From Sholem Shtern, *The White House: A Novel in Verse*, Max Rosenfeld, trans. (Montreal: Waksbroehe Publishers, 1974), 161.

Even today, the community remains caught in the interstices of the three Quebec solitudes — the English, the French, and the Jews — and its intellectuals ponder their future. In a thoughtful article in Montreal's *La Voix Sépharade* in June 1987, Haim Hazan stressed the need for the Sephardi community's continuing adaptation to Jewish social politics in North America. In contrast to the North African respect for authority and hierarchical structures, he observed that "[in North America] freedom is absolute. For the first time in our history we face religious pluralism, something unknown to us. . . . Everyone is free to join the movement of his choice."[124] To survive, Hazan asserted, they must offer something distinctively Sephardic to their youth. In a conclusion that voiced concerns remarkably similar to those of francophone Québécois, Hazan wrote:

> We are a small, vulnerable community, all the more vulnerable because we are isolated and because, in a continent of six million anglophone Jews, we, 25,000 francophones, want to remain Sephardic in a totally Ashkenazi milieu. . . . The status quo can only lead to suffocation and in time to our disappearance as a distinct community.

In the meantime, efforts to strengthen ties between the two segments of Montreal Jewry were continuing. They were at last learning to work together for common concerns.[125]

Francophone Jews in Toronto

Although Toronto's Sephardic community was less numerous than Montreal's, it was also growing after 1957. Their adjustment, however, was even more difficult. Although JIAS helped the new immigrants find housing and employment, many reported that they felt confused by the process and alienated by the professional and "businesslike" handling, which seemed uncaring and cold.[126] These newcomers to Toronto, self-reliant and in some cases well-to-do in Morocco, which they had fled in the wake of rising Arab nationalism, felt ashamed of having to ask for help from "strangers," even though they were fellow Jews. They would rather have relied on the familiar family networks, as they had done in North Africa. Canadian Jews seemed not only uncommunicative and unsympathetic, but also generally less religiously observant.[127]

One study of the 350 Moroccan Jewish families who settled in Toronto between 1957 and 1965 found that their geographical dispersion was a significant social disability.[128] The costs of transporting children to religious schools was prohibitive, for example, forcing some families to withdraw and provide instruction at home. In addition to the problems associated with isolation in Spartan high-rises, low incomes, cultural uneasiness, and language barriers, generational dissonance was becoming an especially painful concern. Relationships between children seeking emancipation in a multicultural environment and parents with a world-view shaped by their North African experience were strained. But the greatest disappointment was the community's feeling that it had been rejected by Toronto Jewry. As one observer noted, "What they are seeking is a Canadian identity within the Canadian Jewish community, the barriers to which seem hard to overcome."[129] Many felt a much stronger cultural and emotional affinity for Italians, while those from Tangier preferred to associate with local Portuguese.

The Sephardim formed a separate congregation using the Brunswick Street Shomrei Shabbat synagogue in the city's former Jewish quarter. In 1967, 150 families who called themselves Petach Tikvah Anshei Castilia bought this synagogue,[130] but they changed quarters several times thereafter.[131] Wherever they moved, they continued to make their distinctive mark on the city's Jewish scene[132] and gradually evoked some local empathy.[133] Complaints from within the community continued, nevertheless, and were often lodged against JIAS for its perceived insensitivity and against professional bodies that refused to recognize qualifications earned abroad. The latter was a sore point with many Sephardic immigrants.[134]

All the while, they continued to face the dilution of their distinctive culture within the predominantly Ashkenazi milieu, an erosion that affected even their own schools. In Toronto, one parent uttered this *cri de coeur*:

> It's tragic. All this money spent so our kids could get a Jewish education. . . . All these sacrifices on our part and for what? They're not learning what we sent them to school to learn. So, it's arguments, arguments, all the time. They are not Sephardim anymore, really[,] and that hurts a lot.[135]

Religion and Culture

Interesting changes took place in religious life from the 1960s onward. The Hasidim grew in numbers as some of the sects, notably the Lubavitchers, established an energetic, almost missionary, outreach program for all Jews — especially university students. In the same period, alternative Jewish religious expression took new forms, with egalitarian services offered by Conservative and even a few "renegade" Orthodox groups.

While on the whole traditional Judaism remained dominant in Canada, there was a significant increase in the number of Reform congregations. One study revealed that Reform Judaism was growing because "it was less demanding than either Orthodoxy [or] Conservativism from a sacramental point of view and because it emphasized associational ties."[136]

This was especially evident, interestingly enough, in small university cities like Kingston and Kitchener-Waterloo. Newer arrivals to those cities — many of them academics — were unwilling to accept the established synagogues and the existing social institutions of the community. They opted instead to form their own more liberal congregations, which held services in borrowed or rented premises, often university buildings. Rabbis were brought in on a temporary basis, and teachers, some of them qualified university students, were hired locally.[137]

These new congregations were not always welcomed by the older ones, but the Reform groups nevertheless thrived, largely because they offered a flexible and warm alternative to what some perceived to be religiously stiff and socially unwelcoming communities. In 1965 in Kitchener-Waterloo, an informal Jewish fellowship of a dozen mostly professional and academic families began to meet in each other's homes for worship and discussion, "because Orthodox Judaism did not suit them."[138] Assisted by Reform synagogues and rabbis in Hamilton and Toronto, the fellowship, which named itself Temple Shalom, soon grew to thirty families, established an afternoon school, bought a building, and employed a series of student rabbis. In 1996 Temple Shalom established itself as joint occupant with a local United Church congregation in the Cedars Worship and Community Centre.

In Kingston nearly one-third of the members of the new Reform group, which called itself Iyr Hamelech (literally "the city of the king") were married to non-Jews, who in some cases were "the decisive influence in the family's decision to join the congregation."[139] Formed in 1975, Iyr Hamelech's membership grew from a small nucleus to fifty families by 1995, an increase of 163 percent in two decades. It continues to thrive.[140] Since its members are, on average, younger than those in the older congregation (and are still having children), Iyr Hamelech — like its sister Reform congregations in other cities — should continue to offer a viable Jewish religious alternative.

In the larger urban centres, meanwhile, some of the new synagogues formed in the prosperous 1950s were having financial difficulties. Temple Beth Sholom, in Montreal's west end, closed its doors in 1980 and merged with Temple Emanu-el. Others had to economize by operating joint educational programs and amalgamated afternoon schools with other congregations. Some even had to rent out space.[141]

In early 1977 Rabbi Michael Stroh warned that congregations should build more modest structures, owing to mounting costs and the "mobility of the Jewish population." Ailing synagogues, he said, should qualify for broad community support. Some experts predicted a polarization between the super-sized synagogue/community centre, which offered a wide range of facilities, and the tiny local synagogues, which provided space for only prayer and study, (much like the old-time immigrant *shtibl* or Eastern European *bes medresh*, from which the modern North American synagogue had emerged).[142] Perhaps there was some agreeable symbolism in this turn back to religious privatism and tradition.

Such a transformation was not acceptable, however, if it meant the development of a "club mentality" and the sacrifice of communal responsibilities, at least as far as Rabbi Gunther Plaut was concerned.[143] He called for the congregations to restructure themselves to handle community service on a broad scale — not just for their members, but for all Jews — in conjunction with federations and other agencies. Plaut asserted that while many rabbis spoke out for social justice, they often encountered difficulty in bringing their congregations onside:

> They generally do not interfere with the rabbi's freedom of personal action, but they will often insist that the rabbi make clear to the community that he is undertaking these political activities on his own and not in the name of either the Jewish community or the congregation.

Only when the rabbis espoused popular causes, such as support for Israel or freedom for Soviet Jewry, were they certain to be completely backed by their entire congregation.

Jewish Secularism

Jewish liberalism — a broad term describing opinion ranging from the moderate to the radical left — had also become more central in the larger Jewish community. The situation in Canada was perhaps healthier than in the United States, where the introduction of affirmative action programs (which effectively discriminated against Jews and other whites) had alienated many of the old Jewish left and turned some into conservatives.[144] Also, the persecution of alleged leftists, a disproportionately large number of whom were Jews, was less severe in Canada than in the United States, according to Len Scher's *The Un-Canadians: True Stories of the Blacklist Era*.[145]

The thriving secular wing of the Jewish school system is in itself testimony to the fact that the liberal and progressive philosophy on which it had been founded many years earlier is still alive. These schools affirm a "Jewish identity that [is] positive, relevent and meaningful." By emphasizing the prophetic tradition and Jewish history, they teach children "the dynamics of ethnic group formation and development, [which] underscores the similarities as well as the distinctive characteristics common to all minority peoples."[146] While both Zionism and Israel are recognized as important parts of the curriculum, supporters of these secular schools consider their "primary purpose to be the continuity and development of a viable, meaningful, prideful Jewish cultural identity in [their] own countries." Thus secular Judaism has embraced a broadly defined Jewish culture that does not exclude religion, but sees it and its universal values — "love and reverence for life, human worth and dignity, humility, learning and joy" — as essential elements of identity in the modern world. "Being a Jew among Jews is easy," one observer said. "It's being a Jew among Gentiles that's difficult."[147]

This secular perspective, of course, is not new. It harks back to the philosophy of the Bund, the Workmen's Circle, and the UJPO, whose members stressed their solidarity with the Jewish people and embraced Yiddish language and culture, while still seeking integration into the countries where they lived. They saw themselves as "secularists . . . who have emotionally and intellectually chosen to express their Jewish identity in less ritualistic, non-religious ways."[148] This philosophy was based on a fundamental resistance to the Jewish establishment, the monied clique that dominated the community's leadership positions in its major organizations. It implied a critique of Jewish politics, which were becoming increasingly conservative. As what might be called non-Jewish Jews, these liberals followed an unconventional agenda.[149] They rejected the "religious infusion of the Jewish community structure [which] has not only gained the upper hand, but it has become hegemonic in the sense that the organization of ethnicity, in this country and in the U.S., has assumed a religious colouring."[150]

Younger secular and progressive Jewish leftists, according to the sociologist Michael Bodemann, have rejected the idea that ethnicity is "a thing of the past [that] universalistically minded progressives must strive to overcome." They object to the "non-leftists" who dominate the major Jewish organizations, arguing that the "very substantial number of Jews who are disillusioned with the established structures [are left] outside the community and leaderless."[151] The progressives continue to attempt to mobilize these disaffected Jews "to confront the monolithic-conservative domination of Jewry by this tiny group of *haute bourgeoisie* who have their names inscribed in the masthead of the *Canadian Jewish News* or the elevators of the Baycrest Geriatric Centre." Bodemann continues, "One thing seems clear, as leftists of one sort or another, we have to realize the political importance of the factor of ethnicity — especially in a country that decreed multiculturalism. Like it or not, ethnicity's a central building block of the Canadian state, an important tool of political control."[152]

Assertiveness can go only so far in this search for legitimacy for the Jewish left. One adherent asked whether "we secular Jews can match that kind of cement that has bound the religious Jew to a heritage derived from a distant, imperceptible past? We may have to try if we want to have a continuation of what we have achieved to date."[153] He called for "the observance of as many Jewish events as possible in a way that denotes originality while simultaneously denoting sameness." Not all would agree that this course of action was easy, or even possible. Certainly not the New York intellectual Irving Howe, a leading spokesman for the Jewish left. In a major address at the University of Toronto in March 1979, he forecast the end of secular Jewish culture.[154] The Holocaust destroyed the cultural well that had fostered this tradition, he argued, and North American Jews had fallen victim to the "enticements of liberal democracy," an oblique reference to post–Second World War prosperity and materialism. Many Jews, he noted, observed religious externalities, "though they are not actively engaged" in religious life. Others had become enthusiastic champions of Israel, but in his view this translated into only weak support for substantive Jewish continuity.

Times had changed. The old Yiddish-speaking leftists were disappearing just as the social-economic conditions that had kept their cause alive had vanished. Sweatshops had long since given way to better working conditions, and very few children of old activists spoke the language of Yiddish dissent or shared the outlook and commitment to the cause of secular Judaism — if they even understood what it once had meant.[155] In its place, a new Jewish ethnicity firmly grounded on Canadian realities had emerged. This multi-faceted identity, which was still evolving in a context that was itself in transition, reflected the complexity of the Canadian-Jewish interface in a Canada that was now native ground to most Jews. Having in large numbers emerged through schools and universities, Second World War military service, active lives in arts and letters, deep engagement in politics, successful businesses, and, above all, the transforming energy of Israel, Canadian Jews were assertive, confident, and proud.

CHAPTER

12

Complexities and Uncertainties from the 1970s to the 1990s

A growing awareness of the Holocaust became a prominent feature of Jewish life in Canada in the 1980s and 1990s. Memorials to its victims dotted the landscape of synagogues, cemeteries, and community centres. There is even one on the grounds of the Manitoba legislature. Survivors' memoirs of the horrific experiences of the camps came rolling off the presses, and film footage and interviews were recorded for posterity. Rallies were convened to honour the Swedish businessman Raoul Wallenberg and other "Righteous Gentiles," and university courses on the Holocaust proliferated. Conferences on teaching the Holocaust were held and educators' kits distributed to schools. In recent years, hundreds of Jews began to travel to Poland's death camps, mainly Auschwitz, to join the March of the Living and bear personal witness to the Holocaust at its most infamous killing ground.

Every year, on the twenty-seventh day of the Hebrew month of *Nisan* (usually in April), Jews in communities small and large gather to light *yahrzeit* (memorial) candles; recite the *kaddish* and *El Moleh Rachamim*, prayers for the dead; listen to talks by survivors and Nazi-hunters like Beate Klarsfeld; and stand in solemn collective remembrance and reflection. There are no differences between Jews in these moments. Rich or poor, Ashkenazi or Sephardi, they are all Jewish people in hushed assembly, confronting the most painful era in their history. Having been separated by many years from those events, Canadian Jewry embraces them, recognizing that the Holocaust is now part of its collective identity.

As yet, few have pondered the long-term utility of an emphasis such as this. Ruth Wisse, however, writing in *Commentary*, reflected on this issue:

> Now that our children have taken over the job of reciting the texts commemorating the ghetto martyrs, I sometimes wonder what we are doing to them. What have we already done? In France last year I met a lapsed Jew whose grandmother had begged him to have his first child baptized: "*Ca suffit!*" She had had enough, this woman who had spent the war hiding in barns and cellars."[1]

Today, some 40 percent of Canadian Jews are Holocaust survivors or their descendants, probably the highest percentage of any Jewish community outside of Israel. As these survivors began to enter old age in the 1980s, there was a proliferation of memoirs recounting their tragic lives in Eastern Europe.[2] As they reached their final years, many survivors felt obliged to record their experiences for succeeding generations.[3]

Much more is known about the Holocaust and scholars have pieced together its evolution. In 1982, when the historians Irving Abella and Harold Troper published *None Is Too Many: Canada and the Jews of Europe 1933–1948*, the public was made fully aware for the first time that Canada's record in saving Jews was the poorest of any Western country. From 1933 to 1948, Canada kept Jewish immigration to a minimum in deference to widespread antisemitism, which was especially strong in Quebec. The government also refused to override the actions of the director of immigration, F. C. Blair, and numerous other officials who conspired to deny entry to Jews. As a result, fewer than five thousand Jews entered Canada during that entire period.

Holocaust denial and rising incidents of antisemitism also sharpened public awareness. Politicized in the late 1950s and early 1960s by an outburst of swastika-daubings across the country, the trial of Adolf Eichmann in Israel, and the re-emergence of Nazi parties in Canada and the United States, groups of survivors urged the Canadian Jewish Congress to take action.[4] When the Congress refused, these groups formed the Association of Survivors of Nazi Oppression; staged a public march in Montreal in the spring of 1961; and issued their own newspaper, the *Voice of Survivors*, to draw attention to their concerns about Nazi activities in Canada.[5]

In Toronto, they directly confronted Nazis who rallied in downtown parks, forcing the Congress to create an anti-Nazi committee and accept survivors on its councils. In 1965, at the Congress' urging, the minister of Justice, Guy Favreau, created a Special Committee on Hate Propaganda and appointed McGill's dean of law, Maxwell Cohen, to head it. The committee included Pierre Elliott Trudeau, Mark MacGuigan, and Saul Hayes, and it helped bring about federal anti-hate legislation in 1970.[6] When the CBC aired an interview with Eric Von Thadden, the leader of a German political party with links to former Nazis, protests were launched by survivors, who were also agitated by the dangers faced by Israel in May and June of 1967. Creating a link between Holocaust awareness and Israel's security, which was so often threatened in the 1970s and 1980s, became increasingly common among Canadian Jewry. In response to this, the Congress resolved in 1971 to establish a Holocaust memorial; it set up a Holocaust education committee a year later.

This new militancy marked the community's transition from old-style, polite or "whispering" diplomacy to an emphasis on mobilizing "the corporate resources of the community and to encourage a measure of militant and even radical action (save physical violence)."[7] It was this spirit that lay behind the 1970s campaign to free Soviet Jewry, the movement in the 1980s to transfer Canada's Israeli embassy from Tel Aviv to Jerusalem, and later campaigns against shifts in Canadian foreign policy that favoured the territorial interests of the Palestinians. Inspired by a range of organizations and a dynamic and well-informed leadership, the Canadian Jewish community was prepared to engage in "near confrontation" politics to achieve its goals.

While successful in some instances, these tactics failed in others — such as the embassy issue — a clear signal to the community of its limitations and of the potentially significant costs of political stridency. Public patience for such tactics is limited. Perhaps even more serious are the resources wasted on losing battles, such as the drawn-out campaign in Ontario for publicly financed Jewish parochial schools. A basic course in Canadian history should have been enough to inform Jewish leaders of the utter futility of this effort.

Nazis and Their Collaborators in Canada

In this same spirit of assertiveness, many Canadian Jews, like Jews in the United States and Great Britain, confronted the issue of Nazi war criminals living in Canada. Allegations had been circulating for years that among the numerous European immigrants who had arrived after the Second World War, there were many who took an active part in the murder of Jews and others. As early as the 1940s, the Canadian Jewish Congress had complained to government officials that the veterans of the Halychyna (Galicia) Waffen SS Division who were about to be admitted to Canada were Nazis. Although this complaint was set aside, the belief persisted that many war criminals (like Comte Jacques de Bernonville, who found refuge in Quebec briefly) had entered the country as a result of the shockingly permissive attitudes of immigration officials, sloppy RCMP screening, and a Cold War hostility to the Soviets, who made many of the initial charges. The possibility of lingering antisemitism was also considered a reason for the government's unwillingness to proceed on this issue. But it is also clear that the Canadian Jewish Congress did not press it, largely because it had much more urgent business to deal with in the war's aftermath.

In Canada rumours had circulated since the 1940s about alleged war criminals like Dr. Josef Kirschbaum, an official with the Hlinka Slovak People's Party during the Second World War.[8] "We know who they are," one survivor stated in 1973, though he admitted that naming names was a ticklish matter.[9] One major legal obstacle was Canadian law, which made extradition of suspected persons difficult.[10] But allegations continued to surface, some appearing in press releases from the Soviet embassy in Ottawa in 1974.[11] Promises of action from Secretary of State Hugh Faulkner to a Congress delegation in 1975 came to nothing, very likely because of Prime Minister Trudeau's strong reluctance to encourage the opening of old wounds.[12]

One of the alleged war criminals was Albert Helmut Rauca, who was wanted in West Germany for the murder of 10,500 Jews in the Lithuanian city of Kaunas in October 1941.[13] Living quietly in a suburban North Toronto neighbourhood, the seventy-three-year-old Rauca, who had immigrated to Canada in 1950 and gained citizenship in 1956, was arrested by the RCMP on June 17, 1982. The following October, a Canadian court ruled that Rauca be extradited, and after all appeals were denied, he was handed over to the German police on May 17, 1983, and flown to Frankfurt. Charged the following September with the murder of 10,500 Jews, Rauca died in a prison hospital before the case was heard. Although he was the only accused Nazi war criminal to be extradited, he was just one of a considerable number who were named as a result of the activities of a small group of Nazi-hunters, the most persistent of whom was Sol Littman, the Canadian director of the Simon Wiesenthal Center.

The issue of war criminals in Canada would not go away and the Congress urged several approaches, including trials, revocation of citizenship, deportation, and extradition.[14] So strong were the pressures for action that, in February 1985, the Mulroney government asked Justice Jules Deschênes "to inquire into the matter of alleged war criminals in Canada."[15] Hearings began in Ottawa on April 10, 1985, and continued until May 6, 1986. Submissions were heard from not only a number of Jewish individuals and organizations, but also other members of interested Canadian ethnic communities. In his report, which was published on December 30, 1986, Justice Deschênes made eighty-two findings and recommendations, and noted several important factors that had affected Canada's post-1945 policy on war crimes. In 1948, for example, secret suggestions made by the British government to the Commonwealth countries influenced Canada's decision to drop war-crimes prosecutions. Nevertheless,

Deschênes concluded, Canada's policy was no worse than that of several Western countries, "which displayed an equal lack of interest." He also determined that allegations that there were as many as six thousand war criminals living in Canada were unfounded, that charges against the Halychyna (Galicia) Waffen SS Division members who were admitted to Canada "have never been substantiated,"[16] and that, contrary to rumours, Joseph Mengele had never entered Canada.

Justice Deschênes recommended that, of 774 suspects' files, 606 be closed and only twenty be given "urgent attention" for possible revocation of citizenship and deportation or criminal prosecution in Canada. He further recommended that amendments be made to Canadian laws to tighten procedures. He also felt that the government should consider either giving the Department of Justice and the RCMP "a specific mandate" and sufficient staff to continue their investigations, or renewing the commission's authority to summon suspects and other witnesses for interrogation.

In the course of the Deschênes inquiry there were some startling revelations. One was that an inter-departmental committee, which met in 1981 to consider taking action against former Nazis in Canada, had been unable to prove that some of the accused lied, partly because they were unaware of the existence of crucial immigration files, which subsequently were destroyed.[17] This act, Justice Minister John Crosbie claimed, prevented the government from prosecuting many suspected war criminals. Outraged, the Congress' representative at the hearings, Irwin Cotler, protested that these missing documents, together with the 1948 cessation of prosecutions, the sanctuary provided to war criminals, and the quashing of deportation orders issued against alleged Nazi collaborators, constituted "an obstruction of justice."[18]

The Jewish community was right in the middle of the controversy stirred up by the commission. "The political fallout from nearly a year of Deschênes commission hearings is raining down on Parliament Hill," one correspondent, Ruth Rucker, reported to the *Canadian Jewish News* in January 1986.[19] Meanwhile, members of the Ukrainian-Canadian community complained to politicians such as Don Blenkarn, Conservative MP for the suburban Toronto riding of Mississauga South. Ukrainians in Canada were often accused of harbouring war criminals, and they feared that evidence from Soviet sources might become admissible in Canadian war-crimes proceedings. Blenkarn said that he had received more than one hundred written protests and had numerous visits from angry constituents, who, he said, "are coming out with lines that I hoped had disappeared from this country. What is coming out is racial hatred [his code word, presumably, for antisemitism]." He continued, "I hope [Deschênes] can find some evidence that's incontrovertible against some individuals. If he can't the government is going to pay for it heavily politically. . . . And the Jewish community is going to suffer."

Jack Silverstone, national executive director of the Congress, responded forcefully that "bringing Nazi war criminals to justice, is not a 'Jewish issue,' nor is it an ethnic one. Rather it is a case of fidelity to law and justice. And that makes it of concern to all Canadians."[20] An insistence that "no one ethnic or national group had a monopoly on Nazi collaboration, and it is wrong and counterproductive to assert that any one ethnic group is now to be singled out for investigation" did not smooth feelings in some sectors of the affected communities, however. Angry controversy erupted from time to time between Ukrainians and Jews over wartime events in Eastern Europe.[21]

The Ukrainian community was outraged by statements made by some Jews, notably by Sol Littman, alleging that "the Ukrainians, by reason of their larger numbers and historic hatred of Poles and Jews, proved themselves pernicious collaborationists. . . ."[22] The future Supreme Court justice John Sopinka, spokesman for the Ukrainian Canadian Committee, claimed that "comments such as these put Ukrainians in the position of either having to denounce these groups and their leaders or accepting the stain of complicity in Nazi atrocities." He pointed out that Second World War Ukrainian nationalist leaders "[Andrei] Melnyk, [Stefan] Bandera, the OUN [Organization of Ukrainian Nationalists] and the UPA [Ukrainian Insurrectionary Army, a group that included alleged war criminals] were the leaders of the Ukrainian people. They represent a chapter of Ukrainian history which is still cherished today. That is why attacks on the OUN or UPA are seen as attacks on the cultural heritage of which Ukrainians are proud."

Sopinka insisted that suspected individuals be differentiated from the Ukrainian community as a whole. "Failure to make this distinction," he argued, "will only serve to perpetuate the unquestioned acceptance by future generations of the myth of Ukrainian collaboration with the Nazis."[23] Faced with the question of what should be done with those who were accused, Sopinka admitted that "the prospect of up to 3,000 war criminals of Joseph Mengele's ilk remaining at large in Canada calls for stern measures." But he suggested that "the nature of the response . . . should depend on the severity of the problem. . . . If there are only a handful of obscure old men against whom a minor role in Nazi war crimes is alleged, Canada may well be advised to consider less radical action or no action at all, all the more so if the Nazi link to these men's actions appears dubious and if the allegations against them are founded primarily upon unreliable Soviet evidence."

In the end, Deschênes's specific and clear exoneration of the Galician Waffen SS Division may have been influenced by Sopinka's representations.

Once the report was out, however, Rabbi Plaut commented that the "anxiety in the Ukrainian community . . . had exacerbated the tension between Canadian Jews and Ukrainians, and now that it has been allayed we may all return to a relaxed relationship."[24]

The Congress' Manuel Prutschi believed that the Ukrainians' approach had backfired, however, and asserted that the Ukrainian Canadian Committee — and possibly the statements made by Sopinka — "has linked Ukrainians with war crimes in the public's mind."[25] Irwin Cotler saw a greater danger. "If we convert this into an 'ethnic' quarrel or, worse, a Jewish versus Ukrainian configuration, we not only trivialize but [also] distort the issue. . . . We seek justice, not labels; criminals, not communities; individuals, not nationalities."[26]

The controversy over war criminals would not go away. The commission employed the historian Alti Rodal to review Canada's postwar record on the admission of alleged war criminals. Her report was not released to the public at the same time as the commission's because it contained highly sensitive material on various European political groups who collaborated with the Nazis. Nevertheless, "snippets . . . were leaked to the press."[27] When it was published, her study revealed that as late as 1983, two alleged Nazi war criminals were allowed into Canada by a senior RCMP officer "who regarded the war criminals issue as blown out of all proportion by the Jewish lobby."[28] This officer was aided by several key officials who destroyed records and disregarded regulations.

Rodal not only documented official Canadian laxity, if not outright antisemitism, but also suggested that the United States had protected and employed alleged Nazis and key collaborators like Klaus Barbie — the infamous "Butcher of Lyons" — in exchange for intelligence about the Soviet Union. She also revealed that in 1949, Pope Pius XII had pressured Prime Minister Louis St. Laurent to admit Slovakia's Hlinka Guard commander, Karol Sidor. St. Laurent, she charged, was also involved in letting in four Vichy collaborators, including Comte Jacques de Bernonville, who was saved from probable deportation by yet another prime ministerial intervention in 1951. Finally, Rodal asserted that while in office, Pierre Trudeau had opposed action on these matters.

To some extent, Rodal absolved the RCMP of blame for allowing these questionable persons to be admitted. Government officials, as a matter of policy, withheld lists of suspected war criminals from officers charged with screening immigrants. In some instances, these officials even overlooked the SS tattoos on the applicants.[29] An enraged editorialist in the *Canadian Jewish News* called for criminal prosecutions of any officials who destroyed documents and of the RCMP for contravening immigration laws.[30]

In the end, Justice Minister Ray Hnatyshyn indicated that the government would accept only Deschênes's recommendation that the Criminal Code be amended to allow alleged Nazi war criminals to be prosecuted in Canada. By narrowing the path of justice to this single avenue, it would take considerable time to bring anyone to trial.

One prosecution did occur fairly quickly, however: that of a retired Toronto restaurateur, Imre Finta, who was arrested and charged with forcible confinement, kidnapping, and manslaughter in connection with the deportation of about 8,617 Hungarian Jews to Auschwitz-Birkenau in 1944.[31] Because of weak evidence, however, Finta was found not guilty in 1989. His arrest followed a successful libel action brought against him by Sabina Citron, the founder of the Canadian Holocaust Remembrance Association. He had accused Citrón of lying when she alleged that he took part in the deportation.

The Canadian government also followed Deschênes's suggestion that it sign bilateral agreements with Israel, the Netherlands, and the Soviet Union to allow Canadian investigators to "gather evidence there that would be admissible in Canadian courts."[32] But the wheels of justice turned slowly, even in the twenty cases that Deschênes had said required urgent action. Despite the prodding given them by Jewish officials, justice department investigators moved cautiously; they did strip Canadian citizenship from a convicted Dutch collaborator, however.[33] Frustrated by the slow pace, David Matas of B'nai Brith reacted angrily. "Unless the Government moves at once against war criminals in our midst," he said, "the verdict of history will stand. Canada will remain guilty, as charged, on every count — as an accessory after the fact of murder, of obstructing justice, and of providing sanctuary to cold-blooded killers."[34]

Charges were laid in several other cases, but the difficulties involved in gathering credible evidence after a lapse of more than forty years meant convictions were hard to obtain. Meanwhile, some Ottawa officials, the historian Irving Abella later discovered, "were determined to delay, indeed even thwart prosecutions."[35] In 1989 the Simon Wiesenthal Center provided the war-crimes unit of the Department of Justice with a list of twenty-one Lithuanian immigrants who were believed to be members of a police battalion that participated in the mass murder of Jews.[36] In June 1995 charges were laid against five elderly men, two of them Latvian, two German, and one Slovakian.

The Congress continues to press authorities for much more aggressive action, and in early February 1995, Justice Minister Allan Rock promised to quickly launch proceedings against twelve alleged war criminals still living in Canada. By November 1996 only eight had been charged, leading the Congress' president, Irving Abella, to criticize the authorities for proceeding too slowly. "Why have they not named the other four?" he asked.[37] Meanwhile, widely publicized revelations by Steve Rambam, an American private investigator, caused a sensation. Rambam claimed that he had interviewed sixty of the 157 alleged war criminals living in Canada and had secretly recorded some of them actually confessing to murdering Jews.[38] With continuing charges that "war crimes cases [are] crawling ahead at [a] snail's pace," the issue continues to fester.[39]

Hate-Propaganda Trials

Holocaust awareness was also heightened by the activities of deniers like Toronto's Ernst Zundel and the Eckville, Alberta, schoolteacher Jim Keegstra. Zundel was publishing and distributing antisemitic and Holocaust-denial literature in Canada and abroad. He was first charged in 1984 after a complaint was made by Sabina Citron, who was herself a survivor, under Section 177 of the Criminal Code, which makes it a crime to wilfully publish a "false statement likely to cause injury to a public interest."[40] However, some prominent people believed it was misguided to prosecute Zundel. Alan Borovoy, general counsel to the Canadian Civil Liberties Association, stated that the trial lent "legitimacy . . . to a very illegitimate organization. Legitimacy has been conferred on garbage."[41] On the other hand, some believed that prosecuting Zundel, who was North America's leading publisher of hate propaganda, would send the important message that such activity would not be tolerated.

Zundel's trial opened in Toronto in 1985, but it was really the Holocaust that was put on trial. The prosecution had first to prove that the Holocaust had actually happened. Raul Hilberg, a distinguished scholar on the subject, and Rudolph Vrba, a former inmate at Birkenau, gave testimony. Zundel, who was defended by the attorney Douglas Christie, summoned several well-known Holocaust-deniers, including Professor Robert Faurnisson of France, who claimed that Auschwitz-Birkenau inmates enjoyed a theatre, a ballroom, and a swimming pool and that it was scientifically impossible for Zyklon B gas to have killed so many people.[42] The prosecution won, and Zundel was sentenced to fifteen months in jail and three years' probation. This conviction was later overturned on appeal and a second trial was held in 1988.

Zundel's new trial attracted widespread attention from the Canadian media — far less in Quebec, though, than in the rest of the country — and some from foreign newspapers and television stations.[43] This coverage no doubt pleased the defendant, who gloated that he had enjoyed a million dollars worth of publicity. But the trial's effect on the Canadian public, according to the scholars Gabriel Weimann and Conrad Winn, was ambiguous. They found that the "increased public understanding of the Holocaust and increased sympathy for Jews were accompanied by a tendency to believe that other people now have doubts about the Holocaust."[44] Television viewers "were especially apt to report increased sympathy for Jews."

In Red Deer, Alberta, meanwhile, the trial of James Keegstra, town mayor and an experienced teacher of social studies at the Eckville high school, began. He was accused of using his classroom to propagate his hatred of Jews.[45] Former students testified that Keegstra instructed them "about Jewish control of the media and governments, and the Jewish role in fomenting wars and revolution and fomenting communism."[46] Students were given pamphlets that described the Talmud as containing "vicious libelous blasphemies of Jesus, of Christianity and the Christian faith."[47] Keegstra allegedly expressed his agreement with claims that Jews were linked to a mysterious order called the Illuminati (a radical group of Masons in the eighteenth century), and that Jews had assassinated two American presidents, Abraham Lincoln and Franklin Delano Roosevelt.[48]

At the trial, several former students testified that Keegstra rewarded students who regurgitated these beliefs in their essays and produced notebooks filled with virulent antisemitic statements copied verbatim from Keegstra's classroom "lessons."[49] Despite a rigorous defence by Douglas Christie, Keegstra was found guilty and fined. His employment had already been terminated by the local school board and he never entered a classroom again. Even so, there remained a certain local sympathy for him. The foreman of the jury that found him guilty even offered to pay his fine.[50] Still, an analysis of the effect of the Keegstra trial on the Canadian public concluded that editorials and opinion columns had "condemned Keegstra and what he represented."[51]

Another active anti-Jewish publicist who surfaced in the late 1980s was Malcolm Ross, a Moncton schoolteacher. He was charged with promoting hatred against Jews by distributing antisemitic material (which he wrote himself) that both denied the Holocaust and posited the existence of a Jewish conspiracy to dominate the world. Authorities were reluctant to prosecute the case because "there was little chance of getting a conviction in view of the fact that unlike Keegstra, Ross had not disseminated his views in class." Ross was removed from his teaching position, but he appealed.

Antisemitism in Contemporary Canada

Although these were the most dramatic cases of antisemitism, surveys done during the 1980s indicated that a more subtle form was strongly present in Canadian society. A study conducted in 1986 concluded that "anti-Jewish prejudice and admitted ignorance of Jewish issues are serious problems in Canada."[52] Although 63 percent of Canadians were entirely free of anti-Jewish prejudice, according to the survey, it concluded that "young people were strikingly ignorant of the Holocaust and were twice as likely as people in their middle years to blame Jews for their own victimization." It further determined that "among poorly educated Roman Catholic francophones in Quebec or New Brunswick, the number who were prejudiced against Jews rose to approximately half the general population."[53]

On the positive side, however, the study found that "university graduates, especially women, were almost devoid of prejudice"; that "Christian believers were no more apt to be prejudiced against Jews than nonbelievers"; and that "francophones revealed a remarkable ability to jettison [antisemitic] prejudice once they encountered their first Jew."[54] Another study, conducted by the League for Human Rights of B'nai Brith, concluded that 16 percent of Canada's population and 22 percent of Quebec's "could be considered antisemitic."[55]

One dramatic antisemitic incident occurred in 1988 in the Montreal suburb of Outremont, where the Vishnitzer Hasidim's petitions for rezoning an empty lot to allow the construction of a synagogue were turned down.[56] The opposition was led by a city council member who voiced fears about further Hasidic incursion into this quiet, largely French-Canadian, middle-class area. Allegations that there was a "Jewish problem" in Outremont, and that the Hasidim were unfriendly people, who ignored parking laws and bought up homes, only exacerbated the feelings.

Because it came at a time of increased French-Canadian nationalism, the Outremont affair can be seen as a symptom of a general malaise that involved more than just antisemitism. One *La Presse* columnist, Gérald Le Blanc, held Jews responsible for the Outremont problem because he said they failed to integrate into "the Quebec milieu." He also criticized anglophone Jews "for allegedly opposing the survival and protection of the French society."[57] In the end, two provincial Cabinet ministers defended the Hasidim as upstanding citizens, and various attempts at dialogue eventually ended the contretemps. (In a series of incidents that were perhaps unrelated, but nevertheless indicated that antisemitism remained strongly present in Outremont, a gang of youths attacked some local Hasidim. A radio commentator blamed the Jews.)

Antisemitism, though no longer a threat in Quebec, has remained somewhat of a public issue nevertheless. Esther Delisle, a history Ph.D. student at Université Laval, wrote her thesis on 1930s antisemitism in the influential newspaper *Le Devoir* and in the writings of the father of modern French-Canadian nationalism, Abbé Lionel Groulx. Following the submission of her thesis, she was stonewalled for two years with administrative delays before being allowed to take the oral examination. When her thesis was published in 1992, bitter denunciations appeared in the Quebec press.[58]

Has antisemitism been worse in Quebec than elsewhere in Canada? A *New Yorker* exposé of the absurdities of Quebec's language laws by Mordecai Richler in September 1991 drew attacks on his personal integrity by outraged Québécois newspaper writers.[59] But a study which was conducted in the wake of his claim that anti-Jewish bigotry is "a prominent feature of the contemporary Quebec outlook" demonstrated that he was essentially correct.[60] Other surveys found that Quebeckers "exhibit higher levels of anti-Semitism than English-speaking Canadians, . . . in part [because of] the special importance that Quebeckers attach to the value of conformity. . . . [Nevertheless,] the weight of the evidence runs against the suggestion that most Quebeckers are anti-Semitic."[61]

In fact, antisemitic incidents were occurring coast to coast during the 1980s and 1990s. Cemeteries were vandalized, some seriously, with gravestones overturned and painted with swastikas and slogans. The worst attacks took place out West. In Edmonton a synagogue was burned to the ground. One in Vancouver was fire-bombed and seriously damaged, and elsewhere others were daubed with hate messages. Threatening telephone calls were made to community leaders. A more serious threat was the rise of neo-Nazi organizations, which pushed old claims of alleged Jewish-Zionist "domination" and advocated the "elimination" of all Jews. A 1989 hate rally in Minden, Ontario, met with strong resistance from war veterans, Holocaust survivors, B'nai Brith members, and local citizens, and another one was stopped altogether.[62]

In 1990 an upsurge of antisemitic incidents took place all over Canada."[63] Some were believed to be of neo-Nazi origin; others were related to Arab-Israeli tensions. There was even evidence that some incidents were co-ordinated. An inclination among skinheads to adopt "white supremacist and neo-Nazi beliefs" was of serious concern. The Heritage Front, led by Wolfgang Droege, was the most threatening of these white supremacist groups. It operated a racist telephone hotline and plotted attacks on individuals.[64]

In 1994 these outbreaks increased, and included swastika-daubings on several Jewish institutions. A brief but bitter controversy in 1993 over the staging of the musical "Showboat" raised concerns when some spokespersons for the black community made baldly antisemitic charges.[65] A Nation of Islam representative, barred from entry into Canada, delivered his anti-white and anti-Jewish attack over the telephone from the United States. Another speaker fulminated about the alleged Jewish subjugation of blacks. Meanwhile, in August of that year, a Polish-language newspaper in Edmonton published excerpts from the fictitious *Protocols of the Elders of Zion*, a long-discredited diatribe against Jews.[66] Three years later, antisemitic articles appeared in a Toronto Arabic-language newspaper.[67]

Many Canadian Jews are worried. Some 70 to 80 percent of Toronto's Jews, according to one scholar, still view antisemitism as a "potential danger," and have "a sense of foreboding and a pessimistic assessment of the potential for future anti-Semitism in North America."[68] However, it would appear that despite these ugly occurrences and gloomy forecasts, antisemitism is not a serious threat and might well be declining in Canada. A 1984 scholarly survey of the social geography of antisemitism found "surprisingly warm feelings towards Jews on the part of Canadians," 86 percent of whom held positive or neutral opinions.[69] In this survey, antisemitism was found to be highest in Newfoundland, New Brunswick, and Quebec — and lowest in Alberta. Although it was more pronounced among Catholics than in the general population, "it was mainly Catholics of French origin who accounted for the tendency of Catholics to be more anti-Semitic than Protestants."[70] Paradoxically, antisemitism was stronger among the irreligious than among the more observant French-speaking Catholics, especially in Quebec.

The report's authors recognized that while other studies lent "no support to the view that Quebec nationalists were more anti-Semitic than non-nationalists," there were probably historical and cultural factors in that province that affected its citizens' attitudes towards Jews.[71] French-Canadian antisemitism, according to historian Pierre Anctil, may be partly explained by their lack of contact with Jews — plain ignorance, in other words, of Jewish culture and history.[72] Since the 1980s, Anctil has published several major French-language books on Quebec's Jewish history and has translated the classics of Montreal Yiddish literature into French, all in a remarkable effort to make francophones aware of this dimension of their province's past.[73]

Not surprisingly, social class was found to be an even more important determinant of antisemitic attitudes than religion or francophone background, and the study found that "irrespective of religion, the lower one descends in the socio-economic hierarchy, . . . the more antisemitism one finds."[74] Thus the lower one's education and income levels, the more likely one was to be an antisemite (although "sympathy for the NDP and union membership mitigated anti-Semitic feeling among the poorer and less educated"). For reasons unexplained, men had stronger tendencies than women towards antisemitism.[75]

These results confirmed a conclusion reached in an earlier study: antisemitism was marginal in Canada.[76] Nevertheless, there was "a positive correlation between anti-Semitic attitudes and opposition to Israel."[77] So "an individual may well be free of anti-Semitism and still favour the Arab cause over Israel, [but] the proportion of anti-Semites is greater among those opposing

Israel than among those favouring the Jewish state." Generally, English Canadians were more likely to back Israel than French Canadians, although support among educated French Canadians was close to English levels.

A reputable overview of antisemitism in Canada in 1994 concluded that it was "a marginal phenomenon, . . . represented most visibly by isolated individuals . . . or by fringe groups. . . . [It] remains unacceptable in mainstream society."[78] The report concluded that "there is little likelihood of a serious outbreak . . . [partly because] Jews have found a number of allies in the struggle against racism in Canada, a fact which in itself strengthens the sense of security of the community." What remains troublesome to Canadian Jews, nevertheless, is the inability of the government to deal successfully with alleged Nazi war criminals living in Canada, its failure to make lower-court convictions of racists like Zundel stick, and the recent emergence of some manifestations of antisemitism among Canada's black population.[79]

Irving Abella remains concerned about the "new antisemitism," which includes a subtle but pernicious attempt to portray Zionism as racism.[80] In this new antisemitism, he points out, "Israel has become the collective Jew among the nations," which implies "the denial of Jewish peoplehood and Jewish statehood, . . . rights granted to every other people on earth." This, coupled with what he called the "canard . . . [of] the dual loyalty of Jews"; the free use of Holocaust terminology to describe the plight of the Palestinians; and the fact that this new antisemitism is pervasive, subtle, and growing (making it "very difficult for pollsters to measure") causes Abella — and no doubt many others — to be both worried and vigilant.[81]

A B'nai Brith survey showed, however, that antisemitic incidents in Canada registered a very sharp decline in 1996.[82] But in the multicultural context of today's university classrooms, according to Professor Harold Troper, many non-Jews, especially members of the visible minorities, see "racism directed against others [as] more immediate and threatening. . . . Non-Jewish students could not relate to the notion that negative press reports on Israel, if excessive, might well be manifestations of antisemitism. Jewish students engaged in the battle of comparative and competitive victimization to ensure themselves oppressed minority status inevitably lose ground to others."[83]

Still, the battle against antisemitism in whatever form it takes can never relax. Warren Kinsella, who wrote *The Web of Hate*, an exhaustive account of Canadian hate groups, warned that people should be on guard against white supremacists, neo-Nazis, and Holocaust-deniers. "When they suffer setbacks or legal challenges," he warned, "they go underground or form support networks across the country. Sometimes, they turn to foreign governments — or foreign neo-Nazi groups — for funding and support. And they grow."[84]

The Heritage Front and other antisemitic groups remain active, particularly in Western Canada. In 1992 they were especially busy spreading hate through Okanagan Valley towns in British Columbia.[85] Two years later, neo-Nazi groups were reportedly targeting university and college campuses for new members.[86] Clearly, vigilance on this front must remain a priority for the Congress and the Simon Wiesenthal Center.

Organizational Restructuring

Activities within the Canadian Jewish community were just as important as these external factors. Structural changes in several organizations resulted in a reallocation of responsibilities in some of the larger communities. In Toronto, for example, the United Jewish Welfare Fund (UJWF) partially merged with the Central Region branch of the Canadian Jewish Congress, forming a new body, the Toronto Jewish Congress, in January 1976. This new group assumed responsibility for some cultural initiatives, while the Congress continued to direct the Ontario region's "external affairs," its activities for smaller communities, and its formal Jewish education program.[87]

Winnipeg had carried out a similar reallocation of functions in 1974, when it amalgamated the local welfare fund with the Western Region branch of the Congress.[88] This new body, the Winnipeg Community Council, hoped to eliminate divisiveness, inefficiency, waste, duplication of functions, and tensions between competing organizations and bureaucracies.[89] In this way, both local communities and the Congress, which retained many regional responsibilities, would be strengthened.

Such changes were part of a national pattern of marshalling Canadian Jewry's resources more efficiently to meet new commitments and adjust to the rise of local federations, in whose hands fund-raising was now concentrated.[90] In large and mid-sized communities, these local federations managed the fund-raising drives for all local, national, and Israeli causes. The last of these was funded by the United Israel Appeal (UIA), which, though under the umbrella of other federations in large communities, ran its own fund-raising campaigns in small centres. The federations were supposed to allocate funds to all organizational claimants depending on need, but politics and personalities undoubtedly played a part in the deliberations.

The Council of Jewish Federations was to allocate funds to the Congress, the UJRA, and JIAS. To ensure that it did so appropriately, local groups agreed in 1974 to establish the National Budgeting Conference (NBC), which would decide annually on each community's contribution.[91] The UIA is also a member of the NBC; it contributes to the Canada-wide organizations on behalf of smaller communities, where it is the major fund-raiser. Thus the NBC has a central role to play in the national Jewish community.[92] Its decisions have met with widespread approval — except from the UIA, which has seen its funding levels decline as local needs took priority.

The NBC's highly intricate co-operative structure for handling the community's charity dollars was in place by the late 1970s, and "imposed a remarkable level of community discipline in the financial sphere."[93] This financial federalism worked despite regional differences and ideological and social diversity on substantive issues.[94] It also worked because all its affiliates recognized that it was a significant improvement over what existed before. Political scientist Harold Waller pointed out that the NBC is "a uniquely Canadian phenomenon" that reflects "the strong countrywide organization of Canadian Jewry."[95]

That there is no comparable organization in the United States points to the fact that Canada's national Jewish bodies have always had more moral authority. This was true not just of the Congress, but also of virtually all country-wide organizations. Because of their size, the Toronto and Montreal communities and their respective federations also tended to have great influence in the NBC, in effect making them "national forces."

Waller concluded that "any analysis of the politics of the Jewish community in Canada [today] must include the impact of the major federations."[96] Such financial federalism reflected a strong, nationwide similarity of values, assumptions, and goals, despite regional and socio-economic differences.

Social Transformations in the Jewish Community

The national Jewish agenda was changing in response to new and pressing local needs. The greatest of these was the plight of the poor (most of whom were elderly). In the mid 1970s, it was estimated that some eighteen thousand Montreal Jews were living in poverty. Some families of four existed on an annual income of five thousand dollars.[97] One community activist pointed out that the high costs of kosher food and Jewish education and the difficulties accessing services made matters worse for many. The Allied Jewish Community Services had to increase direct cash assistance to these families by 25 percent in one year. An investigation of the situation in Montreal the following year indicated that the problem was even more widespread and involved 18 percent of the city's Jews.[98] It was forecast that by 1987, "the aged [among whom poverty was widespread] would constitute anywhere from 27 to 37 percent of the Jewish population, or 25,000 – 30,000 persons."[99]

Toronto, with its growing and comparatively young community, was not as seriously affected, but its Jewish Family and Child Services estimated that "about 13,000 people, or 13 per cent [of its] Jewish population, were living at or below poverty level."[100] About one-quarter of the poor were teenagers, and there were many Jews between fifty and sixty-five who "fell into the displaced skills category in millinery, sales, and the fur and textile trades,"[101] including many Sephardic immigrants with low employment qualifications. It was estimated that the number of Jewish elderly in Toronto — increasing numbers of whom were being abandoned by younger family members — would rise to eighteen thousand by 1986, and that the community needed to provide adequate housing and basic social and health services.[102] Of course, these were not the only welfare responsibilities that were increasing. Growing rates of marital breakdown gave rise to single-parent families that required sophisticated and expensive social services.

By 1981 Toronto was Canada's major Jewish metropolis; it had 42 percent of the country's Jews, compared with Montreal's 34 percent,[103] a shift of profound significance for the future of the Jewish community as a whole. Montreal's Jewish population was decreasing significantly. Between 1971 and 1981, it fell by more than eight thousand, primarily because young persons were emigrating, "thereby ensuring that the already distorted age distribution of the city's Jews, with its large proportion of elderly, would continue."[104] Forecasts of population loss in the Montreal Jewish community varied widely. In 1982 the Allied Jewish Community Services had estimated the loss between 1971 and 1981 at twenty thousand persons and projected a further loss of ten thousand persons by 1987.[105] With this decline, the elderly, who once amounted to 20 to 27 percent of the Jewish population, would represent 27 to 37 percent.

A later study asserted that "Montreal's Jews faced specific demographic problems related in part to the political-economic environment in . . . Quebec." In 1989 Harold Waller pointed out that nine thousand Jews aged fifteen to thirty-four and five thousand aged thirty-six to forty-five had departed Montreal between 1971 and 1981, leaving those "age cohorts badly depleted."[106] Aside from the social problems, this distortion placed a very serious financial burden on the rest of Montreal Jewry. A special committee struck by the AJCS in 1984 recommended that the community try encouraging young Montreal Jews not to leave, "attracting immigrants from overseas and finding new ways to provide services to the elderly." The first suggestion was futile, the second probably counterproductive as a solution to the financial crisis, and the third vague.[107]

Winnipeg's community, meanwhile, faced even worse age distortions. As was the case in Montreal, the young were moving, seeking better economic opportunities elsewhere. Consequently, 27 percent of Winnipeg's Jews were over sixty-five (compared with 20 percent in Montreal and 15 percent for all Canadian Jewry). Moreover, many of the young Jews who remained in the city had abandoned its "traditional North End neighbourhood, . . . [which] had implications for Jewish community institutions."[108]

Budgetary appropriations for elder care and other social programs mounted rapidly. In 1981 the Toronto Jewish Congress, which allocated funds for all community welfare agencies, reported that some twelve thousand to fourteen thousand disabled Jewish persons resided in the city. These agencies were also concerned about the mentally handicapped and an "increasing number of elderly people, . . . the majority of [them] women, many of whom were living below the poverty line abandoned by younger family members."[109] The community's welfare budget was strained. By 1984 Montreal's AJCS called the demographic situation "urgent" and demanded "action to maintain the community's viability . . . [and remedy] a severe financial crisis and its impact on services for the aging population."[110]

MIGRATION, FAMILY, AND GENDER ROLES

By the early 1980s, the decline of Jewish life in small outlying centres was evident. This was especially poignant in the centuries-old Jewish community of Quebec City, where the remaining thirty-five families, now unable to meet expenses, were forced to put the synagogue up for sale.[111] St. John's, with only twenty-eight families, could no longer support its rabbi and was also considering selling its synagogue. In Quebec, Shawinigan's last Jewish family moved away. Out West, the towns of Medicine Hat, Prince Albert, Moose Jaw, and Lethbridge were no longer able to sustain either rabbis or synagogues. In Ontario, Brantford, Cornwall, and Guelph were just getting by, while Belleville, once a lively Jewish centre, had only a handful of Jews. This migration of people from many of the smaller centres to Toronto, Ottawa, Calgary, and Vancouver required those communities to enlarge their facilities and provide for the integration of the newcomers.[112]

Through the 1990s, the postwar trend towards smaller families and later marriages has persisted, and the percentage of elderly Jews has continued to grow. As early as the 1950s, the birthrate for Jews was the lowest of all ethnic groups in Canada.[113] Other facts were just as startling. In the mid-1970s, "persons over 65 accounted for 8 percent of the Canadian population, but 11.5 percent of the Jewish population."[114] The median age for Jews was 33.8 years, while the national mean was 26.3 years. Twenty years later, those over sixty-five were an even larger component of the community's population.[115]

At the same time, the rise of single-parent families — estimated in the late

1980s at 12 percent of the Toronto Jewish population — "delayed parenthood, unmarried couples, dual career families, and other developments" led to the need for "a reexamination of conventional assumptions concerning the nature of Jewish families."[116] A growing recognition in recent years that gays and lesbians are part of the community suggests those assumptions have changed radically.

Higher levels of education and a deeper social awareness have been transforming the perspectives of many Jewish women.[117] By the early 1980s, eloquent and moving Jewish feminist expressions such as those in the acclaimed film *Half the Kingdom* were raising searching and significant questions about the virtual exclusion of women from some of traditional Judaism's most important prayers and rituals.[118] Relegated to the balconies or screened off behind curtains in Orthodox synagogues, women saw themselves as little more than observers of the men, who led prayers, read the Torah, and studied the sacred texts. Modern, educated, articulate, and assertive women such as the journalist Michele Landsberg were now expressing anguish and resentment over this secondary role, which applied even in Reform temples. They were also seeking a new openness in Judaism that would allow them full and equal access to, as the film-maker Francine Zuckerman put it, "the pleasure of

---

DEVOTION

Seymour Mayne

I stand before the snow,
January's tallit
bereft of blue stripes

The morning tassels
of icicles gnarl into view
Tefillin chimney tops
hold to the foreheads of homes

The wind, cantorial,
utters benedictions,
urging the housed congregations
who either curse or sing

Spring will be the Passover of God.

From Seymour Mayne, *The Impossible Promised Land* (Oakville: Mosaic Press, 1981), 74.

community [and] the joy of the Jewish spirit." In Landsberg's prophetic words, "one day we will re-nurture Judaism so that it becomes whole."[119]

To aid in their pursuit of greater knowledge of the traditions that excluded them for so long, Jewish women have organized groups for study and prayer. Their movement shows signs of spreading its important message of equity, wholeness, and renewal in Judaism, though differences exist among its advocates. The traditional physical division, the *mechitzah* between men and women in Orthodox synagogues, for example, does not offend the feminist Norma Joseph, who regards it as an opportunity for private prayer and "the challenge of loving God." "The autonomy the *mechitzah* creates," she comments, "makes it possible for women to stand alone on [their] own merits to try to meet God."[120] The feminist perspective and its pursuit of a larger and more recognized role for women in Judaism promises to bear rich rewards for the entire community. The fact that synagogue constitutions adopted in the 1980s and 1990s consider women as well as men to have full voting rights is clear recognition of this promise.[121] Further progress on this front is essential, warns the sociologist-feminist Sheva Medjuck: "If Jewish women's voices are not heard [in communal affairs], the . . . community runs the risk of losing large numbers of young, well-educated, potential leaders."[122]

Still, trends such as these led one expert to predict that Canadian Jewry's very survival was at risk because "the core group," those who identified themselves as Jews by ethnicity rather than by religion, was shrinking.[123] Those who identified themselves as Jews by religion included many assimilated Jews who would eventually lapse. Meanwhile, intermarriage with non-Jews was rising to levels considered "alarming." But a mid-eighties report for the Ontario Region branch of the Congress indicated that about 25 percent of Jews married outside the faith,[124] a rate only slightly higher than that of the late 1960s. Like all such studies, it had no conclusive evidence of the reasons for intermarriage. It did point out, however, that Jews who were not affiliated with synagogues or Jewish organizations were more likely than affiliated Jews to intermarry. Also, those in Ontario and Quebec were less likely to intermarry, presumably because of a greater availability of Jewish marriage partners within their larger populations.

The New Arrivals of the 1980s and 1990s

Concerns about Canadian Jewry's future were not alleviated by the continuing arrival of immigrants — Sephardic North Africans, Israelis, Russians, and South Africans — some of whom were perceived as "problems." One official observed that the 5,500 Soviet Jews living in Toronto in 1982, for example, "know nothing of our system . . . of Jewishness"; he also noted that only half of them had any Jewish affiliation. Only 205 Russian children were receiving any formal Jewish education and only one hundred families attended holiday celebrations at synagogues, according to one survey.[125] Success rates for integrating Russians differed in each region, however. In Edmonton, by 1982, some three hundred families were "absorbed . . . and on the whole . . . established and gainfully employed," but in Calgary problems were reported (partly because of staff "burnout" in handling the one thousand cases).[126] In smaller centres like Halifax and Regina, there were mixed results. Because of limited employment opportunities, integration in Halifax proved more difficult than in Regina. Hamilton, meanwhile, found that "the Russian Jews tend to socialize among themselves, but are slowly coming into the community framework."

While the integration of the Russians was apparently difficult, that of some others proceeded far more easily. The South Africans, for example, came from a richly developed community endowed with a full range of thriving Jewish institutions. Having abandoned a country sunk into a hatefully oppressive, and socially and economically uncertain, regime, the South Africans were delighted to migrate to a more peaceful land.[127] One South African Jewish doctor who spent two years in the southern United States before moving to Canada remembered that "we immediately liked the calmness and order of Canadian society. . . . Everything and every one seemed to have their rightful place with great respect for each other. . . . I also liked the 'British influence' as I was used to that in South Africa. . . . Everyone was so well-mannered and helpful."[128] By the mid-1990s an estimated ten thousand South African Jews were living in Toronto, where they had adapted very well. Among them, however, were many who felt more comfortable socializing mainly with other South Africans. There were two Toronto synagogues primarily made up of South African immigrants.

The Israeli migration to Canada continued. By 1975 it was estimated that there were twenty-five thousand Israelis living in Canada, most of them in Toronto and Montreal.[129] By 1989 there were more than forty thousand, and they constituted nearly 11.5 percent of all Jews in Canada.[130] While these rapidly rising numbers were a concern and an embarrassment to both the Israeli government and the Canadian Jewish community, which was so strongly committed to the Zionist endeavour, this emigration (called Yeridah [going down], as opposed to Aliyah [going up]) continued apace. These Israeli migrants, reported to be "completely alienated" from the organized Jewish communities, were the objects of continuing interest to Jewish communal leaders and, to some, of barely disguised disapproval for their abandonment of Israel, an act that earned them the name *yordim* (those who go down).[131]

Israelis, unlike the other immigrants, held the general expectation, or declared intention, of eventually returning "home."[132] Their stance as expatriates, or sojourners, helps to explain their non-involvement in Jewish community organizations, while their secularism ruled out synagogue membership. "The shared ethnicity does not entail unanimity of vision," one recent analysis contended, "as Israelis and Jews perceive each other as different in regard to values, mentality, culture and definition of Jewishness."[133] And what is especially important about Israelis is that no matter how long they live in Canada, "most do not give up their emotional and legal membership in Israel [and] rarely reconcile themselves to the factors that ultimately make their immigration permanent."[134] Once they realize that their intended temporary stay is permanent, Israelis find themselves torn, their "imaginary suitcases" disappearing even though they have not yet fully adjusted to the new reality. Most participants in one study "reported oscillating emotionally between the poles of connectedness and separatedness."[135]

Canadian Jewry, however, was even more troubled by the fact that considerable numbers of immigrants from Israel were originally from the Soviet Union. Many Russian Jews who had settled in Israel later requested refugee status in Canada, claiming that they had been persecuted because, as children of mixed marriages, they were not recognized as Jews in Israel.[136] Between 1992 and 1995, government tribunals granted refugee status to 726 Israelis; between January and October 1996, a further 710 Israeli "refugees" applied. Even though most claims were denied, this trend was embarrassing for the Jewish community, not to mention Israeli consular officials in Canada.

Challenges in Education

Yet another serious communal responsibility in the 1980s and 1990s was Jewish education. In spite of the community's strong commitment, day-schools were becoming increasingly expensive and conditions for teachers were in need of improvement. Indeed, low salaries had long been a scandal in Jewish parochial schools, and in 1964 the *Canadian Jewish News* commented:

> There definitely is a discrepancy between the living standard of the average family in our affluent society and our teachers. Especially is this difference noticeable when one compares the salary of a Hebrew teacher who carries the responsibility of molding the future Jewish generation to the income of the so-called Jewish civil servant.[137]

Because of its low status and poor remuneration (as well as the lack of fringe benefits, job security, and full-time employment), the job attracted few high-level professionals. One expert noted that "until the Jewish mother can exclaim with pride 'my son, the Jewish teacher' as she does 'my son, the doctor,' the status of Jewish education will not change."[138] In such an environment, the persons attracted to teaching ranged from "the well-intentioned but untrained housewife to the Israeli whose only qualification is that he speaks Hebrew."[139]

It was only in October 1976 that a contract covering tenure, grievance pro-

---

ALL I GOT WAS WORDS

Author Unknown

When I was young and fancy free
My folks had no fine clothes for me.
All I got was words.
"Gott zu danken." (Thank God.)
"Gott vet geben." (God will provide.)
"Zoll men nohr leben und zein gezunt." (Only let us live and be well.)

When I was wont to travel far
They didn't provide me with a car
All I got was words.
"Geh gezunt." (Go in good health.)
"Geh pamelach." (Be careful.)
"Hub a glickleche reize." (Have a pleasant trip.)

I wanted to increase my knowledge
But they couldn't send me to college.
All I got was words.
"Hub saychel." (Use your head.)
"Zei nisht kein nahr." (Don't be foolish.)
"Torah is de beste schoira." (Torah is the best merchandise.)

The years have flown, the world has turned
Things I've forgotten, things I learned.
Yet I remember:
"Zug dem emmis." (Tell the truth.)
"Gib Tzadakah." (Do righteous acts, such as helping the needy.)
"Hab rachmunis." (Be compassionate.)
"Zei a mensch." (Be a decent human being.)

All I got was words.

cedures, and fringe benefits was agreed to by some of the Toronto schools and their general-subject teachers.[140] Other schools refused such concessions and were threatened with job action. But there was just not enough funding. Unprecedented deficits in 1977 — some schools actually went bankrupt — resulted in a 10 percent tuition increase.[141] The situation was so serious in Montreal that in 1984, administrations were trying to force teachers to give up gains made in previous contracts. When the teachers resisted, a lockout ensued and some four thousand students were forced to end their school year two months early.[142] Extreme bitterness developed on both sides, and fears were expressed about the long-term effects of the dispute on the quality of Jewish education. Low salaries remained a sore point for years.

Public funding was usually not available. Instead, financing was secured almost exclusively through the Jewish community. Quebec was easily the most generous of all provinces — especially with the Parti Québécois government, which between 1976 and 1984 subsidized up to 80 percent of general education, provided that a designated portion of it was in French. This requirement, while not unreasonable, resulted in a lengthening of the school day and a reduction in the time allocated to Hebrew and English instruction, a development that raised questions about the efficacy of the subsidy system.[143] In addition to strengthening Jewish institutions in Montreal, this financial support fostered a promising new relationship between the community and the provincial government, whose agenda included "the francisization of private and public schools."[144]

Ontario, on the other hand, adamantly refused to extend funding to Jewish day-schools — as well as those of any other religious denomination — even though the government of Premier William Davis had decided to increase financial support for the Roman Catholic school system far beyond what was required under the existing law. In Alberta, financial aid was available to Jewish day-schools that hired approved teachers and followed the provincial curriculum, subject to the approval of local school boards.[145] In most cases, though, the problem of finding adequate funds forced day-schools to raise tuition fees to such levels that only the well-to-do — or those who qualified for subsidies — could afford to enrol their children.

The pressure for Ontario government support continued through the 1980s and 1990s. The Jewish community (backed by other groups) contended that under the Charter of Rights and Freedoms, it was as entitled as the Roman Catholic community to public monies. In February 1986 the Ontario Court of Appeals found against them, however; and in 1996 the Supreme Court of Canada wisely upheld that judgement. The issue was closed — though perhaps not forever.

The prevailing assumption that Jewish day-school education served as a hedge against intermarriage and as a guarantor of communal vitality was seldom challenged, though Sidney Harris, Congress' president in 1975, thought it ought to be.[146] He asked (unsuccessfully) for a study to be conducted on the relationship between levels of Jewish education and intermarriage rates. Until that is known, the belief that Jewish education will immunize youth against intermarriage will continue to dominate.

Despite its problems, the Jewish parochial day-school movement has continued to grow, so enduring is the faith in its importance in building a strong Jewish identity. In 1979 it was reported that a larger percentage of Jewish children attended these schools in Toronto than in any other North American city.[147] The commitment of the community was reflected in the financial backing provided by local federations. In Montreal in the late 1980s, the AJCS began allocating increasing amounts to the schools, especially for scholarships.

Jewish education became a subject of endless reflection and commentary, periodic investigation, and widespread interest. The *Canadian Jewish News* often carried editorials on its current state, which usually pointed to perilous conditions and the urgent need for reform and improved financing. Other observers stated that better results could be achieved only if the teachers were paid decent salaries.

Most on-lookers had long before noted that the fundamental problems went much deeper, however. For Jewish education to have meaning, it had to involve the entire family and serve as part of an all-encompassing way of life. The central question had become "How could a 'Jewishly-Illiterate' community survive?"[148] The answer was that it could not, various experts noted, if, as was often the case, children who attended Jewish schools "knew more about Judaism than their parents and insisted on a greater degree of observance." Only education would ensure harmony between parents and children. If that education was to be a preparation for life, it not only had to be conveyed by adequately rewarded teachers and encouraged by knowledgeable parents, but also had to take place within a committed family and community structure.

As M. J. Nurenberger, the editor of the *Canadian Jewish News*, shrewdly observed, "there never was, and there never will be a substitute for the traditional upbringing of a Jewish child."[149] At conferences, experts debated how education could be improved, whether it be through the encouragement of "attitudes that will lead [children] back to Yiddishkeit," an emphasis on survival, the imposition of higher standards for bar and bat mitzvah boys and girls, or better teacher training. One rabbi noted that it would be wrong to hark back to the *shtetl*, reminding listeners that "our goal is not a recreation of Eastern Europe in Canada."[150]

Out in the smaller communities, where there was usually only one synagogue conducting an afternoon school (i.e., after public school), the problems of teacher shortages and turnovers were even worse.[151] Moreover, the local synagogue — though usually nominally Orthodox — included among its members many who, out of necessity, belonged but did not follow the full complement of religious observances. In many cases, parents failed to respect certain aspects of the religious instruction their children received. This led to apathy among both children and parents, as well as the effective termination of Jewish education in most cases at age thirteen, immediately after bar and bat mitzvah celebrations.

Task forces and special study groups continued to grapple with issues affecting the quality of Jewish education, including staffing, visual aids, expert consultants, management practices, in-service training, space, salaries, and curricula.[152] Meanwhile, surveys proved that while most Jewish parents took a keen interest in and favoured improved education for their children,[153] experts like Rabbi Irwin Witty, Toronto's head of Jewish education, continued to emphasize that schooling was only part of the solution. At a conference in Kitchener in 1975, he informed delegates that "it is not what is poured into the student at school that counts, but what is planted in him at home."[154] Indeed, family played a far more important role than Jewish schools in forming identity. A study by the sociologist Yakov Glickman showed that "the mammoth resources poured into the Jewish school experience by the community seems, according to data, to have produced meagre results."[155] Adult education and "family life" programs were likely to be far more effective, he believed.

Education: The Road Ahead

The most challenging, and potentially most rewarding, parts of the Canadian Jewish agenda at the end of the 1990s lie within the confines of the community itself: education programs and social service for seniors. By themselves, Holocaust memorials, the pursuit of alleged war criminals, an excessive concern over antisemitism, and mounting worries about intermarriage offer little support for future growth in Canadian Jewish life. Indeed, they may be dangerous and irrelevant distractions. But Jewish schools do offer hope and can activate the real possibility that Jewish culture, in its many forms, will continue.

Although they were growing in every major community, the problems facing Jewish parochial education in day and afternoon schools persisted into the early 1990s. Tuition fees remained high in most communities and only the well-to-do or the most self-sacrificing families could afford them. The terms of the teachers' employment generally were not equal to those in the public sector. Thus there was a serious shortage of competent teachers. Even though community welfare funds were supporting the schools with ever larger grants, this was still not enough to keep them afloat.[156] Still, as sociologists Morton Weinfeld and Susan Zelkowitz observe, this growing dependency may involve communal interference in the "goals, orientations, and content of Jewish schools."[157]

Ironically, the growing popularity of these schools created extreme difficulties. Winnipeg educators reported that "we are getting killed by our own success. The . . . high school program is bursting at the seams and there is no more money left for expansion."[158] Without improvements in funding, teaching, and the students' home atmosphere, the outlook is one of only qualified hope. Meanwhile, the question of the long-term effectiveness of these schools in countering current concerns about the continuity of Canadian Jewry begs answering.[159] Part of that continuity involves the preservation of the Jewish family, which, as noted, faces the same threats as in the general population.[160]

Epilogue

Oyfn Vegg (On the Road)

At the end of the twentieth century and on the eve of the twenty-first, Canada's Jewish community is vastly different from the one that existed in 1920. Its size and composition have changed enormously. There are now an estimated 360,000 Jews, up from 125,197 in 1921, and the overwhelming majority are Canadian-born. Immigrants come from a variety of countries, not just Eastern Europe, as in the early part of the century. Toronto, rather than Montreal, is the great Canadian Jewish metropolis, and Winnipeg, once third in importance, has given way to Vancouver. Ottawa and Calgary have also grown enormously.

The Jewish farm colonies on the Prairies, still modestly promising in 1920, have essentially disappeared. Meanwhile, many of the small town and city communities are heading towards oblivion, and much of the important regional presence in the Maritimes and in northern and western Ontario cities is disappearing. Unused synagogues, some with prayer shawls still ready for service, stand virtually vacant, occupied only for funerals or, possibly, High Holy Day observances. Soon, even that will end.

Canadian Jews live different lives than their grandparents did in 1920. As a collectivity, they are far better off and have the highest average incomes, the best levels of education, and the highest rates of participation in the professions of all ethnic groups. Jews are some of the richest and the most learned Canadians. They are prominent in universities, the arts, and the media. Barriers no longer impede the entry of qualified Jews into any of these fields. Serious antisemitism has virtually disappeared from mainstream Canadian life. In recent years, even the federal Cabinet, the Bank of Canada, and the Supreme Court have had Jewish members.

New-found confidence and assertiveness sprang from a variety of sources, though the most important was simply that Canada became native ground for most Canadian Jews after 1920. About one-tenth of the community, nearly 40 percent of men of military age, were in uniform during the war and, like all Canadians who enlisted (or were conscripted) into the armed forces, shared in the collective experience of national service. The war bound the Jewish community again, as it had a generation earlier, to the fate of the remaining Jews of Europe and Palestine and gave Canadians the responsibility of providing massive assistance for both. And they understood that because the Jewish world of Eastern Europe had been destroyed, they could no longer draw intellectual sustenance from it. The once vital heartland of Jewish life had disappeared. Only the memory remains, and that, too, is rapidly fading.

Meanwhile, the suburbanization of Jewish life continues, with synagogues and major new community centres — like those in Ottawa and Winnipeg — nearing completion. Along with all the usual recreational and athletic facilities, these elaborate centres include a new component — substantial senior-citizen residences. Old-folks homes always existed, but most Jewish communities, with an even greater proportion of elderly members than in Canadian society in general, are forced to devote ever larger resources to their needs.

Canadian Jewry has been transformed from a mostly insecure, poor, lower-middle- to working-class community living in urban immigrant enclaves to an assertive, well-off, confident, and middle-class group generally residing in the better urban areas and fully able to participate in all sectors of Canada's life. Indeed, some super-rich Jews have achieved status among the most powerful international tycoons.

Although Jews have survived the twentieth century, some Canadian Jewish prophets of doom (taking their cue from Bernard Wasserstein and Alan Dershowitz, who forecast the gradual disappearance of European and American Jews through intermarriage and assimilation) have started to predict disaster. Intermarriage rates in Canada, though not as high as those in the United States, are indeed growing, giving rise to serious concerns about the "continuity," or survival, of Canadian Jewish life. This kind of forecast is based on the knowledge that children of intermarried parents are far less likely to identify themselves as Jews than children of two Jewish parents. Indeed, Israel can no longer count on the automatic support of the Canadian Jewish community.[1]

Programs to enhance the Jewish identity — and reduce the propensity for intermarriage among the community's youth — have proliferated in recent years, but it is too early to measure their results effectively. Some of these initiatives, however, seem to be "crash" summer courses in Israel that are often preceded by a tour of Auschwitz. Thus Israel and the Holocaust are posited as the touchstones of a Jewish identity that is supposed to inspire youth to continue as Jews and marry Jewish spouses.

It remains to be seen if this will work, but thoughtful observers may wonder whether the messianic national dream (now realized) and the horrific mass murder (now fading from memory) can be expected to provide a young adult with enough motivation to make a commitment to Jewish "continuity," whatever that may mean. If all there is to Jewish identity is Israel and the Holocaust, two events posited without significant content and context, then why bother? Excessive concern for Holocaust memorials may seriously distort the Canadian Jewish community's priorities and waste energies needed to address the real issues, such as education.[2] As long as substantive Jewish education is a reality for only a minority of the community's youth, continuity may continue to be elusive. Meanwhile, as the debate on this sensitive subject continues, the detailed studies by Jim Torczyner and Shari Brotman, who conclude that, overall, the Canadian Jewish community is "robust and vigorous," and the wise judgement by the sociologist Morton Weinfeld that "Jews should take a collective valium and think positively," strongly suggest that Canadian Jewry should not panic.[3]

Much has been lost in the transformations of Canadian Jewish culture over the years. Between the 1920s and the 1990s, a Canadian Jewish world has slipped away. Yiddish has virtually disappeared. The daily newspapers have folded and their keen readers have died off. The Jewish trade unions, including the International Ladies' Garment Workers, the Amalgamated Clothing Workers of America, and the International Union of Needle Trades Workers, whose feisty leaders led their militant rank-and-file members through the bloody strikes of the interwar period, are now bereft of Jews.

The sons and daughters of the petty tradesmen and storekeepers and the toiling and striking operators, pressers, cutters, and shippers went to university, to professional schools, or into business. Many of them prospered, moved uptown or to the suburbs, and now drive BMWs, shop at Holt Renfrew, dine at La Gioconda (or places with similar names), and holiday in expensive places. The former Jewish neighbourhoods of Montreal's Main, Toronto's Kensington Market, and Winnipeg's old North End are now home to only tiny numbers of Jewish residents. Struggling and upwardly mobile immigrants from other parts of the world live in the houses the Jews once inhabited, and the little synagogues — many with their Hebrew lettering still in place — have been lovingly converted to Baptist and Pentecostal chapels for new Asian or South American Canadians. The spicy smelling delicatessens have disappeared or changed into fashionable ethnic eateries where stylish uptowners occasionally drop in for Jewish "soul food" or stroll through the old neighbourhoods remembering life as it was in the old days.[4]

The Jewish street guys — the ones who could get it for you wholesale; the punchy ex-boxers; the hulking ex-wrestlers; the pool-hall sharks; the bewildered war veterans who fought the good fight in Spain, Europe, and Israel; the racing touts; the gamblers; the bookies who drove chartreuse-coloured Cadillacs, smoked stogies, wore loud suits, and sported various *noms de guerre* — have all vanished. The rude waiters in delis and restaurants — a Jewish speciality, to be sure — no longer wait on tables.

Meanwhile, a new generation of Canadian Jewish writers is beginning to appear. They will follow those who have superbly recorded the words and music of Canadian Jewish memory, including Leonard Cohen, Adele Wiseman, Miriam Waddington, Jack Ludwig, Morley Torgov, Fredelle Bruser, Mordecai Richler, Norman Levine, and Irving Layton. It has been forty years since the prince of Canadian Jewish letters, Abraham Moses Klein — may his memory serve as a blessing — wrote his poignant verses on the Jewish soul caught in the unyielding web of modernity, while looking back to the past and remembering the sweet smells and Oriental sounds of the olden days. Will the new writers replace him now? If some have the words, do they have the music of his yearning soul? Will they, like him, give voice, by the waters of Canada, to the Jewish longing for the coming of the Messiah? Or will they, like Anne Michaels, link the Canadian Jewish experience to the Holocaust? To what extent will Israel, North Africa, the Soviet Union, and South Africa — the sources of Canada's newer Jewish immigrants — be reflected in the Canadian Jewish literature of future years?

While these literary works continue to enrich the Canadian Jewish canon, the historical record is being greatly enhanced by the publication of memoirs (including a good number by Holocaust survivors), family histories, synagogue and community memorial books, and regional collections.[5] In this latter group, one of the most interesting is Lawrence Guam's *From Belarus to Cape Breton and Beyond: My Family, My Roots*, a compelling look back at the once-thriving Cape Breton Jewish communities of Sydney, Whitney Pier, and Glace Bay, whose sons and daughters (now living in Toronto) proudly celebrate their roots in regular meetings of the Cape Breton Jewish Club — to which mainland Nova Scotians reputedly are not admitted! Edgar Bronfman's memoir, *The Making of a Jew*, is a revealing account of his family and public lives.[6] Harry and Mildred Gutkin's superb *The Worst of Times, the Best of Times* traces the roots of the entertainers, scientists, lawmakers, public servants, prodigal sons, and literary personalities who were produced by the culturally rich Jewish community of

Winnipeg's North End, the "Vilna of Canada."[7] Such works, it is hoped, will multiply; they provide invaluable material for future historians — and are an informative and entertaining perspective on the past for contemporary readers.

ON THE OTHER SIDE OF THE POEM

Rokhl Korn

On the other side of the poem there is an orchard,
and in the orchard, a house with a roof of straw,
and three pine trees,
three watchmen who never speak, standing guard.

On the other side of the poem there is a bird,
yellow brown with a red breast,
and every winter he returns
and hangs like a bud in the naked bush.

On the other side of the poem there is a path
as thin as a hairline cut,
and someone lost in time
is treading the path barefoot, without a sound.

On the other side of the poem amazing things may happen,
even on this overcast day,
this wounded hour
that breathes its fevered longing in the windowpane.

On the other side of the poem my mother may appear
and stand in the doorway for a while lost in thought
and then call me home as she used to call me home long ago:
Enough play, Rokhl! Don't you see it's night?

(Translated by Seymour Levitan)

"Rokhl Korn was born in 1898 in Podliski, a village then in East Galicia. . . . She moved from her birthplace to the larger center of Lvov, and exchanged Polish, the language of her first poems, for Yiddish. She spent some time in Warsaw, escaped to the Soviet Union as a refugee during the Second World War, and went to Montreal in 1948." She died there in 1982. See Irving Howe, Ruth Wisse, and Khone Shmeruk, eds., *The Penguin Book of Modern Yiddish Verse* (New York: Viking, 1987): 524–25.

Meanwhile, ongoing academic studies by historians, sociologists, and political scientists provide rich new insights into the Canadian Jewish experience.

As we approach the end of the twentieth century and mark the 240th anniversary of the founding of Canada's first organized Jewish community, the basic question remains: How can Judaism survive if, as present trends seem to suggest, there might soon not be enough committed Jews to form a strong community? Will the realm of the sacred perhaps redeem the failings of the secular? Those who diligently follow the path of the Almighty are growing rapidly, to be sure. The ultra-Orthodox can easily be seen on the streets of Outremont, Snowdon, and Thornhill with their many children. A recent survey of the ten thousand Hasidim in Montreal, however, revealed a serious economic crunch in a community where poverty and unemployment are rife.[8]

Will the emergence of a constructive Jewish feminism, be it in Reform and Conservative synagogues or in private prayer groups, succeed in reviving Judaism while fulfilling women's eminently just claims for "half the kingdom"? And what will be the effect of immigration, as more new Canadians arrive from the former Soviet Union, South Africa, and Israel?

Although the Yiddish language may be dying, the music, literature, history, and cuisine of the Jewish communities of Eastern Europe have come alive in celebrations like Toronto's popular Ashkenaz festival. Signs such as these can perhaps lead one to safely conclude that the Canadian Jewish community will, therefore, not die off or intermarry itself out of existence.

What is clear, as these pages have shown, is that the Canadian Jewish history from 1921 to the present has been shaped by domestic and international events. But these elements for understanding the Jewish past have never been sufficient, for Judaism exists in time as well as in space. It is collective memory, religious observances, and historical reconstruction that activates Jewish echoes of the covenant at Mount Moriah and its renewal at Sinai, of the continuity of the law, the reality of Diaspora, and the march towards Zion.

To these monumental landmarks of Jewish history we now add the Holocaust and the establishment of Israel. These co-ordinates of the culture that Jews brought with them continue to add to the context of Canada. Over the past nearly eight decades, the interplay between the two has fostered an advancement — indeed an abundance — for both. Jews have added the richness of their chant eternal to the raucous chorus of Canada, and have received in return the ample rewards of peace, freedom, and opportunity in a generous land. To be sure, the passage has not been an easy one. As the twentieth century ends, however, it appears that the major external battles — those for toleration and acceptance — have been won, though vigilance is still needed.

It might be said that if Canadian Jewry was taking root until 1921, the community has spent the last eighty years branching out into the Canadian mainstream. Canadian Jewry is now perhaps in mid-passage, halfway between its past and Klein's "fabled city," an ever-receding messianic ideal that will never die as long as there is one Jew looking for nine others to form a *minyan* (quorum for prayer). It is the past that defines a people, a nation, a culture. History tells us how we got to where we are and provides hints of how our future might evolve. The Canadian Jewish experience evolved at the interface between Jewish culture and Canadian context, a process that took generations and that, though challenged, will continue for generations to come. Jewish culture must be revived and meaningfully lived, and for that to happen, the community needs to recognize that its real frontier of opportunity lies within its own boundaries.

Indeed, there are challenging issues ahead, especially if Quebec separates from Canada. This would, initially at least, put even more pressure on Jews and other anglophones — though not likely on francophone Jews — to leave the province, out of concern for their personal and communal well-being. This would be a sad turn of events, given the centuries-old Jewish presence in Quebec and the fact that, in the words of the writer Merrily Weisbord, "we live here, . . . tied to the soil, having, for better or for worse, taken root."[9] The 1995 referendum, even taking into account alleged vote-tampering, indicates that the next referendum — or the one after that — may carry separatism to victory. In that unfortunate event, the Jewish community, like Canada as a whole, would be sundered.

This is all, of course, speculation on the future, not the province of the historian, except insofar as the Canadian past helps to shape current realities in this country's Jewish life. At the same time, this experience has always been deeply affected by the Jewish world beyond Canada and will increasingly be absorbed into what the historian Zvi Gittelman calls "the global shtetl," a political and technological process drawing Jews around the world into greater contact with each other while activating confrontation and fragmentation over sensitive questions like: "Who is a Jew?"[10]

Meanwhile, the road is open and the journey continues.

Statistical Appendix

Table 1: The Growth of Jewish Population of Canada*

Census Year	Number	Percentage of Total Population
1831	107	0.01
1841	154	0.01
1851	451	0.02
1861	1,186	0.04
1871	1,333	0.03
1881	2,443	0.06
1891	6,501	0.13
1901	16,401	0.31
1911	74,564	1.03
1921	125,197	1.42
1931	155,614	1.5
1941**	168,585	1.5
1951	204,836	1.5
1961	254,368	1.4
1971	276,025	1.3
1981	296,425	1.2
1991	318,060	1.0
1996***	351,700	1.0

* By religion, according to the decennial Census of Canada. *Source:* Louis Rosenberg, *Canada's Jews: A Social and Economic Study of the Jews in Canada* (Montreal: Canadian Jewish Congress, Bureau of Social and Economic Research, 1939), 10.

** *Source:* Daniel J. Elazar and Harold M. Waller, *Maintaining Consensus: The Canadian Jewish Polity in the Postwar World* (New York: University Press of America, 1990), 18.

*** Jews by ethnicity.

Table 2: Jewish Population of Major Canadian Cities, 1911-91 (by religion)

City	1911	1921	1931	1941	1951	1961	1971	1981	1991	1996*
Montreal	28,807	45,802	57,997	63,721	80,829	102,724	109,480	101,365	96,155	89,905
Toronto	18,300	34,770	46,751	49,046	66,773	88,648	103,730	123,725	150,100	156,305
Winnipeg	9,023	14,837	17,660	17,027	18,514	19,376	18,315	15,350	13,160	14,140
Ottawa	1,781	3,041	3,482	3,809	4,558	5,533	6,385	8,470	9,665	12,000
Hamilton	1,763	2,592	2,667	2,597	3,236	3,858	4,115	4,300	4,370	5,190
Windsor	309	1,118	2,517	2,226	2,444	2,419	2,420	2,025	1,575	1,625
Vancouver	982	1,399	2,458	2,812	5,467	7,301	8,940	12,865	14,160	22,195
Calgary	604	1,247	1,622	1,794	2,110	2,881	3,275	5,580	5,355	6,935
Edmonton	171	821	1,057	1,449	1,753	2,495	2,475	4,250	3,930	5,830
Regina	130	860	1,010	944	740	817	795	710	490	665
Saskatoon	77	599	691	703	687	793	490	540	585	895
Saint John	642	848	683	569	580	514	320	—	195	420
London	571	703	683	731	969	1,315	1,565	2,095	2,165	2,730
Halifax	254	585	582	756	1,012	1,186	1,315	1,220	1,440	2,270
Quebec	398	375	436	376	408	495	365	—	145	295
Sydney	162	398	425	445	407	437	—	405	195	—

Note: Figures for 1911 through 1941 are from Rosenberg, *Canada's Jews*, 308–309. See also Louis Rosenberg, "The Jewish Population of Canada: A Statistical Summary from 1850 to 1943," AJYB 48 (1946–47): 35; and the Census of Canada from 1951 to 1996.

* Jews by ethnicity.

Notes

List of Abbreviations

The following abbreviations appear in the notes.

Publications

ACWA	*Documentary History of the Amalgamated Clothing Workers of America*
AJYB	*American Jewish Year Book*
CES/EEC	*Canadian Ethnic Studies/Études Ethniques au Canada*
CHR	*Canadian Historical Review*
CJC	*Canadian Jewish Chronicle*
CJE	*Canadian Journal of Economics*
CJHSJ/SHJCJ	*Canadian Jewish Historical Society Journal/Société de L'Histoire Juive Canadienne Journal*
CJN	*Canadian Jewish News*
CJO	*Canadian Jewish Outlook*
CJR	*Canadian Jewish Review*
CJS	*Canadian Journal of Sociology*
CJS/EJC	*Canadian Jewish Studies/Études Juives Canadiennes*
CRSA/RCSA	*Canadian Review of Sociology and Anthropology/Revue Canadienne de Sociologie et d'Anthropologie*
CWS/CF	*Canadian Woman Studies/Cahiers de la Femme*
EJ	*Encyclopedia Judaica*

HS/SH	*Histoire sociale/Social History*
JCS/REC	*Journal of Canadian Studies/Revue des Études Canadiennes*
JSS	*Jewish Social Studies*
KA	*Keneder Adler*
LG	*Labour Gazette*
L/Let	*Labour/Le travail*
QQ	*Queen's Quarterly*
RCPSMB	*Royal Commission on Price Spreads and Mass Buying*

Archives and Institutions

CJCNA	Canadian Jewish Congress National Archives, Montreal
CSIS	Canadian Security Intelligence Service
CZA	Central Zionist Archives, Jerusalem, Israel
GLEN	Glenbow Museum and Archives, Calgary
JHSWC	Jewish Historical Society of Western Canada
JPLM	Jewish Public Library, Montreal
MHSO	Multicultural History Society of Ontario, Toronto
NAC	National Archives of Canada
OJA	Ontario Jewish Archives, Toronto
PAM	Public Archives of Manitoba, Winnipeg
PANS	Public Archives of Nova Scotia, Halifax
WA	Weizmann Archives, Rehovot, Israel

Introduction

1. Robert Harney, *If One Were to Write a History: Selected Writings by Robert Harney* (Toronto: Multicultural History Society of Ontario, 1991.)
2. Ibid.

Chapter 1/Jewish Geography of the 1920s and 1930s

1. Louis Rosenberg, *Canada's Jews: A Social and Economic Study of the Jews in Canada* (Montreal: Canadian Jewish Congress, Bureau of Social and Economic Research, 1939). A photoreproduction of the book was published in 1993 by McGill-Queen's University Press in its Studies in Ethnic History series, which is edited by Donald H. Akenson, as *Canada's Jews: A Social and Economic Study of Jews in Canada in the 1930s*, edited and with an introduction by Morton Weinfeld and a foreword by Seymour Martin Lipset. The addition of "in the 1930s" is misleading because, except for some data on a few subjects such as immigration and criminality during the 1930s, no use was made of the 1941 census, which would have provided a statistical portrait of Canadian Jewry in the 1930s. The book is really about the 1920s.
2. Ibid., 31–34.
3. Concerning the same transformation in one Northern Ontario community, see Lise C. Hansen, "The Decline of the Jewish Community in Thunder Bay: An Explanation" (M.A. thesis, University of Manitoba, 1977).
4. Rosenberg, *Canada's Jews*, 16.
5. Ibid., 308.
6. Ibid., 17.
7. Ibid., 43.
8. Ibid., 31.
9. Ibid., 19.
10. Ibid., 45, 47.
11. Ibid., 59.
12. Ibid., 83.
13. Ibid., 86.
14. Ibid., 100–01.
15. Ibid., 153. Ten years of age and over.
16. Sheldon Levitt, Lynn Milstone, and Sidney T. Tenenbaum, *Treasures of a People: The Synagogues of Canada* (Toronto: Lester & Orpen Dennys, 1985), 58, 66.
17. Ibid., 53.
18. Ibid., 61.
19. Similar patterns of Jewish residential clustering existed in Thunder Bay. See Hansen, "Thunder Bay," 17.
20. See Cyril H. Levitt and William Shaffir, *The Riot at Christie Pits* (Toronto: Lester & Orpen Dennys, 1987).
21. Avi Aharon Habinski, "Assimilation and Residential Location: Jews in Vancouver" (M.A. thesis, Simon Fraser

University, 1973), 33. See also Myer Freedman, "Growing Up in Vancouver's East End," *The Scribe* 11, no. 2 (1989): 4–7.

22. Ibid., 34–41.
23. See Alan F. J. Artibise, *Winnipeg: A Social History of Urban Growth, 1874–1914* (Montreal: McGill-Queen's University Press, 1975).
24. Louis Rosenberg, *A Population Study of the Winnipeg Jewish Community* (Montreal: Canadian Jewish Congress, Bureau of Social and Economic Research, 1946), 14.
25. Alan Artibise, *Winnipeg: An Illustrated History* (Toronto: James Lorimer, 1977), 202.
26. Rosenberg, *Winnipeg*, 45.
27. Ibid., 69.
28. Ibid.
29. Harry Gutkin, with Mildred Gutkin, *The Worst of Times, the Best of Times: Growing Up in Winnipeg's North End* (Toronto: Fitzhenry and Whiteside, 1987), 268.
30. Jack Ludwig, "Requiem for Bibul," in Robert Weaver, ed., *Ten for Wednesday Night: A Collection of Short Stories Presented for Broadcast by CBC Wednesday Night* (Toronto: McClelland and Stewart, 1961): 107–20.
31. Rosenberg, *Winnipeg*, 72.
32. Ibid., 73.
33. Ibid., 75.
34. Ibid.
35. PAM, MG 10, F 3 (MG6A6), "Memoirs of Berel Miller."
36. JHSWC, List of Winnipeg Jewish Organizations, compiled January 1986.
37. See Harvey H. Herstein, "The Growth of the Winnipeg Jewish Community and the Evolution of Its Educational Institutions," *Transactions of the Historical and Scientific Society of Manitoba*, 3d ser., no. 22 (1965–66): 28–66.
38. Henry Trachtenberg, "The Winnipeg Jewish Community and Politics: The Inter-War Years, 1919–1939," *Transactions of the Historical and Scientific Society of Manitoba*, 3d ser., nos. 34 and 35 (1977–78, 1978–79): 115–153, 120; Gregory S. Kealey, "State Repression of Labour and the Left in Canada, 1914–20: The Impact of the First World War," CHR 73, no. 3 (1992): 281–314, 295, 307. See also Jeff Keshen, "All the News That Was Fit to Print: Ernest J. Chambers and Information Control in Canada, 1914–1919," ibid.: 315–343, 328.
39. Quoted in J. E. Rea, "Parties and Power: An Analysis of Winnipeg City Council, 1919–1975," app. 4, *The Rea Report* (Winnipeg, 1976), 124.
40. J. K. Johnson, ed., *The Canadian Directory of Parliament 1867–1967* (Ottawa: Public Archives of Canada, 1968): 265–66. Eli Gottesman, ed., *Who's Who in Canadian Jewry*. Compiled and prepared by the Jewish Literary Foundation for the Jewish Institute of Higher Research of

the Central Rabbinical Seminary of Canada (Montreal, 1965): 314.

41. Herstein, "Winnipeg," 49.
42. Ibid., 50.
43. Ibid., 55.
44. JHSWC, List of Winnipeg Jewish Organizations.
45. PAM, MG 10, F 3 (MG2B3), *Achdus Free Loan Association: 25th Silver Jubilee Souvenir 1924–1949* (Winnipeg: Yiddishe Vort, 1949).
46. I am grateful for these insights from my colleagues Peter Goheen and Brian Osborne (Queen's Geography), during seminars in February 1998.
47. Rosenberg, *Canada's Jews*, 225.
48. See Gerald Friesen, *The Canadian Prairies: A History* (Toronto: University of Toronto Press, 1984), 382–417.
49. Rosenberg, *Canada's Jews*, 227.
50. Arthur A. Chiel, *The Jews in Manitoba: A Social History* (Toronto: University of Toronto Press and Historical and Scientific Society of Manitoba, 1961), 56.
51. Rosenberg, *Canada's Jews*, 227. Some, like the tiny colony of Trochu, Alberta, had disappeared by 1926. See Max Bercovitch, "I Stayed Here: 85 Years in Southern Alberta," *Western States Jewish History* 26, no. 3 (1994): 259–63.
52. Rosenberg, *Canada's Jews*, 227.
53. Y. Katz and J. Lehr, "Jewish and Mormon Agricultural Settlement in Western Canada: A Comparative Analysis," *The Canadian Geographer/La Géographie Canadienne* 35, no. 2 (1991): 128–42. See also the works of Cyril E. Leonoff, *The Jewish Farmers of Western Canada* (Vancouver: Jewish Historical Society of British Columbia and Western States Historical Society, 1948); *The Architecture of Jewish Settlements in the Prairies: A Pictorial History* (Winnipeg: JHSWC, 1975); *Wapella Farm Settlement (The First Successful Jewish Farm Settlement in Canada)* (Winnipeg: JHSWC and Historical and Scientific Society of Manitoba, 1975).
54. Rosenberg, *Canada's Jews*, 240. These figures were based on "total gross assets."
55. Ibid., 243.
56. NAC, RG 76, Records of the Immigration Branch, vol. 82, F. C. B. (Blair) to Gillmour, 22 Apr. 1930.
57. Vladimir Grossman, *The Soil's Calling* (Montreal: Eagle Publishing Co., 1938), 47.
58. Ibid., 48.
59. The strength of the Mormon colonies stemmed in part from their being clustered together, making mutual support much easier. See Katz and Lehr, "Jewish and Mormon": *passim*.
60. Grossman, *Soil's Calling*, 42.
61. Michael Usiskin, *Uncle Mike's Edenbridge: Memoirs of a Jewish*

Pioneer Farmer, Marcia Usiskin Basman, trans. (Winnipeg: Peguis Publishers, 1983).

62. See Anna Feldman, "Yiddish Songs of the Jewish Farm Colonists in Saskatchewan, 1917–1939" (M.A. thesis, Carleton University, Institute of Canadian Studies, 1983).
63. Usiskin, *Uncle Mike's Edenbridge*, 140.
64. Clara Hoffer and F. H. Kahan, *Land of Hope*, William Perehudoff, ill. (Saskatoon: Modern Press, 1960), 131ff. See also Esther Ghan, "The Hoffer Colony: A Memoir," *The Scribe* 9, no. 3 (1987): 5, for a fascinating account of a suitor who shot his beloved for failing to return his affections. She recovered and married another man, who demonstrated his love for her in more traditional ways.
65. *Personal Recollections: The Jewish Pioneer Past on the Prairies*, vol. 6 of *Jewish Life and Times* (Winnipeg: JHSWC, 1993), 13.
66. Anna Feldman, "Sonnenfeld — Elements of Survival and Success of a Jewish Farming Community on the Prairies, 1905–1939," CJHSJ/SHJCJ 6, no. 1 (1982): 33–53, 45.
67. NAC, RG 76, Records of the Immigration Branch, vol. 82, Enclosure "Jewish colonization and the work of the Jewish Colonization Association in Western Canada," June 8/30, F. C. Blair memorandum, 12 June 1930. The article was identified as being from the *Canadian Jewish Eagle* of 21 Nov. 1929.
68. KA, 27 Nov. 1929. NAC, RG 76, Records of the Immigration Branch, vol. 82, I. Finestone to F. C. Blair, 9 Jul. 1930.
69. Ibid., KA, 19 Nov. 1929.
70. This description is derived from Richard Bartlett, *The New County: A Social History of the American Frontier 1776–1890* (New York: Oxford University Press, 1974), 182–84; Harold Kalman, *A History of Canadian Architecture* (Toronto: Oxford University Press, 1994), 519; and William Wanders, "Log Houses," *The Canadian Encyclopedia*, vol. 2, 2d ed. (Edmonton: Hurtig, 1988): 238.
71. See Cyril E. Leonoff, *The Architecture of Jewish Settlements in the Prairies: A Pictorial History* (N.p., n.d.), 28–29.
72. *Jewish Pioneer Past*, 27.
73. Ruth Bellan, "Growing Up in a Small Saskatchewan Town," in *Jewish Life and Times: A Collection of Essays* (Winnipeg: JHSWC, 1983): 199.
74. See Fredelle Bruser Maynard, *The Tree of Life* (Toronto: Penguin Books, 1989) and *Raisins and Almonds* (Toronto: Penguin, 1985).
75. Anna Feldman, "'Her Voice Is Full of Wisdom': Jewish

Saskatchewan Women in a Small Urban Setting," CWS/CF 16, no. 4 (1996): 100–02, 100.

76. Ibid.: 101–02.
77. For a superb account of Jewish life and insights into the experiences of a Jewish girl reaching maturity in a small Saskatchewan town, see Molly Lyons Bar-David, *My Promised Land* (New York: Putnam, 1953), 3–30.
78. Robert England, *The Central European Immigrant in Canada* (Toronto: Macmillan, 1929), 92.
79. See Uri Hescher, *Jewish Agricultural Utopias in America, 1880–1910* (Detroit: Wayne State University Press, 1981) and Ann Usishkin, "The Jewish Colonization Association," EJ, vol. 10 (Jerusalem: Keter Publishing Co., 1972): 46.
80. NAC, RG 76, Records of the Immigration Branch, vol. 82; KA, 13 Nov. 1929.
81. Bercovitch, "I Stayed Here," 263.
82. For general background see James Lemon, *Toronto Since 1918: An Illustrated History* (Toronto: James Lorimer and National Museum of Man, National Museums of Canada, 1985). The most thorough study of Toronto's Jewish history is Stephen A. Speisman, *The Jews of Toronto: A History to 1937* (Toronto: McClelland and Stewart, 1979). Insight into the community can be gained from a delightful essay by Ben Kayfetz, "The Toronto Yiddish Press," CJHSJ/SHJCJ 7, no. 1 (1983): 39–54.
83. Rosenberg, *Canada's Jews*, 308, and Louis Rosenberg, *The Jewish Population of Canada: A Statistical Summary from 1851 to 1941. Containing Statistical Supplement for Period 1951 and 1954* (Montreal: Canadian Jewish Congress, Bureau of Social and Economic Research, 1954), 17. Also Louis Rosenberg, "Population Characteristics of the Jewish Community of Toronto," in *Canadian Jewish Population Studies*, Jewish Community Series no. 3, 1 Feb. 1955 (Montreal: Canadian Jewish Congress, Bureau of Social and Economic Research, 1955): 1.
84. Daniel Joseph Hiebert, "The Geography of Jewish Immigrants and the Garment Industry in Toronto, 1901–1931. A Study of Ethnic and Class Relations" (Ph.D. thesis, University of Toronto, 1987), 289ff.
85. Ibid., 328. Hiebert's findings, based on samples drawn from directories and City of Toronto assessment rolls, were that 65.7 percent of "blue-collar," i.e., working-class, and 59.4 percent of "white-collar" Jewish families were house owners, indicating that middle-class families tended

to husband their resources for business purposes.

86. Lynne Marks, "*Kale Meydelach* or *Shulamith* Girls: Cultural Change and Continuity Among Jewish Parents and Daughters — A Case Study of Toronto's Harbord Collegiate Institute in the 1920s," CWS/CF 7, no. 3 (1986): 85–89, 88.
87. P. F. Munro, *An Experimental Investigation of the Mentality of the Jew in Ryerson Public School, Toronto* (Toronto: University of Toronto Press, 1926).
88. Ibid., 10, 22, 36, 40, 44, 54.
89. Ibid., 23.
90. Peter Oliver, *Unlikely Tory: The Life and Politics of Allan Grossman* (Toronto: Lester & Orpen Dennys, 1985), 11.
91. Levitt and Shaffir, *Christie Pits*, 34; Speisman, *Jews of Toronto*, 90.
92. Richard Dennis, "Property and Propriety: Jewish Landlords in Early Twentieth-Century Toronto" (unpublished manuscript), table 2, Summary statistics from probate for Jewish landlords in Toronto. See also Richard Dennis, "Landlords and Housing in Depression," *Housing Studies*, no. 3 (1995): 305–24, 317.
93. See Deena Nathanson, "A Social Profile of Peddlers in the Jewish Community of Toronto, 1891–1930," CJS/EJC 1 (1993): 27–40. The Ontario Jewish Archives, Toronto, possesses numerous photographs of proud proprietors.
94. NAC, MG 30, C 119, Louis Rosenberg Papers, vol. 26, no. 19, "Jewish Mutual Benefit and Friendly Societies in Toronto: The First Fifty Years, 1896–1945."
95. Ibid., 21.
96. Ibid., 22.
97. Ibid., 33.
98. Ibid., 35.
99. Ben Kayfetz to Gerald Tulchinsky, 16 Jul. 1997.
100. NAC, MG 30, C 119, Rosenberg Papers, Card catalogue of Toronto Burial Societies.
101. This group was made up of clothing workers who moved seasonally between Toronto and New York until the early 1920s, when, because of tough U.S. immigration rules, they could not get back to New York. Stuck in Toronto, they formed their own *landsmanshaft*, presumably yearning for Seventh Avenue. Ben Kayfetz to Gerald Tulchinsky, 16 Jul. 1997.
102. The author's grandmother, Rivka Stemeroff, always answered questions about her origins by saying proudly "from England," although she lived there only a few years after migrating from Russia, her birthplace, and spoke an imperfect version of the King's English.
103. For that matter, which Ontario

town or city was without its "New York Café"?

104. See Leah Rosenberg, *The Errand Runner: Reflections of a Rabbi's Daughter* (Toronto: John Wiley and Sons, 1981).

105. NAC, MG 30, C 119, Louis Rosenberg Papers, vol. 26, no. 19, "Jewish Mutual Benefit and Friendly Societies in Toronto."

106. Ibid., 39.

107. Ibid., 41, 41a. Jewish per capita outlays for funeral, sick, medical, and hospital benefits were substantially higher, especially for the last of these.

108. Ibid., 44.

109. See Shelly Tenenbaum, *A Credit to Their Community: Jewish Loan Societies in the United States 1850–1945* (Detroit: Wayne State University Press, 1994).

110. *Hebrew Free Loan Association: Seventh Annual Report*, Montreal, 1 May 1918: 8. Photocopy supplied by Dr. Shelly Tenenbaum.

111. "Resources, Operation, and Policies of 14 Free Loan Societies, 1932." Photocopy supplied by Dr. Shelly Tenenbaum.

112. CJR, 9 Jul. 1937.

113. "Summary 1925–1937." Photocopy supplied by Dr. Shelly Tenenbaum.

114. Isidore Sobeloff, Detroit, to Lillian G. Ledeen, Los Angeles, 9 Nov. 1938. Photocopy supplied by Dr. Shelly Tenenbaum.

115. Rosenberg, *The Jewish Population of Canada*, 17.

116. Gerald Tulchinsky, "The Contours of Canadian Jewish History," JCS/REC 17, no. 4 (1982–83): 46–56, 48.

117. Paul-André Linteau, *Histoire de Montréal depuis la Confédération* (Montreal: Boréal, 1992), 361ff.

118. Ibid., 366–67.

119. Judith Seidel, "The Development and Social Adjustment of the Jewish Community in Montreal" (M.A. thesis, McGill University, 1939), table 37 A.

120. Ibid., table 39 A, "Percent which each type of newspaper forms of reading material of three generations, for four areas, 1938."

121. Ibid., table 50 A.

122. Ibid., table 53 A.

123. Ibid., table 54 A.

124. Ibid., table 63, "Number and percent in each area of settlement who attended synagogue, by frequency of attendance for 3 male generations in a sample of 512 families, 1938."

125. Ibid.

126. Ibid., table 34 A, "Families in each area who buy meat, fish, and bread in Jewish stores, showing frequency of purchase, by percent, 1938."

127. See Speisman, *Jews of Toronto*, 276–303; PAM, NG 10, F 3 (MG5D29); H. E. Wilder, "The

Maturing of Winnipeg Jewry," *Israelite Press: 50th Jubilee Edition*, 23 Jun. 1961.

128. Ira Robinson, "Towards a History of Kashrut in Montreal: The Fight Over Municipal By-Law 828 (1922–1924)," in Ira Robinson and Mervin Butovsky, eds., *Renewing Our Days: Montreal Jews in the Twentieth Century* (Montreal: Véhicule Press, 1995): 10–29; Moshe S. Stern, "Communal Problem Solving: The Winnipeg VA'AD HA-IR 1946," CJHSJ/SHJCJ 4, no. 1 (1980): 4–24; Speisman, *Jews of Toronto*, 276–303.
129. See Speisman, *Jews of Toronto*, 297–99.
130. Ibid., 299.
131. Daniel J. Elazar and Harold Waller, *Maintaining Consensus: The Canadian Jewish Polity in the Postwar World* (New York: University Press of America and the Jerusalem Center for Public Affairs, 1990), 70.
132. Speisman, *Jews of Toronto*, 265.
133. PAM, MG 10, F3 (MG2K6), *The History of the YMHA*, n.p. On Winnipeg Jewish sports activity, see also Leible Hershfield, "The Contribution of Jews to Sports in Winnipeg and Western Canada," *Jewish Life and Times: A Collection of Essays*: 84–89.
134. Eleanor Gordon Mlotek and Joseph Mlotek, *Pearls of Yiddish Song: Favorite Folk, Art and Theatre Songs* (New York: Education Department of the Workmen's Circle, 1988), 260.
135. Translated by Eleanor Gordon Mlotek and Joseph Mlotek.
136. Ibid., 14.
137. *Kammen Folio of Famous Jewish Songs: A Collection of Favorite Old-Time Song Hits*, vol. 2 (New York: J. Kammen Music Co., 1953), 15–17.
138. *Kammen Folio of Famous Jewish Theatre Songs: A Collection of Popular Song Hits of Yesteryear*, vol. 1 (New York: J. Kammen Music Co., n.d.), 4–8.
139. Norman H. Warembud, ed., *The New York Times Great Songs of the Yiddish Theatre* (New York: Quadrangle/The New York Times Book Co., 1957): 175–81.
140. Mark Slobin, *Tenement Songs: The Popular Music of the Jewish Immigrants* (Urbana: University of Illinois Press, 1982), 99–103. To date there is no study of Jewish "low life" in Canada, though some tantalizing possibilities for such investigations exist. See Andrée Lévesque, *Making and Breaking the Rules: Women in Quebec, 1919–1939* (Toronto: McClelland and Stewart, 1989), 122.
141. Slobin, *Tenement Songs*, 125.
142. See Stephen Speisman, "Yiddish Theatre in Toronto," *Polyphony* 5, no. 2 (1983): 95–98, and Jean-Marc Larrue, *Le Monument inattendu: Le Monument-National 1893–1993* (Lasalle: Éditions Hurtubise HMH Ltée, 1993.

Cahiers du Québec—Collection Histoire), 183–94. Le Monument-National was the most popular venue for Yiddish theatre in Montreal in the interwar years. On the history of Yiddish theatre in Montreal, see Jean-Marc Larrue, *Le Théâtre yiddish à Montréal* (Montreal: Éditions Jeu, 1996).

143. Rosenberg, *Canada's Jews*, 308.
144. Sheva Medjuck, *The Jews of Atlantic Canada* (St. John's: Breakwater Press, 1986), 25. See also Arthur D. Hart, ed., *The Jew in Canada: A Complete Record of Canadian Jewry From the Days of the French Regime to the Present Time* (Montreal: Jewish Publications Limited, 1926): 164–65.
145. These and other matters have been examined recently in Jack N. Lightstone and Frederick B. Bird, *Ritual and Ethnic Identity: A Comparative Study of the Social Meaning of Liturgical Ritual in Synagogues* (Waterloo: Wilfrid Laurier University Press, 1995).
146. *Baron de Hirsch Congregation, 1890 to 1990: 100th Anniversary Commemorative Book* (Halifax: Beth Israel Synagogue, 1990), 25–26.
147. This was accomplished by one individual, according to the congregation's official history, "in spite of threats to his personal safety." Ibid., 26.
148. Medjuck, *Jews of Atlantic Canada*, 33.
149. Alison Kahn, *Listen While I Tell You: A Story of the Jews of St. John's, Newfoundland* (St. John's: Memorial University, Institute of Social and Economic Research, 1987), 19.
150. Ibid., 36.
151. See Samuel Rothschild, "A Reminiscence by Samuel Rothschild," *Polyphony* 5, no. 1 (1983): 93–99, a fascinating memoir of pioneering Jewish enterprise in Northern Ontario cities and towns in the early 1900s.
152. See John H. Thompson, with Allen Seager, *Canada 1922–1939: Decades of Discord*, Canadian Centenary Series, no. 15 (Toronto: McClelland and Stewart, 1985).
153. Ira Robinson, "'A Letter from the Sabbath Queen': Rabbi Yudel Rosenberg Addresses Montreal Jewry," in Ira Robinson et al., eds., *An Everyday Miracle: Yiddish Culture in Montreal* (Montreal: Véhicule Press, 1990): 101–14.
154. Nachman Shemen, *Tsvishn Kreig Un Friden* (Toronto: Zhurnal Press, 1939).
155. Pierre Anctil, *Yidishe Lider/Poèmes yiddish, de Jacob Isaac Segal* (Montreal: Le Noroît, 1992).
156. Hart, *The Jew in Canada*.
157. Abraham Rhinewine, *Looking Back a Century on the Centennial of Jewish Political Equality in Canada* (Toronto: Kraft Press, 1932).

Chapter 2/Narrowing the Gates of Immigration, 1919-45

1. Roz Wolodarsky Usiskin, ed., *A Lifetime of Letters: The Wolodarsky Family, The Period of Separation, 1913–1922* (Winnipeg, 1995).
2. Ibid.: 124.
3. Gerald Tulchinsky, *Taking Root: The Origins of the Canadian Jewish Community* (Toronto: Lester Publishing, 1992), 274.
4. CJCNA, ZA 1920, 12/11, H. M. Caiserman to A. B. Bennett, 23 Mar. 1920.
5. Ibid., 12/7.
6. Ibid.
7. Ibid., 12/4.
8. ". . . illiterate Italians, Belgians, Jews or Russians, can work just as well in the construction of railroads, dig sewers, blast rocks, make roads, mine coal, cut trees, lay bricks, paint houses, load freight trains, and that, even where skilled labor is necessary, the ability to read and write does not necessarily add to his powers." Ibid.
9. Valerie Knowles, *Strangers at Our Gates: Canadian Immigration and Immigration Policy, 1540–1990* (Toronto: Dundurn Press, 1992), 76ff.
10. See Robert C. Brown and Ramsay Cook, *Canada 1896–1921: A Nation Transformed* (Toronto: McClelland and Stewart, 1974), 321–38.
11. Knowles, *Strangers*, 88.
12. J. K. Johnson, ed., *The Canadian Directory of Parliament 1867–1967* (Ottawa: Public Archives of Canada, 1968): 289–90; Bernard Figler, *Biography of Sam Jacobs (Samuel William Jacobs, K.C., M.P.)* (Montreal, 1959). Two other Jews were elected to the House of Commons later: Abraham A. Heaps, for Winnipeg North in 1925, and Samuel Factor, for Toronto West Centre in 1930.
13. CJC, 18 Jun. 1920.
14. KA, 14 Apr. 1927.
15. NAC, RG 76, Records of the Immigration Branch, vol. 54, file 2240, H. M. Caiserman to J. A. Calder, 13 Apr. 1921.
16. Ibid.
17. Deena Nathanson, "The Role of the Jewish Immigration Aid Society in the Immigration Process, 1919–1931" (unpublished manuscript), chapter 1, 7.
18. Ibid., 13.
19. Ibid., 18.
20. Henry L. Feingold, *A Time for Searching: Entering the Mainstream 1920–1945*, Jewish People in America Series (Baltimore: Johns Hopkins University Press, 1992), 25–29. Many Jews, desperate to rejoin their families, turned to Canada.
21. KA, 13 Nov. 1927.
22. Ibid.
23. Ezra Mendelsohn, *The Jews of East Central Europe Between the World*

Wars (Bloomington: Indiana University Press, 1983), 25.

24. B. Garncarska-Kadary, "Some Aspects of Life of the Jewish Proletariat in Poland in the Interwar Period," in Antony Polonsky, Ezra Mendelsohn, and Jerzy Tomaszewski, eds., *Polin: Studies in Polish Jewry* (London: Littman Library of Jewish Civilization, 1994): 238–54, 243.
25. NAC, RG 76, Records of the Immigration Branch, vol. 485, file 751357, part 1, Report from A. M. M., 7 Dec. 1907.
26. Ibid., F. C. Blair to Thomas Gelley, 12 Oct. 1920.
27. Ibid., high commissioner for Canada to Under-Secretary of State for External Affairs, 21 Apr. 1921.
28. Ibid., F. C. Blair to Canadian National Railways, 23 Dec. 1920; British Consul, Czernowitz, to British Foreign Secretary, 4 May 1921.
29. Ibid., F. C. Blair to Mr. Cory, 30 Oct. 1920.
30. Ibid., John A. Cameron to Sir Herbert Dering, H. M. Minister, Bucharest, 27 Sept. 1921.
31. Ibid., John A. Cameron to Lionel E. Keyser, H. M. Consul, Bucharest, 22 Aug. 1922.
32. Dworkin Papers, in possession of Professor Harry Arthurs, York University. Harry to Dorothy Dworkin, 25 Apr. 1920. "I will tell you that the women here are very ignorant [*sic*] and stupid and absolutely helpless."
33. Ibid., Harry to Dorothy Dworkin, 19 Mar. 1920.
34. Ibid., 15 Mar. 1920.
35. Ibid., 25 Apr. 1920. See also 17 Sept. 1920.
36. Bernard Figler, *Lillian and Archie Freiman: Biographies* (Montreal, 1962), 50.
37. Simon Belkin, *Through Narrow Gates: A Review of Jewish Immigration, Colonization and Immigrant Work in Canada (1840–1940)* (Montreal: Eagle Press, 1966), 95.
38. CJCNA, ZA 1920, 12/7.
39. Belkin, *Through Narrow Gates*, 94–98.
40. See Harold M. Troper, *Only Farmers Need Apply: Official Canadian Government Encouragement of Immigration from the United States, 1896–1911* (Toronto: Griffin House, 1972).
41. Jack Lipinsky, "The Apprenticeship of an Executive Director: M. A. Solkin, A. J. Paul and the Jewish Immigrant Aid Society of Canada," CJHSJ/SHJCJ 9, no. 2 (1985): 67–81, 82.
42. Ibid.: *passim*.
43. Ibid.: 72ff.
44. KA, 15 May 1927.
45. Ibid., 12 Dec. 1926.
46. Ibid., 5 Jan. 1927.
47. Ibid., 6 Mar. 1927.
48. Robert Harney, "The Commerce of Migration," *If One Were to Write*

a History: Selected Writings by Robert Harney (Toronto: Multicultural History Society of Ontario, 1991): 19–36.

49. See "La politique antijuive du gouvernement de Denikine," *Bulletin du comité des délégations juives auprès de la conférence de la paix* (Paris, 19 Feb. 1920). CJCNA, ZA 1920, 12/9. "Facts About the Pogroms," CJC, undated.
50. "Jewish War Orphans Committee," in Arthur D. Hart, ed., *The Jew in Canada: A Complete Record of Canadian Jewry From the Days of the French Regime to the Present Time* (Montreal: Jewish Publications Limited, 1926): 513. The author of this unsigned article, according to Simon Belkin, was Harry Hershman. CJCNA, Belkin Papers, box 1, Publications, Simon Belkin to Ben Lappin, 21 Jul. 1959. These conditions persisted for several years. In June 1923 the Jewish World Relief Conference reported that "thousands and thousands of Jewish children from 7 to 8 years of age . . . traffic and speculate in the streets [of Ukraine] and . . . are enlarging constantly the army of young wretches and criminal children. . . . thousands of young Jewish girls, from 11 to 12 years of age, are compelled to sell themselves in the streets and multiply thus the already dreadfully high number of Jewish prostitutes. . . . We have buried thousands of fathers and mothers who left to our care 150,000 orphans and 30,000 violated women and young girls." CJC, 12 Apr. 1922.
51. PAM, MG10, F3 (MG2J24), F. Shnay, Prince Albert to Leon Goldman, 10 Sept. 1920.
52. Quoted in Lawrence Freiman, *Don't Fall Off the Rocking Horse* (Toronto: McClelland and Stewart, 1978), 33.
53. CJC, 17 Sept. 1920.
54. Ibid., 3 Sept. 1920; see "Jewish War Orphans Committee": 513–20, 513. To date, this is the most complete account of this rescue effort.
55. CJCNA, Hershman Papers, S. Levine to Mrs. Freiman, n.d.
56. Nathanson, "Role of the Jewish Immigrant Aid Society," chapter 3, 1–27.
57. CJC, 26 Nov. 1920, 10 Dec. 1920.
58. Ibid., 1 Oct. 1920.
59. Ibid., 15 Oct. 1920.
60. Ibid., 22 Oct. 1920.
61. Ibid., 24 Dec. 1920.
62. Ibid., 28 Apr. 1921.
63. CJCNA, ZA 1921, 13/4, Hershman to Freiman, 8 Jul. 1921.
64. Ibid., Leavitt to Hershman, n.d.
65. Ibid., Hershman to Leavitt, 5 Jul. 1921.
66. Ibid., "Itinery [*sic*] of Journey," n.d.
67. "Jewish War Orphans Committee": 518.
68. CJC, 21 Jan. 1921.

69. Ibid., 28 Apr. 1921.
70. Quoted in Figler, *Freiman Biographies*, 60.
71. CJCNA, Belkin Papers, Belkin to Lappin, 21 Jul. 1959.
72. CJCNA, Hershman Papers, name of correspondent withheld.
73. CJC, 28 Apr. 1922, 20 Oct. 1922, 15 Jun. 1923.
74. Ibid., 15 Jun. 1923, 13 Jul. 1923.
75. Belkin, *Through Narrow Gates*, 105–06.
76. A. Ulmy, "Helpless Jewish Immigrants in Canada," CJC, 25 Jun. 1920.
77. Ibid., 2 Jul. 1920.
78. Ibid., 6 Aug. 1922.
79. Nathanson, "Role of the Jewish Immigrant Aid Society." Nathanson provided a detailed study of JIAS's work in the 1920s.
80. CJCNA, ZA 1921, 13/11, "In the Matter of Certain Complaints Made Against J. L. Lunney, Dominion Immigration Officer, Saint John, N.B.," 3 Mar. 1921.
81. Ibid.
82. Ibid., ZA 1920, 12/2, E. J. O'Connell to W. I. Little, 13 Oct. 1920.
83. Ibid., A. C. Kaplansky to F. C. Blair, 20 Dec. 1920.
84. Ibid., Leon J. Rosenthal to Minister of Colonization and Immigration, 26 Nov. 1920.
85. Belkin, *Through Narrow Gates*, 108.
86. CJCNA, ZA 1920, 12/6, Caiserman to President, HIAS, 8 Oct. 1920.
87. Ibid., James L. Rodgers to JIAS, 14 Oct. 1920.
88. Ibid., S. B. Haltrecht to HIAS, 15 Oct. 1920.
89. Ibid., Haltrecht to Fain, 28 Oct. 1920.
90. Ibid., ZA 1920, 12/5, Caiserman to HIAS, Danzig, Europe [*sic*], 2 Nov. 1920.
91. CJCNA, JIAS Papers, Isadore Stein to H. M. Caiserman, 27 May 1921, CA1303, quoted in Nathanson, "Role of the Jewish Immigrant Aid Society," chapter 2, 29–30.
92. CJCNA, ZA 1920, 12/6, S. B. Haltrecht to John L. Bernstein, 16 Sept. 1920.
93. Ibid., Caiserman to President, HIAS, 8 Oct. 1920.
94. Ibid., John L. Bernstein to JIAS, 24 Nov. 1920.
95. Ibid., Secretary, JIAS, to J. R. Fain, 29 Nov. 1920.
96. Ibid., 12/4, "Jewish Immigration into Canada: H.I.A.S. Takes Steps to Remedy Conditions," Report of Max Meyerson and Dr. B. B. Berkowitz.
97. Ibid., 8–9.
98. NAC, MG 26I, Arthur Meighen Papers, vol. 30, file 96, J. F. Boyce to Arthur Meighen, 1 Dec. 1921, 017478.
99. Ibid. See telegrams from H. A. Drapeau, Major Paquet, and Charles C. Ballantyne.

100. Ibid., Ballantyne to Meighen, 1 Nov. 1921, 017436-8.
101. Ibid., Rosenbloom to Meighen, 11 Nov. 1921, 017398-9.
102. R. MacGregor Dawson, *William Lyon Mackenzie King: A Political Biography,* vol. 1: 1874–1923 (Toronto: University of Toronto Press, 1958), 350.
103. Henry Paetkau, "Particular or National Interests? Refugees and Immigration Policy in Canada in the 1920s" (University of Western Ontario, Department of History Research Paper, History 509, Profs. Avery and Igastua, Apr. 1978).
104. Quoted in ibid., 16.
105. The best source on this initiative is Belkin, *Through Narrow Gates*, 132–43 and app. 4, 214. See also Johnson, *Canadian Directory of Parliament*: 493–94.
106. Paetkau, "Particular or National Interests," 25.
107. Harold Troper, "Jews and Canadian Immigration Policy, 1900–1950," in Moses Rischin, ed., *The Jews of North America* (Detroit: Wayne State University Press, 1987): 44–58, 53.
108. NAC, RG 76, Records of the Immigration Branch, vol. 51, file 2183, part 3, F. C. Blair to Larkin, 2 Dec. 1921. The Canadian Alliance of Ukrainian Jews and Simon Belkin, who toured Ukraine on their behalf in 1920, made overtures to the Soviet government to allow Jews to emigrate to Canada. Belkin, *Through Narrow Gates*, 111–21.
109. NAC, RG 76, vol. 51, file 2183, part 3, Blair to Larkin, 2 Dec. 1921.
110. Ibid., Blair to S. B. Haltrecht, 5 Nov. 1921.
111. Ibid., J. A. Calder to Hon. George Perley, 3 Feb. 1921.
112. Ibid., Wolf to Canadian high commissioner, London, 2 Aug. 1922.
113. Michael R. Marrus, *The Unwanted: European Refugees in the Twentieth Century* (New York: Oxford University Press, 1985), 89.
114. NAC, RG 76, vol. 51, file 2183, part 4, Philip Baker to W. L. Mackenzie King, 27 Jul. 1923. Baker included a note "which . . . has been written from the League of Nations point of view rather than from that of Poland or Canada. I know that such a friend of the League as yourself will forgive that defect."
115. Ibid., King to Robb, 18 Aug. 1923.
116. NAC, MG 26J, King Papers, W. L. M. King to Philip Baker, 18 Aug. 1923, 70449–70550.
117. NAC, RG 76, vol. 51, file 2183, part 4, Blair to Black, 7 Sept. 1923.
118. Louis Rosenberg, *Canada's Jews: A Social and Economic Study of the Jews in Canada* (Montreal: Canadian Jewish Congress, Bureau of Social and Economic Research, 1939), 136. Between 1921 and

1931, Canada received 44,810 Jewish immigrants and lost 27,095 Jewish emigrants, 24,271 of them to the United States.

119. NAC, RG 76, vol. 51, file 2183, part 4, quoted in Blair to Black, 17 Jul. 1923.
120. See Kristi Corlett, "Arthur Lower's National Vision and Its Relationship to Immigration in Canada, 1920–1946" (M.A. thesis, Queen's University, 1995).
121. See Belkin, *Through Narrow Gates*, 137–38.
122. But see Nathanson, "Role of the Jewish Immigrant Aid Society," chapter 7, 4–5.
123. CJCNA, ZA 1924, 17/6, [Lyon Cohen?] to Barondess, 7 Nov. 1924.
124. The correspondent pointed to other reasons why the quota was cancelled. Skittish officials, chiefly William Egan, were pressured by shipping companies that were not benefiting from the traffic, while the expenses for maintaining Canadian offices for this project in Bucharest were mounting. Ibid.
125. Ibid., General Secretary to M. Kozlovsky, 14 Jan. 1925.
126. PAM, MG2, I1 (J), "Report of Distribution Committee," n.d.
127. Ibid., General Secretary to H. E. Wilder, 1 Sept. 1924.
128. Ibid., General Secretary to Mrs. M. Margulies, 12 Nov. 1924.
129. Ibid.
130. CJCNA, Belkin Papers, box 1, JIAS Reports, 9.
131. The author's father, Harry Tulchinsky, was in one of the last transports, aboard the S.S. *Madonna*, which arrived in Halifax from Constanza on 30 Aug. 1924.
132. Troper, "Jews and Canadian Immigration Policy": 53.
133. J. Murray Beck, *Pendulum of Power: Canada's Federal Elections* (Toronto: Prentice Hall, 1968), 188.
134. Troper, "Jews and Canadian Immigration Policy": 55.
135. NAC, MG 26, King Papers, J1, 61334.
136. Jacobs to Bennett, 7 Oct. 1925, quoted in David Rome, ed., *Our Archival Record of 1933: Hitler's Year*, Canadian Jewish Archives, New Series, no. 5 (Montreal: Canadian Jewish Congress National Archives, 1976): 21.
137. House of Commons, Select Standing Committee on Agriculture and Colonization, *Minutes of Proceedings and Evidence and Report*, app. 8 (Ottawa: King's Printer, 1928), 77.
138. F. C. Blair to Edouard Oungre (Jewish Colonization Association), 30 Jul. 1921, quoted in Rome, *Our Archival Record of 1933*: 21.
139. See Irving Abella and Harold Troper, *None Is Too Many: Canada and the Jews of Europe 1933–1948* (Toronto: Lester & Orpen Dennys, 1982), 7–10.

140. NAC, RG 76, Records of the Immigration Branch, vol. 83, Memorandum (signature illegible) to F. C. Blair, 2 Jun. 1937.
141. Ibid., H. Allam to director, Soldier Settlement of Canada, 24 Mar. 1937.
142. See Gerald Friesen, *The Canadian Prairies: A History* (Toronto: University of Toronto Press, 1984), 382–417, for a fine description of the collapse of the wheat economy.
143. NAC, RG 76, vol. 83, Unsigned to Blair, 2 Jun. 1937.
144. Ibid.
145. Abella and Troper, *None Is Too Many*, 12.
146. Vladimir Grossman, *The Soil's Calling* (Montreal: Eagle Publishing Co., 1938), 42.
147. The best discussion of this debate and of the national context in which it took place is in H. Blair Neatby, *1924–1932: The Lonely Heights*, vol. 2 of *William Lyon Mackenzie King* (Toronto: University of Toronto Press, 1963), 99–100, 238–42, 246–49.
148. Ibid., 239–40.
149. Ibid., 293.
150. Abella and Troper, *None Is Too Many*, 9.
151. See Paula Draper and Harold Troper, eds., *National Archives of Canada, Ottawa. Canadian Jewish Congress Archives, Montreal*, vol. 15 of *Archives of the Holocaust: An International Collection of Selected Documents* (New York: Garland Publishing, Inc., 1991). This collection of documents is an essential source for a systematic and detailed examination of the subject.
152. On Cairine Wilson's work for refugees, see Valerie Knowles, *First Person: A Biography of Cairine Wilson, Canada's First Woman Senator* (Toronto: Dundurn Press, 1988), 195–224.
153. Kenneth Craft, "Canada's Righteous: A History of the Canadian National Committee on Refugees and Victims of Political Persecution" (M.A. thesis, Carleton University, 1987), 23, 73, 119. This thesis argues that the CNCR "also had an effect on Canada's postwar policy concerning displaced persons," and demonstrates that activist Charlotte Whitton was not antisemitic, though she lobbied for a pro-British policy. Ibid., 5, 16, 60, 70, 120.
154. Cyril E. Leonoff, "Farming in the 40s: The Sussels' Experience," *The Scribe* 12, no. 2 (1991): 5–11.
155. J. E. Rea, *T. A. Crerar: A Political Life* (Montreal: McGill-Queen's University Press, 1997), 185.
156. It is interesting that a recent poll of senior Canadian political historians ranked King as Canada's best prime minister since Confederation. Norman

Hillmer and J. L. Granatstein, "Historians Rank the Best and the Worst Canadian Prime Ministers," *Maclean's*, 21 Apr. 1997, 34. But see Dalton Camp, "A Dissenting View," who ranks King second to Sir John A. Macdonald. Ibid., 40.

157. Rosenberg, *Canada's Jews*, 134.
158. See Abella and Troper, *None Is Too Many*, 34.
159. H. Blair Neatby, *1932–1939: The Prism of Unity*, vol. 3 of *William Lyon Mackenzie King* (Toronto: University of Toronto Press, 1976), 305.
160. Neatby, *King*, vol. 2, 242.
161. Ibid., 249.
162. See Paula Draper, "The Accidental Immigrants: Canada and the Interned Refugees: Part 1," CJHSJ/SHJCJ 2, no. 1 (1978): 1–38; "Part 2," CJHSJ/SHJCJ 2, no. 2 (1978): 80–112; and "The Politics of Refugee Immigration: The Pro-Refugee Lobby and the Interned Refugees 1940–1944," CJHSJ/SHJCJ 7, no. 2 (1983): 74–88, which examines the fractiousness within the Jewish leadership over the internees and other issues. Dr. Draper's superb but as yet unpublished Ph.D. thesis, "The Accidental Immigrants: Canada and the Interned Refugees" (Ontario Institute for Studies in Education, 1983), should also be consulted for a full account of this episode. Eric Koch's *Deemed Suspect: A Wartime Blunder* (Toronto: Methuen, 1980) is a valuable personal account by one of the internees.
163. Draper, "Accidental Immigrants, Part 1": 21.
164. Ibid.: 29.
165. Draper, "Accidental Immigrants, Part 2": 82.
166. Quoted in ibid.: 84.
167. Ibid.: 85.
168. Ibid.: 90.
169. Ibid.: 99.
170. See Koch, *Deemed Suspect*, app. "Who's Who," 264–72, for a history of many of the detainees and their occupations.

Chapter 3/The "Jewish Problem" in Montreal Schools in the 1920s

1. The most comprehensive account of this long-standing issue is contained in Leon D. Cresthol's five articles, entitled "The Open Forum on the School Question," CJC, 26 Mar., 2 Apr., 9 Apr., 16 Apr., 14 May 1926. William Nadler's "The Jewish-Protestant School Problem," compiled in 1925, is a valuable collection of documents, as is Louis Rosenberg's "Source Material: The Jewish School Problem in Quebec," NAC, MG 30, C 119, Louis Rosenberg Papers, vol. 27. See also Antonin Dupont,

Taschereau (Montreal: Guérin, 1997), 253–73.

2. The background is covered in Gerald Tulchinsky, *Taking Root: The Origins of the Canadian Jewish Community* (Toronto: Lester Publishing, 1992), 138–44, 243–48.
3. See Ira Robinson, "Kabbalist and Community Leader: Rabbi Yudel Rosenberg and the Canadian Jewish Community," CJS/EJC (1993): 41–58, on the acrimonious disputes involving kosher meat in Montreal.
4. Elson I. Rexford, *Our Educational Problem: The Jewish Population and the Protestant Schools* (Montreal: Renouf Publishing Company, 1924).
5. Ibid., 29.
6. Cited in George E. Fowler, "A Study of the Contributions of Dr. E. I. Rexford to Education in the Province of Quebec" (M.A. thesis, McGill University, 1939), 196.
7. Rexford, *Our Educational Problem*, 32.
8. Ibid., 34.
9. Ibid., 35.
10. KA, 5 Dec. 1927.
11. Rexford, *Our Educational Problem*, 40.
12. Ibid., 41.
13. Ibid., 35. Rexford's data did not go uncontested, however. Various Jewish spokesmen pointed out that taxes paid indirectly by Jewish renters in Protestant-owned buildings were disregarded. Professor Michael Brown to Gerald Tulchinsky, 15 Nov. 1997.
14. CJC, 28 Sept. 1923.
15. In these discussions it was revealed that the Protestant board was also providing, at a substantial loss, schooling for thousands of other non-Protestants and non-Catholics, mainly "members of the various Eastern Churches [and] . . . numbers from China and Japan, etc., . . ." Rexford, *Our Educational Problem*, 42. It was estimated that Jewish-owned property in Montreal was worth about $36 million. Rabbi Max J. Merritt, "Educational Divisions Fatal to Strong Canadianism," CJC, 5 Oct. 1923.
16. In the hearings on the constitutionality of the 1903 Act before the Quebec Court of Appeal, in February 1925, Mr. Justice R. E. A. Greenshields remarked that "the Protestants were educating fourteen thousand Jewish children and were not being fully reimbursed," while George A. Campbell, K.C., a lawyer representing the Protestant board, pointed out that although per pupil costs were sixty-eight dollars (per annum) the board received only sixty dollars. Thus, he said, "the Jewish taxes were low." CJC, 27 Feb. 1925.

Various Jewish spokesmen argued that statistics proved otherwise. In 1929 Peter Bercovitch pointed out that the school taxes "show a surplus of revenue from . . . Montreal and Westmount derived from districts where there is much Jewish property." He calculated that Jews contributed 14 percent more revenue than the Protestants in Montreal. CJC, 29 Mar. 1929.

17. In August 1924, the *Chronicle* pointed out that while thirty-seven qualified Jewish teachers could not get jobs in Montreal, the Protestant board was importing teachers from England. CJC, 29 Aug. 1924.
18. I. Rabinowitz, "Organization Shine By Their Absence at Hearings on School Question," M.I.R., trans., CJC, 3 Sept. 1924.
19. CJC, 5 Sept. 1924.
20. Michael R. Marrus, *Mr. Sam: The Life and Times of Samuel Bronfman* (Toronto: Viking, 1991), 113, 245–47.
21. Maxwell Goldstein, "The Status of the Jew in the Schools of Canada," in Arthur D. Hart, ed. *The Jew in Canada: A Complete Record of Canadian Jewry from the Days of the French Regime to the Present Time* (Montreal: Jewish Publications Limited, 1926): 498.
22. Ibid.
23. Hart, *The Jew in Canada*: 120.
24. CJC, 5 Oct. 1923.
25. Ibid., 29 Dec. 1922.
26. Comments on the issue in the New York Yiddish press were sometimes not appreciated. In May 1927—following the re-election in St. Louis of Peter Bercovitch, who supported an accommodation with the Protestants—the *Chronicle* observed: "It is futile for even one of these Jewish New York [d]ailies to remind us that we are not living in Poland or Roumania, and that it is wrong to inject Jewish nationalism into the elections of a free [*sic*] country. If this is a free country, as the *Jewish Morning Journal* implies, it is precisely because its constitutional basis is the recognition of more than one national entity within its framework." CJC, 27 May 1927.
27. Ibid., 9 Nov. 1923.
28. Ibid., 18 Apr. 1924. The *Chronicle*, at one point, supported this proposal. Ibid., 29 Aug. 1924. Cohen's plan called for a Jewish sub-committee to be in charge of "creating a Jewish atmosphere" in schools where Jews represented 75 percent or more of the pupils. William Nadler, "Jewish-Protestant School Question" (manuscript, 1925), 24. Nadler was the secretary of the Montreal Jewish Community Council.

29. Nadler, "Jewish-Protestant School Question," 28.
30. Ibid., 347–49.
31. Bernard Figler and David Rome, *Hananiah Meir Caiserman: A Biography with an Essay on Modern Jewish Times by David Rome* (Montreal: Northern Printing and Lithographing, 1962), 153.
32. See Bernard Figler, *Biography of Louis Fitch, Q.C.*, Canadian Jewish Profiles (Ottawa, 1968).
33. See KA, 7 Oct. 1926, for a lengthy article by Israel Rabinovitch on this problem.
34. Figler and Rome, *Caiserman*, 157.
35. Nadler, "Jewish-Protestant School Question," 30.
36. Ibid., 31–32.
37. See KA, 26 Feb. 1928.
38. CJC, 29 Aug. 1924.
39. Bernard L. Vigod, *Quebec Before Duplessis: The Political Career of Louis-Alexandre Taschereau* (Montreal: McGill-Queen's University Press, 1986), 254.
40. Nadler, "Jewish-Protestant School Question," 23.
41. Ibid., 157–58.
42. Hart, *The Jew in Canada*: 194, 429.
43. CJC, 14 Mar. 1952.
44. Ibid., 1 Aug. 1924.
45. Ibid.
46. Ibid., letter to editor.
47. Ibid., 3 Oct. 1924.
48. Ibid.
49. Ibid., 10 Oct. 1924.
50. Ibid., 17 Oct. 1924.
51. Ibid., 3 Oct. 1924.
52. One letter to the *Chronicle* pointed out that there were more Jewish students than Protestants in the city's high schools. Even the poorest Jews would send their children to them because "the Jewish child must get a high school education even more than the Gentile child, because of the difficulties the Jewish child encounters in getting a position. Without a high school education, the Jewish child cannot get anywhere except into the semiskilled or unskilled trades. . . ." CJC, 5 Sept. 1924.
53. Ibid.
54. Ibid., 12 Sept. 1924.
55. Ibid., 9 Jan. 1925. The *Chronicle* published a two-page digest of the commission's report.
56. Ibid., 9 Jan. 1925.
57. Ibid.
58. Ibid., 16 Jan. 1925.
59. Ibid., 27 Mar. 1925.
60. Goldstein, "Status of the Jew": 498. See CJC, 27 Feb. 1925, for a lengthy report of the proceedings before the court and 13 Mar. 1925, for an extended analysis of the court's decision.
61. See ibid., 13 Nov. 1925, "The School Problem Before the Supreme Court" and "Quebec School Case Presented to the Supreme Court of Canada for Decision."
62. Ibid., 5 Feb. 1926.

63. *Répertoire des parlementaires Québécois 1867–1978* (Quebec: Bibliothèque de la Législature Service de Documentation Politique, 1980), 41, 207–208.
64. Jack Jedwab, "Uniting Uptowners and Downtowners: The Jewish Electorate and Quebec Provincial Politics 1927–39," CES/EEC 18, no. 2 (1986): 7–19, 9.
65. Ibid.: 10–11.
66. CJC, 2 Dec. 1927.
67. Ibid., 10 Feb. 1928.
68. Ibid., 24 Feb. 1928.
69. See ibid., 1 Feb. 1929.
70. Ibid.
71. See David Roskies, "Yiddish in Montreal: The Utopian Experiment," in Ira Robinson, Pierre Anctil, and Mervin Butovsky, eds., *An Everyday Miracle: Yiddish Culture in Montreal* (Montreal: Véhicule Press, 1990): 22–38.
72. CJC, 1 Feb. 1929.
73. Ibid., 29 Mar. 1929.
74. Ibid.
75. Ibid., 10 Jan. 1930.
76. Ibid.
77. Ibid.
78. Ibid., 24 Jan. 1931.
79. Ibid., 28 Feb. 1930.
80. Ibid.
81. Ibid., 25 Apr. 1930.
82. Ibid.
83. Ibid., 2 May 1930.
84. Ibid.
85. Ibid., 5 Dec. 1930. The commissioners should, the *Chronicle* observed in early December, consult the major Jewish community organizations, such as the Jewish Community Council, Va'ad Ha'ir, or the Jewish Separate School Committee.
86. See ibid., 6 Feb. 1931.
87. Ibid., 12 and 19 Dec. 1930.
88. Quoted in Antonin Dupont, *Les Relations entre l'église et l'état sous Louis-Alexandre Taschereau* (Montreal: Guérin, 1972), 259.
89. Ibid.
90. *La Semaine réligieuse de Montréal* 89 (Mar. 1930): 180; quoted in ibid., 259.
91. Ibid., 261.
92. Ibid., 262–63.
93. Richard Jones, *L'Idéologie de l'Action Catholique (1917–1939)*, Histoire et sociologie de la culture, no. 9 (Quebec: Les Presses de l'Université Laval, 1974), 26. See also Jean Hulliger, *L'enseignement social des évêques Canadiens de 1891 à 1950* (Montreal: Fides, 1957).
94. The third of these editorials, from 19 May 1926, was reprinted as "Questions des écoles à Montréal," *L'Action Française* 15, no. 6 (1926): 379–81. See also Antonio Huot, *La Question juive: Quelques observations sur la question du meurtre rituel* (Quebec: Action Social Catholique, 1914).
95. "Questions des écoles": 380.
96. Marc Hébert, "La Presse de

Québec et les juifs 1925–1939: Le cas du *Soleil* et du *Quebec Chronicle Telegraph*" (Mémoire présenté à la faculté des études supérieures de l'Université Laval pour l'obtention du grade de maitre d'art, Oct. 1994), 23.

97. *Le Soleil*, 3 Feb. 1926; quoted in ibid., 23.
98. *Le Soleil*, 5 Feb. 1926; quoted in ibid., 25.
99. Jones, *Action Catholique*, 293.
100. Ibid., 295.
101. Dupont, *Les Relations*, 261.
102. Quoted in Jones, *Action Catholique*, 295.
103. Quoted in ibid., 264.
104. Vigod, *Taschereau*, 160.
105. David Rome, "The Political Consequences of the Jewish School Question, Montreal, 1925–1933," CJHSJ/SHJCJ 1, no. 1 (1977): 3–15, 12–13.
106. Cornelius J. Jaenen, "Thoughts on French and Catholic Anti-Semitism," CJHSJ/SHJCJ 1, no. 1 (1977): 16–23, 22–23.
107. CJC, 17 Apr. 1931.
108. See Rosenberg, *Canada's Jews*, 270; Dupont, *Les Relations*, 272–73.
109. For an excellent brief survey of some of these controversies, see Donald Swainson, "Franklin Walker, Separate Schools and the Question of Canadian Identity," QQ 96, no. 1 (1989): 14–21.
110. CJC, 27 May 1927.
111. Ibid., 10 Jan. 1930.
112. Ibid., 20 Mar. 1925.

Chapter 4/"Rag Trade": The Clothing Industry in Flux

1. See Jacques Rouillard, "Les travailleurs juifs de la confection à Montréal (1910–1980)," L/Let 8/9 (1981/82): 253–59.
2. These transformations are described and carefully analysed in Veronica Strong-Boag, *The New Day Recalled: Lives of Girls and Women in English Canada, 1919–1939* (Toronto: Copp Clark, 1988), especially 61–63, 85–86, 14–15. See also Graham S. Lowe, "Women, Work, and the Office: The Feminization of Clerical Occupations in Canada, 1901–1931," in Veronica Strong-Boag and Anita Clair Fellman, eds., *Rethinking Canada: The Premise of Women's History*, 2d ed. (Toronto: Copp Clark, 1991): 269–85.
3. David Monod, "Store Wars: Canadian Retailing in Transition, 1919–1939" (Ph.D. thesis, University of Toronto, 1988), 5.
4. Salo W. Baron, *The Russian Jew under Tsars and Soviets* (New York: Macmillan, 1964), 98.
5. Ruth Frager, *Sweatshop Strife: Class, Ethnicity, and Gender in the Jewish Labour Movement of Toronto 1900–1939* (Toronto: University of Toronto Press, 1992), 43.
6. I am indebted to L. G. Laviolette, former director of the Montreal Men's Clothing Manufacturers' Association, for this memorable phrase.

7. See Mercedes Steedman, "Skill and Gender in the Canadian Clothing Industry," in Craig Heron and Robert Storey, eds., *On the Job: Confronting the Labour Process in Canada* (Montreal: McGill-Queen's University Press, 1986): 152–76, 153.
8. Alan Wilson, *John Northway: A Blue Serge Canadian* (Toronto: Burns & MacEachern, 1965); *Report of the Royal Commission on Price Spreads and Mass Buying* (Ottawa: King's Printer, 1935), *passim*.
9. Gerald Tulchinsky, "Hidden Among the Smokestacks," in David Keane, ed., *Essays in Honour of J. M. S. Careless* (Toronto: Dundurn Press, 1990): 257–84.
10. Gerald Tulchinsky, *Taking Root: The Origins of the Canadian Jewish Community* (Toronto: Lester Publishing, 1992), 133.
11. RCPSMB, *passim*.
12. An excellent examination of this problem can be found in Robert McIntosh, "Sweated Labour: Female Workers in Industrializing Canada," L/Let 32 (1993): 105–38.
13. NAC, DLP, V, 333, folder 24 (81), S. Gariepy to Deputy Minister of Labour, 29 Dec. 1924; quoted in Veronica Strong-Boag, "The Girl of the New Day: Canadian Working Women in the 1920s," L/Let 4, no. 4 (1979): 131–64, 154.
14. Michael Brecher, "Patterns of Accommodation in the Men's Garment Industry of Quebec, 1914–1950 (with Special Reference to the Urban Sector of the Industry)," in H. D. Woods, ed., *Patterns of Industrial Dispute Settlement in Five Canadian Industries* (Montreal: McGill University Industrial Relations Centre, 1958).
15. RCPSMB, *Evidence*, 4315.
16. Arthur D. Hart, ed., *The Jew in Canada: A Complete Record of Canadian Jewry from the Days of the French Regime to the Present Time* (Montreal: Jewish Publications Limited, 1926): 343.
17. Ibid.: 357, 199.
18. Ibid.: 357.
19. Ibid.: 199; see also Zvi Cohen, ed., *Canadian Jewry: Prominent Jews of Canada—A History of Canadian Jewry, Especially of the Present Time, through Reviews and Biographical Sketches* (Toronto: Canadian Jewish Historical Publishing Company, 1933): 255.
20. Cohen, *Prominent Jews*: 124, and Hart, *Jew in Canada*: 565, 134.
21. Cohen, 126.
22. Arthur A. Chiel, *The Jews in Manitoba* (Toronto: University of Toronto Press, 1961), 60.
23. Ibid., 61.
24. "In a Dress Factory," *The Worker*, 12 Sept. 1925; quoted in Strong-Boag, "Girl of the New Day": 141.
25. Minutes of ILGWU Convention, Philadelphia, 1916, 46–47.

26. Minutes of ILGWU Convention, Cleveland, 1914, 162.
27. Lewis Levitzki Lotwin, *The Women's Garment Workers: A History of the International Ladies' Garment Workers Union* (New York: B. W. Huebsch, 1925), 320–29.
28. Ibid., 351.
29. *Montreal Star*, 23 Jan. 1925.
30. *La Presse*, 3 Feb. 1925.
31. Ibid.
32. Ibid., 20 Feb. 1925.
33. *Mail and Empire*, 5 Feb. 1925.
34. *Toronto Telegram*, 6 Feb. 1925.
35. *Globe*, 9 Feb. 1925.
36. *Montreal Star*, 6 Feb. 1925.
37. *La Presse*, 2 Mar. 1925.
38. According to Louis Rosenberg, *Canada's Jews: A Social and Economic Study of the Jews in Canada in the 1930s*, Morton Weinfeld, ed. (Montreal and Kingston: McGill-Queen's University Press, 1993): 365, there was a total of 5,059 Jewish workers in the whole Montreal "textile goods and clothing" industry, or 28.68 percent of all workers. Jacques Rouillard estimated Jewish participation at around 30 percent in "Les travailleurs juifs": 254. But as Ruth Frager points out, Rosenberg lumped together textile goods and clothing "despite the fact that relatively few Jews were involved in the production of textile goods" (*Sweatshop Strife*, 233, fn. 25). She calculates that Jewish participation in the Toronto clothing industry (not including the textile-goods industry) in 1931 was 46.04 percent (compared with Rosenberg's estimate of 36.09 percent for clothing and textile goods, a difference of 27.56 percent). A careful calculation of disaggregated census data supplied by Statistics Canada shows that male and female Jews constituted 35.3 percent of all workers in the Montreal clothing industry (Statistics Canada, Microfilm 11-016-107).
39. *La Patrie*, 17 Feb. 1930; *Montreal Star*, 14 Feb. 1930.
40. *Montreal Star*, 27 Feb. 1930.
41. Ibid., 25 Feb. 1930.
42. *Toronto Telegram*, 13 Mar., 1930; see also LG (1930): Apr., 379; May, 447.
43. LG (1933): 627.
44. Ibid.: 217.
45. Ibid.
46. One of the best brief accounts of the Depression in Canada is contained in Robert Bothwell, Ian Drummond, and John English, *Canada 1900–1945* (Toronto: University of Toronto Press, 1987), 245–77. Much fuller treatments are provided by H. Blair Neatby, *The Politics of Chaos: Canada in the Thirties* (Toronto: Macmillan, 1972); and John Herd Thompson and Allen Seager, *Canada 1922–1939* (Toronto: McClelland and Stewart, 1985), 193–302.

47. CJC, 2 Jan. 1931.
48. Ibid., 30 Oct. 1931.
49. Ibid., 13 Nov. 1931.
50. David Rome, ed., *Our Archival Record of 1933: Hitler's Year*, Canadian Jewish Archives, New Series, no. 5 (Montreal: Canadian Jewish Congress National Archives, 1976): 61, 64.
51. Ibid.: 67.
52. CJC, 23 Nov. 1934; CJR, 16 Nov. 1934.
53. CJC, 23 Jan. 1931.
54. RCPSMB, 109, 112.
55. Bernard Vigod, *Quebec Before Duplessis: The Political Career of Louis-Alexandre Taschereau* (Montreal: McGill-Queen's University Press, 1986), 132–35.
56. Bernard Shane, "Great Moments," in *Les Midinettes 1937–1962* (Montreal: Montreal Joint Board International Ladies' Garment Workers Union, 1961): 110.
57. LG (1926): 167; (1927): 204; (1929): 215.
58. RCPSMB, *Evidence*, 4313.
59. *Statistical Yearbook of Quebec* (1924), 359; (1932), 356.
60. RCPSMB, *Evidence*, 4311.
61. Ibid.
62. Among the manufacturers of higher-quality men's clothing, the use of these contractors was limited and the controlled "inside shop" was prevalent.
63. RCPSMB, 115–16.
64. "Interview by B. Ferneyhough with Leah Roback," in Irving Abella and David Millar, eds., *The Canadian Worker in the Twentieth Century* (Toronto: Oxford University Press, 1978): 198–203.
65. CJC, 13 Mar. 1931.
66. Ibid., 6 Feb. 1931.
67. Ibid., 24 Apr. 1931.
68. Ibid., 1 May 1931; 27 Jul. 1934.
69. Ibid., 23 Oct. 1931.
70. Stephen A. Speisman, *The Jews of Toronto: A History to 1937* (Toronto: McClelland and Stewart, 1979), 336.
71. LG (1933): 1183.
72. For a detailed study of the Communist IUNTW's organizing drive and its ability to provide its members, especially women, with control over shop issues, see Mercedes Steedman, "The Promise: Communist Organizing in the Needle Trades, the Dressmakers' Campaign, 1928–1937," L/Let 34 (Fall 1994): 37–73; and Mercedes Steedman, *Angels of the Workplace: Women and the Construction of Gender Relations in the Canadian Clothing Industry, 1890–1940* (Toronto: Oxford University Press, 1997), 142–89.
73. LG (1935): *passim*.
74. Yvette Charpentier, "Emancipation," in *Midinettes*: 18, 80.
75. See Rose Pesotta, *Bread Upon the Waters* (New York: Dodd, Mead & Co., 1941), 253–77; and Rose Pesotta, "The Beginning," in *Midinettes*: 70–71.

76. CJC, 6 Jul. 1934.
77. Andrée Lévesque, *Virage à gauche interdit: Les communistes, les socialistes et leurs ennemis au Québec 1929–1939* (Montreal: Boréal Express, 1984), 54. On the Workers' Unity League see Bryan D. Palmer, *Working Class Experience: Rethinking the History of Canadian Labour, 1800–1991* (Toronto: McClelland and Stewart, 1992), 228–29, 253–55.
78. *The History of the Labour Movement in Québec* (Montreal: Black Rose Books, 1987), 129.
79. CJC, 9 Mar. 1934.
80. Ibid.
81. Eli Gottesman, ed., *Who's Who in Canadian Jewry* (Montreal: Central Rabbinical Seminary of Canada, 1965): 95. Rabbi Bender was the editor of the *Chronicle* from 1931 to 1936. But see Lewis Levendel, *A Century of the Canadian Jewish Press: 1880s–1980s* (Ottawa: Borealis Press, 1989), 59.
82. CJC, 9 Mar. 1934.
83. CJR, 2 Mar. 1934; see also "Every Friday" and "More About Jewish Anti-Semitism," CJR, 23 Feb. 1934.
84. CJR, 9 Mar. 1934.
85. CJC, 29 Jun. 1934.
86. Ibid., 11 Jan. 1935.
87. Irving Abella, ed., "Portrait of a Jewish Professional Revolutionary: The Recollections of Joshua Gershman," L/Let 2 (1977): 201.
88. Jack Cohen, "Shmatas, Syndicates and Strikes: The Organization of the Dress Industry in Montreal Between 1930 and 1940" (B.A. Honours thesis, Concordia University, 1984), 48.
89. Ibid., 35, 45.
90. CJC, 11 Jan. 1935.
91. Ibid., 27 Sept. 1935.
92. David Rome, ed., *The Jewish Congress Archival Record of 1934*, Canadian Jewish Archives, New Series, no. 6 (Montreal: Canadian Jewish Congress National Archives, 1976): 13.
93. Ibid.: 18.
94. Ibid.: 21.
95. Workmen's Circle of Hamilton to Caiserman, 18 Mar. 1935; quoted in ibid.: 63.
96. Ibid.: 80.
97. David Rome, ed., *The Jewish Congress Archival Record of 1936*, Canadian Jewish Archives, New Series, no. 8 (Montreal: Canadian Jewish Congress National Archives, 1978): 5, 28.
98. Ibid.: 105.
99. CJC, 5 Jun. 1936.
100. Louis Rosenberg, "Montreal Jews in Industry," CJC, 17 Jan. 1936; see also Louis Rosenberg, "How Montreal Jews Earn a Living," CJC, 27 Dec. 1935.
101. Interview with Rabbi Harry J. Stern in Montreal, Jul. 1981.
102. CJC, 17 Mar. 1933.
103. Ibid., 23 Apr. 1937.
104. LG (1934): 302.

105. CJC, 8 Jan. 1937.
106. Ibid., 23 Apr. 1937.
107. Ibid.
108. Ibid., 30 Apr. 1937.
109. "Dressmakers Strike Is on the Verge of Being Settled," KA, 18 Apr. 1937; quoted in Cohen, "Shmatas, Syndicates and Strikes," 71.
110. "Why I Left the Manufacturers' Guild," KA, 28 Apr. 1937; quoted in ibid., 79.
111. Gemma Gagnon, "La Syndicatisation des femmes dans l'industrie Montréalaise du vêtement, 1936–1937" (M.A. thesis, Université du Québec à Montréal, 1990), 23.
112. Evelyn Dumas, *The Bitter Thirties in Québec* (Montreal: Black Rose Books, 1975), 58.
113. Ibid., 59.
114. Pesotta, *Bread*, 253.
115. Ibid., 261.
116. Ibid., 266–67.
117. Ibid., 161. Gagnon, "Syndicatisation," 123.
118. CJC, 30 Apr. 1937.
119. Aldea Guillemette, "Forward," in *Midinettes*: 65, 66.
120. Pesotta, *Bread*, 261.
121. CJR, 1 Jan. 1937.
122. Shane, "Great Moments," in *Midinettes*: 118.
123. CJCNA, Caiserman Papers, vol. 2, 2/13, "Amalgamated Clothing Workers Union, 1936–1943," F. White to Allan Bronfman, 11 May 1937.
124. Catherine Macleod, "Women in Production: The Toronto Dressmakers' Strike of 1931," in Janice Acton, Penny Goldsmith, and Bonnie Shepard, eds., *Women at Work in Ontario, 1850–1930* (Toronto: Women's Press Publications, 1974): 309–29, 310. On the Toronto clothing industry see Daniel Hiebert, "Discontinuity and the Emergence of Flexible Production: Garment Production in Toronto, 1901–1931," *Economic Geography* (July 1990): 229–53.
125. Macleod, "Women in Production": 312.
126. Ibid.: 314.
127. NAC, RG 27, vol. 351, file 79. Microfilm T-2762.
128. Ibid., vol. 361, file 62. Microfilm T-2971.
129. See ibid., vol. 359, file 6. Microfilm T-2969.
130. Ibid., vol. 363, files 165, 166, 171, 173, 174. Microfilm T-2974.
131. Erna Paris, *Jews: An Account of Their Experience in Canada* (Toronto: Macmillan, 1980), 140–41.
132. *Toronto Telegram*, 21 Jul. 1934.
133. *Toronto Weekly Sun*, 28 Jul. 1934.
134. NAC, RG 27, vol. 367, file 10. Microfilm T-2977.
135. Louis Rosenberg, *The Jewish Community of Winnipeg* (Montreal: Canadian Jewish Congress, Bureau of Social and Economic Research, 1946), 59.

136. H. Trachtenberg, "The Role of the Manitoba Jewish Community in Canadian Politics and Labour, 1900–1975" (unpublished paper), 2–3; H. Trachtenberg, "The Winnipeg Jewish Community and Politics: The Interwar Years, 1919–1939," *Historical and Scientific Society of Manitoba Transactions*, ser. 3, nos. 34 and 35 (1977–78 and 1978–79): 138. See also Bruce F. Donaldson, "Sam Herbst, the I.L.G.W.U., and Winnipeg," (Undergraduate essay, University of Manitoba, 1976) and Harry Gale, "The Jewish Labour Movement in Winnipeg," in *A Selection of Papers Presented in 1968–69* (Winnipeg: JHSWC, 1970), 1–14.
137. Interview with Max Enkin, Toronto, 15 Jul. 1976.
138. Ben Dunkelman, *Dual Allegiance* (Toronto: New American Library, 1977), chapter 2.
139. RCPSMB, *Evidence*.
140. A resident of Westmount, Rubin nevertheless retained his membership in a downtown synagogue. He was a member of the Masonic Lodge, B'nai Brith, the Elm Ridge Golf and Country Club, and a strong supporter of the labour-oriented Folk Schule.
141. ACWA (1920–1922).
142. Ibid.: 210.
143. Ibid.: 217.
144. Ibid.: 266.
145. Max Swerdlow, *Brother Max: Labour Organizer and Educator*, Gregory S. Kealey, ed. (St. John's: Committee on Canadian Labour History, 1990): 11–13.
146. CSIS file on Mike Buhay, p.o. 21 RCMP, "Secret and Confidential Re—O.B.U.—General Conditions in Montreal. 18 Dec. 1920." RCMP observers thought that the Amalgamated was "the most radical of all unions" on the continent, and that it included "several members [who] are also very active . . . in the O.B.U. movement. . . ."
147. ACWA (1922–1924): 130–41; (1924–1926): 114–19; *Programme of Seventh Biennial Convention: Amalgamated Clothing Workers of America* (10–15 May 1926): 12.
148. ACWA (1926–28): 48–54, 72–79; (1928–1930): 79–86. See also Adhémar Duquette, "French Canadian Workers Join the Union," in *From Drudgery to Dignity 1915–1955: Montreal Joint Board Fortieth Anniversary* (Montreal, 1955).
149. F. R. Scott and H. M. Cassidy, *Labour Conditions in the Men's Clothing Industry* (Toronto: Thomas Nelson & Sons for the Institute of Pacific Relations, 1935), 5–36.
150. RCPSMB, *Evidence*, 107.
151. Ibid., 114–17.
152. Ibid., 115.
153. Ibid., 121.
154. Ibid., 121, 122.
155. Ibid., 123.

156. Quoted in ibid., 125.
157. RCPSMB, 109.
158. A. E. Grauer, *Labour Legislation* (Ottawa: King's Printer, 1941), 50. See also ACWA (1934–36): 216–22.
159. KA, 17 Jun. 1927, 25 Aug. 1927.
160. ACWA (1932–34): 76–83.
161. Ibid.: (1936–38).
162. See Bruno Ramirez, "Ethnic Studies and Working-Class History," L/Let 19 (1987): 45–48, for an interesting discussion of these issues.

Chapter 5/"The Earth Shall Rise on New Foundations": The Jewish Left in the Interwar Years

1. Irving Abella, ed., "Portrait of a Jewish Professional Revolutionary: The Recollections of Joshua Gershman," L/Let 2 (1977): 185–213, 204.
2. Ibid.: 186.
3. George Seldes, ed., *The Great Quotations* (New York: Lyle Stewart, 1960): 572.
4. Hugh MacLennan, "Canada and the Spanish Civil War," in Bruce Hodgins and Robert Page, eds., *Canadian History Since Confederation: Essays and Interpretations* (Georgetown: Irwin Dorsey, 1979): 549.
5. Donald Avery, *Reluctant Host: Canada's Response to Immigrant Workers, 1896 –1994* (Toronto: McClelland and Stewart, 1995), 65.
6. NAC, RG 146, CSIS, Mike Buhay, 021, RCMP, "Secret and Confidential Re—O.B.U.—General Conditions in Montreal. 18 Dec. 1920." The report stated that "several members of this organization [the Amalgamated] are also very active members in the O.B.U. movement. . . ." See also David J. Bercuson, *Confrontation at Winnipeg: Labour, Industrial Relations and the General Strike* (Montreal: McGill-Queen's University Press, 1990).
7. NAC, RG 146, CSIS, Kon, 39, RNWMP, "Secret and Confidential Report Re:—Louis Kon—Suspect, 5 Sept. 1919."
8. Ibid., 139, "*C.I.B. Memorandum* Ottawa, 17 May 1921. Re:—Louis Kon alias Louis Cohen."
9. NAC, RG 18, vol. 1314, file W.G.S and Riot 1919, I, W. H. M. McLaughlin, *Report Re:—General Conditions of Winnipeg Strike*, 27 May 1919.
10. Ibid., Albert Reames, Report Re:—*General Strike in Winnipeg*, 25 May 1919.
11. Ibid., Courtland Starnes, Crime Report Re: *General Strike in Winnipeg*, 23 Jun. 1919.
12. Ibid., "Secret Memorandum on Revolutionary Tendencies in Western Canada."
13. Gregory S. Kealey and Reg Whitaker, eds., *R.C.M.P. Security Bulletins: The Early Years 1919–1929*

(St. John's: Committee on Canadian Labour History, 1994): 47.

14. Quoted in ibid.: 233.
15. Ibid.: 267.
16. See Lorne and Caroline Brown, *An Unauthorized History of the RCMP* (Toronto: James Lewis and Samuel, 1973), 50–86.
17. Kealey and Whitaker, *Security Bulletins: Early Years*: 316.
18. Suzanne Rosenberg, *A Soviet Odyssey* (Toronto: Oxford University Press, 1988), 31ff.
19. Lita-Rose Betcherman, *The Little Band: The Clashes Between the Communists and the Political and Legal Establishments in Canada, 1928–1932* (Ottawa: Deneau, 1982), 7–8; and Ian Angus, *Canadian Bolsheviks: The Early Years of the Communist Party of Canada* (Montreal: Vanguard Publications, 1981), 77. See also William Rodney, *Soldiers of the International: A History of the Communist Party of Canada 1919–1929* (Toronto: University of Toronto Press, 1968), *passim*; *Toronto Daily Star*, 13 Aug. 1968; CSIS file on Spector, 427.
20. Bryan D. Palmer, *Working Class Experience: Rethinking the History of Canadian Labour, 1800–1991* (Toronto: McClelland and Stewart, 1992), 227.
21. Angus, *Canadian Bolsheviks*, 77.
22. Tim Buck, *Yours in the Struggle: Reminiscences of Tim Buck* (Toronto: NC Press, 1977), 99, 104.
23. See Angus, *Canadian Bolsheviks*, 339–56.
24. Ivan Avakumovic, *The Communist Party in Canada: A History* (Toronto: McClelland and Stewart, 1975), 23.
25. Angus, *Canadian Bolsheviks*, 178.
26. Quoted in ibid., 104.
27. NAC, RG 146, CSIS, Spector, 193; E. G. Frere "Secret Report Re YCL–Toronto, Ont. International Youth Day, 8 Sept. 1924," 193.
28. Ibid., 053, A. W. Duffus, "Secret and Confidential Report Re Young Jewish Socialist Club—216 Beverley Street, Toronto," 22 Nov. 1921.
29. Ibid., 072.
30. Ibid., E. G. Frere "Secret Report Re YCL."
31. Avakumovic, *Communist Party*, 57.
32. Buck, *Yours in the Struggle*, 99, 104.
33. Avakumovic, *Communist Party*, 55.
34. Buck, *Yours in the Struggle*, 130–31.
35. *Workers Vanguard*, 26 Aug. 1968; NAC, RG 146, CSIS, Spector, 433.
36. NAC, RG 146, CSIS, Spector, 193; C. D. LaNauze, "Secret Re Maurice Spector," 3 Dec. 1929.
37. Spector to Shachtman, Oct. 1932, Max Shachtman Papers, Tamiment Institute, New York University, *passim*. I am indebted to my colleague, Bryan Palmer, for providing me with photocopies of this correspondence.
38. *New York Times*, 2 Aug. 1968.

See also Angus, *Canadian Bolsheviks*, 201–24, for an extended discussion of this transformation.

39. This paragraph is based on the research of Joan Sangster, *Dreams of Equality: Women on the Canadian Left, 1920–1950*, Canadian Social History Series (Toronto: McClelland and Stewart, 1989), and Louise Watson, *She Never Was Afraid: The Biography of Annie Buller* (Toronto: Progress Books, 1976).
40. See Catherine Vance, *Not by Gods but by People: The Story of Bella Hall Gauld* (Toronto: Progress Books, 1968), which provides useful information on the early years of the Montreal Labour College.
41. Sangster, *Dreams of Equality*, 67.
42. NAC, RG 146, CSIS, Mike Buhay, 103. RCMP Toronto, 10 Jun. 1923, "Report Re M Buhay—Communist Party of Canada—Montreal, Quebec.
43. Ibid., 031. F. S. Belsher, "Crime Report Re:—Communist Party—Ottawa, Ont., 7 Sept. 1921." See also Gregory S. Kealey and Reg Whitaker, eds., *RCMP Security Bulletins: The War Series, Part 2, 1942–45* (St. John's: Committee on Canadian Labour History, 1993): 150.
44. Ibid.: 359–61.
45. Ibid.: 361. See also Gregory S. Kealey and Reg Whitaker, eds., *R.C.M.P. Security Bulletins: The Depression Years, Part 2, 1935* (St. John's: Committee on Canadian Labour History, 1995): 84–85.
46. Ruth A. Frager, *Sweatshop Strife: Class, Ethnicity, and Gender in the Jewish Labour Movement of Toronto 1900–1939* (Toronto: University of Toronto Press, 1992), 160.
47. Ibid., 174–76ff.
48. Ruth A. Frager, "Politicized Housewives in the Jewish Communist Movement of Toronto, 1923–1933," in Linda Kealey and Joan Sangster, eds., *Beyond the Vote: Canadian Women and Politics* (Toronto: University of Toronto Press, 1989): 258–75, 260.
49. Ibid.: 261.
50. Robert Bothwell, Ian Drummond, and John English, *Canada 1900–1945* (Toronto: University of Toronto Press, 1987), 248; James Struthers, "Great Depression," *The Canadian Encyclopedia*, vol. 2, 2d ed. (Edmonton: Hurtig, 1988): 933.
51. Ibid.: 934.
52. See Max Swerdlow, *Brother Max: Labour Organizer and Educator* (St. John's: Committee on Canadian Labour History, 1990), 1–18.
53. Gregory S. Kealey and Reg Whitaker, eds., *R.C.M.P. Security Bulletins: The Depression Years, Part 1, 1933–34* (St. John's: Committee on Canadian Labour History, 1993): 290–91, 298.
54. NAC, RG 146, CSIS, 85-A-88, H. A. R. Gagnon to Commissioner, 15 Feb. 1940;

quoted in Paul Axelrod, "Spying on the Young in Depression and War: Students, Youth Groups and the RCMP, 1935–1942," L/Let 35 (spring 1995): 43–63, 54. For an excellent, though irreverent, overview of the RCMP and its rigorous surveillance of Communists and other Canadian leftists, see Brown, *Unauthorized History*.

55. Avakumovic, *Communist Party*, 35.
56. Betcherman, *The Little Band*, 164.
57. NAC, RG 146, CSIS, ICOR, S. T. Wood, "Secret Memorandum Re Edmonton 'ICOR' Committee," 13 Dec. 1934. See also Robert Weinberg, *Stalin's Forgotten Zion: Birobidjan and the Making of a Soviet Jewish Homeland: An Illustrated History, 1928–1956* (Berkeley: University of California Press, 1998); and Henry Srebrnik, "Red Star over Birobidjan: Canadian Communists and the 'Jewish Autonomous Region' in the Soviet Union" (Paper delivered to the Canadian Jewish History Conference, York University, Jun. 1998).
58. NAC, RG 146, CSIS, ICOR, 497 "R.C.M.P., 'D' Division. Manitoba district. Winnipeg, Man., 14 Oct. 1927. Secret: Man. Dist. 100 W-28. Report Re Workmen's Circle-Jewish Organization Winnipeg. Re Article taken from the Israelite Press of 7 Oct. 1927," 480.
59. Srebrnik, "Red Star," 2.
60. NAC, RG 146, CSIS, Society to Aid Jewish Colonization to the USSR, ICOR file: Wm. MacDonald "Report Re ICOR Committee Edmonton, Alberta," 10 Dec. 1931.
61. Srebrnik, "Red Star," 4.
62. Kealey and Whitaker, *Security Bulletins: Depression, Part 1*: 175.
63. NAC, RG 146, CSIS, Society to Aid Jewish Colonization to USSR, ICOR, S. T. Wood, Secret Memorandum Re ICOR (Jewish Colonization Organization in Russia), 14 Nov. 1935.
64. Ibid., F. W. Davis, Secret Re ICOR, 6 Nov. 1935.
65. Ibid., J. C. Bain, Secret Re ICOR (Jewish Colonization Organization in Russia), 11 Nov. 1935. Ibid., R. W. Buchanan, Secret Re ICOR (Jewish Colonization Organization in Russia), 12 Nov. 1935.
66. Ibid., R. R. Tait, "Secret Re Edmonton ICOR Committee," 13 Dec. 1934.
67. Ibid., S. T. Wood, "Secret Re Edmonton ICOR Committee," 13 Dec. 1934.
68. Ibid., S. C. Coggles, "Secret Re Edmonton ICOR Committee," 24 Oct. 1934.
69. Ibid., J. H. McBrien, "Secret and Personal Re ICOR Committee," to Commissioner of Customs, Department of National Revenue, Ottawa, 28 Dec. 1931.

70. Ibid., Spector, 367.
71. Ibid.
72. Candace Falk, ed., *Emma Goldman: A Guide to Her Life and Documentary Sources* (Cambridge: Chadwyck-Healey, 1995): 93. Ben Kayfetz to Gerald Tulchinsky, 17 Jul. 1997.
73. Richard Drinnan, *Rebel in Paradise: A Biography of Emma Goldman* (Chicago: University of Chicago, 1961), 261.
74. Quoted in Alice Wexler, *Emma Goldman in Exile: From the Russian Revolution to the Spanish Civil War* (Boston: Beacon, 1989), 120.
75. Falk, *Emma Goldman*: 94.
76. Justice Robert Taschereau and Justice R. L. Kellock, *Report of the Royal Commission Appointed Under Order-in-Council P.C. 411 of February 5, 1946, to investigate the facts relating to and the circumstances surrounding the communication, by public officials and other persons in positions of trust, of secret and confidential information to agents of a foreign power. June 27, 1946*. (Ottawa: King's Printer, 1946), 112.
77. Ibid.
78. Fred Rose, *Spying on Labor* (Toronto: New Era Publishers, 1939).
79. Ibid. This pamphlet was published by the Dominion Committee of the CPC and printed in Toronto.
80. Fred Rose, *Hitler's Fifth Column in Quebec* (Toronto: Communist-Labor Total War Committee, 1942). The French edition, *La Cinquième colonne d'Hitler dans Québec* (Progrès de Villeray, n.d.), included a lengthy, detailed letter from Rose rebutting an editorial in *Le Devoir* (7 Dec. 1942) that denied Rose's charges. He had published an earlier pamphlet, *Fascism Over Canada*, covering the subject in the 1930s.
81. CJC, 15 Feb. 1946.
82. See Myer Smiatycki, "Communism in One Constituency: The Election of Fred Rose in Montreal-Cartier, 1943 and 1945" (Graduate essay, York University, 1978); and J. K. Johnson, ed., *The Canadian Directory of Parliament, 1867–1967* (Ottawa: Public Archives of Canada, 1968): 505.
83. CJCNA, Fred Rose Papers, "Letter from a hero's mother to the mothers and fathers of Cartier" (Leaflet, 1943).
84. Ibid., "You and Fred Rose Can Build a Better Cartier" (Leaflet, 1943).
85. Ibid., *Fred Rose in Parliament* (in Yiddish); *Le Masque Tombé*; and *La Menace du chaos: Le Complot Tory contre le Canada*.
86. Taschereau and Kellock, *Royal Commission*, 116.
87. Johnson, *Canadian Directory of Parliament*: 505.
88. For the case of Professor Israel Halperin of the Department of Mathematics at Queen's

University, see Frederick W. Gibson, *1917–1961: To Serve and Yet Be Free*, vol. 2 of *Queen's University* (Kingston and Montreal: McGill-Queen's University Press, 1983), 277–84.

89. Taschereau and Kellock, *Royal Commission*, 97.
90. Ibid., 98.
91. Ibid., 102–03.
92. J. L. Granatstein and David Stafford, *Spy Wars: Espionage and Canada from Gouzenko to Glasnost* (Toronto: Key Porter, 1990), 48.
93. See Reg Whitaker and Gary Marcuse, *Cold War Canada: The Making of a National Insecurity State, 1945–1957* (Toronto: University of Toronto Press, 1994), 71–73, 97, 209, 239.
94. Shloime Perel, "History of the UJPO in Canada, 1926–1949," chapter 12, 2. This work is part of a Ph.D. thesis in progress at McMaster University, Department of Sociology.
95. Kealey and Whitaker, *Security Bulletins: Depression, Part 2*: 92–93.
96. Ibid.: 635–36.
97. Gregory S. Kealey and Reg Whitaker, eds., *R.C.M.P. Security Bulletins: The Depression Years, Part 3, 1936* (St. John's: Committee on Canadian Labour History, 1996): 210.
98. Ibid.: 52, 66, 180, 361, 396, 434.
99. Ibid.: 296, 319, 344, 354.
100. Gregory S. Kealey and Reg Whitaker, eds., *R.C.M.P. Security Bulletins: The Depression Years, Part 4, 1937* (St. John's: Committee on Canadian Labour History, 1997): 291–92.
101. Ibid.: 10, 17.
102. Perel, "UJPO in Canada," chapter 13, 5.
103. Ibid., chapter 16, 16.
104. Abella, "Jewish Professional Revolutionary": 204, 208.
105. Gregory S. Kealey and Reg Whitaker, eds., *R.C.M.P. Security Bulletins: The War Series, 1939–1941* (St. John's: Committee on Canadian Labour History, 1989): 27.
106. Ibid.
107. Ibid.: 106.
108. Eli Gottesman, ed., *Who's Who in Canadian Jewry* (Montreal: Central Rabbinical Seminary of Canada, 1965): 335.
109. Kealey and Whitaker, *Security Bulletins: War Series, 1939–1941*: 120.
110. See Doug Smith, *Joe Zuken: Citizen and Socialist* (Toronto: James Lorimer, 1990).
111. As late as 1995, the Canadian Security Intelligence Service exempted many sections of its 769-page file on the UJPO from the Access to Information Act, presumably still wanting to protect its sources for information on Jewish radicals of the 1930s and 1940s. It is important to note that those sources were almost certainly Jewish and other involved unidentified persons who

were employed on a continuing basis to translate from Yiddish to English. In discussing the identity of M. H. A., who translated Yiddish documents for the RCMP, Ben Kayfetz writes, "When I lived in Ottawa [in] 1943–1945 I met a man named Arnoni who was employed by the RCMP as translator of Yiddish and various other languages. . . . Arnoni was a Jew from Eastern Europe who attended university in Belgium and migrated to Canada. He was a Zionist and attended Zionist meetings. . . . Could he be MHA? Sounds likely." Ben Kayfetz to Gerald Tulchinsky, 17 Jul. 1997.

112. NAC, RG 146, CSIS, UJPO, "Second National Convention of the United Jewish People's Order. Held in Montreal, Que., on 20–22 Jun. 1947. Convention Book . . . Editor: H. Guralnick."
113. Ibid., 49. "Jewish Aid Society of Montreal, 23-9-46, Re: *Canadian Jewish Weekly*, vol. 6, no. 308, Toronto, Ont., 19 Sept. 1946."
114. Abella, "Jewish Professional Revolutionary": 185–213.
115. See Helmut Kallman, Gilles Potvin, and Kenneth Winters, eds., *Encyclopedia of Music in Canada* (Toronto: University of Toronto Press, 1981): 921.
116. NAC, RG 146, CSIS, UJPO, 51, "Jewish Aid Society of Montreal, 23-9-46, Re: *Canadian Jewish Weekly*, vol. 6, no. 308, Toronto, Ont., 19 Sept. 1946."
117. Perel, "UJPO in Canada," Conclusion, 4.
118. Ibid., 5.
119. NAC, RG 146, CSIS, UJPO, 51, "Jewish Aid Society of Montreal, 23-9-46, Re: *Canadian Jewish Weekly*, vol. 6, no. 308, Toronto, Ont., 19 Sept. 1946." "United Jewish People's Order Re: *Canadian Jewish Weekly*, vol. 7, no. 322, Toronto, Ont., 26 Dec. 1946."
120. Ibid., 43, N. Courtois, Re Albert E. Kahn, Speaker at Meeting of the United Jewish People's Order Montreal, P.Q., 8-10-46.
121. Ibid., 331. "Yiddish language, Summarized by MHA at R.C.M.P. Headquarters, News 665, 20-1-39. *Der Kamf* (The Struggle), vol. 14, no. 735, Toronto, 27 Jan. 1938."
122. Ibid., 380. "Yiddish language, Summarized by MHA at R.C.M.P. Headquarters, News 1911, 6-5-48. *Canadian Jewish Weekly*, vol. 8, no. 392, Toronto, 29 Apr. 1948."
123. Ibid., 42. "United Jewish People's Order, Re: Albert E. Kahn (Speaker at Meeting of United Jewish People's Order, Montreal, P.Q., 8-10-46)."
124. Ibid., 53. J. E. M. Barrette, "United Jewish People's Order, 7-9-46, Re: Laurentian Vacation Club, Lac des Quartoze [*sic*] Iles, Terrebonne Co., P.Q."

125. Ibid., 70. "Memorandum for File Re: United Jewish People's Order, Canada General, 6-4-45."
126. Ibid., 78. "Communists Organize National Jewish Order."
127. Ibid.
128. Ibid., 89. N. E. McFadyen, "Memorandum to Inspector Leopold Re: United Jewish People's Order, 19-1-45."
129. Ibid., 55. "Yiddish language, Summarized by MHA at R.C.M.P. Headquarters, News 1911, 18-6-46. *Canadian Jewish Weekly*, vol. 6, no. 294, Toronto, 13 Jun. 1946."
130. Kealey and Whitaker, *Security Bulletins: Depression Years, Part 3*: 330.
131. Ibid.: 261. "Yiddish language, Summarized by MHA at R.C.M.P. Headquarters, *Der Kamf* (The Struggle), vol. 13, no. 655, 13 Aug. 1937."
132. Perel, "UJPO in Canada," chapter 23, 5.
133. Ben Kayfetz to Gerald Tulchinsky, 5 Jun. 1998.
134. See Maximilian Hurwitz, *The Workmen's Circle: Its History, Ideals, Organization and Institutions* (New York: Workmen's Circle, 1936); and C. Bezdel Sherman, "Workmen's Circle," EJ, vol. 16: 635.
135. Raphael Patai, *Encyclopedia of Zionism and Israel* (New York: Herzl Press, 1971), vol. 1: 151–52; vol. 2: 893–94.
136. Bernard Figler, "Zionism in Canada," *Encyclopedia of Zionism*, vol. 1: 174–79, 176.
137. Ben Lappin, "May Day in Toronto in the 1930s," *Commentary* 19, no. 5 (1955): 476–79.
138. See David Lewis, *The Good Fight* (Toronto: Macmillan of Canada, 1981), 198.
139. Ibid., 27.
140. Charles Taylor, "Introduction," in Lewis, *The Good Fight*, xi.
141. David Lewis and Frank Scott, *Make This Your Canada: A Review of C.C.F. History and Policy* (Toronto: Central Canada Publishing, 1943).
142. Lewis, *The Good Fight*, 107.
143. Ibid., 107–08.
144. Ibid., 143.
145. Ibid., 151.
146. See Mark Zuehlke, *The Gallant Cause: Canadians and the Spanish Civil War 1936–1939* (Vancouver: Whitecap Books, 1996); Myron Momryk, "'Canadian Jewish Boys in Spain,' Jewish Volunteers from Canada in the Spanish Civil War 1936–39: A Profile" (unpublished paper, 1995), 6.
147. Ibid., 39, fn. 34.
148. Myron Momryk, "Jewish Volunteers from Canada in Loyalist Armed Forces, Including the International Brigades, Spain, 1936–39" (Paper for Canadian Jewish Historical Association meetings in Montreal, 1995).

149. John English, *Shadow of Heaven: The Life of Lester Pearson*, vol. 1: *1897–1948* (Toronto: Lester & Orpen Dennys, 1990), 303, 306.
150. Ivan Avakumovic, *Socialism in Canada: A Study of the CCF–NDP in Federal and Provincial Politics* (Toronto: McClelland and Stewart, 1978), 111.
151. Sandra Djwa, *A Life of F. R. Scott: The Politics of the Imagination* (Vancouver: Douglas and McIntyre, 1987), 171, 176.
152. CJR, 8 Oct. 1937.
153. *Jewish Standard*, Jun. 1937.
154. "Mit Der Kanader Yiddisher Volunteer fun Shpania," *Der Kamf*, n.d. Goldberg fought with the Dimitrov Battalion, which was composed of volunteers from the the Balkans.
155. Momryk, "Jewish Boys in Spain," 6.
156. Quoted in ibid., 19.
157. Ibid., 27.
158. David Rome, ed., *Canadian Jews in World War II, Part 2: Casualties* (Montreal: Canadian Jewish Congress, 1948): 22.
159. The Jewish Legion was made up of three battalions of Jews recruited mainly in North America, Britain, and Egypt to fight in General Allenby's army in Palestine in 1917 and 1918.
160. Yank Levy, *Guerrilla Warfare* (New York: Penguin Books, 1942).
161. CJN, 9 Mar. 1981.
162. CJCNA, Series ZB, S. H. Abramson Papers, Abramson to H. M. Caiserman, 10 Mar. 1938.
163. Ibid., Abramson to Caiserman, 9 May 1938.
164. Ibid., Abramson to Caiserman, 4 Oct. 1938.
165. CJCNA, Series ZB, S. H. Abramson Papers, Abramson to Caiserman, 29 Oct. 1938.
166. Ibid., Abramson to Caiserman, 7 Nov. 1938.
167. Henry L. Feingold, *A Time For Searching: Entering the Mainstream 1920–1945*, Jewish People in America Series (Baltimore: Johns Hopkins University Press, 1992), 221.
168. Ibid., 222.
169. Ibid., 223.
170. Geoffrey Alderman, *The Jewish Community in British Politics* (Oxford: Clarendon Press, 1983), 115.
171. Geoffrey Alderman, *Modern British Jewry* (Oxford: Clarendon Press, 1992), 316.
172. David Cesarani, "The Transformation of Communal Authority in Anglo-Jewry, 1914–1940," in David Cesarani, ed., *The Making of Modern Anglo-Jewry* (London: Basil Blackwell, 1990): 131.
173. Sharman Kadish, *Bolsheviks and British Jews: The Anglo-Jewish Community, Britain and the Russian Revolution* (London: Frank Cass, 1992), 242.
174. Alderman, *Jewish Community in British Politics*, 110.

175. Djwa, *F. R. Scott*, 173.
176. Donald H. Avery, *Reluctant Host: Canada's Response to Immigrant Workers, 1896–1914* (Toronto: McClelland and Stewart, 1995), 114.
177. Gordon Lunan, *The Making of a Spy: A Political Odyssey* (Montreal: Robert Davies, 1995), 29.
178. Ibid., 98. See also 100, 103, 109, 133, 139, on the Jewish radical left in Montreal during the 1930s and 1940s.
179. Kadish, *Bolsheviks and British Jews*, 243.
180. Ibid.

CHAPTER 6/"NOT COMPLEX OR SOPHISTICATED": CHEQUE-BOOK ZIONISM BETWEEN THE WARS

1. See Gerald Tulchinsky, *Taking Root: The Origins of the Canadian Jewish Community* (Toronto: Lester Publishing, 1992), 181–203.
2. See Bernard Figler, *Lillian and Archie Freiman: Biographies* (Montreal, 1962); Arthur D. Hart, ed., *The Jew in Canada: A Complete Record of Canadian Jewry from the Days of the French Regime to the Present Time* (Montreal: Jewish Publications Limited, 1926): 276.
3. Hart, *Jew in Canada*: 317.
4. See Bernard Figler, *Louis Fitch, Q.C.* (Montreal, 1963).
5. Hart, *Jew in Canada*: 318.
6. PAM, MG 10, F3 (MG2J2), Harry Wilder to Chaim Weizmann, 20 Jan. 1932.
7. CZA, KKL5/365, "Minutes of ZOC Convention, 1924," 30; Louis Rosenberg, *Canada's Jews: A Social and Economic Study of the Jews in Canada* (Montreal: Canadian Jewish Congress, Bureau of Social and Economic Research, 1939), 197.
8. See Michael Brown, "The Americanization of Canadian Zionism, 1971–1982," in Geoffrey Wigoder, ed., *Contemporary Jewry: Studies in Honor of Moshe Davis* (Jerusalem: Hebrew University of Jerusalem, 1984): 129–58; "Divergent Paths: Early Zionism in Canada and the United States," JSS 44, no. 2 (1982): 149–68; and "Canada and the Holy Land: Some North American Similarities and Differences," in Moshe Davis and Yehoshua Ben-Arieh, eds., *With Eyes Towards Zion III: Western Societies and the Holy Land* (New York: Praeger, 1991): 77–91.
9. See Michael Berkowitz, *Western Jewry and the Zionist Project, 1914–1933* (Cambridge: Cambridge University Press, 1997), iii.
10. CZA, KKL5/365, "Minutes of the Nineteenth Convention Zionist Organization of Canada Inc., 1924."
11. Archie Freiman's presidential address spoke of the necessity

"to avoid all contentious little differences . . . because of the solidarity which we must present to the world at large."

12. See Gideon Shimoni, *The Zionist Ideology* (Hanover: University Press of New England, 1995).
13. Tulchinsky, *Taking Root,* 181–203.
14. Zachariah Kay, *Canada and Palestine: The Politics of Non-Commitment* (Jerusalem: Israel Universities Press, 1978), 34.
15. WA, 10.7.22, Freiman to Joseph Cowen, 10 Jul. 1922.
16. CZA, Z4/1402, Leon Goldman to Chaim Weizmann, 8 Apr. 1919.
17. Ibid., KKL5/L5/318, Menachem M. Ussishkin to Zlotnick, 11 Mar. 1929.
18. Ibid., Z4/1405, Goldman to Levin, 17 Dec. 1919.
19. Ibid.
20. Ibid., Goldman to Zionist Organization, Central Office, London, 25 Feb. 1920.
21. Ibid., Goldman to B. Goldberg, 24 Dec. 1919.
22. Ibid.
23. See Ibid., KKL5/319'2, Julius Berger to KKL, 27 Dec. 1927; KKL5/379, JNF (New York) to KKL (Jerusalem), 9 Apr. 1926 and 21 Apr. 1926 (translated from the German by Tom Wien).
24. Quoted in Michael Brown, "A Case of Limited Vision: Jabotinsky on Canada and the United States," CJS 1 (1993): 1–25, 3.
25. Ibid.: 4.
26. CZA, KKL5/365, "Minutes, 1924," 3.
27. Ibid.
28. WA, Weizmann to Dr. D. Feiwel, London, 21 Dec. 1923.
29. Ibid., Weizmann to Freiman, 14 Dec. 1922.
30. Ibid., Weizmann to Freiman, 5 Feb. 1923. Weizmann later wrote, "I might add that [Beaverbrook] has somewhat moderated his activities since I wrote to you before, but at the same time, it is very desirable that we should have authentic information about him in reserve, to be used as occasion may demand."
31. Ibid., Freiman to Weizmann, 27 Feb. 1928.
32. Ibid., Freiman to Weizmann, 8 Sept. 1936.
33. Ibid., Freiman to Weizmann, 14 Aug. 1936.
34. Bernard Figler, *History of the Zionist Ideal in Canada* (n.p., 1962). Reprinted from CJC, 3–17 Nov. 1961; George G. Greene, "The Hadassah Organization in Canada," in Louis Rasminsky, ed., *Hadassah Jubilee, Tenth Anniversary Toronto: Hadassah Achievement in Palestine* (Toronto: Hadassah Council, 1927): 136.
35. Greene, "Hadassah Organization": 145; and

"Activities of Hadassah: Girl's Domestic and Agricultural Science School," in Hart, *Jew in Canada*: 282–87.

36. See Frances Swyripa, *Wedded to the Cause: Ukrainian-Canadian Women and Ethnic Identity, 1891–1991* (Toronto: University of Toronto Press, 1993), 13–19.
37. PAM, MG10, F3 (MG2J31), *Canadian Hadassah Silver Jubilee, Western Division 1917–1942* (Winnipeg, 1942).
38. CZA, KKL5/365, "Minutes, 1924," 41.
39. NAC, MG 28, V74, vol. 1, "Minutes of the Third Convention of the Hadassah Organization of Canada. Toronto, 9 Jan. 1924. King Edward Hotel."
40. Rachel Schlesinger, "Volunteers for a Dream," CJHSJ/SHJCJ 10, no. 1 (1988): 20–33.
41. NAC, MG 28, V74, vol. 15, "General Correspondence, Hadassah-WIZO, Jan.–May 1935."
42. Quoted in Schlesinger, "Volunteers": 25.
43. NAC, MG 28, V74, vol.15, "National Executive, 1939," Minutes, 14 Mar. 1939.
44. Quoted in Schlesinger, "Volunteers": 29.
45. Paula J. Draper and Janice B. Karlinsky, "Jewish Women as Volunteers," *Polyphony* 8, nos. 1–2 (1986): 37–39. Janice B. Karlinsky, "The Pioneer Women's Organization: A Case Study of Jewish Women in Toronto" (M.A. thesis, University of Toronto, 1979), 18, 21, 106, 117.
46. Karlinsky, "Pioneer Women's Organization," 145.
47. *Pioneer Women* (Oct. 1935). Quoted in Karlinsky, "Pioneer Women's Organization," 47.
48. Ibid., 51.
49. Ibid., 56.
50. Ibid., 76.
51. Ibid., 62.
52. Moe Levitt, "The Federation of Young Judaea of Canada," in Hart, *Jew in Canada*: 289.
53. CZA, KKL5/365 "Minutes, 1924," 43.
54. Ibid.
55. PAM, MG 10, F3 (MG2J6), *Year Book of Young Judaea, 1931* (Montreal: Federation of Young Judaea, 1931), 7.
56. Ibid., 10.
57. *Jewish History Must Centre on Palestine (A Handbook on Club Leadership for Leaders of Young Judaea and Other Jewish Youth Clubs*, rev. ed. (Montreal: Federation of Young Judaea, 1927), 22.
58. Lionel M. Gelber, "Young Judaea in Canada," in *Hadassah Jubilee*: 177.
59. Ibid.
60. See Samuel Grand, "A History of Zionist Youth Organizations in the United States from Their Inception to 1940" (Ph.D. thesis, Columbia University, 1958).

61. See Ezra Mendelsohn, *Zionism in Poland: The Formative Years, 1915–1926* (New Haven: Yale University Press, 1981), 72, 278–79, 285–99.
62. CJCNA, *Souvenir Program*, Second Annual Dance: Hashomer Clubs of Montreal, 19 Oct. 1924.
63. CJCNA, CJN clipping, 1980.
64. Ariel Hurwitz, ed., *Against the Stream: Seven Decades of Hashomer Hatzair in North America* (Tel Aviv: Hadfush Hachadash, 1994): 7.
65. Ibid.: 51–52.
66. I thank my colleagues, Karen Dubinsky, Marguerite Van Die, and Bryan Palmer, for these insights.
67. Hurwitz, *Against the Stream*: 256.
68. Mendelsohn, *Zionism in Poland*, 320.
69. See Moshe Cohen, "An American Labor Zionist Youth Movement: Yunge Poalei Zion, the 'Young Workers of Zion'," in B. J. Goldberg and Elliot King, eds., *Builders and Dreamers: Habonim Labor Zionist Youth in North America* (New York: Herzl Press, 1993): 39.
70. EJ, vol. 11: 109–11; CZA, KH1/15/1, *Report to Congress* Sept. 1921, "Canada."
71. CZA, KH1/15/1, Keren Hayesod Resolutions of the Convention of the Canadian Zionists in Montreal, 31/1/21.
72. Melvin Urofsky, *American Zionism from Herzl to the Holocaust* (Garden City, N.J.: Anchor Books, 1976), 268–69.
73. See Thomas P. Socknat, *Witness Against War: Pacificism in Canada, 1900–1945* (Toronto: University of Toronto Press, 1987), 125–26.
74. Maurice Eisendrath, *The Never Failing Stream* (Toronto: Macmillan, 1939), 232.
75. Stephen A. Speisman, *The Jews of Toronto: A History to 1937* (Toronto: McClelland and Stewart, 1979), 242.
76. Meyer Weisgal, *So Far: An Autobiography* (Jerusalem: Weidenfeld and Nicholson, 1971), 92.
77. Shloime Perel, "History of the UJPO in Canada, 1926–1949," chapter 9, 8. This work is part of a Ph.D. thesis in progress at McMaster University.
78. Philip Halperin, "Down with the Religious Mold," *Der Kamf* 11 (1929); quoted in ibid., chapter 10, 5.
79. Ibid., 10.
80. CZA, KKL5/318, Dr. M. S. Rady to M. Ussishkin, 20 Feb. 1929.
81. Ibid., KKL5/466, J. L. Zlotnick to M. Ussishkin, 11 Aug. 1931.
82. Ibid.
83. Ibid., National Council of the Z.O.C., 5 Jan. 1931.
84. CZA, S6/1758, Rabbi J. Schwartz to A. Dobkin, Immigration Department of the Jewish Agency, Jerusalem, 10 Jan. 1936.

85. Walter Laqueur, *A History of Zionism* (London: Weidenfeld and Nicholson, 1972), 326–27.
86. CZA, KKL5/318, Zlotnick to Ussishkin, 9 Feb. 1928.
87. In 1923 Rabbi Brickner was reported to have told Arthur Ruppin "that there is a favourable disposition for investments [in Palestine] in Toronto." WA, Arthur Ruppin to Chaim Weizmann, 15 Mar. 1923.
88. Zvi Cohen, ed., *Canadian Jewry: Prominent Jews of Canada — A History of Canadian Jewry, Especially of the Present Time, through Reviews and Biographical Sketches* (Toronto: Canadian Jewish Historical Publishing Company, 1933): 258.
89. Irit Amit, "Business and Zionism" (Paper delivered at the Jewish Geography Conference, University of Maryland, Apr. 1995).
90. I am indebted to Professor Yossi Katz and Dr. Irit Amit, of the geography department at Bar-Ilan University, Israel, for some of this information and for taking me on a tour of the Gan Chayim and Tel Asher areas in July 1993.
91. See Yossi Katz, *The Business of Settlement: Private Entrepreneurship in the Jewish Settlement of Palestine, 1900–1914* (Jerusalem and Ramat-Gan: Magnes Press and Bar-Ilan University Press, 1994), 208, 214.
92. CZA, S6/3814, Jesse Schwartz to J. N. Behar, 30 Apr. 1936.
93. Ibid., Jesse Schwartz to C. Barlas, 25 Oct. 1935 and 1 Nov. 1935.
94. Ben Dunkelman, *Dual Allegiance: An Autobiography* (Toronto: New American Library, 1976), 35, 39.
95. Chaim Weizmann, *Trial and Error: The Autobiography of Chaim Weizmann* (London: H. Hamilton, 1949), 272.
96. WA, Freiman to Weizmann, 22 Dec. 1921.
97. CZA, KH1/15/1, Secretary of Board of Directors, KH to ZOC, 7 Nov. 1922.
98. Ibid., Goldman to KH, London, 20 Nov. 1922.
99. Ibid., KH4/15/2, Goldstein to KH, London, 7 Mar. 1923.
100. Ibid., KH1/15/1, Goldstein to KH, London, 13 Apr. 1923.
101. Ibid., Goldstein to KH, London, 23 Mar. 1923.
102. CJC, 6 Apr. 1923. He criticized his congregants for being "the cause that life's very necessities have been denied to the poor. At this very Passover, when our own Seder tables groan with plenty, the self-respecting Jewish citizen would feel shame and humiliation, if he knew with what miserable parsimony Federation [of Jewish philanthropies] has had to dole out Passover supplies to the poor."
103. CZA, KH4/15/2, Minutes of

Executive Committee, ZOC, 26 Mar. 1923.

104. Ibid., KH4C/763, Goldman to KH, London, 11 Mar. 1924.
105. Ibid., KH to ZOC, 19 Mar. 1924; Leon Goldman to KH, 7 Apr. 1924.
106. Ibid., KH1/15/A2.
107. Ibid.
108. Ibid., KH4C/763, Rebelsky to KH, London, 19 Mar. 1925, translated from the Hebrew.
109. Ibid., KH1/15/1, Dr. Zweig, KKL, The Hague, to KH, London, 3 Mar. 1922.
110. Ibid., Leon Goldman to JNF, The Hague, 22 Mar. 1922.
111. Ibid., Leon Goldman to KH, London, 10 Apr. 1922.
112. Ibid., KKL5/364, KKL to Zlotnick, 14 Feb. 1924.
113. Ibid., Goldman to JNF, Jerusalem, 12 Mar. 1924.
114. Ibid., Head Office of KKL to Leon Goldman, 18 Mar. 1924.
115. Ibid., Zlotnick to JNF, Jerusalem, 29 Jul. 1924.
116. Ibid., KKL5/366, "Report of the Jewish National Fund in Canada for the Period 7 Dec. 1923–8 Dec. 1925."
117. Ibid., "Report to the XIV Congress of the Zionist Organization of Canada, Inc., for the Period 1 Jun. 1923 to 31 May 1925."
118. Ibid., KKL5/364, "Jewish National Fund Activities in Canada for the First Three Months of 1924."
119. Ibid., KKL, Norman Shiffer to Dr. Julius Berger, JNF Bureau, New York, 2 Mar. 1926.
120. Shiffer identified more than two hundred places on the Prairies where only one or two Jewish families lived. CZA, KKL5/375, Shiffer to JNF Bureau, Jerusalem, 8 May 1927.
121. Ibid., "Jewish National Fund Conference: Resolutions Adopted at the Second Annual Conference Held in Watrous, Sask., 1 and 2 Aug. 1926."
122. Ibid., Shiffer to JNF Bureau, Jerusalem, 30 Nov. 1926.
123. Ibid., KKL5/379, Zlotnick to Berger, New York, 16 Mar. 1926.
124. Ibid., KKL5/366, Epstein, Jerusalem, to Caiserman, Montreal, 29 Jun. 1925.
125. Ibid., KKL5/367 and KKL5/366, JNF Bureau, Jerusalem, to Zlotnick, 11 Nov. 1925.
126. Ibid., KKL5/368, Printed reports of Zionist activity in Canada for Winnipeg Convention of ZOC.
127. Ibid., Z4/3589, vol. 6, Memorandum to the Members of the Executive from Colonel Kisch, 28 Aug. 1927.
128. Ibid., KKL5/319, Ussishkin to ZOC, 3 May 1929.
129. Ibid., KKL5/466, Zlotnick to JNF, Jerusalem, n.d.
130. Ibid., KKL5/465, Zlotnick to Elias Epstein, New York, 31 Dec. 1930.
131. Ibid., KKL5/466, Freiman to Ussishkin, 7 Apr. 1932.

132. There is no mention of a Canadian organization in Judah L. Fishman, *The History of the Mizrachi Movement*, Harry Karp, trans. (New York: Mizrachi Hatzair of America, 1928).
133. Ibid., Z4/1405, Leon Goldman to Zionist Organization, Central Office, London, 9 Jun. 1920.
134. Ibid., KH4, B/1548, Note to Mr. Hermann.
135. Ibid., KKL5/318, "Minutes of the Meeting of the National Council of the Zionist Organization of Canada, 19 Dec. 1927."
136. Ibid., KKL5/3192.
137. See A.B.B. [probably Archie Bennett], "The Mizrachi Holdup," CJR, 22 Mar. 1929.
138. CZA, KKL5/3192, Zlotnick to Ussishkin, Jerusalem, 23 Apr. 1929.
139. Ibid., KH4, B/555, Samuel Schwisberg to Leib Yaffe, London, 9 Mar. 1940.
140. Brown, "Case of Limited Vision": 9–10.
141. In 1931 even the ZOC's executive director, Rabbi Judah Zlotnick, supported Jabotinsky at a Zionist Congress meeting. Ibid., 13.
142. CZA, KH4, B/555, extracts from *Jewish Daily Bulletin*, 9 Mar. 1936.
143. Beit Jabotinsky, Archives (Tel Aviv), 2/1/40 G, Executive Committee, World Union of Zionist Revisionists to Union of Zionist-Revisionists Canada, 9 Oct. 1931.
144. Ibid., A.J.F. to Zionist-Revisionists of Canada, 29 Dec. 1932.
145. Ibid., 1/1/40 G, "Programme for the Winter Activities," Zionist-Revisionists of Canada, Central Committee.
146. PAM, MG10, F3 (MG6A10), Extracts from the diary of H. L. and M. Wiedman, *Impressions of Eretz Israel 1923* (Winnipeg: Israelite Press, 1923).
147. Kenneth I. Cleator and Harry J. Stern, *Harry Joshua Stern: A Rabbi's Journey* (New York: Bloch Publishing Company, 1981), 97.
148. WA, Freiman to Weizmann, 10 Jun. 1929.
149. CZA, KH4/B/548, Minutes of the National Council of the Zionist Organization of Canada, 21 Nov. 1927. Report of Mr. Meyerson.
150. Ibid., KKL5/366, "Summary of Report Western Trip. 6 Aug. to 13 Dec. 1925," enclosed by Hananiah Caiserman to Mr. Epstein, Jerusalem, 25 Dec. 1925.
151. Ibid.
152. Ibid., KKL5/374, E. M. Epstein, Jerusalem, to H. Caiserman, 20 Aug. 1925.
153. Ibid.
154. Ibid., S5/468, "Joint Statement of the Zionist Organizations in Canada," Special Meeting of the National Council of the ZOC and the National Executives of the Poale-Zion-Zeire Zion

Organization of Canada and the Mizrachi Organization of Canada, 10 Jul. 1938.

155. WA, Weizmann to Freiman, 8 Jul. 1934.
156. See Jacob Katzman, *Commitment: The Labor Zionist Lifestyle in America* (New York, 1976).
157. See Rosenberg, *Canada's Jews*, 160 and chapter 19.

Chapter 7 / Antisemitism from the Twenties to the Forties

1. CJC, 26 Jun. 1925.
2. Ibid., 2 Jul. 1920; 1 Apr. 1927; 30 Sept. 1927; 1 Jul. 1921; 31 Dec. 1926.
3. Ibid., 17 Feb. 1922.
4. Ibid., 17 Jun. 1921; 1 Jul. 1921; 4 May 1923.
5. Ibid., 12 Nov. 1920.
6. Ibid., 15 Dec. 1923.
7. Ibid., 1 Feb. 1924.
8. Ibid., 2 Nov. 1923.
9. Ibid., 26 Aug. 1921.
10. H. Murphy to S. W. Jacobs, 13 Mar. 1924. Quoted in CJC, 28 Mar. 1924.
11. Henri Leroux, *L'Actualité économique* 2, no. 3 (1926): 9–11.
12. Ibid.: 10.
13. Ibid.: 11.
14. J. E. Sansregret, "La Part des Canadiens-Français dans le commerce et l'industrie," *Le Détaillant* 1, no. 12 (1927): 14.
15. Ibid.: 15.
16. Ibid.: 16.
17. *Le Duprex* 1, no. 5 (1927): 4. I thank Mary Matthews for bringing this material to my attention.
18. David Monod, *Store Wars: Shopkeepers and the Culture of Mass Marketing, 1890–1939* (Toronto: University of Toronto Press, 1996), 92.
19. Ibid., 94.
20. CJC, 11 Apr. 1924.
21. For valuable information on the Ligue du Dimanche's attacks on Jews, see David Rome, ed., *The Jewish Congress Archival Record of 1936*, Canadian Jewish Archives, New Series, no. 8 (Montreal: Canadian Jewish Congress National Archives, 1978): *passim*.
22. This paragraph is based on Richard Jones, *L'Idéologie de l'Action Catholique (1917–1939)* (Quebec: Les Presses de l'Université Laval, 1974).
23. Édouard V. Lavergne, "Haine aux juifs," *L'Action Catholique*, 21 Sept. 1921; quoted in ibid., 71.
24. Ibid., 91.
25. J. Albert Foissy, "Autour du monde," *L'Action Catholique*, 4 Feb. 1921; quoted in ibid., 73.
26. J. Albert Foissy, "Impressions d'un vétéran," *L'Action Catholique*, 23 Aug. 1920; quoted in ibid., 74.
27. Ibid., 76.
28. Ibid., 80.
29. Abbé Nadeau, "Chronique de la guerre," *L'Action Catholique*, 19 May 1917; quoted in ibid., 81.

30. "La Pologne livrée aux juifs," *L'Action Catholique*, 25 Sept. 1919; quoted in ibid., 83.
31. Lavergne, "Haine aux juifs"; quoted in ibid., 85.
32. Jules Dorion, "Le fascisme: il lui faut quelqu'un, et une situation," *L'Action Catholique*, 26 Aug. 1933; quoted in ibid., 87.
33. Donald J. Horton, *André Laurendeau: French Canadian Nationalist* (Toronto: Oxford University Press, 1992), 36.
34. Quoted in ibid., 37.
35. CJR, 28 Apr. 1933.
36. CJC, 28 Apr. 1933.
37. Ibid., This *Chronicle* editorial blasted *Le Devoir*, "in whom the germs of the *Goglu* are multiplying at a fast rate," for its "meticulous devotion to the cause of Jeune Canada."
38. Horton, *André Laurendeau*, 37.
39. CJC, 26 May 1933.
40. Ibid., 2 Jun. 1933.
41. Ibid., 30 Jun. 1933.
42. Ibid., 11 Aug. 1933.
43. André-J. Bélanger, *L'Apolitisme des idéologies québécoises: Le grand tournant de 1934–1936*, Histoire et Sociologie de la Culture, no. 7 (Quebec: Les Presses de l'Université Laval, 1974), 263.
44. André Laurendeau, *Politiciens et juifs* (Montreal: Les Cahiers des Jeune-Canada, no. 1, 1933); quoted in ibid., 264.
45. CJR, 10 Jan. 1931.
46. CJC, 10 Apr. 1931; 8 Dec. 1931.
47. CJR, 29 Sept. 1931.
48. CJC, 29 Sept. 1933; 6 Oct. 1933.
49. Ibid., 28 Jul. 1933; 6 Oct. 1933.
50. Ibid., 25 Aug. 1933.
51. Ibid., 12 May 1933.
52. Ibid., 30 Jun. 1933.
53. Irving Abella and Frank Bialystok, "Canada," in David Wyman, ed., *The World Reacts to the Holocaust* (Baltimore: Johns Hopkins University Press, 1996): 749–81, 752.
54. The most recent and complete surveys of antisemitism in Canada are Martin Robin, *Shades of Right: Nativist and Fascist Politics in Canada* (Toronto: University of Toronto Press, 1992); Lita-Rose Betcherman, *The Swastika and the Maple Leaf* (Toronto: Deneau, 1975); Irving Abella, "Anti-Semitism in Canada in the Interwar Years," in Robert F. Harney and Moses Rischin, eds., *The Jews of North America* (Detroit: Wayne State University Press, 1987): 235–46; Stephen Speisman, "Antisemitism in Ontario: The Twentieth Century," in Alan Davies, ed., *Antisemitism in Canada: History and Interpretation* (Waterloo: Wilfrid Laurier University Press, 1992): 113–33.
55. Norman Cohn, *Warrant for Genocide: The Myth of the Jewish World Conspiracy and the Protocols of the Elders of Zion* (New York: Harper Torchbooks, 1969), 158–62.

56. Plans for the development of Hamilton's Westdale area in the 1920s included the following restriction: "None of the lands described . . . should be used, occupied by or let or sold to Negroes, Asiatics, Bulgarians, Austrians, Russians, Serbs, Roumanians, Turks, Armenians, whether British subjects or not, or foreign-born Italians, Greeks, or Jews." Quoted in Michael Doucet and John Weaver, *Housing the North American City* (Montreal: McGill-Queen's University Press, 1991), 123.
57. Dominion of Canada, *Debates of the House of Commons* (Fifth Session, Seventeenth Parliament), vol. 2, 1934 (Ottawa: King's Printer, 1934), 1661.
58. CJCNA, Caiserman Papers, vol. 2, Membership campaign, 1935–37; Caiserman to Bernard Gardner, 21 Jun. 1935.
59. Ibid., Boycott of German products, 1936–37, Caiserman circular letter, 10 Oct. 1935. The letter was marked "Very Important, Very Urgent."
60. Ibid., Reitman to Congress, 16 May 1934.
61. Ibid., Boycott committee, 1933–35, Caiserman circular letter, 20 Aug. 1935.
62. Ibid., S. D. Cohen circular letter, 28 Jan. 1935.
63. Ibid., Cohen and Mrs. Florence Levy, Chairman, Vigilance committee, n.d.
64. Ibid., vol. 2, 2/21, Boycott committee bulletin, Apr. 1939.
65. Ibid., 2/2, Correspondence with government bodies, 1937–39, Club Ouvrier Maisonneuve.
66. Ibid., vol. 1, 1/6, Membership campaign, Eastern division, Books and pamphlets, Caiserman circular letter, 25 Oct. 1937.
67. Ibid., enclosure.
68. Ibid., Congress circular, 22 Sept. 1938.
69. Ibid., vol. 1, 1/3, Membership drive, 1938, Congress circular.
70. Ibid.
71. Rabbi Eisendrath's Canadian career, which spanned 1929 to 1942, is covered briefly in Avi M. Schulman, *Like a Raging Fire: A Biography of Maurice N. Eisendrath* (New York: Union of American Hebrew Congregations Press, 1993), 15–25. The flavour of Eisendrath's forthright views on Jewish, Canadian, and world affairs can be captured by reading his published lectures, *The Never Failing Stream* (Toronto: Macmillan, 1939).
72. CJCNA, Caiserman Papers, vol. 2, 2/21, Boycott committee, 1938–39, Mimeographed material, Printed circular of the Committee on Jewish-Gentile Relations.
73. Donald Warren, *Radio Priest: Charles Coughlin, the Father of Hate*

Radio (New York: Free Press, 1996), 237.

74. Mary Vipond, "London Listens: The Popularity of Radio in the Depression," *Ontario History* 88, no. 1 (1996): 49–63, 52.
75. See Geoffrey S. Smith, *To Save a Nation: American Extremism, The New Deal, and The Coming of World War II*, rev. ed. (Chicago: Ivan R. Dee, 1992), *passim*, and Warren, *Radio Priest*.
76. Jonathan Wagner, "Nazi Party Membership in Canada: A Profile," HS/SH 14, no. 27 (1981): 233–38, 234.
77. Jonathan F. Wagner, *Brothers Beyond the Sea: National Socialism in Canada* (Waterloo: Wilfrid Laurier University Press, 1981), 30.
78. Quoted in ibid., 38.
79. Jean Gerber, "Canadian Jewish Congress: Pacific Region, Part I," *The Scribe* 10, no. 2 (1988): 4–8, 13–14, 5.
80. Wagner, *Brothers*, 73.
81. Herbert A. Sohn, "Human Rights Laws in Ontario: The Role of the Jewish Community," CJHSJ/SHJCJ 4, no. 2 (1980): 99–116, 104.
82. Ibid.: 106.
83. CJCNA, Caiserman Papers, vol. 1, 1/7, Membership campaign, Eastern division, 1938, Address for members of the Speakers' Committee, Mimeographed.
84. Irving Abella, *A Coat of Many Colours: Two Centuries of Jewish Life in Canada* (Toronto: Lester & Orpen Dennys, 1990), 190–91.
85. Michael R. Marrus, *Mr. Sam: The Life and Times of Samuel Bronfman* (Toronto: Viking, 1991), 261.
86. Ibid., 264.
87. Ibid., 271.
88. Esther Delisle, *The Traitor and the Jew: Anti-Semitism and the Delirium of Extremist Right-Wing Nationalism in French Canada from 1929–1939*, Madelaine Hebert, trans. (Montreal: Robert Davies Publishing, 1993), 36; and Michael Oliver, *The Passionate Debate: The Social and Political Ideas of Quebec Nationalism* (Montreal: Véhicule Press, 1991), 180–95.
89. Delisle, *Traitor and Jew*, 25–29.
90. Ibid., 25.
91. Ibid., 26. See "Lionel-Adolphe Groulx," in Norah Storey, ed., *The Oxford Companion to Canadian History and Literature* (Toronto: Oxford University Press, 1967): 332–33; Susan Mann Trofimenkoff, "Lionel-Adolphe Groulx," *The Canadian Encyclopedia* vol. 2 (Edmonton: Hurtig, 1988): 941–42; and Susan Mann Trofimenkoff, *Action Française: French Canadian Nationalism in the Twenties* (Toronto: University of Toronto Press, 1975), 23, 78–79.
92. Everett C. Hughes, *French Canada in Transition* (Chicago: University of Chicago Press, 1963), 216–18. Delisle, *Traitor and Jew*, 39.
93. Quoted in Delisle, *Traitor and Jew*, 41.

94. Oliver, *Passionate Debate*, 181. Bourassa returned from a European tour in the summer of 1938 as an admirer of Hitler. Betcherman, *Swastika and Maple Leaf*, 131.
95. Edmond Turcotte, "Sur la voie patriote," *Le Canada*, 20 Jun. 1934; quoted in Pierre Anctil, *Le Rendez-vous manqué: les juifs de Montréal face au Québec de l'entre-deux guerres* (Montreal: Institut Québécois de Recherche sur la Culture, 1988), 137–38.
96. Olivar Asselin, "La Grève de l'internat," *L'Ordre*, 22 Jun. 1934, 23 Jun. 1934; quoted in ibid., 137.
97. Ibid., 249.
98. Marcel Hamel, "Tu mens, juif," *La Nation*, 12 Nov. 1936; quoted in Oliver, *Passionate Debate*, 184–85.
99. Delisle, *Traitor and Jew*, 43.
100. J. K. Johnson, ed., *The Canadian Directory of Parliament 1867–1967* (Ottawa: Public Archives of Canada, 1968): 519; CJC, 22 Sept. 1933.
101. Herbert F. Quinn, *The Union Nationale: A Study in Quebec Nationalism* (Toronto: University of Toronto Press, 1963), 49; CJC, 24 Jul. 1936.
102. Quinn, *Union Nationale*, 38; CJC, 7 Aug. 1936.
103. CJC, 21 Aug. 1936.
104. Ibid., 19 Mar. 1937.
105. Ibid., 2 Apr. 1937.
106. Ibid., 23 Oct. 1936.
107. Ibid., 30 Oct. 1936.
108. Ibid., 16 Aug. 1937.
109. Ibid.
110. The situation for Montreal Jews vacationing in the Laurentians in the late 1920s was so menacing that the *Keneder Adler* was advising its readers to "check with the [local] priest and mayor about their attitude towards Jews before renting. . . ." (KA, 1 May 1927.)
111. Jack Jedwab, "Uniting Uptowners and Downtowners: The Jewish Electorate and Quebec Provincial Politics 1927–39," CES/EEC 18, no. 2 (1986): 7–19, 12. The St. Louis riding was held by the Liberal Peter Bercovitch, who resigned to contest the federal riding of Cartier after the death of long-time MP Sam Jacobs in 1938.
112. *Répertoire des parlementaires québécois 1867–1978* (Quebec: Bibliothèque de la Législature, Service de Documentation Politique, 1980), 207–208.
113. Jedwab, "Uniting Uptowners": 14.
114. Abraham M. Klein, "The Twin Racketeers of Journalism," CJC, 8 Jul. 1932; quoted in M. W. Steinberg and Usher Caplan, eds., *A. M. Klein, Beyond Sambation: Selected Essays and Editorials 1928–1955* (Toronto: University of Toronto Press, 1982): 26–29, 27.
115. Ibid.: 29.

116. Brian McKenna and Susan Purcell, *Drapeau* (Toronto: Penguin Books, 1980), 37.
117. David Rome, "Canada", AJYB 44 (1942): 181.
118. *Congress Bulletin*, Aug. 1943, 7.
119. Abraham M. Klein, "Quebec City Gets Another Park," CJC, 18 Jun. 1943; quoted in Steinberg and Caplan, *Beyond Sambation*: 190–91.
120. Ibid.: 191.
121. Abraham M. Klein, "Incendiary Antisemitism," CJC, 26 May 1944; quoted in ibid.: 219, 220.
122. CZA, Z4/10/74, "Quebec Authorities Charged with Indifference to Acts of Violence Against Jews," Jewish Telegraphic Agency, 25 Jun. 1944.
123. *Congress Bulletin*, Aug. 1943, 7.
124. Quoted in Paul Axelrod, *Making a Middle Class: Student Life in English Canada during the Thirties* (Montreal: McGill-Queen's University Press, 1990), 33.
125. R. D. Gidney and W. P. J. Millar, "Medical Students at the University of Toronto, 1910–40: A Profile," *Canadian Bulletin of Medical History* 13 (1996): 40.
126. A. Brian McKillop, *Matters of the Mind: The University in Ontario 1791–1951*, Ontario Historical Studies Series (Toronto: University of Toronto Press, 1994), 360.
127. Interview with Phillip Stuchen, 29 Oct. 1996.
128. Percy Barsky, "How 'Numerus Clausus' Was Ended in the Manitoba Medical School," CJHSJ/SHJCJ 1, no. 2 (1977): 75–81, 76.
129. Axelrod, *Making a Middle Class*, 33.
130. Ernest Sirluck, *First Generation: An Autobiography* (Toronto: University of Toronto Press, 1996), 32.
131. Ibid., 33.
132. Lesley Marrus-Barsky, "History of Mount Sinai Hospital" (unpublished manuscript), 27–28, 43–45.
133. Axelrod, *Making a Middle Class*, 34.
134. KA, 21 Dec. 1927, 27 Dec. 1927.
135. Peter B. Waite, *1925–1980: The Old College Transformed*, vol. 2 of *The Lives of Dalhousie University* (Montreal: McGill-Queen's University Press, 1998), 83.
136. Sirluck, *First Generation*, 35, 42.
137. *Silhouette*, 30 Jan. 1936. I am grateful to Catherine Gidney, a history doctoral candidate at Queen's University, for this material.
138. Lawrence D. Stokes, "Canada and an Academic Refugee from Nazi Germany: The Case of Gerhard Herzberg," CHR 57, no. 2 (1976): 150–70, 159.
139. Leopold Infeld, *Why I Left Canada: Reflections on Science and Politics* (Montreal: McGill-Queen's University Press, 1978).

140. Eli Gottesman, ed., *Who's Who in Canadian Jewry* (Montreal: Central Rabbinical Seminary of Canada, 1965): 354–59.
141. Michiel Horn, "The Exclusive University" (unpublished manuscript), chapter 18.
142. Axelrod, *Making a Middle Class*, 33.
143. Michael Bliss, *Banting: A Biography* (Toronto: McClelland and Stewart, 1984), 101, 159, 179.
144. Ibid., 252.
145. Michael Brown, "Lionel Gelber," in Geoffrey Wigoder, ed., *New Encyclopedia of Zionism and Israel*, vol. 1 (Madison: Farleigh Dickinson University Press, 1994): 460.
146. Horn, "Exclusive University." Regarding Bora Laskin, see also Jerome E. Bickenbach, "Lawyers, Law Professors, and Racism in Ontario," QQ 96, no. 3 (1989): 585–98, 595.
147. Frederick W. Gibson, *1917–1961: To Serve and Yet Be Free*, vol. 2 of *Queen's University* (Montreal: McGill-Queen's University Press, 1983), 199.
148. Ibid., 200.
149. Ibid., 202.
150. Alfred Bader, *Adventures of a Chemist Collector* (London: Weidenfeld and Nicholson, 1995), 43.
151. Waite, *Lives of Dalhousie University*, vol. 2, 119.
152. Robin, *Shades of Right*, 14.
153. CJC, 7 Oct. 1921.
154. Robin, *Shades of Right*, 85.
155. CJR, 18 Jun. 1937. Rev. G. Stanley Russell, of Deer Park United Church, protested that "when Gentiles kick Jews out of a tennis tournament, it doesn't hurt the Jews, but it does hurt the Gentiles. . . ."
156. Ibid., 25 Jun. 1937.
157. Ibid., 11 Oct. 1935.
158. J. E. Rea, *T. A. Crerar: A Political Life* (Montreal: McGill-Queen's University Press, 1997), 132.
159. Howard Palmer, *Patterns of Prejudice: A History of Nativism in Alberta* (Toronto: McClelland and Stewart, 1985), 153. See also C. B. Macpherson, *Democracy in Alberta: The Theory and Practice of a Quasi-Party System*, Social Credit in Alberta Series (Toronto: University of Toronto Press, 1953), the standard work on Social Credit theory; and Alvin Finkel, *The Social Credit Phenomenon in Alberta* (Toronto: University of Toronto Press, 1989), the most comprehensive treatment of the Alberta Social Credit phenomenon from the 1930s to the defeat of the Social Credit government in 1971.
160. Finkel, *Social Credit*, 82.
161. Janine Stingel, "Social Credit and the Jews: Anti-Semitism in the Alberta Social Credit Movement and the Response of the Canadian Jewish Congress,

1935–1949" (Ph.D. thesis, McGill University, 1997). This thesis provides a superb analysis of the great extent of antisemitism in the movement, the failed responses of the Canadian Jewish Congress, and the key role played by Louis Rosenberg in maintaining a close watch on it.

162. Palmer, *Patterns of Prejudice*, 152.
163. Ibid., 153.
164. Ibid., 155–56.
165. Ibid., 157. See also Janine Stingel, "Responding to the Alberta Experiment: Social Credit Anti-Semitism and the Canadian Jewish Congress" (Paper delivered to the Canadian Jewish Historical Society Conference, Montreal, Jun. 1995; to be published in a forthcoming issue of *Canadian Jewish Studies*).
166. Johnson, *Canadian Directory of Parliament*: 48, 291.
167. Finkel, *Social Credit*, 105.
168. Michael B. Stein, *The Dynamics of Right-Wing Protest: A Political Analysis of Social Credit in Quebec* (Toronto: University of Toronto Press, 1973), 50–52.
169. See David Bercuson and Douglas Wertheimer, *A Trust Betrayed: The Keegstra Affair* (Toronto: Doubleday, 1985), 2–44, *passim*.
170. Sirluck, *First Generation*, 8.
171. Ibid., 21.
172. Ibid., 23.
173. Ibid., 60.
174. Ibid., 67.
175. Robert England, *The Central European Immigrant in Canada* (Toronto: Macmillan, 1929), 92.
176. Orest T. Martynowych, *Ukrainians in Canada: The Formative Period, 1891–1924* (Edmonton: Canadian Institute of Ukrainian Studies Press, University of Alberta, 1991), 89.
177. Ibid., 91.
178. Quoted in ibid., 238.
179. Ibid., 294.
180. Ibid., 204.
181. Stingel, "Social Credit and the Jews," 77; Johnson, *Canadian Directory of Parliament*: 272.
182. Sonia Riddoch to Gerald Tulchinsky, 15 Jul. 1997.
183. *Ukrainian Canadian*, 29 Aug. 1923.
184. Daniel Stone, "Winnipeg's Polish-Language Newspapers and Their Attitude Towards Jews and Ukrainians Between the Two World Wars," CES/EEC 21, no. 2 (1989): 27–37, 38.
185. Ibid.: 29–30.
186. Ibid.: 30–31.
187. This account is based on Cyril H. Levitt and William Shaffir, *The Riot at Christie Pits* (Toronto: Lester & Orpen Dennys, 1987).
188. Circular letter from the public-relations committee of the Congress, 13 Jun. 1934; quoted in David Rome, ed., *The Jewish Congress Archival Record of 1934*, Canadian Jewish Archives, New

Series, no. 6 (Montreal: Canadian Jewish Congress National Archives, 1976): 48.

189. See Irving Abella and Harold Troper, *None Is Too Many: Canada and the Jews of Europe 1933–1948* (Toronto: Lester & Orpen Dennys, 1982).
190. Ibid., 18–19, 41–42.
191. Stingel, "Social Credit and the Jews," 138.
192. Abella and Bialystok, "Canada": 756.
193. Stanley M. Cohen, "An Interview with Saul Hayes," *Viewpoints* 9, no. 4 (1976): 5–25, 23.
194. Abella and Bialystok, "Canada": 758.
195. Alan Davies and Marilyn F. Nefsky, *How Silent Were the Churches? Canadian Protestantism and the Jewish Plight during the Nazi Era* (Waterloo: Wilfrid Laurier University Press, 1997), 37; see also Davies and Nefsky, "The United Church and the Jewish Plight during the Nazi Era 1933–1945," CJHSJ/SHJCJ 8, no. 2 (1984): 55–71.
196. Cited in Davies and Nefsky, "United Church and the Jewish Plight": 61.
197. Cited in Jack Lipinsky, "'The Agony of Israel': Watson Kirkconnell and Canadian Jewry," CJHSJ/SHJCJ 6, no. 2 (1982): 57–72, 58.
198. Quoted in Reuben Slonim, *Family Quarrel: The United Church and the Jews* (Toronto: Clark Irwin, 1977), 2. In the same address, Howse criticized pre-war restrictions on Jews but revealed his lack of understanding of their unique plight:

   > *It is most peculiar blindness for us to think of this horror as a Jewish horror. Some of the appalling complacency which a few years ago greeted the spectre of the refugee, had its roots in the cold and stupid objectiveness with which the rest of us contemplated the phenomenon as being inherently Jewish. But before this war began, for every Jewish refugee there was a Gentile refugee beside him.*

199. L. T. Evans and N. C. Quigley, "Discrimination in Bank Lending Policies: A Test Using Data from the Bank of Nova Scotia 1900–1937," CJE 23, no. 1 (1990): 210–23.
200. See Sam A. Sharon, "Tolerance Was Common in Rural Quebec," *Montreal Gazette*, 6 Mar. 1997. I am grateful to Gérard Bouchard for drawing my attention to this article. See also Mordecai Richler, *Oh Canada! Oh Quebec! Requiem for a Divided Country* (Toronto: Penguin Books, 1992), 79–80, for interesting reminiscences of his early — generally friendly — encounters with French Canadians.

Chapter 8/Canada's Jews at War

1. Henry Feingold's recent excellent work on American Jewish history between 1920 and 1945, *A Time for Searching: Entering the Mainstream 1920–1945*, Jewish People in America Series (Baltimore: Johns Hopkins University Press, 1992), devotes only a few lines to the Jewish contribution to the United States military during the Second World War and the bibliography contains only one reference to U.S. Jewry's contribution to the American military. In this major historical analysis of a community of some six million Jews, which contributed 550,000 persons to the U.S. armed services and suffered approximately eight thousand deaths, the subject is given only brief treatment.
2. Louis Rosenberg, Canadian Jewry's indefatigable historian, compiled much information on the Jewish contribution to the Dominion's military effort in the First World War. He showed that 37.81 percent of Jewish males twenty-one years and older served in the CEF, compared with 31.02 percent of males of "all origins." The study apparently was never published. NAC, MG 30, Louis Rosenberg Papers, vol. 26, "Jews in Canadian Defence Forces" (1943). Barbara Wilson points out that many Jews living in Canada could not enlist, even if they wanted to, because they were not British subjects. Barbara Wilson to Gerald Tulchinsky, 17 Nov. 1995.
3. Michael R. Marrus, *Mr. Sam: The Life and Times of Samuel Bronfman* (Toronto: Viking, 1991), 279–81.
4. There was only one Jewish chaplain in the Canadian army during the First World War: Herman Abramowitz of Sha'ar Hashamayim Synagogue of Montreal, rabbi for the Quebec and Valcartier troops. Canadian Jewish soldiers overseas were visited by Rabbi Michael Adler, a Jewish chaplain in the British army. See Duff Crerar, *Padres in No Man's Land: Canadian Chaplains and the Great War* (Montreal: McGill-Queen's University Press, 1995), 38, 68, 276, 301.
5. "The War Efforts Committee of Canadian Jewish Congress," in Vladimir Grossman, ed., *Canadian Jewish Year Book*, vol. 3 (Montreal: Canadian Jewish Publication Society, 1942): 67–76.
6. Marrus, *Mr. Sam*, 281, 284.
7. CJCNA, DA 18, 3/8, Memorandum to War Efforts Committee from William Abrams, 14 Jul. 1942.
8. Their correspondence, preserved in the Congress' archives in

Montreal, is very revealing about the provision of these services between 1942 and 1946.

9. See Henry Feingold, *The Politics of Rescue: The Roosevelt Administration and the Holocaust, 1938–1945* (New Brunswick, N.J., 1970); and David Wyman, *The Abandonment of the Jews: America and the Holocaust* (New York: Pantheon Books, 1985).
10. Cyril Levitt and William Shaffir, "The Press Reports: Toronto Learns about Nazi Atrocities in 1933," in Paul R. Bartrop, ed., *False Havens: The British Empire and the Holocaust* (New York: University Press of America, 1995): 21–51, 21.
11. Ibid.: 22.
12. J. L. Granatstein, "A Half-Century On: The Veteran's Experience," in Peter Neary and J. L. Granatstein, eds., *The Veterans Charter and Post–World War II Canada* (Montreal: McGill-Queen's University Press, 1998): 224–34, 227.
13. Ernest Sirluck, *First Generation: An Autobiography* (Toronto: University of Toronto Press, 1996), 97.
14. Ibid., 104.
15. Martin Roher, *Days of Living: The Journal of Martin Roher* (Toronto: Ryerson Press, 1959), v.
16. Ben Dunkelman, *Dual Allegiance* (Toronto: New American Library, 1976), 45–46.
17. Harold Rubin, *Those Pesky Weeds: An Autobiography* (Ottawa: Ottawa Jewish Historical Society, 1992), 101.
18. Monty Berger, with Brian J. Street, *Invasion Without Tears: The Story of Canada's Top-Scoring Spitfire Wing in Europe during the Second World War* (Toronto: Random House, 1994), 209.
19. Ibid.
20. CJCNA, Fred Rose Papers, "Letter from a Hero's Mother to the Mothers and Fathers of Cartier" (Leaflet, 1943).
21. Peter Oliver, *Unlikely Tory: The Life and Politics of Allan Grossman* (Toronto: Lester & Orpen Dennys, 1985), 32.
22. Irving Layton, *Waiting for the Messiah* (Don Mills: Totem Press, 1985), 207–208, 213–14.
23. Wayne E. Edmonstone, *Nathan Cohen: The Making of a Critic* (Toronto: Lester & Orpen, 1977), 17.
24. David Lewis, *The Good Fight: Political Memoirs 1909–1958* (Toronto: Macmillan, 1981), 168.
25. Lawrence Freiman, *Don't Fall Off the Rocking Horse* (Toronto: McClelland and Stewart, 1978), 75.
26. Mordecai Richler, "Montreal, 1947: 'We Danced the Hora in the Middle of the Street,'" from "My Sort of War," *New Statesman*, 4 Sept. 1964; reprinted in B. J. Goldberg and Elliot King, eds.,

Builders and Dreamers: Habonim Labor Zionist Youth in North America (New York: Herzl Press, 1993): 126–29, 127.

27. "War Efforts Committee": 68.
28. GLEN, A. I. Shumiatcher Papers, "Report submitted by Mr. M. H. Myerson, Director of Recruiting Activities, Eastern Division," n.d. [1941?].
29. Interview with Rabbi David Monson, Jun. 1995.
30. Shloime Perel, "History of the UJPO in Canada, 1926–1949," chapter 17, 4. This work is part of a Ph.D. thesis in progress at McMaster University, Department of Sociology. See also Irving Abella, ed., "Portrait of a Jewish Professional Revolutionary: The Recollections of Joshua Gershman," L/Let 2 (1977): 185–213, 208.
31. Ben Lappin, "When Michoels and Feffer Came to Toronto," *Viewpoints* 7, no. 2 (1972): 43–64, 55–56.
32. CJCNA, Finding Aid to War Efforts Committee Records, Statistical Highlights, CJC "Yearboxes," ZA 1945, box 3, file 46. This figure does not include the 1,631 Canadian Jews who served in other Allied armed forces. See David Rome, "Canada," AJYB 49 (1948): 288.
33. Charles P. Stacey, *Arms, Men and Governments* (Ottawa: Queen's Printer, 1971), 416.
34. Census of Canada (1941), vol. 3, 14, 204; Stacey, *Arms, Men and Governments*, 590; Max Bookman, "Canadian Jews in Uniform," in Eli Gottesman, ed., *Canadian Jewish Reference Book and Directory* (Ottawa: Jewish Institute of Higher Research, 1963): 111.
35. Frank Lewis, of the Queen's University Department of Economics, drew my attention to the fact that "of Canadian males 18 to 39, a slightly smaller percentage of the Jewish population was aged 20 to 29 (46.8 vs. 48.4 percent). This might account for the lower enlistment rate. To the extent that some servicemen were over the age of 39, these percentages are high and would probably favour non-Jews who would be career soldiers." Frank Lewis to Gerald Tulchinsky, 14 Jun. 1995.
36. These calculations are based on the above figures for enlistment rates of Jewish males and on NRMA data given in Daniel Byers, "Canada's 'Zombies': A Portrait of Canadian Conscripts and Their Experiences during the Second World War" (unpublished paper, 1997), app. 5: Religion of NRMA Recruits.
37. Stacey, *Arms, Men and Governments*, 66.
38. Louis Rosenberg, *Canada's Jews: A Social and Economic Study of the Jews in Canada* (Montreal: Canadian Jewish Congress, Bureau of

Social and Economic Research, 1939), 265. On general education levels in the army, see Brian Nolan, *King's War: Mackenzie King and the Politics of War* (Toronto: Random House, 1988), 117.

39. Rosenberg, *Canada's Jews*, 271.
40. Ibid., 272.
41. According to Dr. Jack English, in the Canadian army's Italian and Normandy campaigns "the infantry incurred 76% of all casualties, the armoured 7%, and the artillery 8%." Jack English to Gerald Tulchinsky, 4 Dec. 1995.
42. Sirluck, *First Generation*, 93.
43. See Salo Baron, *The Russian Jew under Tsars and Soviets* (New York: Macmillan, 1964), 35–38.
44. Sirluck, *First Generation*, 68, 83.
45. "Military Service," EJ, vol. 2: 1550–68.
46. GLEN, A. I. Shumiatcher Papers, box 6, file 49, *Winnipeg Free Press*, 6 Sept. 1940.
47. Ibid.
48. Gregory S. Kealey and Reg Whitaker, eds., *RCMP Security Bulletins: The War Series, 1939–1941* (St. John's: Committee on Canadian Labour History, 1989): 311.
49. Ibid.: 311–12.
50. Ibid.: 381–82.
51. CJCNA, DA 18, 5/3B, Saul Hayes to CJC members, n.d.
52. David Rome, "Canada," AJYB 45 (1943): 225.
53. Byers, "Canada's 'Zombies'," app. 5.
54. There were an additional 163 Canadian Jewish personnel in the Allied forces. These calculations are based on figures given in Bookman, "Canadian Jews in Uniform": 111, and Stacey, *Arms, Men and Governments*, 590.
55. GLEN, A. I. Shumiatcher Papers, box 7, file 50.
56. Ibid., file 49.
57. CJCNA, Caiserman Papers, vol. 4, Reports about immigration (1920–1950), antisemitism (1949), education (1934).
58. CJCNA, Pamphlet Collection.
59. Translated by Ellen Tulchinsky.
60. See Kenneth I. Cleator and Harry J. Stern, *Harry Joshua Stern: A Rabbi's Journey* (New York: Bloch Publishing, 1981); Reuben Slonim, *To Kill a Rabbi* (Toronto: ECW Press, 1987); Abraham L. Feinberg, *Storm the Gates of Jericho* (Toronto: McClelland and Stewart, 1964); and Aron Horowitz, *Striking Roots: Reflections on Five Decades of Jewish Life* (Oakville: Mosaic Press, 1979). There is virtually nothing about the Second World War among the many important events recorded in the memoirs of the *Keneder Adler* publisher Hirsch Wolofsky, *Journey of My Life: A Book of Memories* (Montreal: Eagle Publishing, 1945), and the Montreal rabbi Harry J. Stern's published speeches, *One World or*

No World: A Collection of Sermons, Essays and Addresses (New York: Bloch Publishing, 1973), include nothing about the war. Bernard Figler and David Rome, in *Hananiah Meir Caiserman: A Biography with an Essay on Modern Jewish Times by David Rome* (Montreal: Northern Printing and Lithographing, 1962), include virtually nothing specific on the Jewish community and the war.

61. Abraham M. Klein, "The Plebiscite," CJC, 24 Apr. 1942; quoted in M. W. Steinberg and Usher Caplan, eds., *A. M. Klein, Beyond Sambation: Selected Essays and Editorials 1928–1955* (Toronto: University of Toronto Press, 1982): 141–43, 142.
62. Ibid.: 142–43.
63. J. L. Granatstein, *Canada's War: The Politics of the Mackenzie King Government, 1939–1945* (Toronto: Oxford University Press, 1975), 227.
64. W. Victor Sefton, "The European Holocaust — Who Knew What and When — A Canadian Aspect," CJHSJ/SHJCJ 2, no. 2 (1978): 121–33, 128–29.
65. This raises interesting questions about the extent to which antisemitism had penetrated Canadian society during the 1930s. Perhaps the antisemitism of the 1930s was essentially circumstantial or rhetorical (i.e., related to specific issues such as immigration) or, if general, was not necessarily transferred to the military.
66. CJCNA, DA 18, 3/14A, Rabbi Babb to H/Capt. Cass, 21 Jun. 1943. Babb requested instructions on how to proceed with this complaint.
67. Ibid., 6/6, Levy to H/Capt. H. H. MacSween, Chaplain (P) HQ Command, 2 Corps, Tpt. Coln. RCASC, 7 Mar. 1944.
68. Rubin, *Pesky Weeds*, 104.
69. CJCNA, DA 18, 1/3, N. J. Direnfeld to Gershon Levi, 22 Nov. 1942.
70. J. L. Granatstein, *The Generals: The Canadian Army's Senior Commanders in the Second World War* (Toronto: Stoddart, 1993), 153.
71. Interview with Maj.-Gen. Robert Rothschild, 18 Jul. 1994.
72. NAC, MG 30, D225, Rabbi Cass Papers, vol. 9, app. 3, section 1, 25.
73. Interview with Edwin A. Goodman, Q.C., 30 Jun. 1994.
74. Edwin A. Goodman, *Life of the Party: The Memoirs of Eddie Goodman* (Toronto: Key Porter, 1988), 18.
75. Interview with Ephraim Diamond, 19 Jun. 1995.
76. Dunkelman, *Dual Allegiance*, 46.
77. Interview with Sam Finkelstein, 29 Jun. 1994.
78. Barney Danson to Gerald Tulchinsky, 28 Aug. 1994.
79. Interview with Lt. Col. Ian Hodson, RCR (Retired), 25 Feb. 1997. See also "The Jewish

Captain," in Barry Broadfoot, *Six War Years: Memories of Canadians at Home and Abroad* (Toronto: Doubleday Canada Limited, 1974), 326–27, for information on Jews in the Royal Canadian Regiment.

80. NAC, MG 30, D225, vol. 9, app. 1, 24.
81. Interview with Rabbi David Monson, Jun. 1995.
82. See Rabbi S. Gershon Levi, *Breaking New Ground: The Struggle for a Jewish Chaplaincy in Canada* (Montreal: Canadian Jewish Congress Archives, 1994).
83. *Prayer Book for Jewish Members of H. M. Forces* (London: H. M. Stationery Office, 1940), 4.
84. Ibid.
85. CJCNA, DA 18, 3/3, Abe Halpern to Gershon Levi, 11 Nov. 1942.
86. Ibid., Louis Roter to Gershon Levi, 2 Oct. 1942.
87. Ibid., Herbert Vineberg to Gershon Levi, 6 Feb. 1942.
88. Ibid., S. S. Berlin to Gershon Levi, 3 Feb. 1942.
89. Ibid., John Marcus to Gershon Levi, 23 Mar. 1942.
90. Ibid., J. M. Roe to Gershon Levi, 12 Aug. 1942.
91. Ibid., Levi to Commanding Officer, No. 5 Equipment Depot, RCAF, Moncton, 7 Apr. 1942. Levi to Flt./Lieut. David J. Lane, 7 Apr. 1942.
92. Ibid., Harry R. Nobles to Senior Jewish Chaplain, 7 Apr. 1942.
93. Ibid., H. A. R. Keith to Gershon Levi, n.d.
94. Ibid., Levi to Flt./Lieut. L. B. Merrell, C.O., No. 16 "X" Depot, RCAF, 7 Apr. 1942.
95. Ibid., M. C. P. Macintosh to Levi, 31 Mar. 1942; Flt./Lieut. J. N. Smith, Adjutant for Commanding Officer, No. 5 Equipment Depot, to Gershon Levi, 26 Mar. 1942.
96. Ibid., David J. Lane to Gershon Levi, 24 Mar. 1942.
97. For a poignant story of one encounter between a Jewish RCAF officer and a host family, see Norman Levine, "In Quebec City," in Gerri Sinclair and Morris Wolfe, eds., *The Spice Box: An Anthology of Jewish Canadian Writing* (Toronto: Lester & Orpen Dennys, 1981): 166–76.
98. CJCNA, DA 18, 3/3, Unsigned to Gershon Levi, 14 Apr. 1942.
99. Ibid., Jack Bernstein to Gershon Levi, 8 Sept. 1942.
100. Deborah Osmond, "Tzedakah: Jewish Women and Charity in Halifax, 1920–1945" (Undergraduate essay, Department of History, Dalhousie University, 1996), 63.
101. CJCNA, DA 18, 3/3, Monson to Gershon Levi, 24 Mar. 1942.
102. Ibid., Bernard Saipe to Gershon Levi, 14 Feb. 1942.
103. Ibid., Jacob Feldman, 2 Sqd., 2 Wing, TTS, RCAF, to Gershon Levi, 10 Feb. 1942.

104. Ibid., Sarah Lacle to Gershon Levi, 28 Nov. 1941.
105. Ibid., Gershon Levi to LAC B. R. Woloshin, No. 3 B&G School, RCAF; Levi to Rfm. J. Fogelbaum, "C" Coy, Royal Rifles of Canada, Vernon, B.C., 26 May 1942; L./Cpl. I. Capland to Levi, 30 Apr. 1942.
106. Ibid., Max Greenberg to Gershon Levi, 29 Apr. 1942.
107. Ibid., M. Charton to Gershon Levi, 1 Apr. 1942.
108. Interview with Aaron Palmer, 23 Jun. 1994.
109. CJCNA, DA 18, 3/3, John Marcus to Gershon Levi, 23 Mar. 1942.
110. Rubin, *Pesky Weeds*, 127.
111. Interview with Barney Danson, 30 Jun. 1994.
112. Interview with Morris Lazarus, 30 Jun. 1994.
113. CJCNA, Moses Usher Papers, Moe Usher to Abe and Rose Usher, 8 Jun. 1941.
114. CJCNA, DA 18, 3/6A, Fitterman to Gershon Levi, 12 Aug. 1941.
115. CJCNA, D 18, 5/7, Mrs. F. Levine to Isaac Rose, 18 Sept. 1944.
116. Ibid., Ruth Dankner to Isaac Rose, 15 Sept. 1944.
117. Ibid., Morris Klein to Isaac Rose, 12 Sept. 1944.
118. Ibid., Mrs. A. Solway to Isaac Rose, 11 Sept. 1944.
119. Ibid., Mrs. H. Bach to Isaac Rose, 3 Oct. 1944.
120. CJCNA, DA 18, 6/4, Mary Nidelman to Rabbi David Eisen, 9 Jul. 1942.
121. Ibid., 6/3, Mary Lozdon to Rabbi Samuel Cass, 12 Jan. 1942 [1943].
122. NAC, MG 30, D225, Rabbi Samuel Cass Papers, vol. 9, app. 1, 25.
123. Ibid., app. 3, section 1, 17.
124. Ibid., 18.
125. Ibid., 14.
126. Ibid., DA 18, 3/9, Levine to Canadian Chaplain Service, 31 Aug. 1942.
127. Ibid., 3/10, Cass to H/Capt. and Chaplain E. E. Brandt, 2 Sept. 1942.
128. Ibid., Brandt to Cass, 2 Sept. 1942.
129. Ibid., Fleishman to Cass, 31 Aug. 1942.
130. Ibid., Cass to Rosner, 2 Sept. 1942.
131. Ibid., 3/6 B, Archie Dover to CJC, Montreal, 11 Mar. 1943.
132. Ibid., 2/Lt. Gordon Miller to Samuel Cass, 19 Mar. 1943.
133. Ibid., Gershon Levi to Officer Commanding, RCAF Station, Mountain View, Ont., 2 Feb. 1942.
134. Ibid., DA 18, 3/13, Gershon Levi to Sam Cass, 22 Jan. 1945.
135. Reuben Slonim, *To Kill A Rabbi*, 156.
136. Ibid., 154–55.
137. Aaron Palmer to Mrs. S. Palmer, 22 Dec. 1944.
138. Aaron Palmer to Mary (name illegible), 13 Sept. 1944.
139. Rubin, *Pesky Weeds*, 140.

140. Doug Wilkinson to Gerald Tulchinsky, 25 Sept. 1995.
141. CJCNA, DA 18, 3/10, Cass to OC Infantry Training Brigade, Debert, N.S., 3 Apr. 1944.
142. Ibid., H. Gevantman to B. Wollow, War Efforts Committee, 26 Mar. 1945.
143. Barbara Wilson to Gerald Tulchinsky, 17 Nov. 1995.
144. NAC, MG 30, D225, Samuel Cass Papers, vol. 9, app. 1, 14.
145. *The Battle of Brains: Canadian Citizenship and the Issues of the War* (Ottawa: King's Printer, 1944), 80, 83. I am grateful to Norman Hillmer for informing me of this book.
146. Ibid, 84.
147. CJCNA, DA 18, 6/7, Chaplain, (O/S) (P), Canadian Military Headquarters, 8 Jan. 1945.
148. Ibid.
149. NAC, Photo Collection, DND 1967-52, PA 116331, Photo by Lt. G. B. Gilroy, 30 Apr. 1945.
150. CJCNA, DA 18, 6/7, Cass to Principal Chaplain, (O/S) (P), Canadian Military Headquarters, 8 Jan. 1945, "Report on Activities of Canadian Jewish Chaplains Centre Submitted to H/Capt. I. B. Rose, Resident Dean."
151. NAC, MG 30, D225, Samuel Cass Papers, vol. 9, app. 2, section 2, 6/6, 2.
152. CJCNA, DA 18, 6/6, Cass to Officer Commanding AAG (Pers), 7 Nov. 1945.
153. Ibid., file 5/6, Guardsman Julius Gosevitz, 21 CAR, (GGHG), 1 Sqdn., to Isaac Rose, 6 Jun. 1945.
154. Ibid., Cass to Officer Commanding, No. 1 Canadian Vehicle Company, RCOC Canadian Army, England, 30 Oct. 1945.
155. NAC, MG 30, D225, Samuel Cass Papers, vol. 9, app. 3, section 1, 32.
156. Robert Engel, "My First Canadian Rabbi," preface to Cecil Law, "Camp Westerbork, Transit Camp to Eternity: The Liberation Story" (unpublished manuscript). Engel, a Westerbork survivor, recalled, "I'll never forget [Rabbi Cass's] sermon, the sincerity of warmth. He spoke in Yiddish and English; we loved him. He was one of us."
157. NAC, MG 30, D225, Samuel Cass Papers, vol. 9, app. 3, section 1, 27.
158. Ibid., 27–28.
159. Ibid., vol. 16, Cass to H. Abramowitz, 16 Jan. 1945.
160. See Alex Grobman, *Rekindling the Flame: American Jewish Chaplains and the Survivors of European Jewry, 1944–1948* (Detroit: Wayne State University Press, 1993). Grobman concludes that the American Jewish response to the postwar needs of the survivors, as reported by the chaplains, was inadequate.
161. NAC, MG 30, D225, Samuel

Cass Papers, vol. 9, app. 1, Daily Record, 685, 5 Dec. 1945.

162. Ibid., app. 3, section 1, 37.
163. CJCNA, DA 18, 3/8, Cass to H. Bud Weiser, 6 Jul. 1943.
164. Bookman, "Canadian Jews in Uniform": 111.
165. NAC, MG 30, D225, Samuel Cass Papers, vol. 9, app. 1, 18.
166. Rubin, *Pesky Weeds*, 142.
167. See David J. Bercuson, *The Secret Army* (Toronto: Lester & Orpen Dennys, 1983), 60–64.
168. Author's note: judging by my limited personal experience with RCN cooks in peacetime, I am doubtful.
169. NAC, MG 30, D225, Samuel Cass Papers, vol. 9, app. 1, 35.
170. Mordecai Richler, "Benny, the War in Europe, and Myerson's Daughter Bella," in J. L. Granatstein and Peter Neary, eds., *The Good Fight: Canadians and World War II* (Toronto: Copp Clark, 1995): 426–30.

Chapter 9/The Struggle for Israel, 1943-52

1. Michael Brown, "Samuel Jacob Zacks," in Geoffrey Wigoder, ed., *New Encyclopedia of Zionism and Israel*, vol. 2 (Madison: Farleigh Dickinson University Press, 1994): 1429.
2. Christopher Armstrong, "Moose Pastures and Mergers: The Ontario Securities Commission and the Evolution of Share Markets in Canada, 1940–1980" (Toronto: University of Toronto Press, forthcoming), 17–18.
3. NAC, MG 31, H113, Steven Barber Papers, vol. 27, file 9, Weizmann to Harry Batshaw, 19 May 1941.
4. NAC, MG 30, C144, Samuel J. Zacks Papers, vol. 5, "Chaim Weizmann," Zacks to Weizmann, 25 Jan. 1943.
5. Ibid., Weizmann to Zacks, 16 Apr. 1943.
6. Ibid., vol. 2, "Sam Drache, Winnipeg 1943," Zacks to Drache, 22 Sept. 1943.
7. Ibid., vol. 3, "Sam Jacobson, 1943," Zacks to Jacobson, 22 Dec. 1943.
8. Michael Brown, "Zionism in Canada: World War II and the War of Independence," in Wigoder, *Encyclopedia of Zionism*, vol. 1: 245.
9. See Bernard Wasserstein, *Britain and the Jews of Europe 1933–1945* (Oxford: Oxford University Press, 1979).
10. Dr. I. M. Rabinovitch, who gave a lecture to the Canadian Club of Montreal in October 1946 on the "Menace of Political Zionism," was condemned by the local rabbinical association for attacking "the greatest recreative force in Jewish life today." The rabbis claimed to "speak in the name of all our colleagues when we express our determination to continue

espousing the cause of a legally and publicly recognized national home for the Jews in Palestine as inspired by our Torah and reaffirmed by the Zionist ideal." NAC, MG 30, C144, Samuel J. Zacks Papers, vol. 7, "Oct.–Dec. 1946," Statement by Montreal Rabbinical Association.

11. See Zachariah Kay, *Canada and Palestine: The Politics of Non-Commitment* (Jerusalem: Israel Universities Press, 1978). David J. Bercuson, *Canada and the Birth of Israel: A Study in Canadian Foreign Policy* (Toronto: University of Toronto Press, 1985), also provides a comprehensive treatment of this subject.
12. Walter Laqueur, *History of Zionism* (New York: Schocken Books, 1978), 551.
13. Bercuson, *Canada and the Birth of Israel*, 23.
14. NAC, MG 30, C144, Samuel J. Zacks Papers, vol. 6, "Henry F. Janes, Canada-Palestine Committee, 1943–46," Confidential Report from Henry F. Janes — The Rt. Hon. W. L. M. King's Meeting with Delegation from the Canadian Palestine Committee, the Canadian Christian Council and the Zionist Organization of Canada on 31 Mar. 1944.
15. Ibid.
16. Ibid., "Memorandum on the Jewish National Home in Palestine," 14 Jul. 1945.
17. Bercuson, *Canada and the Birth of Israel*, 23.
18. Kay, *Canada and Palestine*, 88.
19. NAC, MG 30, C144, Samuel J. Zacks Papers, *passim* and especially vol. 10, "Henry F. Janes." Janes's reports to Zacks carefully documented press coverage.
20. Ibid., vol. 1, "Harry Batshaw 1944," Minutes of Public Relations Committee Meeting, 13 Jan. 1944, 2.
21. Ibid., vol. 2, "Irwin Dorfman, Winnipeg," Irwin Dorfman to Zacks, 24 Nov. 1943.
22. Ibid.
23. Ibid.
24. Ibid., Henry F. Janes to Zacks, 13 Jan. 1944. Rabbi Stern, the spiritual leader of Temple Emanu-el in Montreal since 1928, was an ardent and active Zionist, unlike most of the Reform rabbinate. See his book *The Jewish Spirit Triumphant: A Collection of Addresses* (New York: Bloch Publishing, 1943), and Kenneth Irving Cleator and Harry J. Stern, *Harry Joshua Stern: A Rabbi's Journey* (New York: Bloch Publishing, 1981).
25. NAC, MG 30, C144, Samuel J. Zacks Papers, vol. 2, Zacks to Dorfman, 16 Dec. 1943.
26. Ibid., vol. 10, "Canadian Palestine Committee, 1944."
27. Ibid., "Henry F. Janes," Janes to Rabbi Schwartz, 9 Dec. 1943.
28. Ibid., "Canadian Palestine Committee, 1944."

29. NAC, MG 26, J4, William Lyon Mackenzie King Papers, Ellsworth Flavelle to King, 9 Oct. 1945, 321723 (Microfilm C-9873).
30. NAC, MG 30, C144, Samuel J. Zacks Papers, vol. 2, "Sam J. Drache," Zacks to Sam Drache, 9 Nov. 1943.
31. Ibid., vol. 1, "Harry Batshaw, 1944," David Rome to Harry Batshaw, 10 Nov. 1944.
32. Ibid., "Harry Batshaw, Montreal 1946–47," Report #4 on Palestine and Zionism.
33. Ibid., vol. 3, "J. M. Goldenberg," J. M. Goldenberg to Zacks, 20 Jun. 1946.
34. Ibid., "I. M. Gringorten," Gringorten to Zacks, 11 Oct. 1945.
35. Ibid., Mowat to Zacks, 21 Nov. 1944.
36. Ibid., Zacks to Mowat, 23 Nov. 1944.
37. Ibid., Mowat to Zacks, 26 Nov. 1944.
38. Ibid., vol. 11, "Canadian Palestine Com. 1947," Mowat to Harry Batshaw, 21 Feb. 1947.
39. Ibid., vol. 1, "Harry Batshaw, 1945," Canadian Editors Look at Palestine, 2 Oct. 1946, Memorandum from Harry Batshaw, K.C., no. 2.
40. Ibid., 2.
41. Ibid., "Canadian Editors look at Palestine," 25 Oct. 1946, Memorandum on Publicity no. 5.
42. Bercuson, *Canada and the Birth of Israel*, 37, 41.
43. Ibid., 43.
44. Ibid., 47.
45. NAC, MG 30, C144, Samuel J. Zacks Papers, vol. 7, "Jan.–Mar. 1947."
46. Ibid., vol. 1, "Canadian Palestine Committee," Mowat to Zacks, 7 Apr. 1948.
47. Ibid., vol. 4, "Harry Rosenthal, Windsor," Harry Rosenthal to R. M. Harrison, 28 May 1947.
48. Shabtai Teveth, *Ben-Gurion: The Burning Ground, 1886–1948* (Boston: Houghton Mifflin, 1987), 764.
49. NAC, MG 30, C144, Samuel J. Zacks Papers, vol. 6, "Oct.–Dec. 1944," Jesse Schwartz to S. J. Zacks, 4 Oct. 1943.
50. Ibid., Schwartz to Zacks, 13 Oct. 1944.
51. Ibid., Schwartz to Zacks, 7 Nov. 1944.
52. Ibid., Schwartz to Zacks, 10 Nov. 1944.
53. Ibid., Zacks to Schwisberg, 4 Nov. 1944.
54. Ibid., Schwisberg to Zacks, 6 Nov. 1944.
55. Ibid., vol. 4, "Jacobson, 1944," Jacobson to Zacks, 14 May 1944.
56. Ibid., "Samuel Jacobson, 1946," Sam Jacobson to Zacks, 3 Jan. 1944.
57. Ibid., vol. 3, "Samuel Jacobson, 1943," Jacobson to Zacks, 26 Jul. 1943.

58. CJCNA, "Hechalutz Bulletin," Mar. 1941, n.p.
59. CJCNA, *Toward a Positive Zionism* (Hashomer Hatzair, Canadian Region, n.d.), 11.
60. Ibid., "Genesis . . . the First Month at the Shomria Farm, Prescott, Ontario."
61. CZA, S6/2169, Joseph Israeli, New York, to Abe Herman, Jerusalem, 15 Feb. 1944.
62. NAC, MG 30, C144, Samuel J. Zacks Papers, vol. 9, "National Executive Board," Minutes, 17 Jul. 1944.
63. Ibid., "Meyer Weisgal," 3 Sept. 1944.
64. See Mordecai Richler, "Montreal, 1947: 'We Danced the Hora in the Middle of the Street,'" from "My Sort of War," *New Statesman*, 4 Sept. 1964, in B. J. Goldberg and Elliot King, eds., *Builders and Dreamers: Habonim Labor Zionist Youth in North America* (New York: Herzl Press, 1993): 126–29.
65. Mordecai Richler, *This Year in Jerusalem* (Toronto: Knopf Canada, 1994), 31.
66. *Camp Kadimah: The First Fifty Years 1943–1993* (Halifax, 1993), 6.
67. Sheva Medjuck, *The Jews of Atlantic Canada* (St. John's: Breakwater Press, 1986), *passim*.
68. Interview with Professor Mervin Butovsky, 27 Nov. 1996.
69. NAC, MG 30, C144, Samuel J. Zacks Papers, vol. 9, "1946–7," "Midwestern Region."
70. Ibid., "Minutes of the Executive Board of the ZOC, 22 Feb. 1944."
71. Ibid.
72. Ibid., "National Executive Board Meeting," 17 Jul. 1944.
73. Ibid., vol. 2, "Devor," Devor to Zacks, 6 Feb. 1944. See also Devor to Zacks, 30 Oct. 1944.
74. Ibid., Devor to Zacks, 12 Apr. 1945.
75. Ibid., Zacks to Devor, 3 May 1945.
76. Ibid., vol. 9, "National Council of the ZOC," 10 Sept. 1944.
77. Ibid., vol. 6, "Jesse Schwartz, Jul.–Sept. 1945," Nathan Shuster to Rabbi Schwartz, 18 Sept. 1945.
78. Ibid., vol. 1, "Max Bookman," Bookman to Zacks, 30 Jan. 1946.
79. Ibid., Bookman to Zacks, 21 Feb. 1946; 6 Mar. 1946.
80. Ibid., vol. 3, "S. Hart Green," Green to Zacks, 10 Apr. 1947.
81. Ibid., vol. 7, "Apr.–Jun. 1947," Kibbutz Aliyah by National Young Judaea Committee, 11 May 1947.
82. Ibid.
83. Ibid., "1949–1958," *Presidential Report of Samuel J. Zacks to the 30th National Convention*, Zionist Organization of Canada, 22 Jan. 1950, Montreal.
84. Ibid., vol. 1, "Harry Batshaw," Zacks to Batshaw, 24 Jun. 1949.
85. Ibid., vol. 6, "Jan.–Mar. 1945," Abe Herman to Schwartz, 24 Mar. 1945.

86. Ibid., vol. 7, "Minutes of the Executive Board of the ZOC," 19 Aug. 1946.
87. Ibid., vol. 12, "The Jewish Agency, 1948–49, 1970," Zacks to Gershon Asculai, 8 Jun. 1949. See also Hugh Garfinkle and Yosef Kohn to Zacks, 9 Jun. 1949.
88. There were exceptional small communities in which organizations other than the ZOC or Hadassah existed briefly. During the 1940s, Welland had a Labour Zionist group for some years; Kingston had a Mizrachi nucleus at the same time.
89. NAC, MG 30, C144, Samuel J. Zacks Papers, vol. 2, "Joseph N. Frank, Montreal," Zacks to Frank, 12 Nov. 1946.
90. Mordecai Richler, *This Year in Jerusalem*, 33–34.
91. See David J. Bercuson, *The Secret Army* (Toronto: Lester & Orpen Dennys, 1983), and "Illegal Corvettes: Canadian Blockade Runners to Palestine, 1946–1949," CJHSJ/SHJCJ 6, no. 1 (1982): 3–16; Ben Dunkelman, *Dual Allegiance* (Toronto: New American Library, 1976); and Samuel J. Zacks Papers, vol. 12, File Israel Supply, 1948–56, Teddy Kollek to Sam Zacks, 14 Sept. 1948.
92. NAC, MG 30, C144, Samuel J. Zacks Papers, vol. 1, "Leon D. Crestohl," Zacks to Leon D. Crestohl, 26 Aug. 1948.
93. Bercuson, *The Secret Army*, 45; J. K. Johnson, ed., *The Canadian Directory of Parliament 1867–1967* (Ottawa: Public Archives of Canada, 1968): 143.
94. NAC, RG 146, CSIS file on UJPO, 179–80, W. M. Brady Re Montreal Jewish Youth Council "United Palestine Appeal," 15 Mar. 1948.
95. Eddy Kaplansky, *The First Flyers: Aircrew Personnel in the War of Independence* (Israel Defence Forces, Air Force History Branch, 1993), 24–25, 34–35.
96. See Bercuson, *The Secret Army*, *passim*, and Dunkelman, *Dual Allegiance*, *passim*.
97. Bercuson, *The Secret Army*, 103.
98. NAC, MG 30, C144, Samuel J. Zacks Papers, vol. 8, H. Olyan to Appel, 7 Oct. 1948 (enclosure).
99. Ben-Zion Shapiro Papers, Ben-Zion Shapiro to family, 29 Sept. 1951.
100. Shapiro to family, 11 Oct. 1951.
101. L. Greenspan to Gerald Tulchinsky, 2 Apr. 1998.
102. Ben-Zion Shapiro Papers, Resolution of the Formation of Garin Aleph shel Yehuda Hatzair B'Canada, 22 Aug. 1951.
103. NAC, MG 30, C144, Samuel J. Zacks Papers, vol. 1, "Harry Batshaw," Zacks to Batshaw, 10 Dec. 1951.

Chapter 10/Postwar Adjustments, 1945-60

1. Interview with Phillip Stuchen, 29 Oct. 1996.
2. Phillip Stuchen, "Mass-Employment for Displaced Persons," QQ 54, no. 3 (1947): 360–65, 365.
3. Bernard Figler and David Rome, *Hananiah Meir Caiserman: A Biography with an Essay on Modern Jewish Times by David Rome* (Montreal: Northern Printing and Lithographing, 1962), 290; Hananiah Meir Caiserman, "H. M. Caiserman's Report on Poland," *Congress Bulletin*, Mar. 1946, 6. Caiserman was accompanied on this mission by Sam Lipshitz of the UJPO, who reported for Toronto's *Yiddisher Zhurnal*.
4. CJCNA, Caiserman Papers, vol. 4, "Jews in Poland, 1946," Bialystok, 16 Jan. 1946, Typescript, 2.
5. Ibid.
6. Figler and Rome, *Caiserman*, 291.
7. Ibid., 272.
8. Nancy Tienhaara, *Canadian Views on Immigration and Population: An Analysis of Post-War Gallup Polls* (Ottawa: Manpower and Immigration, 1974), 59.
9. NAC, RG 76, vol. 443, file 673831, pt. 12, Molson to Immigration, Microfilm C-10323; quoted in Jean Gerber, "Immigration and Integration in Post-War Canada: A Case Study of Holocaust Survivors in Vancouver, 1947–1970" (M.A. thesis, University of British Columbia, 1989), 26.
10. Irving Abella and Frank Bialystok, "Canada," in David Wyman, ed., *The World Reacts to the Holocaust* (Baltimore: Johns Hopkins University Press, 1996): 749–81, 759. See Ben Lappin, *The Redeemed Children: The Story of the Rescue of War Orphans by the Jewish Community of Canada* (Toronto: University of Toronto Press, 1963). For an excellent description and analysis of the reception given Jewish refugee youth in Montreal, see Greta Fischer and Pearl Switzer, "The Refugee Youth Program in Montreal 1947–1952" (M.S.W. thesis, McGill University, 1955). A recent and most affecting overview of the project is provided in Fraidie Martz's *Open Your Hearts: The Story of the Jewish War Orphans in Canada* (Toronto: Véhicule Press, 1996).
11. CJCNA, UJRA Collection, vol. 27, War Orphans Immigration Project, E. Ostry Correspondence, 1947–48.
12. David Rome, "Canada," AJYB 50 (1949): 290.
13. Louis Rosenberg, "Canada," AJYB 54 (1953): 221; Abella and Bialystok, "Canada": 759–60. See also Gerber, "Immigration and Integration," table 4.2,

"Total Immigration to Canada, General Displaced and Jewish Displaced, 1948–1953," 39.

14. Gerber, "Immigration and Integration," 33.
15. Ibid., 36.
16. *Vancouver News Herald*, 18 Dec. 1944, and *Jewish Western Bulletin*, 4 Jan. 1946; quoted in ibid., 41.
17. Lappin, *Redeemed Children*, 158.
18. Ibid., 166.
19. Gerber, "Immigration and Integration," 19.
20. Myra Giberovitch, "The Contributions of Montreal Holocaust Survivor Organizations to Jewish Communal Life" (M.S.W. thesis, McGill University, 1988), 52.
21. Ibid.
22. Percy Abrams, "A Study of the Jewish Immigrants in Hamilton and their Relationship with the Jewish Community Centre" (M.S.W. thesis, University of Toronto, 1955), 29.
23. Ibid., 79.
24. Ibid., 98.
25. Ibid., 38.
26. Gerber, "Immigration and Integration," 93.
27. Ibid., "Abstract," 12, 76, 83.
28. Ibid., 63.
29. Ibid., 80.
30. Ibid., 71.
31. Giberovitch, "Montreal Holocaust Survivor Organizations," 74.
32. Ibid., 77.
33. See Frank Bialystok, "The Politicization of Holocaust Survivors in Toronto and Montreal, 1960–1973" (Paper delivered to the Canadian Historical Association, Jun. 1996).
34. Gerber, "Immigration and Integration," 31.
35. Ibid., 76, 93.
36. Abella and Bialystok, "Canada": 760.
37. Rosenberg, "Canada," AJYB 57 (1956): 303.
38. Ibid., AJYB 58 (1957): 230; AJYB 66 (1965): 323.
39. See Ibolya (Szalai) Grossman, *An Ordinary Woman in Extraordinary Times* (Toronto: Multicultural History Society of Ontario, 1990).
40. For a penetrating analysis of the complex transformations in post-war Quebec society and politics, see Michael D. Behiels, *Prelude to Quebec's Quiet Revolution: Liberalism versus Neo-Nationalism, 1945–1960* (Montreal: McGill-Queen's University Press, 1985), and René Lévesque, "For an Independent Quebec," in Michael D. Behiels, ed., *Quebec Since 1945: Selected Readings* (Toronto: Copp Clark, 1987): 265–73, and other articles in this useful collection.
41. David Rome, "Canada," AJYB 44 (1942): 181; AJYB 45 (1943): 230.
42. Ibid., AJYB 46 (1944): 203; AJYB 47 (1945): 361, 363. In 1937 Father Valiquette, while

still a student, had consulted Hananiah Caiserman on Jewish affairs (Jacques Langlais and David Rome, *Jews and French Quebecers: Two Hundred Years of Shared History* [Waterloo: Wilfrid Laurier University Press, 1991], 123). Supported by fellow Jesuit Father Joseph Paré of Collège Ste. Marie and encouraged by Rabbi Harry J. Stern of Montreal's Temple Emanu-el, Valiquette continued his research on Judaism and laboured to convey his liberal views to other French-Canadian Catholics. In 1954 he established the Quebec branch of the Canadian Council of Christians and Jews (ibid., 124).

43. David Rome, "Canada," AJYB 48 (1946): 277.
44. Ibid., AJYB 50 (1949): 292–93.
45. Jack Jedwab, "The Politics of Dialogue: Rapprochement Efforts Between Jews and French Canadians: 1939–1960," in Ira Robinson and Mervin Butovsky, eds., *Renewing Our Days: Montreal Jews in the Twentieth Century* (Montreal: Véhicule Press, 1995): 42–74, 54.
46. André Laurendeau, "Bloc Notes," *Le Devoir*, 28 Nov. 1952; quoted in ibid.: 57.
47. Ibid.: fn. 20.
48. Betty Sigler, "Montreal: The Bonds of Community, the Town Within the City," *Commentary* 20, no. 4 (1950): 345–53, 352.
49. Everett C. Hughes, *French Canada in Transition* (Chicago: University of Chicago Press, 1963).
50. See Behiels, *Prelude*, 8–19, and his "Quebec: Social Transformation and Ideological Renewal, 1940–1976," in Behiels, *Quebec Since 1945*: 21–45.
51. Michael D. Behiels, "Georges-Henri Lévesque," *The Canadian Encyclopedia*, vol. 2, 2d ed. (Edmonton: Hurtig, 1988): 1205.
52. Pierre Elliott Trudeau, "Separatist Counter-Revolutionaries," *Federalism and the French Canadians* (Toronto: Macmillan of Canada, 1968), 206.
53. Jean Pierre Gaboury, *Le Nationalisme de Lionel Groulx: aspects idéologiques* (Ottawa: Éditions de l'Université d'Ottawa, 1970), 35–36.
54. See Richard Jones, *L'Idéologie de l'Action Catholique* (Quebec: Les Presses de l'Université Laval, 1974).
55. See Pierre Elliott Trudeau, in collaboration, *La Grève de l'amiante* (Montreal: Les Éditions Cité Libre, 1956), app. 2, Le Rapport Custos, 407–08.
56. Yves Lavertu, *The Bernonville Affair: A French War Criminal in Quebec After World War II*, George Tombs, trans. (Montreal: Robert Davies Publishing, 1995).
57. Ibid., 58.
58. Quoted in Sol Littman, "Barbie's

Buddy in Canada," *Canadian Dimension* 21, no. 6 (1987): 13–15, 14.

59. Ibid. See also CJN, 2 Jun. 1994. I am grateful to Sol Littman for bringing this material to my attention and for allowing me to read a portion of the manuscript of his forthcoming book on war criminals in Canada.
60. Xavier Gélinas to Gerald Tulchinsky, 4 Dec. 1997. See also Xavier Gélinas, "Le droit intellectuel et la Révolution tranquille: le cas de la revue *Tradition et progrès*, 1957–1962," CHR 77, no. 3 (1996): 353–87.
61. See Jedwab, "The Politics of Dialogue": 42–74.
62. Ibid.: 61.
63. Quoted in ibid.: 65.
64. Claude Ryan, "How French-Canadians See Jews," in Robert Guy Scully and Marc Plourde, eds., *A Stable Society* (Montreal: Éditions Héritage, 1978): 322.
65. Ibid.: 321.
66. Yogev Tzuk, "Challenge and Response: Jewish Communal Welfare in Montreal," *Contemporary Jewry* 6, no. 2 (1983): 43–52, 49.
67. Janine Stingel, "Social Credit and the Jews: Anti-Semitism in the Alberta Social Credit Movement and the Response of the Canadian Jewish Congress, 1935–1949" (Ph.D. thesis, McGill University, 1997), 257–303.
68. David Rome, "Canada," AJYB 52 (1951): 237.
69. Ibid., AJYB 51 (1950): 274.
70. Ibid., AJYB 53 (1952): 262.
71. Ben Kayfetz to Gerald Tulchinsky, 17 Jul. 1977.
72. See Irwin Pollock, "Civil Rights and the Anglo-Jewish Press in Canada: 1930–1970" (M.A. thesis, McGill University, 1979).
73. See John C. Bagnall, "The Ontario Conservatives and the Development of Anti-Discrimination Policy: 1944 to 1962" (Ph.D. thesis, Queen's University, 1984), 20–22, 35, 71–72. In an editorial in February 1944, the *Toronto Star* attacked antisemitism as a secret and powerful weapon of democracy's enemies, and argued that "particularly at this time, as an aid to the war effort, it is essential to use every means to fight racial discrimination"; quoted in ibid., 32.
74. Roger Graham, *Old Man Ontario: Leslie M. Frost,* Ontario Historical Studies Series (Toronto: University of Toronto Press, 1990), 263. See also Ben Kayfetz, "On Community Relations in Ontario in the 1940s," CJS 2 (1994): 57–65, 63.
75. Lesley Marrus-Barsky, "History of Mount Sinai Hospital," (unpublished manuscript), 105, 112. One of the conditions under which Mount Sinai

exchanged some prime land with the Hospital for Sick Children for a slightly less desirable site was that Sick Children stop excluding Jewish interns and residents. Ibid., 54.

76. Donald Creighton, *The Forked Road: Canada 1939–1957* (Toronto: McClelland and Stewart, 1976), 181–82.
77. NAC, RG 33, Royal Commission on National Development in the Arts, Letters and Sciences, vol. 14, Brief 132 (Submission . . . by the Canadian Jewish Congress, 14 Nov. 1949), Microfilm C-2005.
78. Creighton, *The Forked Road*, 2.
79. NAC, RG 33, Royal Commission on National Development in the Arts, Letters and Sciences, vol. 14, Brief 132.
80. Leo Driedger and Glenn Church, "Residential Segregation and Institutional Completeness: A Comparison of Ethnic Minorities," CRSA/RCSA 11, no. 1 (1974): 30–52, 39.
81. Gerber, "Immigration and Integration," 43–44.
82. While a student at the University of Toronto in the mid-1950s, I took my shoes for repair to an elderly Jewish cobbler on Harbord Street, just west of Spadina Avenue. He insisted on speaking to me in Yiddish after learning my name: "*Tulchinsky, dos iz a yiddisher numen*." On my last visit to his shop, just before graduation, he told me in a tearful whisper that because of his advancing age, he had decided to sell out. But he stayed there for weeks, proudly introducing all of his former customers to the new owner, a young Italian immigrant.
83. George Gamester, "College and Spadina Gang Prove They're Pals for Life," *Toronto Star*, 15 Mar. 1998.
84. John R. Seeley, R. Alexander Sim, and Elizabeth W. Loosley, in collaboration with Norman W. Bell and D. F. Fleming, *Crestwood Heights* (Toronto: University of Toronto Press, 1956), 212–15, 219, 286–87, 307.
85. Ibid, 287.
86. Ibid, 308.
87. Louis Rosenberg "Canada," AJYB 54 (1953): 228.
88. See *Baron de Hirsch Congregation, 1890 to 1990: 100th Anniversary Commemorative Book* (Halifax: Beth Israel Synagogue, 1990); *Agudas Israel Congregation Dedication Volume 1905–1963* (Saskatoon: Saskatoon Jewish Community, 1963).
89. Harvey Meirovitch, "The Rise and Decline of a Toronto Synagogue: Congregation Beth Am," CJHSJ/SHJCJ 1, no. 2 (1977): 97–113, 99–100.
90. Ibid.: 110.
91. Ben Lappin, "May Day in

Toronto: Yesteryear and Now," *Commentary* 19, no 5 (1955): 476–79, 479.

92. See Kim Ellen Levis, "Keeping the Flame Alive: The Story of the Toronto Jewish Folk Choir," CJO (Dec. 1997): 20.
93. Bessie W. Batist, ed., *A Treasure for My Daughter: A Reference Book of Jewish Festivals with Menus and Recipes* (Montreal: Herald Woodward Press, 1950).
94. Ibid.: 3.
95. Erna Paris, "Growing Up a Jewish Princess in Forest Hill," in Gerri Sinclair and Morris Wolfe, eds., *The Spice Box: An Anthology of Jewish Canadian Writing* (Toronto: Lester & Orpen Dennys, 1981): 243–50, 246–47. The snobbishness and materialism present in the Forest Hill Reform Holy Blossom Temple during the 1940s is effectively discussed by Michele Landsberg in Francine Zuckerman, ed., *Half the Kingdom: Seven Jewish Feminists* (Montreal: Véhicule Press, 1992): 57–69, 58, 60.
96. Yael Gordon-Brym, "The Changing Role of Canadian Jewish Women," in Edmond Y. Lipsitz, ed., *Canadian Jewish Women of Today: Who's Who of Canadian Jewish Women* (Downsview: JESL Educational Products, 1983): 11–21, 14.
97. Rachel Schlesinger, "Changing Roles of Jewish Women," in Edmond Y. Lipsitz, ed., *Canadian Jewry Today: Who's Who in Canadian Jewry* (Downsview: J.E.S.L. Educational Products, 1989): 60–70, 62.
98. Ibid.: 63.
99. Louis Rosenberg, "The Jewish Population of Canada: A Statistical Summary to 1943," AJYB 48 (1947): 50; Ibid., AJYB 56 (1955): 301.
100. Louis Rosenberg, "A Study of the Changes in the Population Characteristics: The Jewish Community in Canada 1931–1961," *Canadian Jewish Population Studies*, Canadian Jewish Community Series 2, no. 2 (Montreal: Canadian Jewish Congress, Bureau of Social and Economic Research, 1965): 15.
101. *Report of the Royal Commission on Bilingualism and Biculturalism*, book 4, *The Cultural Contribution of the Other Ethnic Groups* (Ottawa: Information Canada, 1969), 103.
102. Ibid., 40. They were followed most closely by Italians and Asians.
103. See ibid., 61–63.
104. Ibid., 63. See also 267.
105. Ibid., 103.
106. Ibid.
107. These figures are Jews by religion. Daniel J. Elazar and Harold M. Waller, *Maintaining Consensus: The Canadian Jewish Polity in the Postwar World* (New York: University Press of America, 1990), 18.

108. Louis Rosenberg, "Canada," AJYB 65 (1964): 163.
109. Ibid., AJYB 56 (1955): 299.
110. Ibid., AJYB 52 (1951): 231; AJYB 58 (1957): 229.
111. Ibid., AJYB 68 (1967): 269.
112. See Morton Weinfeld, "Intermarriage: Agony and Adaptation," in M. Weinfeld, W. Shaffir, and I. Cotler, eds., *The Canadian Jewish Mosaic* (Toronto: John Wiley and Sons, 1981): 365–82, 381.
113. Ibid.: 361.
114. Ibid.: 382.
115. Louis Rosenberg, "Canada," AJYB 53 (1952): 260–61.
116. Louis Rosenberg, "Two Centuries of Jewish Life in Canada, 1760–1960," AJYB 62 (1961): 42; Elazar and Waller, *Maintaining Consensus*, 18.
117. See Edward S. Shapiro, *A Time for Healing: American Jewry Since World War II*, vol. 5 of Jewish People in America Series (Baltimore: Johns Hopkins University Press, 1992), 125–26, where the estimated number of post-war Jewish refugee immigrants to the United States is 160,000.
118. Ibid., 126.
119. Louis Rosenberg, "Canada," AJYB 62 (1961): 41.
120. All Conservative and Reform congregations had rabbis, though in 1951 only 96 of 146 Orthodox congregations had their own rabbis. Rosenberg, "Canada," AJYB 52 (1951): 238.
121. Ibid., AJYB 62 (1961): 42.
122. William Shaffir, *Life in a Religious Community: The Lubavitcher Chassidim in Montreal*, Cultures and Communities: Community Studies (Toronto: Holt Rinehart and Winston, 1974), 12.
123. Rosenberg, "Canada," AJYB 58 (1957): 234–35.
124. Ibid. Thirty-five attended Orthodox yeshivot, ten the Jewish Theological Seminary, and three Hebrew Union college.
125. Rosenberg, "Two Centuries of Jewish Life": 42.
126. Rome, "Canada," AJYB 44 (1942): 180.
127. Ibid., AJYB 45 (1943): 228.
128. Ibid., AJYB 47 (1945): 358.
129. Rosenberg, "Canada," AJYB 55 (1954): 169.
130. Mordecai Richler, "This Year In Jerusalem," *Hunting Tigers Under Glass: Essays and Reports* (London: Granada Publishing, 1971): 143–76, 163–64.
131. Elazar and Waller, *Maintaining Consensus*, 71, 161.
132. Rosenberg, "Canada," AJYB 53 (1952): 263–64.
133. See Morton Weinfeld, "Introduction," and "Bibliography of Works by Louis Rosenberg," in Louis Rosenberg, *Canada's Jews: A Social and Economic Study of Jews in Canada in the 1930s*, Morton Weinfeld, ed. (Montreal: McGill-Queen's University Press, 1993).

Chapter 11/Jewish Ethnicity in a Multicultural Canada, 1960–80

1. J. K. Johnson, ed., *The Canadian Directory of Parliament 1867–1967* (Ottawa: Public Archives of Canada, 1968): 243; AJYB 71 (1970): 364.
2. Stephen Clarkson and Christina McCall, *The Magnificent Obsession*, vol. 1 of *Trudeau and Our Times* (Toronto: McClelland and Stewart, 1990), 416.
3. Census of Canada (1961), vol. 3, part 1, 94–515; Ibid. (1971), vol. 3, part 3, 94–731.
4. See Louis Greenspan and Graeme Nicholson, eds., *Fackenheim: German Philosophy and Jewish Thought* (Toronto: University of Toronto Press, 1991).
5. See Richard Menkis, "A Threefold Transformation: Jewish Studies, Canadian Universities and the Canadian Jewish Community," in Michael Brown, ed., *A Guide to the Study of Jewish Civilization in Canadian Universities* (Toronto: The International Center for University Teaching of Jewish Civilization of the Hebrew University of Jerusalem and the Centre for Jewish Studies at York University, Toronto, 1998): 43–69.
6. Ann Gibbon and Peter Hadekel, *Steinberg: The Breakup of a Family Empire* (Toronto: Macmillan, 1990), 2.
7. Ibid., 11.
8. Ibid., 63.
9. Anthony Bianco, *The Reichmanns: Family, Faith, Fortune, and the Empire of Olympia & York* (Toronto: Vintage, 1997), 257.
10. Ibid., 369.
11. Louis Rosenberg, "Canada," AJYB 65 (1964): 168.
12. Ibid., AJYB 66 (1965): 325.
13. Ibid., AJYB 68 (1967): 269.
14. Ibid.: 269–70.
15. Ibid.: 270.
16. See Ben Kayfetz, "Canada," AJYB 69 (1968): 282.
17. Ibid.
18. Ibid.: 283.
19. Ibid.
20. Harold Troper, "The Canadian Jewish Polity and the Limits of Political Action: The Campaign on Behalf of Soviet and Syrian Jews," in Harold Troper and Morton Weinfeld, eds., *Ethnicity, Politics, and Public Policy in Canada: Case Studies in Canadian Diversity* (Toronto: University of Toronto Press, forthcoming).
21. Mitchell Sharp, *Which Reminds Me . . . A Memoir* (Toronto: University of Toronto Press, 1994), 211.
22. See Wendy Eisen, *Count Us In: The Struggle to Free Soviet Jews: A Canadian Perspective* (Toronto: Burgher Books, 1995).
23. Ibid., 45. See also Mindy B. Avrich-Skapinker, "Canadian-

Jewish Involvement with Soviet Jewry, 1970–1990: The Toronto Case Study" (Ph.D. thesis, University of Toronto, 1993).

24. Eisen, *Count Us In*.
25. Quoted in Troper, "Canadian Jewish Polity": 13.
26. Ibid.: 32.
27. Roberta L. Markus and Donald V. Schwartz, "Soviet Jewish Emigrés in Toronto: Ethnic Self-Identity and Issues of Integration," CES/EEC 16, no. 2 (1984): 71–88. Roberta L. Markus, *Adaptation: A Case Study of Soviet Jewish Immigrant Children in Toronto, 1970–1978* (Toronto: Permanent Press, 1979), 15–16.
28. Markus, *Adaptation*, 17.
29. Ben Kayfetz, "Canada," AJYB 69 (1968): 385.
30. Mordecai Richler, *This Year in Jerusalem* (Toronto: Knopf, 1994), 115.
31. Ibid., 115–16.
32. Melvin Fenson, "Canada," AJYB 75 (1974–75): 348.
33. Ibid.: 350.
34. Ibid.
35. Sharp, *Which Reminds Me*, 209.
36. Bernard Baskin, "Canada," AJYB 80 (1980): 179.
37. J. L. Granatstein and Robert Bothwell, *Pirouette: Pierre Trudeau and Canadian Foreign Policy* (Toronto: University of Toronto Press, 1990), 211.
38. Bernard Baskin, "Canada," AJYB 76 (1976): 257.
39. Ibid., AJYB 77 (1977): 332.
40. Ben Kayfetz, "Canada," AJYB 69 (1968): 363.
41. W. Gunther Plaut, *Unfinished Business: An Autobiography* (Toronto: Lester & Orpen Dennys, 1981), 281–82.
42. The best account of this controversy by a participant is Rabbi Plaut's in *Unfinished Business*, 278–94. An excellent scholarly overview is David Taras, "A Church Divided: A. C. Forrest and the United Church's Middle East Policy," in David Taras and David H. Goldberg, eds., *The Domestic Battleground: Canada and the Arab-Israeli Conflict* (Montreal: McGill-Queen's University Press, 1989): 86–101.
43. Warren Bass, "'I Am Surprised You Still Speak to Me': The United Church *Observer* and the Jews, 1948–1987" (Undergraduate essay, Queen's University, 1990), 8.
44. I am indebted for this insight and many others on the CJN in the 1960s to my former student, Richard Kicksee, who carried out an extensive analysis of its contents in "The *Canadian Jewish News*: An Overview," 2 Sept. 1993, a private communication.
45. CJN, 7 Jun. 1968.
46. Bass, "I Am Surprised," 12–13.
47. CJN, 12 Dec. 1969.
48. Ibid.
49. Ibid., 13 Mar. 1970.
50. Plaut, *Unfinished Business*, 286.
51. Taras, "Church Divided": 86.

52. Reuben Slonim, *Family Quarrel: The United Church and the Jews* (Toronto: Clarke Irwin, 1977), vii. See also Gary A. Gaudin, "Protestant Church/Jewish State: The United Church of Canada, Israel and the Palestinian Refugees Revisited," *Studies in Religion/Sciences Réligieuses* 24, no. 2 (1995): 179–91.
53. Canadian policy on the Palestine question and the birth of Israel has been treated superbly in David J. Bercuson's *Canada and the Birth of Israel: A Study in Canadian Foreign Policy* (Toronto: University of Toronto Press, 1985); for Israel's first decade, see Zachariah Kay's insightful *The Diplomacy of Prudence: Canada and Israel, 1948–1958* (Montreal: McGill-Queen's University Press, 1997).
54. See David H. Goldberg, *Foreign Policy and Ethnic Interest Groups: American and Canadian Jews Lobby for Israel* (New York: Greenwood Press, 1990), 112–22.
55. Ibid., 121.
56. Bernard Baskin, "Canada," AJYB 79 (1979): 197.
57. Ibid., AJYB 80 (1980): 180.
58. Granatstein and Bothwell, *Pirouette*, 213–14.
59. Ibid., 218.
60. Ibid., 217.
61. Goldberg, *Foreign Policy*, 140.
62. The analyst David Goldberg points out that Americans were much more successful in securing anti-boycott legislation.
63. Ronnie Miller, *From Lebanon to the Intifada: The Jewish Lobby and Canadian Middle Eastern Policy* (Lanham, MD: University Press of America, 1991), 97.
64. Harold Waller, "Canada," AJYB 90 (1990): 311.
65. Bernard Baskin, "Canada," AJYB 79 (1979): 196.
66. Ibid.: 198.
67. Ibid.: 199.
68. Jack Wertheimer, "The Disaffections of American Jews," *Commentary* 105, no. 5 (1998): 44–49.
69. Ruth R. Wisse, "Between Passovers," *Commentary* 88, no. 6 (1989): 42–47, 47.
70. Michael Brown, "The Push and Pull Factors of Aliyah and the Anomalous Case of Canada: 1967–1982," JSS 48, no. 2 (1986): 141–62, 143.
71. Richler, *This Year in Jerusalem*, 237–38.
72. Michael M. Solomon, "Canada," AJYB 71 (1970): 362.
73. See Stuart E. Rosenberg, "Canada," AJYB 73 (1972): 398.
74. Ben Kayfetz, "Canada," AJYB 69 (1968): 362.
75. See Zailig Pollock, *A. M. Klein: The Story of the Poet* (Toronto: University of Toronto Press, 1994); Miriam Waddington, *A. M. Klein*, Studies in Canadian Literature (Toronto: Copp Clark, 1970); and Adam G.

Fuerstenberg, "The Poet and the Tycoon: The Relationship Between A. M. Klein and Samuel Bronfman," CJHSJ/SHJCJ 5, no. 2 (1981): 49–69. See also Ruth R. Wisse, "Jewish Participation in Canadian Culture" (a study for the Royal Commission on Bilingualism and Biculturalism, n.d., manuscript).

76. Michael Greenstein, *Third Solitude: Tradition and Discontinuity in Jewish-Canadian Literature* (Montreal: McGill-Queen's University Press, 1989), 53.
77. Norman Ravvin, *A House of Words: Jewish Writing, Identity, and Memory* (Montreal: McGill-Queen's University Press, 1997), 33–47.
78. Ruth R. Wisse, "My Life Without Leonard Cohen," *Commentary* 100, no. 4 (1996): 27–33, 33.
79. See Mervin Butovsky, "An Interview with Irving Layton," in Chaim Spilberg and Yaacov Zipper, eds., *Canadian Jewish Anthology/Anthologie Juive du Canada* (Montreal: National Committee on Yiddish, Canadian Jewish Congress, 1982): 59–74.
80. Rosenberg, "Canada," AJYB 73 (1972): 396.
81. Ibid.: 397.
82. Ibid.
83. Ibid.: 397–98.
84. Ibid., "French Separatism: Its Implications for Canadian Jewry," AJYB 73 (1972): 407–27, 427.
85. Quoted in ibid.: 409.
86. Melvin Fenson, "Canada," AJYB 75 (1974–75): 320.
87. *Montreal Gazette*, 17 Oct. 1979.
88. Graham Fraser, *P.Q.: René Lévesque and the Parti Québécois in Power* (Toronto: Macmillan, 1984), 153–54.
89. Fenson, "Canada," AJYB 75 (1974–75): 321.
90. Bernard Baskin, "Canada," AJYB 78 (1978): 281.
91. Fraser, *René Lévesque*, 67.
92. Mordecai Richler, "Language (and Other) Problems," *Home Sweet Home: My Canadian Album* (Toronto: Penguin Books, 1986): 224–64, 241–42.
93. Ruth R. Wisse and Irwin Cotler, "Quebec's Jews: Caught In the Middle," *Commentary* 64, no. 3 (1977): 55–59.
94. Michel Laferrière, "Quebec's Jews," *Commentary* 65, no. 1 (1978): 4–5.
95. Ibid.
96. Irwin Cotler, "Le Fait français et le fait juif: First Encounters," *Report on Confederation* 1, no. 8 (1978): 26–28, 27.
97. Ibid.: 28.
98. Jean-François Lisée, "Interview with Pierre Anctil," in William Dodge, ed., *Boundaries of Identity: A Quebec Reader* (Toronto: Lester Publishing, 1992): 151–56, 153.
99. Naim Kattan, "Jewish Characters

in the French-Canadian Novel," *Viewpoints* 1, no. 3 (1966): 29–32, 29.

100. Ibid.: 30.
101. J. L. Granatstein, *Canada 1957–1967: The Years of Uncertainty and Innovation* (Toronto: McClelland and Stewart, 1986), 248.
102. NAC, RG 33/80, Royal Commission on Bilingualism and Biculturalism, vol. 45, file 740-252.
103. Ibid., 4.
104. Harold Waller, "Canada," AJYB 86 (1986): 237.
105. Lisée, "Pierre Anctil": 154. But it was the law and it was enforced.
106. Harold Waller, "Canada," AJYB 97 (1997): 252.
107. Jean-Claude Lasry, "A Francophone Diaspora in Quebec," in M. Weinfeld, W. Shaffir, and I. Cotler, eds., *The Canadian Jewish Mosaic* (Toronto: John Wiley and Sons, 1981): 221–40. See also Jean-Claude Lasry, "Sephardim and Ashkenazim in Montreal," in Robert J. Brym, William Shaffir, and Morton Weinfeld, eds., *The Jews in Canada* (Toronto: Oxford University Press, 1993): 395–401.
108. See Marie Berdugo-Cohen, Yolande Cohen, and Joseph Levy, *Juifs maroccains à Montréal: Témoinages d'une immigration moderne* (Montreal: VLB Éditeur, 1987).
109. Ibid., *passim*.
110. Rosenberg, "French Separatism: Its Implications": 407–27, 420.
111. Melvin Fenson, "Canada," AJYB 75 (1974–75): 317–57, 321.
112. CJN, 27 Dec. 1963.
113. Ibid., 30 Aug. 1968.
114. Jean-Claude Lasry and Evelyn Bloomfield Schacter, "Jewish Intermarriage in Montreal, 1962–1972," JSS 37, nos. 3–4, (1975): 267–78, 272.
115. Harold Waller, "Canada," AJYB 86 (1986): 234.
116. Ibid., AJYB 89 (1989): 261.
117. Lasry, "A Francophone Diaspora": 227.
118. Ibid.: 231.
119. CJN, 28 Jan. 1972.
120. Ibid., 22 Jun. 1973.
121. CJO (Apr. 1975).
122. CJN, 22 Nov. 1979.
123. This paragraph is based on Berdugo-Cohen et al., *Juifs maroccains à Montréal*.
124. CJN, 25 Jun. 1987.
125. See Janice Arnold, "Plans Created for Ashkenazi-Sephardic Programmes" and "Montreal Dialogue Boosts Sephardi-Ashkenazi Ties," CJN, 9 Jan. 1986 and 11 Sept. 1986.
126. Margaret Spack, "Integration of Jewish Immigrants from Morocco into the Toronto Community: The Use of Attitudes Towards the Social Services" (M.S.W. thesis, University of Toronto, 1965), 2–3.
127. Ibid., 5.

128. Sylvia K. Baker, "Integration of Jewish Immigrants from Morocco into the Toronto Community: A Comment on the Relationship between Integration and Disciplinary Problems with Their Children Experienced by Parents from Morocco" (M.S.W. thesis, University of Toronto, 1965), 2.
129. Thomas H. Zador, "Integration of Jewish Immigrants from Morocco into the Jewish Community: An Exploratory Study of Sephardic Jewish Immigrants Who Came to Canada After Morocco Gained Independence in 1956, with Special Reference to Psychological-Emotional as well as Socio-Economic Satisfactions and Dissatisfactions in Canada" (M.S.W. thesis, University of Toronto, 1965), 7.
130. CJN, 27 Jan. 1967.
131. Ibid., 15 Mar. 1968, 20 Mar. 1973, 24 Aug. 1973.
132. See Ruth Teitel, "The Sephardim Now Are Here," CJN, 15 Mar. 1968.
133. "Don't Overlook Mitzvah of Aiding Sephardim with Life, Death Struggle," CJN, 19 Apr. 1974.
134. CJN, 6 May 1977.
135. Quoted in Sarah Taieb-Carlen, "Monocultural Education in a Pluralist Environment: Ashkenazi Curricula in Toronto Jewish Educational Institutions," CES/EEC 24, no. 3 (1992): 75–86, 83.
136. Sheldon Kirshner, "School's Role in Instilling Jewish Identity Exaggerated, Research Claims," CJN, 4 Mar. 1977.
137. See Marion E. Meyer, *The Jews of Kingston: A Microcosm of Canadian Jewry?* (Kingston: Limestone Press, 1983), 101–08.
138. Laura Wolfson to Gerald Tulchinsky, 25 Apr. 1997.
139. Meyer, *Jews of Kingston*, 107.
140. Marion E. Meyer, "Ten Years Later: Another Look at Our Community" (unpublished manuscript, 1997), 2.
141. Toba Korenblum, "Expensive Synagogues, Lavish Programs Must Be Ruled Out in the Future, Warns Rabbi," CJN, 25 Feb. 1977.
142. Rabbi Stuart Rosenberg made some interesting observations on transformations in the modern synagogue in "Looking Ahead: The Synagogue's Future," CJN, 14 Jan. 1972.
143. CJN, 10 May 1972.
144. Norman Tollinsky, "Liberalism Has Deserted Jews: Our Golden Age Is at an End," CJN, 3 Nov. 1972.
145. Len Scher, *The Un-Canadians: True Stories of the Blacklist Era* (Toronto: Lester Publishing, 1992).
146. "Secular Jewish Schools: Proposed Statement of Principles," CJO (Mar. 1973).
147. Marvin Klotz, quoted in Jack

Cowan, "Secular Jewish Life," CJO (Jun. 1973): 12.

148. Jerald Bain, "Secular Jewish Viewpoint," CJO (Aug.–Sept. 1973): 9.
149. See M. J. Olgin, "In Defense of Progressive Jewish Culture," CJO (Mar. 1973): 5, 6, 13; Harold Benson, "Some Aspects of Jewish Secular Identity," CJO (Jul.–Aug. 1974): 3–4; and Maxine and Sol Hermolin, "Searching for Meaning of Jewish Secularism," CJO (Jul.–Aug. 1976): 8–9.
150. Michael Bodemann, "Does the Jewish Left in Canada Have a Future?" CJO (Mar. 1981): 3, 4, 15; and Bodemann, "Jews in Canada: What Place for Progressives?" CJO (Oct. 1981): 10–12.
151. Bodemann, "What Place for Progressives?": 10–12, 11.
152. Ibid.
153. Jerald Bain, "A Vision for the Future," CJO (Dec. 1982): 13–16, 16.
154. Sheldon Kirshner, "Secular Jewish Culture Ending Is Gloomy Forecast of Irving Howe," CJN, 29 Mar. 1979.
155. See Ben Lappin, "May Day in Toronto: Yesteryear and Now," *Commentary* 19, no. 5 (1955): 476–79, for a poignant look at the remnants of this old left and one of their intellectual's mordant views of the younger generation, and Merrily Weisbord, *The Strangest Dream: Canadian Communists, the Spy Trials and the Cold War* (Montreal: Véhicule Press, 1994), 214–30.

Chapter 12/Complexities and Uncertainties from the 1970s to the 1990s

1. Ruth R. Wisse, "Between Passovers," *Commentary* 88, no. 6 (1989): 42–47, 46.
2. See Morton Weinfeld and John J. Sigal, "The Effect of the Holocaust on Selected Socio-Political Attitudes of Adult Children of Survivors," CRSA/RCSA 23, no. 3 (1986): 365–82.
3. See Jack Kuper, *Child of the Holocaust* (Toronto: General Publishing, 1967).
4. See Leslie Ann Hulse, "The Emergence of the Holocaust Survivor in the Canadian Jewish Community" (M.A. thesis, Carleton University, 1979). Irving Abella and Frank Bialystok, "Canada," in David Wyman, ed., *The World Reacts to the Holocaust* (Baltimore: Johns Hopkins University Press, 1996): 749–81, 766.
5. Frank Bialystok, "The Politicization of Holocaust Survivors in Toronto and Montreal, 1960–1973" (Paper delivered to the Canadian Historical Association, St. Catharines, 1996), 6–7.

6. See William Kaplan, "Maxwell Cohen and the Report of the Special Committee on Hate Propaganda," in William Kaplan, ed., *Law, Policy, and International Justice: Essays in Honour of Maxwell Cohen* (Montreal: McGill-Queen's University Press, 1993): 243–74.
7. Quoted in Yaacov Glickman, "Ethnicity and National Allegiance in the Canadian Body Politic," *Canadian Review of Studies in Nationalism* 11, no. 2 (1984): 219–29, 226.
8. CJN, 28 Jun. 1963.
9. Ibid., 30 Mar. 1973.
10. S. Joshua Langer, "War Criminals: How Long Can They Hide Here?" CJN, 23 Apr. 1971.
11. CJO (Jan.–Feb. 1975): 21–22.
12. CJN, 7 Feb. 1975; Harold Troper and Morton Weinfeld, *Old Wounds: Jews, Ukrainians and the Hunt for Nazi War Criminals in Canada* (Toronto: Viking, 1988), 383.
13. See Sol Littman, *War Criminals on Trial: The Rauca Case* (Markham: PaperJacks, 1984).
14. Harold Waller, "Canada," AJYB 86 (1986): 235.
15. Jules Deschênes, *Commission of Inquiry on War Criminals Report: Part 1* (Ottawa: Minister of Supply and Services, 1986), iii.
16. Ibid., 3–14.
17. Harold Waller, "Canada," AJYB 87 (1987): 199.
18. Ibid.
19. CJN, 16 Jan. 1986.
20. Ibid., 30 Jan. 1986.
21. See Troper and Weinfeld, *Old Wounds*, for a superb comprehensive study of Jewish-Ukrainian relations in Canada, including developments during the Deschênes Commission inquiry.
22. Quoted in John Sopinka, Q.C., *Ukrainian Canadian Committee Submission to the Commission of Inquiry on War Criminals* (Toronto: Justinian Press, 1986), 6.
23. Ibid., 7.
24. CJN, 2 Apr. 1987.
25. Ibid., 6 Feb. 1986.
26. Ibid., 27 Nov. 1986.
27. Troper and Weinfeld, *Old Wounds*, 304.
28. Quoted in CJN, 13 Aug. 1987.
29. Ibid.
30. Ibid., 20 Aug. 1987. See also Harold Waller, "Canada," AJYB 89 (1989): 259–60.
31. Waller, "Canada," AJYB 89 (1989): 260.
32. Ibid., AJYB 90 (1990): 306.
33. Ibid.: 308; see David Matas, with Susan Charendoff, *Justice Delayed: Nazi War Criminals in Canada* (Toronto: Summerhill Press, 1987).
34. Ibid., 264.
35. Irving Abella, "Eluding Justice: Nazi War Criminals in Canada" (Paper to Conference on Canadian Jewish Studies, York University, Jun. 1998).
36. Harold Waller, "Canada," AJYB 91 (1991): 234.

37. CJN, 7 Nov. 1996.
38. Ibid., 5 Dec. 1996.
39. See Arnold Fradkin, "Canada Ignored War Criminals for 27 Years" and "War Crimes Cases Crawling Ahead at Snail's Pace," CJN, 2 and 9 Jan. 1997; see also R. Paltiel, "Canada Portrayed as Sanctuary for War Criminals," *Globe and Mail*, 31 Jan. 1997.
40. Harold Waller, "Canada," AJYB 86 (1986): 236.
41. Quoted in Gabriel Weimann and Conrad Winn, *Hate on Trial: the Zundel Affair, the Media and Public Opinion in Canada* (Oakville: Mosaic Press, 1986), 29.
42. Harold Waller, "Canada," AJYB 87 (1987): 198.
43. Weimann and Winn, *Hate on Trial*, 35–37.
44. Ibid., 163.
45. See David Bercuson and Douglas Wertheimer, *A Trust Betrayed: The Keegstra Affair* (Toronto: Doubleday, 1985). See also David R. Elliott, "Anti-Semitism and the Social Credit Movement: The Intellectual Roots of the Keegstra Affair," CES/EEC 17, no. 1 (1985): 78–89.
46. Harold Waller, "Canada," AJYB 87 (1987): 198.
47. Bercuson and Wertheimer, *Trust Betrayed*, 56.
48. Ibid., 60.
49. Ibid., 62–63, 213–23.
50. Harold Waller, "Canada," AJYB 87 (1987): 198.
51. Ibid., AJYB 88 (1988): 247.
52. Weimann and Winn, *Hate on Trial*, 164.
53. Ibid., 125, 165.
54. Ibid., 164–65.
55. Harold Waller, "Canada," AJYB 88 (1988): 248.
56. Ibid., AJYB 90 (1990): 313.
57. Ibid.
58. For an excellent synopsis of the controversy, see Michael Brown, "Introduction: The Contemporary Campus Setting," in Michael Brown, ed., *Approaches to Antisemitism: Context and Curriculum* (New York: American Jewish Committee and the International Center for the Teaching of Jewish Civilization, 1994): 1–9, 7.
59. Mordecai Richler, *Oh Canada! Oh Quebec! Requiem for a Divided Country* (Toronto: Penguin, 1992), 251–60.
60. Paul M. Sniderman, David A. Northrup, Joseph F. Fletcher, Peter H. Russell, and Philip E. Tetlock, "Psychological and Cultural Foundations of Prejudice: The Case of Antisemitism in Quebec," CRSA/RCSA 30, no. 2 (1993): 242–70.
61. Ibid.: 243, 265.
62. Harold Waller, "Canada," AJYB 91 (1991): 233.
63. Ibid., AJYB 92 (1992): 289.
64. Ibid., AJYB 96 (1996): 198.
65. See Howard Adelman, "Blacks and Jews: Racism, Anti-

Semitism, and *Show Boat*," in Howard Adelman and John H. Simpson, eds., *Multiculturalism, Jews, and Identities in Canada* (Jerusalem: Magnes Press, 1996): 128–78, and Eugene Kaellis, "Jews and Blacks: An Uneasy Interface," CJO (Jan.–Feb. 1998): 15, 28.

66. Harold Waller, "Canada," AJYB 96 (1996): 199.
67. CJN, 16 Jan. 1997.
68. Yaacov Glickman, "Anti-Semitism and Jewish Social Cohesion in Canada," in Ormond McKague, ed., *Racism in Canada* (Saskatoon: Fifth House, 1991): 45–63, 212–15.
69. Robert J. Brym and Rhonda L. Lenton, "The Distribution of Anti-Semitism in Canada in 1984," CJS 16, no. 4 (1991): 411–18, 411.
70. Ibid.: 413.
71. Ibid.: 414.
72. Jean-François Lisée, "Interview with Pierre Anctil," in William Dodge, ed., *Boundaries of Identity: A Quebec Reader* (Toronto: Lester Publishing, 1992): 149–56, 153.
73. See Pierre Anctil, *Le Devoir: Les Juifs et l'immigration de Bourassa à Laurendeau* (Quebec: Institut Québécois de Recherche Sur la Culture, 1988); *Le Rendez-vous manqué: Les Juifs de Montréal face au Québec de l'entre deux guerres* (Quebec: Institut Québécois de Recherche Sur la Culture, 1988); *Montreal foun Nekhtn/Le Montréal juif d'autrefois, de Israël Medresh* (Sillery, QC: Éditions du Septentrion, 1997); *Yidishe Lider/Poèmes yiddish, de Jacob Isaac Segal* (Montreal: Le Noroît, 1992).
74. Brym and Lenton, "Distribution of Anti-Semitism": 415.
75. See also Simon Langlois, "The Distribution of Anti-Semitism in Canada: A Hasty and Erroneous Generalization by Brym and Lenton," CJS 17, no. 2 (1992): 175–78, which is an attack on these findings, and the response by Brym and Lenton, "Anti-Semitism in Quebec: Reply to Langlois," CJS 17, no. 2 (1992): 179–83.
76. Werner Cohn, "English and French Canadian Public Opinion on Jews and Israel: Some Poll Data," CES/EEC 11, no. 2 (1979): 31–48.
77. Ibid.: 34.
78. *Antisemitism World Report 1995* (London: Institute of Jewish Affairs and the American Jewish Committee, 1995): 14–23, 22.
79. Ibid.: 23.
80. Irving Abella, "Antisemitism in Canada: New Perspectives on an Old Problem," in Brown, ed., *Approaches to Antisemitism*: 46–56, 53.
81. Ibid.: 53–54.
82. CJN, 13 Mar. 1997.
83. Harold Troper, "Ethnic Studies and the Classroom Discussion of Antisemitism," in Brown, ed.,

Approaches to Antisemitism: 193–203, 203.

84. Warren Kinsella, *Web of Hate: Inside Canada's Far Right Network* (Toronto: HarperCollins, 1994), 349.
85. CJO (Sept. 1992).
86. CJN, 3 Nov. 1994.
87. Bernard Baskin, "Canada," AJYB 77 (1977): 324.
88. Ibid., AJYB 76 (1976): 253.
89. Ibid.
90. See Daniel J. Elazar and Harold Waller, *Maintaining Consensus: The Canadian Jewish Polity in the Postwar World* (New York: University Press of America, 1990), 4, 32, 46–49, on which this paragraph is based.
91. Ibid., 47.
92. Ibid., 48.
93. Ibid., 54.
94. Ibid., 56.
95. Ibid., 49.
96. Ibid., 50.
97. Bernard Baskin, "Canada," AJYB 77 (1977): 326.
98. Ibid., AJYB 78 (1978): 279.
99. Ibid., AJYB 84 (1984): 176.
100. Ibid., AJYB 79 (1979): 193.
101. Ibid., AJYB 80 (1980): 174.
102. Ibid.: 176.
103. Leo Davids, "Canada: Canadian Jewry: Some Recent Census Findings," AJYB 85 (1985): 193.
104. Harold Waller, "Canada," AJYB 86 (1986): 232.
105. Bernard Baskin, "Canada," AJYB 84 (1984): 176.
106. Harold Waller, "Canada," AJYB 89 (1989): 261.
107. Ibid., AJYB 86 (1986): 232.
108. Ibid., AJYB 90 (1990): 309.
109. Bernard Baskin, "Canada," AJYB 83 (1983): 190.
110. Harold Waller, "Canada," AJYB 86 (1986): 232.
111. Ibid.
112. For a careful examination of the decline of communities in Northern Ontario, see Lise C. Hansen, "The Decline of the Jewish Community in Thunder Bay: An Explanation" (M.A. thesis, University of Manitoba, 1977); and Gerald L. Gold, "A Tale of Two Communities: The Growth and Decline of Small-Town Jewish Communities in Northern Ontario and Southwestern Louisiana," in Moses Rischin, ed., *The Jews of North America* (Detroit: Wayne State University Press, 1987): 224–34. For a superbly insightful — and brilliantly humorous — novel about Jewish life in Sault Ste. Marie, see Morley Torgov, *A Good Place to Come From* (Toronto: Lester & Orpen Dennys, 1974).
113. Melvin Fenson, "Canada," AJYB 75 (1974–75): 350–51.
114. Bernard Baskin, "Canada," AJYB 76 (1976): 251.
115. Harold Waller, "Canada," AJYB 96 (1996): 201.
116. Ibid., AJYB 89 (1989): 262.
117. See Rachel Schlesinger, "Changing Roles of Jewish Women," in Edmond Y. Lipsitz,

ed., *Canadian Jewry Today: Who's Who in Canadian Jewry* (Downsview: J.E.S.L. Educational Products, 1989): 60–70.

118. Francine Zuckerman, ed., *Half the Kingdom: Seven Jewish Feminists* (Montreal: Véhicule Press, 1992).
119. Ibid.: 9, 67.
120. Ibid.: 102.
121. Michael Brown, "Signs of the Times: Changing Notions of Citizenship, Governance and Authority as Reflected in Synagogue Constitutions" (Paper for Conference on Canadian Jewish Studies, York University, 1998).
122. Sheva Medjuck, "If I Cannot Dance to It, It's Not My Revolution: Jewish Feminism in Canada Today," in Robert J. Brym, William Shaffir, and Morton Weinfeld, eds., *The Jews in Canada* (Toronto: Oxford University Press, 1993): 328–43, 341.
123. Harold Waller, "Canada," AJYB 91 (1991): 234.
124. Ibid.: 235.
125. Bernard Baskin, "Canada," AJYB 83 (1983): 189.
126. Ibid., AJYB 84 (1984): 177. Calgary had received some Soviet Jewish families since the early 1970s. See Arthur Levin, "A Soviet Jewish Family Comes to Calgary," CES/EEC 6, nos. 1–2 (1974): 53–66. See also Roberta L. Markus and Donald V. Schwartz, "Soviet Jewish Emigrés in Toronto: Ethnic Self-Identity and Issues of Integration," in Brym, Shaffir, and Weinfeld, eds., *The Jews in Canada*: 402–20.
127. Writing to his wife, Marion, in London, England, in 1962, the South African born Dr. Gerald Marks, newly appointed professor of pharmacology at the University of Alberta, thought he had arrived in the "promised land . . . [and] he felt people should be made to pay an entrance fee to get into Canada." On arriving in Winnipeg, Marion Marks went through Canada Immigration, where she saw that the typed forms that gave information about her and her children had the word *Jewish* written on them boldly in blue ink. Marion Marks to Gerald Tulchinsky, 24 Mar. 1997.
128. Dr. Aubrey Groll to Gerald Tulchinsky, 30 May 1997.
129. Bernard Baskin, "Canada," AJYB 78 (1978): 283.
130. Harold Waller, "Canada," AJYB 92 (1992): 293.
131. See Bernard Baskin, "Canada," AJYB 83 (1983): 189.
132. See Ruth Linn and Nurit Barkan-Ascher, "Imaginary Suitcases in the Lives of Israeli Expatriates in Canada: A Psychological Look at a Unique Historical Phenomenon," CJS/EJC 2 (1994): 21–40, 21.

133. Ibid.: 22.
134. Ibid.: 23.
135. Ibid.: 37.
136. Peter Kruitenbrower, "Fleeing the Promised Land," *Maclean's*, 13 Jan. 1997, 58–59.
137. CJN, 19 Jun. 1964.
138. Mark Medicoff, "Teaching Manpower Crisis," CJN, 4 Feb. 1972.
139. David Kaufman, "Survey Expected to Change Entire Face of Toronto Jewish Education," CJN, 25 Aug. 1972.
140. Bernard Baskin, "Canada," AJYB 78 (1978): 280.
141. Ibid., AJYB 79 (1979): 200.
142. Harold Waller, "Canada," AJYB 86 (1986): 233.
143. Ibid., AJYB 88 (1988): 253.
144. Michael M. Rosenberg and Jack Jedwab, "Institutional Completeness, Ethnic Organizational Style and the Role of the State: The Jewish, Italian and Greek Communities of Montreal," CRSA/RCSA 29, no. 3 (1992): 266–87, 276. See also Michael M. Rosenberg, "Ethnicity, Community, and the State: The Organizational Structures, Practices and Strategies of the Montreal Jewish Community's Day School System and Its Relations with the Quebec State" (Ph.D. thesis, Carleton University, 1995).
145. Harold Waller, "Canada," AJYB 86 (1986): 233.
146. Bernard Baskin, "Canada," AJYB 77 (1977): 325.
147. Ibid., AJYB 81 (1981): 188.
148. Abraham G. Duker, "Can a 'Jewishly-Illiterate' Community Survive?" CJC, 19 Sept. 1952.
149. CJN, 12 Jan. 1962.
150. Patricia Rucker, "Committee Members Dosed with Educational Philosophy," CJN, 29 Jun. 1973. Rucker covered the sessions of the Toronto Study Group on Jewish Education for the CJN.
151. Dorothy Lipovenko, "Educator Attacks Parental Indifference," CJN, 11 May 1973.
152. Patricia Rucker, "Board Says Small Staff Is Problem" and "Task Force Recommends Improvement in Salaries," CJN, 22 and 31 Aug. 1975.
153. Mark Medicoff, "Parents Favour Jewish Education," CJN, 18 Oct. 1974; Patricia Rucker, "Survey Shows Keen Interest Taken in Jewish Education," CJN, 26 Nov. 1975.
154. Jeffrey Lipsitz, "Role of Jewish Home Vital," CJN, 9 May 1975. See also Rabbi Meir Gottesman, "The Best Way to Teach Children Is by Example, So Share with Them Great Mitzvahs of Purim," CJN, 1 Feb. 1975.
155. Sheldon Kirshner, "School's Role in Instilling Jewish Identity Exaggerated, Researcher Claims," CJN, 4 Mar. 1977.

156. See Morton Weinfeld, "Jewish Education: Some Modest Proposals," *Viewpoints* 14, no. 1 (1986); Sam Maister, "Jewish Education's Greatest Problem: Teacher Shortage Decried," CJN, 27 Aug. 1987.
157. Morton Weinfeld and Susan Zelkowitz, "Reflections on the Jewish Polity and Jewish Education," in Brym, Shaffir, and Weinfeld, eds., *The Jews in Canada*: 142–52, 152.
158. Daniel Acks, "Education Funding Greatest Problem, Conference Told," CJN, 15 Dec. 1979.
159. Myron Love, "There's More to Continuity Than School, Says Witty," CJN, 28 Apr. 1994; Len Butcher, "Jewish Continuity: Education of Children Plays Important Role," *Covenant*, 24 Mar. 1994.
160. Judy Platt, "Rash of Runaway Youths Confront Family Workers," CJN, 10 Mar. 1972.

EPILOGUE/ *Oyfn Vegg* (On the Road)

1. Irving Abella, "Family Ties," *Saturday Night* (Jun. 1988): 16–17; Sherry Aikenhead, Maureen Argon, and Cindy Barrett, "A Community's Torment," *Maclean's*, 4 Apr. 1988, 13–14.
2. The controversy in 1998 over a proposed Holocaust exhibit at the National War Museum is a case in point.
3. Jim L. Torczyner and Shari Brotman, "Jewish Continuity in Canada," *Viewpoints* 22, no. 2 (1994): 3–5, 5; Morton Weinfeld, "Between Quality and Quantity: Demographic Trends and Jewish Survival" (Paper for conference, "Creating the Jewish Future," Centre for Jewish Studies, York University, Oct. 1996), 27.
4. Moses Milstein, "Memories of Montreal — and Richness," *Globe and Mail*, 28 Apr. 1998.
5. One of the most recent and widely distributed of these books is the richly illustrated anthology *Growing Up Jewish: Canadians Tell Their Own Stories*, Rosalie Sharp, Irving Abella, and Edwin Goodman, eds. (Toronto: McClelland and Stewart, 1997).
6. Edgar Bronfman, *The Making of a Jew* (New York: G. P. Putnam & Sons, 1996).
7. Harry Gutkin, with Mildred Gutkin, *The Worst of Times, the Best of Times* (Toronto: Fitzhenry and Whiteside, 1987).
8. *Globe and Mail*, 5 Feb. 1998.
9. Merrily Weisbord, "Being at Home," in William Dodge, ed., *Boundaries of Identity: A Quebec Reader* (Toronto: Lester Publishing, 1992): 157–59, 159.
10. Zvi Gittelman, "The Decline of the Diaspora Jewish Nation: Boundaries, Content, and Jewish Identity," JSS 4, no. 2 (1998): 112–32, 127.

Index